The Organization
and Control
of American Schools

The Organization and Control of American Schools

FIFTH EDITION

Roald F. Campbell
The University of Utah

Luvern L. Cunningham
The Ohio State University

Raphael O. Nystrand
The University of Louisville

Michael D. Usdan
*Institute for Education Leadership
and Fordham University*

Charles E. Merrill Publishing Company
A Bell & Howell Company
Columbus Toronto London Sydney

Published by
Charles E. Merrill Publishing Company
A Bell & Howell Company
Columbus, Ohio 43216

This book was set in Century Oldstyle.
Cover design: Cathy Watterson
Cover photo: Baron Wohlman
Production coordination: Martha Morss

Library of Congress Catalog Card Number: 84-061744
International Standard Book Number: 0-675-20386-4
Printed in the United States of America
1 2 3 4 5 6 7 — 91 90 89 88 87 86 85

Contents

Preface

Our main purpose in this book is to examine the nation's schools in terms of the complex milieu in which they are embedded. Such an approach is essential to an understanding of the American school, for in a democratic society the state and its educational system stand in a reciprocal relationship with society as a whole: the school not only exerts influence, but influence in many forms is exerted upon it.

Our perspective for viewing these relationships is that of open systems theory. From this perspective control is much more than a legal concept. The variables affecting the school are numerous and complex; they are both obvious and subtle, formal and informal. The more understanding school administrators have of these variables, the more effectively they can perform. Although specific events and actors in educational systems change over time, certain structures and processes persist.

The roles of individuals within the open systems are emphasized. The roles of school administrators, school board members, teachers, students, and citizens as they participate in the processes of school governance are described and analyzed. Special attention is given to the superintendency and the importance of this office in the future of American education. The function of the school board and the significance of the school board–superintendent relationship are examined in the context of local control and administration of schools.

Since the appearance of the fourth edition five years ago, our country has witnessed a resurgence of interest in education comparable to that which followed the launching of *Sputnik* by the Soviet Union in the late 1950s. The subsequent emphasis on improving education, particularly in science and mathematics, has been explained as a reaction to a perceived challenge. The current interest is an outgrowth of the perceived need to retool the American economy in order to compete more effectively in world markets and in a highly technological world society. A number of distinguished commissions at the state and national levels have issued reports that indict American schools for a range of shortcomings and urge a new commitment to excellence. Many of these reports note the relationship between education and economic productivity, acknowledge the dramatically changing economy, and call for educational improvements to insure that our society keeps pace.

This reawakening of public interest in schooling has intensified the amount of activity at all levels of school governance. The action has been particularly intense at the state level where numerous legislatures have enacted reforms dealing with such matters as requirements for high school graduation; certification, evaluation, and compensation of teachers and administrators; essential skills testing; and programs for gifted and talented students. Despite some reversion at the federal level, the formal involvement of both federal and state government in schooling continues to be substantial, and much of this involvement has had a regulatory emphasis. Likewise, court decisions continue to be a prominent influence on school policymaking.

The federal and state presence in school affairs has often come at the behest of citizen groups. The diversity of interests represented by such groups is greater than ever before. Moreover, many of these groups possess considerable political sophistication and realize that they can pursue their objectives not only by petitioning school officials but by appealing to public opinion and to various agencies that have some jurisdiction regarding schools. As a consequence, school policy matters are increasingly caught up in interagency conflicts, jurisdictional disputes, and appellate reviews.

For many years, it has been recognized that education is more than schooling. Recent developments, such as the renewed interest of the business community in education, have brought this point into sharp focus, and they are addressed in a chapter entitled "Extended Educational Programs and New Collaborations." As in other chapters, we examine the effect of these developments on the control of schools.

In studying the control of education, the administrator is increasingly dependent on the social and behavioral sciences. This book draws upon concepts and research findings from the disciplines of psychology, sociology, political science, and economics. The schools are institutions designed to serve particular social purposes. They are part of a larger social system, linked to society through formal structures of government which legitimize educational policies. Formal governmental structures are subject to a vast array of influences that affect the course of decision making. The many influences exerted by the larger world are mediated by the subsystem, the schools.

As in past editions, we have tried once again to make predictions about the course of future events. Each chapter closes with a brief overview of coming developments as we see them and a summary of major control factors discussed in the chapter. The final chapter recapitulates and synthesizes these factors in a general discussion of control elements affecting schools.

This book has been written essentially for students of school administration, administrators in public and nonpublic schools, the academic community, and interested lay persons, especially school board members. This volume will also be useful as a source book for any teacher or other professional who wishes to understand the dynamics of school operation. Since this work deals with the stresses and strains present in most local school environments, much of our analysis will be of value to nonschool people responsible for thinking through and acting upon school issues.

Our gratitude is extended to the many scholars and practitioners who have helped with this manuscript in various ways, especially those who have offered thoughtful criticisms, among them John Sullivan (Georgia State University) and Max Abbott (University of Oregon). We are also grateful to the many researchers and practitioners from whom we have acquired data and new ideas. We are particularly indebted to Roderick F. McPhee, coauthor of the first and second editions, whose contributions continue to be evident in this edition.

1
Schools in the American Scene

On October 17, 1979, President Jimmy Carter signed Public Law 96–88 which established the Department of Education. He commented at the time, "My guess is that the best move for the quality of life in America in the future might very well be this establishment of this new Department of Education, because it will open up for the first time some very substantial benefits for our country."[1] His formal statement noted that the department bill "will increase the Nation's attention to education . . . make Federal education programs more accountable . . . streamline administration of aid to education programs . . . (and) ensure that local communities retain control of their schools and education programs."[2]

Less than two years later, Ronald Reagan replaced Jimmy Carter in the White House and declared his intention to dissolve the new Department of Education. Although the department remained intact after Reagan's first three years of office, he did reduce federal spending for education and cut back government regulations in some areas during the period. These developments will be considered in more detail in chapter 2. Here it is sufficient to note that they raise questions about the federal interest in education that have continuing relevance, Why was the Department of Education established? What does it do? Why did President Reagan want to terminate it? Why was he unsuccessful in this regard? What import does the presence of the Department of Education have for local and state control of education? Answers to these questions suggest that education is a national as well as a state and local concern as indicated by the following vignettes.

During the middle and late 1970s the Cleveland, Ohio, public schools experienced a series of events that produced great strife in the city and demonstrated the complexities of intergovernmental relationships in education. Two issues, school desegregation and school finance, were intertwined.[3] In December 1976 a federal district court found the Cleveland and Ohio Boards of Education liable for unconstitutional

1. "Remarks by President Jimmy Carter at the Department of Education Organization Act Bill Signing Ceremony," 17 October 1979, Administration of Jimmy Carter, 1979, p. 1956.
2. Statement on Signing S210 into Law, Administration of Jimmy Carter, 1979, p. 1979.
3. For more detail, see D. W. Proctor, "Update on *Reed* vs. *Rhodes*" (Cleveland: Study Group on Racial Isolation in the Public Schools, 23 December 1977).

1

school desegregation and ordered that a desegregation plan be prepared. The court subsequently ordered that no school was to be closed without prior permission of the court because of a finding that past closings had increased segregation. In late 1977 the Cleveland Board anticipating a shortfall in operating revenues and faced with a state law that prohibits deficit spending asked the state superintendent of public instruction for permission to close for the remainder of 1977 when these funds were exhausted. The state auditor indicated that funds would last until October 17. However, the district court which had issued the desegregation order mandated that the Cleveland Schools remain open "while public schools are open and operating anywhere in the State of Ohio."

At this point the only funds available to the Cleveland Schools had already been obligated to pay tax anticipation notes held by Cleveland banks. When it appeared that the schools would spend this money for other purposes, the banks asked the Ohio Supreme Court to set aside the funds due them. A confrontation between the state and federal courts was averted by emergency action of the state legislature which extended the due date on the bank notes for another year. This action was accompanied by a decision to place a property tax levy before Cleveland voters for their approval in early 1978. It was widely publicized that failure of voters to approve this levy would leave Cleveland with insufficient funds to complete the school year. Antitax sentiment and opposition to the desegregation order of the federal court produced an overwhelmingly negative vote. Once again the Cleveland schools were confronted with the prospect of fiscal collapse. Again this was averted by special action of the legislature which advanced the remainder of 1978 state aid to the district but also placed the district in a form of financial receivership which required all district expenditures to be authorized by the state superintendent of public instruction. Another attempt to pass a local tax increase for schools failed by an even greater margin. State officials were confronted with the prospect of continuing to subsidize Cleveland schools beyond conventional levels in the face of considerable public sentiment that the schools should be allowed to close if local voters refuse to support them.

What does this incident suggest about the relationships between the federal courts and local school districts, between federal courts and state officials, and between local districts and the state legislature? Who has the responsibility for financing local schools? Some other kinds of local issues are suggested by the following vignette.

A surburban board of education voted 4–3 not to renew the contract of their superintendent of schools when it would elapse the following spring. Many community residents were displeased by this action and charged that it was taken primarily because the superintendent had exercised strong leadership toward integrating local schools. Members of the board asserted that their action had nothing to do with integration for they too supported this policy. They contended, however, that they found it difficult to work with the superintendent. An estimated fifteen hundred persons, most of them sympathetic to the superintendent, attended the meeting at which the board voted. Before taking this action the board heard from more than fifty speakers, most of whom praised the superintendent and urged the board to retain him. The audience applauded speakers who supported the superintendent, jeered those who spoke against him, and reacted angrily when the decision of the board was announced. Following this action the superintendent reportedly asserted that he had been "hung in a kangaroo court" and demanded an opportunity to defend himself against written charges in an open hearing.

In the days following the board meeting, supporters of the superintendent held demonstrations, wrote letters to newspapers, held press conferences, distributed buttons and bumper stickers, and collected signatures on petitions urging his retention. Seven black members of the caucus which traditionally screens local board of education candidates resigned, charging that "black representation on the caucus does not serve well the interest of the black community." The local teachers' association criticized the manner in which the board acted, threatened to withhold cooperation from any new superintendent selected by the board, and noted the possibility of action "that might preclude the opening of school in the fall."

Finally, after meeting with the local human relations commission, the board unanimously agreed not to act upon the superintendent's contract until after the election in the following spring at which three members (two of whom voted to dismiss the superintendent) would be candidates for reelection.

What are the issues here? Why did the board of education choose not to exercise its legal prerogative by holding to its original decision? How and why was such widespread support for the superintendent mobilized? Will carrying the issue over to the next board election resolve the problem? What will be the impact of these events upon interracial and other group relationships in the community? It is with questions like the ones provoked by these vignettes that the authors of this book are concerned.

A Statistical Picture of American Schools

A statistical picture of American elementary and secondary schools is difficult to develop and becomes obsolete in a short time. Even so, a rough approximation of that picture seems necessary at this point. The United States contains both public and nonpublic schools. The public schools are organized into approximately 16,000 operating school districts or basic administrative units. The number of school districts varies widely among the states. For example, there is only one district in Hawaii, 24 in Maryland, and more than 1,200 in Nebraska. In the public school districts of the nation there were in 1980 an estimated 63,400 elementary schools and 22,700 secondary schools.[4] In the same year there were an estimated 14,000 nonpublic elementary schools and 3,700 nonpublic high schools. Nonpublic schools include those organized under church auspices as well as those under other private agencies.

Estimated enrollments in public and nonpublic schools for 1981 are shown in Table 1.1. Although enrollments have declined recently in both public and nonpublic schools, the rate of decline has been considerably faster in public schools.

TABLE 1.1

Estimated Enrollments in Public and Nonpublic Schools for 1981

	Public		Nonpublic	
	Number	Percentage Change since 1975	Number	Percentage Change since 1975
Elementary (1–8)	27,665,000	−11	3,692,000	−1
Secondary	13,319,000	−6	1,357,000	−.3

4. U.S. Bureau of the Census, *Statistical Abstract of the United States,* 103rd ed. (Washington D.C.: Government Printing Office, 1982), 132.
5. Ibid., 135.

TABLE 1.2

Estimated Education Staff in Public and Nonpublic Schools for 1980

	Public	Nonpublic
Elementary teachers	1,175,000	187,000
Secondary teachers	988,000	89,000
Principals and Supervisors	135,000	16,500
Total	2,298,000	292,500

The number of teachers in public schools in 1980 was approximately 1,175,000 in elementary schools and 988,000 in secondary schools.[6] Nonpublic schools employed approximately 187,000 teachers in elementary schools and 89,000 teachers in secondary schools. We also estimate that there are 135,000 administrators and supervisors in public schools and that approximately 16,500 persons hold similar positions in nonpublic schools. These figures are shown in Table 1.2.

Estimates for 1981 indicate that public schools expended $97.5 billion for current operation and $6.3 billion for capital outlay and debt service—a total of $103.8 billion. This was more than twice the 1970 expenditure level. The financing of nonpublic schools at the same time was estimated to be $12.2 billion for current operation and $900 million for capital outlay and debt service. These estimates are shown in Table 1.3. When combined with expenditures for higher education, these costs represent approximately 6.5 percent of the gross national product.

Schools as Open Systems

We view the organization and control of schools from the perspective of open systems. This view emphasizes the interdependence between an organization and its environment, and is based upon the work of David Easton, who developed a model of political systems which is helpful in understanding the organization and control of schools.[8] The key concepts in such a model are *system, environment, response,* and

TABLE 1.3

Expenditures in Public and Nonpublic Schools for 1981

	Public	Nonpublic
Current operation	97.5 billion	12.2 billion
Capital outlay	6.3 billion	.9 billion
Total	103.8 billion	13.1 billion

6. Ibid., 153.
7. Ibid., 135.
8. David Easton, *A Framework for Political Analysis* (Englewood Cliffs, N.J.: Prentice-Hall, 1965), and David Easton, *A Systems Analysis of Political Life* (New York: John Wiley & Sons, 1965). For another discussion of American schools from this perspective, see Frederick Wirt and Michael Kirst, *Schools in Conflict* (Berkeley: McCutchan, 1982)

feedback. A *system* can be defined as any set of variables (e.g., individuals, agencies, governments) which interrelate. It is a political system if it produces authoritative decisions. The *environment* refers to all other systems outside the boundaries of the system under scrutiny. *Response* refers to the actions a system takes in response to stimuli from other systems in its environment, and *feedback* refers to the effect of the system response upon other environmental systems.

The relationship among these concepts is shown in Figure 1.1. The environment produces inputs to the political system which, in an effort to persist, responds by making decisions or policies that result in outputs. These outputs act as feedback to environmental systems which accordingly modify their demands and supports to the political system.

Recall the vignette about Cleveland which appeared earlier in this chapter. If we regard the Cleveland schools as a system for analytic purposes, we can say that the federal court demand that the schools remain open despite their fiscal problems produced a system response to spend the money earmarked to repay bank loans for current operating expenses. This decision prompted local banks to go to court to force schools to meet their contractual obligations. This feedback to an environmental system (local banks) created new and conflicting demands upon the political system (the schools and state officials).

The open system perspective contrasts with the literature which argues that schools traditionally have been bureaucratic systems which are nonresponsive to their

FIGURE 1.1

A Simplified Model of a Political System

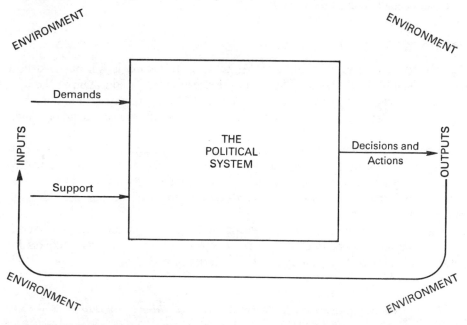

SOURCE: David Easton, *A Framework for Political Analysis* (Englewood Cliffs, N.J.: Prentice-Hall, Inc., 1965). Used by permission of the author.

environment.[9] As subsequent chapters will show, administrators, teachers, and others within school systems often have considerable effect upon policy decisions and school activities. But other individuals, groups, and agencies influence these decisions as well. We will explore many facets of this general theme in the following chapters. As we shall see, the model is made more complex by the fact that actors within the system (e.g., teachers) often have affiliations with groups outside the system (e.g., unions and professional associations).

Schools are open systems in another respect which deserves mention at this point. In Karl Weick's terms they are "loosely coupled."[10] Weick says that "coupled events are responsive but . . . each event preserves its own identity and some evidence of its physical or logical separateness."[11] In terms of the organization and control of schools, this suggests that different events in the environment may have different effects for various schools within a single system. For example, parent concerns about textbooks or extracurricular activities at one school will not necessarily affect conditions at other schools. Or, faculty concerns at any given school may differ substantially from those at other schools. Loose coupling also means that it is difficult for the central administration to enforce uniform compliance with many policies across the entire district. Even if desired, it would be very difficult, for example, to ensure that all third-grade teachers across a city district are teaching the same things at the same time and in the same way.

The concept of system is a general one which can be applied to many phenomena at different levels. It is possible to refer to a single school as a system, to a school district as a system, to a state educational system, or to the educational system in the United States. The term will be used in each of these ways throughout this book. Within the context of open systems we will give particular attention to the concepts of organization, control, and schools. The following paragraphs provide explicit meanings for and delimitations to these terms.

Organization

The word *organization* is a broad term. At times in this book it will be used in a formal, legal sense. Thus, we shall speak of the organization of education at the federal, state, and school district levels. We shall also deal with the organization of intermediate units, most often at the county level, and of attendance areas or single schools.

At other times we shall speak of organization in an extralegal or less formal sense. Thus, we shall deal with the organization of the board of education, the administrative structure of a school system, and the formal and informal organizations of teachers. Despite these many uses of the word *organization,* we shall do our best through modifiers and context to clarify our usage of the term.

Perhaps we should share one predilection we have about organization: we see it as a means and not an end. In other words, to speak of how we organize schools for a moment, we think that argument about the merits of 6–3–3 versus an 8–4 organi-

9. See, for example, Marilyn Gittell and T. Edward Hollander, *Six Urban School Districts* (New York: Praeger, 1968).
10. Karl E. Weick, "Educational Organizations as Loosely Coupled Systems," *Administrative Science Quarterly* 21 (March 1976): 1–19.
11. Ibid., 3.

zation is largely beside the point. More important to us is what kind of program goes on when schools are organized in these or other ways. Likewise we know of no administrative organization which, per se, we would defend above all other forms of organization. More important than the formal organization chart are the work patterns which chief administrators and their subordinates have been able to establish.

In keeping with our conviction that organization is a means and not an end, we do suggest that organizations can be managed to facilitate or obstruct the achievement of goals. For instance, some students of the problem conclude that it is easier to provide an adequate instructional program in school districts enrolling 10,000 pupils than in those enrolling 1,000 pupils. But organization of larger districts alone will not achieve the end; the resources of the larger units must be used for school purposes. In like manner, the division of a large high school into "houses" may permit, but does not guarantee, more intimate student personnel arrangements. Again, what is done within the organization is more significant than the organization itself.

Control

Control is also a word of many meanings. We shall speak of both legal and extralegal control. Legal control tends to be more formal, and as the name implies, grows out of the law. In each of the fifty states there is a formidable body of school law—constitutional provisions, statutory enactments, court decisions, and administrative regulations. The law specifies or implies the powers and duties of the legislature, state boards and state departments of education, local boards of education, and other official bodies. Thus a local board of education often has some tax discretion within limits set by state statute. Or, a local board of education may employ teachers, provided they meet certification standards established by the state board of education under power given by state statute.

Legal control also resides at the federal level. While no specific mention of education appears in the United States Constitution, the general welfare clause is sufficiently broad to provide the basis for legislation on the part of the Congress. The general welfare clause and Amendments I, V, and XIV have also supplied the United States Supreme Court with adequate grounds for a number of decisions having to do with education. Administrative regulation on the part of the executive branch of the federal government or federal court decisions also constitute a form of legal control.

But legal control, whether exercised at the local, state, or federal level, is only part of the picture. We shall also consider extralegal control, which some may prefer to call extralegal influence. We do not wish to quibble about words. We are interested in examining how decisions pertaining to American education actually are made and implemented rather than simply how they are formalized. Thus, any force or movement which in the end affects the decision is, in our judgment, an aspect of control and thus within the purview of this book.

Many people do not view control in this broad context and their limited definition of control has led to naive citizenship and inept school management. Equating control with its legal manifestations leads to a rather superficial focus on the formal expression of policy and overlooks the motives and processes which produce that policy. Since we are interested in control as it concerns not only policy decisions but also the implementation of policy, we have chosen to deal with formal structures of school government, with the activities of interest groups, and with any other forces which appear to control the schools.

Schools

We shall use the term *schools* in its customary sense to include institutions established to provide elementary and secondary education. We shall not attempt to describe the organization and control of colleges, although to be sure, some of the legal controls pertaining to schools also pertain to colleges, and many of the extralegal controls affect colleges in much the same way they do schools.

The growth of the junior or community college and programs of adult education makes the distinction between school and college less clear-cut. A number of these colleges are established by local school districts as extensions of their programs in elementary and secondary education. In these cases organization and control tend to be even more like that found in elementary and secondary schools but again no explicit treatment of the college will be included.

We shall treat private and parochial as well as public schools. While the book as a whole will deal with public schools more fully than with private and parochial schools, these alternatives to public education will be examined specifically and the relationship between the public and alternative arrangements for schools will be noted at many points.

This choice reflects our conviction that to understand the schools of America one must look at the public *and* the nonpublic schools. The presence of the nonpublic school affects in many ways the organization and control of public schools. Also, events in some public school systems have given impetus to nonpublic alternatives. It is time that as complete a picture as possible of all American schools be drawn because alternatives to traditional public as well as nonpublic school programs are being considered more frequently by educators and lay persons alike.

The Development of American Schools

A Brief Overview

American schools during the seventeenth and eighteenth centuries, despite the passage of the Massachusetts laws of 1642 and 1647, were essentially private or church institutions. Such schools were few in number; attendance was usually selective; and control rested in the hands of individual or church groups. About 1800 there began a growing demand for public education in America. Thomas Jefferson, in Virginia, was among the first to propose a system of free public elementary schools. His proposal was not adopted, but a little later, largely as a result of the work of Horace Mann in Massachusetts and Henry Barnard in Connecticut, the public schools movement of America was launched.

The small community district became the unit in which the public school, usually a one-room elementary school, was established. Early state laws permitted school districts to be formed almost anywhere a half-dozen families wished to establish one. The simplicity of the plan was appealing. A community wishing to establish a school and pay taxes to support it could establish one; a community not desiring a school or not wishing to pay taxes for its support could let matters alone. To be sure, as the nineteenth century progressed, the states became more adamant about the establishment of public schools and tax support for them. The small district pattern of organization, with some modification in the county-unit states of the South and in the cities, remained for that century and even much of the twentieth century the predominant pattern of organization.

The development of control mechanisms for the schools of Massachusetts has been reported in some detail.[12] Using Massachusetts as a prototype, we find that for two hundred years the schools were under the direction of the town meeting and later of the town selectmen or a committee of the selectmen. For this entire period, school government was very much a part of other local government. In 1826 and 1827 the Massachusetts General Court (legislature) established the town school committee (school board) as a separate governmental body. This action was approximated in other states and school government came to be separated from other government at the local level.

During our early history, school management was a function performed by lay citizens. However, with the growth of cities and the merger of school districts within cities, the problems of school administration became too demanding for part-time, lay school board members. This led to the creation of the office of superintendent of schools. The evolution of this office is noted in chapter 9.

In the cities, one-room schools tended to give way to two-room, four-room, eight-room, and even larger schools. The increase in school size and the grading of pupils provided the need for a head or principal teacher in each school. We find that Cincinnati established a principal-teacher in each school as early as 1838.[13] The Quincy School of Boston reported in 1847 that all departments had been placed under a single principal. St. Louis had placed each of its schools under a single principal by 1859.

Initially, the duties of the principal were essentially clerical in nature, such as the compilation of enrollment and attendance figures. Later, the principal was relieved of teaching so that he might give full time to organization and management duties. The classification of pupils by grade levels was not the least of these duties. In recent decades, the principal has tended to become, or is at least thought of as, an instructional officer in the school.

Our early schools, largely under the control of the local communities, seemed to serve a rural, homogeneous society rather well. As noted previously, in the growing cities these small districts were combined, in time, into city school systems. Moreover, for much of the nineteenth and some of the twentieth century secondary education was available, for the most part, only in the academies which remained under private and parochial auspices. Gradually public education came to be viewed as important to the political and economic progress of America. The growth of secularization and of egalitarianism also became forces which served to promote the extension of public education.

The schools of today are not only the product of the forces noted above; they also exist in a complex, largely urban, and pluralistic society. Moreover, world-wide ideologies and practices affect today's schools beyond the wildest dreams of the citizens of this nation during the last century.[14] Under these circumstances, the questions

---

12. Henry Suzzallo, *The Rise of Local School Supervision in Massachusetts,* Teachers College Contribution no. 3 (New York: Columbia University, 1906).
13. Paul R. Pierce, *The Origin and Development of the Public School Principalship* (Chicago: University of Chicago Press, 1934).
14. See David Tyack and Elizabeth Hansot, *Managers of Virtue* (New York: Basic, 1982) and Diane Ravitch, *The Troubled Crusade* (New York: Basic, 1983).

of organization and control of American schools have new meanings and require fresh analyses.

Some Legal Milestones

In the development of public education, as we have previously suggested, there have been a number of legal milestones which deserve some mention. The first of these was the establishment of the legal basis for public education in the various states. By 1820 thirteen of the twenty-three states then in existence had constitutional provisions and seventeen had statutory provisions pertaining to public education. All except two of the states had either constitutional or statutory provisions and nine states had both.[15] Today, most states have firm constitutional mandates regarding public education as is illustrated by the Ohio constitution:

> The General Assembly shall make such provisions, by taxation, or otherwise, as, with the income arising from the school trust fund, will secure a thorough and efficient system of common schools throughout the State; but no religious sect, or sects, shall ever have any exclusive right to, or control of, any part of the school funds of this State.[16]

Provisions for compulsory attendance and tax support for schools as found in the constitutions or the statutes of the various states became particularly important in the establishment of public education. Beginning with Massachusetts in 1852, each of the 50 states enacted compulsory education laws. The question of minimum school attendance for the child was no longer a decision for the parent but for the state.

To begin with, the laws providing tax support for schools were often permissive, and in some cases schools for pauper children were the first schools for which money was mandated. New York in 1812 became the first state to pass a permanent law for the organization of public schools. New Jersey provided for the education of pauper children in 1820 and for all children in 1838. Ohio and Delaware authorized taxation for education in 1821 and Illinois followed in 1825. Cubberley notes that "the battle for the establishment of tax supported schools was a bitter one, but after about 1850 it had been won in every Northern state."[17] Thus, tax support and required attendance became important steps in establishing the public schools of America. Both reflected the growing power of the state over a function once left to individuals and the church.

Fundamental questions of tax support for schools were again brought before the courts in the early 1970s. A series of cases filed in both state and federal courts challenged school funding arrangements based principally upon local property taxation.[18] It was contended that states which promulgated such systems did not guarantee equal educational opportunity to children in the state because this opportunity was a function of the taxable property located within their particular school district. Some state courts found that such systems violated their respective state constitutions.

---

15. Lee M. Thurston and William H. Roe, *State School Administration* (New York: Harper & Row, Publishers, 1957), 59–60.
16. Ohio Constitution, Art. VI, sec. 2.
17. Elwood P. Cubberley, *Public School Administration* (Boston: Houghton Mifflin, 1929), 10.
18. The best known were *Serrano* v. *Priest*, 96 Cal. Rptr. 601, 487 P 2nd, 1241, 5 Cal 3rd, 584 (1971), *Robinson* v. *Cahill*, 62 N.J. 473 (1973), and *San Antonio Independent District et al.* v. *Rodriguez et al.*, 411 U.S. 1 (1973).

However, the U.S. Supreme Court held that they did not violate the Constitution because education is not a "fundamental" right guaranteed by it.[19] Even so, the Court noted the imperfections in current finance systems and indicated that their reform was a matter for the attention of state legislatures. This issue is discussed in more detail in chapter 7.

While state laws generally came to require the establishment and support of "common schools," there still remained some doubt that common schools included secondary schools. This question became the heart of the Kalamazoo case.[20] In 1874 the Supreme Court of Michigan said:

> We content ourselves with the statement that neither in our state policy, in our constitution, or in our laws, do we find the primary school districts restricted in the branches of knowledge which their officers may cause to be taught, or the grade of instruction that may be given, if their voters consent in regular form to bear the expense and raise the taxes for the purpose.[21]

This and similar decisions in other states made it clear that local boards of education had powers to establish schools and levels of instruction and to use tax money in support of those schools even though the state laws did not specifically provide for such schools and levels of instruction.

With the growth of public schools it is not surprising that the idea of eliminating all nonpublic schools should have evolved. Major arguments for schools seemed, in many cases, to be arguments against nonpublic schools. This question was ruled on by the U.S. Supreme Court in the now famous Oregon case.[22] The court held that the statute which required all children to attend only public schools was unconstitutional as being an undue infringement on the rights of parents to control the education of their children. While the state had the right to inspect and reasonably regulate private schools, it did not have the right to abolish them. Since 1925 it has been clear that nonpublic schools may be an acceptable alternative to public schools.

But the question of public versus nonpublic schools was not yet settled. Louisiana passed a law providing free textbooks for children attending public and parochial schools alike. The law was challenged and eventually reached the U.S. Supreme Court. In the Cochran case, the Court declared the Louisiana law constitutional and in so doing created a new doctrine called the "child benefit" theory.[23] This theory has not always been accepted by state courts, and it was vigorously contested in the Everson case in the U.S. Supreme Court.[24] In a 5–4 decision, however, the Court ruled that the New Jersey law permitting boards of education to provide transportation for any school pupil, public or private, was constitutional. Again, a number of state courts have ruled that state constitutions do not permit the expenditure of public money for transportation of pupils to private schools. Despite the division of judicial opinion on this matter, the "child benefit" idea has become a powerful one.

The separation of church and state was the basic issue in the Pierce, Cochran, and Everson cases noted briefly in the preceeding paragraphs. A number of other

19. *San Antonio Independent School District et al.* v. *Rodriguez et. al.*
20. *Stuart* v. *School District No. 1 of Village of Kalamazoo*, 30 Michigan 69 (1874).
21. Ibid.
22. *Pierce* v. *Society of the Sisters of the Holy Names of Jesus and Mary*, 268 U.S. 510 (1925).
23. *Cochran et al.* v. *Louisiana State Board of Education et al.*, 281 U.S. 370 (1930).
24. *Everson* v. *Board of Education of Ewing Township et al.*, 330 U.S. 1 (1947).

cases have dealt with other aspects of this issue. In 1948 the U.S. Supreme Court ruled, in a split decision in the McCollum case, that the "released time" religious education program being conducted in the Champaign, Illinois, schools was not constitutional.[25] The chief objections to the practice seemed to be the use of the school buildings for the program and the administrative assistance given to the program by the school officials. Justice Black, who wrote the opinion for the majority, contended that these practices were contrary to the First Amendment of the Constitution.

About four years later, the Zorach case in New York State, which again raised the question of released time religious education, reached the U.S. Supreme Court.[26] In this instance, the Court sustained the New York law permitting released time religious instruction. The chief differences between the New York and Illinois practices appeared to be that in New York the religious classes were not held in the school buildings and the school officers exercised less control over the attendance of pupils in the religious program. Again, however, there was a split decision and in this instance Justice Black found himself in the minority.

During the late 1960s and early 1970s, some states enacted legislation which extended aid to nonpublic schools for teachers' salaries and other expenses related to specified "secular" courses. The U.S. Supreme Court held that such aid was unconstitutional because its implementation would foster "excessive entanglement" of government and religion.[27] Subsequent legislation to achieve the same purpose by providing partial reimbursements for tuition expenses to parents of nonpublic school pupils was also declared unconstitutional.[28]

The issue of relationships between public and nonpublic schools became more intense in the 1980s as a result of proposals for tuition tax credits, nondenominational prayer in public schools, and teaching creationism as a theory contrary to evolution. Attention to these relationships was encouraged by public statements of support for tax credits and school prayer by President Reagan. However, the constitutionality of both these issues remained in doubt in the mid-1980s, and laws that would require the teaching of creationism were held unconstitutional in court tests below the Supreme Court level.

These cases and others not cited here suggest that although schools may not require students to participate in religious observances, a degree of cooperation between the public schools and religious groups will be found to be constitutional. Should that cooperation go too far, however, the Court will declare the matter contrary to the principle of separation of church and state.

Perhaps the most notable decisions of the U.S. Supreme Court having to do with education are the Brown case of 1954[29] and the implementing decision one year later.[30] In the initial decision the long accepted "separate but equal" doctrine was declared inadequate in the field of public education. Forced segregation of black pupils into separate schools was found to be contrary to the equal protection of the law as guaranteed by the Fourteenth Amendment. The Court recognized that many difficul-

25. *People of the State of Illinois ex rel. McCollum* v. *Board of Education of School District No. 71, Champaign Co., Ill., et al.,* 333 U.S. 203 (1948).
26. *Zorach* v. *Clauson,* 343 U.S. 306 (1952).
27. *Lemon* v. *Kurtzman,* 403 U.S. 602 (1971).
28. *Committee for Public Education* v. *Nyquist,* 413 U.S. 756 (1973) and *Sloan* v. *Lemon,* 413 U.S. 825 (1973).
29. *Brown* v. *Board of Education of Topeka,* 347 U.S. 483 (1954).
30. *Brown* v. *Board of Education of Topeka,* 349 U.S. 294 (1955).

ties would arise in implementing the decision and that these problems might vary by location. Hence, in 1955 the enforcement of the decision was remanded to the appropriate federal courts. The lower federal courts were instructed to accept "reasonable progress" toward the ultimate goal of desegregated schools.

Efforts to achieve desegregation concentrated first on those southern states where dual school systems were in existence. Resistance to these efforts was considerable. Each plan of resistance resulted in additional court cases, and in most instances plans which proposed to achieve indirectly what had been forbidden directly were struck down. Probably the most widespread plan in the South was "freedom of choice" in which students were allowed to choose enrollment in schools outside their immediate neighborhood if space were available there. The U.S. Commission on Civil Rights reported that factors such as residential segregation, segregated teaching staffs, administrative judgments as to what constitutes overcrowding, and transportation policies limited the amount of desegregation resulting from such plans.[31] Indeed, the Commission found that, in the North and South alike, more blacks attended segregated schools in 1965 than at the time of the 1954 Brown decision.[32]

The Supreme Court subsequently held that more positive action was required to dismantle dual school systems. In October 1969 the Court ruled that a number of school districts in Mississippi could no longer postpone desegregation and called for the immediate termination of dual school systems.[33] In a later decision, *Swann* v. *Charlotte—Macklenburg Board of Education,* the Court authorized compulsory busing as a method to achieve this purpose.[34] Thus the Court clearly indicated the need for school districts to initiate affirmative remedial action where the law had previously tolerated or encouraged dual systems.[35]

Left unsettled by the court, as it reviewed desegregation cases emanating from the South and other areas where official efforts were made to segregate schools, was the matter of state responsibility to desegregate school districts where segregation was a product of residential patterns rather than legal action. Moreover, these instances of *de facto* segregation became more numerous as urban residential patterns became more segregated. A series of lower court decisions suggested that affirmative action may be required in this regard also and posed the issue for the Supreme Court. Among the alternatives considered favorably by lower courts was the possibility of busing students across city district lines in metropolitan areas. However, the U.S. Supreme Court held that federal courts could not mandate such action unless the state or one or more of the surrounding districts could be shown to have caused interdistrict segregation.[36]

Let us summarize these legal milestones as they pertain to the public schools. In response to social, economic, and political developments in this country, there was first the establishment of public schools by constitutional and statutory provisions. As time went on, attendance of pupils in school and payment of taxes for school purposes

---

31. U.S. Commission on Civil Rights. *Racial Isolation in the Public Schools,* vol. 1 (Washington, D.C.: Government Printing Office, 1967), 66–70.
32. Ibid., 2–10.
33. *Alexander* v. *Holmes County,* 369 U.S. 19 (1969).
34. *Swann* v. *Charlotte-Mecklenburg Board of Education,* 402 U.S. 1 (1970).
35. For discussion of this and related decisions, see John C. Hogan, "School Desegregation—North, South, East, West: Trends in Court Decisions, 1849–1973," *Phi Delta Kappan* 55 (September 1973): 58–63.
36. *Bradley* v. *Milliken,* 345 F Supp 914 (1972). 42 LW 5249 (July 25, 1974). A more extended discussion of litigation pertaining to desegregation will be found in Chapter 7.

were required. In the latter half of the nineteenth century the public school program was extended to include the secondary level. Convictions about the importance of public schools, however, were not sufficient to eliminate the nonpublic school. While the doctrine of separation of church and state still pertains, it does not rule out the use of some public money for the benefit of pupils in nonpublic schools, nor does it prohibit a limited amount of cooperation between school and religious bodies. Finally, the obligation of the public school to serve all children without regard to race or color has been given rigorous interpretation by our highest court.

In these developments it seems quite clear that public schools and schools in general do not enjoy a protected status. Schools take shape in response to the ideological and practical demands of the society of which they are a part. In fact, they have been battlegrounds in the resolution of social conflict. What is meant by separation of church and state may have been clarified more through school decisions than by any other means. Certainly the extension of civil rights to blacks and other minorities is being attempted through the schools as much as through any other realm of activity. With school decisions being part of the mainstream of life, there is little wonder that school control is a matter of consequence.

Contemporary Issues

In addition to adopting a historical perspective, in order to understand the organization and control of schools we must examine the contemporary issues which face the schools. A few of those issues will be noted here as a preface to more extensive treatment in subsequent chapters.

The first issue is what the tasks of the schools are. Should the schools emphasize intellectual, social, personal, or vocational objectives? Twenty-five years ago, a surprising amount of agreement was found among educators and lay citizens in their perceptions of the task of the school.[37] All groups considered intellectual tasks to be most important, but many individuals saw social, personal, or vocational goals as more important.

A recent survey indicated that 42 percent of American citizens believe the current school curriculum is sufficient to meet contemporary needs.[38] This reflects a slight shift from 1970 when 46 percent of citizens indicated satisfaction with the curriculum. Among the 1982 respondents who believed curriculum changes were needed, the most frequent suggestions were for more emphasis on "basics," more practical instruction, more vocational instruction, and higher academic standards.[39] Spurred by concern about the competitiveness of American economy and encouraged by well-publicized government and foundation reports,[40] citizens and educators directed attention to identifying those elements and standards essential to high-quality education.

---

37. Lawrence W. Downey, *The Task of Public Education* (Chicago: Midwest Administration Center, University of Chicago, 1960).
38. George H. Gallup, "The 14th Annual Gallop Poll of the Public's Attitudes Toward the Public Schools," *Phi Delta Kappan* 64 (September 1982): 41.
39. Ibid.
40. See for example, National Commission on Excellence in Education, *A Nation at Risk: The Imperative for Educational Reform* (Washington, D.C.: U.S. Government Printing Office, 1983), and Task Force on Education for Economic Growth, *Action for Excellence* (Denver: Education Commission of the States, 1983), and Ernest L. Boyer, *High School: A Report on Secondary Education in America* (New York: Harper & Row, 1983).

The current concern for quality in American education underscores the relationship between educational purposes and national social problems. It now appears that the United States' economy is on the threshold of a change that will parallel the industrial revolution in significance.[41] The shift from an economy based principally on manufacturing and hardware to one dominated by services and information development and dissemination has important implications for education. Economic competition with Japan and other countries that depends upon technological advances has led business and government leaders to call for school improvement. Other social developments such as changes in family structure, the growing number of Spanish-speaking, school-age children, and high rates of youth and minority unemployment also concern educational policymakers. In addition, questions of what constitutes equal educational opportunity in an increasingly heterogeneous society are especially complex.

Moreover, it is increasingly clear that education takes place in many settings outside the school. For example, the media now disseminate much information which was traditionally included within school curricula. The diffusion of educational activities and programs raises a number of questions. What priorities are to be established for the schools? How can agreements regarding these priorities be reached? In what ways should the purposes and programs of schools be related to the purposes and activities of the home, the church, and other community agencies? What alternatives should exist to schools as we presently know them? To what extent should school programs be adapted to local conditions and priorities, and to what extent should national purposes be served?

Actions to resolve the above questions necessarily involve local, state, and federal governments, and other official agencies. What then should be the relationship of local, state, and federal governments regarding school questions? The day of extreme localism is clearly at an end. On the other hand, few people would place actual operation of schools in the hands of federal agencies. During the past decade state involvement in education has become more critical particularly with regard to finance reform and the expansion of state-wide program mandates. Recent years have also made clear the intensifying tensions between different levels and branches of government. For example, local board of education members and state legislators sometimes blame each other for difficulties in financing schools or implementing state-mandated programs. Both local and state officials may resent the regulations which federal officials believe necessary to achieve compliance with federal laws.

Before us is the task of determining the most appropriate partnership of local, state, and federal governments for education. How can we achieve a balance between local, state, and national goals in education? How can state responsibility for education be harmonized with national interests and local priorities? To be sure, these questions about education are not unrelated to the provision for and control of other services in our society such as health, welfare, law enforcement, transportation, and communication. Again, the possibility of competition exists between education and these agencies at local, state, and federal levels.

A third issue is the financial support of schools. This issue has several aspects. The first of these pertains to the amount of the school tax bill. As noted earlier, the support of public and private education at elementary, secondary, and college levels requires approximately 6.5 percent of our gross national product (GNP) each year. If

41. See John Naisbitt, *Megatrends* (New York: Warner, 1982).

all adult education, publicly and privately supported, and all education programs of governmental departments and research grants of those departments to universities and other agencies are included, the total educational share of the GNP is appreciably increased. The question of what part of our resources should be used for education has always been complex and must be addressed at various governmental levels.

A second aspect of the finance issue has to do with the source of funds. Are local funds, largely dependent upon the property taxes, to be the primary source of revenue for schools? Or are state funds, chiefly dependent upon sales and income taxes, to be the main financial support for schools? Or might federal revenues, now about 61 percent of all taxes collected at all levels of government and largely dependent upon personal and corporate income taxes, become a major source of school support?

The 1970s has witnessed considerable controversy concerning present financing arrangements. Extensive litigation, citizen initiatives to repeal tax measures, and refusal to support taxes in public referenda have provided evidence of public dissatisfaction with current school funding arrangements. It remains to be seen if these arrangements can be modified in ways which make them both more effective and politically palatable. The Reagan administration reduced both federal taxes and spending for education. The administration asserted that the reduction in federal taxes enabled state and local officials to raise taxes for education if they wished to do so. They also said that the same cuts should increase the likelihood of private gifts to schools. A number of school districts established local education foundations to attract such contributions in the 1980s.

A third aspect of the finance issue is that of prudent allocation and effective use of funds. This concern, in combination with growing doubts about the effectiveness of schools and the credibility of school officials, gave rise to the accountability movement in the 1970s. For many years, most school systems experienced steady enrollment increases which provided a strong rationale for increases in school expenditures. This is no longer the case, and school officials find it increasingly difficult to convince the public to spend more for schools. Moreover, widespread publicity about dropouts and low achievers has made legislators as well as the general public more concerned about forcing schools to be accountable for particular results. This has led to more state mandates, greater emphasis upon legislative oversight, increased emphasis upon program and performance audits, and minimum competency requirements in many states. While educators may find some comfort in the fact that citizens are also challenging the credibility of and calling for greater accountability from other professionals and government employees, the issue is one which portends changes in the organization and control of schools.

The fourth and last issue we shall present here has to do with the roles of lay citizens and professional educators in determining school purposes and procedures. The concern for accountability has brought increased attention to this issue. The proliferation of citizen advisory committees indicates the possibility of new lay-professional relationships. However, the functioning of most such groups is largely perfunctory and often dissatisfying to both citizens and professionals. The underlying issue here is that of how to share control of an organization between constituents who pay for and benefit from it and professionals who are specially trained and pursue their careers in it.

This is not an easy problem to solve. In a complex, technological society there is always the question of how the specialist and the generalist can work together. Despite the insistence of some special interest groups, there seems to be no way that public policy can be turned over to the specialists—public health to the doctors or foreign affairs to the military, for instance. Yet the generalists, or the public at large, if they are to have a hand in determining public policy, must somehow come to possess much of the specialists' knowledge. There is a great need for generalists who can assess the significance of the knowledge of the specialists, who can convey their assessments to lay citizens, and who can secure a measure of agreement in terms of the commonweal. This need exists in the realm of school operation as truly as it does in other areas.

The brief presentation of these issues suggests the setting for this book. Basic questions of public policy regarding our schools are before us. These policies have to be determined within our organization structures and our control mechanisms. We need to see clearly what the structures and processes are by which basic educational decisions are now made. Neither structures nor processes may be adequate to the demands of the times. Therefore, in addition to analyzing what is, we will suggest what ought to be in light of current developments in the organization and control of American schools.

Plan for the Book

Beginning with the work of Mayo and Roethlisberger, the behavioral scientists have developed some useful concepts about organizations and much empirical work has been done to test these concepts. As a result the in-organization or interpersonal relationships of organizations have been described with considerable accuracy. We shall make use of some of that work when we speak of organization within the school and when we deal with the controls exercised by the organized profession. The major focus of this book, however, is not on internal organization.

Instead, we wish to focus on the out-organization relationships. In Parson's terms we shall deal less with the technical level of the school organization, more with the managerial level, and most of all with the institutional level. [42] In other words, we are less interested in how things are done in schools than we are in the processes through which policies or general directions are established for the schools. Our principal thesis is that the schools are open systems influenced by a broad range of forces, both governmental and nongovernmental, and that school policies are developed through interaction of these forces with school officials. Our purpose is to describe and explain these relationships. The discussion will view school organization and control chiefly in social, political, and economic terms. In short we are attempting to look at the school in its total environment.

In the chapters to follow, we will begin with a description of the formal structure at federal, state, and local levels. Next the internal and interstitial organization segments, such as board of education, administration, teachers, and students will be examined. The social matrix within which the school operates will then be analyzed. A picture of nonpublic and alternative schools as an influential part of the American school system will then be presented. Finally, we will summarize the many kinds of controls which affect American schools.

---

42. Talcott Parsons, "Some Ingredients of a General Theory of Formal Organization," in *Administrative Theory in Education,* ed. Andrew W. Halpin (Chicago: Midwest Administration Center, University of Chicago, 1958), ch. 3.

This book will be descriptive, analytical, and interpretative. Where research data are available, we will make use of them. Where research evidence appears skimpy, we shall resort to the best commonsense analyses we can muster. Our arguments will be made on the basis of the research evidence and our experience with the phenomena under study. We hope that this kind of treatment will increase the understanding of school administrators, school practitioners, students of school administration, and others interested in the nation's schools.

2

American Schools and the Federal Government

The federal Constitution adopted in 1788 contained no mention of public education or public schools. At least two circumstances may explain the absence of any such reference. In the first place, the Constitution created a federal government which was to have delegated to it only certain enumerated powers and those implied by such enumeration. As made clear in Amendment X, "the powers not delegated to the United States by the Constitution, nor prohibited by it to the States, are reserved to the States respectively, or to the people." The spirit of the time as well as the official language made for a carefully limited federal government.

A second condition of the Constitution should also be noted: the states had not yet established any genuine public school systems. Some beginning steps had been taken, but it was to be fifty to a hundred years before public schools were finally established in the several states. In 1789 schools were still very much in the private and parochial domain. Since provisions to place schools in the public domain were as yet either weak or nonexistent in state constitutions, there appeared to be little need to transfer such an incipient matter to the federal government.

While the federal Constitution did not address the subject of public schools in specific language, the federal government has always had a hand in public education. Beginning with the land grant acts, which actually antedated the federal Constitution, and continuing until the last session of Congress, certain provisions for public schools have been enacted. The general welfare clause of the federal Constitution, Article I, Section 8, authorizes Congress "to lay and collect Taxes, Duties, Imports and Excises, and to pay the Debts and provide for the common Defence and the general Welfare of the United States." This clause has been interpreted as giving Congress power to tax for broad social purposes. Moreover, this power has been upheld by the United States Supreme Court in *Helvering* v. *Davis,* which concerned the Social Security Act.[1]

While there seems to be no case on record involving the power of Congress to tax for public education, the language of other cases makes it clear that the national

1. *Helvering* v. *Davis,* 301 U.S. 619 (1937).

government may tax and spend in support of schools and school programs. Moreover, our history suggests that the national government may enter into agreements with the states for the mutual support of education and may exercise whatever controls are necessary to the accomplishment of the purposes for which federal funds are provided.

In this chapter we will describe the context within which the federal government has related to schools, note how federal relationships have evolved over our history, indicate the nature of the controls exercised by the federal government, and consider probable future developments in federal relationships.

From Dual to National Federalism

The relations of the federal government to state and local governments for any purpose cannot be understood without recognizing that over the years there has been a shift from dual to national federalism. We use the term *dual federalism* to mean the historical separation of powers between state and national governments. Power, as we shall show, has shifted more and more toward the national government; *national federalism* has come to prevail, despite some recent slowing of this trend.

Dual Governments

Early American government was a very limited one at both state and national levels. Government dealt with civil and political matters, and had little to do with social or economic problems. Jefferson spoke for his generation when he contended that less government was better government. The founding fathers intended to limit government at all levels and to leave much to the individual's discretion.

When the framers of the United States Constitution met in 1787 to revise the Articles of Confederation, with which they had become dissatisfied, they cast aside the old document and wrote a new one. Clearly they wanted to create a national government and not just a league of separate states. At the same time they wished to limit the powers of the national government, as Amendment X stipulates. Prior sections of the Constitution prescribed the powers of Congress, and these powers included the right to tax, to coin money, to establish post offices and post roads, to provide armed forces, to regulate commerce with other nations, and to declare war. There was also the famous provision that Congress could "provide for the . . . general welfare of the United States."

The Constitution did represent an attempt to separate the powers of government between the states and the nation. To be sure, there was disagreement from the beginning as to just what this attempted separation meant. Hamilton advocated a strong federal government, particularly a strong executive branch. Jefferson tended to emphasize states' rights more than federal responsibility. He was also disposed to place more faith in legislative than in executive action.[2] In terms of today's developments, however, both Hamilton and Jefferson might be seen as exponents of dual federalism.

The economic and political circumstances of the United States in its first decade or so of existence affected the design of American government. The economy was predominantly rural in nature. In the South, particularly, there were large landholders,

2. Leonard D. White, *The Federalists* (New York: The Macmillan Company, 1948), 512.

but the corporate form of business had not yet evolved. While war was seen as a possibility, and indeed became a reality in 1812, armed conflict on a worldwide scale was not imagined. The thought that the new nation would one day devote a major portion of its budget to defense would have seemed preposterous. In other words, dual federalism seemed quite adequate for a nation chiefly concerned with its own domestic problems, the expression of which tended to be somewhat unique to each of the states. Logical as the separation of power between the state and the national governments appeared to our founding fathers, Grodzins has contended that there never was a genuine separation.[3] Instead of comparing federalism to a layer cake— one layer representing local government, the second layer state government, and the third layer national government—Grodzins has used the model of a marble cake. Each function, he contends, is mixed in the American federal system. Each level of government is seen as interacting with and influencing each other level of government. In fact, Grodzins maintains that federalism is a plan for sharing the functions of government and not a plan for separating them.

In terms of the actual operation of government, he may be correct. His description of shared functions may be even more accurate for today's government than for government of almost two centuries ago. Even so, the original concept of federalism did attempt to delegate to a national government certain necessary but limited functions and to reserve for the states or for the people the remaining functions. This concept, never one upon which there was complete agreement and one still invoked by some politicians, has been subject to many changes as we shall now see.

National Federalism

A number of circumstances contributed to the demise of dual federalism and to the development of national federalism. Many of these circumstances were social and economic in character. The rural economy of the early nineteenth century gave way to industrialization and urbanization. These developments were national in scope. Communication and transportation increased greatly in volume and efficiency. A great depression and two world wars required action that only the national government was in a position to take. In growing numbers, people were beginning to think of the nation as a single political entity.

Governmental provisions reflected these changes in social and economic circumstances. The Civil War was fought to preserve the Union. Following the Civil War, the Fourteenth Amendment was added to the U.S. Constitution. This amendment made citizens of the states also citizens of the United States and forbade the states from depriving "any person of life, liberty, or property without due process of law." By the time the U.S. Supreme Court upheld the social security legislation of the 1930s, the superior position of the national government on social as well as civil matters was well established.[4]

Grodzins does not decry this shift from dual to national federalism; he suggests that the national government, instead of doing too much, is actually doing too little.[5] He points out that national deficiencies in education, health, housing, urban development, air pollution, water supply, and mass transportation require additional, not less,

3. Morton Grodzins, "The Federal System," in *Goals for Americans,* Report of the President's Commission on National Goals (Englewood Cliffs, N.J.: Prentice-Hall, 1960), ch. 12.
4. *Helvering* v. *Davis,* 301 U.S. 619 (1937); also *Stewart Machine Co.* v. *Davis,* 301 U.S. 548 (1936).
5. Grodzins, "The Federal System," 282.

attention on the part of the national government. Most of these problems extend beyond the boundaries of local government and in many cases beyond the boundaries of state government. The extent of the problems, coupled with the fact that most of the tax resources accrue to the federal government, makes it apparent that even with some revenue sharing, national action is required.

Import for Education

The shift from dual to national federalism has had great import for education. Historically education was interwoven with the concept of dual federalism, or separation of powers. Education was seen as one of those matters left to the states. To be sure, the national government never ignored schools and colleges completely, but for the most part, the state legislatures exercised plenary power over education, particularly the public elementary and secondary schools. The desire to retain this state of affairs has been expressed strongly by many. As late as 1962 the American Association of School Administrators contended:

> The Executive Committee of AASA reaffirms its belief in the principle long held in the United States that education is a state function, and that the principle works exceedingly well when the responsibility of the state is delegated in large measure to local boards of education who operate with close sensitivity to the needs of developing young people and adults in a given community. Although the record is never perfect, and not even good in some instances, the Executive Committee holds to the concept that on the whole the educational needs of the local community, the state, and, indeed, the nation can best be served when the control of education rests at the state and local levels rather than at the national level.[6]

In recent years, AASA has been less explicit about local control. For instance, their 1978 and 1983 resolutions emphasized the "urgent need to increase the level of federal financial support of public education" through general aid, revenue sharing, and categorical aid. The establishment of a partnership with local, state, and federal governments, each providing financial support was also urged.[7]

In spite of the current preoccupation with reappraisal of the federal role in education, national involvement continues. Some of those who resist the growth of national government have devised another argument which is often employed in connection with attempts to secure federal aid for schools. They attack the federal government's reputed wasting of money. The claim is sometimes made that five dollars are sent to Washington for every dollar's worth of service received from the federal government. Wealthy states, to be sure, never receive from Washington services equivalent to the taxes collected by the federal government from those states. Poor states, on the other hand, tend to receive services in excess of federal taxes collected within their borders.

These circumstances provide those who would keep all taxes low with an excellent opportunity to lament the takeover by the national government and to decry the waste of the bureaucrats in Washington. Actually, the national government, more than local and state governments, can collect taxes where the resources are and can provide services where they are needed. Thus, if schools or any other service for the

6. *The School Administrator* 20 (November 1962): 3.
7. Report of the Resolutions Committee of AASA, February 1978 and February 1983.

entire nation are to be brought up to a minimum standard, some action on the part of the federal government is necessary. Moreover, federal tax collection costs are much lower than state and local tax collection costs.

The issue of general versus categorical aid also figures in the growth of national federalism. If educational policy is seen as the major province of the states, the argument for federal grants of money without stipulation as to purpose seems to make sense. But if educational policy is also seen as the province of the national government, it is clear that categorical aid, not general aid, should be provided by the federal government.

Attempts to secure general aid began in 1870 and have continued with little success in intervening years.[8] On the other hand, Congress has a long record of providing categorical aid to the schools and colleges of the various states. The legislative record provides concrete evidence of the growth of national federalism. The Morrill Act of 1862, the Smith-Hughes Act of 1917, Public Laws 815 and 874 (designed to assist federally impacted areas), the National Defense Education Act of 1958, the Elementary and Secondary Act of 1965, and other actions of the Congress all reflect a desire on the part of the national government to assist education—but to assist it in particular ways. While categories may be revised or consolidated, reversal of this policy seems unlikely.

This shift from dual to national federalism is unrecognized in some quarters, causes concern in others and strong resistance in others. The nature and magnitude of the social, economic, political, and technological problems facing the nation have made this shift inevitable. Education has some relationship to all these problems and thus is caught up in the increasing scope of government at the national level.

Early Federal Relations

Land Grants

Early federal legislation pertaining to education had to do chiefly with land grants and the establishment of land grant colleges. In the Ordinance of 1785 Congress declared that in the land of the Northwest Territory, later to become the states of Indiana, Illinois, Michigan, Ohio, Wisconsin, and part of Minnesota, "there shall be reserved the lot No. 16 of every township, for the maintenance of public schools, within said township."

The Ordinance of 1787 dealt with the sale of one and one-half million acres of land to the Ohio Company and might properly be described as a governmental and not a land act. Nevertheless, one clause of the Ordinance was destined to have a salutary effect on education. That clause reads, "Religion, morality and knowledge, being necessary to good government and happiness of mankind, schools and the means of education shall forever be encouraged."

With the admission of California to the Union in 1850, sections sixteen and thirty-six were set aside for school purposes. Fourteen states entered the Union under this provision of two sections of each township being reserved for school purposes. In Utah, Arizona, and New Mexico, where land was cheap, four sections of each township were so reserved. Thus, with the thirteen states which came into statehood

8. Frank J. Munger and Richard F. Fenno, Jr., *National Politics and Federal Aid to Education* (Syracuse, N.Y.: Syracuse University Press, 1962).

under the Ordinance of 1785, a total of thirty states received grants of this kind, and some 80 million acres of land were granted.

The Michigan legislature in 1850 petitioned Congress for a grant of public land to establish a college of agriculture. Illinois made a similar request in 1853, and Michigan renewed its request in 1857. Senator Justin Morrill of Vermont introduced a bill in 1857 which granted 20,000 acres of land to each state for each senator and representative in Congress for the purpose of establishing colleges of agriculture. Congress approved the bill, but it was vetoed by President Buchanan. In 1862, however, the Morrill Act passed, and the grant increased to 30,000 acres for each senator and representative. The act provided for the

> endowment, support, and maintenance of at least one college where the leading object shall be, without excluding other scientific and classical studies, and including military tactics, to teach such branches of learning as are related to agriculture and the mechanic arts—in order to promote the liberal and practical education of the industrial classes in the several pursuits and professions of life.

Other legislation pertaining to the land grant colleges included the Hatch Act of 1887, which established the experiment stations; the so-called second Morrill Act of 1890; the Nelson Amendment of 1907, which allowed the training of teachers; and the Bankhead-Jones Act in 1935, which extended some of these functions.

Vocational Education

In 1917, influenced to some extent by World War I, Congress passed the Smith-Hughes Act for the support of vocational education. In its own language, the act was

> for the purpose of cooperating with the states in paying the salaries of teachers, supervisors, and directors of agricultural subjects, and of teachers of trade and industrial subjects, and in the preparation of teachers of agricultural, trade, and industrial, and home economics subjects—and for the purpose of making studies, investigations, and reports to aid in the organization and conduct of vocational education.

The act originally required that the states and the local school districts match federal funds. Public interest in vocational education grew until many high schools in practically every state had vocational agriculture and vocational home economics as established parts of the high school curriculum. A number of trade or vocational high schools were established in large cities, and trade and industry programs were also established in some comprehensive high schools. The initial legislation was later extended by the George-Reed Act of 1929, the George-Ellzey Act of 1934, the George-Deen Act of 1937, and the George-Barden Act of 1946.

Depression Legislation

Spurred by the depression of the 1930s, the national government enacted a great many relief measures, and many of these measures affected school operation. The Civil Works Administration (CWA) and later the Public Works Administration (PWA), for instance, set up grants and loans and in some instances supplied materials to help with the construction, alteration, and repair of school buildings. The two relief measures which seemed to have most influence on school programs were probably the Civilian Conservation Corps (CCC) and the National Youth Administration (NYA).

The CCC was created by an act of Congress in 1933. The act was designed chiefly to relieve unemployment through "the restoration of the country's depleted natural resources and the advancement of an orderly program of useful public works." Young men between the ages of 17 and 22 years, most of them in the larger cities, were sent to camps in remote areas of the country where they made trails, planted trees, built bridges, and performed many other useful tasks. For this service, the men were housed, fed, provided with medical care, and paid a small wage.

Learning opportunities existed in the program from the start, but in 1937 Congress stipulated that "at least ten hours per week may be devoted to general educational and vocational training." In time each camp was provided with an educational adviser appointed by the United States Office of Education. These advisers recruited a staff of part-time teachers from among the personnel of the camp and they also often enlisted the help of teachers in nearby high schools and colleges. More than 3 million young men were enrolled in the CCC program and 2.7 million participated in some kind of organized educational activity during its ten-year history.

The NYA was established by executive order of the president in 1935 and received congressional appropriations until its liquidation in 1944. The purpose of NYA was to provide full-time employment for youths 16 to 24 years of age who were in high school and college. While most of the young people in the program lived at home, a number of states did establish NYA resident centers. In many instances, young people performed useful services in the construction of public buildings, in the performance of clerical tasks, in augmenting services performed by public libraries and museums, in assisting with research projects, and in other ways.

For most of its history, NYA was an independent federal agency and had its own federal, state, and local administrative organization. In 1939 NYA, along with CCC, was placed in the Federal Security Agency, and in 1940 part of its budget was channeled through the United States Office of Education. The out-of-school work program reached a peak employment of about 470,000 youths in February 1941. The maximum employment under the student work program was 482,000 in April 1940. Peak appropriations for the program were for the 1940–41 fiscal year and amounted to $157,159,000.[9]

Other Federal Programs

Federal relationships are too numerous to be described in full here, but a few additional federal activities in education will be noted. For example, the federal government has a long history of providing schools in areas under special jurisdiction. Since 1804 Congress has provided for the schools in Washington, D.C. The Bureau of Indian Affairs since 1824 has been charged with providing schools for Indians and Eskimos. The schools of the territories have often been administered by federally appointed officials. The federal government has also established and operated schools on reservations where it maintains "forts, magazines, arsenals, dockyards, and other needful buildings." The creation of defense bases around the world has also created a sizable school system under the various military jurisdictions.[10]

9. Hollis P. Allen, *The Federal Government and Education* (New York: McGraw Hill Book Company, 1950), 94–97.
10. See "List of Accredited Schools by States and Overseas," *North Central Association Quarterly* 57 (Fall 1982): 298–305.

Another example of federal activity in education is found in the provisions made for federally impacted areas. Beginning with the Lanham Act in 1941, Congress appropriated money to aid local government in the construction and operation of schools and other facilities where war-incurred federal activities had created burdens on local government. Many of these provisions were continued with the enactment of Public Laws 815 and 874 in 1950 and with their extensions since that time.

The United States Office of Education

Federal programs for education have been organized in many ways, some under a separate agency, some under other agencies of government such as the Department of the Army or the Navy, and some under the United States Office of Education. The United States Office of Education, first known as the Department of Education, was created by act of Congress in 1867. An early report of the Commissioner states the department's purpose as follows:

> to collect such statistics and facts as shall show the condition and progress of education in the several States and Territories, [and] to diffuse such information respecting the organization and management of schools and school systems, and methods of teaching, as shall aid the people of the United States in the establishment and maintenance of efficient school systems, and otherwise promote the cause of education throughout the country.

For many years, the U.S. Office of Education was in the Department of the Interior. In 1939 the office was transferred to the Federal Security Agency and in 1953 to the Department of Health, Education, and Welfare. The office was headed by a commissioner of education, appointed by the president. Over most of its history, the office exercised a very modest role in American education. In recent years, as will be shown later, the education agency has become the Department of Education and its functions somewhat modified. In no sense, however, has or is the agency a national ministry of education as that term is understood in many other countries.

Nature of Early Federal Activities

This historical background of federal relations with education might be summarized by brief reference to the findings of two studies completed about 1950. Allen, as a member of the Hoover task force on the reorganization of the federal government, had a unique opportunity to examine the character and extent of federal programs in education. His report suggested that at least twenty federal agencies were engaged in bona fide educational programs, that the annual expeditures for these programs amounted to over $3 billion, and that only 1 percent of that amount was channeled through the United States Office of Education.[11]

In 1951 Quattlebaum prepared a report for the Congress in which federal activities in education were carefully assessed.[12] His summary of federal allocations for fiscal year 1950 totaled $3.6 billion. Of this amount, 81 percent was for expenditures

---

11. Allen, *Federal Government and Education.*
12. Charles A. Quattlebaum, *Federal Educational Activities and Educational Issues Before Congress,* 3 vols. (Washington, D.C.: Government Printing Office, 1951).

through the Veteran's Administration. Nineteen other departments or agencies of the federal government were also shown to have funds allocated for education.

Data from both Allen and Quattlebaum permit us to draw a number of conclusions regarding federal activities in education as of 1950. One, these activities were extensive and widespread. Two, the money appropriated for such activities was appreciable. Three, the U.S. Office of Education had meager influence and even less control over this vast program. Four, there was apparently little, if any, coordination of the programs of the several federal agencies.

Rapid Expansion of Federal Influence

While federal participation and influence in education has been with us since the founding of the nation, the twenty-year period from 1950 to 1970 is particularly noteworthy as a time of rapid growth of federal involvement. The federal courts may have done as much as Congress to create a national policy for education. Their role is discussed in chapter 7. We shall now examine some of the major programs established during that period and give some attention to the federal structure created to administer those programs.

The GI Bills

Congressional authorization of educational benefits for veterans has come chiefly through the Vocational Rehabilitation Act of 1943 (Public Law 16), the Servicemen's Readjustment Act of 1944 (Public Law 346), and subsequent legislation made to apply to veterans of the Korean and Vietnam conflicts.

Under Public Law 16, the Veterans' Administration emphasized the need of vocational advisory service to the disabled veteran. This service was given by the regional offices of the Veterans' Administration and also by more than 300 educational institutions under contract with the Veterans' Administration. The policy was also adopted that, if possible, the veteran would be trained in his own community and in existing accredited schools and colleges. By July 1, 1959, 675,000 disabled veterans had taken vocational rehabilitation training.[13]

Under the provisions of Public Law 346, practically all veterans were eligible for educational benefits. The veteran was free to elect a course of study, to enter any approved school or college, and to pursue that course for one year plus the number of months he or she was in service (not in excess of 48 months).

The federal government made payments directly to the veteran and also to the school or college the veteran attended. In 1955 the 82nd Congress in Public Law 550 simplified the method of payments and required that the veteran be responsible for payments to the educational institution. Increased benefits for Vietnam veterans were provided by the passage of PL 92–540 in 1972. Educational assistance for single veterans enrolled in a full-time program was set at $220 per month. Additional allowances were provided for veterans with dependents.

Altogether the IOUs represented by all of the GI bills have been collected by some 27.5 million men and women. Counting all forms of educational benefits—college, secondary, and on-the-job training—about 48 percent of the World War II vet-

---

13. Charles A. Quattlebaum, *Federal Educational Policies, Programs and Proposals*, Part 2 (Washington, D.C.: Government Printing Office, 1960), 221.

erans claimed benefits, about 42 percent of the Korean veterans claimed benefits, and responses from Vietnam veterans indicate that the percentage claiming benefits may well go beyond that of World War II.[14] By 1956 the education of veterans had cost the federal government $14.5 billion.[15] By now, the total cost is more than double that amount.

The full impact of veteran enrollment and federal money on school and college programs cannot be assessed here, but certain facts are noteworthy. The federal government did assume responsibility for interrupting the school or college careers of the young people who served in the war. Approved existing schools and colleges were utilized and subsidized by the federal government. Public and private schools and colleges alike were approved for the veteran programs and hence for federal subsidy. In effect veteran benefits established a far-flung system of federal scholarships at the college and graduate school level. These scholarships tended to go to the academically talented.

The National Science Foundation

The establishment of a National Science Foundation in 1950 was essentially an outgrowth of American experience in World War II; the scientific resources of the nation had been mobilized by the federal government. The foundation was created "to promote the progress of science; to advance the national health, prosperity, and welfare; to secure the national defense; and for other purposes." As such, the act was a response to meet a need described in terms of the national welfare.

Among the eight functions the foundation was authorized and directed to perform, those pertaining to education are listed as follows:

1. to develop and encourage the pursuit of a national policy for the promotion of basic research and education in sciences;
2. to initiate and support basic and scientific research in the mathematical, physical, medical, biological, engineering, and other sciences; . . .
4. to award . . . scholarship and graduate fellowships in the mathematical, physical, medical, biological, engineering, and other sciences; . . .

While functions (2) and (4) in the list have specific educational import, it is clear that the broad wording in (1) provides considerable latitude for interpretation. The several kinds of educational programs initiated by the foundation in the past years can be justified on the basis of the discretionary powers granted therein. In 1959 it was expressly the existence of these programs that resulted in the amendment of function (2) to include support for "programs to strengthen scientific research potential . . . by making contracts and other arrangements . . . to support such scientific activities."[16] These changes were viewed by the sponsoring legislators as making "explicit the Foundation's authority to support programs designed to stimulate improved scientific teaching and to encourage the undertaking of careers in science."[17]

14. Story Moorefield, "The Remarkable GI Bill," *American Education* 10 (August–September 1974): 25.
15. "World War II G.I. Bill Expires," *Higher Education* 13 (September 1956).
16. "An Act to Amend the National Science Foundation Act of 1950," *U.S. Statutes at Large* (Washington, D.C., 1959), LXXIII, 467.
17. "Amendments to NSF Act—HR 8282, Sectional Analysis of Bill," *U.S. Code Congressional Service* (86th Congress, 1st Session, 1959), II, 2245.

Control of the organization was vested in a National Science Board consisting of twenty-four members and the director. Only the board could make policy decisions, and it had to approve all contracts and grants pursuant to the statutory functions of the foundation. Thus, the National Science Foundation, in keeping with the dominant thinking of the Congress, was established as a quasi-independent agency in the executive branch of the government.

The Cooperative Research Program

In 1954 the 83rd Congress passed Public Law 531 establishing the cooperative research program. The U.S. Commissioner of Education was authorized to enter into contracts with universities, colleges, and state education agencies for the conduct of research, surveys, and demonstrations in the field of education. There was the further stipulation, however, that these contracts could not be made until the Commissioner had obtained the advice of educational research specialists on the merit of the proposals. No money was appropriated for this program until 1956–57.

The Cooperative Research Program was begun in fiscal 1957 with an appropriation of $1 million. By fiscal 1965 the appropriation had reached $16 million. In that year the program was incorporated in Title IV as part of the Elementary and Secondary Education Act. Research support was broadened to include research and development centers, regional laboratories, and the training of researchers, as well as project support. Estimated expenditures for successors to these programs for fiscal 1979, though hard to isolate in the 1979 budget, totaled about $300 million.[18]

A few observations about the cooperative research program are appropriate. First, the program was lodged in the U.S. Office of Education and not established as an independent agency as was the National Science Foundation. Second, the money, while relatively small in amount as compared to other federally supported research programs, has given great impetus to educational research. Scholars in many basic disciplines, particularly the social sciences, as well as those in education have turned their attention to research problems in education. Third, the project approval procedure and more recently the approval of research and development centers and regional laboratories have inevitably influenced the nature and course of educational research.

The National Defense Education Act

The National Defense Education Act, Public Law 85–864, provided for loans to college students, fellowships for graduate study, centers for research and study of foreign languages, experimentation with television and related media, and improvement of statistical services in state departments of education.

In many ways NDEA served as a precursor for subsequent legislation. For instance, the student loan program, Title II, was enlarged to include many more students largely on the basis of need; and curriculum improvement, Title III, originally limited to science, mathematics, and foreign languages, was broadened to include many other school subjects. Several titles in NDEA have also been incorporated into more recent legislation. Area vocational education, Title VIII, became part of the Vocational Education Act of 1963. Help for statistical services for states, Title X, was

18. *Special Analyses, Budget of the US, FY 1979* (Washington, D.C.: Government Printing Office, 1978), 220.

merged with the Elementary and Secondary Education Act of 1965. Institutes for teachers and other school personnel, Title XI, was incorporated into the broadened Educational Professions Development Act of 1967. NDEA contributed to local-state-national partnership in education and also set a precedent for assisting nonpublic as well as public schools. In a decade total appropriations for NDEA were about $3 billion.

Vocational Education

The Vocational Education Act of 1963 represented a new emphasis for the federal government in the area of vocational training. The purpose of the legislation, as stated in Section 1 of the act, follows:

> It is the purpose of this part to authorize Federal grants to States to assist them to maintain, extend, and improve existing programs of vocational education, to develop new programs of vocational education, and to provide part-time employment for youths who need the earnings from such employment to continue their vocational training on a full-time basis, so that persons of all ages in all communities of the State—those in high school, those who have completed or discontinued their formal education and are preparing to enter the labor market, those who have already entered the labor market but need to upgrade their skills or learn new ones, and those with special educational handicaps—will have ready access to vocational training or retraining which is of high quality, which is realistic in the light of actual or anticipated opportunities for gainful employment, and which is suited to their needs, interests, and ability to benefit from such training.

Whereas appropriations to the states for vocational education under the Smith-Hughes and George-Barden acts had been about $52 million per year, the new legislation provided $60 million for fiscal 1964, and $225 million for fiscal 1967 and each year thereafter. These provisions take on added significance when they are viewed in connection with the Area Redevelopment and the Manpower Training Acts, both of which authorized vocational training programs for the unemployed and for the underemployed.

The Vocational Education Act of 1963 and its subsequent revisions not only provided additional financial support but represented an attempt to broaden and redefine the area of vocational and technical education. Each state was required to submit a plan to the United States Commissioner of Education.

The Elementary and Secondary Education Act of 1965

The most sweeping extension of federal involvement in education was provided in the Elementary and Secondary Education Act of 1965. Bailey and Mosher have contended that the act "mandated a series of programs and priorities which involved a massive shift in the locus of policy-making power in American education.[19] The law directed federal attention to local educational agencies for the education of children of low-income families (Title I). It provided a continued federal "impact on poverty" and allocated $1.06 billion for the first year toward a program of assistance. The act also provided for a five-year expenditure of about $100 million for school library resources,

---

19. Stephen K. Bailey and Edith K. Mosher. *ESEA—The Office of Education Administers a Law* (Syracuse, N.Y.: Syracuse University Press, 1968), 3.

textbooks, and other instructional materials (Title II). ESEA called for the establishment of supplementary educational centers and services of a wide variety—academic enrichment, guidance, counseling, health services, and remedial instruction (Title III). Title IV subsumed PL 83–531 and called for the extension of cooperative research programs sponsored by universities and state departments of education; it also authorized research and development centers and regional educational laboratories. ESEA Title V was designed to strengthen state departments of education by improving planning, research, and personnel.

After a few years of operation, Berke and Kirst had this to say of ESEA:

> It is true that the pupil achievement results on Title I are at best unknown and at worst very discouraging. But to evaluate whether a program that reaches nine million children "works" on the single dimension of achievement test scores is to ignore the multitude of other political objectives embeded in Title I. Title I's defenders point to such positive outcomes as the fiscal equalization impact of Title I funds and the concern it has generated among educators all over the nation for the previously neglected disadvantaged child. Others have contended Title I funds were intended to be "a sugar solvent" to help ease acceptance by the South of black children rather than forsake the federal financial windfall. In effect, Title I held out so many different aspirations to so many different constituencies that inevitably several of these aspirations were never met. Perhaps multiple objectives in large-scale federal programs is a formula for insuring that no single objective will be substantially accomplished.[20]

Other Federal Programs

A number of other federal programs which affect elementary and secondary schools have been enacted by Congress. These include the Manpower Development & Training Act of 1962, the Economic Opportunity Act of 1964, the Civil Rights Act of 1964, the Higher Education Act of 1965, and the Education Professions Development Act of 1967. For the most part, these acts are directed toward institutions other than the schools and in some instances have purposes other than education. Even so, implementation of these programs has required considerable effort on the part of school agencies at all levels of government.

Vacillation During the 1970s

The rapid increase in number of federal programs for education began to slow down about 1970. The 1970s became a time of vacillation and even retrenchment on one hand and a time for even more extended federal intrusion on the other. We shall now examine some aspects of this seeming paradox.

Reappraisal of Programs

During the 1950s and the 1960s there seemed to be no deficiency in American life that could not be corrected by education, particularly by federal intervention in education. As might be expected, the time came when questions about the effectiveness of these programs were raised. One of the first of these inquiries was authorized by the Civil Rights Act of 1964, which charged the commissioner of education to conduct

---

20. Joel S. Berke and Michael W. Kirst, *Federal Aid to Education—Who Benefits, Who Governs?* (Lexington, Mass.: D. C. Heath, 1972), 392.

a survey "concerning the lack of availability of equal educational opportunities for individuals by reason of race, color, religion, or national origin." It seemed appropriate, ten years after the Brown decision had ordered an end to desegregated schools, to find out what had been accomplished.

The survey became a monumental task. Under the general direction of James S. Coleman, scores of scholars in and out of the U.S. Office of Education were engaged in the effort. The major report was over 700 pages in length and there was a supplement almost as long.[21] In brief, the great majority of American children were found to attend segregated schools. Moreover, schools serving primarily blacks and other minorities were generally inferior, as measured by accreditation, class size, and teacher background, to schools attended by whites. With the exception of some oriental Americans, achievement of minority pupils was distinctly below that of whites. However, when characteristics of schools were related to pupil achievement, with the socioeconomic background of students held constant, a small fraction of the differences in pupil achievement appeared to be related to school characteristics. This has been the subject of much controversy and other scholars, employing different methods of analyses, have found school factors somewhat more important.[22]

The Coleman report was an early attempt to marshall the resources of the social scientists to determine the outcomes of a policy enactment. The highest federal court and the Congress had taken policy positions in the area of school desegregation. The politicians were now turning to the scholars and asking what difference desegregation had made. The scholars, in turn, at least in measurable outcomes, suggested that the power of schooling was less than had been popularly supposed.

Another study on the effects of schooling was done by Christopher Jencks and his colleagues at the Harvard Center for Educational Policy Research.[23] In large part, three years of work by Jencks and others was devoted to a careful examination of other studies and frequently a reanalysis of the data generated by those studies. As part of this examination Jencks called attention to the Piccariello study which suggested that in terms of cognitive skills students in Title I programs, to which substantial federal money had been channeled, did not do appreciably better than similar students not in such programs.[24] Also noted in the Jencks report was the Westinghouse study of Head Start graduates.[25] This study concluded that neither year-round nor summer Head Start programs had significant long-term effects on cognitive growth.

The Jencks report and many of the individual studies cited in the report became controversial.[26] Our purpose here is not to continue the argument. Rather, we shall note some of their consequences. The studies, regardless of the limitations surround-

21. James S. Coleman et al., U.S. Department of HEW, Office of Education, *Equality of Educational Opportunity* (Washington, D.C.: U.S. Government Printing Office, 1966).
22. See Samuel Bowles and Henry M. Levin. "The Determinants of Scholastic Achievement—An Appraisal of Some Recent Evidence," *Journal of Human Resources* 3 (Winter 1968): 3–24.
23. Christopher Jencks et al., *Inequality: A Reassessment of the Effect of Family and Schooling in America* (New York: Basic, 1972).
24. See Harry Piccariello, "Evaluation of Title I," Mimeographed (Washington, D.C.: U.S. Office of Education, 1969).
25. Westinghouse Learning Corporation, Ohio University, *The Impact of Head Start* (Springfield, Virginia: Clearing House for Federal Scientific and Technical Information, U.S. Department of Commerce, June 12, 1969).
26. For instance, see David E. Wiley and Annegret Harnischfeger, "Explosion of a Myth: Quantity of Schooling and Exposure to Instruction, Major Educational Vehicles," *Educational Researcher* 3 (April 1974): 7–12.

ing them, cast doubt upon the capacity of the schools to make a difference. Some have noted that the objectives of federal programs, expressed in political terms by politicians, who were often joined by educators, represented overclaiming from the beginning. Others have pointed out that the results of the studies may be suspect because of limitations in methods of measurement and the great difficulty of doing research with human subjects. But policymakers at the federal level and the general public were nevertheless disappointed with the results of these studies. The contrast between two decades of oversell and a decade of measurable results was just too great. Faith in the schools gave way to doubt.

The President and the Congress

The nature of the real and potential conflicts between the president and Congress was clearly revealed in the Nixon administration. The position of the Nixon administration with regard to federal support of elementary and secondary schools was epitomized in the Better Schools Act of 1973. Since earlier attempts at revenue sharing contained no specific provisions for education, the Better Schools Act was seen as a special form of revenue sharing for the schools. In some ways "revenue sharing" was simply new rhetoric for federal aid, but the act did make explicit the position of the administration on certain matters. For instance, the act proposed to consolidate federal assistance to schools into 30 programs. Before the act the U.S. Office of Education had been administering some 100 categorical programs affecting the schools. The broad national purposes to be served by the consolidated program included the following: aid for the disadvantaged, aid for the handicapped, vocational education, assistance for schools in federally affected areas, and supporting services.

The Better Schools Act did not receive approval in the Congress for a number of reasons. Consolidation of grants obviously meant that some specific forms of federal aid would no longer be sustained. Also, there seemed to be some uncertainty as to how much control the governors of the states might exercise over the money to be allocated to the states. Moreover, there was an initial attempt to sell the formula to the Congress without specifying dollar amounts for the program.

National Assessment

Another movement begun in the 1960s, the National Assessment of Educational Progress (NAEP), has been continued. National Assessment was encouraged in 1963 by Francis Keppel, then U.S. commissioner of education. The first chairman of the exploratory program was Ralph W. Tyler, then director of the Center for Advanced Study in the Behavioral Sciences at Stanford, California. The early funding for national assessment came from the Carnegie Corporation of New York. Funds also were received from the Ford Foundation's Fund for the Advancement of Education. Major funds for national assessment were later provided by grants to the Education Commission of the States from the U.S. Office of Education. Federal funding in the early 1970s shifted from OE to the National Institute of Education. To implement such a program appropriate achievement tests had to be developed and a testing schedule established. Initially, it was planned that over a three-year cycle about 140,000 persons would take sections of the tests. The procedures used did not make it possible to compare individuals, schools, and school systems. Groups to be tested in the assessment program were classed by region (Northeast, South, Midwest, and Far West), age level (9, 13, 17, and 30), community type (rural, urban fringe, medium-sized city, and large city), race, and economic level. Students in public, private, and parochial schools, and persons no longer in school were to be tested. The areas to be assessed were reading, writing, science, mathematics, social studies, citizenship, music, literature, vocational education, and art. Assessment techniques were to include paper-and-pencil tests, interviews, and observations.

The projected program has been implemented: tests have been formulated and administered, the results analyzed, and reports made to the public. On reading tests, for instance, it was found that pupils in the Northeast did better than pupils elsewhere, that girls did better than boys, that whites did better than blacks, that suburban pupils did better than inner city pupils, and that pupils with educated parents did better than those without. With results such as these in hand, policymakers could ask why something was so and what could be done about it. Assessment was becoming the basis for policy decisions. Indeed, assessment data have been widely quoted in *A Nation At Risk* and other recent national reports of education.[27] It should be noted that in 1983 the contract for the administration of NAEP was shifted from the Educational Commission of the States to the Educational Testing Service.

Reorganization of the Federal Agency

What should be the purpose of the U.S. Office of Education had long been debated.[28] With the Keppel interest in reform the mission and effectiveness of the office became the subject of even more controversy. Developments requiring that the office support and monitor programs in research and development as well as in the operation of schools and colleges contributed to the complexity of the issue. One suggested course of action, growing quite logically out of the development of regional laboratories and research and development centers, was that an institute, or institutes, of education be established. Such an institute, it was thought, might be given the research and development functions, and the distribution of aid to operational programs might be left to the Office of Education. This reorganization of education at the federal level received the support of the president and Congress, and the Institute of Education was established in 1972. At the same time a new Division of Education was to be created in the Department of HEW. The Office and the Institute were to be "separate, coequal" units in this new division. The reorganization was apparently facilitated by making the commissioner of education, chief executive officer of USOE, the assistant secretary for the new division in HEW.

This reorganization was typical of the period under consideration. The institute moved ahead on the basis of its new authority. After some delay the president nominated, as provided by law, the members of the National Council on Educational Research which was to be the general policy body of the new institute. After still more delay council members were approved by the Congress. In the meantime most of the research and development programs had been transferred from the office to the institute and the institute found it necessary to move ahead with many of these activities. Under these circumstances the institute became operational even before its policies had been approved by the new council.

27. National Commission on Excellence in Education, *A Nation at Risk* (Washington, D.C.: U.S. Department of Education, 1983).
28. For instance, see Donald R. Warren, *To Enforce Education* (Detroit, Mich.: Wayne State University Press, 1974).

To go forward with its several functions the institute established a rather complex organization. Several offices, each with an assistant director and staff, were created for each of the following functions: research grants, exploratory studies, development, resources, administration, planning and management, external relations, human rights, and public information. For fiscal 1973 institute plans were based on a $110 million budget and a personnel allocation of about 350 persons. The president requested an appropriation of $162 million for fiscal 1974.

But the institute ran into hard times with Congress. The House shaved the $162 million request to $142 million and the senate shaved it further to $75 million. Apparently, relationships between NIE and the Congress had not been friendly; many congressmen saw NIE as an administration program and not a creature of their own making. A few senators were critical of the turnback of $3.5 million in fiscal 1973 funds.

In the late 1970s a more significant reorganization of the federal structure in education was considered. President Carter, strongly supported by the National Education Association and some other groups in education, proposed that a cabinet-level department of education be established. Such a department, he said, would be designed to consolidate education functions found in other departments of government. For example, the programs found in USOE and NIE, then located in Health, Education, and Welfare, would be transferred to the new department. Proponents of the reorganization plan contended that educational concerns became lost among other concerns of HEW such as welfare reform, social security. and national health insurance. Supporters believed that the new department would give education first-class status and the full-time attention of cabinet level policymakers. Rufus Miles made a strong case for the new department.[29] However, not all students of the problem were convinced that a new department would make much difference. Gerald Sroufe, for instance, maintained that members of the president's cabinet have little to do with policymaking.[30]

These considerations aside, a Department of Education was approved by the Congress and the president in 1979. The proposal passed the House by only four votes but was approved in the Senate by a vote of 72 to 21. The reorganization bill was signed by the president and became effective early in 1980. By July of that year, the first Secretary of Education, Shirley Hufstedler, was appointed. Since Hufstedler was a California jurist and largely unknown to the education world, the appointment came as something of a shock to some educators. Even so, many education groups, including the National Education Association and the American Association of School Administrators, saw merit in the appointment and voiced their support for the new secretary.

Initially, the new department was to be responsible for 152 programs in education, the employment of approximately 17,000 personnel, and a $14 billion budget. The department's personnel structure would include six assistant secretaries—one each for elementary and secondary education, post-secondary education, vocational and adult education, educational research and improvement, special education and rehabilitative services, and civil rights. In addition, there was to be an administrator for overseas education and an office for bilingual education and minority affairs.

29. Rufus E. Miles, Jr., *A Cabinet Department of Education: Analysis and Proposal* (Washington, D.C.: American Council on Education, 1976).
30. Gerald E. Sroufe, "The Case Against the Department of Education," Phi Delta Kappan 58 (April 1977): 597–600.

The election of 1980 had severe repercussions on the new department. President Reagan was pledged to eliminate the department. By January 1981, Terrell H. Bell was the new Secretary of Education, and a program of reversion, described later, was begun.

Greater Federal Intrusion. Before considering in detail the record of the Reagan administration in education, it is well to note that the schools have had a long and varied relationship with the federal government. For most of our history the federal government exercised relatively little control over school programs. From about 1950 to 1970 federal influence increased rapidly. The 1970s represented a period of vacillation in federal influence. We have discussed reappraisal and retrenchment aspect of this vacillation in the preceeding sections. We turn now to the phenomenon of even greater federal intrusion. Brief treatments of Title IX and Public Law 94–142 will be offered as illustrations.

Title IX (PL 92–318) was but one part of a legislative explosion in the 92nd Congress (1971–72) designed to end sex discrimination in schools and colleges.[31] For instance, Title VII of the Civil Rights Act of 1964 was amended to cover employment in all institutions whether or not they received federal funds. Also, the U.S. Commission on Civil Rights was given jurisdiction over sex discrimination. Finally, Title IX of the Education Amendments of 1972 forbidding sex discrimination against students and employees in federally assisted education programs was passed. Title IX covers only about two pages in the U.S. Code and was little noticed at the time of its enactment.

A major provision in Title IX reads: "No person in the United States shall, on the basis of sex, be excluded from participation in, or be denied the benefits of, or be subjected to discrimination under any educational program or activity receiving federal financial assistance." In other sections of the act, virtually all programs affecting students are covered including classes once designed for one sex only and participation in athletic programs. No longer can girls be kept out of a shop program nor can the sports program for boys dominate use of the gymnasium.

Whereas the initial legislation was relatively brief, the rules and regulations governing Title IX, which appeared June 23, 1974, are extensive. They occupy 27 three-column pages in the *Federal Register* and cover in great detail what schools and colleges must do in order to prevent sex discrimination.

Federal control is implicit not only in the language of the act itself but also in the detailed nature of the regulations. At this point, it seems pertinent to note the place of administrative law, in this case at the federal level, in the control of schools. Unless challenged and reversed in the courts, the stipulations of a federal agency force compliance as truly as the statutes themselves. For the most part, the regulations for enforcing all types of legislation have increased in length and specificity in recent years.

But in the case of Title IX, there are other and more far-reaching elements of control. To begin with, Title IX is patterned after Title VI of the Civil Rights Act of 1964, which prohibits discrimination on the basis of race, color, and national origin. Moreover, Title IX and Title VI are both enforced by the Office of Civil Rights of the Department of Health, Education, and Welfare. Individuals and organizations can challenge any discriminatory practice by writing a letter directly to the secretary of HEW. Since Title IX is patterned after Title VI, individuals also have the right to bypass

31. See Bernice Sandler, "Title IX: Antisexism's Big Legal Stick," *American Education* (May 1977): 6–9.

HEW and carry suits alleging discrimination directly to the courts. Moreover, as noted earlier, Congress also amended Title VII of the Civil Rights Act of 1964 to cover employment in *all* educational institutions whether or not they receive federal money. It is one thing to have the federal government regulate school practice as a condition incident to the acceptance of federal money. It is a new order of regulation to have federal regulations imposed on schools even if they accept no federal money. The latter condition is, of course, sustained only because education has been identified as a civil right. But even with this new attitude, the impact of federal control on local schools and state education agencies is nonetheless considerable.

In some ways Public Law 94–142, passed in 1975, extends federal control over schools even further than Title IX or legislation on vocational education. The law itself is long and detailed, requiring 23 pages in the U.S. Code. The purpose of the law is comprehensive: "to assure that all handicapped children have available to them . . . a free appropriate public education which emphasizes special education and related services designed to meet their unique needs. . . ." The meaning of the terms used in the statement of purpose are not left to the conjecture of school officials or OE rule makers; they are specified. For instance, *special education* means "specifically designed instruction, at no cost to parents or guardians, to meet the unique needs of a handicapped child, including classroom instruction, instruction in physical education, home instruction, and instruction in hospitals and institutions," and *related services* means "transportation, and such developmental, corrective, and other supportive services (including speech pathology and audiology, psychological services, physical and occupational therapy, recreation, and medical and counseling services, except that such medical services shall be for diagnostic and evaluation purposes only) as may be required to assist a handicapped child. . . ."

To meet these very specific requirements the federal government does provide some money, 5 percent of the average per pupil expenditure in the United States the first year and up to 40 percent by the fifth year of operation. Note that the money is allocated on the basis of average expenditure *per pupil*, not on the basis of expenditure *per handicapped child* which would obviously be a much higher figure. Moreover, to implement the program the states and local districts, even after the fifth year, must provide most of the financial support.

A notable part of PL 94–142 is the detail specified for the state plan, which must be submitted to the U.S. commissioner of education if the state is to qualify for federal assistance. For instance, the plan must include: a statement of the goal of providing full educational opportunity to all handicapped children, a detailed timetable for accomplishing such a goal, and a description of the facilities, personnel, and services necessary to achieve the program. The plan must also give assurance that the state education agency is responsible for seeing that all educational programs for handicapped children, including those provided by any local agency, meet the education standards of the state education agency. Indeed, the state agency is required to prescribe rules and regulations for local agencies and to oversee compliance with these rules.

With the specificity found in the law, one might assume that the rule makers in the U.S. Office of Education could have done with fewer words, but such was not the case. The rules run 44 three-column pages of fine print in the *Federal Register*, under the date of August 23, 1977. More legislative detail seems to require more rules interpretation. For instance, the rules stipulate eight categories of handicapped: deaf, deaf-blind, hard of hearing, mentally retarded, multi-handicapped, orthopedically impaired, other health impaired, and seriously emotionally disturbed. For each of these categories a detailed definition is given. The rules also devote over ten columns to specifying the content of the annual program to be submitted by the state. The program must include: a description of public hearings and public participation regarding the plan; a copy of each state statute, court order, attorney general's opinion, and other state documents that show the source of the state policy on the handicapped; in detail, the policies and procedures the state will undertake to insure full educational opportunity to the handicapped; in detail, the policies and procedures the state will undertake to insure that the handicapped are identified, located, and their needs evaluated; and a list of administrative positions and a description of the duties for each person in such a position whose salary is paid in whole or in part with PL 94–142 funds.

Five columns in the rules are devoted to the requirements for local school districts. They specify: procedures to be used to identify the handicapped; facilities, personnel, and services to be used in the program; provisions for participation of and consultation with parents; the nature of records to be kept on the handicapped; and the contents of reports to be made to the state agency.

The rules give considerable attention to the independent evaluation of each handicapped child. Each public agency, on request of the parents, must provide information about where such an evaluation may be obtained. *Independent educational evaluation* in the rules means "an evaluation conducted by a qualified examiner who is not employed by the public agency responsible for the education of the child in question." This evaluation is to be done at public expense and at no cost to the parent. Recollection of the eight categories of handicapped suggests something about the extent of the program designed for the evaluation of pupil disabilities, particularly when other provisions of the evaluation program are taken into account. For instance, tests and other evaluation procedures are to be administered in the child's native language, they are to be given by trained personnel, and they are to be selected and administered so as best to insure that "the test results accurately reflect the child's aptitude and achievement level . . . rather than reflecting the child's impaired sensory, manual, or speaking skills. . . ."

The rules speak not only to the nature of identification and evaluation procedures for the handicapped but also to the nature of the school environment in which instruction is to be offered. The term used is *least restrictive environment.* To implement such a concept two specific requirements are set forth. The first requirement is "that to the maximum extent appropriate, handicapped children . . . are educated with children who are not handicapped. . . ." The second is "that special classes, separate schooling, or other removal of handicapped children from the regular educational environment occurs only when the nature or severity of the handicap is such that education in regular classes . . . cannot be achieved satisfactorily."

The rules also make provision for an impartial due process hearing. A parent or a public agency may initiate a hearing. Any party to a hearing has the right to be accompanied and advised by counsel and by specialists in the area of the handicapped and to obtain a written or electronic version of the hearing. Parents also have the right to have the child in question present and to have the hearing open to the public. After the hearing the public agency is required to transmit the findings and decisions to the state advisory panel on the handicapped, about which more will be said later. The result of any hearing may be appealed to the state education agency and such appeal requires the state agency to review the hearing record, seek additional evidence if needed, and make an independent decision upon completion of the review. If still not satisfied, the aggrieved party may bring civil action in the courts.

Both the law and the rules require the state to establish a state advisory panel on the education of the handicapped. Members of the panel are to be appointed by the governor or other state official authorized to make such appointments. The membership of the panel must include at least one person from each of the following groups; handicapped individuals, teachers of handicapped children, parents of handicapped children, state and local education officials, and special education program administrators. The state may include other persons on the panel. The advisory panel has been given specific duties including the following: to advise the state education agency on the unmet needs of the handicapped; to comment publicly on the annual program of the state, the proposed rules and regulations of the state, and the proposed distribution of funds; and to consider any appeal by an aggrieved parent or guardian.

Finally, the state is required to monitor and evaluate the programs established for the handicapped and to make annual reports to the commissioner. As to monitoring, the procedures must include: collection of data and reports from operating agencies, on-site visits to those agencies, audits of federal fund utilization, and a "comparison of a sampling of individualized education programs with the programs actually provided."

As prescriptive as the language of PL94–142 is, the real "teeth" of the law are in Section 504 of the Rehabilitation Act as amended in 1974. The section reads as follows: "No otherwise qualified handicapped individual in the United States . . . shall, solely by reason of his handicap, be excluded from participation in, be denied the benefits of, or be subjected to discrimination under any program receiving federal assistance."

The rules set up for the administration of this brief section require 27 three-column pages in the *Federal Register* under the date of May 4, 1977. Obviously these rules have broad application to both education and employment, but subpart D has specific reference to preschool, elementary, and secondary education. These provisions have been explicitly coordinated with those of PL 94–142. Some of the specific language follows:

> While the Department does not intend to review individual placement decisions, it does intend to insure that testing and evaluation required by the regulations are carried out, and that school systems provide an adequate opportunity for parents to challenge and seek review of these critical decisions. And the Department will place a high priority on pursuing cases in which a pattern or practice of discriminatory placements may be involved.

Much of the strength of Section 504 derives from the fact that it is related to the Civil Rights Act. In the language of that section, "the procedural provisions applicable to Title VI of the Civil Rights Act of 1965 apply to this part." School practices concerning handicapped students have been specified in great detail. According to Section 504, departure from those practices could constitute discrimination. Schools or persons guilty of such discrimination could, if the case went to court, be found guilty of denying the civil rights of a student. The sanctions for discrimination against the handicapped when placed within the civil rights context are very powerful.

In recent years, the U.S. Department of Education, in keeping with Reagan administration policy of decentralization, has proposed changes in regulations governing the operation of Public Law 94–142. Public pressure from those interested in the handicapped has been mounted against such changes, hence, as of this writing, none of those proposals have been implemented.

The Reagan Reversion

Over our history, the nature of federal influence on American education can be characterized as follows: a long period of modest influence, a rapid expansion of influence during the 1960s, a vacillation between retrenchment and even greater intrusion during the 1970s, and then the Reagan reversion. Reagan described his program as "new federalism", although he was actually advocating a return to dual federalism. We now turn to this last period. We shall examine the major proposals set forth by President Reagan, report actual legislative action and other responses to his proposals, and suggest some implications related to these changes.

The Proposals

As a candidate and later as president, Ronald Reagan made it clear that he intended to restructure the federal government. He believed social and human services, including education, should be delegated to state and local governments rather than undertaken at the federal level. One observer noted that as a candidate, "Reagan had reacted negatively to the formation of the Department of Education, stating that he thought it ought to be abolished. He stood strongly for 'deregulating' education, and, more radical yet, favored tuition tax credits."[32]

Thomas has provided even more detail with respect to the Reagan position on education:

> President Reagan's definition of the federal role in education has been manifested in such developments as: (1) sharp reductions, on the order of 20% to 25%, in spending for elementary and secondary education programs and college student aid; (2) support for antibusing legislation and reduced willingness of the Justice Department to bring or aid in desegregation suits; (3) a proposal, as part of President Reagan's New Federalism, to consolidate all federal aid to education into two block grants that would be disbursed by the states and would not be subject to federal requirements or standards; (4) proposed regulations that put "reasonable limits" on the rights of handicapped students and on the services that schools must provide to them; (5) Reagan's strong personal endorsement of tuition tax credits for parents of children attending private schools; and (6) the proposal to abolish the Department of Education.[33]

President Reagan himself made his proposals quite clear. For instance, as part of his "A Program for Economic Recovery" under date of February 18, 1981, he made specific recommendations to the Congress regarding several education programs. The then current budget authority and proposed budget authority for these programs, taken from the message, are shown in Table 2.1. The proposed reductions are dramatic.

After interviewing members of the new administration and examining many pertinent documents, Clark and Amiot said that the hallmarks of the administration's efforts to disassemble the federal educational establishment were:

---

32. James W. Guthrie, "The Future of Federal Educational Policy," *Teachers College Record* 84 (Spring 1983): 683.
33. Norman C. Thomas, "The Development of Federal Activism in Education," *Education and Urban Society* 15 (May 1983): 284–85.

Diminution—to reduce the size and scope of federal expenditures in education;

Deregulation—to reduce federal control and monitoring in the field of education;

Decentralization—to accomplish a transfer of responsibility for education from the federal to the state and local levels;

Disestablishment—to eliminate the bureaucratic structure for education at the federal level, that is, the Department of Education; and

Deemphasis—to remove educational policy from a position of priority on the federal agenda.[34]

While some might demur about the nature and magnitude of Reagan's proposals, it seems clear to us that a new policy shift was being advocated.[35] In some ways, it is remarkable that a new administration could make proposals plausible to Congress and others that countered decades of federal interest and involvement. Thomas has suggested that the restructuring of national educational policy was a product of several factors. These are paraphrased as follows: (1) the ideological convictions and persuasive talents of Reagan himself, (2) a recognition by elite groups that education alone could not solve social problems, (3) a substantial decline in the power of education interest groups, and (4) an appeal to popular feelings regarding race, religion, and federal control.[36] We would add one other factor. The federal intrusion, particularly with respect to Title IX and Public Law 94–142, discussed previously and Public Law 94–482, having to do with vocational education, did seem to be excessive. The laws themselves were long and detailed and the regulations were even more extensive. Compliance had become a complex and time-consuming task on the part of state and local educational agencies.

Response to Proposals

Despite opposition from some quarters, the Reagan reversion succeeded remarkably well. Let us examine a few of the specifics. Chapter 2 of the Educational Con-

TABLE 2.1

Current and Proposed Budget Authority for 1986 for Certain Education Programs

	Budget Authority for 1986 in Millions	
Program	Current	Proposed
Student assistance	6,004	3,717
Impact aid	1,178	546
Vocational education	1,104	810
National Institute of Education	105	78
Elementary and Secondary Education	7,983	5,366

SOURCE: "Presidents Proposals for Tax Reductions" in *America's New Beginning: A Program for Economic Recovery* (Washington, D.C.: The White House, office of the Press Secretary, February 18, 1981), 2–4, 6-4, 6–5, and 7–2.

34. David L. Clark and Mary Anne Amiot, "The Disassembly of the Federal Educational Role," *Education and Urban Society* 15 (May 1983): 368–69.
35. See Chester E. Finn, Jr., "Reflections on the Disassembly of the Federal Role," *Education and Urban Society* 15 (May 1983): 389–96.
36. Thomas, *Development of Federal Activism*, 285.

solidation and Improvement Act (ECIA) did consolidate some 28 federal programs in elementary and secondary education. Also, state and local agencies were given some authority to determine just how the federal funds for these programs were to be expended.

In addition to the consolidation of a number of federal programs, there has also been an actual reduction in the dollar amounts for many of those programs. As Table 2.2 illustrates, expenditures for the major programs in elementary and secondary education were, over a two-year period, reduced by almost 30 percent. It is appropriate to note that the Congress followed the lead of the president in authorizing these reductions.

In addition to persuading Congress to accept his program, President Reagan also made use of his appointment powers. For instance, in 1982, he replaced 10 members of the 15-member National Council on Educational Research (NCER), the policy-making arm of the National Institute of Education (NIE), even though terms of many of the incumbents had not yet expired. Observers reported that the president had given NCER a "conservative cast with the naming of George Roche as chairman" and by appointing Onalee McGraw as a member of the council.[37] Roche was president of a private college that had refused to accept federal funds. McGraw was an outspoken critic of federal social research and on the staff of the conservative Heritage Foundation. President Reagan made an additional change in Council membership by appointing a new director of NIE. These changes were apparently made on ideological grounds and without counsel from the research community in education.

Anne Lewis, executive editor of *Education USA*, and a close observer of the political scene, has suggested that the "administration seems willing to turn back both the clock and the Consitution on civil rights".[38] She supported this indictment by citing a number of specifics. For instance, the Justice Department did not appeal a federal district court ruling in *University of Richmond* v. *Bell* which seemed to prevent the

TABLE 2.2

Federal Expenditures for Certain Programs in the Department of Education, 1981 and 1983

	Expenditures in Millions of Dollars	
Program	1981	1983
Vocational education	682	500
Impacted aid	682	287
Disadvantaged	3,104	1,942
Bilingual education	158	95
Handicapped	1,025	846
Other programs	216	407
State block grants	538	433
TOTAL	6,405	4,510

Adapted from Paul E. Peterson and B.G. Rabe, "The Role of Interest Groups in the Formation of Educational Policy: Past Practice and Future Trends," *Teachers College Record* 84 (Spring 1983): 715.

37. "President Names Conservatives to Policymaking Education Research Panel," *Education Times,* 7 June 1982.
38. Anne C. Lewis, "Washington Report," *Phi Delta Kappan* 64 (April 1983): 523.

Office of Civil Rights in the Education Department from requiring a college to correct a Title IX violation. She noted, as well, the administration's blind opposition to busing in the East Baton Rouge Parish. She maintained that:

> There are other fires all over the battlefield: the Administration's legal fiasco over withholding tax-exempt status from schools that discriminate, its proposals to turn compensatory education into a voucher system, its support of efforts to overturn affirmative action plans, its recent efforts to diminish the role of the Office for Civil Rights (by causing it to focus more on "technical assistance" and less on compliance review).[39]

Members of the Civil Rights Commission who objected to such action and non-action were later fired from their positions by the president.

On two matters, strongly recommended by the president, there has not been favorable action. T. H. Bell, Secretary of the Department of Education, as directed by the president, did, as early as October, 1981, develop four possible replacement arrangements for the department. He made it known that he favored converting the department to a foundation, somewhat like the National Science Foundation, to preside over the federal role in education.[40] The Congress has taken no action on this proposal nor does the administration now seem intent on pushing the proposal. On the other hand, President Reagan's proposal for tuition tax credits was brought to a Senate vote in November, 1983, and was defeated. But only one defeat and one matter deferred still leaves the president with a good box score in achieving his program.

Indeed, one development in the Department of Education seemed to provide a surprising plus for the administration. In August, 1981, Secretary Bell created the National Commission on Excellence in Education and directed it to present a report to him and the American people by April, 1983. A distinguished group of educators and lay citizens were appointed to the commission. David P. Gardner, then president of the University of Utah, was selected as chairman. The commission was given several specific charges including: the assessment of the quality of teaching and learning in the nation's schools and colleges, a comparison of American schools and colleges with those of other advanced nations, and a definition of the problems that must be overcome if the nation is to pursue a course of excellence in education. While the charge was broad, the commission focused its attention on the high school. The commission held a number of hearings across the country, commissioned papers from experts on schools and colleges, used the assistance of a competent staff, and then published a succinct report, *A Nation at Risk*, subtitled *The Imperative for Educational Reform*.[41] The language of the report was, in some instances, dramatic as the following excerpt illustrates:

> If an unfriendly foreign power had attempted to impose on America the mediocre educational performance that exists today, we might well have viewed it as an act of war. As it stands, we have allowed this to happen to ourselves. We have even squandered the gains in student achievement made in the wake of the Sputnik challenge.

---

39. Ibid., 524.
40. Martha Snyder, "Federal Dateline," *The School Administrator* (October 1981): 25.
41. National Commission on Excellence in Education, *A Nation at Risk* (Washington, D.C.: U.S. Department of Education, April 1983).

Moreover, we have dismantled essential support systems which helped make those gains possible. We have, in effect, been committing an act of unthinking, unilateral educational disarmament.[42]

Whether it was the nature of the report or the tenor of the times, or both, the report provoked widespread attention and response. We should note that several other major reports on education, sponsored by authoritative bodies, also appeared in 1983. Education became a major national concern. In general, there was widespread support for the recommendations set forth in *A Nation at Risk*. The media and citizens generally agreed that something should be done to rescue the nation from "a rising tide of mediocrity". Scores of state legislatures and hundreds of school boards prepared their own responses on excellence in the schools.

There were a few more discerning voices. For instance, Meg Greenfield in *Newsweek* had this to say,

You give a child nothing, I think, when you give him this joyless, driven concept of learning. But alas, there are plenty among us who think this is just fine. Following the great cackles of the political antipermissiveness crowd when this report was released, I was struck again by how much such people, who claim to be champions of education, implicitly view education as a disagreeable thing.[43]

In a thoughtful commentary on the recent studies on education, Harold Howe makes the following point,

It is important to add, however, that we must settle one issue soon: the role of the federal government in education. The recent studies and reports, including that of the National Commission on Excellence in Education, generally agree that the federal government should play a strong role in identifying national priorities in education, in doing something about them through legislation and appropriations, in supporting research on education, and, particularly, in dealing with issues of equity and equal opportunity. Right now we face a major political division on these matters. Both houses of Congress lean in the direction that the reports suggest, but the President tilts in the other direction.[44]

Even though *A Nation at Risk* and the other reports failed to mention President Reagan's own agenda for education—such matters as school prayer and tuition tax credits—the president soon saw that education was a politically viable issue. He responded to Secretary Bell's invitation to appear at several regional meetings where implementation of the report's recommendations was considered. Public acceptance of *The Nation at Risk* apparently provided the president with an opportunity to appear as a champion of education.

Some Implications

While, at this writing, it is too early to assess the full impact of the Reagan policies on education, some implications growing out of recent federal action and current debate can be suggested.

42. Ibid., 5.
43. Meg Greenfield, "Creating a Learning Society," *Newsweek,* 16 May 1983, 100.
44. Harold Howe II, "Education Moves to Center Stage: An Overview of Recent Studies," *Phi Delta Kappan* 65 (November 1983): 169–70.

First, federal action can make a difference. Michael Knapp and his colleagues at SRI International examined, in a number of school districts, the impact of federal aid programs from 1965 to 1980 dealing with student populations with special educational needs.[45] Specifically, their study dealt with Title I of ESEA, which discusses the educationally deprived; P.L. 94–142, which discusses the handicapped; Title VII of ESEA, which discusses limited English proficiency; the 1968 amendments to the Vocational Education Act, which discuss support for handicapped and disadvantaged; and the civil rights laws—Title VI of the Civil Rights Act of 1964, Title IX of the Education Amendments of 1972, and Section 504 of the rehabilitation Act of 1973—all of which were designed to prohibit discrimination against students and staff. The general conclusions of the study are shown in the following list:

Collectively, federal and state policies for special populations have substantially improved and expanded the array of educational services for the intended target students.

These policies have increased the structural complexity of schools and districts, which appears to represent a necessary consequence of providing targeted services.

Over time, local problem solving, federal and state policy adjustments, and gradual local accommodation have generally reduced to a manageable level the costs associated with special services.[46]

In further comment on the findings, the authors say,

Despite the vagaries of state and local handling of specific program provisions, the overall effects of federal involvement in the education of target students have been relatively clear and consistent.[47]

We recognize that the Knapp study covered the fifteen-year period prior to the Reagan administration. We have two reasons for including reference to it here. First, the study made its appearance in 1983 and will probably become important to further consideration of the nature and consequences of federal educational policy. Second, the presence of federal programs, even though they required modifications in local school organizations, were found to be compatible to these organizations. In short, it has been demonstrated that federal aid can achieve national goals and, at the same time, not abridge or destroy local initiative. This evidence for a partnership between federal, state, and local levels seems quite in contrast to some of the recent rhetoric about the dire consequences of federal aid.

As a second implication, recent federal legislation appears to have reduced the equity provisions of federal programs. Two studies support such a conclusion. The American Association of School Administrators surveyed a random sample of 2,500 large, medium-sized, and small school districts with respect to the impact of block grants—money from Chapter 2, passed by the Congress in 1981—on school district operation.[48] Responses from these districts led to two conclusions. First, Chapter 2

---

45. Michael Knapp et al., *Cumulative Effects of Federal Policies on Schools and Districts,* SRI Project 3590, (Menlo Park, Calif.: SRI International, January 1983).
46. Ibid., 159.
47. Ibid., 162.
48. AASA, "The Impact of Chapter 2 of the Education Consolidation and Improvement Act on Local Education Agencies" (Washington, D.C.: AASA, 1983).

funds were being used to help districts move into the high-technology era. Second, the block grant system was creating a serious equity problem. In effect, block grants were being dispersed to a larger number of school districts. In this process, however, small districts received an increase in federal funds while large districts received a decrease. Larger districts with average grants of $941,299 before block grants received average grants of $105,463 after block grants. This decrease had crippled desegregation and other equity projects. This neglect of equity concerns was further exacerbated by a decrease in total appropriations.

Stephen Barro, under the sponsorship of the Institute for Research on Educational Finance and Governance at Stanford University, also did a study assessing the equity of federal education grants.[49] Again, the focus was on the programs consolidated under ECIA Chapter 2. In this case, the study dealt with the language of the statutes and the program regulations, not with their actual implementation. The major conclusion of the study is shown below:

> The present federal aid allocation formulas are not so much inequitable as insensitive. They take into account too few of the relevant educational and fiscal factors to satisfy widely shared standards of distributional justice. Specifically, most of the present interstate and intrastate allocation formulas (1) distribute aid according to person counts that are only loosely linked to the program's goals, (2) take no account of other dimensions of educational need, (3) do nothing to compensate (equalize) for differences in revenue-raising ability, and (4) fail to adjust for variations in costs, fiscal effort, and other fiscal factors.[50]

While block grants may have simplified administrative procedures in the Department of Education and possibly have permitted more state and local discretion, they seem to be found wanting in terms of equity provisions. If equity is still a national concern, Chapter 2 apparently should be revised.

As a third implication, and contrary to President Reagan's initial proposals, there is a federal role in education. As we've noted, Howe, after examining *A Nation At Risk* and other recent reports on education, was convinced that the elements of a federal role in education must be confronted. Anne Lewis also found that all of the recent reports on school reform, despite their differences in practicality and tone, emphasized a federal role in education.[51] Moreover, Lewis found that the reports supported the type of federal involvement that has been shaped over the past several years with a focus on equity and a recognition of other national interests. She contended that recommendations from the several reports require an increase, not a decrease, in federal funding.

In view of the conclusions just cited, it is not surprising to note that large school improvement proposals are, as of this writing, being considered in Congress. The most notable of these seems to be the American Defense Education Act. This legislation is reported to have 175 cosponsors in the House and 40 in the Senate. President Reagan himself, in his recent awakening to the political viability of education issues, may even find certain educational efforts at the federal level to his liking. At the very least, *A Nation at Risk* has called attention to certain educational problems and has encouraged states and local districts to do something about them.

49. Stephen M. Barro, *Federalism, Equity, and Distribution of Federal Education Grants,* Project Report no. 83–A6 (Stanford, Calif.: Stanford University Institute for Research on Educational Finance and Goverance, February 1983).
50. Ibid., 78.
51. Anne C. Lewis, "Washington Report," *Phi Delta Kappan* 65 (November 1983): 163–66.

By way of summary, Ronald Reagan, as a candidate and later as president, made it clear that the role of the federal government in education should be diminished. Overall, his proposals were approved by Congress and seemed, at least initially, to elicit the approval of most citizens. Some of the measures instituted by President Reagan seem to counter prior efforts to provide more equity in the system. Despite the Reagan posture, many observers are convinced that national interests cannot be served adequately unless the federal government is a vigorous partner in the educational enterprise.

Summary and Future Prospects

Let us summarize the kinds of federal controls now being exercised and suggest the probable nature of future federal relationships. Federal control or influence is frequently denied. Indeed, many of the bills enacted by Congress contain a specific stipulation that nothing in the act shall be construed as giving the federal agency control over local and state education agencies. And at least until recently, local and state agencies presumably were free to turn down federal money. But the matter is not that simple. Controls are of many kinds and include those suggested below:

Federal Controls

1. *Law.* Congress can and does enact a great many laws having to do with education. Title IX on sex discrimination in education and PL 94–142 on education of the handicapped are two examples. Not only must schools cope with the statute as enacted by the Congress, schools must also follow the regulations which are prepared by the U.S. Office of Education or other federal agencies. When law and regulation are further fortified by civil rights enforcement, as is true particularly under Title IX and PL 94–142, control at the federal level is enhanced.
2. *The Courts.* The federal courts exercise great and growing control over the operations of schools and state education agencies. In particular, the courts exercise jurisdiction in matters pertaining to civil rights in areas such as desegregation and sex discrimination.
3. *Money.* For the most part federal dollars are for categorical purposes such as aid to the disadvantaged and funds for vocational education. The very nature of these subventions constitutes control; in no way can local or state agencies use the money for other than the specified purpose.
4. *State Federal Offices.* Federal control is also exercised through the establishment of specific offices and divisions with federal support in state departments of education. Thus, state education agencies have divisions devoted to vocational education, disadvantaged pupils, sex discrimination, the education of the handicapped, and for other federally funded programs. While these divisions are nominally under the direction of the state board of education and the chief state school officer, their existence, their operation, and their funding hinges on federal initiative and support. Such units are established to "help" local districts comply with federal directives.
5. *Regional Resource Centers.* Regional resource centers designed specifically to promote federal programs at state and local levels also foster federal control. In the case of education for the handicapped, 17 regional centers have been established, are well staffed, and are vigorously at work. Any local or state

education agency that wishes to be "with it" will see that teachers and administrators participate in the workshops and other activities of these centers.

6. *Teacher Training.* Some federal legislation contains specific provision having
to do with the preservice or the in-service training of teachers. The special
requirements such as those found in vocational education are intended to help
provide the understandings and skills needed in special fields of teaching but
these experiences also do much to socialize teachers into the norms of the
particular field in question.

7. *Professional Interest Groups.* Still another aspect of federal control is the use
of federal money to foster the growth of specialized professional groups. This
form of control has long been present in vocational education. For instance:
teachers in that field have part of their salaries paid from federal money; much
of their training is provided with the aid of federal money; in each state agency
for education there are special supervisors and directors, largely supported
from federal money; and these state officers are frequently convened in special
workshops and conferences sponsored by the National Center for Vocational
Education, a creature that awards sizable federal grants. Communication
among persons at local, state, and national levels is frequent and continuous.
All of this builds a powerful group of professionals ready to support vocational
education at all levels of government. Similar arrangements are found in other
areas of major federal involvement.

8. *Special Interest Groups.* Perhaps even more significant than the building of
special interest groups in the profession is the building of special interest
groups among citizens. Federal programs have frequently identified citizens
with special interests, made those interests legitimate, and utilized such interests in promoting federal programs. This process is frequently fostered by the
establishment of citizens' advisory committees made up almost entirely of citizens who have special interests and is clearly exemplified in the law on education for the handicapped. Federal legislation often specifies powers for these
advisory committees that tends to make them much more than advisory. Indeed, these advisory bodies often determine the decisions officially enacted by
the boards of state and local agencies.

Outlook for the Future

The controls enumerated above represent pervasive federal influence. What about the
future? The following predictions are offered as highly likely. First, despite the Reagan
reversion, the federal presence in education will continue. Federal influence of one
kind or another has been with us for a long time; it is part of our tradition. Also there
are great disparities among the states and within the states in the economic ability of
states and school districts to support programs of education. Although current programs designed to alleviate these disparities have not always been effective,[52] such
programs will continue to appear. Certain problems in education of national impact,
such as education of the disadvantaged, will continue. Many policymakers will support
federal action to alleviate what appear to be national deficiencies. Within the federal
system bucking problems to the next level of government is a common strategy of
interest groups. When minority groups, for instance, find that they do not get redress
at the local level, they may buck the problem to the state or even the national level.

52. See Berke and Kirst, *Federal Aid to Education: Who Benefits? Who Governs?*

Second, with other demands on the federal budget and reduced allocations for education already in place, increased money for education will be hard to come by. For the most part, money that is made available for education will probably go to meet national needs or to effect reforms in current practices. In both cases the federal aid will be for specific categorical purposes, and this specificity acts as a control mechanism.

Third, many actors will continue to participate in policymaking at the federal level. The president and the Congress, of course, are major policy actors. In addition, the federal bureaucracy, particularly the Office of Management and Budget, has emerged as a very powerful determiner of federal policy. The courts, too, are becoming more and more influential. No single policy decision has affected schools as much as the Brown decision in 1954. The pervasive influence of the courts in many areas will probably continue. These formal actors, we are convinced, will continue to be joined by a host of informal actors or interest groups who wish to affect federal decisions.

Fourth, federal agencies have taken a reform stance with respect to education. This reform objective is reflected in much of the legislation passed by Congress, in the federal guidelines developed by the department, in the evaluation procedures required of support programs, and even in the decisions of the judiciary. The push for reform as exemplified by Title IX and PL 94–142 is likely to continue, but some reduction in regulations, begun by the Reagan administration, may also continue.

Fifth, federal agencies exert influence through evaluation and assessment. We have noted the continued but reduced support of the National Assessment Program. While federal support for this program has been shifted from the Education Commission of the States to the Education Testing Service, the program will probably continue. Federal influence is also sustained through the allocation of federal money to state education agencies. Most of these agencies now receive about half of their operating funds from federal sources. One purpose for which much of this money is allocated has to do with the "improvement" of state departments of education through the establishment of greater capability in the areas of planning, research, and evaluation. In part, this is an attempt to implement the evaluation requirements made a part of all federal grants. This increased emphasis on evaluation implies a conviction that there ought to be greater correspondence between costs and benefits. We suspect that the emphasis on costs and benefits will continue to motivate federal policy makers.

With the Reagan reversion, as noted above, federal intrusion has been somewhat reduced. But, for the most part, the statutory language for most federal programs remains unchanged, hence federal influence will continue. Moreover, the long-term shift from dual to national federalism, while slowed, will likely continue. Indeed, the current studies of education, including *A Nation at Risk,* all identify a significant role in education for the federal government.

3

American Schools and State Government

Although the Constitution of the United States contains no direct reference to education, most state constitutions have specific provisions which make education a legal responsibility of the state. Moreover, the statutes of most states stipulate in considerable detail how schools are to be governed. Much of this control is delegated to district boards of education and to other bodies all of which become a part of the state system of education. In a sense, then, we have 50 systems of education in America, but in many respects these various systems are similar. In this chapter we will review how a state structure for education developed, note the emerging shift of power to the state level, examine current organizational arrangements for schools found in the states, consider the types of decisions made by state school agencies, indicate the major functions of state school agencies, and suggest the types of controls states exercise over schools.

The Development of a State Structure

Early Movements

Education in colonial America was closely allied with religion. This alliance took different forms in the various colonies. In most of New England early government was a theocracy. In these church-states it was thought necessary that all children learn to read the Bible and the laws of the colony. Compulsory education laws, of which the famous acts of 1642 and 1647 in Massachusetts are examples, were passed by all New England colonies except Rhode Island.

While compulsory school laws were passed, compulsory attendance laws were not. In effect these Puritan commonwealths required that parents and masters assume responsibility for the education of their children. This was a reflection of the colonists' English background, in which education was conceived as a private and not a public matter. Only in later years did New England towns begin to contribute to the support of schools.

The middle colonies presented another picture. Instead of the relative homogeneity of the Puritans, there were Dutch, French, Irish, Scotch, Germans, and many other national groups. Religious sects included Presbyterians, Jews, Lutherans, Catholics, Quakers, Mennonites, and Moravians. Some of these colonies also passed early laws requiring that parents and masters instruct their children in reading and writing for religious and governmental reasons. Examples were the "Great Law" in Pennsylvania in 1682 and the Public School Act in New York in 1732.

Unlike New England, however, the middle colonies lacked singleness of purpose, and little seems to have been done to enforce such laws. As time went on, primary education became essentially a church or parochial responsibility and secondary education became a private matter. In neither case was educational opportunity widespread.

Conditions were different still in the southern colonies. Whereas many groups in New England and in the middle colonies were motivated by the Reformation, leaders in the southern colonies were for the most part adherents of the Anglican Church and were willing to support it as long as it did not interfere with their way of life. The well-to-do believed education to be a private matter. Virginia did pass legislation in 1642 providing for the education of orphans, but it was at least a century later before the opportunity to learn to read and write was provided for dependent children and children of pauper parents.

The Society for the Propagation of the Gospel in Foreign Parts, an auxiliary of the Anglican Church, began sending missionaries to America in 1702. These missionaries came to be numbered in the hundreds, most of them settled in the middle and southern colonies. Their purpose was to establish and revive the Anglican Church, but they also organized schools as a means of training children in religious worship.

While these colonial activities with regard to schools may seem meager by today's standards, Thurston and Roe suggest that some important concepts were beginning to emerge.[1] Among these were the following: the belief in the worth of the individual regardless of wealth or lineage, the realization that education is necessary for successful government, the notion of education as a state function, and the recognition that church and state are not one.

Following the colonial period, it took at least two generations before the outlines of state school administration, as we know it today, began to emerge. The leaders of the first generation included Thomas Jefferson, Alexander Hamilton, George Washington, and Benjamin Franklin. They helped establish the United States as a nation and they were also deeply interested in education.

Jefferson offered the most definitive plan for a state school system. In 1779 he and Wythe reported to the Virginia assembly "A Bill for the More General Diffusion of Knowledge." Under the plan each county was to be divided into "hundreds" of such size that all children living in these subdivisions could conveniently attend the school which was to be established in each. All free children, girls as well as boys, were to attend school for three years without paying tuition and for longer than that at private expense if their parents, guardians, or friends thought proper.

The Jefferson plan also provided for a statewide system of secondary schools. Twenty districts, each composed of two to seven counties, were to be organized and a grammar school was to be organized in each. Promising boys who had finished the "hundred" schools were to have an opportunity to attend the grammar school tuition-free. The best scholars in the grammar schools were to be selected and sent to William and Mary College for three years at the expense of the state.

---

1. Lee M. Thurston and William H. Roe, *State School Administration* (New York: Harper & Row, 1947), ch. 2.

One notable feature of Jefferson's plan was the provision that all free children attend the primary school for three years at public expense. But the plan was ahead of the times; the bill did not pass in 1779. A somewhat similar measure, again drafted by Jefferson, presented to the Virginia assembly in 1817, also failed to pass. The colonies were not yet ready for universal education, but the concept by no means died.

The work of Jefferson, Washington, and other leaders of the revolutionary period was carried on by Horace Mann of Massachusetts, Henry Barnard of Connecticut, John D. Pierce of Michigan, Calvin H. Wiley of North Carolina, Caleb Mills of Indiana, and John Swett of California. Each of these men marshalled the forces in his state behind a plan for the development of schools open to all children and paid for out of the public treasury. Each of these leaders deserves recognition, but the work of Horace Mann set a precedent for others.

Mann was trained as an attorney and served for ten years in the Massachusetts legislature. In 1837 he was made secretary of the newly formed State Board of Education in Massachusetts. For the next twelve years he attempted to inform and unify the people regarding public education. He held many meetings for teachers, head masters, and the public at large. His annual reports still stand today as distinguished documents on education. He also founded and edited for many years the *Common School Journal.*

Mann had to contend with indifference, conservatism, political opposition, and sectarian bigotry. To his task he brought considerable ability and great dedication. Not content with existing knowledge about education, he studied educational programs in Europe. Perhaps most important for this work, he made the state board of education and the state superintendency respected and necessary agencies for education and for government.

Some revisionist historians question the motives of the early public school founders. For instance, Katz says, "What they did not admit . . . was that the bureaucratic structure, apparently so equitable and favorable to the poor, would in fact give differential advantage to the affluent and their children, thereby reinforcing rather than altering existing patterns of social structure."[2] We believe, however, that the early champions of the public schools were motivated by a genuine desire to extend educational opportunity.

From General to Special Government

Early school laws passed by the colonies suggested that education in the beginning was controlled by general government. The general assembly made regulations for education as it saw fit. There were no state boards of education, no chief state school officers. When towns, upon direction from the general assembly, began to take some responsibility for schools, the town selectmen dealt directly with educational matters. There were no separate boards of education for the first 200 years of our history.

The basis for state control over education was pretty well established as early as 1820 by constitutional and statutory provisions of the states which made up the Union. As can be seen in Table 3.1, 13 of the 23 states had constitutional provisions for education, 17 had statutory provisions, 9 had both constitutional and statutory provisions, and only 2 states—Rhode Island and Tennessee—had neither constitutional nor statutory provisions for education.

Lack of special government for education probably stemmed from two conditions. First, government was just beginning to recognize that it had a direct role to play in

2. Michael B. Katz, *Class, Bureaucracy, and Schools!* (New York: Praeger, 1975), xxi.

providing schools. Though many of the constitutional provisions indicated that govern-ment was to "protect and encourage" schools, the concept of establishing and sup-porting schools was not as yet well developed. Second, schools for the most part were still simple institutions. Their purposes were straightforward, enrollments were small, each teaching staff was composed of one or just a few persons, and no great specialization of subject matter or pedagogy had as yet developed. Thus members of the general assembly and the town selectmen felt equal to any educational governing required of them.

But special government for education was soon to emerge, first in the form of a chief state school officer, often called a state superintendent of public instruction, and later in a state board of education. The first state superintendency was established in New York in 1812. Shortly thereafter, however, the office was abolished and was not reestablished until 1854. Maryland went through a similar experience: the office was established in 1826, then abolished, and reestablished in 1864. Michigan, Kentucky, and Massachusetts established the state superintendency in 1836 or 1837, and the office has been maintained in those states since that time. By 1870, 36 of the states had created such a position; by 1900 all states admitted to the Union—44 in number—had chief state school officers; and all states since admitted to the Union also have such officials.

TABLE 3.1

Statutory and Constitutional Provisions for Public Education in States Prior to 1820

State	Date Admitted to Union	Statutory Provisions for Education	Constitutional Provisions for Education
Delaware		Yes	Yes—Direct establishment
Pennsylvania		Yes	Yes—Direct establishment
New Jersey		Yes	No
Georgia		Yes	Yes—Direct establishment
Connecticut		Yes	No
Massachusetts	Original	Yes	Yes—Protect and encourage
Maryland	States	Yes	No
South Carolina		Yes	No
New Hampshire		Yes	Yes—Protect and encourage
Virginia		Yes	No
New York		Yes	No
North Carolina		No	Yes—Direct establishment
Rhode Island		No	No
Vermont	1791	Yes	Yes—Protect and encourage
Kentucky	1792	No	Yes—Direct establishment
Tennessee	1796	No	No
Ohio	1803	Yes	Yes—Protect and encourage
Louisiana	1812	Yes	No
Indiana	1816	Yes	Yes—Protect and encourage
Mississippi	1817	No	Yes-Encourage schools
Illinois	1818	Yes	No
Alabama	1819	No	Yes—Protect and encourage
Maine	1820	Yes	Yes—Protect and encourage

SOURCE: Ellwood P. Cubberley and Edward C. Elliot, *State and County School Administration* (Macmillan Company, 1915), 12–17, and from a study of early state statutes, as prepared by Thurston and Roe, *State School Administration,* 59.

Mann, Barnard, Pierce, Wiley, Mills, and Swett were all chief state school officers in their respective states. Their careers illustrate that such officials can be very effective in marshalling public opinion for a program of public education, in convincing a state legislature that schools should be organized and supported, in establishing teacher training facilities, and in providing professional leadership to teachers and school administrators.

Many chief state school officers who have followed the pioneers in this office, however, have not had the vision or influence of their predecessors. In fact, as will be shown later, one of the problems surrounding the office at present is that of attracting able people to it. Although this state of affairs has changed recently in a growing number of states, some local superintendencies are still accorded more prestige than the office of the chief state school officer.

Almost coordinate with the development of the state superintendency for education was the evolution of the state board of education as a second expression of special government for education at the state level. New York is usually credited as the first state to establish this agency, which it did in 1784.[3] Actually, the legislature created the Board of Regents of the State of New York and gave it some jurisdiction over the academies and colleges of the state. It was not until 1904 that the board was given control over the public schools of the state.

North Carolina created a state board in 1825 under the name of President and Directors of the Literary Fund, and Vermont and Missouri soon after established state boards of education. However, the main impetus for this movement was the action of Massachusetts in 1837 and the demonstration in that state, under the leadership of Horace Mann, of the efficacy of a state board of education. By 1900, 34 states had state boards of education, and by 1960, 46 states had state boards exercising general supervision over elementary and secondary schools. Today, only Wisconsin has no such body.[4] In Wisconsin, powers ordinarily lodged with the state board of education are given to the state superintendent of public instruction. In Hawaii, also somewhat of an exception, the state board of education is a district board of education; the schools in Hawaii are operated much as they are in a single city school district.

In the beginning, membership on most state boards of education was *ex officio* and often included the governor, the attorney general, and the state superintendent of public instruction. Gradually this was changed and board members came to be appointed by the governor or elected by the people. In 1982 board members in 34 states were appointed by the governor; in 12 states they were elected by the people; and in 3 states they acquired office in other ways.[5]

To recapitulate, during the past century forms of government designed specifically to cope with education have developed in every state. In nearly all states a state board of education composed of lay citizens, most often appointed by the governor but in a number of cases elected, has come into being. All states have a chief state school officer. In over half of the states the chief state school officer is selected by the state board of education and serves as its executive officer while in the remaining states the relationship of the chief officer to the state board of education is less well defined.

---

3. W. W. Keisecker, *State Boards of Education and Chief State School Officers,* Office of Education Bulletin 1950, no. 12 (Washington, D.C.: Government Printing Office, 1950).
4. Council of Chief State School Officers, *Educational Governance in the States* (Washington, D.C.: U.S. Department of Education, 1983).
5. Ibid.

But the development of this special government has not taken education away from general government. The state legislature retains plenary power for education. The legislature may create special machinery, may charge state boards and state superintendents with particular functions, as it has done, but it may also alter the machinery and call back the functions. Moreover, the governor's budget is still a most persuasive instrument with most legislatures. State boards and state superintendents must recommend to the governor a budget for the schools of the state, but neither the governor nor the legislature is required to accept their recommendations. Special government for education, then, supplements but does not replace general government.

The Emerging Role of the States

In recent years the place of the state in the governance of education has received increasing attention. This shift runs counter to our long tradition of local control and represents an interesting turn of events since the 1960s when great emphasis was placed on the federal role in education. We shall note some of the conditions which seem to have contributed to the emerging importance of the states and some of the ways through which increasing state influence is now being expressed.

Conditions Stimulating Change

A number of trends in recent years seem to have converged to require that the state exercise a more definitive role in the governance of education. The first of these is a matter of money. School expenditures have increased much faster than the gross national product. Census figures show that for the period from 1960 to 1980 school expenditures for the nation as a whole went up 600 percent whereas the gross national product increased 419 percent.[6] With expenses increasing faster than income, most school districts have found that local revenue resources are inadequate and that more money must be secured from state sources.

As states have been pressed to provide more money for school purposes, they have found that state finance programs are often inadequate. In some cases state revenues were meager and new funding plans, often requiring use of an income tax, had to be devised. Equally inadequate have been state plans for the allocation of funds to school districts. While most states have had so-called equalization programs designed to provide more money to poor districts and less to wealthy districts, many of these programs were of doubtful merit in the first place and often, like the federal tax structure, they have been subjected to continuing amendments until they no longer serve an equalizing function.[7]

The shortcomings of state school finance programs have been dramatically demonstrated in the state and federal courts. Many of these decisions, such as *Serrano* in California, *Rodriguez* in Texas, and *Cahill* in New Jersey, have now provided household words. Some important principles have emerged from the court litigation. For instance, it now seems clear that the wealth of the state, not the wealth of a school district, determines the resources behind a pupil's education. While the U.S. Supreme

---

6. *Statistical Abstract of the United States* (Washington, D.C.: Government Printing Office, 1982): 154, 149.
7. For instance, see Joel S. Berke, Alan K. Campbell, and Robert J. Goettel, *Financing Equal Educational Opportunity* (Berkeley: McCutchan, 1972.

Court did not see education as a "fundamental interest," the Court did suggest that school finance reform was an appropriate activity for the state legislatures. The New Jersey Supreme Court, in *Cahill,* placed the task in perspective. If the mandate of the state constitution that there be a "thorough and efficient system of free public schools" were not observed for any reason, the matter was to be rectified by the state legislature.[8] In a sequel to the Cahall decision, the state supreme court found it necessary to close all public schools in 1976 in order to force the legislature to act. As a result, a graduated income tax, designed to meet constitutional requirements, was enacted.[9]

Still another concern of the state is the increasing demand for accountability in education. To be sure, accountability means different things to different people, but basically more and more people want to know what schools are attempting to do and how well they are succeeding. When people do not get satisfactory answers to these questions at the local level, they frequently raise the same questions at the state level. These demands have resulted in specific accountability legislation in almost half of the states.[10] While some states may move more rapidly than seems warranted in terms of our knowledge and technology in the field and other states may delay by taking recourse in the difficulties inherent in implementing a program, the fact remains that people are going to insist that states require school districts to give attention to the outputs and not merely to the imputs of school programs.

Teacher power also leads to more state jurisdiction. Teachers' organizations often find that the coffers of many school districts are quickly emptied. If more money is to be had for increased salaries and other benefits, it must be secured at the state level. Little wonder that Aufderheide found that teachers' organizations in many states were the most powerful education interest group.[11] On the political front teachers' organizations employed two resources: votes and money for campaign purposes. Leaders of teachers' organizations were quick to acknowledge that they wished to influence the legislature because "that is where the action is." While some legislators were not sympathetic with the efforts of teachers to shape legislation, few denied their influence with the state legislative body.

Teachers have also been moving forward on another front. For the sake of controlling their own profession, teachers organizations in state after state have pushed hard for the establishment of a professional practices board composed chiefly of teachers. A recent survey reports that 40 of the 50 states have some type of professional practices board or commission.[12] In 35 states these boards serve in an advisory role to the state education agency. In five states—Arizona, Illinois, Indiana, Minnesota, and Oregon—the professional practices boards have been given authority for some governmental functions such as establishing certification standards and approving preparation programs. In Arizona and Illinois, however, authority may be limited for their budgets are controlled by the state education agency. Whether the professional

8. See Arthur E. Wise, "Legal Challenges to Public School Finance," *School Review* 82 (November 1973): 1–27.
9. Allan Odden et al., *School Finance Reform in the United States, 1976–1977.* (Denver, Colo.: Education Finance Center, Education Commission of the States, December 1976, 4
10. Phyllis Hawthorn, *Legislation by the States: Accountability and Assessment in Education* (Denver: Co-operative Accountability Project, Colorado Department of Education, 1972).
11. JAlan Aufderheide in Roald F. Campbell and Tim L. Mazzoni, Jr., *State Policy Making for the Public Schools* (Berkeley: McCutchan, 1976), ch. 5.
12 *Standards and Certification Bodies in the Teaching Profession* (Washington, D.C.: National Education Association, 1983).

practices board, the established state board of education, or the legislature is currently responsible, control has shifted to the state level.

Both the Nixon and the Carter administrations suggested a decreased federal role in education and stressed the need for a more prominent state role. While these expressions supported the emergence of the state as an important partner in education, it remained for the Reagan administration to insist upon a decreased role on the part of the federal government.

New Expressions of the State Role

The augmented role of the state in the governance of education is expressed in many ways. In 1983 alone, several states, including California, Florida, Illinois and Mississippi, passed major reform legislation. Earlier, as shown in the Governance Project, governors and legislators were playing a much greater part in policymaking for education.[13] At least four of these governors made educational reform the key to their campaigns. In Florida, Michigan, and Minnesota school finance reform became the overriding issue. Inevitably school finance reform requires more money; hence tax reform becomes a necessary concomitant of such a program. These governors did not shy away from the larger question. These findings were confirmed in a case study showing the great influence of the governor of Wisconsin on educational policy making in that state.[14]

School finance and tax reform obviously require legislative action, so legislators are always involved in the education arena. While the involvement of legislators and governors in the area of finance is necessary, the nature of that involvement represents a departure from past decades. Governors and legislators are not merely reacting to what is presented by others—they are taking the initiative in school finance reform. Moreover, issues other than finance have prompted legislative action. As noted above, almost half of the state legislatures have taken some kind of action in the accountability area. Frequently, this action was taken despite the opposition of educators.

As a wider range of actors have begun to play important roles in state policy making for education, government offices added to their staffs persons who can supply them with information basic to policy decisions. Whereas governors and legislators once relied on interest group organizations, chiefly teacher groups and state departments of education for information, they now turn increasingly to their own staffs. Every governor in the twelve states included in the Governance Project had at least one staff person in education and most had more than one. Every legislature in those twelve states had a staff of some kind in education, and staffs in California and New York were extremely large and reflected a wide range of expertise. These staffs still make use of information from the state education agency and from interest groups, but they submit that information to much more sophisticated analysis than was done a decade or two ago.

Another sign of the new emergence of state governance in education is the disappearance of most of the state coalitions in education. Bailey noted that in the fifties and sixties in the northeastern states where school finance reform was achieved, the

13. Edward R. Hines, "Governors and Educational Policy Making" in *State Policy Making for the Public Schools,* ed. Roald F. Campbell and Tim L. Mazzoni, Jr. (Berkeley, Calif.: McCutchan, 1976), ch. 4.
14. Terry G. Geske, "State Educational Policy Making: A Changing Scene," *Administrator's Notebook* 26, no. 2 (1977–78).

influence of an effective education coalition was always present. This coalition ordinarily included the education interest groups-teachers, administrators, school board members, representatives of citizen groups (particularly the Parent Teacher Association), and representatives of the state education agency. The coalition frequently had easy access to legislative leaders and to the governor.

By the early 1970s most of these arrangements were no longer in existence. Of the twelve states in the Governance Project, educational coalitions retained some degree of their former power in only Colorado and Tennessee.

Recently, in a number of states there have been attempts, some successful, to reestablish these coalitions. Despite these attempts, the labor-management split between teachers' organizations and organizations representing school boards and school administrators is not easy to heal. Moreover, even where such healing has taken place these new coalitions are confronted with the increased influence of governors and legislators in the educational·policymaking process.

In their study of *Legislative Education Leadership in the States,* Rosenthal and Fuhrman note that the governance of education changed in the 1970s: ". . . by the end of the decade legislatures were in the thick of policy making in education. Many had wrested the initiative from state departments and interest groups; and most had started to exercise control over the design, funding, implementation, and assessment of education in their states."[15]

The most dramatic change in this direction was the establishment in the early 1970s of the office of secretary of education in at least four states.[16] The most complete reorganization took place in Pennsylvania, but the transition was partially achieved in Massachusetts, South Dakota, and Virginia. In each case the secretary was appointed by and responsible to the governor. The secretary was usually a member of the governor's cabinet and thus the formal structure required that educational concerns be considered in a total state context.

Not all states moved education as far into general governance as those noted above. In the recent reorganization of the state structure for education in Illinois, for instance, the state board of education members are appointed by the governor with the consent of the senate. The board has jurisdiction over a number of matters, specifically those delegated by the legislature. The board selects and employs its own executive officer. But even in states where the structure of the government has not been changed, it seems doubtful that the autonomy once ascribed to the state agency for education will continue.

Current Organizational Arrangements

Responsibilities of the Legislature

Most state constitutions contain language whereby the state legislature is charged with the responsibility of establishing and maintaining a system of free public schools. In the Utah constitution, for instance, the provision reads as follows: "The Legislature shall provide for the establishment and maintenance of a uniform system of public schools, which shall be open to all children of the State, and free from sectarian

15. Alan Rosenthal and Susan Fuhrman, *Legislative Education Leadership in the States* (Washington, D. C.: Institute for Educational Leadership, 1981), 1.
16. See Roald F. Campbell and Tim L. Mazzoni, Jr., *State Policy Making for the Public Schools.* (Berkeley, Calif.: McCutchan, 1976), ch. 10.

control" (Article X, Section 1). The courts of the several states have consistently interpreted such language as ascribing plenary power to the legislature. In a Florida case in which the jurisdiction of school districts was in question, the plenary power of the legislature was reiterated:

> County school boards are part of machinery of government operating at local level as agency of state in performance of public functions, and character of their functions and extent and duration of their powers rest exclusively in the legislative discretion.

Powers of county school boards may be enlarged, diminished, modified or revoked, and their acts set aside or confirmed, at pleasure of the legislature.[17]

This plenary power does not mean that there are no restrictions upon the legislature. To begin with, the legislature cannot take action contrary to the state constitution, or the federal constitution. The courts also have consistently ruled that the legislature cannot exercise its power in an unreasonable manner, nor can the legislature delegate its plenary power to other governmental agencies.

Constitutional and statutory language, court interpretations, and long practice make it clear that the legislature of each state is the "big school board." The dismay with which many state legislatures view the school bills of each legislative session is, in a sense, inevitable; the basic decisions regarding education cannot be made anywhere else. To be sure, state boards of education and appropriate state commissions can do much to screen and improve the proposed legislation, but only the legislature can decide basic policy questions regarding the schools.

Another development in many legislatures is the desire to exercise legislative oversight. This was recently demonstrated dramatically in Florida where the legislature was particularly concerned about the implementation of three of its policy enactments: management at the school site level, the establishment of citizens advisory councils for each school, and the effects of the Florida school finance program. Rather than depend entirely upon reports from the State Department of Education and from school district officers regarding these matters, the legislature decided to employ a group of consultants to help determine the extent and nature of the impact of these legislative actions. The legislature also sought recommendations about how to improve their general oversight procedures for educational legislation. The consultants did provide the legislature with a comprehensive report of its findings and recommendations.[18]

The work of the legislature is done through committees, and the finance and education committees of the senate and the house are crucial bodies in regard to legislation affecting schools. But these committees do not sit and deliberate in an aseptic environment. Every special interest group in the state interested in education or in expenditures, and some beyond the state, attempt to influence the education and finance committees.

In a study of the role of education interest groups in state policymaking for education, Aufderheide found that teacher associations were the most effective interest groups, particularly in terms of influence on the legislature.[19] Only in three of the

17. *Buck* v. *McLean*, 115 So. (2d) 764 (Fla. 1959).
18. Luvern L. Cunningham et al., *Improving Education in Florida: A Reassessment* (Tallahassee: Select Joint Committee on Public Schools of the Florida Legislature, February 1978).
19. Alan Aufderheide, "The Place of Educational Interest Groups in State Educational Policy-Making Systems" (Ph.D. diss., Ohio State University, 1973).

twelve states studied did school board associations appear to come near to matching the influence of teacher groups. Generally, school administrator associations were found to have still less influence in policymaking. Moreover, in most states noneducation interest groups did not match teachers in terms of influencing the legislators although, when educational issues also became tax issues, particularly in the area of school finance, business, labor, and agricultural groups exerted more influence than normal.

The state legislature, then, has plenary power in making basic policy decisions regarding the schools. This power is exercised amid the welter of forces which constitute American society. In a sense, the legislature is the arena within which these forces make the best case they can and marshall all the influence they can muster. Any realistic appraisal of controls imposed on American schools must consider not only the arena but all of the actors who contend for influence within that arena.

State Executive Arrangements

Control over education is also exercised by the executive branch of state government. The governor, the chief state school officer, the state board of education, the staff of the state department of education, and other state agencies all participate in school government.

The governor exerts influence in several ways. Because the governor is head of a political party at the state level, his or her position on educational questions is crucial, particularly if the governor's party controls the state legislature. The viewpoint of the governor on education is usually set forth in the messages submitted to the legislature. Provisions for education in the budget recommended by the governor to the legislature are often the most fateful expression of the governor's control over education. The governor also has the power to veto educational legislation. Finally, in a majority of the states the governor appoints, often with the approval of the senate, the members of the state board of education. In recent years more and more governors are insisting upon an increased role in educational matters.

As noted earlier, all states now have chief state school officers. Eighteen of these officials are still elected by popular ballot, twenty-seven are appointed by state boards of education, and five are appointed by the governor.[20] In the case of those appointed by the governor and those elected by popular ballot, the chief state school officer is legally an officer of the state and as such exercises the sovereignty of the state. Most chief state school officers appointed by state boards of education are legally employees and not officers of the state. In these cases, the sovereignty of the state has usually been lodged with the state board of education.

In actual practice all chief state school officers can exercise considerable influence over education in their respective states. In many cases the chief state school officer influences state policy for education by giving public expression to educational needs, by enlisting grassroots support, by recommending action to the state board of education, and by influencing the legislature and the governor as they consider educational problems. Moreover, this official is usually charged by statute or state board of education regulation to exercise general supervision over the schools of the state, to organize a staff of professionals in the state department of education, and to actually

---

20. Council of Chief State School Officers, *Educational Governance in the States* (Washington D.C.: U.S. Department of Education, 1983), 23–25.

direct the operation of certain special schools, such as those for the deaf and the blind, which may be under state jurisdiction.

We have noted that forty-nine states have a state board of education charged with the general supervision of elementary and secondary schools within the state. In those states where the chief state school officer is still elected by popular ballot, there is often confusion between the basic responsibility of the state board of education and that of the state superintendent of public instruction. In states where the state board of education selects its own chief executive, this confusion does not ordinarily exist.

Most state boards of education are composed largely of lay citizens rather than professional educators. In a majority of the states, these members are appointed by the governor. A number of states have provided for the election of state board members by popular ballot. In most cases state board members serve without salary, although a per diem and expenses for attending meetings may be allowed. Ordinarily, state boards of education meet at least once every three months.

In one sense, state boards of education are administrative agencies, usually charged with exercising general control over the elementary and secondary schools of the state and in a few cases also given some jurisdiction over higher education. State boards are also seen as having a policymaking function, specifically in those areas delegated to them by the legislature, and also in terms of supporting policy positions to the governor and the legislature. Based on a study of the state governance of education the policymaking role of most state boards is more fiction that fact.[21] For the most part, state boards of education tended to legitimize the policy recommendations of the chief state school officer and exercised little policy initiative on their own.

The governance study also supported the earlier conclusions of Sroufe that state board members were much alike whether appointed or elected.[22] He thought this might be due to the low visibility of the board in most states which makes it unlikely that the governor will appoint candidates who might be controversial. The governor tends to rely on selected advisors or representatives of educational professions for assistance. In states where board members are elected, the voters, like the governor, find it impossible to make choices for membership among candidates who seem to have no positions on substantive issues, and must rely upon educational reputation and general status. These are the only criteria available to the governor or to the electorate and explain why board composition is so predictable.

The state department of education is the professional arm of the chief state school officer and the state board of education. In recent years, new and expanded functions of state departments have required an increase in professional personnel. This growth in departmental staff has been facilitated by expansion of federal assistance for state departments which began in the 1960s.

In 1982, the average number of full-time professionals on staff in the headquarters of state departments of education was 273.[23] The highest number of staff members was 1233 in California and the lowest was 34 in North Dakota. Ten years earlier, the average number of staff members in state departments of education was 191. Ordinarily, these people are organized into divisions such as administration and finance, teacher certification, instructional services, junior colleges, vocational and adult edu-

21. Campbell and Mazzoni, *State Policy Making for the Public Schools,* ch. 2.
22. Gerald E. Sroufe, "Selection Procedures and Self-role Expectations of State School Board Members: An Exploratory Description and Analysis" (Ph.D. diss., University of Chicago, 1970).
23. Council of Chief State School Officers, *Educational Governance in the States.*

cation, and vocational rehabilitation. These divisions suggest the areas in which members of the professional staff give supervision to the schools of the state.

In many cases state department personnel are required to enforce the regulations of the state imposed either by statute or by state board action. Sometimes enforcement duties are thrust upon state boards of education but no supporting budget to permit implementation of such responsibilities is provided. In recent years most state departments have tried to give increased emphasis to the leadership role of the department. While state departments appear to have been strengthened in recent years, many of them are still too overburdened with regulatory duties to exert much leadership.

In terms of enforcing minimum standards upon the schools of the state, however, state departments of education are rather effective. These standards may apply to such practices as the adoption of textbooks, the certification of teachers, and the distribution of state money. In all instances state department personnel are charged with following statutory provisions or state board of education regulations.

Ordinarily, a number of other state agencies have some control over the schools. These agencies may have jurisdiction over certain aspects of the health and the safety of school pupils, the auditing of school funds, the employment of minors, and other matters. In Illinois, for example, these agencies include the following: the auditor of public accounts, who apportions state school funds; the attorney general, who may give legal opinions on educational questions; the State Teachers Certification Board, which administers the teacher certification function; the Department of Labor, which exercises some control over the employment of minors; the Board of Trustees of the Retirement Fund, which administers the teacher's retirement program; the Scholarship Commission, which awards scholarships to high school graduates; and the School Building Commission, which allocates state funds to "needy" school districts for school building purposes. While these agencies have only those powers granted to them by the legislature, the exercise of these powers inevitably requires some discretion and thus represents a measure of control.

In summary, the execution of educational government at the state level is performed by the governor, a chief state school officer, a state board of education, a state department largely composed of professionals in education, and a number of other state agencies to which certain kinds of educational functions have been delegated by the legislature. In some cases, these officers and agencies seem to understand rather clearly what their respective duties are and they perform these duties satisfactorily. In other cases, neither perception nor performance appear to be adequate. Emphasis upon local government of education, even among state officials, has undoubtedly weakened state government of education, a condition now undergoing some change but which still demands attention.

Delegation to Local Agencies

While the legislature and certain executive agencies have much to do with the government of education, responsibility for the actual operation of most of our schools has been delegated to district boards of education. The nature of the power of these boards has been set forth in chapter 8. In brief, the duties of school board members include the right to establish schools, to build school houses, to employ a superintendent, to establish necessary rules to manage and govern the schools, and to raise and expend money. The courts have consistently held that such delegations by the state legislature to district boards of education are appropriate. An excerpt from a New Jersey case follows:

> Recent years have witnessed an increasing liberality in the approach of our courts toward the construction of legislative delegations of power. The keynote was struck in *Ward* v. *Scott,* 11 N.J. 117, 123–4, A 2nd 385 (1952), where Justice Jacobs observed that "the exigencies of modern government have increasingly dictated the use of general rather than minutely detailed standards in regulatory enactments under the police power.[24]

This extensive delegation to district boards of education is always within the framework established by the state legislature. While local boards of education may, for instance, raise and expend money, they do this within the limits prescribed by law. Often the ceiling on the local tax rate is set by law. Nearly always, expenditures for capital outlay are possible only after approval is secured by a referendum in the district, a procedure stipulated by state law. Nearly all other operational powers of school boards are circumscribed in similar fashion.

Many states establish an additional agency to assist with educational government. As noted in chapter 5, over half the states have organized intermediate units of school administration. The intermediate units may be represented in the office of the county superintendent of schools, in the county board of education, or in both. While the function of the intermediate unit is not always clear, the county superintendent or the county board is usually charged with preparing information and making reports to the state department of education, assisting in the reorganization of school districts, registering teachers' certificates, assisting in the supervision of rural schools, assisting with the in-service education of teachers, and providing some special services in weak districts. The stipulation of the functions of these intermediate units is another clear example of the delegation of power by the state legislature to agencies nearer the scene where the school is in actual operation. The county superintendent throughout most of U.S. history has been charged with seeing that school districts, particularly those in rural areas, operate schools as the legislature intended.

States, then, have delegated powers—within stipulated limits—to district boards of education to operate schools. In many states, particularly those with numerous rural districts, the state has established an inspection office to see that schools are operated according to the law. Both legislative and executive branches of state government play a part in the control of the schools. The judicial branch of state government, too, particularly through the decisions rendered by the state courts, affects school operation. The nature of our state and federal courts, and the role the courts play in school matters are treated at length in chapter 7.

At this point is seems appropriate to ask if the structure of state government, including the state education agency, has a bearing on the capacity of that agency to conceptualize and implement its functions. In 1976 Campbell and Mazzoni dealt extensively with that question and we will refer briefly to that discussion.[25] They explicated three possible models for state governance of education: the centralized executive model, the separate agency model, and some combination of the two. Each of the three models stressed particular values in governance. The centralized executive

---

24. *Schinck* v. *Board of Education of Westwood Consolidated School District,* 159 A. (2d) 396 (N. J. 1960).
25. Roald F. Campbell and Tim L. Mazzoni Jr., *State Policy Making for the Public Schools.* ch. 10.

model, for example, emphasized the role of the governor as the chief executive of the state, in education as in other state functions. While no state employed a complete centralized model, some states, such as Massachusetts and Pennsylvania, had moved in that direction. Whereas the centralized executive model would make education a part of general governance, the separate agency model emphasized considerable independence of educational governance. This independence was to be achieved through separate educational arrangements: a state board of education and a chief state school officer. Many states employed some variation of this model with New York, where education was almost a fourth branch of government, having the most independent arrangement. At the other extreme, found in several states, was the elected-chief model where the chief state school officer was publicly elected. Several variations of the combination model were also discussed by Campbell and Mazzoni. One of these variations, also found in several states, was the governor-appointed authoritative board with the board selecting the chief state school officer.

After analyses of these various models and consideration of the expressed preferences of persons knowledgeable about state structures for education, Campbell and Mazzoni came to the following conclusion:

> We reiterate our two major concerns: *(1) formal structure must be seen as one of many variables in any plan for the reorganization of state governance for education, but undue reliance cannot be placed on structure alone, and (2) at the same time there should be a recognition that structure can make some difference.* It is quite clear that how people choose to work within a structure makes a difference. It also seems that formal structure may permit, may actually encourage, certain kinds of behavior on the part of policy makers. Even if changing structure does not guarantee desirable changes in behavior, the fact that it might encourage such changes seems to be sufficient inducement to consider structural arrangements.[26]

It seemed quite clear, for instance, that an elected chief state school officer and a governor-appointed state board of education could often invoke political and jurisdictional issues in place of dealing with the substantive functions of the state education agency.

Decisions Made at the State Level

We have touched on a number of the types of educational decisions which are made at the state level. We shall now take a closer look at these decisions. While states vary somewhat in their practices, a number of decisions are rather common among the states.

The Instructional Program

Most states make a number of decisions having to do with the instructional program. They usually determine the scope or the extent of the program. The common school for which states take responsibility now refers to both the elementary and the secondary school. In some states the kindergarten is recognized as part of the state program, but in many states the kindergarten is optional and its organization is left to the discretion of local districts. A number of states now have permissive junior college

26. Roald F. Campbell and Tim L. Mazzoni Jr., *State Policy Making for the Public Schools.* p. 433

legislation, including some state financial support, but most states have not yet included the junior college as part of the public school program. The extent to which vocational education, education for the handicapped, preschool education, and adult education are given attention is often dependent upon decisions made at the state level. Prescriptive federal programs, as noted in chapter 2, have come near to forcing states to take action in vocational education and in education for the handicapped.

In addition to determining or at least influencing the scope of the instructional program, most states exercise some authority in establishing standards for the program. A few states actually write these standards into the statutes. A more common practice is for the legislature to delegate the establishment of standards to the state board of education or to the office of the chief state school officer. In Ohio, for instance, the state board of education is given specific authority to formulate and prescribe minimum standards for elementary and secondary schools. These standards pertain to the curriculum, instructional materials, pupil admission and promotion, and graduation requirements. Formulation of standards under such authority makes these standards a part of the administrative law under which the schools of the state operate. With the recent stress on accountability, the establishment of standards or criteria against which to measure performance has taken on a new importance.

All states have passed laws requiring all children, except those who are physically or mentally incapable, to attend school. While the period of compulsory attendance varies somewhat among the states, and as part of the integration struggle the provisions were modified in Mississippi, South Carolina, and Virginia, a common required attendance period is from age 8 to age 16 or graduation from the eighth grade. Most states also prescribe the minimum school term, usually nine months or about 180 school days. Many states also define a minimum school day. One legislature recently set the minimum school day at no less than five hours.

Some states require their state boards to specify a course of study for the schools of the state to follow. The state board of education in North Carolina, for instance, is required to adopt a standard course of study upon the recommendation of the state superintendent of public instruction. To meet a requirement such as this, most state boards appoint a committee of professional school workers to prepare the course, or courses, of study. The materials prepared by these groups would then be approved by the state board of education and made available to the schools of the state.

In some states the course of study provided by the state is binding only on rural school districts; city school districts may have authority to prepare their own courses of study. In other states the county superintendent's office is charged with specifying a course of study for all rural districts. In most states, however, the statutes affect the course of study in some way. A common stipulation is the requirement of United States history and government for graduation from high school.

Many states also have requirements governing the selection and uses of textbooks. For example, the Texas Education Agency is required to purchase and distribute textbooks to the schools of the state. To aid in the performance of this function the agency appoints a state textbook committee and charges it with the examination and recommendation of the books to be used. Ordinarily, the agency accepts the recommendations of the committee. A few states still have single textbook adoptions for elementary schools, but a number of states adopt multiple lists from which school districts may select books. Some states leave selection of books to local school districts or to the county office, but they do require that each book so selected be reported to the state education authority.

State decisions concerning the instructional program may deal with the scope of the program, the establishment of standards, the requirement of a course of study, or the approval of books to be used. Some of these decisions are specified in the statutes, but more often they emanate from the state board of education or the office of the chief state officer in keeping with statutory authority. The financial support program of the state may, in effect, also control the program. For instance, many districts would find it difficult to provide kindergarten and junior college programs unless they were included in state aid provisions.

Certification of Personnel

More definitive than program decisions are state regulations having to do with the certification of teachers. Haberman and Stinnett report that all states have set up controls governing teacher certification and administer these regulations directly.[27] Forty-five years ago, about half of the states left the administration of certification to other agencies, most often the county superintendents of schools. A few large city school districts still have authority to examine and certify teachers, but for the most part this function has been taken over by the states. Most states stipulate the length of the training program and something about its content in order for prospective teachers to meet certification standards.

A growing practice among states is the approval of institutions and programs for teacher education and the acceptance of graduates from such programs for certification without further individual appraisal. This practice requires that the state department of education have staff members who can examine teacher education programs, make judgments about them, and ultimately recommend to the appropriate state authority what programs be accepted or rejected. Recently, in some states there has been political pressure to "open up" some certification requirements. This pressure has frequently been stimulated by the shortage of math and science teachers and the need to recruit as teachers, even on a part-time basis, persons with math and science backgrounds who have difficulty meeting rigid certification requirements.

Another development is the growth of reciprocity of certification among the states. About three-fifths of the states grant certificates to teachers of other states provided they have graduated from institutions accredited by the National Council for the Accreditation of Teacher Education. NCATE is a voluntary organization composed chiefly of representatives from teachers' colleges and teachers' organizations, and its influence is an example of how private groups can exercise as much or more control than public government.[28] In 1983, NCATE began the process of revising their accrediation system to coordinate state approval with national accreditation and to insure more quality control of teacher education.[29]

Facilities Standards

Almost all states exercise some control over school facilities. Such control may include the establishment of school plant standards, approval of school sites, and the approval of plans and specifications for new buildings. The school plant standards may actually

27. Martin Haberman and T. M. Stinnett, *Teacher Education and the New Profession of Teaching* (Berkeley: McCutchan, 1973), 18.
28. For a study of NCATE, see John R. Mayor and Willis G. Swartz, *Accreditation in Teacher Education— Its Influence on Higher Education* (Washington, D.C.: National Commission on Accrediting, 1965).
29. *AACTE Briefs* 4 (June 1983), 1–3.

appear in the statutes, but more commonly an administrative body has statutory authorization for the establishment of standards. This body in many cases is the state board of education; in other cases it is the industrial commission or some similar agency in the state. In New York the State Education Department and the State Department of Public Works collaborate on some aspects of this function.

In some states grants or loans from the state for school plant outlays are available to school districts under some circumstances. Often these districts have to appear needy in order to qualify for any of the state aid. Moreover, school districts in these circumstances are often required to accept an austerity building. Since these districts are often the ones with rapidly expanding school enrollments and depleted local funds, they ordinarily have no recourse but to accept the conditions stipulated by the state agency. Thus a more severe form of control sometimes follows the dollar. A number of states have established special agencies to administer these special grants for school plants.

Financial Support

State control over education is often the strongest in matters of money for school operation and for capital outlay. In some states, particularly in New England, and in some large cities school districts are fiscally dependent upon some other agency, such as the city council, for the approval of their budgets. In a majority of school districts, however, boards of education need not submit their budgets to another agency; hence they are considered fiscally independent.

Even in fiscally independent school districts, however, numerous state controls are imposed. Boards of education may have the power to determine their own budgets, but the tax rate necessary to provide the revenue to meet the budget must ordinarily fall within the tax limits set by the state. Sometimes, by means of a referendum, these limits may be extended, but even then the upper limit for the operating levy is usually set by the state legislature. Sometimes special levies are permissible for supplementary purposes, such as transportation.

Most states not only set a ceiling on school district taxes, but they also stipulate how the school budget is to be prepared, what budget breakdowns must be shown, and how budget approval must be sought. Often the board of education is required to advertise the budget and hold a hearing on it.

Crucial to the financial operation of the school districts are the assessment practices applied to real estate and other property. As with other taxing jurisdictions, state goverment and often county government determine the nature of these practices. Some states have established strong equalization boards which influence the local assessment practices and which apply corrections among counties designed to equalize assessments. Most local school districts are very dependent upon these equalization boards.

The state exerts control over capital outlay funds as well as operating funds. Nearly every state sets limits upon the borrowing capacity of school districts for capital outlay purposes. Michigan and Virginia do not appear to impose debt limits upon certain types of districts. There is usually a limit, often expressed in precentage of assessed valuation, beyond which bonds may not be floated even by vote of the people. In Illinois, for instance, this limit is 5 percent of the assessed valuation of the school district. In most states, the percentage must be approved by a simple majority of qualified electors voting; in other states, a two-thirds majority of electors is required. In some states, electors must also be property holders in order to vote in a bond election, and in a few states a two-thirds majority of property holders is required to pass the bond referendum.

In most states, financial controls imposed upon school districts are stipulated in detail in the statutes. An administrative board, often the state board of education, may be required to allocate the money among the school districts of the state; but ordinarily these bodies can exercise little, if any, discretion.

Nonpublic Schools

Most of the state-level decisions mentioned thus far apply specifically to public elementary and secondary schools of the state. The role of the state in regulating nonpublic schools is not as plain. Opinions on this issue are varied: some would make such schools illegal while others would have states take a "hands-off" policy. The United States Supreme Court made it clear in the Oregon case that states could not require all pupils to attend the public schools. An excerpt follows:

> No question is raised concerning the power of the State reasonably to regulate all schools, to inspect, supervise and examine them, their teachers and pupils; to require that all children of proper age attend *some* [italics added] school, that teachers shall be of good moral character and patriotic disposition, that certain studies plainly essential to good citizenship must be taught and that nothing be taught which is manifestly inimical to the public welfare.[30]

Following the decision of the Court, it seems clear that the compulsory education laws of states can also be oberved by attendance at nonpublic schools. It seems equally clear that states can and in fact are obligated to see that nonpublic schools meet appropriate standards. A number of states still have legislation to pass if they are to meet this obligation; still others are not enforcing existing statutes.[31] Should Congress enact any form of tuition tax credit for nonpublic schools, as advocated by the Reagan administration, the need for state regulation of nonpublic schools would become even greater.

This discussion has not covered all types of state-level decisions for education. Enough has been said, however, to indicate the nature of state school decisions for education. We shall next turn to some broad functions of the state education agency.

Suggested Functions of the State Education Agency

As we have seen, many decisions for schools are made at the state level. Governors, legislators, the state education agency, and other actors participate in this decision-making process. We will look now at the functions assigned specifically to the state education agency. In so doing, we are defining the state agency to include the state board of education, the chief state school officer, and the professional staff of the department. Our description of these elements is based on actual practice in some of our more advanced states as well as what practice needs to be in all of our states. In a sense we are suggesting that, if schools are to be conducted in keeping with Amer-

---

30. Donald A. Erickson, "Nonpublic Schools in Michigan" in *School Finance and Educational Opportunity in Michigan*, ed. J. Alan Thomas (Lansing: Michigan Department of Education, 1968), ch. 7.
31. *Pierce* v. *Society of Sisters*, 268 U.S. 510 (1925).

ican values and in the American scheme of government, state education agencies have a unique and crucial function to perform.

State departments of education, as we have shown, have a regulatory function. Minimum standards are an important area of regulation. Personnel in the state department of education should have a hand in developing such standards. The formulation of these standards should take into account professional knowledge in the area whether that knowledge is gained from looking at educational practice in other states or from relevant research.

Ordinarily the process of arriving at a statement of the minimums should be a cooperative one. In attempting to develop a state program on teacher certification, for instance, teachers, administrators, school board members, and professors in teacher education institutions should be consulted. Also the views of people who will be affected by the state program should be ascertained and any special insights these people have should be noted.

Once standards have been established, they should be enforced. Ordinarily this will be done through explanation and persuasion. The emphasis should be on achieving excellence rather than merely conforming to the minimum standards. When state minimum standards are clearly ignored, however, the state should have legal recourse to require compliance. This may be done through such measures as denying approval of schools, withholding state funds, and, if necessary, by means of mandamus action and recourse to the courts. State departments represent the people of the state and, in terms of minimum standards, the state, not the locality, is sovereign.

A second function of state departments of education is direct operation of schools. In the past a number of states have been charged with operating special schools for the blind and deaf. Sometimes special vocational or technical schools and junior colleges have been set up under the immediate control of the state board of education. In recent years, however, there has been a tendency to distribute these special school functions among existing school districts or to create special school districts for such functions. For example, many city school districts now conduct their own classes for the blind and hard of hearing. It is not unusual either to find special districts or combinations of districts organized for slow learners. Special junior college or technical institute districts are also common in some states.

State departments of education, we believe, should give up the direct operation of schools wherever they can find or establish a local agency to take over such a function. Direct operation of schools is inconsistent with the other functions a state department is called upon to perform. For instance, states operating schools for the deaf might be more reluctant to examine alternative programs for such people than states which do not have such vested interests.

Most state education agencies try to help the schools of the state improve their operation. Thus, service is a third appropriate function of these agencies. In the past, this service was extended more frequently to the rural than to the urban districts of the state but that condition is undergoing some change. One of the first services provided by many state agencies was the preparation and distribution of instructional materials. Some of the early visual aids libraries and testing centers, for instance, were located in state departments of education. Most state agencies have also prepared, usually with the assistance of teachers and administrators from the schools of the state, courses of study and teaching guides for the use of the schools.

A recurring question is how a supervisory agency can be helpful to an operating agency, particularly when the supervisory agency also has regulatory duties to perform. In an attempt to solve this problem most state agencies in education have made staff available to consult with teachers and administrators on an individual basis. State agencies may anticipate the need to provide consultation on new programs or new demands being made on the schools. For instance, in the area of computer education, a state agency might have one or two very knowledgeable people on call for advice throughout the state. Or, the new demands growing out of the implementation of Title IX forbidding sex discrimination and the new provisions of the law on the education of the handicapped might warrant special staff in the state agency to advise school people.

Obviously, in populous states the one-to-one appraoch to consultation is not sufficient to serve thousands of school people. Therefore, state agency staff members have set up in-service education workshops for groups of teachers and administrators or for key personnel in local school systems, who would carry the message to others in their own school districts.

Planning, research, and evaluation is a fourth responsibility incumbent upon state departments of education. Each state department of education should have a strong division of planning and research responsible for the collection and analysis of relevant statistics on the operation of the schools. This unit would investigate numerous questions such as how many high school graduates took advanced placement courses, how many school districts have introduced the school mathematics study materials, and how many teachers are teaching in their major fields.

State education departments should not stop with status research; evaluative research should also be done. Objectives for experimental programs should be set, then evidence should be gathered in order to ascertain the extent to which the objectives had been achieved. For instance, a number of school districts with nongraded primary schools might cooperate with the state department in determining to what extent the objectives for such a plan were accomplished.

A few state departments may also find it possible to do basic studies wherein relationships among variables are ascertained. However, most basic research will probably still be done on university campuses or in special research organizations. In many ways this separation of research functions is desirable, for it permits both universities and state departments to do the type of research for which they are best fitted and in which the members of the respective organizations have the most interest.

While funds are not as plentiful as they were in the 1960s, some money for research and evaluation is available from the U.S. Department of Education and from other agencies. State departments should also seek state funds for such purposes. In addition to actually doing research, state departments should encourage and give leadership to research and evaluation activities among the school districts of the state. Unfortunately, very few school districts have either the staff or the budget for such purposes. Moreover, professional workers in these districts are confused about the meaning of research, about how to apply the results of research, and about what research can and cannot do. State departments should provide education on these matters at the local level.

Perhaps the most important aspect of the research function in the state department of education is the communication of research. Research personnel should not only be informed about the studies done in their own department, but they should know what is going on in important research agencies across the nation. Ways of summarizing this knowledge and transmitting it to all state department personnel and to many school and college workers in the state should be developed. This information could be used by the state board of education and the legislature as they consider basic educational problems.

If state departments expanded their role in planning, research, and evaluation and left operation to the schools themselves, the state departments would become more useful in the government of education. Such a shift in emphasis would give substance to the leadership which departments provide to the schools. Leadership is the fifth function of state education departments. Major problems confront us: How can urban schools be improved? How can teacher education be improved? How can schools be more adequately financed? How can schools be appropriately desegregated? To answer these and many more questions, we need additional research knowledge, but even more we need the judgment of competent people who know what the facts are, who ask the right questions, who are sensitive to probable consequences, who reflect the basic values of our culture, and who can point to a course of action designed to improve our lot. Hopefully, some of this vision will come from the membership of the state board of education, some from the chief state school officer, some from professionals within the state department, and some from other lay citizens and professional school workers over the state. The state agency should have a means of utilizing the contributions from these sources to develop goals and directions for education in the state.

State departments of education should lead not only by helping people to do better what they are now doing but also by helping them to see new and important things to do. This means that long-range planning should be an important task of the state department; it means that the best brains among lay people and professionals in the state should be involved in this long-range planning. It means that consultants outside the state may be sought to stimulate thinking about goals and programs to be undertaken. Finally, it means that state agencies—boards, chief state school officers, and departmental specialists—should play a part in policymaking for education.

The question arises, What is the appropriate balance among these five functions for a state education agency? Or, if the operation of schools is eliminated, what is the appropriate balance among the four remaining functions? That very question was raised by the State Board of Education in Delaware.[32] In Delaware the effort devoted to regulation, service, and leadership was under review. While measurement was difficult, there seemed to be evidence to suggest that, in terms of staff time expressed in person-weeks, 48 percent of the department's effort went to regulatory activities, 14 percent to leadership activities, and 38 percent to service activities. There are no magic formulas for computing what these percentages ought to be, but the consultants did suggest that the effort going into leadership was less than it should be. The effort going into regulation confirmed the reality of that obligation for state education agencies. Delaware, perhaps more than many other states, emphasized the service function and that effort was met with widespread approval among the teachers and administrators in the schools.

This effort to map out directions cannot be dominated by a small group. Goals must make sense to lay citizens and to professional school workers. Ultimately, if these programs proposed to meet goals are to be implemented, they, or rather the money to support them, must be approved by the legislature. The marshalling of

32. Henry M. Brickell and Roald F. Campbell, *An Evaluation of the Delaware Department of Public Instruction* (Denver, Colo.: Education Commission of the States, 1978).

positive public opinion so necessary to legislative action is a prime leadership task of the state education agency.

Summary and Future Prospects

State controls over the schools take numerous forms. Many of these controls are implemented by the state education agency, but some may be exercised directly by the governor, the legislature, the attorney general, the state auditor, or by other state agencies, such as those that consider new buildings or establish health standards. The major state controls operating in most states are summarized below.

State Controls

1. *Control of Information.* The state education agency, and to a lesser extent other state agencies, require school reports and conduct studies of school practices and in the process build data banks about the schools of the state. For the most part, these agencies determine what data are to be collected, what uses are to be made of such data, and to what extent reports of data analyses are to be made public. At times, state legislatures require specific studies and federal agencies often require specific reports.

2. *Technical Services.* The state education agency determines, in large part, what technical services are to be made available to the schools of the state. Decisions on services influence the staffing required in state departments of education and the establishment of relationships with local school districts. Whatever that staffing whether in reading, evaluation, or computer education the influence of the state department is tipped in that direction

3. *Regulation of Standards.* By constitution and statute legislatures are required to set certain standards for the schools of the state. Legislatures then generally require that the state agencies, most often the education agency, check up on the implementation of those standards. Thus, the state agencies may be required to check on such matters as school attendance, the use of books and other instructional materials, and the keeping of certain fiscal records. In each case, school districts are required to obey the law.

4. *Allocation of Money.* The state education agency is usually required to allocate money made available by the legislature to the schools of the state. While the allocation formula is usually found in the law, the state education agency must often interpret what the law means, and sometimes some portion of the state appropriation is left to the discretion of the chief state school officer or to the state agency to meet emergency needs in the state. The allocation of money is a sanction of some importance.

5. *Certification of Personnel.* All states have now taken over the function of certifying persons who may teach or administer in the schools of the state. Some states delegate most of this function to the teacher education institutions of the state, but in many states education agencies determine the nature of preservice preparation programs for the teachers and administrators and the requirements for the renewal of certificates. State agency control is frequently challenged by the universities and also by teacher organizations but in most states the right to determine those who enter and those who stay in the profession is a state prerogative.

6. *Coalitions.* Many state agencies have solidified their influence through the maintenance of coalitions with educators and related groups in the state. In the past, these coalitions often included teacher organizations, school administrator organizations, the state school board association, the parent teacher association, and other groups. With the advent of collective bargaining by teachers, many of these coalitions have been partially dismantled, but most chief state school officers still find that their strength with the legislature and governor is enhanced through alliance with some of the education interest groups.

7. *Legislative Oversight.* The determination of legislatures to see that their enactments are implemented represents another increasingly important aspect of state control. As noted earlier, the Florida legislature went so far as to employ consultants from outside the state to determine to what extent three legislative mandates were being implemented. In many states the legislature depends upon its agencies or a staff employed by the legislature itself to conduct these implementation studies

8. *The Courts.* In the many relationships between officials at the state level and those at the school level, it is quite normal that differences in interpretation and judgment would emerge. Frequently, these differences have been carried into court; while those cases based on the federal constitution such as school desegregation, have gone to federal courts, many state issues have ended up in the state courts. These issues may include compulsory attendance, teacher fitness, and the use of public money. The courts must often say what the law is and insist that it be obeyed.

9. *The State as Federal Proxy.* States are frequently asked to allocate federal funds to the school districts and to enforce the federal regulations pertaining to those allocations. To achieve these ends, one-half to two-thirds of the staff members of many state departments of education are paid from federal funds. These staff members are found in the administration of funds for such programs as those pertaining to the disadvantaged, the handicapped, planning and evaluation, and vocational education. In the process, the state is helping to establish special interest groups among professionals and also among lay people. These special interest groups in turn are becoming strong and influential advocates for their own narrow concerns.

Outlook for the Future

Let us now shift to some consideration of future prospects at the state level. Control of schools at the state level will probably grow. Several considerations lead us to this conclusion. First, by constitutional and statutory provisions, education is a state and not a local function. School districts have delegated, not plenary, power. The growing interest of state legislatures in the operation of schools, particularly in legislative oversight, is another expression of the plenary power of the legislature.

Another factor leading to more state control is the increasing demand for more money from state sources. As current state funding programs are found to be unconstitutional, states are ordinarily required to provide additional revenues to equalize educational opportunities throughout the state. While money and control do not stand in a one-to-one relationship, it is difficult to envision added state funding without some increase in state control.

Still another condition leading to more state control rests in the attempt of the Reagan administration to shift some educational decisions from the federal to the state level. While that attempt has met with uneven success, it does further enhance the role of the state. With increased presence of the state in education, we suggest that in many states structural arrangements for the governance of education need examination.

But the enhancement of the state role in education has a somber side. In terms of money, many states will find it most difficult to meet the additional responsibilities thrust upon them. The Education Commission of the States, after examination of funding prospects of the states through the year 2000, came to the conclusion that "the fiscal condition of the states is, on the whole, bad."[33] Lack of money coupled with a waning of legislative support, as noted by Rosenthal and Fuhrman,[34] does not augur well for the future. Thus, our second prediction is that resources for education in many states will be limited and their procurement will require hard choices, well supported requests, and capable management on the part of state officials.

In spite of this bleak outlook, a third prediction for the future is that state education agencies will not be able to escape their regulatory function. The demands for more regulation are probably on the increase. For instance, many state legislatures have mandated competency standards for promotion or for high school graduation and require that the state education agency implement such standards. As to service, most state education agencies will continue to provide technical assistance to the schools and school districts of the state. State agencies may become selective in the nature of these services and in the strategies employed, but the service function will continue.

As the state is called upon to exercise a greater role in regulation, service, and leadership, it will be very difficult to meet those demands without a more extensive knowledge base which can be had only with more planning, more research, and more evaluation. Thus planning, research, and evaluation as a state agency function will grow in importance. States will be required to provide more leadership. Some traditional service functions will probably have to be reduced in order that more attention can be given to planning, research, and evaluation.

Our fourth projection is that state departments of education will need to increase personnel to cope with the challenges facing those bodies. The day of almost exclusive recruitment of state department personnel from the rural schools of the state seems to be coming to an end. State agencies, in need of technically competent people, must recruit such people wherever they may be found—in the schools, in the universities, in business, in law, and in government.

With more prudent regulation, more extensive planning and evaluation, and more discerning leadership in state agencies, many chief state school officers, members of state boards of education, and even legislators and governors will see the need for competent personnel. Moreover, the chief clients of the state agency, the schools and school districts of the state, will demand competence. While the state agency was once relevant to the rural districts and largely ignored by the urban districts, that day is passing. Districts with competent leadership will be able to expect the same from the state education agency.

33. Allan Odden et al., *School Finance Reform in the States: 1983*, Report no. 783-1 (Denver, Colo.: Education Commission of the States, 1983), 5.
34. Alan Rosenthal and Susan Fuhrman, *Legislative Education Leadership* (Washington, D.C.: Institute for Educational Leadership, 1981), 102.

4

The Local School District

The local school district is the basic administrative unit in school organization. In this chapter we will examine local school government through the perspective of history; we will review the current status of school districts and school district reorganization; we will contemplate the future of local school districts in keeping with contemporary as well as what appear to be emerging developments in local government in the United States; and we will suggest, at least by implication, ways by which district structure may affect the control of American schools.

The School District in Local Government

Local school government in the United States is not an historical accident. The deep belief in freedom of our founding fathers as well as the exigencies of a rigorous environment led quite naturally to a reliance upon local government. As Dewey said, describing the newcomers to this continent, "The imagination of the founders did not travel beyond what could be accomplished and understood in a congeries of self-governing communities."[1] Local government today is undoubtedly a grotesque representation of the image of government held by the framers of our federal and state constitutions. In the past two centuries we have witnessed a steady movement away from the sharp separation of powers among the three levels of government. The oft-cited changes in our way of life, including rising expectations for governmental services, have contributed to a new national federalism. Some activities of government, once essentially local, are now blended with strong state and federal interest; and some revenue sources, which were once the property of only one level, are now shared.

Because of the interdependence of the levels of government as well as the complex mixing of local units, it is difficult to understand local units without comprehending the intricacies of intergovernmental affairs. The function of local governments in the total mosaic of governments is expressed aptly in the quotation that follows:

1. John Dewey, *The Public and Its Problems* (Denver, Colo.: Alan Swallow, 1957), 111.

A study of intergovernmental relations without adequate attention to local government would be as invalid as a physical examination by a doctor who examined only the exterior of the body and the limbs and assumed that the tissues and the muscles had no bearing on the body as a whole. Local governments are to total government what basic tissues are to the human body. Without them, government would have no vitality. The counties, cities, towns, villages, and boroughs serve as training schools for the leaders of government, and in the affairs of local government are tried those who aspire to State and National office. More important still is the use of local government to soften the impact of arbitrary State and National laws and regulations and to modify them to fit a population quite diverse in its cultural, economic, geographic, and political elements.[2]

The school district is very much a part of local government and thus is affected markedly by other layers and units of government including the courts. As a government unit unto itself, however, the school district does have some distinguishing characteristics.

What a School District Is

A school district is the basic governmental unit through which the exercise of local control of schools is effected. It is a unit of government, possessing quasi-corporate powers, created and empowered by state law to administer a public school or a public school system. A school district is controlled by a governing board; it has taxing power, the right to make contracts, and the right to sue and be sued. It may or may not employ a superintendent; thousands of common school districts, the one-room rural schools, do not have superintendents.

School districts are the most numerous units of local government with approximately 16,000 separate school districts still in existence in the United States.[3] To characterize properly this unit of local government one must say that local districts are at once the most common and at the same time the most diverse of all local jurisdictions. They range from districts comprising great cities such as New York, Los Angeles, Chicago, and Detroit to nonoperating districts that number in the thousands and include a conglomeration of sizes, classes, and types in between. Their diversity illustrates the tenaciousness with which Americans hold to these remnants of localism and grassroots expression of the public will.

Education is a legally constituted responsibility of each state and is subject to the direction and sometimes the vagaries of state government. Local school districts are the instruments through which education is overseen and managed; they are extensions of state governments. Any state, within its unique constitutional and statutory framework, can destroy, modify, or proliferate these units. It is remarkable, however, how unwilling legislatures have been to change school district structure. Modifications that are made are most often the result of long, arduous, and carefully organized efforts of special interest groups working for school district reorganization.

School districts, along with townships, municipalities, fire districts, sanitary districts, park districts, and a number of other local governments, are considered by most Americans to be essential units in the effective administration of public services.

2. "An Advisory Committee Report on Local Government," (Washington, D.C.: Commission on Intergovernmental Relations by the Advisory Committee on Local Government, June 1955), 9.
3. *Digest of Education Statistics 1982* (Washington, D.C.: National Center for Education Statistics, 1982), 59.

Through school districts, local decisions on the management and operation of the schools are reached. Likewise, through these districts the policy of the state is implemented. The local district is expected to be a servant of the public interest, and in this case the public interest is as broad as the state itself.

The municipal character of the school district's responsibility is discussed in detail later in this chapter. The school district has many characteristics of the municipality and at times is expected to observe laws which pertain to municipal government. The autonomy enjoyed by school districts differs among the states and frequently among classes of districts within states. The statutes provide the framework and the specifications to govern the formal relationships among local units of government. But independent of the formal relationships there exists a strong set of informal liaisons among units of local government irrespective of the special purposes for which they were created and designed.[4]

Important connections exist between local districts and the federal government. In the 1960s and 1970s local school districts were often involved directly or indirectly with federal agencies. Affirmative action directives, mainstreaming requirements for the handicapped, mandatory citizen involvement, and guidelines involving acquisition and expenditures of federal monies are illustrations. The economic policies and decentralization philosophy of the Reagan administration altered past practice in intergovernmental relationships. As a result, more of the responsibility for education and attendance control shifted to the states and local districts. Ironically, this is where responsibility and control rest constitutionally. Since the new federalism affected all local governments similarly, new competition for local and state revenue sources occurred, altering relationships between and among local units of government.[5]

In the public mind, school districts have been set apart from other governmental bodies. They have enjoyed this distinction primarily out of public refusal to associate anything as fundamental as education with the supposed muck and mire of practical politics. Corruption, graft, and cynicism are assumed to be trademarks of politics at all levels, and while they are tolerated in some arenas of public concern, they are not acceptable when attached to the shaping and training of the immature minds of the public's progeny. For this reason school districts in the majority of cases enjoy considerable autonomy in the management and control of their fiscal affairs and in retaining nonpartisanship in the selection of citizens to serve on local school boards. This separation has been perpetuated and reinforced by professional educators.

Educators have tended to treat school districts as something unique, almost to the point of divinity, in the operation of schools and the conduct of school affairs. Political scientists, on the other hand, have resisted philosophically the setting apart of school districts from other units of local government and made a plea for incorporating education into the broad range of public services provided locally.

Peterson believes that local governments (including school districts) have limited ability as individual units to achieve equity in the distribution of benefits and services.[6] Even with the aid of federal and state policy interventions, the prospect of genuine and far-reaching achievement of equity is doubtful. National politics, Peterson observes, have produced a range of welfare-state policies, including low-income housing,

---

4. A persuasive case for integrating local governments, formally and informally, is made in Roscoe C. Martin, *Government and the Suburban School* (Syracuse, N.Y.: Syracuse University Press, 1963), 102–5.
5. For a useful analysis of intergovernmental relationships see Donald Phares, "Federalism, State-Local Sector, and Education: A Look to the 1980s," *Issues in Education* (1983), 31–55.
6. Paul E. Peterson, *City Limits* (Chicago: The University of Chicago Press, 1981), ch. 11.

compensatory education, food stamps, and unemployment compensation. As appealing as these concepts and their accompanying programs are in theory, they fail in practice to assure fairness and non-discrimination in the availability of public services such as education. Given the disparaties in the quality of educational programs that exist between and among school districts, the question of what can be done to achieve equity becomes singularly important. The generic tension between equality on the one hand and control on the other is at the center of debates regarding improvement in services provided by local school districts.

Admittedly some of the control of public schools that heretofore resided with local district officials has been shifted to other levels of government or is being shared to some extent with agencies and interests outside of government. Some years ago Campbell suggested that local control was more folklore than fact:

> It is quite clear that the public schools of this country have always operated within a framework established by the various states and that federal influences of some kind have always been prevalent. In recent decades, state controls over schools have been strengthened and federal activities in education, widely dispersed among many agencies, have multiplied. Federal influence has been piecemeal, haphazard, perhaps even surreptitious and often clothed in pious affirmation of state and local control. But inevitably the national stake in education and the growing social and economic interdependence of the nation have required congressional action and United States Supreme Court interpretation on educational questions. The time seems ripe for a realistic view of circumstances as they are and the forging of an honest local-state-federal partnership in education.[7]

Despite interference in local control by outside forces, the citizens for the most part appear to value the local district and the opportunity to participate in educational decisions which have significance for the welfare of the people of their community. Some have attributed the desire to retain local control simply to the reluctance of citizen-taxpayers to relinquish one of the few remaining opportunities to affect directly the expenditures of public funds and thus control the tax rate. No doubt this is true; many citizens are rightly concerned about mounting educational costs. On the other hand, many citizens value local control because it does permit some local discretion; it does permit the local district to be responsive to local needs; it does allow local districts to exceed minimum standards established by the state; it does allow for the participation of large numbers of citizens in the consideration of the objectives and directions of local schools.

Public sentiments regarding local control appear to ebb and flow. In the 1950s there was substantial resistance to federal aid on the grounds of encroachment. A surge of interest in "community control" took place within large urban districts in the early 1960s. Deeply embedded in this movement was the realization that, for whatever reason, thousands of inner-city residents were not having an adequate say in how their schools were performing. Statewide ground swells of support for local control occurred in several states in the late 1970s. Revisions in the Florida Constitution reflected a strong "home rule" theme. California passed the much publicized Jarvis-Gant Amendment to the California Constitution in June of 1978, which substantially reduced the property tax and was in large measure a populist revolt against big and centralized state government. In 1981, voters in Massachusetts, through initiative,

7. Roald F. Campbell, "The Folklore of Local School Control," *The School Review 68* (Spring 1959): 15.

passed Proposition 2½ which limited total local property tax levies to 2.5 percent of full and fair cash value of a municipality's taxable property. This statewide initiative had a severe impact upon local school districts, many of which suffered drastic budget cuts. Furthermore, Proposition 2½ introduced intense strain between and among local governments. The Massachusetts' example illustrates how one form of grassroots control, the initiative, can serve to constrain local governments. Considerable control was exercised over school districts, themselves instruments designed to reflect the preferences of local citizens.[8]

Origin and Development of School Districts

The school district, as a unit of school government, was created in Massachusetts, but it existed for nearly a century and a half before it was legally recognized. Dexter explains how the school district began:

> As each little settlement extended its boundaries, it became convenient for families so far removed from the centre of population as to make it difficult for them to send their children to the town school, to form a separate nucleus of educational interests and establish a separate school. The region contributing to the separate school formed the school district. In Massachusetts it arose without legal recognition, for the General Court Act of 1647 established the schools upon a town basis; but as the district plan worked well under colonial conditions, it was fully legalized by the act of 1789, and continued to be the dominant school power within the state until well into the nineteenth century, and was not legally abolished until 1882.[9]

The celebrated Act of Massachusetts General Court in 1647 required the towns to establish schools. This legislation was important not only because it provided for the formal education of colonial children but because it enunciated the principle of state authority in the control of schools.[10] This principle was adopted in all of New England and ultimately spread throughout the United States. The town in Massachusetts was the local unit of government responsible for schools. This arrangement was satisfactory for those who lived in the town itself or near enough to walk to school each day. But it failed to meet the demands of the rural residents, and it was out of the need for schooling for these people that the districts emerged. The districts were actually subdivisions of the towns; the town in New England contained the "town," or population center, as well as a considerable farming area on the periphery. These areas were carved into smaller units, and provisions were made to provide schooling in each of the new "districts." Various schemes were devised to carry on instruction in the districts; the "moving school" and the "divided school" were common in New England.[11] The control of the schools remained with the towns under these arrangements; likewise, the responsibility for supporting the schools rested with the towns. It was not until the end of the eighteenth century that the districts were granted power to conduct and control their own schools. Horace Mann described the Massa-

8. Lawrence Susskind and Cynthia Horan, "Proposition 2½: The Response to Tax Restrictions in Massachusetts," *The Property Tax and Local Finance*, Proceedings of the Academy of Political Science, vol. 35, (1983): 158–171.
9. Edwin Grant Dexter, *A History of Education in the United States* (New York: Macmillan, 1922), 183.
10. R. Freeman Butts and Lawrence A. Cremin, *A History of Education in American Culture* (New York: Holt, Rinehart and Winston, 1953), 103.
11. Ibid, 100–8.

chusetts Act of 1789, which granted legal rights to school districts, as the most unfortunate legislation on common schools enacted in Massachusetts. The act provided for the appointment of school committees within the districts and was followed by legislation in 1801 granting the local districts the power to raise money through taxation for the support of district schools. This privilege had heretofore resided only with the towns.

Horace Mann's concern was founded not on opposition to the principle of local control per se but was based on the demonstrated inability as well as unwillingness of these very small units to provide adequate schools. Dexter writes about the situation in Massachusetts:

> The really disastrous legislation came, however, in 1801, granting the district the power to raise moneys by taxation, a right which had heretofore been vested in the larger social unit, the town. In actual practice, the district proved too small to be intrusted with final legislation in money matters, in many cases the sentiment among the limited number of voters within a single district being the opposite of generous toward the schools or the district too poor to do much; and although the acts of 1789 and 1801, and similar laws passed in the neighboring states a little later, gave to New England the "little red schoolhouse" in great numbers, they were frequently not very red for want of paint, nor was the teaching within their walls of a very high order. Yet it cannot be denied that much good came from them.[12]

Either because the district system worked reasonably well in New England or because the conditions which spawned the system were present in other places, it was adopted and adapted in other parts of the United States. As the country developed and populations migrated westward, the district system seemed to move west too. Except in the South, the New England pattern ultimately spread across the land, partially because the nation, until the twentieth century, was a rural nation dependent upon agriculture economically. Even though the responsibility for and control of schooling was with the states, the creation of subdivisions within the states was necessary for them to fulfill their responsibilities for education. The Midwest, Far West, and Northwest were marked by the early proliferation of local districts, a condition which many states have been trying to modify through school district reorganization and consolidation legislation.

In the South the basic unit of school government became the county. The principal reason for the difference between the New England affinity for a town and district system and the South's proclivity for a county system stems from a fairly fundamental difference in church-state relationships in the colonies of New England and the colonies of the South. The Church of England, predominant in the South, assumed authority over education in the southern colonies; this pattern was transferred to those colonies directly from England, where the authority and control of public and private schools had been placed in the hands of the bishops by the Canons of the Church of England in 1603.[13] As a consequence, church affairs and school affairs in the southern colonies were closely related. The parish and its officials and the county and its officials became the administrative arms of the Church of England as well as of the colonial government. Teaching was often the responsibility of the clergy, and, as in England, importance was placed upon provisions for educating or training or-

12. Dexter, *A History of Education in the United States,* 184.
13. Butts and Cremin, *A History of Education in American Culture,* 104–7.

phans, indigents, and other unfortunates. The responsibility for schooling was centralized, and this feature of school organization has persisted through the years. The influence of the church was marked in the South; although the church and the state were separated by the ratification of the federal constitution, the centralization that prevailed in the colonial period still characterizes the South today. The county unit has persisted and had even been adopted in other parts of the country, notably Utah and Nevada.

Legal Basis of School Districts

School districts are arms of state government created to implement the mandates of the state and to ensure the rights and privileges of a free education to the people. School districts are the instruments through which the state can fulfill its constitutional obligations; they are the legally established and authorized subdivisions of government constructed for the purpose of maintaining a system of public schools. As noted in chapter 3, legislatures of the several states, within consitutional limitations, have plenary power over school district organization; they can create, modify, consolidate, reorganize, or destroy school districts; they can make these subdivisions autonomous, independent fiscal units, or they can make them dependent units, subject fo fiscal control resident in other subdivisions of government.

Legislatures can classify districts, even charter districts under special circumstances, and can differentiate duties, obligations, or amount of discretion among the classes of districts they create. If state legislative bodies are so disposed, they may actually require counties, cities, towns, or townships to assume the responsibility locally for providing schools; or the legislatures may simply constitute the geographical area of some subdivision as a school district and vest it with independence. Legislatures may also establish separate school districts covering the same geographical area but for different purposes. For example, in California and Illinois separate elementary and secondary districts frequently serve the same area.

The supremacy of the legislature has been well established.[14] Unless the constitutions of the various states stipulate to the contrary, the legislatures can establish or alter school districts without the consent of the people. As will be noted later, the legislatures have been reluctant to change school district arrangements in the face of widespread public opposition, but they do possess the power to do so. In the same way, they possess the power to delegate authority to establish school districts; this delegation could be to a special committee or to another governmental subdivision or to an official. The specific statutes which have created school districts are numerous. The laws providing for one class of school district, the community unit district in Illinois for example, take eighteen pages in the code book of that state.[15]

School Districts and Municipalities

Because of the peculiar nature of the public service they render, school districts are commonly called quasi corporations, and in some cases, as determined by the courts, they are held to be municipal corporations. The corporate statuses of school districts are not uniform among the various states although there are some similarities. The

---

14. For further elaboration see Newton Edwards, *The Courts and the Public Schools* (Chicago, Ill.: University of Chicago Press, 1955), 63.
15. *School Code of Illinois*, Art. 11, Secs. 6–10.

distinctions between consideration of a school district as a quasi corporation and a municipal corporation are important, and each school administrator needs to know the interpretation of the courts of his state in reference to the corporate status of districts. Edwards has described school districts as municipal corporations in this way:

> Strictly speaking, a school district is not a municipal corporation; it is a quasi-corporation. A municipal corporation proper is a city or town incorporated primarily for purposes of local government. While such a corporation is in part an agency of the state established to assist in the affairs of civil government, it is created, in the main, to enable the locality to regulate and administer its own local concerns. Local interest and advantage rather than execution of state policy are its determining characteristics. In order to effectuate the purposes of their creation, it is obvious that municipal corporations must be granted considerable powers of a legislative and regulatory nature. A quasi-corporation, on the other hand, is purely a political or civil division of the state; it is created as an instrumentality of the state in order to facilitate the administration of government.[16]

Considerable confusion has arisen because school districts and other governmental units often comprise the same geographical area but are autonomous subdivisions. Cities, townships, towns, and counties have been determined by legislatures to be fit and convenient geographical entities within which school systems can be organized, and thus school districts have been created to serve these same subdivisions. Cities and incorporated towns are municipal corporations established for the purpose of local self-government, and the statutes of the state pertaining to municipal corporations are applicable to these subdivisions. The school districts serving the same areas are quasi-corporations, created for administrative purposes to enable the state to fulfill its constitutional responsibility for education. As a quasi-corporation, the school district, and its governing board, is limited to the exercise of powers specifically granted in the law plus such discretionary powers designated by the law or determined necessary to meet reasonably the state's obligation to provide an educational system.

Only a few municipal corporations have responsibilities for providing schools or managing schools. Only those municipal corporations which have been delegated responsibilities for education by state legislatures have these obligations. In other words, there is nothing inherent in the municipal corporation which requires this subdivision to provide and manage a system of public schools. At the same time there is no prohibition against legislatures fixing responsibility for schools upon municipal corporations.

Some school districts and municipalities provide services to one another. Purchasing, warehousing, libraries, recreation facilities, personnel administration, levying and collecting taxes are examples. On occasion conflicts and misunderstandings have occured. For example, the San Francisco Unified School District was established in 1917. Prior to 1917 the administration of education was the responsibility of the city of San Francisco. At the time of the establishment of the new district, however, the city of San Francisco retained responsibilities such as purchasing, warehousing, legal services, and health services. Over the years, tensions grew related to these services and led to the complete or partial transfer in the 1970s of many of those responsibilities to the San Francisco Unified School District. In addition, there was controversy

---

16. Edwards, *The Courts and the Public Schools*, 54. See also E. Gordon Gee and David J. Sperry, *Education Law and the Public Schools* (Boston: Allyn and Bacon, 1978), S–16.

over the ownership of school sites since clear title to school sites had not been transferred in 1917. Eventually such property titles will be clarified by the courts since the value of land is appreciating and is sought for other private and public purposes.[17]

The courts in the several states have been called upon to clarify the corporate nature of local school districts. Disputes have arisen involving the police power of municipalities when exercised against school boards, the local financing of schools, the control of school buildings, the interpretation of home rule charters, and the relationships between school and municipal officials. The numerous cases involving the determination of the municipalities' rights, privileges, and obligations and the school districts' rights, privileges, and obligations have failed to provide clarification. The decisions of the courts lack consistency and uniformity. For example, controversies have been generated by attempts of municipalities to apply their building codes to school structures over the objections of school district officials. In some instances, the courts have ruled that municipalities have the right and indeed the obligation to apply building codes to school district facilities. In other cases, the courts have decided that school districts, as extensions of the state, are immune from the application of municipal codes and regulations, unless the statutes have stipulated that local school districts are to abide by municipal building standards. When the laws are explicit and the relationships between these subdivisions are stated, the courts have only to adjudicate in terms of the statutes. In the absence of clear positions, the courts are forced to decide on other bases, such as precedent or the supremacy of the state in educational matters.

It is not surprising that the courts are frequently called upon to adjudicate disputes arising out of questions involving school finance and, most often, the control of school district budgets. It is in this area of budget approval and control that an important distinction between two types of school districts must be made.

Fiscal Independence

The independent or dependent nature of school districts continues to be subject to extensive debate. On the one hand, there are the professional educators, supported by a substantial number of lay leaders, who believe strongly that school districts should be independent or autonomous; that is, they should maintain control over their budgets, they should have taxing authority, and they should have board members selected by the citizens of the districts they serve.

On the other hand, there are some political scientists, and citizens sympathetic to their general position, who believe that there is no justification for autonomous governmental units to carry on the business of providing schools. They argue that provisions for schools should be managed in the same way and within the same governmental structure as other public services are provided; they hold that there should be some unity in local government and that much of the proliferation of local subdivisions is accounted for in local school districts; they maintain that fiscal control should remain with the municipality and that separation of school fiscal policy from other local governmental fiscal policy leads to waste and inefficiency; they believe further that the independence of local school districts coupled with the increasing professionalizing of school administration has given unwarranted advantage to local school districts in

17. San Francisco Public Schools Commission, *School District: City and County of San Francisco, An Analysis of Relationships* (San Francisco: San Francisco Public Schools Commission, 1976), 25.

the competition for local fiscal resources. Eliot elaborates this latter point when he says:

> School administration, as a profession, is a latecomer, but in terms of understanding the politics of the public schools it is perhaps the most important of all. School administration is a decidedly hierarchical and disciplined business, and the top administrator, the local school superintendent, holds the key position in each school district. Indeed, there seems to be professional agreement that the most significant duty of the people's representatives on the local school board is the selection of the superintendent.[18]

The argument is advanced also by proponents of independence that school affairs should not become political affairs; that the special nature of schooling sets it apart from other governmental services; that the fundamental importance of schools justifies a special structure which places school affairs close to the citizenry; that the run-of-the-mill municipal official is not prepared to make important policy decisions for schools, and that under dependent arrangements the fixing of responsibility may be elusive.

It is most interesting to note that, while most school professionals support independence and rely heavily on the unwholesome manifestations of some political activities as the basis of their argument, these same professionals are dependent upon political activity in the administration of schools. Bailey makes the point that the success of school people in eight northeastern states in acquiring state aid has been directly related to the sophistication of their understanding of the political instruments available to them.[19] These same political skills are necessary at the district level.

One of the most fundamental points upon which decisions about independence or dependence should turn is whether or not one structure permits demonstrably better schools than the other. And it is on this point that we are woefully short of evidence. If one is in fact better than the other, it is not obvious on the basis of superficial analyses. James and his colleagues at Stanford University found that fiscally independent or dependent districts did not differ greatly in their patterns of expenditure.[20] The range of factors which contribute to or detract from excellence are numerous but this should reduce in no way the desirability of comparing further the two district types.

The Stanford group has challenged the traditional definitions of dependence and independence and has proposed some useful comparative analyses of local school governments. They contend that there are actually very few, if any, independent local school governments. There are instead, these educators believe, various types of dependent school districts, more reasonably conceived of as falling along a continuum of more dependence to less dependence. These writers suggest thirty-two models of local school government which hopefully will lead to some productive research on local school governments.

Ninety percent of all school districts in the United States are fiscally independent, as defined by the Bureau of the Census. There are four states—Hawaii, Maryland,

---

18. Thomas H. Eliot, "Toward an Understanding of Public School Politics," *The American Political Science Review* 53 (December 1959): 1034.
19. Stephen K. Bailey et al., *Schoolmen and Politics: A Study of State Aid to Education in the Northeast* (Syracuse, N.Y.: Syracuse University Press, 1962), 104.
20. H. Thomas James, J. Alan Thomas, and Harold J. Dyck, *Wealth, Expenditure and Decision-making for Education* (Stanford, Calif: School of Education, Stanford University, 1963), 99.

North Carolina, and Virginia—which have only dependent units. Hawaii, in fact, has one school district and it is coterminus with the state; the schools of Hawaii are administered through a department of state government. In twenty-three states there are only independent districts, and the remainder of the states have both types.

Reorganization of Districts

Legislators have generally been reluctant to act arbitrarily in the alteration of existing units or in the establishment of new districts. The existence of hundreds of small, inefficient districts is testimony to the fact that legislators have been slow, in many states at least, to reorganize their districts. It is significant, however, that the number of school districts in the United States was reduced by nearly 79,000 in the thirty-five year period, 1947–1981 (see Table 4.1). Since 1967 the rate of reduction in numbers has slowed tremendously to the point where some stabilization seems to have occurred.

Some legislatures have taken action. The decrease in these numbers is all the more important when examined in the light of the severe political wrestling that normally surrounds most changes in the statutes governing district organization. It would be erroneous to imply that gross reductions in numbers automatically result in better district organization. Obviously this is not true; many consolidations of small, poor, inefficient districts have resulted in larger, poor, inefficient districts. And as those who have worked hard for reorganization of districts know, the second try for reorganization is much more difficult than the first.

Legislation to encourage or to realize school district reorganization is usually classed as permissive, semipermissive, or mandatory. Permissive legislation simply permits districts to merge, to consolidate, or to reorganize. There are no prescriptions, no real teeth in the laws of this kind; districts are given the opportunity to rearrange themselves and the ground rules to guide these changes are stipulated. In many states, laws permitting changes have been on the books for years; as one would suspect, relatively few significant reorganizations have grown out of permissive legislation. Too many barriers and too few incentives were present; large-scale satisfac-

TABLE 4.1

Numbers of Local School Districts in the U.S., 1947–48 through 1980–81

Year	No. Districts*
1947–48	94,926
1951–52	71,094
1955–56	54,859
1959–60	40,520
1963–64	31,705
1967–68	19,977
1971–72	16,838
1975–76	16,376
1979–80	15,929
1980–81	15,912

SOURCE: Data are drawn from official publications of the National Center for Educational Statistics, U.S. Office of Education.
*Totals include both operating and nonoperating districts with the exception of 1967–68 and 1971–72 which include only operating districts.

tion with the status quo, fear of the loss of local control, transportation problems, and general conservatism have mitigated against purely voluntary reorganization.

Some states, in efforts to accelerate district reorganization, passed laws which were semipermissive. In other words, local districts were free to reorganize within limits incorporated in the law, but reorganization, acceptable to the state, would have to be proposed within a specified number of years. The initiative for reorganizing was taken from the local districts; the states became the initators but the residents of local districts were free to express their voice in the reorganizations to be effected. Many of the laws of this type were not effective because they included many checkpoints where proposed reorganization could be defeated. Failures of early permissive legislation led to strengthening of reorganization statutes and to the incorporation of financial incentives for reorganization. The linking of financial advantages to the creation of more efficient districts stimulated reorganization to some extent, but even laws of this type did not generate rapid changes.

The imposition of the will of the state in the form of mandatory reorganization laws characterized post-World War II reorganization legislation. These acts combined the formation of local committees, usually at the county level; the establishment of specific time schedules for the submission of reorganization proposals to state agencies for review, recommendations, and appraisal, and for the vote of citizens; the incorporation of financial incentives for reorganization; and the inclusion of financial penalties to be exacted against small, inefficient units which failed to reorganize. Much of the legislation enacted since World War II has been patterned after the recommendations of the National Commission on School District Reorganization.[21] Laws which forced reorganization usually had some safeguards built into them to avoid poor or ill-advised rearrangements. The opportunity for local participation was provided and sufficient checks were incorporated to ensure the approval of the citizenry. There was, however, one important proviso: if the machinery for some reason broke down, if citizens failed to agree or if they submitted what were determined to be weak proposals for reorganization, the state would step in and arbitrarily effect reorganization. Such action was considered drastic in most cases, but it could be done and was done. The reorganization in those instances was decided by a state agency authorized by the legislature to make such decisions.

School district reorganization is often necessary as a result of shifting population trends. The South and the West were the only regions in which metropolitan areas as a group grew faster than nonmetropolitan territory during the 1970s. In the Northeast and North Central regions, the metropolitan areas experienced very little change during the decade; in sharp contrast, the metropolitan areas in the South and West grew substantially (21.5 and 22.6 percent, respectively).[22]

However, this is not evidence of a significant migration of metropolitan dwellers back to farms. In fact, the farm population declined by about one-quarter between 1970 and 1980 and numbered only about 6 million in 1980.[23]

School districts were markedly affected during the period of rapid post-World War II population growth, including the large-scale rural to urban migrations. School administrators and school board members were growth-conscious in that period and took

21. *Your School District* (Washington, D.C.: Department of Rural Education, 1948).
22. U.S. Bureau of the Census, *Population Profile of the United States, 1981* (Washington D.C.: Government Printing Office, 1982), 8.
23. Ibid.

great pains to project enrollment trends accurately. Now the demographic picture is less clear overall and there are important trend differences within and between regions of the United States as well as within and between metropolitan and nonmetropolitan areas. The implications of such changes are not clear nor are they likely to be the same in all parts of the United States. We can say, however, that these changes do exist and have meaning for those responsible for educational planning at all levels.

Desegregation may also be linked to school district reorganization. In Kentucky, where the Louisville and Jefferson County school districts were involved in a school desegregation lawsuit, the Louisville school board voted to dissolve the Louisville school district and to merge with the county district, forming a single county district. Implementation of a desegregation remedy plan then involved children from the entire county, in fact most of the metropolitan area, because Jefferson County includes most of the Standard Metropolitan Statistical Area. In contrast, the courts forged a new school district in Delaware, the New Castle County district. It covered one-third of the land area of the state; had the former Wilmington, Delaware, district at its center; and inherited simultaneously the desegregation of schools and the reorganization of what formerly were eleven independent school districts. The New Castle County district was again reorganized in 1980 into four districts, each of which contains part of the city of Wilmington. District structures may be altered in other metropolitan areas where school desegregation litigation involving suburban districts and city districts is still in the federal courts. St. Louis and nearby suburban districts have just been ordered to cooperate, short of district reorganization, in ways specified by the court to achieve desegregation.[24] The case of *Jenkins v. Missouri,* came to trial in 1983 to achieve a similar objective in Kansas City.

Despite the magnitude of the assignment, the question of reforming educational government has been placed directly before the people in several metropolitan areas.[25] A few changes were effected in the 1960s. Nashville-Davidson County, Tennessee is one example of how city and county districts were consolidated through a voting proess. Another federation was established in Detroit during the 1970s and early 1980s which involved eight sub-districts each with its own school board. Those districts and their boards were discontinued in 1982. Costs, problems of communication, and lack of clarity regarding the sharing of authority and responsibility between the control board of education and the eight regional boards were factors in the decision to return to a more centralized structure.

Problems of district organization in rural areas are different from those in urban areas. In analyzing school district reorganization in terms of a rural-urban dichotomy, one is guilty to some degree of establishing an unrealistic, if not false, division. It may be more defensible to conceive of an urban to rual continuum along which one could place communities or areas according to criteria of urbanism or ruralism. Obviously the rapidly increasing areas of rural-urban fringe are difficult to classify as either urban or rural. We recognize the limitations inherent in our approach but believe that the extremely rural and the extremely urban are unlike enough to warrant independent discussion.

24. *Craton Liddell, et al., v. The Board of Education of the City of St. Louis, no. 72-100C (3) (E.D. Mo. July 5, 1983).*
25. The theory of a federated structure is elaborated in Raphael O. Nystrand and Luvern L. Cunningham, "Federated Urban School Systems: Compromising the Centralization-Decentralization Issue" in *Toward Improved Urban Education* ed. Frank Lutz (Worthington, Ohio: Charles A. Jones, 1970).

Reorganizing Districts in Rural Areas. The small districts, those that often have few pupils enrolled and inadequate financial resources, are usually in rural areas. They may be one-room rural school districts, offering elementary education only; they may be districts that attempt to provide secondary education only; or they may be unit districts offering both elementary and secondary school programs. Four states—California, Illinois, Nebraska, and Texas—accounted for over 25 percent of the school districts in the nation in 1980–81.[26] Each of these states had over 1,000 local school districts. Despite the elimination of thousands of districts in recent years, many reorganized districts fall short of meeting reasonable criteria of adequacy.

Population in rural sectors has decreased in the past several decades with little evidence that the decline will be arrested. Technological changes have affected agriculture as sharply as any other segment of our industry. The productivity of the farm worker has risen appreciably, the demand for farm workers has decreased correspondingly, and the size of the "family size farm" has increased.

Among the barriers to reorganizing districts in rural areas have been the persistence of the idea of home rule; resistance to tax increase for any public service; the fact that many people simply do not realize that the quality of the educational program in their districts is inferior; and, as Kammeyer reported, the degree of heterogeneity reflected in rural populations.[27] Kammeyer studied 110 small Iowa communities which had made decisions on reorganization involving secondary schools between 1956 and 1959. Ethnically homogeneous communities displayed less opposition to the loss of their high schools than did heterogeneous communities.

It is extremely difficult to pinpoint reasons why citizens in any given area resist changes in local districts. Undoubtedly a range of factors influences decisions about reorganization, not the least of which are sentiment or strong feelings about the "old school" and the nature of the people themselves. In rural sections where population movement in and out of school districts, at least among community leaders, is not so pronounced, traditions are maintained, and the feelings of identification with a given institution are strong. Although tax considerations are also important, and in many cases may outweigh other reasons for resisting changes, the sentiments of local citizens cannot be discounted. In urban areas where population movement is pronounced and where new neighborhood and communities are springing up annually, traditions are very difficult to maintain and in many cases nonexistent. The much touted role of the schools as centers of community activity—cultural, recreational, and social—is important, and modification in what seemingly have been very satisfactory arrangements are examined cautiously in rural districts.

Substantial improvements in educational opportunity have been realized in many rural areas. Fine new schools have been constructed, marked strengthening in school programs has been effected, and important increases in the level of preparation of professional personnel have been realized. But the job is far from complete.

Reorganizing Districts in Urban Areas. As impressive as the need for reorganizing rural districts has appeared to be, the problems may be even more critical in urban areas. The urbanization process has introduced innumerable demands for public services which government is often inadequately prepared to provide. It is an immense undertaking in areas undergoing urbanization to meet needs for such things as police

26. *Digest of Education Statistics, 1982,* 59.
27. Kenneth C. W. Kammeyer, "Community Homogeneity and Decision Making," *Rural Sociology* 28 (September 1963): 238–45.

and fire protection, parks and recreation facilities, libraries, sanitation and water supply, roads, and schools.

Growth rates during the 1970s were lowest in the largest metropolitan areas. The New York metropolitan area, the largest of all, experienced a loss of more than 900,000 persons between 1970 and 1980. Of the six other metropolitan areas with a 1970 population of more than 3 million, Philadelphia, Detroit, and Boston had small losses, while Chicago had a small gain. Only the Los Angeles and San Francisco metropolitan areas grew significantly during the period (15.2 and 11.9 percent, respectively). Together these seven very large areas had a net growth of only 1.1 million (2.1 percent) in the 1970s, compared with 7.1 million (15.5 percent) for the same areas in the 1960s.[28] These changes reflect the "Sun Belt" growth patterns as well as the decline of the older cities of the East, South, and Midwest. The phenomenon of relatively uncontrolled growth on the peripheries of central cities is continuing in many places where land will be used indiscriminately, overburdening the existing local governmental structures. Mushrooming subdivisions, irregular location of industry, businesses, and residences, destruction of natural drainage systems, speculation in land values, which are characteristic of areas in the process of urbanization, will continue. "Urban sprawl" is the term attached to this kind of growth; in most cases there are no controls operating to guide or order land usages on the urban fringes. In the few places where planning bodies exist, they have notable records of ineffectiveness in regulating the growth and development of areas over which they ostensibly have jurisdiction.

The "big city" districts, usually chartered by the state, are important units of local school government and cannot be ignored in reorganization planning. However, these districts offer special problems, primarily of decentralization rather than centralization; these issues will be considered later in this chapter.

Existing districts on the outskirts of our central cities are studies in extremes.[29] The haves and the have-nots can be found side by side. The haves possess taxable wealth either in the form of industrial property, business property, or residences owned by upper-class families with sufficiently high personal incomes to afford generous local levies for schools as well as other local services. The have-nots usually have little industrial or business valuation; the taxes for local purposes must be assessed against middle- or lower-income family residences owned by families which more often than not are struggling to meet payments on their houses, automobiles, home furnishings, and other obligations. The have districts, often serving mostly upper-middle- and upper-class citizens, normally have high expectations for their schools and consider the tasks of the public schools somewhat differently than the residents of the have-not districts. The people who live in the have-not districts also have expectations for their schools but these may be of a different order. Whereas the residential suburbanite may prefer emphasis on aesthetic and intellectual goals for his schools, the blue-collar citizen wants applied arts such as home economics and vocational education stressed.[30] Between these extremes are districts of modest wealth, differential states of development, mixed expectations for schools which are reflec-

28. U.S. Bureau of the Census, Current Population Reports, series P-20, no. 374, *Population Profile of the United States: 1981* (Washington, D.C., U.S. Government Printing Office, 1982).
29. For a thoughtful analysis of the equality of educational opportunity problem as it relates to district structure see Arthur E. Wise, *Rich Schools, Poor Schools* (Chicago: University of Chicago Press, 1968).
30. Lawrence W. Downey, *The Task of Public Education* (Chicago: Midwest Administration Center, University of Chicago, 1960).

tions of the heterogeneous character of the citizens who live there. The variety of circumstances which prevails defies adequate description. There are districts with exceptional concentrations of industrial wealth and few school-age children; the tax valuation behind each youngster of school age is sizable. At the same time, the residents of these districts may have relatively modest expectations for their schools. Close by may be districts with middle- and upper-middle-class families, most of whom are caught up in the upward mobility patterns characteristic of business and professional people, and who hold expectations for schools which are extraordinarily high with respect to the districts' abilities to finance schools.

The district structure in suburban areas is something to behold. The range of variables to be considered in suggesting improved district organization for urban America is almost incomprehensible. For example, these factors must be considered: aspirations of the public, including its many subpublics, for schools; present and potential capacity to finance local government including schools; tax assessment practices; present and potential provisions for planning; role of the state and federal governments in school support; present and potential relationships among local units of government; locations of transportation routes such as superhighways or commuter railroads; and the social stratification of urban residents.

One criterion for organizing school districts that has received acclaim has been the plan of arranging school district boundaries around "natural" communities. Districts in suburban areas and in the rural-urban fringes frequently overlap several municipalities or population centers. The "natural" community, if it exists at all, is at best hard to discover. The expectation that school district or attendance area boundaries can somehow accommodate communities or neighborhoods has been sharply debated. The issues in attendance area decisions are examined in chapter 6.

The problem of defining criteria of school district adequacy is troublesome. To date, universally acceptable criteria or universally applicable criteria are not available. It is clear that adequate districts in sparsely populated sections of rural America will differ from what should be defined as adequate districts in urban areas. The AASA Commission on School District Reorganization in 1958 listed nine points to be examined in determining the effectiveness of existing school districts. They are educational program, pupil population, financial resources, educational leadership provisions, instructional personnel, use of personnel, school plant provisions, framework for operation, and provisions for community participation.[31] The 1958 AASA Commission statement is the most recent statement available despite the continuing importance of achieving sound, defensible local units.

The Current Scene

The elimination of a vast number of school districts has contributed little to reducing the kinds, classifications, or types of districts. In fact, new classes have been created. The array of district types has caused confusion among those who wish to understand better the arrangements of districts in the states. Each state classifies its own districts legally. In Nebraska, for example, there are six classes of districts which are differentiated in a number of ways, such as school census enumeration, scope of program to be offered, number of school board members, and amount of discretion per-

---

31. American Association of School Administrators, *School District Organization,* Report of the AASA Commission for School District Reorganization (Washington, D.C.: AASA, 1958), 122.

mitted school officials. Other states have similar systems with some having but one legal class, as in Nevada, and others having as many as eight.

Two other useful ways of categorizing districts were used by the AASA Commission on School District Reorganization.[32] One scheme was to describe districts in terms of the scope of school program they provide; the other method was to classify districts in terms of their geographical or territorial characteristics. There were five types within each of these two categories. When districts are regarded in terms of the scope of the program they provide, one of the most familiar is the elementary unit. In 1977 there were approximately 4,121 elementary districts variously classified as K–6, 1–6, K–8, or 1–8, K–9, 1–9 in scope.[33] Although most of these districts are of the one-room rural school variety, there are many elementary districts in metropolitan areas. Most of the elementary pupils in Cook County, Illinois, exclusive of the Chicago School District which is unified, are enrolled in elementary districts. Likewise, there are numerous elementary units in Arizona and California. The extremes in quality of education are exemplified in this category. On one end of the continuum are the thousands of rural districts with small enrollments, frequently with poorly trained teachers, narrow programs, and in some cases weak financing; at the other extremity are the historically prominent, widely known elementary districts such as Winnetka and Glencoe, Illinois. Reorganization in rural areas is reducing the number of elementary districts rapidly in many states, but considerable work remains to be done.

There were 608 school systems that offered only secondary education programs in 1977.[34] Such high school districts overlay elementary districts and receive their students from one or more of these "feeder" units. They are most numerous in California, Illinois, and Montana. Some of the high schools, many of which are located in the suburbs of our metropolitan areas, reflect the finest in secondary education to be found in the United States. At the other end of the scale there are high school districts which run secondary schools enrolling fewer than 100 pupils, offering grossly inadequate programs, costing more than they are worth, and persisting to exist despite efforts to reorganize these units into more desirable districts.

Most of America's pupils attend schools in unified districts—those which provide both elementary and secondary education and, in a few cases, junior college programs as well. In 1977 there were approximately 10,897 unified districts, more than two-thirds of all school districts.[35] The large number of pupils attending is explained by the fact that most of our large cities such as Chicago, New York, Detroit, Cleveland, and Baltimore are unified districts. In every state at least one unified district exists; all districts are unified in nine states; and in several others, almost all districts are unified.

The number of small, unified districts in some states is further illustration of the need for continuing district reorganization. The AASA Commission on School District Reorganization has contended: "The unified, or 12-grade, school district which is adequate in size has proven to be the best system of school government devised by the American people."[36] The success of this unit is premised upon sufficiently large en-

32. AASA, *School District Organization*, 88–103.
33. National Center for Educational Statistics, U.S. Department of Health, Education, and Welfare, *Education Directory 1977-78 Public School Systems* (Washington, D.C.: Government Printing Office, 1978).
34. Ibid.
35. Ibid.
36. AASA, *School District Organization*, 92.

rollments as well as sufficiently generous local resources. Both of these are currently lacking in thousands of unified districts. In some places the landscape is dotted with numerous inefficient unified districts that could be reorganized into much more efficient units which could provide correspondingly more effective programs.

Districts offering junior college or community college programs, special education, and vocational-technical education have been established in many of our states. Each year the number of such districts increases. Justification for these special units is based on the inability of many other districts to provide post-high school, special, or vocational-technical programs. Often larger areas can reasonably support such offerings and serve an important public need. In rural areas, the special district is often the only way local government can provide such educational opportunities.

One of the little known types, described in terms of scope of program, is the nonoperating district. These are bona fide governmental subdivisions, and they provide no program at all. In 1981 there were 311 of these districts.[37] They have school boards which meet in accordance with the law, but they do not operate schools. In some of these districts in rural areas there may be no children of school age; or there may be so few pupils that it is more economical to contract with neighboring districts for the schooling of these youngsters; or it may be that most or all of the school age pupils are enrolled in nonpublic schools. Some states have succeeded in doing away with these units, but where they continue to exist there is usually strong opposition to their elimination. The nonoperating district serves to protect the tax interests of its residents. It is much less expensive to contract for the education of a very few pupils than to maintain a school for them. At the same time it is advantageous to keep property out of reorganized districts that provide comprehensive and more expensive educational programs. Any attempt to reorganize nonoperating units or to consolidate them with neighboring districts is automatically viewed as a threat to the tax advantage which nonoperating districts enjoy. These units are anachronisms, and in due time, they will be eliminated.

Districts classed by geographical or area characteristics[38] are usually treated as follows: (1) community districts—those which are organized around "natural" communities and labeled as such in the law, (2) city districts—those which are coterminous with city boundaries, (3) county districts—the county can be designated as a basic unit of school government, (4) towns or townships—hundreds of districts exist coterminous with towns or townships, particularly the township high school districts are good example, and (5) common school districts—there are thousands of these found in twenty-seven states, and they include the remaining one-room rural schools. A large portion of the elementary districts described in the scope of program classification are also common school districts, in many cases identified as "common schools" in the laws of the states.

Local school districts as governmental units vary in several ways. Districts do not exercise control as unified political units; control comes from people within the districts, such as school board members, superintendents, citizens groups, teachers, professional organizations, and civic associations. Nevertheless, the characteristics of school districts do affect the range and quality of educational programing that school districts are able to provide. Wealth is one obvious attribute that is linked with educational opportunity.

---

37. *Digest of Education Statistics, 1982,* 59.
38. Approximately 80 percent of all school districts have areas differing from those of other units of local government.

The financial circumstances of districts affect the scope and quality of educational programs. Thus wealth, either its presence or absence, helps define the limits of schooling and is a controlling or determining factor in district-level decision making. Similarly, the characteristics of the population that resides within the districts are limiting factors. Bainbridge found that a high percentage of the population over 25 years of age with less than five years of formal education, a low birth rate, and large numbers of middle income families were present in Ohio school districts that were voting down millage rate increases or bond issues for new construction.[39] Population characteristics likewise determine the eligibility of districts for federal and state funds which often make it possible to meet the specific needs of large numbers of children. From another perspective, the characteristics of the student populations are frequently reflected in special demands that are made of school officials, through, for example, multicultural, bilingual, vocational-technical, and academically talented education programs.

Reference has been made to the extremes present in existing district structures. Some districts serve no pupils at all (nonoperating units) or just a very few, while others serve hundreds of thousands. For example, two districts in Nevada—Elko and Nye—both cover an area over 18,000 square miles, yet Elko County serves about 3,900 and Nye enrolls about 1,100. There are in other states extremely small districts covering only one, two, or three square miles; some enroll very few pupils, but others equally small may serve large concentrations of population and thus large numbers of students. San Francisco City Unified School District in California, for example, covers but forty-five square miles yet has an enrollment of over 60,000 pupils.

Districts vary too in their capacities to finance schools, in the quality of programs offered, in the scope of educational needs provided for, in the training, experience, and performance of teachers and school administrators employed. These variations are notable within states and even within counties. Quality differences are so important that many people select their residences in terms of what local districts provide or fail to provide. These contrasts have existed for decades; it will take decades more to reduce these differences and to construct more adequate local units.

Summary and Future Prospects

Our concern thus far has been essentially structural and not operational. Although some generalizations have been made about the relative performance of different types of districts, these were introduced to make the structural descriptions more meaningful. Obviously the decisions made by public officials who serve in these units of government are political decisions. It is apparent to the professionals in education and to thoughtful lay people that the attainment of educational objectives depends upon the successful operation of our political system. The future of local school districts appears to be caught up in the question of whether or not our political system, functioning through the mechanisms of local districts, can carry its burdens. Banfield has offered a basis for judging the "effectiveness" of a political system:

> In judging how a political system will work over time, increases and decreases in the burdens upon it are obviously extremely relevant. They are not all that must be considered, however. Changes in the "capability" of a system, that is, in its ability to

39. William L. Bainbridge, "An Analysis of the Relationship Between Selected Economic, Social, Demographic, and Election Variables and Voter Behavior in Outer City School District Property Tax Elections" (Ph.D. diss., Ohio State University, 1979).

manage conflict and to impose settlements, are equally relevant. The "effectiveness"
of a political system is a ratio between burdens and capability. Even though the burdens upon it increase, the effectiveness of a system will also increase if there is a
sufficient accompanying increase in its capability. Similarly, even though there is an
increase in capability, the effectiveness of a system will decrease if there is more than
commensurate increase in burdens.[40]

What are the burdens that local districts must carry in the years ahead? We
believe the most crucial burden will be informed decision making; it is at this point
that local districts seem most vulnerable. As indicated in chapter 8, we believe that
improved processes and approaches to decision making can be adopted that respect
the limits of local descretion and at the same time maximize the opportunities for the
exercise of local control.[41] Dror argues that the quality of policy can be improved in
the public sector if public officials will use policymaking knowledge and allocate resources to that end.[42]

Knowledge about policy making can profitably be applied in our judgment to questions of local control or the allocation of responsibilities to levels of government. Lieberman charged twenty years ago that "local control of education has clearly outlived
its usefulness on the American scene. Practically, it must give way to a system of
educational controls in which local communities play ceremonial rather than policymaking roles: *Intellectually,* it is already a corpse."[43]

Furthermore, he argued that the mobility and interdependence of our society
undermined the idea that local communities should have a free hand in educating their
children; that national survival required policies and programs not subject to local vote;
that local control in practice could not be reconciled with the ideals of a democratic
society; and that local control was the major cause of "the dull parochialism and attenuated totalitarianism that characterizes public education in operation."[44] This was not
an idle charge nor a passing, whimsical allegation; Lieberman believed that local control was passé.

This posture stands in sharp contrast to the plaintive cries for community control
which issued forth from ghettoes in most large cities. Parents and other neighborhood
leaders genuinely desired a larger role in educational decision making. Many ghetto
residents wanted in on the act, at home, in the neighborhood, not in state houses or
in Washington. Implicit in Lieberman's reasoning was the assumption that another
type of structure may be more efficient as well as more effective—and of course the
alternative to local control was some kind of centralization: state, regional, or national.
Following Banfield's notion of "capability," the centralization of control asked for by
Lieberman rested upon the assumption that central control is able "to manage conflict
and to impose settlements"—or to utilize maximum intelligence in decision making.

At the moment there is little evidence that our political system produces more
rational or more beneficial decisions about education at the state or federal level than
at the local level. Granted that the effects of a good state decision are pervasive, it is

---

40. Edward C. Banfield, "The Political Implications of Metropolitan Growth," *Daedalus* 9 (Winter 1961):61.
41. Luvern L. Cunningham, "Policy About Policy: Some Thoughts and Projections" *Executive Review* 1,
    (Nov. 1980).
42. Yehezkel Dror, *Public Policymaking Reexamined* (San Francisco: Chandler, 1968), ch. 1.
43. Myron Lieberman, *The Future of Public Education* (Chicago: University of Chicago Press, 1960), 34.
    (Italics in original.)
44. Ibid.

also true that the repercussions of a bad state decision are far-reaching. Decisions at all levels of government depend upon the capacities, the values, and the interests of the decision makers involved. Therefore, it serves little purpose to debate the quality of decisions at different levels in the absence of policy output criteria.[45]

The problem appears to be one of searching out the responsive publics, the people and the groups in society, broadly conceived, who are most capable of charting the course for public schools and then creating the means for converting their expressions into public decisions. The converting process is a governmental process. Dewey has given almost poetic description to the problem:

> An inchoate public is capable of organization only when indirect consequences are perceived, and when it is possible to project agencies which order their occurrence. At present, many consequences are felt rather than perceived; they are suffered, but they cannot be said to be known, for they are not, by those who experience them, referred to their origins. It goes, then, without saying that agencies are not established which canalize the streams of social action and thereby regulate them. Hence the publics are amorphous and unarticulated.[46]

As indicated earlier, the ultimate choice of local versus nonlocal control may well rest upon whether substantive quality in decisions relative to local problems can be attained. It is doubtful that a public inarticulate at the local level will be more articulate at the state level. Transfer of core decisions to the state or national government means that the responsibility for policy in education may be shifted to professional educators and administrators—not by design necessarily but by public default. Professionals keep schools going; they are always around; they know the problems, they are consulted immediately by official policymakers, the school board members; they cannot but affect policymaking. The canalization of the public will at higher levels of policy formulation may be as illusive as it is at the local level. Again Dewey is insightful when he suggests that the ramifications of the issues before the public are so comprehensive and delicate, the technical matters so specialized, the details so many and so elusive that "the public cannot for any length of time identify and hold itself." He continues:

> It is not that there is no public, no large body of persons having a common interest in the consequences of social transactions. There is too much public, a public too diffused and scattered and too intricate in composition.[47]

The structure of governance for schools cannot be considered in isolation. The future of the local unit of school organization seems to hinge upon what the body politic decides to do about local government affairs in general. The scope and complexity of problems facing local units of government are staggering, particularly in the urban setting. Those problems have worsened to some extent as a consequence of President Reagan's "new federalism." Reductions in federal support for human services programs, including education, linked with the allocation of increased responsibilities to state and local authorities for meeting "social" problems have intensified

---

45. For a useful review of the function of criteria in policy appraisal see Yehezkel Dror, *Public Policymaking Reexamined* (San Francisco: Chandler, 1968).
46. Dewey, *The Public and Its Problems,* 131.
47. Ibid., 137.

competitiveness for local resources, especially the property tax. In the past, bargaining to receive federal resources for local services was essentially a vertical process. Under the new federalism, bargaining is becoming a horizontal process between and among local units of government.[48]

One alternative to such intergovernmental competitiveness is some kind of consolidation of disparate authorities, some kind of powerful central control over cities, metropolitan areas, even regions, that would be able to effect a patterned, planned sequence of development. But such centralization seems to be almost impossible: the job is too big; the conflicting interests are too strategic and powerful; the fear of centralization resident in the citizenry is too pervasive; and the capacity of our political system to focus adequate intelligence upon the job of creating a "super" local government is too limited. The prospect of such centralization seems remote, at least in the near future.

The federated notion described in chapter 5 is a form of decentralization and to some extent a step closer to community control. No one should view it as a panacea for its possesses the weakness of further extending the structure of government and introducing another layer of decision making between the citizen and the state. Nevertheless, it is an alternative.

The theory of governance prominent in federated proposals calls for a structure that will accommodate the advantages of bigness and smallness simultaneously.[49] The design is expected to meet the general need for efficiency that large-scale enterprise provides; at the same time it allows for extended opportunities for political access. Theoretically, it opens up the political system; practically, it remains to be seen whether or not interested citizens would participate more actively in school affairs given such structural change.

The rural scene is quite another matter. Farmers are relatively self-contained with respect to provisions for water, sanitation, and other utilities. Their local governments provide roads, schools, modest police and fire protection, and some other special services. Villages and towns provide more services of course, but these needs have been met in most instances without undue hardship or even delay. The school districts in many places, as we have described them earlier, are archaic and need examination. But the dimensions and complexity of local government problems in rural areas do not approach those of the urban environment. It does not follow that these units of government are any less important or that they can be ignored. Wherever inadequacies in district structure exist they are reflected in inadequacies of educational program; the shortcomings in program manifest themselves immediately in less than satisfactory educational opportunity.

In the past concern for school district reorganization has been focused on reducing the number of districts in rural America. We maintain that, although further progress of this nature is warranted, the focus in the future must be shifted to improving district organization in the urban areas as well as in the expanding rural-urban fringes around our metropolitan centers. The remaking of district structures should include evaluation of the place of intermediate units in the total milieu of educational government.

48. See Richard P. Nathan, "State and Local Governments under Federal Grants," *Political Science Quarterly* 98 (Spring, 1983), 56–57.
49. Peterson defines federalism as a system of government in which powers are divided between higher and lower levels of government in such a way that all levels have substantial responsibilities for their constituencies. Peterson, *City Limits,* 67.

The 1970s and early 1980s were marked by paradox. Many school districts accustomed to rapid and sustained growth since World War II, faced decline for the first time. Increasing enrollments, new facilities, and program extensions gave way to retrenchment, reductions in force, and program cutbacks. The pronounced nature of these changes coupled with school finance uncertainties and the impact of the courts on the schools placed new stresses on the governance and management of education. The future of local school districts appears to be caught up in the question of whether or not our political system, functioning through the mechanisms of local districts, states, and federal centers of responsibility can carry its burdens.

Thus we see three fundamental challenges confronting local school districts in the years ahead. The most basic is operational responsibility for the conduct of instruction. The state and federal centers of responsibility are structurally remote from the day-to-day activities of teaching and learning. Thus they essentially set directions and follow through by facilitating and supporting programs to meet stated objectives. Because local districts carry the principal responsibility for school effectiveness, the pressures for instructional accountability from parents, students, and the citizenry in general are likely to affect local district officials even more severely in the future than in the past. The seeds of structural change may be falling all around them and may, in fact, take root in the soils of continued discontent. Consequently, the existing patterns of school districts may be examined in light of the public's assessment of their effectiveness.

A second challenge, therefore, is the specification of comprehensive criteria to use in the appraisal of school district effectiveness. Organizations of professional educators, school board groups, interested lay people, and researchers will need to address the criteria problem. It will be difficult to identify useful indications of effectiveness. This is not a new problem but we are hopeful that neither its complexity nor its political nature will deter concerted efforts to identify such indications of effectiveness. Educational government should never become so rigid that it fails to respond to the needs confronting society.

A third challenge is the integration of diverse community interests and resources into formulating educational policies. It is likely that mediating public structures, such as the Twin Cities Metropolitan Council of Minneapolis and St. Paul, and planning organizations, such as the Citizens' League of Minneapolis and St. Paul, will have a growing impact upon local governments, including school districts. In fact there is evidence that new bonds are being developed between the public and private sectors as well as between and among citizens organizations and both sectors.[50] Cleveland notes that the reactive mode of modern government requires that most new ideas originate outside in "nongovernments." Nongovernments involve thinkers, nongovernmental experts, and advocates linked with government officials and legislators.[51] Such bridging mechanisms may increase the amount and improve the quality of information upon which many critical school district decisions will be based.[52]

50. Judith Getzels, Peter Elliott, and Frank Beal, *Private Planning for the Public Interest* (Chicago: American Society of Planning Officials, 1975).
51. Harlan Cleveland, "People Lead Their Leaders in an Information Society," in *Communications and the Future*, Howard F. Didsbury, Jr. (Bethesda, Md.: World Future Society, 1982), 173.
52. For a detailed account of third party mediating structures in education see Luvern L. Cunningham, "Third Parties As Problem Solvers," in *Communities and Their Schools*, Don Davies (New York: McGraw-Hill, 1981), ch. 5.

The locus of school control in the future must depend upon the structure of government which can most successfully translate the informed public will into effective public policy. Our concern is not with state or federal or local control per se; rather, we are interested in perfecting our public capacity to select the most appropriate level for focusing our collective intelligence on public educational problems.

5
The Intermediate Unit of School Administration

Historically, the term *intermediate unit of school administration* refers to the office or agency in an intermediate position between the state department of education and local school districts. Within the past decade or two, intermediate units in many states have undergone substantial change. Initially, their primary function was regulation and control as instrumentalities of state educational agencies. A major objective was to ensure that state policies and programs were administered in local districts, many of which were too small to provide the necessary educational services. In more recent times, however, as we shall discuss, the paramount purpose of intermediate units has evolved to be that of providing needed educational services.[1] The importance of these units will likely increase as demands for greater efficiency in the public sector intensify in the face of declining enrollments, inflation, and increased competition for resources. Within the immediate future these somewhat "invisible" units may become more focal centers of attention as educators are compelled to develop more efficient delivery systems and structures.[2]

Thirty-nine states have some form of intermediate unit. In most states, mainly in the Midwest and West, the intermediate unit of school administration is often coterminous with the county. In New York there is a Board of Cooperative Educational Services which serves essentially as an intermediate unit, and this organization is not coterminous with county boundaries. The remaining 11 states have no intermediate unit of school administration; many of them have operating school districts which for the most part are country-wide in area.

The supervisory unions found in the New England states have often been treated as intermediate units of school administration. Actually, these supervisory unions serve chiefly as a way of promoting cooperative action among the boards of the local districts (towns). The union is composed of board members who, in many unions, meet to select a superintendent of schools and attend to other joint business. The

1. Harold S. Davis, *Educational Service Centers in the U.S.A.*, (Hartford, Conn.: Connecticut State Department of Education, 1976), 72.
2. Rae M. Levis, *The Education Service Agency—Where Next?* (Washington, D.C.: American Association of School Administrators, 1983).

101

superintendent tends to work with each district board instead of in an intermediate district capacity.

In some of the literature on intermediate units the county school district is treated as though it were one type of intermediate unit. Such a concept is an erroneous one for in some states which have county districts the county district is the basic operating unit of school government and does not stand in an intermediate position. Reference is also made in the literature to regional subdistricts of large cities as intermediate units. We do not include these organizational arrangements here for they are variations effected within basic operating school districts and not intermediate between the state and local districts.

Development of the Intermediate Unit

Each of the 39 states with intermediate units of school administration has a somewhat unique history of the unit's development. Louisiana, Montana, Virginia, Indiana, and Minnesota are among the states in which intermediate units have been created relatively recently. Obviously, this is not the place for detailed state-by-state discussion. Instead, we shall note the development of the office in two states and make a few generalizations which seem to characterize the growth of the office generally. Michigan is one of the states in which the intermediate unit has been coterminous with the county until recently, and the history of the intermediate unit in Michigan can be used as an illustrative case for this group of states.

In Michigan the territorial laws of 1827 and 1829 provided for township officials who would have some jurisdiction over schools and who were required to divide the township into school districts. Thus, the township became the first intermediate unit in Michigan. The Michigan constitution of 1835 provided only for local officials to supervise the schools but the law of 1837 created school inspectors for each of the townships. In 1867 Michigan provided for an elective office of county superintendent of schools. This plan was repealed in 1875 and the plan of township inspectors was reestablished. It was 1891 before the plan of having a chief county school officer was reestablished under the title of the county school commissioner. For fifty years, 1841 to 1891, there was a constant tug-of-war to determine whether the county or the township would become the intermediate unit of school administration in Michigan.[3]

During this period there was constant criticism of township officials as politicians attempted to deal with such problems as certification, supervision, and reporting to the state school office. At the same time, the township was reluctant to relinquish any control to the larger unit, the county. This controversy was finally ended in Wayne County (Detroit area) in 1937 when board members of local school districts were authorized to select a county board of education and that board in turn was to select a county superintendent of schools. The county board became the creature of local boards of education and the county board operation was limited to those functions favored by local school districts. This plan was made uniform for the state in 1947. In 1962 the Michigan legislature strengthened the intermediate school district financially and administratively and provided a means whereby as many as three counties might be combined into one unit.

Since 1962 the Michigan legislature has repeatedly strengthened the intermediate district. In 1976, out of 83 counties, Michigan had 58 intermediate districts, which

---

3. Harlan D. Beem and H. Thomas James, *Report of the Michigan Committee for the Study of the Intermediate Unit of School Administration* (Chicago: Midwest Administration Center, University of Chicago, 1956).

included all of the operating local school districts of the state. The boundaries of the intermediate districts were no longer determined by county lines but by the boundaries of the constituent local districts. By the 1970s there were 15 multi-county intermediate school districts; nine served two counties, four served three counties, one served four counties, and one served a five-county region. In consolidated intermediate districts, board members were elected at large while in regular intermediate districts they were elected by representatives of local boards of education. In all cases the intermediate superintendent was appointed by the intermediate district board.

The intermediate unit in New York is not coterminous with the county. In New York State as early as 1795 the law established a body known as the town commission which was to apportion state school money among the several school districts of the town, to confer with district trustees about the qualifications of teachers, and to exercise a modicum of supervision over the course of study. This early provision was strengthened in 1812, and two years later the town commissioners served as a sort of board and the inspectors actually did more of the school visitation.

This arrangement continued until 1841 when legislation created a deputy superintendent, apparently deputy to the state superintendent, who was to be appointed by the county board of supervisors. Half of the deputy superintendent's salary was to be paid from state funds, an arrangement which smacked of state control. In 1843 town commissioners and town inspectors were eliminated and a town superintendent was created. For a time both the town superintendent and the deputy superintendent, operating at the county level, served intermediate functions. Shortly, however, the deputy superintendent was eliminated. This left the town superintendent to represent the intermediate unit until 1856. In that year the town superintendency was eliminated and an elected county superintendency was provided. Almost all duties of the town superintendent were transferred to the new office which remained in effect for more than fifty years.

In 1910 the elected county superintendency was abolished and supervisory districts, each comprised of a number of towns, were established. All territory outside cities of 4,500 or more in population was to be included in supervisory districts. Initially, there were 208 such districts and each supervisory district had a district board of school directors which selected the superintendent of schools. Even so, the superintendent appeared to be responsible directly to the state commissioner of education.

After extended study an intermediate unit law was passed in 1948. As an interim step, provision was made for boards of cooperative services to be composed of representatives of local district boards. These boards selected their own superintendent of schools and had general supervision over the services to be provided to component districts. Within two years after this permissive legislation there were 90 boards of cooperative school services and about 1,200 professional workers providing services in some 25 categories to many thousands of pupils in the state of New York. As of 1973 the supervisory districts had been reduced to 46 in number, boards of school directors had been abolished, and each of the districts was governed by a Board of Cooperative Educational Services (BOCES). Each of these boards selected a district superintendent. The district superintendent, while responsible to the state commissioner of education, also served as the Executive Officer of the Board of Cooperative Educational Services. The 44 BOCES's in New York now serve all but 21 of the state's 740 school districts.

New York, like Michigan, has a long history of intermediate unit expressions which began in 1795 and continued until 1948 when the present arrangement emerged. Much of this controversy centered on whether the town or the county should be the intermediate unit. Finally, groups of towns were formed into supervisory districts and became, in effect, the intermediate units. The creation of the deputy superintendent in 1841, however, sparked another controversy which continues today. The question is whether the intermediate office stands midway between the local school districts and the state department of education or whether the intermediate office actually represents the state department of education.

Cooper and Fitzwater some years ago examined the evolution of the intermediate district over 150 years of American history,[4] and their conclusions suggest the summary of trends below:

1. There has been a growing recognition of education as a state function and the need for a workable number of intermediate offices to facilitate communication between the state and a great number of local school districts.
2. In the early stages the intermediate unit was seen essentially as an extension of the arm of the state department of education.
3. Over the years there has been a gradual transfer of the functions of the intermediate office from a lay board to a professional or semiprofessional officer.
4. Progress toward making the intermediate office more than a perfunctory one has been slow because people resisted any encroachments upon their exercise of control of education at the local district level.
5. In recent years the intermediate unit has come to be viewed by many people as an agency to provide to small local school districts services which they cannot ordinarily provide for themselves.

There is considerable variety in the organizational arrangements of the intermediate unit of school administration as found in the 39 states. In 19 states there are only two levels of school government: the state and the basic operating school district. Hawaii seems to stand alone and actually operates as one large centralized school district.

In most of the 39 intermediate unit states, boards of education are the governing body of the intermediate unit. In some states the traditional practice of reposing legal responsibility in the county superintendent of schools alone has been retained. For the most part, these board members are elected at large by popular vote. In Iowa and Washington they are elected from wards. In New York and Pennsylvania the members of the intermediate boards are elected by representatives of the local boards of education. In Pennsylvania intermediate board members must actually be serving on local boards at the time of election. In a number of states superintendents of intermediate districts are appointed, in most cases by the intermediate boards and in New Jersey by the state commissioner. However, intermediate superintendents are elected by popular vote in many states. In a number of these states intermediate boards of education are also elected by popular vote. Presumably, these superintendents are supposed to serve as administrators for these intermediate boards, but it is clear that the boards have no ways of holding the superintendents responsible. These states probably represent partial reorganization of the intermediate office, which has been retarded because of timidity or lack of understanding.

A look at the intermediate unit of school administration raises a number of questions. What should be the structure and function of the intermediate unit? If 11 states

4. Shirley Cooper and Charles O. Fitzwater, *County School Administration* (New York: Harper & Row, 1954), 108–9.

have managed without recognized intermediate units, can the other states do likewise? If an intermediate unit is needed, what can we learn from the wide variety of practices that now exist? Is it possible that the functions which were necessary in a rural America of a century ago are no longer needed? We shall now turn to these questions.

The Intermediate Unit Today

In the past decade or so, substantial changes have been made in more than 20 states in the organization of intermediate units. In one case, Kansas, the county as an intermediate unit was eliminated entirely. In other cases the number of intermediate units was reduced either by elimination or by combining counties for intermediate purposes. In Nebraska, even though the county superintendency was retained, 19 service units were created. Texas, in a sweeping reorganization, created a statewide network of 20 educational service centers for its 254 counties. Iowa created Joint County School Systems, Georgia established a statewide network of Cooperative Educational Service Agencies, and West Virginia in 1972 established multi-county Regional Educational Service Agencies. In 1975 Montana mandated the creation of five Special Education Regional Services and Virginia enacted legislation to create voluntary Regional Education Service Agencies. In 1976 Indiana passed enabling legislation for the creation of Educational Centers, and Minnesota established ten Educational Cooperative Service Units.

These and other actual and pending changes receiving serious study in numerous other states suggest that the intermediate unit is on trial. Possibly the intermediate unit of school administration has always been evolving. It may be that any unit which attempts to find a place between the legally fixed responsibility for education at the state level and the jealously guarded operation of schools at the local district level is inevitably in flux. In any case this is an issue which needs to be examined closely.

Needed or Not?

The first consideration revolves around the question of whether the intermediate unit is or is not needed. Those who favor retention of the intermediate unit point out that in most states we have hundreds and even thousands of local school districts, the majority of which are too small or too poor to offer complete educational programs; therefore, some intermediate office must provide a number of services, such as supervision and guidance, or else rural children will be deprived of adequate educational opportunity. To those who suggest that districts should reorganize into larger and more efficient units, the supporters of the intermediate unit reply that such arrangements decrease local control and local identification, and that rural citizens are opposed to any such arrangements.

Those who favor abolition of the intermediate unit say there are better solutions. One, local districts can be reorganized into adequate units of school administration wherever possible, with pupil enrollments in grades 1 through 12 of no less than 10,000 or 12,000, and such units can provide, in most cases, adequate elementary and secondary school programs. To those who say that rural people resist such reorganization, it is pointed out that with proper leadership reorganizations have been effected and that after a few years experience in the reorganized districts, most people do not favor a return to the old plan.

A second alternative, if districts are to remain small and there is to be no intermediate unit, is a plan of cooperation among districts. One or more cooperative plans might be established. For instance, an audiovisual center might be established through the voluntary cooperation of several districts and the cost prorated among the districts. Or, small districts might contract with a larger district to provide some service, such as classes for the mentally handicapped, which small districts find impractical to establish on their own. Actually, a number of county superintendents, who do not have service staffs of their own, are facilitating agreements among districts in order to provide some of these services on a cooperative basis. One wonders, however, if many cooperative plans will be fostered without the vision and encouragement of professional persons not ordinarily found in small rural districts.

The third possible solution is the decentralization of the state department of education. It is conceivable that, in place of establishing an intermediate layer of school government with more boards, administrators, and staff, the state department might establish a number of regional offices throughout the state and equip each office with personnel who could provide consultative services to local district board members, administrators, and teachers.[5] Such consultants could provide the leadership necessary to establish cooperative programs among the districts. These regional offices might also provide specialized personnel in instruction, guidance, and other areas. To be sure, such a plan might be perceived as coming close to actually centralizing school operation under state auspices, a program hardly in keeping with school development in this country.

Decentralized regional offices established by the state department of education would be a new arrangement, and these offices could probably be established where needed, not necessarily in every county. Much recent thinking about the intermediate school district has suggested that in sparsely settled areas such districts might embrace more than one county. Whether an intermediate service be provided by a reorganized intermediate district or by a decentralized state department of education, it seems clear that it should not be tied inevitably to county lines. Parenthetically, we might add that county lines are obsolete for a number of other governmental services as well.

The Question of Function

The discussion above suggests that the general question of providing or not providing an intermediate unit of some type is by no means settled. What the function of such a unit should be is another question that is debated. Traditionally, proponents of the intermediate unit have suggested that the chief functions of such a unit are: general educational leadership, specialized educational services, and certain management and purchasing services for small districts.

The school codes of most intermediate unit states are replete with references to the duties of county boards of education and the duties of the superintendents who serve such areas. These seemingly are broad grants of power and responsibility, but actual practice suggests that they tend to be pious affirmations, little more. This may be accounted for in several ways. The wording of such injunctions tends to be so general that each person can interpret them as he or she sees fit, at least as long as the incumbent county or district superintendent does not take the provisions too seriously. By contrast, state legislatures have given local boards of education very specific powers and duties having to do with school operation, and there is a body of case

5. Stephens Associates, *Education Service Agencies: Status and Trends* (Burtonsville, Md.: Stephens Associates, 1979), 2.

law making it clear that most operating decisions rest with local boards. While local boards may listen to the advice of the county or district superintendent, they are more apt to seek the advice of their own employee, the local superintendent of schools.

To be sure, county or district superintendents do perform certain legal functions, but by and large these have to do with recordkeeping and reporting often required by the state department of education. In the rural school districts of some states, the power of the county superintendent may extend, as it does in Ohio to the recommendation of all teaching and administrative personnel. Even in Ohio, however, the exercise of this function is often *pro forma* in nature, ignored altogether, or dispensed with by a majority vote of the local board. It is clear to see why county boards of education and their superintendents feel frustrated about the roles they are to perform.

Despite the general confusion regarding the traditional function of the intermediate unit, increasing numbers of intermediate organizations, usually those in metropolitan settings, have forged ahead with new and expanded programs. New York's BOCES in Southern Westchester County, for example, projected for 1983–84 a budget of $24.7 million servicing the needs of 29 component districts, 6 non-component districts and school districts in several other BOCES areas. The Southern Westchester BOCES provides a wide variety of occupational education, special education, computer education, teacher and administrator training, and other instructional and related services.[6]

Ohio's 87 county offices of education provide supervisory, special educational, administrative and other services to 793,000 students and 40,000 educators in the state's 381 local school districts.[7] The Cuyahoga County Board of Education in the Cleveland area, for example, offers a wide variety of services and programs and in 1981–82 had a staff of 220 with a budget of approximately $5 million.[8]

A growing number of states have accepted the service function of the intermediate unit and have provided, over a period of time, state funds to the unit for services. By combining federal, state, and county funds with school district funds through contractual arrangements, many California county departments of education, for example, have been able to finance a wide range of services for local school districts. Thus, an increasingly influential movement that clearly perceives service, not regulation and control, as the primary function of the intermediate or middle-echelon unit of school administration is already underway. Numerous models of these recently rejuvenated units can be cited. Although their names and structures vary considerably between states and even within states, entities such as Michigan's Regional Dissemination Centers, New Jersey's Educational Improvement Centers, and Connecticut's Educational Service Centers are becoming more vital mechanisms within the educational infrastructure.[9] Advocates of these regional service centers cite the following to illustrate the benefits they provide:

1. They can facilitate the provision to local districts of easily accessible and definite self-determined supplemental and supportive services of high quality.

6. *1983–84 Estimated Budget: BOCES Southern Westchester,* (Port Chester, New York; BOCES Southern Westchester, 1983).
7. *The County Office of Education: Ohio's Vital Learning Link,* (Columbus, Oh.: Ohio County Superintendents Association, 1978), 1.
8. *Annual Report of the Cuyahoga County Board of Education 1981–1982,* (Bedford Heights, Ohio: Cuyahoga County Board of Education, 1982).
9. See, for example, Frank R. Yulo, *Educational Service Centers in Connecticut,* (Hartford, Conn.: Connecticut State Department of Education, 1977).

2. They can facilitate the development and/or provision of required programs and services to local districts in the event the local unit is unable to do so.

3. They can contribute substantially to the equalization of educational opportunities for all children by minimizing the accident of geography and neutralizing artificial barriers as important determinants of the kind of educational programs available.

4. They can promote the better utilization of known applications and force a systematic search for new applications of cost-benefit/cost-effectiveness principles in the delivery of educational programs and services within the state school system.

5. They can contribute to the healthy interface between urban, suburban, and rural interests in the search for solutions to areawide educational and educationally related issues.

6. They can contribute significantly to the development of a statewide research, development, evaluation, and dissemination network in the state and promote the concentration of and best use of resources to foster the network once it is in place.

7. They can contribute significantly to the establishment of a statewide network of resident change agents possessing both authenticity in the eyes of their principal constituencies and legal mandates, where necessary; they can also more readily implement the staffing and resources necessary to effect fundamental change in the workings of the state school system on a regular and planned basis.

8. They can substantially promote meaningful local school district involvement in statewide and regional planning and decision-making processes:[10]

While this discussion of function could be extended, enough has been said to illustrate that the purposes of the intermediate unit vary from state to state. This confusion seems to reside in a few general areas. There is first the area of direct service to small local districts aimed at strengthening the total educational program. Thus, for example, film libraries, counseling services, and supervisory services were provided, where budgets permitted, by the intermediate unit and made available to local school districts. Now many local districts have grown to the point where their own film libraries, counselors, and supervisors are superior to those available in the county or intermediate office. What does this suggest about direct service for the future?

A second area of confusion is often referred to as the leadership role of the intermediate unit. At one time, and possibly in many places still, the county superintendent or members of his staff, if he were fortunate enough to have a staff, might provide useful advice to rural school boards and administrators. Again, with the reorganization and increased size of school districts, and possibly, too, with the increased specialization of education, county superintendents often find they have little advice to give or that local boards and local superintendents do not seek such advice. What should be the leadership role of the intermediate unit in the future?

10. E. Robert Stephens, *Regional Educational Service Agencies* (Arlington, Va.: Educational Research Service, Inc., 1975), 57–58.

The Question of Structure

Just as basic questions are being raised about the functions of the intermediate unit, basic questions are also being raised about the organization and financing of such units.[11] The question of the geographical area to be contained in the intermediate unit has already been referred to. In most cases the intermediate unit is now coterminous with the county. While there are some conveniences in having the county as the intermediate unit, in terms of having a unit large enough and with resources enough to perform many functions, the county, at least in sparsely settled areas, will not suffice.

A tendency to reject the county as the appropriate geographic area for the intermediate unit may be noted in recent legislation in Iowa and Wisconsin, where two or more counties were permitted to join units; several such combinations have been made. Legislation in Michigan requires that counties be joined to form intermediate units if any single county contains less than 5,000 population. The actual and proposed structural changes represented by these and other states have a long tradition to overcome, but the question does appear to be a live one.

Whether or not the intermediate unit should have a board and, if so, how that board should be selected, are also major questions at this time. A number of states have no county board of education even though they have county superintendents of schools who perform some intermediate unit services. Should the intermediate unit become more significant as a part of the educational structure of these states, intermediate boards will probably be established.

In states which have intermediate unit boards of education, board members are selected in a number of ways. In some states, members are elected from the intermediate unit at large. In a few states board members are elected from areas or wards within the intermediate unit. In other states intermediate board members are elected by local board members or by representatives of local board members. Recent legislation in Michigan altered this arrangement somewhat and in New York the plan was initially seen as an interim arrangement. In any case these and other practices suggest that the manner of selecting intermediate unit board members still varies widely.

The structure of the intermediate unit office must also take into account the professional staff provided by such an office. Near one end of the scale, we find that San Diego County, California, employs many professionals including administrators, coordinators, and special teachers. Somewhere in the middle of this continuum, largely due to legislation passed during the last decade or so, is Ohio, where every county school district now has at least one professional person in addition to the county superintendent of schools; many county school districts have a rather diversified staff of professional workers. On the other end of the scale, however, some county school superintendents are pleased to have just a secretary. Indeed, the county superintendent may even look upon the job as part-time employment. In some states the lack of professional staff may signify quite clearly the tenuous position of the intermediate unit.

Financial support for the intermediate unit includes state appropriations, a tax levied by or at the behest of the intermediate unit, and contracts with local school districts. In California all three plans are in operation. One concern of school people

---

11. Stephens Associates, *Education Service Agencies: Status and Trends,* 88–125.

in California is that county school funds are under the control of the county supervisors, thus making the intermediate unit dependent fiscally for at least the county share of its budget.

In Iowa, on the other hand, legislation has conferred taxing power and thus fiscal independence upon the intermediate unit. The intermediate unit in Washington, however, and in a number of other states has no tax-levying authority. In both Washington and California the intermediate unit may enter into contracts with local school districts for services to be provided. In any state where the intermediate unit is taken seriously, its financing becomes an important problem.

Socioeconomic Forces Affecting the Intermediate Unit

To understand more fully what has been happening to the intermediate unit of school administration over the last several decades, it is necessary to examine some of the socioeconomic forces operating in our society. Certainly a plan for the future must take into account such forces. A brief discussion of some of these influences and their possible implications for the intermediate unit follows.

Growth in Technology

The growth of technology in America has affected rural as well as urban life. With increased farm mechanization, each farm owner attempts to get more acres to cultivate and this gives rise to displacement of some farm laborers and to increased size of farms. Thus, in the past half century or so farm population decreased even though total population increased. In 1920 farm population was 30 percent of total population while sixty years later it was less than 5 percent.

Mechanization, of course, has played a major role in the rapid demographic movement away from farms. The great and rapidly increasing capital investment now characteristic of agriculture has driven small farmers off the land and given the remaining, more prosperous farm owners no choice but to make a heavy investment in machinery to work as many acres as possible.

Along with farm mechanization have come improved transportation and communication. Most farm roads have been surfaced to accommodate the automobile. Aided by the Rural Electrification Administration in the 1930s, most farms now have electric current. This, in turn, has meant that radio and televison are as common in farm homes as they are in city homes. Many farmers hold jobs in industrial plants and often drive 30 to 50 miles to such plants, thus becoming part-time farmers. Good roads also have enabled city dwellers to move to the suburbs and retain their jobs in the city. In short it is becoming more and more difficult to draw a line between rural and urban areas. Indeed, recent demographic analyses indicate, as we will amplify shortly, that the massive migration to urban areas is being reversed and a perceptible population shift to rural and smaller communities has been underway in the past decade.[12]

The migration resulting from these developments has affected schools and school organization. Most notably, people in farm areas are fewer in number. These people often find reorganization of local school districts essential if an adequate educational program, particularly at the high school level, is to be provided. These reorganizations would not be possible without school bus transportation, but good roads have made

12. Calvin L Beale, *Where Are All the People Going—Demographic Trends* (Washington, D.C.: Rural Housing Alliance and Rural America, Inc., 1975)

that feasible. Even with these local school district reorganizations, it is often difficult to form a rural high school attendance area with more than two or three hundred pupils. With such an enrollment, and ordinarily with the financial resources available in such an area, a complete educational program is an impossibility. Under these circumstances, an intermediate unit of some kind may be the most feasible way of complementing the limited programs of the component local districts within such a unit.

School District Reorganization

School district reorganization over the last four decades has affected the nature and function of the intermediate unit. The intermediate unit, up until the end of World War II, particularly as reflected in the office of the county superintendent, was a product of rural America. Many counties in the Midwest contained 75 to 100 small school districts, most of which operated a one-room, eight-grade school. Each district had a board of trustees or directors who knew little about schools, and each district had a teacher who had completed the eighth grade and passed the county teacher's examination in the school subjects.

The schools, the teachers, and the board members the county superintendent was to visit, often by stipulation, no less than once a year. The county superintendent acted as the arm of the state in seeing that minimum legal requirements were met, in distributing small amounts of state funds usually derived from school lands, and in supplying simple statistics to the state superintendent of public instruction.

With improved roads, the one-room school, often located within walking distance for all pupils, made less sense. With the growth of high schools, it was clear that not every district could support a high school. These circumstances led in some states to reorganization of school districts even in the early decades of this century. Many of these reorganizations resulted in the establishment of elementary schools of 100 to 200 pupils and of high schools of 50 to 100 pupils. Often these schools were located in the villages adjacent to the farm areas. As some of the villages grew into towns and cities, school enrollments increased. Other villages and the open country actually decreased in population, and this created the need for a new round of district reorganization.

This movement received genuine impetus in the years following the close of World War II. As noted in chapter 4, school districts have been reduced from over 100,000 to about 16,000. Some people have suggested that this process should be continued until there are no more than 10,000 school districts in the nation. Even the attainment of this goal would leave us with many school districts enrolling as few as 2,000 pupils.

A district of 2,000 pupils would not be, in our judgment, self-sufficient. While it could support elementary and secondary schools, it could probably provide only limited programs for gifted pupils, for slow learners, for the vocationally oriented, and for the physically handicapped. It could probably provide no post-high school program in technical curricula or in college-preparatory curricula. Total pupil enrollments of at least 10,000 are necessary if complete educational programs are to be provided.[13] In rural areas, even if school districts are reduced to 10,000 pupils, some intermediate level of organization will be necessary if a comprehensive educational program is to be made available.

13. A minimum of 30,000 pupils is recommended in E. Robert Stephens et al., *The Multi-County Regional Educational Service Agency in Iowa* (Iowa City, Ia.: Iowa Center for Research in School Administration, College of Education, University of Iowa, 1967).

Demographic Trends

Until relatively recently, only demographic changes in rural areas were considered. More recently, the growth of urban areas, and its implications for educational organization, has been recognized. In the past few decades, while the total population has been increasing, many of the central cities have been declining in population. The population in the suburban areas surrounding these cities grew as core cities lost residents. The 1980 census indicated that most of the central cities were continuing to lose population. Indeed, in the mid-1960s American society reached a demographic watershed when the suburban population for the first time surpassed the central city population.

More recent demographic trends reflect changing population patterns that will have significant ramifications for educational governance, particularly for intermediate districts. In the 1970s the nation's largest metropolitan areas experienced a marked decline in the rate of their population growth, a development without precedent since the first census was compiled in 1790. Moreover, the nation's large metropolitan centers—New York, Los Angeles, Chicago, Philadelphia, and Detroit—showed net population losses during the 1970s while many small towns in many less populous areas experienced considerable growth. These trends, of course, reflect the widely acknowleged shift of population away from the Northeast and North Central regions to the "Sun Belt" areas of the South and West.[14]

These data also reflect the embryonic stages of a reverse migration back away from the urban centers into rural America. Indeed, from 1970 to 1974 population growth in rural areas was 5.6 percent in comparison to national and metropolitan area growth of 4 percent and 3.4 percent respectively.[15] Of particular significance is the fact that this nonmetropolitan growth is not limited to adjacent "spillover" or "sprawl" areas, but is also found in regions that are nonadjacent and frequently quite distant from populous metropolitan areas.[16]

These trends, not foreseen even a few years ago, reflect a series of private, personal, and business decisions which are significantly different and have profound implications for educational governance. What it may augur are profound changes in rural life as one-time urban dwellers alter their life-styles and antiurban feelings escalate. Economic diversification also has been a vital factor in reducing rural poverty and altering the realities of country life. While rural poverty still abounds in our society, the massive migration of the less affluent to the industrial centers of the North in recent decades has substantially altered the geographical distribution of the nation's poor. In 1959, for example, 56 percent of poor people lived in rural areas. By 1975, 60 percent of the poor lived in metropolitan areas.[17]

Another salient point is that racial, social, and economic segregation is pronounced in most metropolitan areas, frequently along school district lines. Bluntly stated, the cities are increasingly black and the suburbs are white. City schools are becoming pauper schools for poor and often minority children. Although progress was made in the decade of the 1960s to close the gap between black and white city workers with similar educational backgrounds, blacks today still earn only approximately 65 percent as much as their white counterparts. These are some of the reasons why

14. Harold L. Hodgkinson, *Guess Who's Coming to College: Your Students in 1990*, (Washington, D.C.: National Association of Independent Colleges and Universities, 1983).
15. *Education Daily*, 11 May 1977, 4.
16. Beale, *Where Are All the People Going—Demographic Trends*.
17. Jon Nordheimer, "America's Rural Poor: The Picture is Changing," *New York Times*, 17 August 1975.

reformers are urging closer suburb-city or "metro" relationships in education. Of course, other problems, such as transportation, housing, air and water pollution, energy conservation, and airport congestion, are also regional in nature and are becoming more acute.

Although suburban communities are predominantly white, they are no longer the exclusive places of residence for upper- and upper-middle-class people. Since World War II lower- and middle-class people have also fled to the suburbs. The desire to have more living space, combined with the decentralization of industry and improved expressways into the cities, has led to this influx to the suburbs. Many of the suburban communities for working-class people, however, have been poorly planned and are often short on public services; the result has been the random and irregular growth known as urban sprawl.[18]

The changing composition of large central cities, the migration to the suburbs, and incipient rural growth have many implications for school organization. School systems in central cities, often cumbersome, bureaucratic, and impersonal organizations, are beset with very serious problems. School districts in suburban areas have grown so much in size that relationships with intermediate units are no longer appropriate. Rural districts, on the other hand, traditionally understaffed and poor in programs, may well be on the threshold of an exciting new era of enrichment and growth if the aforementioned demographic trends persist. Such developments may create enlarged roles and responsibilities for intermediate units of school administration. For example, a study of the fiscal impacts of declining enrollments (while admittedly limited in its explanatory capacity) did report that in four states—Michigan, Missouri, South Dakota, and Washington—school districts with the largest enrollment increases were located in non-metropolitan areas.[19]

Summary and Future Prospects

We have reviewed briefly the development of the intermediate unit of school administration in its various forms; we have made some assessment of its current operation; and we have noted the socioeconomic forces which may bring about a new role for the intermediate unit. Some alternative solutions and some directions for the future will now be suggested.

While there are notable exceptions, by and large the intermediate unit still is not performing a vital role in American education, and we believe it should either be eliminated or reconceived. If the intermediate unit were eliminated, a massive reorganization of school districts, far beyond anything now contemplated, would be required. If a minimum student enrollment of 10,000 is needed to support a comprehensive educational program, sparsely populated states would suffer under such an arrangement. In Wyoming, for instance, it would mean dividing the state into four or five school districts. The closest approximation of this arrangement we have is in Alaska where, except for a few city school districts, everything is included in District #1.

Another alternative which might also involve elimination of the intermediate unit would be a decentralization of the state department of education into regional offices.

18. See, for example, *Modernizing Local Government* (New York: Committee on Economic Development, 1966).
19. Education Finance Center, *The Fiscal Impacts of Declining Enrollments* Education Commission of the States Report no. F76–5 (Denver, Colo.: Education Commission of the States 1976), 10.

New Jersey already has moved in this direction. The county superintendent is considered a member of the state department of education staff and is appointed by, paid by, and responsible to the state board of education. More than a decade ago the New Jersey legislature provided for area service programs including state funds to help finance such programs. These centers now exist in nearly all of the state's 21 counties, and the great majority of New Jersey's school districts receive their services.

For a small, highly industralized state like New Jersey, this plan seems to have many advantages. One level of government is eliminated, services complementary to those provided by local school districts are available, and coordination with the state department of education appears to be complete. Whether or not our larger and more diversified states are ready for such a plan is still a question. If people in these states resist centralization of government at the state level, movement in this direction would be very slow. To make the New Jersey plan work in populous states such as Ohio and Illinois would require a very large number of professionals on the staff of the state department of education and hence a generous state department budget. The decentralized state department plan does not seem to be the best solution for many states.

There are very tangible signs that the intermediate unit movement is already well on the way to being reconceived and revitalized. There appears to be a new dynamism inherent in the movement as administrative entities once known as intermediate units are being restructured and renamed "regional educational service agencies." The change in terminology reflects the belief that these units are now "essentially organizations intended to serve constituent local school districts (rather than agencies designed primarily to perform administrative and regulatory functions for the state education agency as was true of the dominant historical middle-echelon unit—the county school system)."[20]

The concept of regional educational service agencies has grown considerably since the mid-1960s and the fact that approximately one-half of the states have recently reorganized their former middle-echelon units along these lines is ample testimony to their potential and viability. A recent study of emerging regional educational service agencies in a dozen states (Colorado, Georgia, Iowa, Michigan, Nebraska, New York, Oregon, Pennsylvania, Texas, Washington, West Virginia, and Wisconsin) reports that elements such as the following are found in these units:

1. Comprehensive programs and services for exceptional children in virtually all the states
2. Comprehensive educational media programs and services in virtually all the units
3. Curriculum subject matter consultant services in a majority of the units
4. Comprehensive data processing services in many of the units
5. Staff development activities in a majority of the units
6. Vocational-technical programs and services[21]

This growing grassroots restructuring of middle-echelon administrative units has triggered the creation of a new organization in Washington, D.C. to represent the

20. Stephens, *Regional Educational Service Agencies,* 1.
21. Ibid.

interests of the nation's educational service agencies. In February 1977 the American Association of Educational Service Agencies was created at the national convention of the American Association of School Administrators (AASA). This new organization, a contract agency of AASA with a membership of 193 contracted educational service agencies, has established a working national office and is engaged in such activities as publishing a newsletter, conducting regional workshops on career education for small school districts through the resources of educational service agencies, representing the agencies in the Congress and in the executive branch, and disseminating information about the regional service agencies through research and publications.[22]

These recent developments are impressive. This exciting reconceptualization of traditional intermediate units augurs well for their future, but even the most ardent advocates of the movement recognize that such progress has been spotty and that most units are still in an embryonic stage with respect to services provided and students reached. In the rural setting, especially, many districts will continue to depend upon the traditional intermediate unit for certain services. Such rural intermediate units should continue to meet the following criteria:

1. The major functions of the intermediate unit should be: planning for local district reorganization; determining the location of school plants; providing supplemental financing designed to further equalize educational opportunity; offering specialized instructional programs such as technical and junior college programs; providing specialized educational services such as psychiatric help to pupils in local districts, and providing educational leadership to local school districts.
2. Whenever possible, there should be a minimum enrollment of 10,000 pupils in the public schools of the areas included in an intermediate unit. An enrollment of 20,000 to 30,000 pupils would be even better.
3. The boundaries of the intermediate unit should be coterminous with the outer boundaries of a logical combination of local school districts which are to constitute the area of the intermediate unit. There should be no required relationship between the boundaries of the intermediate unit and the boundaries of the counties.
4. Each intermediate unit should be under the direct control of a board of education elected at large by the residents of the intermediate area. The board should appoint the intermediate superintendent and determine salary and tenure for that position. The board should adopt policies to govern the operation of the intermediate unit, employ the necessary personnel upon recommendation of the superintendent, and appraise the effectiveness of the policies as they are carried out by the employed personnel. An advisory committee to the intermediate unit board should be elected from the membership of the local district boards of education.
5. The intermediate board of education should be fiscally independent; it should have independent taxing power and the authority to determine its own budget. State funds should also be made available to intermediate units. The intermediate-unit board should also have power to contract with local district boards to provide certain services.

---

22. *American Association of Educational Service Agencies, Annual Report, 1982–83* (Washington, D.C.: 1983, Mimeographed).

6. The intermediate superintendent should be a person with the qualifications and competence to earn and deserve high professional recognition by administrators in all types of local school districts. In order to obtain a superintendent of such quality, an intermediate board of education should not be limited in its choice of a superintendent by residence requirements.

7. Both in structure and functions the intermediate unit should be sufficiently flexible to adapt to changing educational conditions and needs. There should be legal provisions for the reorganization of intermediate units similar to those presently applicable to local districts. As local districts become capable of providing more of their own services, it should be possible for an intermediate unit to discontinue a function no longer needed and to assume another which changing conditions indicate to be desirable.

As we contemplate the future of urban areas, it seems clear that the fates of the central cities and their suburban fringes are closely interrelated. Integrated planning for the inside and outside of these metropolitan areas is a clear necessity. It also becomes very plain that planning for education must be coordinated with the planning that is being done for housing, parks, fire and police protection, transportation, water and sewage disposal, and other services. Moreover, the well-being of more than two-thirds of our people is affected by what is done in these metropolitan areas.

The general issue of metropolitanism has been raised frequently throughout the country in recent years and is discussed in some detail in chapter 4, but metropolitan governance of education has rarely been achieved: Nashville in Tennessee's Davidson County, is the outstanding example. "Metro" solutions are proposed, but they are very rarely adopted. Why is metropolitanism less popular with voters and politicians than it is with planners, social scientists, and "ivory tower" professors? There are a number of reasons that can be briefly cited. As the more affluent and largely white population has moved to suburbia and as the minority and lower-income classes have stayed in the cities, there has been a growing racial and economic polarity. Metropolitanism would mean a basic redistribution of resources with suburbanites being taxed more heavily. Social class factors, of course, are also significant. The move to suburbia often means "we have made it." The fear of tax increases is pervasive. Thus the future of metropolitan government is not particularly bright politically—we will never have many examples of metropolitan government unless there are massive financial incentives for this specific purpose.

Many may think of regionalism and metropolitanism as additional examples of the disturbing trend towards centralization. A view more in keeping with reality might be to see the regional approach as perhaps the only means through which we can now create workable and responsive governmental entities of reasonable size in the United States. If we do not develop imaginative regional approaches, major decisions will necessarily be made at the state and federal levels. We have seen some manifestations of suburb-city cooperation, such as Operation Exodus in Boston, in which ghetto children have been bused to schools in the suburbs, and Project Wingspread in Chicago, where there have been suburban-urban exchanges. We have seen cities, such as Hartford, Connecticut, involved in suburban-city pupil exchanges. But these few tiny programs affect only a handful of youngsters.

In the 1970s, of course, the desegregation thrust lost much momentum, and many of the integration initiatives have either disappeared or remain rather limited. The volatile issue of busing and the concomitant racial and social-class tensions make it unlikely that metropolitan area approaches to school governance will have political viability. Indeed, metropolitanism probably will stay dormant, for the short run at least, unless the courts act, as they recently have in decisions involving Wilmington, Delaware; St. Louis, Missouri; and Louisville, Kentucky. The sustaining of lower court decisions compelling the merger of predominantly black city school systems with largely white suburban districts, for example, probably offers the best, and perhaps only, opportunity for meaningful metropolitanism to occur in the next decade or so. The U.S. Supreme Court's 5 to 4 decision in the summer of 1974 rejecting a metropolitan school desegregation approach in Detroit, will serve, of course, as a major deterrent to similar efforts to create such regional districts.

While the formation of viable intermediate units in rural areas will often involve combining all or parts of two or more counties, the problem is quite different in urban areas. In our central cities, particularly those over 200,000 in population, we may need to break the city school district into several legally autonomous school districts. Each of these districts might contain one or more high schools and several elementary schools, represent a recognized division within the city, and contain a population of 100,000 to 200,000 people or 20,000 to 40,000 pupils in elementary and secondary schools. Thus, a city of one million people might be divided into five to ten school districts.

We are convinced that some such division, coupled with plans to rehabilitate central cities and make them once more habitable for all classes of people, will go far toward eliminating the bureaucratic outlook among the professionals and restoring a feeling of local responsibility among lay citizens. It seems clear that early attempts to decentralize huge school districts into subdistricts, as in New York and Chicago, achieved neither of these ends. One must acknowledge, however, that these attempts did not have the benefit of overall city planning and rehabilitation.

The breakup of large city school districts is necessary to the organization of the most effective intermediate unit in the urban setting. Once this is done, the phenomenon of a single giant district in the center surrounded by scores of smaller districts is gone. In many respects school districts in the city and outside the city will be on a somewhat equal footing. Moreover, if both central city and suburban rings have been made habitable for all classes of people, the way for cooperation among all districts in a metropolitan area will be cleared. Thus, each metropolitan area should establish an intermediate unit to include all school districts in the entire area.[23]

This intermediate unit might correspond in area to other metropolitan authorities established to provide water, police protection, highways, and other services. The intermediate unit in the urban setting should meet many of the criteria suggested above for the intermediate unit in the rural setting. The intermediate school district should have independent taxing power and authority to determine its own budget. State funds should also be made available to intermediate units. The way should also be open for the intermediate board to contract with local school districts to supply certain services.

The major functions of the urban unit would be similar to those of the rural unit except that fewer specialized services to local districts would probably be necessary. There would be no problem with minimum enrollments in the intermediate unit. Boundaries would not be too difficult to determine. With respect to the controlling

23. Stephens Associates, *The Role of Education Service Agencies in Metropolitan Areas* (Burtonsville, Md.: Stephens Associates, 1980).

board, professional staff, and flexibility of organization, the two plans would be quite similar.

Variations of the intermediate district both in the urban and rural settings may well become more vital forces within the educational governance structure. In many ways this middle tier of administration represents a logical compromise between fragmented local districts, which are too small to provide quality educational programs in an increasingly complex social, economic, and political environment, and overly centralized city, state, or federal systems, which are cumbersome and unresponsive to local needs.

Escalating demands for greater efficiency in the delivery systems which provide educational and other public services might serve to buttress and enlarge the role of intermediate, or regional, educational service agencies in the difficult years ahead. Education, its problems exacerbated by shrinking enrollments and inflation is a singularly labor-intensive enterprise. Regional approaches are a rational means for reducing school costs; the political and economic reasons for strengthening intermediate units may become compelling.[24]

Indeed, as the country continues to experience economic and technological change in an interdependent world economy, regional mechanisms which can be flexible in meeting ever-changing training and employment needs will become more important not only in meeting the needs of youth but also the escalating retraining needs of adults.

The impact of technology and computers is increasingly reflected in the programs being offered by intermediate or regional units. The Twin Cities Metropolitan Study Council, for example, provides leadership by reviewing educational software and data processing equipment. Growing numbers of intermediate units such as the Board of Cooperative Educational Services of Nassau County in New York State are providing programs that prepare individuals for the changing job market in a fluid, technological economy.[25] Escalating numbers of regional service units are offering services similar to those provided by the Merrimack Education Center Technology Lighthouse Project which serves as a clearinghouse in computer technology for 22 school districts in northeastern Massachusetts.[26]

These technological changes and the other economic and demographic factors discussed in this chapter have significant implications for the influence and the nature of control exercised by the intermediate district. Although legal, ideational, structural and, to a great extent, financial control elements continue to place intermediate units in a relatively invisibile and ostensibly uninfluential role, basic changes in the economic and social needs of the society will in all likelihood increase substantially the types of control these districts will exercise in the years ahead. In other words, intermediate districts will be uniquely and increasingly positioned not only to manifest more voluntary forms of leadership but also might well be in a position to exercise their control more directly because of the society's profound need for more coherent, economical, and effective means of networking knowledge and allocating scarce resources.

A particularly important development which possibly portends more control and influence for intermediate districts is the fact that the rapid technological changes and economic challenges confronting American society have helped recently to rekindle

24. "Regionalism: Help in Cutting School Costs," *The School Administrator* 34 (November 1977), 6.
25. Board of Cooperative Educational Services of Nassau, *The 1982–1983 Skills for Success Planner* (Westbury, N.Y.: BOCES of Nassau, 1982).
26. "A Lighthouse on Computers", *AAESA Report: Perspectives on Service* 1 (March–April 1983), 2.

the interest of business and industry in schools, training, and employment issues. There is a growing recognition, as we shall discuss in chapter 18, that all segments of the society have a collective stake in developing educational delivery systems which foster collaborative or bridging efforts between and among the various sectors. Regional service centers and intermediate units are uniquely positioned to provide the more flexible programs which will be needed if we are to thrive economically in the face of strong foreign competition.

6

School Attendance Areas

The determination of an attendance area for a particular school seems to be a rather straightforward administrative problem—one that could be resolved with dispatch permitting school leaders to move ahead with important matters of teaching and learning. But such is not the case, at least not today. Few school problems have elicited such continued public outcry as those associated with school attendance areas. The word "busing" alone has created large scale community turmoil and intense debate in state legislatures and the U.S. Congress. School closings, often necessary as enrollments decline, produce similar responses.

The issues related to the social, racial, and ethnic fabric of a school's population which were once thought to be simple administrative matters, subject to professional judgments of school administrators, are now policy matters and demand resolution at the level of the board of education and even the courts. The segregation of pupils on a racial basis violates the federal Constitution, but the action of the U.S. Supreme Court in 1954 has not resolved the thousands of attendance area problems across the land. In fact, the reverse is true. The action of the courts and the spirited drive of minority groups seeking their civil rights have catapulted the attendance area question into one of national interest and importance.

There are two main problems of definition regarding attendance areas. One is essentially geographical or territorial; the other is administrative and political. In this chapter we will acknowledge both and highlight some of the recurring attendance area problems facing school officials and their communities.

What an Attendance Area Is

An attendance area or attendance district, as it is sometimes called, is that portion of a school district in which pupils are required to attend a particular school as designated by the local school board. In a more general sense, an attendance area could be defined as the geographical area from which a school's population is drawn. Within an operating school district there is always at least one attendance area, and in large districts there are many attendance areas. If we said that for every school building there is an attendance area, we would be right most of the time but not always, for

121

in some instances there may be different attendance areas for different grade levels within a single building. Attendance areas are far from uniform, and defining them is not a simple matter.

There is a tendency, particularly on the part of lay people, to confuse an attendance area with a school district. Many people believe the area served by a given school building is a school district and fail to understand the difference between the two units of school organization. Citizen naiveté about this distinction is often revealed in discussions of community control. Prominent issues in citizen participation debates turn on legal differences between the prerogatives of professionals and citizens located at the district and the attendance area levels. The school district is the total area under the jurisdiction of the school board whereas the attendance area is ordinarily the territory served by a particular school building.

A rural school district, the typical one-room rural school at least, has the entire geographical area of the district as its attendance area. Every youngster wishing to attend a public school is expected to attend the school within that district. But even here exceptions are made where geographical barriers such as rivers or mountains or dangerous highways and railroads intervene. In these cases young people may be permitted to attend other schools in other districts on a reciprocal exchange or a tuition-payment basis. For the most part, however, the attendance area boundaries and rural school district boundaries are coterminous. Similar circumstances prevail in thousands of small town districts which may have but one public elementary school and one public secondary school. The boundaries of the district are also the attendance area boundaries for each of the two schools.

The number of public schools in the United States has decreased substantially since 1929–30 while the number of nonpublic schools increased. The attendance area concept does not apply to the nonpublic school in the same sense as to the public school, but the shifts in numbers of schools are still noteworthy. If each public school is considered to have a single attendance area, there were 85,733 attendance areas in 1981 in the United States.[1] (This total is at best an approximation, however, because, as was explained earlier, a single school may have more than one attendance area.) In 1931–32, there were 312,812 public schools. The elimination of 168,007 schools by 1975–76 was due primarily to school district reorganization throughout the nation. The decline came for the most part in one-teacher schools; in 1975–76 only 1,166 of these remained, whereas there were 143,000 in 1931–32.[2]

When districts are of sufficient size to warrant more than one building at a given level, attendance boundaries within a district must be established—unless a district chooses to try an open enrollment policy, permitting students to attend anywhere they choose within the district.

Boundaries for attendance areas in the nation's large districts can be confusing to citizens. A family might reside in a different attendance area for each school level. In other words the attendance areas for an elementary school, a junior high school, a senior high school, and possibly a junior college would not be identical. A family might even have second- and fifth- grade children in one school and third- or fourth-grade children in another school. For elementary school purposes alone, this family would be living in two attendance areas.

1. *The Condition of Education, 1983 Edition, A Statistical Report* (Washington D.C.: National Center for Education Statistics, 1983), 27.
2. Ibid.

Attendance areas are important, and professional educators as well as interested lay people are increasingly concerned about how they are established. The decisions about where to draw the lines among schools are difficult, and the consequences of such decisions are far-reaching. The nature of a given school population is determined frequently by where attendance lines fall. In many school districts in recent years controversies over racial balance often have focused upon whether plans to redraw attendance lines either increase or decrease integration.

The right of school boards to establish attendance areas is implicit in their authority to require attendance at a given school. A school board can designate the place of attendance of all pupils as long as it acts reasonably and does not abuse its discretion, especially as such discretion applies to the constitutional rights of children.[3]

The authority of school boards to establish attendance boundaries or to assign pupils to schools has been challenged frequently in recent years. Much of the litigation has grown out of school district reorganization. Following reorganization, pupils, and in some cases whole classes, have been transferred to other schools. In some instances these transfers have involved movements from small town and village schools to schools in rural areas. Parents, fearful that their children so transferred might be deprived of educational advantages, have contested such school board decisions. Other cases involve parents who demand that their children be transferred to another school.[4] In a case in Mississippi, parents requested that their daughter be transferred because she was reported to have headaches brought on by the butane gas heat at the school to which she had been recently assigned. Furthermore, the girl had purchased a class ring, helped raise funds for a senior class trip, and had been elected to the yearbook staff in the school she had attended the year before as a junior. The court held that these were not sufficient reasons for the girl to be transferred back to her former school and that the assignment by the school board would stand.[5]

The 1954 decision in *Brown et al.* v. *Board of Education* denied the use of race as a criterion for the assignment of pupils to the public schools. This historic decision found segregation on the basis of race to be in violation of the Fourteenth Amendment. The court ruled that children so segregated were deprived of equal educational opportunity and that the doctrine of "separate but equal" had no place in American public education. As a consequence of this action, the question of attendance areas has become one of the most significant and controversial issues in American education in this century. The black American in 1954 regarded the decision as a second Emancipation Proclamation although the battle of segregated schools was far from over. The spirited optimism of blacks and other minorities turned to cynicism in many sections of the United States as communities complied with great reluctance to court-ordered desegregation orders and to directives from the U.S. Department of Health, Education, and Welfare. Although desegregation has been implemented grudgingly and the effects are still under appraisal, conservative scholars such as Thomas Sowell believe that there are many objective indicators that " . . . ethnicity is changing in a changing America" and for the better.[6]

---

3. Newton Edwards, *The Courts and the Public Schools* (Chicago: University of Chicago Press, 1955), 540.
4. For a discussion of the authority of school boards to assign pupils see E. Edmund Reutter, Jr. and Robert R. Hamilton, *The Law of Public Education* (Mineola, N.Y.: Foundation Press, 1970), 117–20. A more recent statement on the establishment of attendance areas and assignment of pupils can be found in Leroy J. Peterson, Richard A. Rossmiller, and Marlin W. Volz, *The Law and Public School Operation*, (New York: Harper & Row, 1978), 289–90.
5. Ibid, 45.
6. Thomas Sowell, "Ethnicity in a Changing America," *Daedalus* (Winter 1978): 215–37.

Derrick Bell, a prominent black civil rights legal authority, is less sanguine. Bell argues that "merely integrating schools, in a society still committed to white dominance, does not insure black parents and their children equal educational opportunity."[7]

During President Nixon's and President Ford's terms in office, the national posture on school desegregation remained confused. Nixon showed ambivalence and inconsistency on the desegregation issue. While the executive branch openly opposed busing as a means of forcing racial desegregation, a number of the federal courts actively sought to eliminate deliberate attempts to segregate school pupils on the basis of race.[8] Ambivalence marked the early history of the Carter administration too but it was of a different order. The executive branch supported school desegregation including busing while the U.S. Supreme Court, reflecting the sentiments of its several Nixon appointees, remanded cases for reconsideration to the lower courts in several instances (Dayton, Omaha, Milwaukee) where large numbers of students were to be bused.[9]

The Nixon and Ford administrations failed to support affirmative legislative or executive branch initiatives which would actively require racial desegregation. Their postures generated widespread public antibusing feeling which turned school desegregation into a political football. Violence erupted most dramatically in Boston and Louisville. The early and mid-1970s were difficult especially in Northern school districts. The backlash against actions to desegregate, court-ordered or otherwise, contributed to the uneasiness of many already troubled school districts, some of which were trying in their own way to achieve better racial balance in their attendance areas.

President Reagan, openly hostile to busing as a remedy, supported proposals within the Congress that would restrict "forced" busing as a means to achieve school desegregation. The nation received contradictory messages from the White House; although Reagan claimed to support justice and equality, he consistently opposed measures such as busing that would make desegregation possible.

Members of the 97th Congress introduced several bills designed to limit the authority of the federal courts in cases involving desegregation. Such legislation, supported by President Reagan, provoked the Citizens Commission on Civil Rights to issue a strong protest arguing that such proposed legislation reflected a critical misunderstanding of the role of the courts and would elminate vital protections against government abuse of the rights of citizens.[10] Despite the reluctance of the president's office to locate and support means to ensure equality of educational opportunity, the federal district courts continued to endorse remedy plans requiring busing. The Columbus, San Francisco, Indianapolis, Omaha, and Cleveland remedy plans during the late 1970s and early 1980s are examples that involved extensive transportation to achieve desegregation. Large numbers of school closings also occurred in those school districts engendering attendance area problems resulting from declining enrollments.

7. Derrick Bell, "Learning from Our Losses: Is School Desegregation Still Feasible in the 1980s?" *Phi Delta Kappan* 64 (April 1983): 575.
8. For a discussion of changes in the desegregation situation that occured in the Nixon administration and the impact of the courts upon educational policy, see Donna E. Shalala and James A. Kelly, "Politics, the Courts, and Educational Policy," *The Teachers College Record* 75 (December 1973): 225–26.
9. Arthur S. Miller, "The Politics of the American Judiciary," *The Political Quarterly* 49, (April-June 1978): 200–207.
10. *"There is no Liberty . . . " A Report on Congressional Efforts To Curb the Federal Courts and To Undermine the Brown Decision.* (Washington, D.C.: Citizens Commission on Civil Rights, 1982).

Cases pertaining to desegregation will be discussed in greater detail in chapter 7 which focuses on the importance of the courts in determining educational policy.

Decisions on Boundary Formations

Two types of issues must be considered in the determination of attendance areas: geographical-organizational and political-social. The more mechanical and less troublesome decisions pertain to geographical-organizational issues; the difficult decisions usually grow out of political-social issues associated with boundary formation.

Geographical-Organizational Problems

One set of decisions relates to size—the size of enrollment to be accommodated in a building and the size of the geographical area to be served. The actual dimensions, measured in square miles or square blocks, are functions of population density and the availability of transportation. Size, however, is not the only consideration; it is one of several factors. Since 1954, for example, racial and ethnic criteria became particularly significant. Attempts were made to define optimum unit sizes in terms of preferred total enrollments and distances from school. These ideal conditions proved to be extremely difficult to achieve, and usually the recommendations in regard to size ended up as very general statements based on ease of transportation for students, suitability of the school facility as a community center, and the attendance area's capacity to provide an adequate staff and a flexible program.

A primary attendance area problem of the 1970s and early 1980s was school closings and the resultant redrafting of attendance boundaries. "The 10 percent decline in public elementary/secondary enrollment between 1970 and 1980 was not uniform across the States. During that period four states—Delaware, Rhode Island, North Dakota, and South Dakota—and the District of Columbia registered decreases of more than 20 percent. In eight States there were actually increases: Arizona, Nevada, Utah, Wyoming, Idaho, Florida, New Hampshire, and Texas. In most States that had significant enrollment declines, the number of schools also declined during the 1970s."[11]

"Although the number of schools declined during the 1970s, it was primarily a result of a drop in the number of very small and very large schools. The number of schools with fewer than 50 students and with 50 to 99 students dropped by 13 and 16 percent, respectively. Schools with 1,000 to 1,999 students and those with 2,000 students or more declined in number by 11 and 5 percent, respectively. At the same time, schools with 250 to 499 students increased by 16 percent. By type of school, the changes in number reflected both enrollment changes and changes in policy. The number of elementary schools dropped by more than 5 percent reflecting the severe declines in enrollment at that level. The number of schools in the "other" category, which consists primarily of combined elementary/secondary schools, dropped by more than 27 percent. This decline was a result of the movement toward separate schools for younger and older age groups, and a recognition of the need for such specialized facilities as laboratories and gymnasiums for secondary school students. Schools not classified by grade level include those serving special education and handicapped students. These more than doubled in number during the 1970s as policies supporting

11. *The Condition of Education, 1982 Edition, A Statistical Report,* (Washington D.C.: National Center for Education Statistics 1982).

the need to educate all children took effect,[12] particularly passage of Public Law 94–142, The Education for All Handicapped legislation."

In cities, enrollment decline combined with school desegregation requirements intensified the geographical-organizational issues and created new social and political dimensions in school attendance area decisions. In Omaha, Nebraska (1983) and Columbus, Ohio (1982), for example, lawsuits were filed in opposition to the closing of high schools based upon the argument that those schools were naturally integrated historically. School officials in both cities maintained that although the enrollments were integrated racially, enrollment decline and costs required the closing of secondary schools. The buildings chosen for closing were losing enrollments and too expensive to maintain. The courts upheld local school officials in both districts.[13]

In some circumstances, geographical characteristics in the district may force school officials to abandon optimum unit size and to determine attendance areas almost totally on the basis of geography. The existence of barriers, natural as well as artificial, cannot be ignored. Small enclaves in large cities or rural environs may be surrounded or hemmed in by railroads, superhighways, rivers, lakes, industrial concentrations, business districts, or airports. Such barriers may preclude the application of other more desirable guidelines for attendance area determination.

If a district is able to transport students or if district policy includes transporting students outside of an established radius of its schools, such conditions affect decisions regarding attendance areas. Of course, transportation decisions and attendance area decisions can hardly be separated in practice. The substantial costs of transportation cannot be ignored in determining school size and the geographic area to be served. Moreover, the emergence of the national energy shortage has made transportation costs a much more visible and important factor. On the other hand, distances and numbers to be transported should not, by themselves, dictate school size and loation.

Finally, there is a relationship between school level and attendance area size. Elementary school attendance areas, in large city districts at least, are usually smaller than junior or senior high school attendance areas. In some dense population sections it is not uncommon to find entire elementary school enrollments coming from two or three large apartment buildings. Elementary units, even though they include more grades as a rule than do junior or senior high schools, are most often smaller in total enrollments than the secondary schools. Secondary schools must draw their populations from a more extensive area because of larger capacities and the decreases in attendance caused by dropouts.

Attendance areas and neighborhood schools are terms often thought to be synonymous. The neighborhood school is essentially a geographical referent rather than an administrative designation. Its significance is primarily psychological; it is cherished by many parents and other citizens and does satisfy many of the criteria for attendance area formation. Recently, the neighborhood school concept has received renewed interest and support from unexpected quarters, namely parents who resist school closings, especially their neighborhood schools.

---

12. Ibid.
13. For summaries of some school districts' responses to school closings see *Surplus School Space—The Problem and the Possibilities* (Columbus Oh.: Council of Educational Facility Planners, International, 1978).

Political-Social Problems

Segregation is most often thought of in relation to blacks and other racial minorities, but segregation occurs when any minority group is set apart from a majority group, whether the minority is defined in terms of race, national origin, creed, intellectual skill, economic status, personal capacity, physical handicap, or some other differentiating characteristic.

We are speaking of "imposed" segregation in contrast to "self-imposed" segregation. If we extend the application of the segregation concept beyond its racial usage, segregation becomes significant in relation to a wide range of school board and administrative decision making. The point has been made frequently that school boards and school officials make few preparations in advance for problems growing out of segregation and are not able to comprehend some of the unanticipated consequences of their acts. Usually this criticism has been leveled when racial issues have arisen, but the lack of preparation for other types of desegregation should be acknowledged too. The segregation of gifted children or any other group for "special" education purposes, that is, imposed segregation, carries with it important social and psychological consequences for the segregated group as well as for the majority group. Bettelheim has cautioned educators to be aware of what they are doing when they segregate the intellectually capable from the less capable.[14] Segregated youngsters learn of their minority status and observe the fact that they are kept apart from others who may be treated with either more or less respect than they are. They may react with feelings of superiority or inferiority, a sense of exhilaration or humiliation, an attitude of acceptance or rejection.

As important as these other segregation issues are, the most compelling problem is racial segregation. The numbers of pupils involved and the social-political implications of the racial issue outstrip all others. The problem is extraordinarily complex and is interwoven with other contemporary social issues. Unquestionably, many honorable men and women facing the racial question at the local school district level have made very bad decisions with the feeling that they were doing the right thing. Few people possess the comprehensive intelligence necessary to consider all the relevant factors at once. Furthermore, decisions about segregation are made in fluid circumstances: each judgment affects subsequent judgments, and decision making continuously alters the landscape for decision.[15]

The opponents of racial segregation and the proponents of integration, for the most part the same people, object to segregation of any kind—de jure or de facto. The perpetuation of the concept of the neighborhood school, it is argued, is antithetical to the interests of the individual student when such attendance area determinations ensure segregated schools.

Powder-keg situations arose throughout the United States in the 1960s. Numerous urban school districts were faced with protests against de facto segregation and discriminatory employment practice. Emotionalism spread in schools in most large cities and lead to attacks upon teachers in classrooms, walkouts, boycotts, and outbursts of violence. As Isaacs contended, blacks throughout the world were caught up in a profound and massive change in their conception of their place in the world, and

14. Bruno Bettelheim, "Segregation: New Style," *The School Review* 66 (Autumn 1958): 251–72.
15. For a thorough review of the policy dimensions of school desegregation see Thomas F. Pettigrew, "Racial Change and Social Policy," *Annals* 441 (January 1979): 114–31.

most important of all, they were being compelled to change their concept of themselves.[16] Isaacs argued further that whites too must develop a new self-concept. The system of western white supremacy no longer exists; it has fallen, he maintains, as white supremacy fell in Asia and Africa: "We are all participating in this great intercontinental rearrangement of power and relationships; whites are being compelled to abandon the habits of mastery, and non-whites the habits of subjection.[17]

Numerous court decisions, social science studies, and community confrontations kept the attendance boundaries of schools in the vortex of the racial turmoil in the late 1960s and the 1970s. The courts, as well as political leaders, continued to push into the public limelight the issue of racial school segregation.[18]

Let us now look briefly at some examples.

The Supreme Judicial Court of Massachusetts unanimously upheld a statute requiring local school districts to submit plans to eliminate racial imbalance when it existed in a public school; *racial imbalance* was defined as "a ratio between non-white and other students in public schools which is sharply out of balance with the racial composition of the society in which non-white children study, serve and work."[19] The Supreme Court of Illinois in a 4–3 decision voted to uphold a similar statue which required local boards of education to consider the prevention of segregation in their determination of attendance units.[20]

The power of state-level educational authorities to attempt to eliminate de facto segregation has also been accepted by the courts and has been viewed as a reasonable educational policy and thus enforceable on local school districts. The Commissioner of Education in New York, for example, ordered specific actions to further integration in a number of local districts and his authority to make such public policy in the field of education has been upheld by the state's highest court.[21] The Supreme Court of New Jersey likewise affirmed the power of the Commissioner of Education to require local school systems to accept particular plans which eliminate racial imbalance and thereby provide greater equality of educational opportunities.[22]

Local boards of education also were deemed by the courts to have been within their powers in correcting de facto segregation on their own initiative. Michigan's Court of Appeals sustained the Flint Board of Education in its use of racial balance as one of four criteria in establishing high school attendance districts.[23]

A federal District Court in Connecticut upheld the initiative of the Norwalk school board in busing black and Puerto Rican youngsters out of their neighborhoods to correct racial imbalance.[24] Interestingly, the plaintiffs in this case were civil rights adherents who reflected in their action the growing dissatisfaction among minority groups with the one-way busing of only black students and other desegregation efforts. This dissatisfaction was, of course, a major cause of the minority group separatist thrust which began to emerge dramatically in the late 1960s.

16. Harold R. Isaacs, "The Changing Identity of the Negro American." in *The Urban Condition,* ed. Leonard J. Duhl (New York: Basic, 1963), 276–77.
17. Ibid.
18. For an analysis of these cases see Karl E. Taeuber, "Housing, Schools, and Incremental Segregative Effects," *Annals* 441 (January 1979): 157–67.
19. *School Committee of Boston* v. *Board of Education,* 352 Mass 693, 227 NE (2d) 729 (1967).
20. *Tometz* v. *Board of Education* 39 Ill (2d) 593, 237 NE (2d) 498 (1968).
21. *Vetere* v. *Allen,* 15 NY (2d) 259, 206 NE (2d) 174 (1965).
22. *Booker* v. *Board of Educ.,* 45 N.J. 161, 212 A(2d) 1 (1965).
23. *Mason* v. *Flint Board of Educ.,* 6 Mich. App 364, 149 NW (2d) 239 (1967).
24. *Norwalk CORE* v. *Norwalk Board of Educ.,* 298 F Supp 213 (D Conn 1969).

The 1970s saw no abatement of judicial decisions which potentially have profound implications for the manner in which school attendance areas are determined. Cases such as *Swann* v. *Charlotte–Mecklenburg Board of Education,*[25] *Bradley* v. *School Board of the City of Richmond, Virginia,*[26] *Bradley* v. *Milliken,*[27] and *Keyes* v. *School District No. 1, Denver, Colorado,*[28] which are discussed elsewhere in this volume, can dramatically influence districting patterns in school systems. For example, the cases establishing the affirmative duty of school boards to dismantle "dual school systems" (*Swann*), the state's obligation to include predominantly white suburban districts in the desegregation of predominantly black metropolitan school districts to remedy discriminatory practices (*Bradley*), and the school board's responsibility to prove the absence of segregative intent throughout the system if intentional segregation has been proven in a substantial portion of the district (*Keyes*), can alter radically the manner in which school attendance areas are determined throughout the United States.

In the late 1970s the United States Supreme Court introduced the concept of "incremental segregative effect" when it remanded a proposed district-wide desegregation plan in Dayton, Ohio, to the U.S. District Court for further hearings.

> The duty of both the District Court and of the Court of Appeals in a case such as this, where mandatory segregation by law of the races in the schools has long since ceased, is to first determine whether there was any action in the conduct of the business of the school board which was intended to, and did in fact, discriminate against minority pupils, teachers or staff. *Washington* v. *Davis, supra.* All parties should be free to introduce such additional testimony and other evidence as the District Court may deem appropriate. If such violations are found, the District Court in the first instance, subject to review by the Court of Appeals, must determine how much incremental segregative effect these violations had on the racial distribution of the Dayton school population as presently constituted, when that distribution is compared to what it would have been in the absence of such constitutional violations. The remedy must be designed to redress that difference, and only if there has been a systemwide impact may there be a systemwide remedy. *Keyes, supra.* at 213.[29]

Justice William Rehnquist, who authored the Dayton decision, later issued a stay in the implementation of a system-wide remedy plan in Columbus, Ohio, in part because in his judgment the Sixth Circuit Court of Appeals, in upholding the decisions of the federal district court, failed to consider properly the meaning of incremental segregative effect.[30] The U.S. Supreme Court in a 7–2 decision on July 2, 1979, denied an appeal by the Columbus defendants, lifted the stay, and ordered implementation of a district-wide remedy plan, thus laying to rest the concept of incremental segregative effect.

Various studies and reports also have kept the issue of school desegregation visible and controversial. The findings of the historic Coleman report continue to receive extensive attention as have some modifications in Coleman's earlier perspectives on the implications of school desegregation. Professor Coleman has expressed concerns

25. *Swann* v. *Charlotte-Mecklenburg Board of Education,* 402 U.S. 1, 15 (1971).
26. *Bradley* v. *School Board of City of Richmond, Virginia,* 462 F. 2d, 1058, 1060 (1972).
27. *Bradley* v. *Milliken,* 345 F. Supp. 914 (1972).
28. *Keyes* v. *School District No. 1, Denver, Colorado* 413 U.S. 189 (1973).
29. *Dayton* v. *Brinkman,* 433 U.S. 406 (1977).
30. *Columbus* v. *Penick,* A-134 U.S. (1978).

more recently regarding the circumstances of school attendance which follow court ordered desegregation. The movement of pupils to achieve racial balance removes the constraints that have been imposed on account of race. Such actions, however, produce additional constraints embedded in hostility and negative feelings toward the different schools to which pupils are assigned.[31]

Sociologist David Armor challenged the purported benefits of school desegregation, claiming that busing had neither improved race relations nor raised the academic achievements, aspirations, or self-esteem of black young people.[32] Armor's analysis, based on studies of busing programs in Boston, Massachusetts; White Plains, New York; Ann Arbor, Michigan; Riverside, California; and the Connecticut cities of Hartford and New Haven, tended to buttress the view that academic achievement is not likely to be raised simply by changing attendance areas to achieve desegregation.

Professor Thomas Pettigrew and his colleagues claimed in rebuttal that Armor's research was distorted and incomplete and that school desegregation was not a static but a dynamic process.[33] Armor, they contended, ignored the critical distinction between desegregation (achieved simply by ending physical segregation) and integration which involves the quality of interracial interaction. Armor retorted that Pettigrew and his associates furthered the prevailing ambiguities and confusions in the field of race relations by not observing the essential distinction "among the findings of science, the results of policy, and the dictates of law or morality."[34] This exchange among prominent social scientists indicates how controversial the sociological and psychological data are on the effects of desegregation and illustrate the issue's intense volatility and pervasive political ramifications. It thus seems safe to predict that the manner in which school attendance areas are drawn will remain a very visible and significant public policy issue in part because of the incontrovertible historial record of racial discrimination in America.[35]

In the late 1970s there were some important new contours in the desegregation terrain which were not formed through the actions of the courts. Andrew Greeley presented two basic options for school desegregation in the future.[36] One is to extend our most recent history of " . . . judicial decision and bureaucratic rule, fashioned and enforced by elites".[37] The other option is to build upon growing public acceptance of the need for racial integration in schools, and in the society as well, and the public's increasing willingness to do something about it. Greeley favors the second option based on his analysis of longitudinal data on public attitudes toward desegregation amassed by the National Opinion Research Center. The number of persons who take a pro-integrationist stance has been growing steadily since the early 1960s. Many support integration and reject busing. Greeley believes that within a climate of acceptance it is possible to achieve substantial integration without imposing involuntary pupil

31. James S. Coleman, "Choice in American Education," in *Parents, Teachers, and Children* (San Francisco: Institute for Contemporary Studies, 1977), 1–12.
32. David J. Armor, "The Evidence on Busing," *The Public Interest* 28 (Summer 1972): 90–126
33. Thomas F. Pettigrew, Elizabeth L. Useem, Clarence Normand, and Marshall S. Smith, "Busing: A Review of the Evidence," *The Public Interest* 30 (Winter 1973): 88–118.
34. David J. Armor, "The Double Double Standard: A Reply," *The Public Interest* 30 (Winter 1973): 119. For an excellent anthology of differing views on the interrelated issues of school desegregation and busing see Nicolaus Mills, ed., *The Great School Bus Controversy* (New York: Teachers College Press, 1973).
35. John Hope Franklin, *Racial Equality in America* (Chicago: University of Chicago Press, 1976).
36. Andrew M. Greeley, "Freedom of Choice: Our Commitment to Integration" in *Parents, Teachers, and Children: Prospects for Choice in American Education* (San Francisco: Institute for Contemporary Studies, 1977), 183–205.
37. Ibid., 185.

assignments and transfers. His is a rather sharp departure from the diehard view that the nation must stamp out racism, prejudice, and discrimination through " . . . a desperate fight for the soul of America," including the use of the school bus to achieve that objective.[38] This view is represented by David L. Kirp and others.[39]

New too is a substantial minority sentiment in favor of voluntary approaches to school desegregation, rather than busing, linked with an emphasis on and genuine concern for quality education.[40] Persons with this view are not separatists; rather they hold tenaciously to the tenets of the Constitution and oppose racism, discrimination, and injustice in all their forms. They believe that the benefits of American society can most effectively be attained by concentration upon quality education accessible to everyone.[41]

Education alternatives within the public schools, such as magnet schools and schools of special emphasis, have support from many parents, including some minority parents. The shifting sentiments of some minority leaders regarding school desegregation and the growing acceptance of integration by whites may affect attendance area decision making. Local districts may be able to implement more approaches to school desegregation that do not require massive busing. Magnet schools may grow in significance though heretofore they have often been viewed with skepticism as desegregation remedies. Such organizational alternatives, initiated simultaneously, have been created in many public school districts. Alternative schools usually develop programs of special emphasis such as mathematics, science, or the arts, and they often attract students from throughout the district. Many advocates of desegregation-integration may find fresh philosophical meanings within a public school setting that provides free choice, quality education, subsidized free-choice transportation, and quotas reflecting districtwide enrollment patterns.

The most far-reaching school desegregation development of the early 1980s occurred in St. Louis. After eleven years of litigation (*Craton Liddell, et al.* v. *the Board of Education of the City of St. Louis, State of Missouri, et al.*), an interdistrict "settlement plan" was negotiated involving 23 St. Louis county suburban school districts and the city of St. Louis school district.

The initial St. Louis school desegregation lawsuit was filed in 1972. From that date through 1980, the litigation was in an intradistrict phase. Beginning in 1980, the lawsuit entered an interdistrict phase, initially involving fifteen St. Louis county school districts and the St. Louis city school district. Three years later (July, 1983), twenty-three suburban districts and the St. Louis city school district were ordered by the federal district court to become parties to an interdistrict desegregation remedy entitled the Settlement Plan. The plan was essentially a negotiated agreement among the parties.

Key provisions of the Settlement Plan call for: (1) voluntary interdistrict transfers of students, with specified ratios and goals for racial balance of student populations in participating districts; (2) a hiring and transfer program, with specified goals for the

---

38. Ibid.
39. David L. Kirp, "School Desegregation and the Limits of Legalism," *The Public Interest,* 47 (Spring 1977): 101–28.
40. Ronald R. Edmonds, "Desegregation and Equity: Community Perspectives," *Harvard Graduate School of Education Bulletin* (Winter 1974 75) See also Ray C. Rist, "Race and Schooling: Key Policy Issues," *Educational Forum* 50 (May 1976): 522.
41. Derrick Bell, "Non-Separation Based Educational Inequalities and the *Brown* Decision." (Paper prepared for the San Francisco Public Schools Commission, May 1976), 15, 572–75.
   See also Mary Anne Raywid, "Schools of Choice: Their current Nature and Prospects," *Phi Delta Kappan* (June 1983) 684–88.

racial balance of administration and teaching staff of the participating districts; (3) the state of Missouri to bear a major share of the costs involved; (4) the establishment of specialized educational programs, including: programs focused on the all-black schools remaining within the city of St. Louis; magnet schools; part-time programs; cooperative programs with paired schools and with local cultural, civic, and business institutions; and (5) an administrative body to coordinate and review implementation of the programs.[42] The agreement has extraordinary significance in regard to pupil assignment, attendance areas, school finance, and interdistrict administrative and coordinative authority.

Community Control and Decentralization

In the late 1960s the related issues of community control and decentralization surfaced dramatically to further compound the problem of determining school attendance areas in large urban districts. Although a number of small cities did desegregate their school systems, these success stories had little relevance for major cities where increasingly a majority, or a large percentage, of the school population was nonwhite and where the sheer number of students, extensive residential segregation, and geographical distance made desegregation efforts logistically and politically very difficult. Minority group members, as we mentioned earlier, became increasingly disenchanted with abortive efforts to achieve widespread or meaningful desegregation. Frustrated by these efforts and spurred by escalating separatist sentiment, growing numbers of urban nonwhites demanded community control and decentralization of big city school systems. Both of these concepts obviously can affect in a profound manner the establishment of school attendance areas.

It is important to clarify at the outset of this discussion the differences between decentralization and community control, two ideas which are often blurred in the public mind. The two concepts, although related, are not the same. Decentralization usually means internal administrative reorganization with very few concessions offered to those who wish to change the locus of educational control. Community control, on the other hand, entails a basic restructuring of governance, with major alterations in the distribution of power and authority. National attention was focused on the issue by the bitter and protracted struggle in New York City which pitted the powerful teachers union against large segments of the black community. This highly publicized and harsh decentralization struggle illuminates the complexities of the issue as they became manifest in urban schools throughout the country.

New York's decentralization law, which was passed in 1969 after an acrimonious legislative debate, divided the city into thirty-one community school boards which received a substantial measure of operating control over elementary, intermediate, and junior high schools. Each of the nine-member elected boards had the right to select its own community superintendent and was empowered to hire employees, submit budget requests to the system's central office, select instructional materials from those sanctioned by the chancellor, operate community centers and school cafeterias, and submit proposals for new schools and the repair of existing schools. The central board, however, maintained control of the high schools and key personnel prerogatives. While the community boards did not have the independence to warrant calling them examples of true community control, they did tend to decentralize and

42. *Craton Liddell, et al.,* v. *The Board of Education of the City of St. Louis.,* No. 72–100C(3) (E.D. Mo. Jul. 5, 1983).

bring somewhat closer to the people some facets of a school system which for years had been criticized for being remote, inefficient, and unresponsive.[43]

The city of Detroit and the state of Michigan, like New York City and New York State, were enmeshed in controversy over decentralization.[44] In 1969 the Michigan legislature, upon urging from a Citizens Committee, enacted a school decentralization bill. The Detroit Board of Education shortly thereafter developed attendance boundaries which would have dramatically increased racial desegregation. A massive backlash set in and the board's authority to create district lines was nullified. The desegregationist board was subsequently recalled as 60 percent of the voters favored its removal from office. New decentralized attendance areas which perpetuated existing segregated patterns were then established by a gubernatorial commission.

When new elections were held for membership on the reconstituted central board and the eight regional boards, the conservative nonintegrationist elements clearly dominated and blacks gained a majority on only two of the eight regional bodies, although there was a majority of black students in six of the eight local districts or regions. Observers attributed these results not only to obvious black-white polarization but also to the damaging split within Detroit's black community between moderates who still advocated desegregation and separatists. Detroit's public schools were beset with a critical financial crisis as well as the strife generated by its decentralization struggle.

Parents and other citizens of Detroit as well as public officials in Lansing criticized the two-tier system. The system was charged with inefficiency, ineffectiveness, poor pupil achievement, over-bureaucratization, and excessive cost. A special citizens committee, named by Governor Milliken in 1977 neither affirmed nor denied the allegations. The committee urged that the decentralization system be continued with some modifications.

After nearly fourteen years of trying to make the two-tier system of decentralization work in Detroit however, it was dropped in 1982. The district returned to a central board of education, a pattern of governance which centralized all attendance area decisions once again.[45]

The New York City and Detroit school vignettes represent only two of the major decentralization battlegrounds. Boston, Los Angeles, Washington, D.C., Chicago, Philadelphia, and numerous other urban school systems, both large and small, were engulfed in decentralization controversies. Citizens, as well as students of urban and educational politics, have understandably wondered whether the bitter fights, which have left festering wounds, and which in some cases still rage, served any constructive purpose. Advocates of community control, of course, contend that schools will become more responsive to student needs only when the community itself controls the institution. Their contention is that the parents are in the best position to know the needs of their children and obviously have the greatest stake in having them succeed in school.

There are few hard data on the impact of school decentralization or community control upon student achievement although adherents of these concepts would argue that the process of participation alone has a salutary attitudinal impact both on parents and students. Involvement in the institution, in other words, breeds familiarity, miti-

43. For observations on decentralization and the status of education in New York City see E. Babette Edwards, "Why a Harlem Parents Union?" in *Parents, Teachers, & Children*, 59–65.
44. William R. Grant, "Community Control vs. Integration: The Case of Detroit," *The Public Interest* 24 (Summer 1971): 62–79.
45. See "Schools," in *Michigan Legislative Bulletin*, 79–1003, (1982): 204.

gates alienation, and thus helps to generate a better learning environment. One of the few systematic studies of local control was undertaken by Professor Marilyn Gittell and several of her associates at the Institute of Community Studies at Queens College.[46] This study analyzed the three decentralized demonstration districts funded by the Ford Foundation in New York City. These three districts—Ocean Hill—Brownsville, IS 201, and Two Bridges—figured prominently in the 1968 teacher strike and subsequently disappeared as they were absorbed into larger districts under the 1969 decentralization legislation. The major findings were that the three experimental districts recruited different types of community school board members. Experimental district boards were usually composed of members who were black, public school parents, female, and high school graduates with experience as poverty workers.[47] Conversely, most other members of community school boards were typically college-educated, middle-class professionals who were white, male, and had children in parochial schools. The boards in the three demonstration districts purportedly were more participative, change oriented and reform minded. These districts ostensibly made special efforts to employ minority supervisory personnel. Ocean Hill—Brownsville's attempts to transfer teachers precipitated the showdown with the teachers union which led to the strike and the ultimate demise of all three demonstration districts. According to the Gittell study these three experimental districts were more innovative than other local boards in generating new programs and in creating a more conducive learning environment in which student educational achievement improved despite declines elsewhere in the city. Gittell and her colleagues considered the three demonstration projects to be relatively successful politically and educationally and felt that the "long-run cumulative impact of the districts" may be "more significant than the immediate results."[48]

Others, of course, have taken a less sanguine view of the effects of the three demonstration projects. Many lay persons and educators contended that the experiment had catastrophic effects from which the New York school system still has not recovered. Supporters of the teachers union, in particular, had little or nothing positive to say about the decentralization projects which led to the cataclysmic strike in 1968. On the other hand, it seems clear that in conjunction with Office of Economic Opportunity, Head Start, model cities, and other social programs of the 1960s, the decentralization thrust helped to facilitate greater public participation in the governance of their institutions.

Also important to the decentralization and community control issue is the emergence of federal- and state-mandated citizen participation, especially at the building level. Most federal legislation enacted since the early 1970s requires citizen consulting and advisory mechanisms. The number of federally mandated advisory councils is staggering: there are approximately 14,000 district-wide Title I Parent Advisory Committees and 44,000 building-level committees with a total of nearly 900,000 members; another 150,000 persons serve on Head Start, Follow Through, and other district and building-level groups.[49]

46. Marilyn Gittell and Associates, *Demonstration for Social Change: An Experiment in Local Control* (New York: Institute for Community Studies, Queens College, 1971).

47. Ibid., 15.

48. Ibid., 137.

49. A comprehensive overview of the status of mandated citizen participation can be found in Luvern L. Cunningham et al, *Improving Education in Florida: A Reassessment* (Tallahassee, Fla.: Select Joint Committee on Public Schools, 1978), 215–95. For further help in understanding the development of local building councils see Jim Stanton, Bobbi Whittaker, and Ross Zerchykov, *Resource Guide and Bibliography on School Councils* (Boston: Institute for Responsive Education, 1978).

The movement to have communities participate more actively in the life of their schools has been reinforced by the recommendations of several prestigious statewide commissions. The Fleishmann Report in New York, for example, recommended the creation of Parent Advisory Councils in every public school "in order to foster and facilitate citizen involvement in the educational process."[50] In Florida, the Governor's Citizens Committee on Education recommended that the Legislature "should mandate local school boards to establish School Advisory Councils at each school" which were "broadly representative of the community served by the school, including parents, teachers, administrators and students, where practicable."[51] These councils were also to assist in the preparation of an "annual report of school progress" which would include "school population data, fiscal data, results of assessment programs, attitudes toward the school as well as plans and programs for school improvement."[52]

In the early 1980s decentralization of schools and citizen involvement in educational decision making appeared to slow in the United States just when participation seemed to be generating momentum in other parts of the world.[53] Mandated citizen involvement seemed to run out of steam. As noted earlier, Detroit abandoned its two-tier decentralization plan in 1982, and there were few, if any, new forms of decentralization adopted in large school districts. Ironically, John Naisbitt identified decentralization of decision making as a major future trend based upon the experience of business and industry in Japan, Europe, and the United States.[54] It remains to be seen whether or not decentralization will again intensify within education in the future.

The significance of these events for school attendance area decisions is fuzzy at best. It would appear, however, that more emphasis will be placed on centralized planning and administration when issues of school closings, desegregation, or changes in organizational structure arise. The involvement of parents and other interested citizens, for these purposes at least, is likely to be orchestrated more fully by boards of education and superintendents in the future than in the recent past.

Despite the seeming stabilization of rates of parent and other citizen involvement at the building level, two initiatives from President Reagan in the early 1980s have significance for educational control and policy at the building level. The first was the establishment in December, 1981 of the President's Task Force on Private Sector Initiatives. Its mission was to encourage the private sector to take a more active role in solving community problems including those in education.[55] The second was the report "A Nation At Risk" issued by the National Commission on Excellence in Education in April of 1983. The Commission was created by Secretary of Education Terrel H. Bell.[56] The formation of these citizen groups had unexpected symbolic meaning for education as well as practical significance at the grassroots. New emphasis was placed on developing partnerships with businesses and industries at the attendance area level, especially in urban school districts.

50. *The Fleishmann Report on the Quality, Cost, and Financing of Elementary and Secondary Education in New York State*, vol. 4 (New York: Viking Press, 1973), 7.
51. *Improving Education in Florida: A Report by the Governor's Citizens Committee on Education* (Tallahassee, Fla.: The Governor's Citizens Committee on Education, 1973), 11.
52. Ibid.
53. George Baron, ed. *The Politics of School Government*. (Oxford, England: Pergamon, 1981): ch. 1, 10.
54. John Naisbitt, *Megatrends* (New York: Warren, 1982), ch. 5.
55. The President's Task Force on Private Sector Initiatives, *Building Partnerships:* (Washington, D.C., The Task Force, 1982.)
56. National Commission on Excellence in Education, *A Nation At Risk* (Washington, D.C., U.S. Department of Education, 1983).

Three Cases

Three school district attendance area cases have been selected to illustrate a number of attendance area issues facing American school districts. Case A describes a rapidly growing rural district in an agricultural state. Case B depicts how a metropolitan school board approached the increasingly common problem of declining enrollments and surplus teachers and classrooms. Case C involves an extended period of desegregation litigation with consequences for attendance area decision making.

Case A

This example reflects not only typical patterns of rapid school district growth but also the special problems of school districts which have private schools in fiscal difficulty within their attendance areas. The situation in Case A is not yet critical, but it illustrates how a decline in nonpublic school enrollment can influence a public school's attendance area boundaries.

The school district is located in a burgeoning rural area of a "farm-belt" state. The system was organized in 1960 when 51 small rural school districts were consolidated. The district, which covers 555 square miles, includes five different counties and has a population of 22,000 citizens. The largest town in this farm area has a population of 3,500.

The student population growth in the district is attributable largely to the closing of a number of Catholic schools. The district originally had only 2 small high schools and 16 elementary units, many of which were one-room rural schools. In 1960 the Catholic school system consisted of 26 schools, 7 of which were high schools. The Catholic enrollment of 5,100 students far exceeded the 711 students attending the public schools. Of the 26 schools which were in the Catholic system, only 13 remain open and 7 of these have shared time arrangements with the public schools wherein students split their day between a parochial and a public school. Almost one-third of the students in the district enroll on a shared time basis.

The public school district's major problem is finding adequate classroom space despite its having built in recent years nine schools or additions, including a junior high school, five elementary schools, and a senior high school. This building program, however, was not adequate to meet the system's escalating space requirements. The district still is compelled to lease 31 portable classrooms and 3 former parochial school buildings.

The uncertainty of the continued existence of the remaining parochial schools hampers efforts to devise long-range space utilization plans or districting patterns which would solve or at least mitigate the district's perpetual space problems. Under existing state law private school youngsters may enroll in public schools in a shared time arrangement. Although relationships have always been excellent between the public and the parochial school systems, long-range planning has been impossible. Shared time is accepted as a fact of life in the district and there is little overt community conflict over the issue. Requests by private school students have never been refused and mutual cooperation and respect between the two systems prevail.

Despite these amicable arrangements, neither system is pleased with the existing situation. The private schools, where massive financial problems have caused attrition, look grimly to the future and feel that only massive state or federal assistance can make them viable. The public school district is disturbed by the administrative problems and the mixed student loyalties caused by shared time. Public school officials, however, would be more concerned if all the parochial schools were compelled to close and the public schools forced to accommodate their students.

School attendance area patterns are complicated because of the relatively large number of students enrolled in parochial schools and the prevalence of shared time. In the school district's largest town, for example, a kindergarten center is the only public school. The largest Catholic high school with an enrollment of more than 800 students is located in this town. The public high school students are bused to the district's single high school. The complexity of the situation is illustrated by what happened to some of this town's fourth graders after the parochial school found that it did not have either the space or resources to accommodate this group. The public school system leased classroom space in a former parochial school and hired a teacher to accommodate these fourth graders. Similar mixed attendance arrangements exist in other areas of the school district with youngsters shifting between the parochial and public schools.

A district covering such a huge geographical area, needless to say, has major busing problems. Indeed, the second largest item in its budget (instruction is first) is to maintain and operate its fleet of 54 buses. Special attempts are made to enroll the younger children in school attendance areas as close to their homes as possible. Both attendance area and transportation policies are affected by the extensive shared time arrangements and the classroom leasing practices found in the district.

Case B

Within the past few years growing numbers of school districts have faced problems relating to declines in enrollment. In many communities the post-World War II expansion boom has stopped abruptly and the growth patterns which characterized so many aspects of public education in recent decades are rapidly vanishing. Indeed, more and more districts, particularly inner-ring suburbs and cities, are faced with attendance area problems which were somewhat unexpected and unprecedented in the experience of many school administrators; these problems relate to shrinking enrollments and the concomitant need for fewer teachers and classrooms. School boards and a skeptical tax-conscious public, accustomed to problems caused by growth and perennial increases in staff size and plant capacity, are now confronted with a new set of politically explosive issues. They must contemplate reducing faculties at a time when there is a shrinking job market for teachers and must face public outcry about plant underutilization when only a few years ago large sums of money were being allocated for the construction of school buildings which could accommodate flexible new programs and growing numbers of students.

The district in Case B is located in a large metropolitan area. The school system's 43 schools enrolled 30,000 students in 1971. Almost 20 percent of these students were from minority groups. White enrollment was decreasing and projections indicated that this trend would continue. Nearly one-third of the school-age young people in the community attended nonpublic schools which were more than 90 percent white. Population growth slowed considerably (0.3 percent annually), as it did in so many urban areas in the latter half of the 1960s. The school population growth of only 1.16 percent in the sixties was much lower than the overall population increase of 7.17 percent during the decade.

Projections for the 1970s and 1980s indicated that birth rates were declining, private housing starts would be relatively few in number, and that economic expansion would be limited because so little unused land remained for development. These analyses indicated that such limited expansion of housing and business construction would stabilize the population and not increase school enrollments. This limited or no-growth pattern in the public schools would also apply to the substantial nonpublic school population.

Confronted with this troublesome prognosis, severe fiscal problems, and the need to provide new or rehabilitated facilities in areas where school buildings were antiquated, the board of education employed a university team to conduct a comprehensive analysis of the school system's facilities, demography, and organization. Extensive data were collected on class size, room utilization, and teacher station efficiency for each of the schools.

At the elementary level it was found that all the schools enrolled fewer students than they could theoretically accommodate. Attendance boundaries had remained fixed for some time and thus did not reflect changes in enrollment patterns. Declining enrollments in some areas had further widened the disparity between actual enrollments and school capacity. These declines were more pronounced in the lower grades. Enrollment imbalances were found not only among attendance areas but also among grade levels within schools. Large numbers of classes were below the maximum class size set forth in district policy. The decrease in class size was expected to continue.

Thus it was clear that a full review of school utilization attendance areas was needed. The university study team advised the board of education to consider measures such as the following to combat the problems of shrinking enrollments and facility underutilization.

1. Some schools could be closed and students assigned to the remaining buildings in numbers that would be in accord with plant capacity.
2. Class size could be reduced throughout the district, a move which would utilize more classrooms.
3. The district's grade plan policy could be altered to achieve enrollments that were more consonant with classroom capacity.
4. A nongraded elementary program might be considered; such a program would offer far greater flexibility in the utilization of available classroom space.
5. "Combination classes" could be established in which students from two different grades would meet as one class.

Case C

Like many Northern school districts, this district (along with the state) was found liable for many discrete racially discriminatory acts. Some were recent, others occurred many years ago. The cumulative pattern of isolated discriminatory actions, many of which were attendance area decisions, was sufficient in the judgment of the court to require a system-wide remedy. The Denver *(Keyes)* case was the principal legal precedent.

The school district at the time of the liability findings had 33 percent minority enrollment and 67 percent white enrollment. The court determined that schools would not be racially identifiable if their minority enrollments were within a range of 15 percent on either side of the 33 percent district-wide minority enrollment. For example, a school that had 90 percent white and 10 percent minority enrollment would not meet the court's criterion of racial representations. A school that was 83 percent white and 17 percent minority would meet the criterion.

More than 160 school buildings were operating prior to the desegregation order. The primary basis for determining attendance areas for elementary purposes was proximity. Junior and senior high school attendance was based essentially on feeder patterns. There were several schools that served the entire district for special education, career education, adult education, or alternative schools purposes. A voluntary desegregation plan in operation was aimed at reducing racial isolation but only about 8 percent (mostly white) of the enrollment was involved. A white school board majority strongly defended the neighborhood school attendance area concepts and resisted the imposition of a system-wide remedy.

The federal district court placed with local school officials the responsibility for preparing a system-wide remedy. Eventually a remedy plan was developed that was satisfactory to the court. That plan included contiguous and noncontiguous pairings and clusterings as well as several school closings. Each attendance area in the school district was affected. More than 42,000 students were to be transported for desegregation purposes. Over 200 new buses were purchased; additional storage and maintenance facilities were acquired, and new drivers were employed and trained.

The remedy plan also required detailed preparation for implementation. School officials (local and state) had one year to make pupil reassignments, acquire transportation, alter programs and prepare students, parents, personnel, and the community. The local board of education met every deadline and fulfilled each requirement of the courts. At the same time the school board availed itself of every available avenue of appeal, even the U.S. Supreme Court.

A stay of implementation was granted by the U.S. Supreme Court less than 30 days prior to implementation. The school board ordered an immediate dismantling of the remedy plan including the reestablishment of all previous attendance areas, the reassignment of pupils to their former schools, and the cessation of all other preparations.

Parents and other citizens registered their feelings in many ways during the litigation that led to the stay. Opposition to desegregation was reflected in the defeat of tax rate increases for example. Conservative, antibusing persons were returned to the school board. Pro-neighborhood schools and antibusing groups sprang up. Groups formed to fight school closings. Celebrations were held when the announcement of the stay of implementation came. At the same time neutral or supportive sentiments were in evidence. New as well as established community organizations provided leadership in preparing for a responsible, law-abiding implementation. The mayor, business leaders, and the media publicly endorsed peaceful implementation although many privately resented the need to bus thousands of students.

School administrators encountered a spate of political, logistical, technical, planning, financial, and other problems. Among the most severe political problems were those engendered by school closings. Groups of parents descended en masse upon board meetings and administrators' offices. *Ad hoc* "save-our-school" committees held public meetings, letter-writing campaigns, and press conferences. The resentment surrounding school closings was based only partially on school desegregation. Most parents objected to the closing of "their schools" but not others. The school board majority tried unsuccessfully to pass the responsibility for school closings to the federal district court. When the stay of implementation was granted, all closed schools were reopened with pupils, principals and staff assigned, even though less than a month remained before schools were to open in the fall. Decisions to reopen the schools and to reestablish attendance areas were made in spite of declining enrollments and severe financial pressures.

The future of this school system and its attendance areas rested with the courts. The United States Supreme Court, after one year, lifted the stay of implementation on June 30, 1979 and remanded the case back to the federal district court. The federal district court immediately ordered implementation of a system-wide desegregation remedy plan.

When schools opened in the autumn of 1979, parents and students found that a new set of attendance areas were in place, reflecting not only the requirements of a system-wide desegregation effort but a number of school closings as well.

The school system, especially its school administrators, encountered many new problems of school-community relations as the system-wide remedy was implemented. Old patterns of parent involvement had to be modified and new ones developed. Daily schedules for employees were altered. New and different faces filled classrooms, many with educational needs unlike those of prior students. Disequilibrium was present for awhile. In 1983, after four years of desegregation, every graduating senior had experienced four years of desegregated education. Remarkable progress had been made in the district despite a complete realignment and redrafting of school attendance areas.

Significance of Cases

In Case A school officials in a rapidly growing rural area were faced with attendance area problems that were difficult to handle because of uncertainty about the continuation of nonpublic schools which enrolled a very substantial proportion of the district's school-age population. External factors over which public school officals had virtually no control frustrated efforts to plan rationally. Political realities dictated the widespread continuation of the administratively cumbersome, if not chaotic, shared time arrangements. The district's entire structure and operations as well as the determination of its school attendance areas were inextricably linked to the rather tenuous financial condition of the parochial school system.

In Case B a board of education chose to avail itself of the best knowledge base possible to arrive at attendance area and school housing decisions. Faced with issues like rising costs, shrinking enrollments, and space underutilization, the board launched with the assistance of a university study team a detailed analysis of the school system's facilities, demography, and organization. The university team presented a series of alternative plans predicated on comprehensive school-by-school data. Any of the options, if implemented, would engender controversy as the district confronted the inevitable need to alter attendance areas in the face of its shrinking enrollments. Racial and private school questions would exacerbate the situation.

In Case C a school district successfully turned to judicial appeal. The United States Supreme Court however, upheld the findings of both the district and the appelate courts returning the responsibility for overseeing implementation of the district-wide remedy plan to the court of original jurisdiction. Every attendance area in the district was changed as a consequence. This case illustrates the prominence of school attendance area decisions in the history of this district as well as the power of the courts in their regard.

These cases highlight a point made at the beginning of this chapter. Attendance area decisions were once rather straightforward administrative decisions. Now, because of widespread social, political, and economic changes in our society, attendance area decisions are political decisions and demand resolution at the several policy levels.[57]

Summary and Future Prospects

Attendance area boundaries, as indicated, are currently much less stable and enduring than school district boundaries. Consequently, changes in attendance boundaries are likely to lay bare the issues of control more often than boundary changes at district levels.

There are several areas of existing or prospective change which have implications for attendance areas.

1. Education returned to the public agenda in the early 1980s, stimulated largely by the report of the National Commission on Excellence in Education. That report, along with several other widely publicized analyses of American education cited elsewhere, elevated the problems of education to national significance and brought fresh recognition of the relationship of education to the national interest. Discussions of the issues highlighted in the Commission's report will likely extend well into the 1980s, including review of the attendance area issue all across the country.

2. School desegregation, although an exceedingly important public problem, will likely enter into a new phase. This phase will reflect the large demographic shifts in the U.S. population and a strengthened commitment to quality education rather than racial balance. The growth of the Spanish population particularly, could shift the concern about equality of educational opportunity away from essentially a black-white focus to a multi-cultural, multi-ethnic focus. Simultaneously, several influential black leaders are emphasizing quality education and non-busing alternatives to achieving school desegregation especially in large school districts. The 1983 Settlement Plan for St. Louis and St. Louis county suburban districts may become a precedent for a small number of other metropolitan areas. Should this occur there will be new implications for interdistrict coordination and control. With fewer intradistrict remedy plans in the offing, desegregation may have less meaning for attendance area decisions in the future.

3. Building-level advisory councils and school site management promises to continue to stimulate new debates regarding local control. The traditional tensions of local control center upon the power and authority of local school boards with respect to state and federal governments. Many who have been apprehensive about the erosion of authority and responsibility from above may become concerned about erosion from below. As school site management and citizen participation become effective, new strength will be added to a district's governance and management system. School officials at the district level need not perceive these developments as a threat. One distinct area for development is

---

57. See Patricia Cayo Sexton, "City Schools," *The Annals of the American Academy of Political and Social Science* 352 (March 1964): 97–98.

collective bargaining vis-à-vis the rights and obligations of attendance area representatives to particpate. School site management and citizen participation at
the building level are concepts with wide application. They are as germane in
rural settings as they are in cities and metropolitan areas.

4. The administrative and policy decentralization movement may be stabilizing.
Feelings about the effectiveness of school district decentralizations are mixed
ranging from advocacy to skepticism to rejection. The meaning of decentralization for attendance area decision making is still not clear. Energy has been
invested in specifying the decision and policy-making prerogatives of central
and subdistrict offices. Not enough attention has been given to such clarification at the building level. Adoption of site management philosophy and practice
will force such clarification and produce improved understanding of the dimension of control that should reside at each level.

5. The expansion of magnet schools, schools of emphasis, and other educational
alternatives will likely continue. These require school officials to reevaluate
traditional attendance areas. Alternative schools can introduce a healthy competitiveness and stimulate education improvements in conventional attendance
areas, but if there are only a few alternative schools and they are highly specialized, negative consequences can result. Often the best students opt for the
alternative programs, draining local schools of high-ability young people.

6. There is extensive soul-searching ahead regarding the nature, forms, and effectiveness of citizen participation. The evidence indicates that school systems
are now more responsive than they were in the past. Nevertheless, there is
some disenchantment with citizen involvement at all levels. School systems
may give the appearance of responsiveness but in fact continue to be heavily
influenced by professional and citizen elites. The control of education is likely
to remain solidly in the hands of whites at the attendance area level with the
exception of the nation's very large cities where minorities will assume more
and more responsibility for educational decision making.

7. Nationally, declining enrollments will continue although about 25 percent of the
school districts still face rapid growth, especially in the Southwest and West.
Furthermore, indications are that elementary school enrollments will soon begin to increase once again. Controversy surrounding school closings, which
often occur because of attendance area changes, creates severe political problems for local school officials. Some superintendents have, in fact, lost their
jobs over school-closing decisions. Given the sustained pattern of enrollment
decline, many more schools will be closed and the tranquility of many local
districts will be disturbed. With experience however, local school officials are
becoming more skillful in dealing with school closings, thus leading to less
controversy and bitterness within local communities.

7

The Courts

The role of the the federal and state courts in shaping school policies is significant. Virtually every school district relies on legal counsel for assistance of some kind, and an increasing number of districts employ one or more attorneys on a full-time basis. It is not uncommon for school districts to be sued and administrators often are named personally as defendants. One administrator remarked recently that he had lost track of the number of lawsuits in which he was named as a defendant. Litigation is both time-consuming and expensive in that attorney's fees are sometimes more than $100 per hour. Everywhere legal issues have become a prominent topic of discussion at meetings of administrators. The courts have had long-standing influence on schools and this influence is becoming more noticeable in a number of areas.

This chapter is not intended to be a primer on school law nor a substitute for detailed material or counsel in any particular area. Instead, it provides an overview of the American court structure and its dynamics as they relate to education and covers the structure of the American judicial system, the premises and the processes of judicial policymaking, some examples of judicial influence, and the outlook for the future.

Structure of the American Judicial System

A fundamental characteristic of the American judicial system is that it is actually comprised of overlapping systems. Each of the states has its own court system as does the federal government. Some questions are a matter of state jurisdiction, others are initiated in the federal system, and still others can be initiated in state courts and reviewed by the U.S. Supreme Court. Moreover, both the state and federal systems have tiered court structures which allow for the appeal of judicial decisions from one level to another.

Some Early History

The origins of the American legal system are found in the British common law.[1] American colonists were expected to be guided by the common law, and the colonies followed the English precedent of making the legislature (in England, the House of Lords) the highest court. However, geographical separation and colonial initiative combined to produce a number of deviations from the English system. Because of a shortage of trained lawyers and judges in the colonies, it was not uncommon for citizens rather than lawyers to be appointed to the bench. The colonists, however, favored this arrangement; they preferred that their neighbors, rather than appointees of the royal crown, serve as judges. In fact, among the criticisms of George III in the Declaration of Independence was that "he has made judges dependent on his will alone, for the tenure of their offices and the amount and payment of their salaries." Thus it was not surprising that postrevolutionary judicial reforms included the legislative election of judges and the expansion of the role of juries to decide questions of law as well as fact.

The colonists had reservations about strong courts and these were manifested in the debates of the Constitutional Convention. While it was agreed that there was a need for a single national, or supreme court, strong reservations were lodged about the desirability of establishing a federal court system. There was fear that such a system would intrude upon the jurisdictions of the respective state courts. Some argued that state courts could serve as lower tribunals to the supreme court. Unable to resolve the issue, the Convention deferred it by providing for "one Supreme Court, and . . . such inferior Courts as the Congress may from time to time ordain and establish."[2]

The matter of the federal court structure was considered by the first Congress. The Judiciary Act of 1789 established the Supreme Court with a chief justice and six associates. It also established three circuit courts and thirteen district courts which were at the bottom of the federal judicial hierarchy. Furthermore, this act established the procedure through which the federal courts could review and, if appropriate, declare void state laws and court decisions which conflicted with federal powers established by the Constitution.[3]

The Federal Court System

Congressional actions since the Judiciary Act of 1789 have expanded the federal court system substantially. The Supreme Court now includes a chief justice and eight associates. There are also twelve circuit courts of appeals and 94 district courts. Each state has at least one federal district court and New York and Texas each have four. Most of the district courts and all of the appeals courts have several judges.

Most scholarly work has focused upon the Supreme Court because it is at this level that decisions have their most general application. However, most federal cases

1. For an early history of the courts see Francis R. Aumann, *The Changing American Legal System* (Columbus, Oh.: Ohio State University Press, 1940). See also Robert A. Koenig, "The Law and Education in Historical Perspective," in *The Courts and Education*, Seventy-seventh Yearbook of the National Society for the Study of Education, Part 1. (Chicago: University of Chicago Press, 1978), 1–26.
2. *United States Constitution*, Article III, Section I. The history of the Constitutional Convention is discussed in Catherine Drinker Bowen, *Miracle at Philadelphia* (Boston: Little, Brown, 1966).
3. Richard Hofstadter, William Miller, and Daniel Aaron, *The United States* (Englewood Cliffs, N.J.: Prentice-Hall, 1957). 142.

are actually heard and decided at lower levels in the system. The so-called inferior courts are the courts of first jurisdiction for all but a very few federal cases. Until the Judiciary Act of 1875, however, these courts served little national purpose. This legislation extended the jurisdiction of these courts to most federal questions and thereby helped these courts become "powerful instruments for the centralizing and unifying tendencies of a national law."[4] These courts are able to promote compliance with Supreme Court doctrines.[5] They also serve a shaping and testing function where new legal positions can be formulated for review by the Supreme Court.

Cases brought under a federal question are first heard in a U.S. District Court. The most frequent federal questions concerning education are alleged violations of First or Fourteenth Amendment rights. More will be said about this later in this chapter. Most cases which enter the district court are resolved at that level although either party has the right of appeal to the court of appeals. In 1982 nearly 240,000 cases were filed in U.S. District Courts. Most of these did not go to trial; however, in the same year, approximately, 24,000 cases were forwarded to one of the courts of appeals and there were 5311 cases on the docket of the Supreme Court.[6] The Court disposes of most of these without a hearing and issues approximately 150 decisions each year. The caseload of the Supreme Court has increased so dramatically in recent years that Chief Justice Burger has called for creation of a new federal court to reduce the high court's workload.[7]

The Supreme Court has original jurisdiction in disputes between the states and in a few other technical matters. Most of its work involves reviewing cases which come to it on appeal. Such cases may come from lower federal courts or from the state supreme courts in the case of state laws which are alleged to be unconstitutional. The Supreme Court has virtually complete discretion to decide which cases it will and will not hear. More than 90 percent of the cases heard by the Court come before it through the process of certiorari. According to this procedure, persons wishing to appeal a case to the Supreme Court submit a petition asking the Court to order the lower court to forward its decision for review. At least four justices must agree to such an order before it is issued. Certain other cases can be appealed to the Court apart from the certiorari procedure, but these too can be declined if the Court holds that they do not present, "a substantial federal question." The power of the Supreme Court to choose which cases it will hear means that it can wait to let a body of law develop on a subject in the lower courts thus providing a broad or closely reasoned context in which to render a decision. This power also allows the court to time its decisions according to public interests.

Judicial decision making and public interests also intersect in the selection and appointment of judges. Federal judges are appointed to lifetime terms, and such an appointment is generally considered a high honor. While it is always difficult to assess criteria for such appointments, it can be safely stated that factors other than excellence in jurisprudence are often considered. The actual procedure for the appointment of federal judges is for the president to make them subject to the "advice and consent"

4. Carl McGowan, *The Organization of Judicial Power in the United States* (Evanston, Ill.: Northwestern University Press, 1969), 30.
5. Ibid., 16–17.
6. *Annual Report of the Director of the Administrative Office of the U.S. Courts* (Washington, D.C.: Government Printing Office, 1982), 92ff.
7. Linda Greenhouse, "Burger Proposes New Panel to Cut High Court's Load," *New York Times*, 7 February 1983, 1.

of two-thirds of the Senate. In recent years at least, the president has been obliged, as a senatorial courtesy, to first clear proposed appointees with the senators of their home state. As the procedure suggests, there is opportunity for the partisan or personal ideological perspectives of the president and the Senate to have some effect. History shows that this has sometimes been the case. In 1801, when the Federalists were about to surrender the presidency to the Republicans, President Adams appointed several Federalists to newly created judgeships. Adams was the last Federalist president, but his newly appointed chief justice (John Marshall) presided over the Supreme Court for more than 30 years.[8]

Lifetime appointments to the federal judiciary have created ideological tensions between the judicial branch on the one hand and Congress and the president on the other. It has not been uncommon in our history for the Court to reflect a conservative bias at a time when the rest of the government showed more liberal tendencies and vice versa. Thus, as newly elected officials come into office, they may find the Court which awaits them to be an impediment to their programs. The most dramatic example occurred during the New Deal period of the 1930s when a holdover Court declared unconstitutional some of the emergency legislation promulgated to fight the depression. President Roosevelt responded by proposing a judicial reform bill which would have allowed the appointment of additional justices to the Supreme Court. This so-called court-packing bill, which was not enacted, aroused great controversy and cost Roosevelt some public prestige. At about the same time, however, one judge retired, enabling Roosevelt to appoint the liberal Hugo Black, and another justice began to cast more liberal votes. Thus the Court began to swing to the liberal posture which characterized it into the 1970s. Most observers believe the Court has subsequently become more conservative as a result of appointments during the Nixon and Reagan Administrations. The composition of the Court is likely to be determined for many years to come by appointments made in the middle or late 1980s.

The Supreme Court in the past forty years has had an important impact upon American social and political life. First the "new" Roosevelt court upheld efforts to extend the government's role in economic life, thereby allowing for the introduction of new regulations on private enterprise. Subsequently the Court under the leadership of Earl Warren issued a series of landmark decisions in the areas of racial equality, electoral equality, and criminal procedure. The pronouncement of these decisions and the response to them by the president, the Congress, and the public have made it clear that the courts are an integral part of the American political process.[9]

As Richard Nixon campaigned for the presidency in 1968 he was critical of the Supreme Court for being unfamiliar with criminal law and procedure and for having " 'gone too far' in imputing its own 'social and economic views' to the rule of decision." [10] He immediately had an opportunity to appoint a new chief justice and selected Warren Burger who was confirmed to this post. Given the opportunity to make another appointment in 1969, the president declared his intention to appoint a southerner, thereby perhaps appealing to those concerned that the courts had been too aggressive in school desegregation. His efforts to appoint first Clement Haynsworth and then Harold Carswell to this post provoked furious controversy in the Senate

---

8. Hofstadter, Miller, and Aaron, *The United States,* 155.
9. For discussion of this view see William F. Swindler, "The Supreme Court, the President, and the Congress," *The International and Comparative Law Quarterly* 19 (1970): 671–92.
10. Ibid., 680.

which failed to confirm either candidate. Senate liberals, smarting some from the forced resignation of Justice Fortas, mounted a strong campaign against both men. Nixon subsequently appointed Lewis Powell, James Blackmun, and William Rehnquist to the Court. Neither President Ford nor President Carter had the opportunity to appoint a Supreme Court Justice before Mr. Reagan selected Sandra Day O'Connor to be the first woman on the court.

The importance of partisanship in federal judicial appointments has been clearly documented. Schmandt reports that over 90 percent of all appointees to the federal courts were members of the president's own party.[11] For example, Eisenhower appointed 190 Republicans and 13 Democrats and Kennedy appointed 141 Democrats and 13 Republicans.

While it is clear that politics and ideological perspectives can influence the nature of appointments to the Court, it is sometimes difficult to predict how a judge will behave once appointed. For example, Hugo Black was once a member of the Ku Klux Klan and Earl Warren supported wartime detention camps for Japanese Americans, yet both became strong advocates for the rights of racial minorities.[12]

The State Court Systems

There are great differences among the states in the way they have organized their court systems.[13] However, they generally follow the hierarchical pattern of the federal system. All states have a court of final jurisdiction which serves as the court of final appeals for state matters. Twenty-three states have intermediate courts of appeals. All states have trial courts of general jurisdiction where cases are initially heard. In addition, all states have one or more trial courts with special jurisdiction such as probate courts, juvenile courts, and courts of small claims.

Consider the state of Illinois. Excluding the special courts, the lowest or general trial level court in Illinois is the circuit court. There are twenty-one circuit court districts in Illinois which have general and original jurisdiction over criminal and civil cases including those pertaining to schools. At the second level there are the appellate courts. In Illinois there are five appellate districts. These courts have no original jurisdiction, but they do hear appeals on the basis of the evidence presented in the lower courts. At the apex of the judicial system is the state supreme court. Ordinarily this body, too, acts in an appellate and not in an original capacity. Crucial questions pertaining to schools, particularly those having to do with the constitutionality of certain legislative actions, often progress through all three levels of the state court system.

The state courts are very concerned with interpreting legislative will or intent. The courts recognize the authority of the legislature, and they are loath to substitute their own judgment for legislative intent. There are cases, however, in which the statutes are contradictory or ambiguous and, when required to do so, the courts will rule in such cases. Then, too, when litigation involves disputes between two or more parties, the courts are required to render judgment. The courts also, when called upon, will rule on the constitutionality of statutory provisions.

11. Henry J. Schmandt, *Courts in the American Political System* (Belmont, Calif.: Dickenson, 1969) 34.
12. Thomas Halper, "Senate Rejection of Supreme Court Nominees," *Drake Law Review* 22 (September 1972): 107.
13. See Henry Robert Glick and Kenneth N. Vines, *State Court Systems* (Englewood Cliffs, N.J.: Prentice-Hall. 1973).

Court procedures reveal a relationship between the lower and the higher courts. For instance, the court of original jurisdiction ordinarily has more to do with the credibility of witnesses since in lower courts witnesses are examined firsthand. Courts tend to examine only those issues which are before them, though they may comment *obiter dictum* on others. If the issue is one of procedure, the substantive nature of the problem will not be considered. Higher courts will not reverse decisions of lower courts unless it is clear that there has been an abuse of discretion. A state court of one state may take cognizance of decisions rendered by the higher courts of other states, but it is not bound to follow them. On the other hand, state courts are subservient to decisions of the United States Supreme Court. This was illustrated in a decision of the Supreme Court of Arkansas as indicated in the following language:

> While we deeply deplore the fact that the Supreme Court of the United States did not follow the clear legal precedents announced in *Plessy* v. *Ferguson,* 163 U.S. 537, 16 S. Ct. 1138, 41 L. Ed. 256, in *Gong Lum* v. *Rice,* 275 U.S. 78, 48 St. Ct. 91, 72 L. Ed. 172, and in numerous other decisions over a period of fifty years, instead of a long list of nonlegal authorities, yet this court will be subservient to the decision it did reach.[14]

When considering education issues, the courts have consistently declared board of education members to be state and not local officers. The court of appeals in Kentucky put it this way:

> We have said that the members of a county board of education and its officers are "state officers," although they are elected locally and function in a local capacity, because education is a state function.[15]

Moreover, the courts traditionally have been reluctant to substitute their judgment for that of the board of education. This principle has been enunciated many times and the language from a United States Court of Appeals case as shown below is but an example:

> The school board, in the operation of the public schools, acts in much the same manner as an administrative agency exercising its accumulated technical expertise in formulating policy after balancing all legitimate conflicting interests. If that policy is one conceived without bias and administered uniformly to all who fall within its jurisdiction, the courts should be extremely wary of imposing their own judgment on those who have the technical knowledge and operating responsibility for the school system.[16]

On the other hand, there are indications that the courts may now take a harder look at the judgment of school officials and overrule them, particularly as school rules affect individual rights. For example, the U.S. Supreme Court held that local school officials legally could not prevent students from wearing black armbands in peaceful protest of U.S. involvement in Vietnam. Part of the opinion delivered by Justice Fortas stated:

14. *Garrett* v. *Faubus,* 323 SW (2d) 877, 880 (Ark. 1959).
15. *Hogan* v. *Glasscock,* 324 SW (2d) 815, 816 (Ky. 1959).
16. *Deal* v. *Cincinnati Board of Education,* 369 F. 2d 55, 61 (6th Cir. 1966).

The record does not demonstrate any facts which might reasonably have led school officials to forecast substantial disruption of or material interference with school activities, and no disturbances or disorders on the school premises in fact occurred. . . . They [the students] neither interrupted school activities nor sought to intrude in the school affairs or the lives of others. They caused discussion outside of the classrooms, but no interference with work and no disorder. In the circumstances, our Constitution does not permit officials of the state to deny their form of expression.[17]

The jurisdiction of state courts extends to any matter except federal statutes and those matters outside their territorial prerogatives brought before them at the trial court level. In the case of issues which involve a federal constitutional question, plaintiffs have a choice of initiating their action in state or federal courts. If brought before a federal court, cases involving the constitutionality of state statutes are heard by a three-judge federal district panel with direct appeal to the U.S. Supreme Court. Cases involving federal statutes are filed in federal courts. Recent years have seen a growing tendency on the part of individuals and agencies to take matters of dispute to court. As a consequence, court dockets have become very crowded and trials often suffer long delays in the state as well as in federal courts.

The rulings of state supreme courts establish guidelines for their respective states but are not controlling for other states. Similarly the decisions of state lower courts are binding upon the particular litigants involved but do not constitute precedents which necessarily will be adhered to by other courts in the state. Thus at the trial court level it is not uncommon to see a series of cases about the same kind of issue (e.g., student dress codes or hair length) decided in different ways.

State judges are selected in a variety of ways and serve terms of varying lengths. Some are appointed by the governor, some elected by the state legislature, some elected on a partisan ballot, some elected on a nonpartisan ballot, and some selected through a combination of these means.[18] Virtually all of these procedures lead to the appointment of persons who have local ties to the areas in which they serve. Thus it is not unusual for a judge to reflect local values and priorities as he presides on the bench. Local preferences may influence his interpretation of statutory enactments and higher court rulings. For example, Schmandt has noted:

Many examples of this situation [local court decisions influenced by local values] exist in the handling of civil rights cases by the local judiciary in those Southern cities that have achieved national notoriety in recent years by their open defiance of integration measures. In many situations, the courts have acted in a distinctly political fashion, showing acute sensitivity and even servility to local feelings and pressures. As a result of this type of differential treatment by the local judiciary, acts considered constitutionally protected in one community are regarded as illegal and punishable in another.[19]

In a sense, the courts stand as a last resort in educational government as they do in general government. They determine, when necessary, the constitutionality of legislative action. They interpret the meaning of statutes, being careful to ascertain legislative intent. The structure of the court system permits appeal for judicial

17. *Tinker* v. *Des Moines Independent Community School District,* 393 U.S. 503, 514 (1969).
18. Glick and Vines, *State Court Systems,* 39.
19. Schmandt, *Courts in the American Political System,* 14.

review to the higher courts from the lower courts where mercy or human frailty may have crowded out justice. While the courts are subject to human foibles, the judges who preside over them do, for the most part, reflect not only the word but the spirit of the law.

Premises and Processes of Judicial Policymaking

A policy is an authoritative decision which guides other decisions. For example, a school district policy which states that all teachers in the district must hold a degree from an accredited college or university offers some guidance to those who recuit teachers. Similarly, a federal policy of making aid available to school districts in federally impacted areas provides guidance to school officials in those districts and to Department of Education officials. In the first example, policy is enacted by a school board resolution and in the second by federal statute. Court decisions also can provide guidance to other decision makers. Some of the best known decisions of this type in education were discussed in chapter 1. While courts do not make laws, their interpretations of laws often have the impact of significant policy decisions. In this section we will explore the process through which the courts exert such influence.

Some Basic Premises

Basic civics books explain that the function of the courts is not to enact laws but to interpret them. In so doing, the courts can act only upon the basis of the facts presented to them. Thus, the essence of a court proceeding, be it civil or criminal, is first to ascertain the facts of the case at hand and second to apply the law to those facts. An important resource of the court as it seeks to apply the law is the body of cases which have been decided on similar matters in the past. The doctrine of *stare decisis* (let the decision stand) is an important legal principle. It means that the court will take into account previous rulings on similar issues as it rules on any particular case. This means that the evolution of judicial policy in any particular area is likely to be incremental as it builds upon previous decisions in related areas. It also means that review of past decisions is an important step in determining whether or not to pursue a case in the courts and in assessing its possible outcomes. However, this body of case law is extremely comprehensive and, as a consequence, the courts are often called upon to mediate among conflicting claims of rights and interests when rendering a verdict.

   A civil case is usually initiated when one party (the plaintiff) files a formal complaint against another party (the defendant). The defendant files a response to the complaint which either denies that all or part of it is true or admits to the allegations but submits legal justification for his or her behavior. At this point the case is ready for trial although it may still be settled by out-of-court negotiations among the parties. While trial may be delayed some time for procedural reasons, a date is ultimately set for a hearing. The court hears evidence about the case and renders a decision. If one or both of the parties are not satisfied with this decision, they may appeal. Testimony is not heard at the appellate level. Rather, the appellate court reviews the record of the trial proceedings as a basis for upholding or reversing the lower court decision or remanding it for further testimony.

Judicial Trends in Education

Hogan reviewed the history of court actions in education and identified five discernible stages.[20] He identified the first period, prior to 1850, as one of "strict judicial laissez faire" in which education was viewed primarily as a local matter and even state courts were reluctant to intervene. The second period, from 1850 to 1950, was identified as the "stage of state control" during which few cases reached the U.S. Supreme Court and "a body of case law developed at the state level which permitted, if not actually sanctioned, educational policies and practices that failed to meet federal constitutional standards and requirements." [21] This period was followed by a third period, a "reformation stage," which continues today and is characterized by federal decisions which bring state-sanctioned policies and practices into conformity with constitutional provisions. Hogan notes that a fourth period, partly concurrent with the third, has been one of "education under supervision of the courts" in which the federal courts took on enforcement responsibilities to ascertain that the minimum reform standards for school administration and programs are implemented. Finally, he suggests that the Supreme Court decision in the *Rodriguez*[22] case marks a fifth, new stage of "strict construction."

A clear example of court policymaking in stages three and four is seen in decisions pertaining to school desegregation. The *Brown* decision and several subsequent decisions set forth the principle of school desegregation and called upon school districts to implement it. The dilatory tactics of many of these districts provoked further litigation in which the courts began to mandate specific desegregation plans for particular districts. For example, court orders have been issued which require districts to implement complex plans to reassign staff members and students and, in some cases, to employ or reemploy minority group personnel.

The Basis of Federal Involvement

Policy formation in education often follows a kind of sequence: basic social forces lead to antecedent movements; these movements in turn lead to political action which may culminate in formal policy enactments. This sequence helps to explain the growing involvement of the federal courts in education since the mid-twentieth century. Probably the most important basic force has been the historic pursuit of equality by black Americans. Various civil rights groups have employed diverse tactics in quest of this goal, but one of the most persistent and effective over time has been the legal efforts of the National Association for the Advancement of Colored People (NAACP). The NAACP Legal Defense Fund led in pressing school desegregation cases up to and including *Brown* v. *Board of Education*.[23] Since the *Brown* decision, the fund has continued to provide financial and technical assistance in support of desegregation litigation.

The press of the civil rights movement has also produced legislation which has strengthened the courts' hands in the area of desegregation. The Civil Rights Act of 1964 facilitated the filing of suits alleging discrimination, forbade the use of federal

20. Reprinted by permission of the publisher, from *The Schools, the Courts, and the Public Interest* by John C. Hogan (Lexington, Mass.: D.C. Heath, 1974), 5–14.
21. Ibid., 5.
22. *San Antonio Independent School District* v. *Rodriguez*, 411 U.S. 1 (1973).
23. 347 U.S. 483 (1954).

funds for discriminatory programs, and empowered the Justice Department to side with plaintiffs in desegregation suits.[24] These developments encouraged civil rights advocates to file additional cases, which led the courts to a series of decisions on desegregation.

The recent past has witnessed the emergence of other advocate groups that have sought changes in public policy through the courts. A number of Community Action Agencies initially funded under the Economic Opportunity Act of 1964 included legal aid services to the poor. Attorneys for such agencies filed numerous suits on behalf of children and their parents against school districts. Other organizations have emerged as advocates of children's rights; they have helped interpret these rights to young people and have initiated legal actions. Shannon identified nine areas in which legal service agencies had challenged local school districts.[25] They included: (*a*) student discipline, (*b*) use of federal funds by local public schools, (*c*) school bus transportation, (*d*) racial integration of pupils, (*e*) school district organization and management, (*f*) school tuition, (*g*) application of one man-one vote principle, (*h*) state aid to local public schools, and (*i*) educational activities about the law. Moreover, as the courts have acted to broaden the rights of juveniles and students, they have opened the possibility for further litigation. The result has been a great increase in the number of education cases heard in the federal courts and consequently rapidly evolving case law. More recently, the Reagan administration unsuccessfully sought to abolish the Legal Services Corporation but limited the effectiveness of this program by reducing its budget.

The constitutional basis for federal involvement in education derives from a limited number of provisions. Those which have been most important are Article I, Section 10, which forbids the impairment of contractual obligations, and the First, Fifth, and Fourteenth Amendments.[26]

The First Amendment guarantees freedom of speech, religion, the press, assembly, and the right of petition. Its importance in education was noted first in a series of cases dealing with religion and the public schools. First Amendment protections regarding speech, the press, assembly, and petition in relation to student, teacher, and citizen rights vis-à-vis schools have also become matters for litigation.

The Fifth Amendment provides protection against self-incrimination and has been the basis for cases dealing with loyalty oaths and testimony of teachers.

The Fourteenth Amendment states in part that "No state shall make or enforce any law which shall abridge the privileges or immunities of citizens of the United States; nor shall any state deprive any person of life, liberty, or property, without due process of law; nor deny to any person within its jurisidction the equal protection of the laws." This amendment was proposed and ratified during the post-Civil War period and some argue that it was intended only to protect the rights of freedmen in a white society. Conversely others have argued that Congress intended for it to apply more generally. Particularly in recent years the courts have been inclined toward a liberal interpretation.

24. For discussion of these developments see Donna E. Shalala and James A. Kelly, "Politics, the Courts, and Educational Policy," *Teachers College Record* 75 (December 1973): 223–37.
25. Address by Thomas A. Shannon, 15th Annual Convention of NOLPE, Cleveland, Ohio, November, 1969, reported in Susanne Martinez, "Poor People in Public Education in America: Issues and Problems," in *Current Trends in School Law* (Topeka, Kans.: National Organization on Legal Problems in Education, 1974), 296–97.
26. E. Edmund Reutter, Jr. and Robert R. Hamilton, *The Law of Public Education*, 2d ed. (Mincola, N.Y.: Foundation Press, 1976), 2–5.

The due process and equal protection clauses of the Fourteenth Amendment have become the two most important means used by the federal courts to invalidate state laws and to overturn state decisions.[27] Examples of decisions in education where the Supreme Court has used the Fourteenth Amendment in this way include a declaration that a state law prohibiting foreign language instruction below the ninth grade was unconstitutional,[28] a declaration that a state could not infringe upon freedom of religion through compulsory attendance laws,[29] and a ruling that dual school systems for the purpose of segregation were unconstitutional.[30]

At the heart of Supreme Court policy-making behavior is the concept of judicial review. This refers to the authority of the Court to review the actions of other governmental bodies, namely the state and federal courts and legislatures. The Constitution did not provide this right explicitly although most scholars argue that it was intended. The concept has developed principally through the actions of the courts. Chief Justice Marshall is given credit for much of the initiative in this area beginning with his decision in *Marbury* v. *Madison* (1803) which said that a provision of the Judiciary Act of 1789 was unconstitutional.

While the precedent of judicial review has been firmly established over the past 150 years, controversy persists over the manner and extent to which it should be used. For example, President Nixon's statement that he would appoint "strict constructionists" to the Supreme Court was evidence of his belief that the concept had been overextended in recent years. Schmandt has categorized views about judicial review as being of three types: restraint, activism, and neutralism.

> The first argues that judges must recognize the primacy of the legislative and executive branches in policy making and must avoid injecting their own socioeconomic preferences into the judicial process. The second approach maintains that courts are policy makers and, as such, should consciously exercise their judicial power to influence the social system in the interest of justice. The third, while showing far less deference for the legislative and executive wills than the advocates of judicial restraint, holds that constitutional judgments may not be based on the court's sympathy toward litigants or their cause but on fundamental and disinterested principles of law.[31]

These terms, of course, are somewhat ambiguous and do more to point up the philosophical issues which grip the Court than to demarcate absolute positions. The historical trend seems to have been toward a more active judiciary. As Kurland[32] points out, however, judicial activism can be conservative as well as liberal; under judicial activism the Court may impose its judgments upon other governmental branches, but the question of whether those judgments should favor the wealthy or the poor, the powerful or the oppressed, the majority or the minorities is left open. One possible consequence of an activist posture of the Court is an opposition stance and efforts to change it by the executive and legislative branches.[33]

27. Philip B. Kurland, "The New Supreme Court," *The University of Chicago Magazine* 66 (July–August 1973): 8.
28. *Meyer* v. *Nebraska*. 262 U.S. 390 (1923).
29. *Wisconsin* v. *Yoder et al.*, 406 U.S. 205 (1972).
30. *Brown* v. *Board of Education*, 347 U.S. 483 (1954).
31. Schmandt, *Courts in the American Political System*, 43.
32. Kurland, "The New Supreme Court", 5.
33. See Swindler, "The Supreme Court, the President, and the Congress."

While the recent Court has tended toward activism, the nature of the judicial system itself, as set forth earlier in this chapter, imposes certain restraints upon court action. It sometimes exercises restraint in determining the grounds on which a case will be decided. For example, the Court was once asked to decide if a law school admissions policy which accepts minority group applicants with lower test scores than white applicants constitutes reverse discrimination.[34] The Court noted that the individual who filed the case had since been admitted to law school and declared the case moot rather than issue an opinion on the principles involved. The Court subsequently considered a similar case involving a white male who was refused admission to medical school. The Court ruled in his favor in a divided decision which demonstrated the tendency to decide cases on narrow grounds.[35] The Court has imposed certain conditions upon itself regarding judicial review. They include the following:

1. The Court will not pass upon the constitutionality of legislation in a friendly non-adversary proceeding, declining because to decide such questions is legitimate only in the last resort, and as a necessity in the determination of real, earnest, and vital controversy between individuals.
2. The Court will not anticipate a question of constitutional law in advance of the necessity of deciding it . . . It is not the habit of the Court to decide questions of a constitutional nature unless absolutely necessary to a decision of the case.
3. The Court will not formulate a rule of constitutional law broader than is required by the precise facts to which it is to be applied.
4. The Court will not pass upon a constitutional question although properly presented by the record, if there is also present some other ground upon which the case may be disposed of.
5. The Court will not pass upon the validity of a statute upon complaint of one who fails to show that he is injured by its operation.
6. The Court will not pass upon the constitutionality of a statute at the instance of one who has availed himself of its benefits.[36]

The point to be emphasized is that as the Court exercises its review function it does so within a context bounded by public values and interests, the positions of other governmental branches, and procedural guidelines which have evolved over time.

Compliance with Judicial Decisions

One school of thought regarding policy analysis holds that it is important to look beyond the making of an authoritative decision to see whether or not anything happens as a consequence of the decision. Thus the question of whether a school district has a policy of individualizing instruction is answered better by observing classrooms than by reviewing the policy manual. The same test can be applied to court-initiated policies by asking to what extent citizens comply with court decisions. History has recorded

34. *De Funis* v. *Odegaard,* 42 US LW 4578 (1974).
35. *Bakke* v. *Board of Regents* 438 U.S. 265 (1978). While five justices ruled that Bakke must be admitted, five also held that race may be used as a factor in admissions decisions. Four of the five who favored Bakke's admission based their decision on their conclusion that the admissions process in question violated the Civil Rights Act of 1964 rather than the *Constitution.*
36. *Ashwander* v. *Tennessee Valley Authority,* 297 U.S. 288, 346–48 (1936), quoted in Edward C. Bolmeier, *Landmark Supreme Court Decisions on Educational Issues* (Charlottesville, Va.: Michie, 1973), 5.

some spectacular examples of noncompliance. For example, President Andrew Jackson reportedly responded to a Supreme Court decision which was sympathetic to Indian claims by saying, "John Marshall has made his decision; now let him enforce it!"

The courts depend heavily upon assistance from the legislative and executive branches of government as well as general public support to promote compliance with their decisions. Where such assistance and support is lacking, decisions may go unheeded. The most dramatic example in education is in the area of school desegregation. Thirty years after the *Brown* decision, school desegregation remains an issue in the nation. Indeed, for a decade following the decision very little progress was noted in desegregating the dual systems of the deep South. Not until passage of the Civil Rights Act of 1964 and the subsequent involvement of the Department of Justice was substantial progress made. However, the Nixon administration then slowed the desegregation litigation filed by the Justice Department and pushed school busing into the limelight as a public issue.[37] Thus pressure mounted once again to slow the desegregation process, particularly in the North.

Despite the slow pace with which school desegregation has gone forward, the Supreme Court has spoken infrequently on this subject since 1954. Wirt and Kirst attribute this to the patience of the Court in waiting for the rest of the nation to accept the principle they had enunciated and steadfastly maintained.[38] While acknowledging the political sensitivity of the Court in this regard, they also rightly credit the Court with establishing the principle which over time was to have major impact upon the nation.

The compliance problem is apparent in other areas of school litigation. For example, Dolbeare and Hammond studied five towns and found that in each of them school prayers, Bible readings, and other religious observances continued five years after the Supreme Court decision declared them unconstitutional.[39] In their words, "Local leaders are not deliberately defying the Court; they have simply found it congenial and possible to continue established local practice without regard to the Court's decisions."[40]

Student rights is another area in which compliance problems may exist. Mandel points out that many legal efforts in this and other areas are intended to change school organizations and hypothesizes that court decisions which would bring such change will be resisted.[41] The frequency with which essentially similar students rights cases are filed in various jurisdictions suggests that administrators in many areas are unaware of or unaccepting of precedents established elsewhere. As noted earlier, the belief that local court officials are in tune with local values may encourage such behavior.

Even though compliance with court rulings may be problematic in some instances, the courts are nonetheless influential policymakers. They do establish directions on a number of important matters, and parties aggrieved with regard to any of them have

37. Shalala and Kelly, "Politics, the Courts, and Educational Policy," 225–26. See also Michael B. Wise, "School Desegregation: The Court, the Congress, and the President," *School Review* 82 (February 1974): 159–82.
38. Frederick M. Wirt and Michael W. Kirst, *Schools in Conflict* (Berkeley, Calif.: McCutchan, 1982).
39. Kenneth M. Dolbeare and Phillip E. Hammond, *The School Prayer Decisions* (Chicago: University of Chicago Press, 1971).
40. Ibid., 5.
41. For discussion of this hypothesis, see Richard L. Mandel, "Judicial Decisions and Organizational Change in Public Schools," *School Review* 82 (February 1974): 327–46

the right to seek a trial and appeal the decision if they wish. Moreover, the decision of the trial court establishes policy in at least a particular instance regardless of the quality of that decision. At the very least such decisions should serve as guides for school officials who realize that departure from such principles may bring another court case. Equally important, the directions established by the courts through the process of judicial review serve to limit the policy-making prerogatives of other governmental bodies.

Examples of Judicial Influence

In chapter 1 we observed that the Supreme Court exerted important influence upon education through a series of milestone decisions. At this point, we will examine the way court influence has evolved in two areas, school desegregation and school finance reform. In the first case, the position of the court has been clarified and its role enlarged as it forced school districts to desegregate their facilities and programs. In the second case, a broadly written Supreme Court decision slowed a movement toward reform which had gained considerable momentum in state and lower federal courts. We have quoted at some length from a number of decisions to illustrate how the courts seek facts, how they reason, and how they build upon precedent.

School Desegregation

The views of the courts regarding school desegregation have evolved slowly since the landmark *Brown* decision and they have been implemented even more slowly. Resistance to implementing the *Brown* decision combined with the continual refocusing of the issue according to particular geographical or legal bases have led the courts to become increasingly specific about what constitutes unlawful segregation.

The 1954 *Brown* decision was based on cases from Kansas, South Carolina, Virginia, and Delaware in which plaintiffs sought to enjoin enforcement of state constitutional and statutory provisions which permitted or required the segregation of black and white children in the public schools. Taking note of the psychological aspects of learning and prejudice, the Supreme Court said:

> We conclude that in the field of public education, the doctrine of "separate but equal" has no place. Separate educational facilities are inherently unequal. Therefore, we hold that the plaintiffs and others similarly situated for whom the acts have been brought are, by reason of the segregation complained of, deprived of the equal protection of the laws guaranteed by the Fourteenth Amendment.[42]

In a subsequent decision setting forth bases for implementing the first *Brown* decision, the Supreme Court remanded the cases to the district courts to monitor progress toward desegregation and rendered the well-known guideline of "with all deliberate speed." The Court also said:

> The courts will require that the defendants make a prompt and reasonable start toward full compliance with our May 17, 1954 ruling. Once such a start has been made,

---

42. *Brown* v. *Board of Education*, 347 U.S. 483, 495 (1954). A useful source on school desegregation that includes most of the cases cited here (as well as others) and related analytical material is David L. Kirp and Mark G. Yudof, *Educational Policy and the Law: Cases and Materials* (Berkeley, Calif.: McCutchan, 1974), ch. 4. Also see Betsy Levin, *The Courts as Educational Policymakers and Their Impact on Federal Programs* (Santa Monica, Calif.: The Rand Corporation, 1977).

the courts may find that additional time is required to carry out the ruling in an effective manner. The burden rests upon the defendants to establish that such time is necessary in the public interest and is consistent with good faith compliance at the earliest practicable date. To that end, the courts may consider problems related to administration, arising from the physical condition of the school plant, the school transportation system, personnel, revision of school districts and attendance areas into compact units to achieve a system of determining admission to the public schools on a nonracial basis and revision of local laws and regulations which may be necessary in solving the foregoing problems. They will also consider the adequacy of any plans the defendants may propose to meet these problems and to effectuate a transition to a racially nondiscriminatory school system.[43]

The next decade was characterized by southern resistance to dismantling dual school systems. For the most part, the Supreme Court was silent as litigation continued at lower levels, although it did uphold lower court enforcement of the *Brown* decisions.[44] In widely noted rulings, the Court held that state legislative, executive, or judicial authorities could not nullify the constitutional rights declared in *Brown*,[45] and that a county could not close its public schools to avoid desegregation.[46]

One procedure employed by school districts to desegregate dual systems was the "freedom of choice" plan. The essence of this plan was that each child would be allowed to attend the school of his or her choosing. In the early stages of the desegregation effort, the court refused to overturn such plans. As time passed, however, it became apparent that "freedom of choice" did not always produce desegregated schools. Against this background, the U.S. Supreme Court accepted a case for review in which freedom of choice had not ended school segregation. The court ruled against the plan in this instance and put the matter in historical perspective:

> For the time immediately after *Brown II* the concern was with making an initial break in a long established pattern of excluding Negro children from schools attended by white children. The principal focus was on obtaining for those Negro children courageous enough to break with tradition a place in the "white" schools. See e.g., *Cooper* v. *Aaron 358, US 1*. Under *Brown II* that immediate goal was only the first step, however. The transition to a unitary, nonracial system of public education was and is the ultimate end to be brought about; it was because of the "complexities arising from the transition to a system of public education freed of racial discrimination" that we provided for "all deliberate speed" in the implementation of the principles of Brown I. . . . The burden on a school board today is to come forward with a plan that promises realistically to work and promises realistically to work *now*. . . .Where it [freedom of choice] offers real promise of aiding a desegregation program to effectuate conversion of a state-imposed dual system to a unitary, nonracial system there might be no objection to allowing such a device to prove itself in operation. On the other hand, if there are reasonably available other ways, such for illustration as zoning, promising speedier and more effective conversion to a unitary, nonracial school system, "freedom of choice" must be held unacceptable.[47]

A year later the Supreme Court refused to accept further delay in implementing desegregation plans for thirty Mississippi school districts. The Court extended the

43. *Brown* v. *Board of Education*, 349 U.S. 294, 300–1 (1955).
44. Wirt and Kirst, *The Political Web of American Schools*, 186.
45. *Cooper* v. *Aaron*, 358 U.S. 1 (1958).
46. *Griffin* v. *County School Board of Prince Edward County*, 377 U.S. 218 (1964).
47. *Green* v. *County School Board*, 391 U.S. 430, 435–36, 439, 440–41 (1968).

position it had taken in the *Green* case and ruled that "all deliberate speed" was "no longer constitutionally permissible. Under explicit holdings of this Court, the obligation of every school district is to terminate dual school systems at once and to operate now and hereafter only unitary schools."[48]

The Court was to speak further about the affirmative responsibilities of a school district in bringing about desegregation. The most far-reaching ruling of this type came in *Swann et al.* v. *Charlotte-Mecklenberg Board of Education et al.*[49] The Court spoke to several points. It stated the obligation of school authorities to "eliminate invidious racial distinctions," and "produce schools of like quality, facilities, and staff." The Court affirmed the power of district courts to order the "assignment of teachers to achieve a particular degree of faculty desegregation." The Court also held that district courts could use their authority to oversee future school construction and abandonment so that they "do not serve to perpetuate or reestablish the dual system."

The central issue in the *Swann* case, however, dealt with pupil assignment. The Court held that it was within the district courts' discretion to establish very limited and flexible ratios for pupil assignment among buildings, that "the existence of some small number of one-race or virtually one-race schools within a district is not in and of itself the mark of a system which still practices segregation by law" but that school officials have the "burden of showing that such school assignments are genuinely non-discriminatory." It also held that the district court can alter attendance zones, that "the pairing and grouping of non-contiguous school zones is a permissible tool," and that it was within the power of the district court to order busing as a remedy. On busing, the court noted that no child would ride a bus for longer than thirty-five minutes under the proposed plan and that "an objection to transportation of students may have validity when the time or distance of travel is so great as to risk either the health of the children or significantly impinge on the educational process."

With the pronouncement in *Swann* the Supreme Court moved from the enunciation of a general principle in the first *Brown* case to a statement of specifics applicable to the dismantling of dual school systems. At the time the courts were considering these cases, they were also dealing with a number of actions filed against northern school districts. Here school officials and others have maintained that segregated schools were not a result of state action and thus segregated de jure but were instead the product of segregated housing patterns and hence de facto. Thus the questions before the courts in the North have been somewhat different than those associated with dual systems in the South.

The New Rochelle, New York schools were the first in the North to be found in violation of the *Brown* provisions. In the 1961 case the federal district court found that the district had deliberately gerrymandered school boundaries to perpetuate segregation. Other early northern cases, however, were decided otherwise. The rationale for such decisions was set forth in *Bell* v. *School City of Gary*.[50] In a ruling affirmed by the court of appeals, the district court held that

> The problem in Gary is not one of segregated schools but rather of segregated housing. Either by choice or by design, the Negro population of Gary is concentrated in

48. *Alexander* v. *Holmes County Board of Education,* 396 U. S. 19, 20 (1969).
49. 402 U.S. 1 (1970).
50. 324 F.2d 209 (7th Cir 1963) cert. denied 377 U.S. 924 (1964). Cf. *Taylor* v. *Board of Education of New Rochelle,* 294 F.2d 36 (2d Cir 1961), cert. denied 368 U.S. 940 (1961).

the so-called central area, and as a result the schools in that area are populated by Negro students. . . . The Court finds no support for the plaintiff's position that the defendant has an affirmative duty to balance the races in the various schools under its jurisdiction, regardless of the residence of students involved.[51]

Similar reasoning was expressed in a case dealing with de facto segregation in Cincinnati. Part of the appeals court decision held,

We hold that there is no constitutional duty on the part of the Board to bus Negro or white children out of their neighborhoods or to transfer classes for the sole purpose of alleviating racial imbalance that it did not cause, nor is there a like duty to select new school sites solely in furtherance of such a purpose . . . the crucial fact to be found is whether the racial imbalance was intentionally caused by gerrymandering or by other alleged discriminatory practices on the part of the Board.[52]

More recently, however, the courts have demonstrated a tendency to rule against northern school segregation. Kirp and Yudof note that this has been done "not by repudiating the *de jure/de facto* distinction, but by expanding the scope of *de jure* segregation." [53] They cite *Kelly* v. *Guinn*[54] as an example of this practice. Here the Court noted that the Clark County, Nevada, schools had recently built four new elementary schools within a predominantly black area, closed two other predominantly white schools on the fringe of this area, and also built a new elementary school in a more distant white area. The Court also noted that most of the teachers in the black area were black. The court of appeals concluded "that there was ample evidence to support the district court's finding that the Clark County School District used its power to aggravate segregation in elementary schools in violation of the Constitution." This finding was in the face of the district's defense that they were "simply adhering to a neighborhood school policy" and that "whatever imbalance exists stems not from any official action of the school district, but rather from the racial composition of the Westside population, which is almost completely black."

A subsequent and more far-reaching decision of this type was set forth by the Supreme Court in a case involving the Denver Public Schools. In *Keyes* v. *School District No. 1 Denver, Colorado,*[55] the high court held that if it could be shown that "school authorities have carried out a systematic program of segregation affecting a substantial portion of the students, schools, teachers, and facilities within the school system, it is only common sense to conclude that there exists a predicate for a finding of the existence of a dual school system." The case was remanded to the district court for hearing on this point with the stipulation that if a "dual school system" was found to exist, then the Board of Education would have the obligation to desegregate the entire school system.

In this case, the court noted that the Denver schools had never been a dual system under constitutional or statutory provision but maintained its distinction be-

---

51. *Bell* v. *School City of Gary,* 213 F. Supp 819, 827–31 (N.D. Indiana 1963). Our analysis of this and the Cincinnati case was aided by an unpublished paper by Roger D. Anderson, "The Constitution and De Facto School Segregation."
52. *Deal* v. *Cincinnati Board of Education* 369 F. 2d 55, 61, 64 (6th Cir. 1966) cert. denied 389 U.S. 847.
53. Kirp and Yudof, *Educational Policy and the Law,* 401.
54. 456 F. 2d 100 (9th Cir 1972).
55. 413 U.S. 189 (1973). For an excellent discussion of this case see Thomas A. Shannon, "The Denver Decision: Death Knell for Defacto Segregation?" *Phi Delta Kappan* 55 (September 1973): 6–9.

tween de facto and de jure segregation, saying that the "differentiating factor" was *"purpose* or *intent* to segregate." However, the ruling in this case substantially broadens the grounds on which northern school districts may be required to take affirmative action to desegregate. Moreover, Justice Powell in a separate opinion suggested that the de facto/de jure distinction was no longer useful and should be discarded. He wrote:

> I concur in the Court's position that the public school authorities are the responsible agency of the state, and that if the affirmative duty doctrine is sound Constitutional law for Charlotte, it is equally so for Denver. I would not, however, perpetuate the *de jure/de facto* distinction nor would I leave to petitioners the initial tortuous effort of identifying "segregative acts" and deducing "segregated intent." I would hold quite simply that where segregated public schools exist within a school district to a substantial degree, there is a prima facie case that the duly constituted public authorities . . . are sufficiently responsible to warrant imposing upon them a nationally applicable burden to demonstrate they nevertheless are operating a genuinely integrated school system.[56]

Powell, however, also let it be known that he believed there might be some limitations on the responsibility of school officials to desegregate. Recalling *Swann* which he said was the "controlling case" in this instance he wrote:

> To the extent that *Swann* may be thought to *require* large scale or long distance transportation of students in our metropolitan school districts, I record my profound misgivings. Nothing in our Constitution commands or encourages any such court-compelled disruption of public education. It may be more accurate to view *Swann* as having laid down a broad rule of reason under which desegregation remedies must remain flexible and other values and interests be considered.[57]

In subsequent cases, the Court has spoken further about the limits of official responsibility to desegregate. In a case involving the Pasadena, California schools, the Court ruled that once a school district had implemented a suitable plan to remedy earlier segregative behavior, the district could not be required to revise the plan regularly in order to account for natural population shifts in the district.[58] Thus the Court held out the possibility that school districts which had implemented desegregation plans under judicial oversight could escape this supervision in time.[59] In other decisions, the Court indicated that the test of whether or not a district acted with segregative intent must include evidence that speaks to the purpose as well as the effects of these actions.[60] Moreover, the Court ruled that a finding of liability for segregation against a district does not necessarily require a district-wide desegregation plan. Instead, the scope of the remedy is to be determined by the extent of the impact of the wrongful acts.[61]

56. *Keyes,* 413 U.S. 189, 224 (1973).
57. *Keyes,* 413 U.S. 189, 238 (1973).
58. *Pasadena City Board of Education* v. *Spangler,* 427 U.S. 424 (1976).
59. Clifford P. Hooker, "Issues in School Desegregation" in *The Courts and Education,* 112.
60. *Austin Independent School District* v. *United States,* 429 U.S. 990 (1976), and *Dayton Board of Education* v. *Brinkman,* 431 U.S. 902 (1977).
61. *Dayton* v. *Brinkman,* 431 U.S. 902 (1977). But also see *Dayton* v. *Brinkman* 443 U.S. 526 (1979) where the Court subsequently held that the facts in Dayton warranted a system-wide remedy. A similar decision was rendered in the case of Columbus, Ohio. See *Board of Education* v. *Penick,* 443 U.S. 449 (1979).

As the focus on desegregation litigation has moved to the North and the courts have expanded the doctrine of affirmative duty to northern cities, another important question dealing with jurisdiction has been raised. It deals with the responsibility of the state to require cross-district efforts at desegregation in metropolitan areas where suburbs have remained white as core cities become increasingly black. The most important case was Detroit. In this case a federal district court had ordered a metropolitan plan for desegregating the Detroit schools which would have involved cross-district busing, and this plan was upheld by the court of appeals.[62] However, the Supreme Court struck down this plan by a vote of 5–4. In doing so, the Court reaffirmed the tradition of local school control, determined that there was no proof of segregative action by the surrounding 85 suburban school districts, and ruled that it would not be appropriate to impose interdistrict remedies for segregation unless it could be shown that such segregation was the result of interdistrict actions.[63] In a vigorous dissenting opinion written by Justice Marshall, the minority argued that the state of Michigan was responsible for the educational system provided in Detroit and that there was "no basis either in law or in the practicalities of the situation justifying the state's interposition of school district boundaries as absolute barriers to the implementation of an effective desegregation remedy."[64] Despite this division, the impact of the decision was to further clarify the responsibility of local school districts regarding desegregation and to deter similar cases being advanced in other metropolitan areas. However, a metropolitan remedy has been upheld where it was shown that state or suburban action contributed to city school segregation.[65]

School Finance Reform

In 1965 Arthur Wise, then a graduate student at the University of Chicago, wrote an article in which he argued that the Fourteenth Amendment could be used as a vehicle for declaring state school finance plans unconstitutional.[66] He contended, later, in a book which amplified his position, that education was a right which must be provided equally and that the existing variations among school districts' expenditures precluded this from happening.[67] This argument provided the theoretical underpinnings for scholars interested in greater equity in school finance and was the basis for some early court cases. Important among these were a case filed by the Detroit City school board but subsequently dropped and a case in Illinois.[68] Both cases argued that the state had a responsibility to meet the "educational needs" of students. In *McInnis* the court held " . . . (1) the Fourteenth Amendment does not require that public school expenditures be made only on the basis of pupil's educational needs, and (2) the lack of judicially manageable standards makes this controversy non-judiciable."[69]

62. *Bradley* v. *Milliken,* 345 F. Supp. 914 (E. D. Michigan S.D. 1972).
63. 418 U.S. 717 (1974).
64. 418 U.S. 717 (1974) at 783.
65. For example, *Evans* v. *Buchanan,* 423 U.S. 963 (1976). and *Morrilton School District No. 32 v. U.S.* 606 F.2d 222 (8th Cir. 1979). cert. denied 100 S. Ct. 1015 (1982). Also see *U.S. v. Board of School Commissioners of the City of Indianapolis* 637 F.2d 1101 (7th Cir. 1980) cert denied 101 S. Ct. 114 (1980)
66. Arthur E. Wise, "Is Denial of Equal Educational Opportunity Constitutional?" *Administrator's Notebook* 13 (February 1965).
67. Arthur E. Wise, *Rich Schools-Poor Schools* (Chicago: University of Chicago Press, 1969).
68. *McInnis* v. *Shapiro,* 293 F. Supp. 327 (N.D. Ill. 1968) affirmed. *McInnis* v. *Ogilvie,* 394 US 322 (1969).
69. Quoted in Joseph A. Williams, Harold W. Gentry and Michael W. LaMorte, "The Attack on Educational Finance Programs—An Overview," NOLPE *School Law Journal* 2 (Fall 1972):6.

The Wise position was modified somewhat by John E. Coons, William Clune, and Stephen Sugarman.[70] They argued that the basic constitutional problem with state finance programs was that they allowed wealthy school districts to spend more than others. Shifting from the educational need argument advanced by Wise, they contended that the equal protection clause of the Fourteenth Amendment required states to adopt a position of fiscal "neutrality," that is, one which did not make it easier for wealthier districts to provide more educational opportunities than a less wealthy district. This theory of "power equalizing" regarding taxation provided the basis for the landmark California case, *Serrano* v. *Priest*,[71] and a series of emulators in states throughout the country.

At the crux of the *Serrano* case were the plaintiff's contentions that the California school financing system violated the equal protection clause because it favored a "suspect classification" (i.e., those who lived in wealthy school districts) and that education was a "fundamental interest" of California citizens. If these conditions could be established as true, then constitutional law required the state finance plan to be declared unconstitutional unless it could be shown "(1) that the state has a 'compelling interest' that justifies the law, and (2) that the particular manner in which the law treats people differently is *necessary* to futher the law's valid purposes." [72] The California Supreme Court found that "the school financing system discriminates on the basis of the wealth of a district and its residents." The court also held that education is a "fundamental interest," and rejected the arguments of local and state officials that the present law was necessary. In remanding the case for further hearings the court observed " . . . that if, after further proceedings, that court [the trial court] should enter final judgment determining that the existing system of public school financing is unconstitutional and invalidating said system in whole or in part, it may properly provide for the enforcement of the judgment in such a way as to permit an orderly transition from an unconstitutional to a constitutional system of financing." [73]

Similar cases dealing with other states proceeded through state and lower federal courts. Within a short time after the *Serrano* decision, "roughly comparable" decisions were rendered in Minnesota, Texas, Kansas, Arizona, New Jersey, and Michigan.[74] It appeared that a substantial reform movement was under way. However, an attorney in the Texas case decided to pursue his case before a three-judge federal district court. In late 1971 this court held that the Texas school finance law did not guarantee equal protection, a decision which the state of Texas appealed directly to the U.S. Supreme Court.

The decision of the high court in *San Antonio Independent School District et al.* v. *Rodriguez et al.*[75] was a severe disappointment to those who hoped the court would add its support to the reform effort. By a 5–4 decision, the court overturned the

70. See their book, *Private Wealth and Public Education* (Cambridge, Mass.: Harvard University Press, 1970). In presenting this historical account, we have relied heavily upon Joel S. Berke, "Recent Adventures of State School Finance: A Saga of Rocket Ships and Glider Planes," *School Review* 82 (February 1974): 183–206 and Williams, Gentry, and La Morte, "The Attack on Educational Finance Programs—An Overview."
71. 5 Cal. 3d 584, 96 Cal. Rptr, 601, 487 p. 2d 1241 (1971).
72. Thomas A. Shannon, "Chief Justice Wright, The California Supreme Court, and School Finance: Has the Fourteenth Done It Again?" (Washington, D.C.: American Association of School Administrators, n.d.)
73. Ibid.
74. Berke, "Recent Adventures of State School Finance."
75. 411 U.S. 1 (1973).

district court holding. The Court did so not on narrow technical grounds but on the basic constitutional questions posed in *Serrano* and subsequent cases. In the majority opinion, Justice Powell set forth the task of the court as follows:

> We must decide, first, whether the Texas system of financing public education operates to the disadvantage of some suspect class or impinges upon a fundamental right explicitly or unexplicitly protected by the Constitution, thereby requiring strict judicial scrutiny. If so, the judgment of the District Court should be affirmed. If not, the Texas scheme must still be examined to determine whether it rationally furthers some legitimate, articulated state purpose and therefore does not constitute an invidious discrimination in violation of the Equal Protection Clause of the Fourteenth Amendment.[76]

The Court held that the plan "does not operate to the peculiar disadvantage of any suspect class" and that the system was not "so irrational as to be invidiously discriminatory." Perhaps most significant, the Court addressed the question of education as a fundamental interest. Noting the historic dedication of the Court to public education and its importance in society, Justice Powell nevertheless wrote:

> But the importance of a service performed by the State does not determine whether it must be regarded as fundamental for purposes of examination under the Equal Protection Clause. . . . It is not the province of this Court to create substantive constitutional rights in the name of guaranteeing equal protection of the laws. Thus the key to discovering whether education is "fundamental" is not to be found in comparisons of the relative societal significance of education as opposed to subsistence or housing. . . . Rather the answer lies in assessing whether there is a right to education explicitly or implicitly guaranteed by the Constitution. . . .
> Education, of course, is not among the rights afforded explicit protection under our Federal Constitution. Nor do we find any basis for saying it is implicitly so protected. . . .[77]

The decision had the effect of closing the federal courts at least temporarily to those who sought redress of inequities in state school finance plans. But it did not destroy their recourse altogether. Justice Powell himself concluded the *Rodriguez* opinion by writing:

> We hardly need add that this Court's action today is not to be viewed as placing its judicial imprimatur on the status quo. The need is apparent for reform in tax systems which may well have relied too long and too heavily on the local property tax. And certainly innovative new thinking as to public education, its methods, and its funding, is necessary to assure both a higher level of quality and greater uniformity of opportunity. These matters merit the continued attention of the scholars who already have contributed much by their challenges. But the ultimate solutions must come from the lawmakers and from the democratic pressures of those who elect them.[78]

Moreover, it is a final commentary on the complexity of our court systems that judical remedies are still possible as well. The fact that the decision was by a 5–4 vote

76. 411 U.S. 1 (1973) at 17.
77. Ibid., 30–35.
78. Ibid., 58–59.

suggests that a change of mind might be possible on the Supreme Court at some later date. In the meanwhile, state courts offer a potential source of judicial remedy in many instances. In contrast to the federal Constitution, 48 state constitutions mention education as a fundamental interest.[79] Moreover, the education clause in some state constitutions may itself be basis for state litigation holding the finance program unconstitutional. This was the finding of the New Jersey Supreme Court in a decision rendered shortly after *Rodriguez.*[80] This court affirmed a lower court ruling that New Jersey statutes which allowed considerable variation in per pupil expenditures according to local tax patterns did not fulfill the state constitutional requirement to provide "a thorough and efficient system of free public schools." The Los Angeles Superior Court in a follow-up to the earlier *Serrano* decision held that California must promulgate a school finance plan which will reduce differences among districts in basic per pupil expenditures to less than one hundred dollars per pupil within six years. Differences among districts in tax rates are to be reduced to "nonsubstantial variations" within the same period. The legislatures in New Jersey and California enacted new school finance laws in response to their respective courts. In the decade since *Rodriguez,* cases involving the constitutionality of financing arrangments for schools have reached the supreme courts of twelve states. In five of these states (New Jersey, California, Connecticut, Washington, and Wyoming), the courts have held the existing system unconstitutional. The present system has been upheld in the remaining seven states largely because of judicial concern over the "fundamental interest" issue and reluctance to override the state interest in preserving local control of schools.[81] Despite the action in some states, it would appear that the Supreme Court decision did have the effect of slowing the momentum which had been building for state school finance reform.

Summary and Future Prospects

The past two decades have been extremely busy ones for court activity in education. In addition to the important cases discussed previously, the courts have also rendered significant decisions in the areas of student rights, church-state relationships, and teacher rights and responsibilities. Such cases have involved the courts in matters which are of day-to-day importance to school administrators, and court involvement is likely to continue. Thus it is important that education officials be informed not only about the substance of the law but about the nature of judicial proceedings as well.

The influence of the courts is rooted in the law and the respect of the American population for it. By constitution and tradition the judicial process is regarded as the ultimate authority for resolving conflicts and redressing injustices. Judicial influence is not without its limits, however. Court decisions must be consistent with constitutional provisions, relevant statutes, and, in the case of lower courts, superior court rulings. They also are guided by past decisions in similar cases. Moreover, the courts may only rule on issues which are brought before them. Despite these limitations, court rulings have had a substantial impact on schools. This impact has been conservative from one perspective because it represents an effort to bring schools into compliance

79. Berke, "Recent Adventures of State School Finance," 173.
80. *Robinson* v. *Cahill,* 62 N.J. 473 (1973).
81. David C. Long, *"Rodriguez:* the State Courts Respond," *Phi Delta Kappan* 64 (March 1983): 481–84.

with existing constitutional and statutory provisions.[82] In their efforts to understand facts and apply the most appropriate laws in an environment which is increasingly complex, the courts rely not only upon the adversarial pleadings of the parties, their counsel, and expert witnesses, but more and more upon their own court-appointed experts, special masters, and advisory bodies.

A review of cases pending before the courts suggests some areas in which future decisions are likely. Certainly there will be further decisions dealing with metropolitan school desegregation and state school finance reform. Another set of finance questions of concern to the courts deals with state aid to nonpublic schools. The 1983 decision of the Supreme Court upholding tuition tax credits for nonpublic school students in Minnesota will likely be followed by legislation and litigation in other states.[83] An apparently critical feature of the Minnesota law is that it allows deductions for education expenses incurred by parents of students in public as well as private schools. The right of states to regulate nonpublic schools is another topic on which further court action is likely.

A major emphasis of litigation in the mid-1980s will be to extend and clarify the principles established by the courts in the past decades with respect to such issues as student rights, the rights of the handicapped, affirmative action, and fair dismissal of employees.[84] In addition, the value clashes of disparate groups in heterogeneous school settings will continue to present the courts with cases that deal with issues like textbook selection, religious observances, and the teaching of creationism. At the same time, new trends in society will bring new issues to the courts. One current example is the controversy regarding the applicability and enforcement of copyright laws to high technology and curriculum products such as software and videodiscs. Another set of questions to be litigated will deal with validity and due process considerations associated with competency testing for students and teachers.

One can only conclude from such developments that the courts will continue to be active in education and that the law will change as a result. It could be, however, that it will change in ways to limit the considerable use of the equal protection clause. Kurland has suggested this and also that the Supreme Court may choose to place more emphasis on another clause in the Fourteenth Amendment which says, "No state shall make or enforce any law which shall abridge the privileges or immunities of citizens of the United States. This remains to be seen. Likewise, we must wait to see if the courts become more conservative in other respects. However, the growing involvement of the courts in education suggests that educators will need to find efficient ways of keeping abreast of legal developments at all court levels.

82. See Raphael O. Nystrand and W. Frederick Staub, "The Courts as Educational Policy-Makers" in *The Courts and Education.*
83. *Mueller* v. *Allen* 103 U.S. 3062 (1983).
84. See Ralph D. Stern, "The Law and Public Education, Projections for the 1980's," *Education and Urban Society* 14 (February 1982): 211–34; M. A. McGhehey, ed., *School Law in Changing Times* (Topeka, Kan.: National Organization on Legal Problems of Education, 1982); and Philip K. Piele, ed., *The Yearbook of School Law 1983* (Topeka, Kan.: National Organization on Legal Problems of Education, 1983).

8

The Board
of Education

Boards of education are policymaking bodies by tradition and legal interpretation. Educational policymaking is a political activity conducted within complex political environments. Some communities possess unique political cultures which must be understood if one is to comprehend the policymaking and the decision making that occurs within them. In this chapter we will focus on policymakers and the political context within which they perform their public services. We will describe the functions of boards of education and their members in relation to the growing complexity of the environment of local school district governance.

In the United States, lay control of public institutions, especially schools, has had a profound impact on society and the nation. We will point out, however, that there are opportunities to strengthen the quality of local control and to direct school boards to spend more time on fundamental issues of educational policy and less time on trivial, often idiosyncratic points of individual board member interest.

The significance of lay governance must not be underestimated. Cremin credits the lodging of the governance of education with ordinary citizens as a critical feature of the revolution in education during the early colonial period. Cremin notes further that, "The laicizing of the sponsorship and the control of education was paralleled by a significant broadening of clientele."[1] This was the beginning of universal free public education. Lay participation was essential in its origins; it is equally critical to its extension and improvement.

Several pages in this chapter are devoted to the origins of boards of education and to their responsibilities. We have done this for several reasons. First, citizens and professionals today are not well informed about boards of education, their functions, and their responsibilities. Second, Americans in recent years have been inclined to turn their backs on the past and ignore its richness. Consequently history no longer acts as a lens for looking at the future. Third, the examination of the history of lay

---

1. Lawrence A. Cremin, *American Education: The Colonial Experience 1607-1783* (New York: Harper & Row, 1970), 170. For a brief, insightful history of school boards see Raymond E. Callahan, "The American Board of Education, 1789-1960," in *Understanding School Boards*, ed. Peter J. Cistone, (Lexington, Mass.: Lexington, 1975), 19-46.

control of education, blended with an analysis of contemporary governance issues, can form the basis for projecting refinements and improvements in the governance of education.

The United States' experience with, and commitment to, lay boards of education is the most far-reaching in the world. Canada, England, and Wales have had a somewhat parallel experience with local control although their histories of lay participation through school boards have been quite different from that of the United States. Many nations, as matters of national policy, are urging more active citizen involvement in education through several participatory forms especially local councils. Local councils, by and large, have very limited power and authority, and are therefore usually only advisory.[2]

There are approximately 95,000 American citizens serving on school boards in the United States. These people make decisions which affect the educational welfare of the millions of school children enrolled in our public schools; they give countless hours of their time to this public service. Some are wealthy, some are poor; some are well educated, some have little formal schooling; some are self-seeking, some are genuinely interested in rendering useful public service. Irrespective of one's point of view about the desirability or undesirability of local school control, the fact is that thousands of board members, men and women, exercise a measure of control over American public schools.

The Control Function

School districts, as described in chapter 4, are extensions of the states, subject to the will of the legislatures. School board members are agents of the state, chosen locally in accordance with constitutional or statutory provisions and derive their authority from the state. The relation of the board member to the state has not always been well understood. The courts have been called on to clarify the relationship of board members in the state, and the decisions of the courts have repeatedly acknowledged the "agent" position of these local officials.

Boards fulfill their control obligations locally in two general ways. First, they are the official link with the public. Boards are to apprehend, understand, and reflect the public will in what they do. Second, boards have internal management responsibilities which are crucial to the enterprise's operation. The selection of top administrative leadership, allocation of fiscal resources, and examination of the system's product are examples. Obviously the external and internal faces of responsibility are related. Public policy bodies such as school boards cannot concentrate on internal affairs at the expense of responding to citizen interest. They must effectively mediate the public will.

Thus school boards are controlling bodies, acting in the interests of the local districts they represent, within statutory and constitutional boundaries existing in their states. The local control tradition has an historical precedent. Yet there is substantial evidence that the scope of local discretion is being increasingly circumscribed. The current status of local control will be described later in the chapter.

Local governments of any type are legal fictions unless power and authority are expressly delegated to specific persons at that level. The famed Massachusetts School

2. For a comparative view of national and local structures for citizen participation including school councils see George Baron, ed., *The Politics of School Government* (Oxford: Pergamon, 1981).

Ordinance of 1642 was quite specific in delegating the responsibility for education to the "townsmen." In the words of the ordinance:

> This court, taking into consideration the great neglect of many parents and masters in training up their children in learning and labor, . . . do hereupon order and decree that in every town the chosen men appointed for managing the prudential affairs of the same shall henceforth stand charged with the care of the redress of this evil, so as they shall be sufficiently punished by fines for the neglect thereof upon presentment of the grand jury, or any other information or complaint in any court within this jurisdiction; and for this end they, or the greater number of them, shall have the power to take account from time to time of all parents and masters, and of their children, concerning their calling and employment of their children, especially of their ability to read and understand the principles of religion and the capital laws of this country.[3]

The words are clear—"in every town the chosen men appointed for managing the prudential affairs of the same" are held responsible for and have the power "to take account from time to time of all parents and masters, and of their children . . . especially of their ability to read and understand the principles of religion and the capital laws of the country." Not only is the state supreme but the delegation to local citizens is specific and binding. The pattern thus established was reinforced in the Massachusetts School Ordinance of 1647 and in amendments to the 1647 ordinance passed in 1671 and 1683. Note, however, that in the 1642 ordinance, control was placed in the "townsmen," persons who also had other local governmental responsibilities. The control of education was not separated from other local regulatory and service functions of the townsmen; the townsmen were both legislative and administrative officials. They made "policies" either as townsmen or through the mechanism of the town meeting at which other citizens could be heard. Reeves credits the townsmen, or selectmen, as they are sometimes called, with deciding such things as the levy of the town taxes, the selection of teachers and the determination of their wages, the length of the school year, and provisions for housing the schools.[4]

Ordinances passed by the General Court of Massachusetts became the models for subsequent actions of other colonial legislatures. In 1677 Plymouth Colony passed an act similar to the Massachusetts Ordinance of 1647. The Plymouth Colony law not only called for the establishment of schools but provided state aid to the local community to be collected from assessments against profits arising from Cape Cod fishing. The Connecticut Laws of 1650 likewise followed the Massachusetts pattern but were considerably more specific and detailed in describing the duties and responsibilities of the selectmen, the nature of the education and apprenticeships to be provided, and the ways and means of supporting local colonial schools. For example, two people were to be appointed in each town of the colony and were empowered to demand that every family give support to the school and to see that the gifts were brought to some central location each March. The responsibility of these two people for this service was to continue until relieved by the local selectmen.

The Connecticut Laws were much stronger than the Massachusetts Ordinances. The language was sharp and the consequences for failure to observe the intent of the law were prescribed. When selectmen found parents or apprentice masters negligent

3. Edwin Grant Dexter, *A History of Education in the United States* (New York: Macmillan, 1922), 584.
4. Charles Everand Reeves, *School Boards, Their Status, Functions, and Activities* (Englewood Cliffs, N.J.: Prentice-Hall, 1954), 17.

in observing the laws, they were directed to take children from their parents or apprentices from masters and place them with acceptable masters until the age of 21 for boys and 18 for girls. The justifications for such arbitrary actions were implied in the act itself: an educated citizenry is imperative if representative government is to survive.

The New England Colonies set the standard for other colonies and subsequently for the states of the union. The control of schools vested in the selectmen continued for nearly two centuries until the task of governing schools became so great that it was separated from the other affairs of local government. Beginning with the appointment of the first permanent school visiting committee in 1721 in Boston, the practice of separating school governing bodies from other local governing bodies began. The Boston visiting committee was a subcommittee of selectmen with a specific task or assignment. The members of the visiting committee were to visit schools and report their observations to the selectmen. This led quite naturally to the delegation of other school responsibilities to this committee until the subcommittee of selectmen was given full legal status and recognized as the governing committee for the schools. Thus the term "school committee" arose and was applied to other local educational control bodies in other colonies and eventually in the states of the United States. Now, of course, local school governing bodies are known under many titles: for example, this body is called the school committee in Massachusetts, the school trustees in Indiana, the board of schoool directors in Oregon, the school board in Nebraska, and the board of education, board of school commissioners, or board of school inspectors in other places. Regardless of what they are titled there are many marked similarities in what they can do.

Today the statutes of the 50 states provide the boundaries within which school boards function and prescribe rather explicitly the frameworks for selecting citizens to serve on boards and for guiding board member behavior after selection. Such matters as the size of the board, length of term of members, procedures for filling vacancies on the board, place and time of regular meetings and special meetings, and the duties and responsibilities of board members are described in the laws of the several states.

As agents of the state, local school board members must fulfill the mandates of the state; at the same time, local board members give expression to the will of local citizens and interpret public interest. Legally, board members owe their allegiance to the state and must abide by and carry out the state's mandate. Practically, board members are either elected or appointed locally and must be responsive to their constituencies.

The board, as a governmental body, is created to perform specified functions. It exists apart from its membership.[5] In other words, the powers and duties of the board must be exercised by the board as a whole. Its members come and go, but the board remains the control center for the school district. The courts have been called on repeatedly to clarify the authority of local boards of education. The powers of local boards as agreed on by the courts are: (1) those expressly granted by statute; (2) those fairly and necessarily implied in the powers expressly granted; and (3) those essential to the accomplishments of the objects of the corporation.[6]

5. Robert R. Hamilton and E. Edmund Reutter, Jr., *Legal Aspects of School Board Operation* (New York: Bureau of Publications, Teachers College, Columbia University, 1958), ch. 1.
6. Newton Edwards, *The Courts and the Public Schools* (Chicago: University of Chicago Press, 1955), 146. See also E. Gordon Gee and David J. Sperry, *Education Law and the Public Schools* (Boston: Allyn and Bacon, 1978), section B–1.

Although the laws frequently specify in some detail the powers as well as the responsibilities of boards, questions of interpretation continue to arise. Whether a power is "necessarily implied" or is "essential" has had to be settled repeatedly in the state courts. The actions of local boards have been classified by the courts as well as by special analysts of school law as acts that are mandatory and as acts that are discretionary. The day-to-day exercise of local control can be examined in terms of these two classes of board action, although, as will be discussed later, classifying an action is sometimes difficult.[7]

Mandatory Powers and Obligations

With specific powers to act go obligations and responsibilities. Not only do boards have the power to build school buildings, to staff them with teachers, and to determine which students will be enrolled at which building; they also have the obligation to meet building construction codes, to employ legally certified teachers, and to abide by court decisions. Not only do local boards possess the power to enforce compulsory education laws, but they must also provide an education for all the children of their districts. Not only do school boards possess the power to transport children to school, they must also observe the safety precautions written into the pupil transportation codes of the states, as well as those passed by local municipal authorities.

The laws are both general and specific. The statutes may empower the local board to make general provisions for educating the mentally handicapped but require every student to pass an examination on the federal Constitution before graduating from high school.

Boards cannot delegate to their administrative officers or to committees of their own members the authority to carry out acts which boards alone are empowered to perform. A classic example is the power to employ teachers; boards cannot delegate this power under any circumstances.[8] The board can request its administrators to make recommendations for employment and then act on those recommendations, but it cannot legally authorize a superintendent to employ teachers.

As the word *mandate* indicates, the board has no choice but to comply with the statutes of the state. When the intent of the law is clear, the board must act in accordance with it. For example, the board cannot refuse to allocate funds to support a local district's financial obligation in a state retirement system. Boards can, however, work through established legislative channels to have statutes amended, abolished, or modified.

Discretionary Powers and Obligations

Reeves defines discretionary acts of boards as "those involving the use of judgment in promoting the legal objectives of the board."[9] He goes on to say that many actions require quasi-judicial decisions on the part of boards and that probably most of the activities of school boards are discretionary rather than mandatory; the acts are "desirable" rather than prescribed by the law. A board exercises discretion when it chooses to participate in programs financed under federal auspices, when it elects to surpass minimum curriculum standards, when it votes to employ teachers who are

7. Ibid., 147.
8. Hamilton and Reutter, *Legal Aspects*, ch. 4.
9. Reeves, *School Boards*, 77.

more highly qualified than state certification standards require, or when it decides to add a new member to the district's central office staff.

School boards involved in school desegregation litigation exercise discretionary authority when they choose to appeal rulings of the courts. Despite the relatively small number of school desegregation cases where the findings of liability or scope of remedy have been overturned, local boards generally avail themselves of every appellate opportunity. They do so most often within a prevailing climate of public support. School boards can take alternative discretionary action through a consent decree. Hooker advocates the increased use of this option, which would reduce costs to local districts and remove the cloud of protracted litigation from the community.[10]

Many mandatory actions taken by boards allow for discretionary choices in their compliance with the law. For example, a board may be required by law to keep the schools open and in session 180 days each year but has the right to determine when the schools are to open and to close as well as in some instances which days of the year are to be observed as school holidays. Similarly, the law directs most local boards to employ only certified teachers, but the board controls the assignment of teachers within the district. The board can assign its best teachers to the "toughest" schools in the district, or it can assign its weakest teachers to the problem schools. It cannot, however, choose to employ noncertified teachers in defiance of the law.

Ethical Responsibilities

School board members do not live in political or social vacuums. As citizens of local communities, board members assume substantial obligations to act in the best interests of their local constituencies. In each school district modes of acceptable school board behavior develop, and each new school board member more or less fits into these patterns. Moreover, there are well developed patterns of board member socialization often involving superintendents of schools, incumbent board members, and school board associations.[11]

Sometimes the public schools become the political arena for reconciling many social differences. Browder has described the behavior of a suburban superintendent who tried to influence the outcomes of a school board election.[12] Commuterville (a fictional community) was a harshly factionalized community. When the progressive leadership of the board was threatened by a conservative group, the superintendent decided to intervene. The behavior of individuals and groups prior to and following this election displays the sweep of community sentiment regarding school affairs. The progressive majority grew comfortable in its control of the board. It proposed a 20 percent increase in the annual budget which aroused the passions of conservatives. A painful battle ensued with the progressives managing to save two of three contested school board seats.

While readers may debate the propriety of a superintendent's political activity, the events in Commuterville reflect the value structures of hundreds of similar Amer-

10. For an insightful discussion of the consent decree see Clifford P. Hooker, "Issues in School Desegregation Litigation" In *The Courts and Education,* Seventy-seventh Yearbook of the National Society for the Study of Education, Part 1, ed. Clifford P. Hooker (Chicago: University of Chicago Press, 1978), 114–15.
11. For a recent analysis of school board member socialization see Luvern L. Cunningham and Joseph T. Hentges *The American School Superintendency: A Summary Report 1982,* (Arlington, Va.: American Association of School Administrators, 1982), 59–61.
12. Lesley H. Browder, Jr., "A Suburban School Superintendent Plays Politics," in *The Politics of Education,* ed. Michael W. Kirst (Berkeley, Calif.: McCutchan, 1970), 191–212.

ican communities. The travail surrounding this school board reveals the depth of feeling that school board members and candidates bring to school board service.

There are numerous situations in which school boards have been replaced due to widespread reactions of citizens. Some cases have resulted in recall elections and reappointments. In 1961 the New York City Board of Education was replaced. The governor and the legislature of the state of New York removed the entire board and asked the mayor of New York City to appoint a new one. The freshly appointed board assumed its responsibilities and was confronted almost immediately with serious problems on several fronts. The civil rights issues, teacher strikes, and eventually decentralization questions led to further membership changes in the board in 1969. Citizens have registered their dissatisfaction in smaller districts too. In 1977 the seven-member La Crosse, Wisconsin, school board was recalled primarily because of public concern about permissiveness and lack of discipline in the schools.[13]

There are local, regional, state, and national associations for school board members. Most of these have codes of ethics which board members tend to observe. To the extent that these are shared as acceptable guides to board member actions, the codes tend to standardize the behaviors of board members. Thus the codes serve as sanctions. The state associations frequently develop handbooks which include the codes and also provide useful information about schools, school laws, and the duties and responsibilities of board members; they are designed to help board members learn and perform their jobs.[14] The codes as a rule address the following topics: relationships with other board members, relationships with the superintendent and members of the school staff, responsibilities of board members to their communities, and the board members' sense of responsibility to children.[15]

The constitutions and statutes of the various states, the expectations of local communities for school board member performance, the shared standards of "good" performance as exhibited in codes of ethics of the school board associations are determinants of what board members do. Obviously though, these are only a few of the forces that influence what board members do.

The essence of all government is decision making; the decisions made by school boards are the fiber of local school government. From the standpoint of public interest, the public must be concerned with maximizing "good" decisions and minimizing "bad" decisions. Board members are powerful because they can apply sanctions that will have consequences for future generations as well as the present one: they exercise enormous influence through their discretionary powers as the following case illustrates.

In 1974 the Detroit Central Board of Education established a residency policy for professional employees. The decision affected nearly 4,000 persons. The action required teachers, administrators, and other professional employees to live within the

---

13. Barbara Parker, "This School Board Learned Seven Lessons in Community Relations—After It Got Sacked," *The American School Board Journal* 165 (July 1978): 30–32.
14. For a recent handbook see Craig Gifford, *Boardsmanship* (Columbus, Oh.: Ohio School Boards Association, 1978). For other discussions of board member skills see Thomas A. Shannon, "Look Here for the Skills You Need to Survive as a School Board Member," *American School Board Journal*, 169, (April 1982): 35, 40, and George Donoian, "Recognize and Acquire These Attributes of a Good School Board Member," *American School Board Journal* 168, (February 1981): 34.
15. The codes are expected to assist with board member socialization, although much socialization into the role apparently occurs well in advance of incumbency. Peter J. Cistone, "The Socialization of School Board Members," *Educational Administration Quarterly* 13 (Spring 1977): 19–33. For more on school board ideology read Raphael O. Nystrand and Luvern L. Cunningham, *The Dynamics of Local School Control* (ERIC Document Reproduction Service, 1974).

boundaries of the Detroit Public School District. The board policy was patterned after earlier Detroit Common Council residency decisions applied to policemen and firemen. The school board policy was immediately challenged by the Detroit Federation of Teachers. The Michigan Supreme Court determined that residency was a "negotiable item," thereby returning the ultimate decision to the public employee bargaining table. Thus, the discretionary power of the Detroit Central Board of Education was exercised in regard to where employees live and pay their taxes. The arguments advanced in support of the residency ruling were that professional employees should live in the environment where they perform their professional services in order to understand fully the problems of children and youth there. Similarly, it was argued that teachers should live in the district so that their tax dollars would benefit Detroit children. Opponents argued that a residency requirement was an infringement on individual rights.

Board members have been cajoled, threatened, harassed, and sometimes applauded for their stances on emotion-laden issues. Public sentiment has often been strong enough to threaten recall elections, mobilize opposition slates, or otherwise effect the outcome of school board elections. Busing, the neighborhood school, prayer in the school, reading methods, and pupil safety are some of the issues capable of arousing widespread interest in who school board members are and how they have been chosen.

Selection of School Board Members

Appointive Systems

People now serving on boards are either appointed or elected to membership. In the American School Board Journal-Virginia Tech Survey, forty-nine percent of the 4,200 board members who responded came from medium-sized school systems (those that enroll from 1,000 to 5,000 pupils). Of that percentage, only 6.3 percent are appointed to their boards.[16] There are some regional differences, however. Appointive systems are more common in the South than in the Northeast, North Central region, and West.

In 1961 when the New York City Board was removed, the governor and legislature of the state of New York took an active part in the removal. The governor called a special one-day session of the New York legislature to consider mounting unrest and dissatisfaction with the New York Public Schools and the school board of that city. The legislature forced the removal of the New York board and instructed the mayor of New York City to appoint a new nine-member board from a slate of 18 names selected by a special eleven-member committee appointed by the legislature itself.[17]

Chicago has an appointed school board. The present system of selecting board members in Chicago emerged from a set of conditions not unlike those leading to the 1961 change in New York City. Chicago's school board was under fire in the early 1940s, and the mayor of Chicago asked a committee of the presidents of several Chicago colleges and universities to recommend a better system of school board con-

---

16. Kenneth E. Underwood, Jim C. Fortune, and James A. Meyer, "Fifth Annual Survey of School Board Members," *The American School Board Journal,* 170 (January 1983): 22–26 and Kenneth E. Underwood, Wayne P. Thomas, and Mark Pace, "Your Portrait: Who You Are, Region by Region," *The American School Board Journal* 168 (January 1981): 21–25.
17. Terry Ferrer. "Commissioner Allen of the Empire State," *Saturday Review,* 16 (September 1961): 66–67.

trol for the city. The special committee rejected recommending an elective system in favor of continuing the appointive system with some marked changes. To rid the existing board selection system of blatant political overtones, the committee recommended that the mayor appoint members to the board of education from a list of names presented to him by a special commission on school board nominations. The special commission was to be created by the mayor and be composed of representatives of organizations reflecting the disparate social interests of the city. The representatives to the commission were not to exceed fifteen in number and were to be selected by the organizations themselves. Labor, the professions, welfare, education, business, and parents were to be represented through organizational representatives. The system was adopted. Each year the commission presents names, usually twice as many names as there are vacancies, to the mayor, who in turn makes appointments from this list.

Among the nation's larger school districts various appointment schemes operate. The National School Boards Association surveyed the fifty-one largest districts in 1973–1974 on school board composition and practices. Ten of these districts had appointed school boards. Appointments were made in four cases by the mayor, in two cases by the mayor with council approval, and in one case by the judge of the court of common pleas. Two other appointment procedures were found: appointment by city councils in two cases and an appointment by the presidents of New York City boroughs in another case.[18] Appointment is often used to fill school board vacancies even where board members are regularly elected. Detroit, San Francisco, and St. Louis are examples of cities where mayors make such appointments and as a consequence exercise substantial influence over school affairs.

Citizens, concerned with educational programs, have shifted attention in recent years to the structure of educational government in many large cities. The methods of selecting board members was the subject of debate among *ad hoc*, as well as established, local citizen groups. Methods were also reviewed within state legislative chambers. New York City's shift to an appointed board is one example of action taken following a study of selection methods. Kansas City remodeled its methods of electing school board members in 1969 allowing for at-large election of a few members and territorial or area representation for others. Seattle, Omaha, Milwaukee, and Boston are other city districts where changes in the size and/or methods of selection of boards have occurred in recent years.

The Michigan legislature mandated several changes in Detroit in 1969 including an enlarged Central Board of Education, decentralization of the district, and the establishment of new regional boards. But in 1982 the eight regional boards were discarded in favor of a single central board of eleven members, four of whom are elected at large and seven of whom represent voting districts.[19]

These changes (reduction in size and movement toward regional representation) are contradictory in part to Tyack's observation about the histories of boards in large cities. He documented the trend toward smaller size and away from ward membership from 1893 through 1923 and concluded that "The campaign to centralize control of urban schools in small boards succeeded for the most part."[20]

18. Survey of Public Education in the Nation's Big City School Districts (Washington, D.C.: National School Boards Association, 1975), 8.
19. Senate Bill No. 635, 75th Legislature, State of Michigan, Regular Session, 1969.
20. David B. Tyack, "Governance and Goals: Historical Perspectives on Public Education," in *Communities and Their Schools*, Don Davies, ed. (New York: McGraw-Hill, 1981), 20.

The changes in Detroit and Seattle were made by state legislatures. In San Francisco, on the other hand, a change in the method of choosing board members was made through a public initiative. A small citizens group obtained more than 45,000 signatures on a petition requesting that a vote on the appointive system be brought before the people. Voters were asked to vote simultaneously on two propositions in 1969. The first was a test of whether there should be an elected board leaving details of at large or area representation to the San Francisco Board of Supervisors. The second called for an elected board and area representation with the areas designated in the call for the vote. Voters approved the first proposal by a narrow margin and soundly defeated the second. The outcome demonstrated how emotional the question of boundary designations had become as well as the difficulty encountered when such proposals are brought to a vote of the people.

Within states there are variations in selection procedures just as there are differences among states in those practices. While most boards in New York are elected, they are appointed in Buffalo and New York City. In Indiana more board members were appointed than elected until Indiana's extensive school district reorganization took place in the 1960s. Now all board members are elected with the exception of those in Indianapolis. In contrast, Oregon elects all of its board members including those in Portland, the state's largest school district.

Elective Systems

In some states all board members are elected and in others only some board members are elected. The percentage of elected school boards in the United States remained rather constant over the years. Of the elected members, 86 percent are selected through nonpartisan elections.[21] Further progress in school district reorganization could lead to a decrease in the proportion of board members chosen through elective systems. However, in some states with large numbers of school districts, the elective system still seems to be the most popular method.

The election laws are certainly not uniform among the states. Within states there are specific provisions under which elections are held, and in some cases the statutes are very precise about the selection of candidates and election procedures. Primarily, board members are elected either at large, or by wards, or at town meetings.

As significant as the legal selection machinery is, the systems of nominating candidates are of equal importance. The sorting of persons that precedes the actual voting has become a highly developed procedure in many districts, less so in others. To qualify for candidacy, persons must observe legal prescriptions for getting their names on the ballot. Some candidates actively seek membership on boards, circulate petitions to have their names placed on the ballots, and campaign for the positions. Other persons are less active and must be sought out and persuaded to run for election. In these instances other people frequently carry petitions, see that the "letter of the law" is observed, and campaign for the candidates of their choice. In some communities caucus systems are used. Caucuses attempt to choose the best possible membership on school boards with the hope that school programs of the highest quality will be achieved.

Some caucuses were called for by statute. Formerly Class-II districts in Nebraska held non-partisan caucuses for the purpose of nominating two candidates for each

21. Stemnock, "Local Boards of Education."

school board position to be filled each year. But that requirement has been abandoned.[22]

Muns defined the caucus committee as "a body of representatives of a school district chosen for the purpose of canvassing, screening, and nominating the best available candidates for school board membership.[23] Muns concluded, in his study of selected counties in Illinois, that superintendents, school board members, and caucus officers considered the caucus committees to be effective and fulfilling their purposes.[24] Most school board candidates nominated by caucus procedures were eventually elected, and frequently highly qualified citizens who would not otherwise consider candidacy for school board positions were secured through the caucus committee procedures. Indeed, the quality of school board members seemed to be enhanced by the caucus system. Political party participation in school board elections appeared to be limited, but about one-sixth of the committees appeared to be controlled by a few organizations or by a few individuals in the district. Board presidents and superintendents in districts where there were no such caucus committees operating were concerned about the political implications of the caucus system.

The caucus, as a procedure, has had both critics and advocates. It has been most frequently attacked on grounds of elitism. It has been most often defended because it is said to choose individuals with ability who are dedicated to schools and the welfare of young people. There appears to be an ebb and flow of interest in the caucus practice. In the 1950s there was a growing interest in caucuses. The viability of the concept seemed to diminish in the 1960s and 1970s in the wake of an expanding commitment to openness and participation. In the future caucuses may be revived through strategies of large-scale community involvement in caucus procedures.[25]

Motives for Seeking School Board Posts

Those persons who are asked to become candidates for school boards and agree to have their names placed on the ballot have various reasons for accepting the invitation to run. Likewise, those citizens who nominate themselves have various reasons for wanting to be board members.

McCarty investigated the motives of fifty-two board members in seeking school board membership—the relationships of motives to the type of community; the relationships of motives to variables such as age, sex, economic level, occupation, religion, and education; and the effects of these motives on the operation of the board.[26] The board members were from seven communities in Illinois and Wisconsin. Fifty-four percent of the board members expressed self-oriented motivations for seeking office; they were interested in achieving personal goals or in representing special interest groups. Forty-six percent had community-oriented motives; they were interested in advancing the objectives of the school system to benefit the community gen-

22. *Reissue Revised Statutes of 1943*, (Lincoln, Neb.: Revisor of Statutes, 1981), 196.
23. Arthur C. Muns, "A Study of Caucus Committee Procedure for Nominating Candidates for Board of Education in Cook, DuPage, and Lake Counties, Illinois" (Ed.D. diss., Northwestern University, 1961), 2.
24. Ibid., 72.
25. Mark W. Hurwitz, "What Works Best: An Elected or an Appointed School Board?" *American School Board Journal* (July 1972): 23.
26. Donald J. McCarty, "Motives for Seeking School Board Membership" (Ph.D. diss., University of Chicago, 1959). For a brief description of this study and a report of major findings and conclusions, see his "School Board Membership: Why Do Citizens Serve?" *Administrator's Notebook* 8 (September 1959), No. 1.

erally. Within each of these two broad classes of motivations, more specific motives were discerned. Some saw board membership as desirable because it would lead to political advancement, offer personal prestige, or provide a means to plead the causes of special interests or to voice disapproval of the way schools were operated. Others saw school board service as an opportunity to contribute to better education, to become more knowledgeable about schools, or as a professional challenge. Boards composed of a majority of self-oriented board members were found to evidence high friction in the everyday conduct of school board business. On the other hand, boards with a majority of their membership made up of community-oriented members displayed low friction in their operations.

Similar conclusions were reached by Gross who analyzed superintendents' descriptions of board member motivations.[27] Approximately 50 percent of the superintendents in Massachusetts described motives of their board members for the study. Gross classified board members according to three motives: to perform a civic duty, to represent some group, and to gain political experience. As one would suspect, the higher the proportion of board members motivated by civic duty, the more likely the board would be to agree on matters confronting it. Similarly, when boards were made up of members predominantly representing interest groups or out to gain political experience, there was substantially less consensus on those boards. Likewise, Gross found that the composition of boards bore a direct relationship to a measure labeled "adherence to professional standards."[28] Professional standards refer to such things as boards appointing only those teachers nominated by the superintendent, helping to sell "good" education to the community, taking full responsibility for decisions, and having a clear statement of the policies under which the school system should be operated. Boards whose members were predominantly motivated by civic duty adhered more directly to professional standards than did boards composed mostly of members with other motives.

It should be noted that McCarty analyzed the statements of board members themselves and Gross summarized interviews with superintendents. The conclusions in large part agree and together contradict the general image of American school board members as altruistic public servants. Reeves for instance, while admitting that some members have selfish motives, states that "there can be no doubt that most school board members have assumed the duties of their office because of a sincere desire to render an important public service."[29] McCarty, on the other hand, concludes, "The school board, even though it is a voluntary association with presumed magnanimous purposes, attracts some people whose motives for this type of service may well be questioned."[30]

Hentges (1984) analyzed large city district board members' preferences for either a trustee or representative orientation to school board service. He found, contrary to expectation, that more than 30 percent of those board members preferred to be viewed as trustees (serving the district at large) rather than representatives of either regions or constituencies.[31]

27. Neal Gross, *Who Runs Our Schools?* (New Yrok: John Wiley and Sons, 1958), ch. 7.
28. Ibid., 87.
29. Reeves, *School Boards,* 106–8.
30. McCarty, "Motives for Seeking School Board Membership.", 163.
31. Joseph T. Hentges, "The Politics of Superintendent-School Board Linkages: A Study of Power, Participation and Control" (Ph. D. diss., Ohio State University, 1984).

Most board members receive little or no compensation for their services. Those who do generally indicate that it is not a factor in seeking board membership. Doughty found, however, that black board members felt they must be economically self-sufficient in order to have the necessary time to be effective.[32] In large cities especially, where poor people of diverse racial background are serving on school boards in larger numbers, per diems and stipends are important. Wage earners and some salaried people cannot afford to take work time for school business. Thus dollar support for serving on school boards makes it possible for broader segments of the population to participate in this form of public service.

The Men and Women Who Serve

Men continue to dominate board membership, but that pattern is changing. In 1927 Counts found only 10.2 percent of all board members to be female.[33] The number rose slightly to 12 percent in 1972 and to 32.8 percent in 1981. There was a drop to 28.2 percent, however, in 1982.

When a comparison is made between 1982 and 1981, the percentage of Hispanics on boards declined slightly; black board members dropped from 3.7 percent to 2.2 percent; and Orientals, included on the survey form for the first time in 1982, constituted .3 percent of board membership nationally. Other trends are toward youth (including 18-year-olds), higher income levels, and higher levels of education.[34]

The results of a 1978 survey of Ohio board members were generally consistent with national trends. Nearly 19 percent were women, the percentage of minorities increased by 35 percent from 1975 to 1978, and length of tenure for all board members was decreasing. Ohio board members were getting younger *and* older; that is, there was a simultaneous increase of 56 percent in the number of board members under the age of 30 and a 133 percent increase in members over the age of 60.[35]

A 1972 survey of female board members conducted by the *American School Board Journal* confirmed some earlier findings regarding female board members and yielded some new results.[36] Most female board members are between 35 and 55, serve at least five years, and are elected. Very few women are appointed. They are almost always a minority on the board, usually a minority of one. According to the survey, women are often motivated to run for boards out of a conviction that governing bodies need a female point of view. Women cite the preoccupation of male members with finance and construction and their disinterest in programs and humanistic problems. Mullins reports that women display coolness under fire, confront tough decisions, and often devote considerable time to their board responsibilities. Some women have felt discrimination. Most reflect a keen awareness of the sentiments of their constituencies.

32. James J. Doughty, "Black School Board Members and Desegregation," *Theory Into Practice 17* (February 1978); 36–37.
33. George S. Counts, *The Social Composition of Boards of Education,* Supplementary Educational Monographs, no. 33 (Chicago: University of Chicago Press, July 1927).
34. Underwood, Fortune, and Meyer, "Fifth Annual Survey of School Board Members", *The American School Board Journal* 170
35. Jerry F. Gumbert, "Survey Reveals Diversity," *Ohio School Boards Journal* 22 (August 1978); 18–20.
36. Carolyn Mullins "The Plight of the Boardwoman," *The American School Board Journal* 159 (February 1972): 27–32.

The National School Boards Association established in 1973 a Commission on the Role of Women in Education Governance.[37] The charge to this commission included a request for recommendations whereby the talents and abilities of larger numbers of women may be drawn upon and utilized more effectively in local lay control of public education. In the Commission's initial report issued early in 1974, three major points were made: (1) the talents of women are grossly underutilized in school governance; (2) attitudes widely held by both men and women are a major impediment to increasing the participation of women; and (3) women currently serving exhibit personal qualities of service comparable to, and sometimes superior to, those of men currently serving. The Commission argued that the population of men and women on school boards is grossly out of balance and that steps should be taken immediately to encourage more women to seek membership on school boards. In *A Survey of Public Education in the Nation's Big City School Districts* during 1973–1974, forty-nine of America's largest cities were included. Of the 398 board members in the 52 largest school districts, 120 (30%) were women.[38] There is also evidence that women are taking on roles as chairpersons and as leaders of state school boards associations.[39]

The social characteristics of school board members described by Counts held true for some 30 years after his study.[40] White reported that in 1958–59 occupations of board members had not changed a great deal since Counts' study. White's work indicated that two broad occupational categories accounted for more than three-fifths of the school board members in his sample.[41] One category including business owners, officials, and managers made up 34.5 percent of the board, and a second category consisting of professionals and technical service people made up 27.4 percent. Farmers ranked third, accounting for 12.4 percent of the total membership, and housewives were fourth with 7.3 percent.

Although White's and Counts's classifications are not identical, they are enough alike to permit comparisons.[42] In Counts's accounting there were more farmers on school boards than any other occupational class. White's study shows farmers in third place. The shift is undoubtedly due in part to consolidation of rural districts with concomitant abolishing of hundreds of rural boards, rather than a result of an abrupt shift away from selecting farmers as school board members. Counts found persons engaged in professional service as the second best represented occupational class ahead of proprietors; White's findings placed the proprietor group (business owners, managers, and officials) in first place ahead of professionals. Thus there appears to be some change here worth noting. And this change may in part be accounted for by what appears to be heightened interest of Chambers of Commerce and businessmen in school district operation, particularly with respect to the tax rate and school finance.

37. Marian Thompson, Commission Chairperson, Memorandum submitted to the National School Boards Association Board of Directors, March 29, 1974.
38. *Survey of Public Education in The Nation's Big City School Districts*, (Washington, D.C.: National School Boards Association), 12.
39. Laura T. Doing, "Women on School Boards: Nine Winners Tell How They Play," *The American School Board Journal* 160 (March 1973): 34–40.
40. Counts, *Social Composition of Boards of Education*, 52.
41. Alpheus L. White, *Local School Boards: Organization and Practices* (Washington, D.C.: U.S. Office of Education, Department of Health, Education and Welfare, Government Printing Office, 1962), 24.
42. White studied boards in districts with more than 1,200 pupils enrolled. Counts included districts of all sizes; more than half of his sample was made up of rural districts, hence the prominence of farmers as an occupational group in Counts's study.

White's data included responses from 4,072 districts in contrast to 1,654 districts in Counts' earlier study.[43] Nearly half the board members, 48 percent, in White's district were college graduates; the percentage of college graduates for appointed and elected members was about the same. Over three-fourths of the boards had no one with less than a high school diploma on the board. Larger districts had more members with higher levels of educational attainment than did smaller districts. Counts collected data on educational level from county, city, state, college, and university boards but omitted local district boards.[44] He found that 61 percent of the members of these four types of boards had education beyond high school; and 19 percent of the members had only elementary school educations. Although school board members have long reflected high levels of educational attainment, the levels appear to be increasing. College graduates, for example, were six times as prevalent among school board members as in the general population.[45]

In the more recent 1982 American School Board Journal-Virginia Tech Survey, Underwood and his associates reported that 63.3 percent of board members have completed four or more years of college. The largest occupational category is professional or managerial occupations (66.6%), followed by homemakers (15%), clerical sales (6.2%), retirees (5.8%), and skilled workers (4.3%).[46]

Despite a slight decrease in the number of minorities on city boards in 1982, the overall trend in recent years has been an increase. In 1978, 24 percent of the membership on urban boards was black and 5 percent was Hispanic.[47]

What about the relative freedom of board members to act independently? To what extent are board members captives of or beholden to individuals or organizations in the community? The autonomy of board members has been of considerable interest to observers of school board functioning. Some favor boards composed of free agents—well-educated, intelligent, unselfish, community oriented, farsighted individuals—who would act rationally in solving the problems and formulating the policies for local districts. Others recommend having school boards composed of representatives from or spokespeople for a broad range of community interests.

Zeigler has emphasized the historical and continuing middle-class representation on boards.[48] He argues that middle-class bias in public service is not unique. What is unique is the political isolation of middle-class board members. They are relatively free of encumbrances to other political systems. As a consequence board members fall prey to the superintedent's claim to expert knowledge and become dependent upon the superintendent's leadership.

The behavior of large city boards during the late 1960s and early 1970s tends to support Zeigler's contention.[49] Superintendents and board members were unprepared

43. White, *Local School Boards*, 18–19.
44. Counts, *Social Composition of Boards of Education*, 47.
45. White, *Local School Boards*, 18.
46. Underwood, Fortune, and Meyer, "Fifth Annual Survey of School Board Members," 22–26.
47. *Survey of Public Education in the Nation's Urban School Districts* (Washington, D.C.: National School Boards Association 1979), 86.
48. Harmon Zeigler, "Creating Responsive Schools," *Urban Review* 6 (1973): 40.
49. Studies of boards of education in Boston, Chicago, Columbus, New York, and Los Angeles were conducted during 1967–70. This research was supported through grants from the Danforth Foundation and was conducted by teams of researchers at New York University, University of Chicago, Claremont Graduate School, Harvard University, and Ohio State University. See, for example, Paul E. Peterson, *School Politics Chicago Style* (Chicago: University of Chicago Press, 1976).

for citizen demonstrations at board meetings, for example. They found it difficult to communicate and understand the sentiments of the poor and underprivileged. Some admitted, in interviews, their anxiety during such encounters. They expressed support for citizen participation publicly but were privately terrified of it; this was especially true for board members from the middle class. Community-oriented representatives on boards were able to communicate easily and sympathize with their constituents. Such board members often became heroes and were visibly inspired by the presence of delegations in attendance. The ease of such board members in their associations with "the people" compounded the uneasiness of middle-class board members who found such associations difficult.

The presence of poor people on school boards in larger numbers has produced another sort of problem, in the short run at least. Middle-class members of boards have limited ties to other centers of influence in the community. The lower-middle-class members have better linkage to their constituencies but are powerless. Thus city boards are often comprised of a politically unencumbered middle class and a powerless lower-middle class.

The absence of external ties to other sources of community power was recognized in Detroit in 1972. A new type of broadly representative citizens task force was formed to aid the Detroit Public Schools in problem solving.[50] Its membership included persons from diverse centers of political, social, and economic power. The task force served as a proxy for diverse centers of public interest and tied the school decision system more fundamentally to influential elements and the grassroots. It was connected directly with neighborhood groups and business and industrial leaders, with the mayor's office and the governor of Michigan, and with the state legislature and the superintendent of public instruction. It became a powerful third party and was able to assist in the solutions of serious financial, management, and learning problems. And it served at the behest of the Detroit central board.

As individuals, few school board members appear in the upper echelons of power in their communities. The studies of power structure reveal few school officials, superintendents, or school board members who possess reputations for unusual political influence. There are exceptions of course, mostly in small towns and rural areas. For a small number of persons, school board membership may be a form of public service that will provide entry into the community power system. For others such as former mayors Richard Lugar of Indianapolis, Joseph Alioto of San Francisco, and Governor James Rhodes of Ohio, it has been the launching point for an active political career. For most board members currently, however, school board membership marks the zenith of their political and public service careers.

In summary, school board members typically have higher than average income and educational attainment. They serve on boards that usually have from three to seven members. The term of office is likely to be three, four, or six years. They are usually nominated through the petition method and elected popularly in nonpartisan, separate elections. They must be qualified voters in order to hold office and most often represent the districts at large rather than geographical subdivisions of districts. They may receive some compensation in the form of reimbursable expenses but seldom receive a salary for services. They may be motivated to serve on a board for

50. Luvern L. Cunningham, "Third Parties As Problem Solvers," in *Communities and Their Schools*, ed. Don Davies (New York: McGraw-Hill, 1981), ch. 5.

various reasons, but they are not always public-service oriented. Personal motives often stimulate desire to be on a board.

In the past the literature about school boards was filled with descriptions of what good school board members are like and what good school board members should do. Much of what was written reflected an idealism that probably contributed to improved education. On the other hand there was less interest in or recognition of the political nature of school board service until Charters challenged social scientists several years ago to inquire into how school boards reach decisions.

Educational research has given us no faithful description—much less an explanation—of the way in which school board members reach decisions. Such descriptions must necessarily include reference to the person-to-person relationships underlying the deliberations and actions of board members, since board decisions are products of an enterprise which is essentially social. One aspect of the decision process which could bear intensive investigation is the matter of social influence. Certain members of a school board, we commonly observe, are more effective than other members in shaping and guiding the formulation of school policy. We know very little about these key people—how they attain their influence, whether or not they are aware of it, and how it affects the process of arriving at decisions. Of critical importance, also, is the question of the school administrator's influence in relation to board members. The board-administrator relationship may turn out to be the crux of understanding school board action.[51] During the more than quarter-century since Charters issued his challenge, a small number of important studies of school boards have been made. Much of the recent research has been done by political scientists, most of whom have witnessed educational politics for a relatively brief period. Their observations of school boards have occurred during an era of extreme turbulence. They see school districts as essentially closed political systems. Tyack notes that many political scientists would like to politicize local school districts to increase their responsiveness, but warns of the possible detrimental effects of such action on education.[52] Wirt and Kirst argue that a broader conceptual framework is needed for understanding boards as small political systems and one that provides for longitudinal analysis and historical perspectives.[53]

Considerable public and professional interest exists currently in the control of local education policy and decision making. One concern is the locus of control—whether at the local, state, or federal level. Another concern is who controls—professionals or lay people. Still another is the characteristics of persons or populations—race, sex, wealth, ethnicity. For example, there are almost no minority persons in key administrative decision making roles regarding finance. Most fiscal officers, comptrollers, and business managers, are white males. The preponderance of school board chairpersons, chief state school officers, superintendents of schools, union officials, state treasurers, and chairpersons of key legislative committees who participate in resource decisions are white and male. These circumstances brought criticism from women, racial and ethnic minorities, and others concerned about who participates in critical decision areas. There has been an awakening to those realities and a mobilization of effort to do something about them. Such events, recent and powerful, are having an impact on school district decision making at all levels.

51. W. W. Charters, Jr., "Beyond the Survey in School Board Research," *Educational Administration and Supervision* 41 (December 1955): 449–52.
52. Tyack, "Governance and Goals: Historical Perspectives on Public Education", 20.
53. Frederick M. Wirt and Michael W. Kirst, *Schools in Conflict* (Berkeley, Calif.: McCutchan, 1981), 130–31.

Many other new influences are affecting educational leaders. Affirmative action directives have transformed personnel decision making, ensuring better opportunities for minorities and women. Affirmative action parallels in its effect the arrival of civil service on the personnel scene several decades ago. The emergence of collective negotiations has altered the decision practices of administrators and school boards in remarkable ways. Decentralization and community control have similarly changed decision practices within education. The result is a new, often confused, pattern of decision making within local school districts and communities.

Community Political Structures and Educational Decision Making

Vidich and Bensman dealt with school politics as part of an extensive analysis of one small, rural community called Springdale.[54] The school board was the focus of attention along with the local school principal who in this instance also served as the district's chief administrator. The school board was credited as being the source of some of the community's most important decisions—decisions which were perceived to have far-reaching consequences in the community at large. The school had the largest budget in the community, which made the school the community's biggest industry.

One value of the study for school leaders is the sharpness of description and the clarity of presentation of the "real" world of decision making in small districts. It focused on the visibility of school board and administrator activity, the social composition of the school board reflecting rural dominance over village interests, role conflict experienced by the principal, and the principal's relationships with the PTA, the board, and the community. The major contribution of the study, however, was the demonstration of how community coordination was achieved through leadership. As the authors pointed out, the overlapping, duplication, and interlocking of leadership roles tended to concentrate community policy into a few hands and provided a high degree of community organization. A wide range of community activities was carried out successfully simply because a small number of individuals occupied a wide range of leadership positions.[55] Four Springdale leaders appeared in several contexts, and together they occupied a great many of the available leadership positions in Springdale.

Only a few studies have been made of power and influence within school districts. Several investigators included educational issues in their analyses of community decision making, but they examined these in the same way as other public issues. Almost all students of community power have failed to differentiate the formal organizational structures within which school decisions must be made from those in which questions such as fluoridation of the water supply, building a new airport, or changing to a city-manager form of government must be settled.

Another study of school politics was made by Goldhammer in the early 1950s.[56] A small Oregon school district was the subject for his study. He observed a board of education over a period of time, noting the formal and informal behavior of board members. He was particularly interested in how school board members were inte-

54. Arthur J. Vidich and Joseph Bensman, *Small Town in Mass Society* (Garden City, N.Y.: Doubleday, 1958). For a review of the value of community studies to the practitioner see Luvern L. Cunningham, "Community Power: Implications for Education," in *The Politics of Education,* ed. Robert S. Cahill and Stephen P. Hencley (Danville, Ill.: Interstate, 1964), ch. 2.
55. Ibid., 263.
56. Keith Goldhammer, "Community Power Structure and School Board Membership," *American School Board Journal* 130 (March 1955): 23–25.

grated into or excluded from the broader community power structure. School board membership in the district was found to be of prime concern to the community's power clique. The school board was to a large extent self-perpetuating, but its capacity to perpetuate itself was contingent upon the acceptability of school board candidates to the dominant community power structure, the general apathy of the voters to school district politics, and the ability of the power structure to sustain its supremacy in the face of challenge. The findings of Vidich and Bensman and those of Goldhammer are similar. Each study reflects the way in which school political affairs become intertwined with other community matters.

Kimbrough and his colleagues at the University of Florida have produced much of the investigative work on the study of power structures within school districts. Analyses of two Florida districts were reported in 1964, and were labeled River County and Beach County.[57] Identical methodologies were adopted in the study of power structures in the two districts. Common instruments were employed and the teams of interviews were jointly coordinated. Quite different power structures were found in the two districts: in River County a complex, competitive power structure existed whereas in Beach County a monopolistic power structure was present.

A more ambitious research effort involving 122 districts in four states (Florida, Georgia, Kentucky, and Illinois) was completed in 1968 at the University of Florida. Johns and Kimbrough analyzed fiscal policy in districts above 20,000 total population in relation to ability to support education and elasticity in demand for education.[58] They also identified factors associated with change in fiscal policy in school districts, and assessed the power system in each district in order to ascertain the relationship of selected behavioral and socioeconomic elements of power and financial effort to support education.[59] Characteristics of local power structures were determined by an adaptation of the reputational and decision analysis techniques. Some relevant findings were: (1) the power structures in low financial effort districts are more monopolistic than those in high effort districts; (2) school administrators in high financial effort districts are more politically active in resolving both educational and general community issues than the superintendents of low effort districts; (3) the tenure of board members and superintendents tends to be shorter in the competitive than in the monopolistic power structures; (4) the power structures of the low effort districts are dominated more by leaders from the economic sector than in high effort districts; (5) leadership in high effort districts is inclined to come from persons in the political category; and (6) community influentials in the low effort districts seem to produce closed social systems whereas the leaders in the high effort districts tend to produce open social systems.

Their research is unique in the sense that they have related power systems to the other significant variables such as records of support for education. Their work is a substantial step forward in the total domain of power analysis. Hopefully it will be augmented by political scientists and sociologists generally.

Crain and several associates from the National Opinion Research Center at the University of Chicago chose school desegregation decision processes as the subject

57. Ralph B. Kimbrough, *Informal County Leadership Structure and Controls Affecting Educational Policymaking*, Cooperative Research Project no. 1324 (Washington, D.C.: Office of Education, 1964).
58. Roe L. Johns and Ralph B. Kimbrough, *The Relationship of Socio-economic Factors, Educational Leadership Patterns and Elements of Community Power Structures to Local School Fiscal Policy* OE–5–10–146 (Washington D.C.: Office of Education, 1968).
59. Ibid., xiii and xiv.

of inquiry in the mid-1960s. Their focus was on structure, process, and product. Desegregation was an issue of unusual public interest, thus their findings and conclusions have substantive as well as methodological importance. Their work represented an attempt to understand more clearly how large city school boards have responded to external pressures. They examined too the relationship between characteristics of boards and the policies they produced. Symbolic and real outputs were described: for example, it is possible to adopt a racial policy which will partially satisfy civil rights leaders without actually making a large impact on the school system. They related the policies enacted by boards to the larger political culture of the cities and concluded that the school board is relatively autonomous in its decision making procedure, yet the tendency to acquiesce to community demands is determined by the overall political structure of the city.[60]

Minar approached his interests in suburban political life through the analysis of decision making within school districts.[61] A comparative study of four suburban districts was stimulated by his earlier work on school system elections and referenda.[62] The four-case comparison was based upon Easton's framework for analyzing political systems.[63] Context, political process, and policy were accepted as the three component parts of a political system. More specifically, Minar was interested in (1) the conditioning effect of social structure on the political system; (2) testing an "input-output" model of political process; (3) assuming a pluralistic rather than an elitist view of what is likely to be found in local community life; and (4) utilizing several techniques and concepts in the study of school district politics.[64] The precise focus was on variations in the style and content of the decision making process and in the division of authority to be found among school systems whose social-structural contexts differ. He distinguishes between high and low conflict districts for example and associated this distinction with variations in administrators' policymaking roles.

There are many specific findings of interest (for example, the relationship between level of urbanism and decision making style) but possibly its most useful product is a set of nine propositions for further testing. Three of these are particularly worthy of investigation: (1) a principal factor that differentiates systems appears to be the degree to which organizational skills are applied to the political process at both the demand-aggregating and decision making levels; (2) low conflict systems appear to have more "orderly," more managed, and more issue-related modes of demand aggregation and presentation; and (3) low-conflict systems grant wider decision latitude to technical-administrative personnel.[65]

The University of Oregon has a long tradition of research focused on school boards, educational decision making, and intraorganizational problems. The most recent school board research has been directed by L. Harmon Zeigler. He and his col-

---

60. For a brief account of Crain's desegregation decision-making research as well as other large city organizational studies see Robert L. Crain and David Street. "School Desegregation and School Decision-Making" *Governing Education: A Reader on Politics, Power, and Public School Policy,* ed. Alan Rosenthal (Garden City, N.Y.: Doubleday, 1969), 342–62.
61. David W. Minar, *Educational Decision-Making in Suburban Communities,* Cooperative Research Project no. 2440 (Washington, D.C.: U.S. Office of Education, 1966) 136–39.
62. David W. Minar, "Community Characteristics, Conflict, and Power Structures," in *The Politics of Education,* ed. Cahill and Hencley, 125–43.
63. David Easton, *A Framework for Political Analysis* (Englewood Cliffs, N.J.: Prentice-Hall, 1965).
64. Minar, *Educational Decision-Making,* 3–4.
65. Ibid., 133.

leagues interviewed respondents from a national sample of school districts. School board members, superintendents, and citizens were included.[66] Zeigler draws an important distinction between schools as service institutions and schools as commonweal institutions. They conclude that the record of schools is better in the service area than in the commonweal.[67] In other words, schools serve the individual interests of children and youth by providing career preparation, entry to higher education, and better lifetime earnings, better than they serve "the public good" by providing equal educational opportunity and ensuring equal access to learning resources in the school district.

Understanding the service-commonweal distinction is necessary for school board effectiveness. Affirmative action, desegregation, equity in educational finance, suspensions and expulsions are commonweal considerations. Had a commonweal perspective been more dominant in the post-World War II years, American public education may have fulfilled its commonweal and service obligations more effectively.

Zeigler and his colleagues have published their findings widely. They have observed a gradual reduction in distance between schools and the public, the continuing importance of constructive school board-superintendent relationships, and the need for broad representation among those who participate in educational decision making.[68] School politics, they emphasize, still do not qualify as democratically governed institutions. In the area of school board selections, for example, "competition is limited, sponsorship and preemptive appointments common. Challenges to the status quo are infrequent; incumbents are but rarely challenged and more rarely defeated."[69] They add that often there are no issue differences at all in an election, and when there are, they seldom concern the educational program per se. They note too that the apolitical myth remains which has traditionally characterized discussions of decisions in education.[70]

An important case study of the Chicago Board of Education appeared in 1976.[71] Peterson focused upon three major issues confronting the Chicago Board of Education in the late 1960s: desegregation, collective bargaining, and political decentralization.[72] His analysis, though emphasizing the school board, addresses the political factors that help shape Chicago educational policy. Peterson applied both bargaining and unitary decision models to case study data and discovered that each had explanatory value.[73] The behavior of the Chicago board reflected Chicago's political history and its attendant political culture. The board was composed of reform-minded and machine-oriented factions, each devoted to ideological perspectives which controlled their positions on Chicago's educational issues. The single sentiment which allowed the factions to coexist was a shared devotion to the central city.

66. L. Harmon Zeigler and M. Kent Jennings with the assistance of G. Wayne Peak, *Governing American Schools* (North Scituate, Mass.: Duxburg, 1974), 269.
67. Ibid., 243–46.
68. Ibid., 242–55.
69. Ibid., 244–45.
70. Harvey J. Tucker and L. Harmon Zeigler, "Responsiveness in Public School Districts: A Comparative Analysis of Boards of Education," *Legislative Studies Quarterly* 3, (May, 1978): 213–37. See also L. Harmon Zeigler and Harvey J. Tucker, "Who Governs American Education: One More Time," in *Communities and Their Schools*, ch. 2.
71. Peterson, *School Politics Chicago Style*.
72. Ibid., ch. 7, 8, and 9.
73. Ibid., ch. 1–6, and 13.

The reform-minded board members were devoted to rational decision making processes and citizen involvement. They believed, too, in collective bargaining and felt that school integration would in the long run serve Chicago best. The machine-oriented faction preferred a balanced budget to collective bargaining, favored present neighborhood configurations over desegregation, and supported the invoking of police power to keep black extremists in line. Each faction defended its perspectives by arguing that their positions were in the best interest of the city.[74]

There are many policy scientists who subscribe to the bargaining model. They hold that public policy is formulated through negotiations among a plurality of individuals, groups, agencies, and interests. Peterson distinguished between pluralist and ideological bargaining. Pluralist bargaining was said to occur when dominant policy makers combined an interest in maximizing votes with an interest in compromising among group demands. Ideological bargaining occurred when the dominant policy makers perceived the issues as major questions of race, social class, or regime interests.[75]

Studies of community decision making with special reference to education seldom specify with precision the linkage between external centers of power and outside centers of influence upon boards of education. Peterson's work is exceptionally thorough in that regard, especially his discussion of the role of the mayor. The mayor is characterized as a pluralist bargainer exercising influence over schools through the political machine as well as through his appointments to the school board and citizens commissions charged with the study and analysis of school problems.[76]

In the late 1960s a comparative analysis was made of the Columbus, Ohio Board of Education and the Columbus, Ohio City Council. These are two independent local governments serving essentially the same geographical area although they are not coterminous. Board members are non-partisan, serve four year terms, and are elected at large. Both bodies are the same size. School board members serve without pay; council members are paid a modest salary. Board members have longer tenure and more council members aspire to higher political office than do board members.[77]

These two policy bodies behave in quite different ways. Council members put in considerably more time than do school board members. School board members meet less often than council members and rely more heavily upon administrative leadership. Board members were more reluctant than council members to substitute their own judgment for that of the chief executive. Not only were board members more accepting of administrative direction, they were less critical of one another and persons in their employ.

Council members were found to be more open than board members. They made themselves available more frequently to their constituencies and provided more regular, publicly announced opportunities for citizens to present their grievances. Council meetings were much less formal and more given to debate than were school board meetings.

From this comparative study several important questions arise. Should board members be paid? Should they be expected to become more expert regarding edu-

74. Ibid., 251–56.
75. Ibid., 254.
76. Ibid., ch. 4.
77. These are unpublished data.

cation? Should new grievance mechanisms be formulated? Do independent governments in other cities resemble those in Columbus? Further comparative studies of this nature seem to be warranted.[78]

Studies directed toward local district politics appear to be fewer in number than was true in the 1960s and 1970s. Slackening of effort may be more a function of decline in available resources for research than diminished interest in local district politics as an area for inquiry.

Local Control and the Contemporary American Scene

Local control no longer reflects the pure localism and relative autonomy that school boards enjoyed or were thought to enjoy in the past. Moreover, local discretion is likely to become even more circumscribed in the years ahead. Still, every effort should be made to resist unnecessary centralization. Citizens must have the opportunity to participate in decisions which affect the welfare of their children.

Opponents of local boards of education recite a long list of failures as justification for discontinuing local control. They point to unequal educational opportunity as manifest in have and have-not school districts, to high dropout rates in some areas, to rejections from military service because of inability to read and write adequately, to poor job performance of high school graduates, to "soft" curriculums, to shoddy teaching, and to shabby college performance. People who oppose local boards frequently feel these bodies are composed of persons who are unable to make sound decisions and who are susceptible to the domination of the superintendent of schools. They lack faith in the system and see centralized control as the essence of good school government. Frequently opponents claim that local control is a luxury and reasons are cited to explain why a centralized system would be more efficient.

Debate about whether or not school boards will or should continue arises from time to time. Callahan in reviewing the history of school boards documents the periodic challenges to the existence of school boards and notes their sources of public and professional support.[79] Superintendents, Callahan says, have politely contended with board members for power and influence, but in the end the concept of lay authority has been sustained. The most powerful current contenders for a share in control are the teachers organizations which Callahan believes have a strong case.[80] Others would agree that lay control is not in jeopardy even though there are ideological and political bases for change.[81] Usdam believes that the viability of school boards is in doubt but maintains that " . . . the local school board will survive in some manner, shape, or form although its basic responsibilities and capabilities must be assessed more realistically."[82] He argues that if school boards were to disappear we would soon set about the task for constructing something similar to replace them. Usdan contends that, "Citizen or lay participation of one form or another in local school affairs is simply too important a part of the 'warp and woof' of America's political and educational traditions to disappear."[83]

78. That opinion is shared by Edith K. Mosher, "The School Board in the Family of Governments" in *Understanding School Boards*, 97.
79. Callahan, "The American Board of Education" in *Understanding School Boards*, 19–46.
80. Ibid., 42.
81. Nystrand and Cunningham, *The Dynamics of Local School Control*.
82. Michael D. Usdan, "The Future Viability of School Boards" in *Understanding School Boards*, 265–76.
83. Ibid., 271.

Those who believe in local boards and local control argue that the nation could ill afford to centralize educational decisions. They grant that local boards sometimes make bad decisions but hasten to add that they often make extraordinarily good decisions and that one poor centralized policy can be much more debilitating than a number of isolated poor policies. Others argue that centralized control is antithetical to the American tradition and that America's educational process to date is founded on locally controlled school systems. Proponents cite the importance of citizen interest in education and maintain that central control will dampen that interest. They also point out that centralized decision making is vulnerable to political machinations in high places.

School board members and administrators have limited experience in many emerging policy and administrative areas. To succeed they will need expert staff help, much of it from legal counsel. The spillover from court actions affects programs, supervision, personnel, pupil information systems, finance, maintenance, and school construction. Local boards will have to become disciplined in the fulfillment of their duties, and the performance of administrators will require extensive knowledge about the policy and administrative decision areas affected by the actions of the courts.[84]

The emergence of collective bargaining in education in the early 1960s produced an interesting set of initial responses. Administrators, especially superintendents, were threatened by it, as were many board members. Principals were often overlooked in the process while teachers gradually came to accept it as an avenue to better salaries and other benefits. Board members and professionals reluctantly accepted the concept and showed themselves to be clumsy, even if successful, negotiators. A consequence of bargaining has been the concentration of power in the hands of teachers organizations. Bargaining has crystallized perspectives and rigidified positions on issues and in many cases has immobilized school boards. Many labor disputes, some of which developed into strikes, have occurred. More disputes can be anticipated as enrollments decrease and resources are reduced. Inflation exaggerates the difficulties involved. At the same time, more and more issues are being placed on the bargaining table to the extent that increasing concern is expressed about protecting the public interest on basic questions of teaching and learning.

Bargaining has become a private, sheltered, almost clandestine activity. Issues on the table become the decision province of a restricted few, essentially the union and the board representatives. The bargaining process is incredibly difficult and energy-draining. The product of bargaining which eventually emerges is often accepted without extensive board scrutiny and participation. With more and more issues on the table and growing difficulties in achieving resolutions, it is inevitable that more and more educational policy will be decided by a very few persons. A bargained agreement becomes almost sacrosanct when produced. It is the result of intensive work behind closed doors, essentially uninformed by public opinion. Citizens are seldom well informed about what issues are being bargained and what progress is being made. And the eventual agreement becomes unassailable as far as many clients of the school are concerned.

The expansion of strikes in the public education sector is likely to provoke a harsh public reaction. The sentiments underlying such reaction will be complex, reflecting discontent with the performance of schools, school closures, and the financial burden

84. Raphael O. Nystrand and W. Frederick Staub, "The Courts as Educational Policy Makers" in *The Courts and Education.* See also Luvern L. Cunningham, "Judicial Mandate and Educational Policy," *Cross Reference* (January-February 1978): 40–55.

imposed by growing school budgets. But the strongest reactions may be to the clumsiness and the clandestine nature of bargaining itself. Board members, school administrators, and labor leaders need to examine negotiating practices and procedures with a view toward making them as public as possible. One approach may be to include a third party in the process.[85] Teachers and other professionals, as Moskow and McLennan point out, in the past had the support of many community groups in their requests for improved salaries and benefits. With the arrival of "teacher power," teachers now often find community groups against them.[86]

The schools are either the beneficiaries or the victims, depending upon one's perspective, of advancing internal and external pluralism.[87] For example, in school systems with strong professional unions or associations there are at least two contending and often contentious authority systems. One is the formal, legal, hierarchial system. It is constitutional and statutory in its origins, reasonably well-known, and provides the framework within which school board members and administrators conduct their affairs. The second is the union or association authority system headed by visible, powerful individuals. Albert Shanker in New York City and John Elliott in Detroit are heads of locals of the American Federation of Teachers. Each is at least as well-known as the superintendents of schools in those cities. Teachers in those and similar systems divide their loyalties between the union heads and the superintendents. Educational changes worthy of note can occur only if supported by both authority systems.

Board members and administrators are facing unusually difficult policy problems. They will have to focus on the present and future simultaneously. Day-to-day leadership has become so demanding that little time or energy is left for looking ahead. A promising method for blending current leadership needs with the intelligent appraisal of future issues is the "decision seminar."[88] The seminar is a device for dispassionate, intensive examination of difficult present and emerging issues confronting school systems. It is designed to combine broad sources of data relevant to issues and to do so in a specially designed decision environment. The seminar permits within-system data to be examined concurrently with significant nonsystem data. It allows for administrators or board members to examine transcendent problems that have implications for individual sectors of administrative or policy responsibility.

Board members are occupied increasingly with issues that are only remotely related to classrooms. These issues are often adult issues, not issues concerning children and youth. In Detroit and Cincinnati boards of education invested hundreds of hours in debate over employee "residency." Philadelphia debated limousines for board members. In dozens of other districts energy was consumed in bickering and in fight-

---

85. Harry H. Wellington and Ralph K. Winter, Jr., *The Unions and the Cities* (Washington, D.C.: The Brookings Institution, 1971), 150–53. See also Sumner M. Roson, "Public Service Unions and Public Service" in *Improving the Quality of Urban Management* eds. Willis D. Hawley and David Rogers (Beverly Hills, Calif.: Sage 1974), 580–81.

86. Michael H. Moskow and Kenneth McLennan, "Teacher Negotiations and Decentralization," in *Community Control of Schools*, ed. Henry M. Levin (Washington, D.C.: The Brookings Institution, 1970), 215.

87. Teachers went out on strike in St. Louis in the autumn of 1983 but returned after four days. Extreme community pressure arose when the strike threatened to stall desegregation. The board, with community support, voted to fire every teacher who failed to return to duty.

88. For a concise summary of the decision seminar concept see Philip M. Burgess and Larry L. Slonaker, *The Decision Seminar: A Strategy for Problem-solving* (Columbus, Oh.: Mershon Center of the Ohio State University, 1978). A comprehensive description is available in Harold D. Lasswell, *A Pre-View of Policy Sciences* (New York: American Elsevier, 1971), 144–59.

ing over inconsequential philosophical differences among board members. The choice of board chairperson or president frequently produces turmoil. That issue is obviously important for the outcome may determine the future course of board policy. Boards would be well advised to examine their own performance and employ reasoned criteria to ensure that the interests of their clients are properly served.

Summary and Future Prospects

As indicated in the 1982 AASA survey of the superintendency, tensions between school boards and superintendents are likely to escalate.[89] The demands upon boards and their chief executives will grow as a consequence of strengthened interest in education. Conflict is probable, especially in regard to educational purposes and priorities. The relationships between superintendents and school boards deserve continued attention in both research and practice. The tension between lay and professional concerns is most visible at the school board level where expectations of citizens blend with professional judgments. Reconciliations of differences about the goals, objectives, and theories of education must be achieved. The ideological and pluralistic bargaining that Peterson has described manifests itself in these exchanges as well as within boards themselves. It is there that the difficult financial and managerial questions must be resolved.[90]

Until these questions are resolved, school board service will continue to be marked by stress and discord. Successful performance of the board member role will be more difficult in the future than in the past due to the increasing complexity of the policy problems that will be encountered as well as the diversity of local community interests. Policy issues will require more study and analysis on the part of school board members and superintendents. In fact, boards may need to develop clear policies to govern their own policy development. Stated differently, board members and administrators need to probe the basic dilemmas of their governance and management practices and locate more effective ways to approach policy problems in the future.

In recognition of the complexity of school board service three proposals are suggested: (1) persons elected or appointed to school boards should have an extended period for learning about their new responsibilities before formally assuming their duties; (2) boards should adopt a formal system for monitoring events and changes occurring in their districts' external environments and set aside time to formally interpret these events and changes; and (3) boards should examine in detail the scope of their responsibilities to discover those activities that are most central to the educational mission of their districts.

Boyd has argued that the record of governance and management of local school districts has been relatively strong.[91] Nevertheless, stronger board and administrative leadership will be necessary as society and its institutions move into the post-industrial era. Paige, following a comprehensive analysis of American political leadership, argues that policymakers and administrative personnel require intensive, planned political leadership experiences.[92] Such experiences should reflect five basic principles: (1) the need for omni-relevant understanding; (2) value clarification; (3) an understanding of

89. Cunningham and Hentges, *The American School Superintendency.*
90. Peterson, *School Politics Chicago Style.*
91. William L. Boyd, "The Public, The Professionals, and Educational Policy Making: Who Governs?" *Teachers College Record,* 77 (May 1976): 539–77.
92. Glenn D. Paige, *The Scientific Study of Political Leadership* (New York: Free Press, 1977), 189–207.

people; (4) development of the capacity for innovation; and (5) engagement in practical problem solving efforts.[93] "Transforming leadership," is a concept described in detail by James MacGregor Burns.[94] Burns emphasizes the leader's need to enable followers to transcend daily affairs, to free themselves from a preoccupation with power, and to build upon man's need for meaning. Peters and Waterman note that leadership transformation is present in successful companies and has equal merit within other forms of enterprise.[95] Paige's five basic principles and Burns' concept of transforming leadership provide a sound basis for school board and administrator leadership development.

Leadership transformation has merit within the community as well. Yankelovich has identified four requirements for creating an informed public which blend well with transforming leadership philosophy. Those requirements are: (1) credible signals to inform the public of existing problems; (2) an incentive for paying attention, (3) analysis of issues so that leaders can understand the relationship between the technical and the moral aspects of a problem; and (4) time for people to work through their decisions. School board members and administrators can benefit from reflecting on this philosophy of leadership and its relationship to creating an informed public.[96]

School boards and superintendents comprise school district governance and management systems. Board members and their chief executives need to understand the flow of legislative-executive activity which is the heart of governance and management responsibility. Often the work of school boards and superintendents has been too simply dichotomized into policy and administration. However, there is some value in preserving the general distinction between the policy responsibility for board members and administration for the professionals.

Six phases in the flow of legislative-executive activity in Florida were analyzed recently; the initiation of legislation, pre-enactment analysis, enactment, preparation for implementation, implementation, and appraisal.[97] Of particular significance was the absence of attention to "preparation for implementation." There was little understanding on the part of legislators of the administrative problems involved in the implementation of major new educational reforms. Similarly, administrators had difficulty articulating legislative intent when implementing policy at the school district level. We suspect that there are similar problems in the flow of legislative-executive activity within school districts that warrant attention.

Belief in hierarchical distributions of power, in which a small number of people at the top of a power pyramid possesses extraordinary power and influence, is now being challenged. Boulding defines decentralization as the antidote to institutional helplessness.[98] She adds that "decentralism and the associated problems of how to increase the number of decision points in the lower reaches of any system and how to increase local involvement in decision making are now important issues." Philosophies of decentralism applied to intra-institutional decision making do not fit well with philosophies

93. Ibid., 198–99.
94. James MacGregor Burns, *Leadership* (New York: Harper & Row, 1978).
95. Thomas J. Peters and Robert H. Waterman, Jr. *In Search of Excellence* (New York: Harper & Row, 1982), 81–85.
96. Daniel Yankelovich, "Information, Judgment, and Consensus." *Kettering Review,* (Summer 1983): 30–31.
97. Luvern L. Cunningham et al., *Improving Education in Florida: A Reassessment, A Summary* (Tallahassee, Fla.: Select Joint Committee on Public Schools of the Florida Legislature, 1978).
98. Elise Boulding, "Learning to Make New Futures" in *Educational Reform for a Changing Society,* ed. Louis Rubin (Boston: Allyn and Bacon, 1978), 57–74.

of centralism applied to extrainstitutional decision making. School systems must cope with the spirit as well as the facts of decentralization. There may be serious practical problems for administrators if they act on the belief that an important community power elite exists as they simultaneously endorse grassroots citizen involvement and the extension of decision points at the school attendance area and classroom levels. To whom do they listen? And how do they reconcile mixed messages when they appear?

School board members and their administrators must identify and utilize more rational approaches to governance and management than have been previously employed. Institutional needs are too important and the problems too complex for school districts to rely on traditional methods of policy preparation, enactment, and implementation. The decision seminar is a helpful policy-planning tool that incorporates substantial board member and staff development potential as well.

The American debate about control will continue. Some issues are new, but many are perennial such as the balance between lay and professional influence in educational policy. National concern about education as reflected in "A Nation at Risk" ensures sustained attention to both the substance and process of education. The National Commission on Excellence in Education reaffirmed the centrality of education to the nation's well-being and specified the roles and responsibilities of school boards in achieving education reforms.[99] The consequence of this reaffirmation of belief in education will be elevated expectations and attendance accountability for boards of education.

In 1983 voices everywhere, including President Reagan's, were speaking out on educational issues. The result of such widespread and diverse concerns was a cacophony of voices, each determined to have a say in how the schools are run. Recent matters at issue such as desegregation, finance, school closings, and teacher contracts are likely to be replaced in the late 1980s by the issues of computer literacy, compulsory lifelong learning, facility in the use of two or more languages, and global economics.

Even as this book is being written, forces are in motion to strengthen local school boards. State-wide school board development proposals are under consideration which emphasize the improvement of school board members as individuals, as well as school boards as collectivities. School boards are likely to remain as the nation's form of local school government sustaining the United States' commitment to public education.

---

99. *A Nation At Risk* (Washington, D.C.: National Commission on Excellence in Education, Department of Education, 1983).

9

The Superintendent of Schools

In most of the 16,000 operating school districts in the United States, the program is large enough to have prompted the board of education to employ a chief executive officer, usually called the superintendent of schools. This chapter focuses on the kinds, numbers, and characteristics of superintendents, the function and professional development of the position, and the role and influence of the superintendent.

Kinds and Numbers of Superintendents

While the term *superintendent,* or *superintendent of schools,* is sometimes applied to the chief state school officer, it usually denotes the chief executive officer of a board of education in an operating school district. In most states, when the term *superintendent of schools* is used without the prefix of state or county, it is the local school official who is meant.

This designation reflects the nature of school organization in the United States. Legally, education has been conceived chiefly as a function of each of the fifty states. Operationally, the legislature of each state, except Hawaii, has divided the state into school districts and created boards of education as the administrative agencies for these districts. These boards, except in those districts where small elementary schools of one or a few rooms are in operation, have employed a chief executive and delegated to that person many of the administrative functions legally assigned to the board itself.

Evolution of the Position

Two movements appear to have created the need for a superintendent of schools. The first was the reorganization of school districts. As long as school districts were organized in the early New England pattern, each district containing a single one-room school, administrative duties could be handled quite adequately by the board of education. However, when many of these districts were combined into a city-wide school district, as was done in numerous cities during the first half of the nineteenth century, management of the entire enterprise became too demanding for a board of education made up of citizens who were volunteering just part of their time to public service.[1]

This problem was accentuated by the growth of cities. Soon the one-room schools located in each ward or section of the city grew into schools of four, eight, or even sixteen rooms each. The work of the several schools in a single city needed to be coordinated. Moreover, the financial resources of the city-wide school district required allocation among the various schools of the city. Again, lay board members were beset with problems and demands that caused them to seek assistance.

Initiative in establishing the new office of superintendent was often taken by the city council. The Buffalo common council appointed a superintendent of common schools on June 9, 1837.[2] On July 31, 1837, the first agent of the public schools of Louisville was elected by the mayor and aldermen.[3] As time went on, boards of education in some states were given statutory authority to appoint superintendents; in other states, the boards proceeded to make such appointments without specific legislative authorization. By 1860 twenty-seven cities or city school districts had established the office of superintendent of schools.[4] Springfield, Philadelphia, Cleveland, Baltimore, and Detroit had to establish the position a second time before it remained, but general acceptance of the new position in city school districts seemed assured.

Establishment of the local superintendency in noncity areas did not occur until the twentieth century. For years noncity schools were rural schools, and as had been true earlier in the cities, each school district generally had a one-room, eight-grade school. Moreover, a structural plan for giving minimum supervision to these schools had evolved in the creation of the county superintendency.

In time, however, the movement to combine rural school districts into larger administrative units took hold. Utah was one of the early states to move toward large, consolidated school districts. The Utah legislature passed an optional reorganization law in 1905 and in 1915 mandated the so-called county unit plan of school district organization. Actually, there were five city school districts and thirty-five county school districts, and these forty school districts are still the operating school units in Utah. Bateman attributes this early action on school district organization to the need for high school facilities and to the quality of leadership the state was able to marshall.[5]

Two movements appeared to affect the organization of school districts outside the major cities. The first of these, already alluded to, was the acceptance of the high school as part of the common school system of the country. This was given legal expression by the Michigan Supreme Court in 1874 in the now famous Kalamazoo case.[6] Within the next five or six decades, not only city school districts but rural areas as well began to consider ways and means by which high school opportunity could be made available to all youth.

A still more recent development affecting school districts outside (and inside) the central cities has been the growth of suburbia. For several decades and particularly since World War II, areas surrounding each of our major cities have become the sites

1. Thomas M. Gilland, *The Origin and Development of the Powers and Duties of the City-School Superintendent* (Chicago: University of Chicago Press, 1935), ch. 2.
2. Theodore L. Reller, *The Development of the City Superintendency of Schools in the United States* (Philadelphia: The Author, 1935), 82.
3. Ibid.
4. Ibid.
5. E. A. Bateman, *Development of the County-Unit School District in Utah* (New York: Bureau of Publications, Teachers College, Columbia University, 1940), 92.
6. *Stuart* v. *School District No. 1 of Kalamazoo,* 30 Michigan 69 (1874).

for suburban communities. In many instances, the possibility of securing "good" schools for their children has been a major motivation for people moving to these suburban communities. Scarsdale, Shaker Heights, and New Trier are three such communities with outstanding school systems.

In rural, consolidated school districts and in most of the newly formed suburban school districts, the board of education has found it desirable to employ a local superintendent of schools. The concept of the position in these more recent organizations has been influenced by the concepts which first developed in the city superintendency.

Four stages can be identified in the development of the superintendency. To begin with, the office was essentially a clerical one; board members needed someone to relieve them of minor details. Frequently, the first superintendents were not trained in the field of education. As educational programs became more complex, board members began to rely more on their superintendents for assistance with educational problems. Thus, in the second stage the superintendent was chiefly an educator, often a scholar of some reputation. Tyack suggests that "superintendents in the nineteenth century conceived of this task in part as an evangelical enterprise" and that this conception "left behind a legacy of millenial optimism and an ideal of heroic leadership." [7]

With the continued growth of the educational enterprise, boards of education often felt it necessary to employ a superintendent of business as well as a superintendent of education. This frequently led to a dual administrative organization—an executive for business and an executive for education, both reporting directly to the board. Dissatisfaction with this plan plus the influence of a business culture led to the third stage in the development of the superintendency in which the superintendent became a business manager.[8] At this time, superintendents were budget builders, managers of property, school plant specialists, and directors of elections to pass tax levies and bond issues. They demonstrated business acumen, but they tended to neglect educational purposes and instructional procedures.

The emphasis on business tended to establish unitary control in most school districts. The superintendent became the chief executive for the board of education. But clearly this was not enough; the board needed professional advice on the purposes and procedures of education itself. Thus, the fourth stage, perhaps still evolving, made the superintendent the chief executive and the chief professional adviser in the school system. This concept of the superintendency will be explored further later in this chapter.[9]

Legal Definition and Status

Cunningham and Hentges identified over 14,000 superintendencies in the United States.[10] In some states the legal definition and the common usage of the term correspond. In Illinois, for instance, any school board employing four or more teachers may employ a superintendent of schools. About 1,000 of the 1,050 districts in the

---

7. David B. Tyack, " 'Pilgrim's Progress Toward a Social History of the School Superintendency, 1860–1960," *History of Education Quarterly* 16 (Fall 1976): 258.
8. For elaboration of this point see Raymond E. Callahan, *Education and the Cult of Efficiency* (Chicago: University of Chicago Press, 1962), 250.
9. For a more complete treatment of the evolution of the superintendency see Daniel E. Griffiths, *The School Superintendent* (New York: Center for Applied Research in Education, 1966).
10. Luvern L. Cunningham and Joseph T. Hentges, *The American School Superintendency, 1982: A Summary Report* (Arlington, Va.: American Association of School Administrators, 1982).

state have employed such an official. Thus, in Illinois there are legally and in common parlance about 1,000 superintendents.

In other states legal definition and common usage of the term are at considerable variance. Until recently in Ohio, for example, legally the term superintendent was reserved for the chief executive officer in city and village school districts, of which there were over 200. Only recently was the so-called executive head of the "local" school district given the legal title *superintendent.* This change in the law confirmed actual practice and thus increased the number of superintendents in Ohio to over 600.

Other titles are still used in some states. For instance, in New York and Wisconsin, the chief executive of some types of school districts bears the title *supervising principal.* In these and in other cases where the officer in question serves as the chief executive for a board of education, we shall apply the more general designation, superintendent of schools.

These figures (see Table 9.1) suggest that only about 7,000 of the superintendents were members of the AASA. There were an additional 7,000 superintendents, chiefly in districts with small enrollments, who were not members of AASA.

Legally, the superintendent of schools seems to have an ambiguous role. There is, to begin with, the question of whether the superintendent is an officer or an employee. An officer, in the reasoning of the courts, usually meets a number of the following criteria: has an official designation, receives salary fixed by law, is usually elected, has duties of a continuing nature, serves in a position created by constitutional or statutory authority; the incumbent is required to take an oath or give a bond, and the position carries with it independence of a superior power other than the law.

Criteria such as these, as applied to the superintendent of schools, have been interpreted differently by the courts of the various states. Gee and Sperry examined the legal status of the superintendent and came to the following conclusion:

> The only generalization that we can reach after careful study of many state laws is that the statutory protection of the job tends to be minimal, with employment conditions dictated primarily by contractual agreement negotiated between the board and

TABLE 9.1

Membership of the American Association of School Administrators

The American Association of School Administrators reported the composition of its membership, as of December 31, 1982, as follows:

Superintendents and deputies	7,623
Assistant superintendents	1,579
Directors and central office staff	1,544
School level staff and principals	1,022
State personnel	149
College personnel	700
Association personnel	209
Federal personnel	15
Others (many retired)	2,939
Institutions	496
Total	16,276[11]

11. "AASA, Membership-Financial Information," *The School Administrator* 40 (March 1983).

the superintendent. Thus, the superintendent who by law may have the right to exercise a good deal of initiative may in fact not be able to survive if the board is determined to restrict or scrutinize his/her every move. Conversely, the superintendent who has little or no statutory authority ascribed to his/her position directly may exercise great liberty and initiative if the board is willing to place faith and trust in the superintendent's judgment and give sustained approval to the administrator's ideas, suggestions, and actions. [12]

The Supreme Court of Kentucky dealt with the same issue and declared that the superintendent was an employee and not an officer. Part of the language of the court appears below:

> The difficulties experienced in defining "officers" are attributable to the court's determination to extend the term beyond the officers named in the constitution. The misgivings expressed in 1896 by Judge Guffy's dissenting opinion in the City of Louisville v. Wilson, supra, proved to be well founded. The term became a creature of the court, not of the constitution itself, resulting in an era of ambiguity and evasion. In the circumstances, a re-examination and reconsideration of the subject are well within the legitimate scope of the judicial process, and we have concluded that the meaning of the word "officers" as it is used in the constitution, Paragraphs 161, 235, and 246 should be restricted to the officers directly named and designated in the text of the constitution. [13]

We are inclined to agree with the Supreme Court of Kentucky that the superintendent is logically an employee, but not all state supreme courts have as yet made such a reassessment.

Another major question having to do with the legal status of the position pertains to the superintendent's official relationship with the board of education. The statutes of almost one-half of the states declare that the superintendent of schools is the executive officer of the board of education. In Illinois, for example, the board of education has power

> . . . to employ a superintendent who shall have charge of the administration of the schools under the direction of the board of education. In addition to the administrative duties, the superintendent shall make recommendations to the board concerning the budget, building plans, the location of sites, the selection of teachers and other employees, the selection of textbooks, instructional material, and courses of study. The superintendent shall keep or cause to be kept the records and accounts as directed and required by the board, aid in making reports required by the board, and perform such other duties as the board may delegate to him. [14]

The fact that school codes in only about half of the states contain language defining the relationship between the board of education and the superintendent is further evidence of the ambiguity of the position. To be sure, individual boards in some of these states have established their own policies and procedures in which the role of the superintendent is given clarification, but there is still considerable indeterminacy about the legal status of the office.

---

12. E. Gordon Gee and David J. Sperry, *Education Law and the Public Schools: A Compendium* (Boston: Allyn and Bacon, 1978), A-19 and A-20.
13. *Board of Education* v. *DeWeese*, 343 S.W. (2d) 598 (Ky. 1961).
14. *Illinois School Code*, 10–21.4.

We have restricted our discussion of the superintendent of schools to the executive employed by a board of education in an operating school district. The evolution of the position in something over a century has been noted. We found considerable variation in titles applied to the position and great variation in the size of school systems employing superintendents. Despite the general acceptance of the position and its professional development, we saw that there remains considerable legal ambiguity pertaining to it.

Characteristics of Superintendents

In 1960 Griffiths completed a study for the American Association of School Administrators in which he described the superintendents as of that time.[15] Superintendents in school districts of 2,500 and above in total population were nearly all men; there was a wide range in age when they assumed their first superintendency with the median age being 35; their average tenure in position was about eight years; salaries varied greatly by population of district, but the average was about $12,000. At the undergraduate level superintendents had strong backgrounds in liberal arts, while at the graduate level their preparation was concentrated in education and educational administration. Most commonly, superintendents had had prior experience as teachers and principals. As districts increased in population, prior experience as a staff member in the central office also became common.

More recently, Cunningham and Hentges directed a study, again for AASA, of the school superintendency, and their findings are shown in Table 9.2. They found that

TABLE 9.2

Summary of Selected Characteristics of the American School Superintendent, 1982

Characteristic	Weighted Mean
I. Age factors	
1. Chronological age	48.0
2. Entry age-first education position	23.9
3. Entry age-first administrative position	30.4
4. Entry age-first superintendency	35.2
II. Professional experience	
5. Years as classroom teacher only	8.8
6. Years as principal only	5.8
7. Years central office only	1.1
8. Years teacher and principal	37.2
9. Years teacher, principal, and central office	30.2
III. Professional preparation	
10. Percentage bachelor's degree only	1.1
11. Percentage masters degree only	48.0
12. Percentage specialist only, 6th year	17.1
13. Percentage doctorate or more	33.4

SOURCE: Luvern L. Cunningham and Joseph T. Hentges, *The American School Superintendency, 1982: A Summary Report* (Washington D.C.: American Association of School Administrators, 1982).

15. American Association of School Administrators, *Profile of the School Superintendent* (Washington, D.C.: The Association, 1960).

the total population of superintendents was 14,260. They divided the population into four categories according to pupils enrolled in the districts where superintendents were employed and sampled each of these population categories. Thus, there were 189 superintendents in Group A, districts with pupil enrollments over 25,000, and all of these superintendents were included in the study. In Group B, districts with 3,000 to 24,999 pupil enrollment, there were 3,360 superintendents and 20.8 percent of these were sampled. In group C, districts with 300 to 2,999 pupil enrollment, there were 8,040 superintendents and 11.1 percent of these were sampled. In Group D, districts with less than 300 pupils enrolled, there were 2,671 superintendents and 18.7 percent of these were sampled. A questionnaire was sent to the study population of 2,342 superintendents. Responses from superintendents varied somewhat in terms of size of school districts. Thus, 59.8 percent of those sampled in Group A responded, 57.7 percent of those in Group B responded, 66.5 percent of those in Group C responded, and 40.6 percent of those in Group D responded. Overall, 57.1 percent of all superintendents sampled responded. A national weighted profile, which took into account statistically the differences in sample size of the four enrollment categories and the percentage of respondents from each category, was computed from these responses. Data reported in Table 9.2 are from the national weighted profile.[16]

The superintendent of schools is typically the executive officer of a relatively small school system; over two-thirds of the superintendents in groups A, B, and C combined are located in school districts that enroll 300 to 2,999 pupils. If these figures are translated into total population, we find that most school systems are in communities with total populations of 1,500 to 15,000 persons. Additional results of their study showed that most superintendents were male, from a rural or small town background, dedicated to the job, and middle-aged. The weighted mean age was 48 years.

Table 10, also adapted from the Cunningham-Hentges study, reports how superintendents ranked a number of educational issues. Many of the responses in Table 9.3 reveal the relentless day-to-day demands of the superintendency. At least one issue, the greater visibility of the superintendent, ranked eleventh, reveals the concern of superintendents with their own status. This concern is understandable when one considers the criticism currently directed at schools and school officials.

Concept of the Position

While the superintendency in American education began in the nineteenth century, attempts to professionalize the position have been most prevalent during the twentieth century. At least four movements have had major impact upon the central concept of the position.

Scientific Management

The first of these influences was that of "scientific management." A major contributor to this movement was Frederick W. Taylor who published *The Principles of Scientific Management* in 1911.[17] Taylor was trained as an engineer, and he worked for the

16. Luvern L. Cunningham and Joseph T. Hentges, *The American School Superintendency, 1982, A Summary Report* (Washington, D.C.: American Association of School Administrators, 1982), 13.
17. This and other works by Taylor are collected in *Scientific Management* (New York: Harper & Row, 1947).

Midvale Steel Company in a wide variety of positions from laborer to chief engineer. He was convinced that there was much waste and inefficiency in industry, and this conviction led him to formulate his principles of management. This formulation included the time-study principle, the price-rate principle, the separation-of-planning-from-performance principle, and the scientific-methods-of-work principle.

The ideas of Taylor had influence on the superintendency through the work of Franklin Bobbitt. In 1913 Bobbitt published an article in a yearbook of the National Society for the Study of Education under the title of "Some General Principles of Management Applied to the Problems of City-School Systems." [18] Bobbitt very deliberately applied Taylor's principles to the schools. He said:

> In any organization, the directive and supervisory members must clearly define the ends toward which the organization strives. They must co-ordinate the labors of all so as to attain those ends. They must find the best methods of work, and they must enforce the use of these methods on the part of the workers. They must determine the qualifications necessary for the workers and see that each rises to the standard qualifications, if it is possible and when impossible, see that he is separated from the organization. This requires direct or indirect responsibility for the preliminary training of the workers before service, and for keeping them up to standard qualifications during service. Directors and supervisors must keep the workers supplied with detailed instructions as to the work to be done, the standards to be reached, the methods to be employed, the materials and appliances to be used. They must supply the workers with the necessary materials and appliances. . . . They must place incentives before the worker in order to stimulate desirable effort. Whatever the nature or

TABLE 9.3

Superintendents' Ranking of Issues and Challenges Facing the Superintendency, 1982

Type of Issue or Challenge	National Weighted Profile
Financing schools	1
Planning and goal setting	2
Assessing educational outcomes	3
Accountability/credibility	4
Staff and administrator evaluation	5
Administrator/board relations	6
Special education/Public Law 94-142	7
Obtaining timely and accurate information	8
Issues such as negotiations, strikes	9
Rapidly decreasing/increasing enrollments	10
Greater visibility of the superintendent	11
Personal time management	12

Source: Cunningham and Hentges, *The American School Superintendency, 1982 A Summary Report,* (Washington D.C.: American Association of School Administrators, 1982).

18. Franklin Bobbitt, "Some General Principles of Management Applied to the Problems of City-School Systems," in *The Supervision of City Schools,* Twelfth Yearbook of the National Society for the Study of Education, Part 1 (Chicago: University of Chicago Press, 1913), 7–96.

purpose of the organization if it is an effective one, these are always the directive and supervisory tasks.[19]

Callahan has analyzed with some care the impact of the scientific management movement on the theory and practice of educational administration between 1910 and 1929.[20] He doubts that superintendents of schools could have resisted the movement since the efficiency ideology was adopted wholeheartedly by school boards, the press, and the general public. Even university leaders such as Bobbitt, Cubberley, and Strayer yielded to the tide. Callahan's observations led him to suggest a thesis of the vulnerability of public school administrators.

Human Relations

The second major influence upon the superintendency evolved in some ways in response to the first. The 1930s and 1940s might be characterized as the human relations period in administration. Again there were major contributors in the larger society, and their influence was soon felt in education. The first exponent of the human relations view was Mary Parker Follett.[21] In her book *Creative Experience,* published in 1924, she reflected upon her experience with industry, government, and education and contended that the fundamental problem of any organization was the building and maintenance of dynamic, yet harmonious, human relationships.

Supplementing the philosophical position espoused by Mary Parker Follett was the empirical work of Elton Mayo and his colleagues of the Harvard Business School. From 1923 to 1932 they performed the now famous experiments at the Hawthorne plant of the Western Electric Company. That work was described in a volume by Roethlisberger and Dickson.[22] To the surprise of the investigators, the long-held assumption that wages and physical working conditions were the chief factors in employee motivation and productivity did not hold.

This finding led to more careful study. The experimenters selected six female employees and studied the factors related to their work patterns and productivity. Again, the findings were surprising. Whenever factors were changed—rest period, length of day, method of payment—even when change meant return to the original condition, productivity increased. Roethlisberger and Dickson state their major findings as follows:

> It became clear to the investigators that the limits of human collaboration are determined far more by the informal than by the formal organization of the plant. Collaboration is not wholly a matter of logical organization. It presupposes social codes, conventions, traditions, and routine or customary ways of responding to situations. Without such basic codes or conventions, effective work relations are not possible.[23]

In a recent study, Thomas Fleming[24] has shown that administration in education was influenced not only by the human relations movement in industry, but by a second

---

19. Ibid., 7–8.
20. Callahan, *Education and the Cult of Efficiency,* 246.
21. Mary Parker Follett, *Creative Experience* (New York: Longmans, Green & Co., 1924), xiii–xiv.
22. F. J. Roethlisberger and William J. Dickson, *Management and the Worker* (Cambridge, Mass: Harvard University Press, 1941).
23. Ibid., 568.
24. Thomas Fleming, "Management by Consensus: Democratic Administration and Human Relations" (Ph.D. diss. University of Oregon, 1982).

progenitor as well: the "democratic" administration movement. John Dewey was an early exponent for this position[25] and the democratic view of administration became a major theme from about 1930 until well into the 1950s.

One prominent book of this period bore the title *Democracy in School Administration*. The authors of this work referred to the Western Electric experiments and to Dewey as they developed their thesis.[26] They suggested that the basic principles of democratic administration were as follows:

1. To facilitate the continuous growth of individual and social personalities by providing all persons with opportunities to participate actively in all enterprises that concern them.
2. To recognize that leadership is a function of every individual, and to encourage the exercise of leadership by each person in accordance with his interests, needs, and abilities.
3. To provide means by which persons can plan together, share their experiences, and cooperatively evaluate their achievements.
4. To place the responsibility for making decisions that affect the individuals.
5. To achieve flexibility of organization to the end that necessary total enterprise with the group rather than with one or a few adjustments can readily be made.[27]

Structuralism

A third major influence on the American superintendency, largely a product of the 1950s and 1960s, was the concept of structuralism. Perhaps the excesses of some human relations disciples gave rise to a more structured view of organizations. An important contributor to this view, though his work was done in Germany from about 1890 to 1920, was Max Weber. Due to translation problems, Weber's ideas had little impact on English-speaking scholars or practititioners for several decades. Weber gave us the concept of bureaucracy. For him its distinctive characteristics included the following: *(a)* a clear cut division of labor to permit specialization, *(b)* positions organized into a hierarchical authority structure, *(c)* a formally established system of rules and regulations, *(d)* an impersonal orientation on the part of officials, and *(e)* career employment in the organization.[28]

March and Simon were also contributors to the structural view of administration. While both men were trained in political science, March at Yale and Simon at Chicago, they approached organizations as behavioral scientists and set forth essentially a social-psychological model. Their concepts were contained in two books, *Administrative Behavior* by Simon[29] and *Organizations*[30] by both authors. March and Simon saw organizational behavior as different from individual behavior. Human beings, they believed were "intendedly rational" but limited by their capacities and their knowledge. As such, people in organizations when making decisions make a limited search for

25. John Dewey, *Democracy and Education* (New York: Macmillan, 1916).
26. G. Robert Koopman, Alice Miel, and Paul J. Misner, *Democracy in School Administration* (New York: Appleton-Century-Crofts, 1943), 107.
27. Ibid., 3–4.
28. See H. N. Gerth and C. Wright Mills, eds. and trans., *From Max Weber: Essays in Sociology* (New York: Oxford University Press, 1946), 196–204.
29. Herbert A. Simon, *Administrative Behavior*, 2d ed. (New York: Macmillan, 1957).
30. James G. March and H. A. Simon, *Organizations* (New York: Wiley, 1958).

alternatives, and they tend to select the first satisfactory alternative that comes along. Thus, organizations do not continue to search for optimal decisions; they settle instead for "satisficing" decisions.

March and Simon also contended that the superior in an organization has the power and the tools to structure the conditions and the perceptions of subordinates. While March and Simon acknowledged the importance of rules, they suggested that most behavior in organizations is dependent more on habit, training, routine, and socialization than on rules. These men did extend the Weberian concept of organizations but in doing so organizations were regarded essentially as closed systems; little attention was paid to the environment in which organizations existed.

Most people who have dealt with superintendents and school systems over the past decade or so will realize that these organizations and their chief administrators have been deeply influenced, knowingly or unknowingly, by structural concepts. The superintendent is at the top of a formal hierarchy. Statements of policies and operating procedures become important documents. Some attempts toward specialization of staff are made. When possible, the problems of employees and patrons are placed in a universalistic context. For the most part, great autonomy for the organization, with little interference from the community, is sought. But we need not rely entirely on impressions; Anderson has supplied us with empirical data in which he found the schools of the 1960s to be organized essentially around bureaucratic concepts.[31]

Open Systems

Within the past decade or so a fourth view of administration, the open systems concept, has emerged.[32] This view stresses the interdependence between an organization and its environment. Whereas structuralism focuses largely on internal organizational arrangements, open systems recognizes the interaction through input and output between an organization and its milieu. Open systems can be viewed two ways: as political systems, as set forth by Easton, and as loosely coupled systems, as explicated by Weick.

As noted in chapter 1, Easton suggested a model for political systems.[33] While Easton probably intended his model to describe the political system at the governance level, it can also help to explain political action at the organization level, including schools and school districts, which continually interact with their environments.

Another approach to open systems (also noted in chapter 1), as set forth by Weick, is to consider them as loosely coupled organizations.[34] Weick states:

> Organizations as loosely coupled systems may not have been seen before because nobody believed in them or could afford to believe in them. It is conceivable that preoccupation with rationalized, tidy, efficient, coordinated structures has blinded many practitioners as well as researchers to some of the attractive and unexpected properties of less rationalized and less tightly related clusters of events.[35]

31. James G. Anderson, *Bureaucracy in Education* (Baltimore: Johns Hopkins University Press, 1968).
32. Roald F. Campbell, "A History of Administrative Thought" *Administrator's Notebook* 26, no. 4 (1977–78).
33. David Easton, *A Framework for Political Analysis* (Englewood Cliffs, N. J.: Prentice-Hall, 1965).
34. Karl E. Weick, "Educational Organizations as Loosely Coupled Systems" *Administrative Science Quarterly* 21 (March 1976): 1–19.
35. Ibid., 3.

Such an organization would appear to permit intrusion by forces in the environment more easily than a tightly structured organization.

While the open systems concept may not yet be fully developed, only such a view can fully describe the interaction between an organization and its environment. To be sure, the environment may be difficult to determine when elements in the organization, labor unions, for instance, combine with elements outside the organization to affect the organization.

We suspect that more superintendents still cling to a structural view of administration than an open systems view. At the same time, the realities of administration, such as interest group demands and governmental intrusions, more and more suggest that administrative behavior can be better understood through an open systems perspective than through a structural perspective. In fact, for many the concept of structuralism makes the superintendency seem untenable.

While the four views affecting the superintendency have been presented in roughly chronological order, none of these views has disappeared. Concepts springing from scientific management, human relations, and structuralism are still with us even though open systems is now affecting thought and practice. Indeed, it may be that each view has some usefulness depending upon the problem at hand. Also, while for the most part the four views originated outside of education, they quickly permeated administrative thought and practice in education. To be sure, education did have some scholars who contributed directly to administrative thought. These included J. W. Getzels who developed a social process model of administration and Andrew W. Halpin who set forth a leadership theory of administration.[36] The work of these and other scholars is evidence of the growth of knowledge in the field of educational administration over the last few decades.

Professional Development of the Superintendency

A profession can be defined as an occupational group that meets the following characteristics: renders a vital social service, possesses an esoteric body of knowledge, requires rigorous intellectual preparation, possesses considerable autonomy in its practice, and is governed by a high sense of ethics.[37] To be sure, as Becker pointed out, this is an idealized concept of a profession to which no group, in reality, quite corresponds. Even so, the growth of the superintendency toward professional status might be examined in terms of such criteria.

Preparation Programs

A major question concerning the growing professionalism of the superintendency is: have requirements for entrance to administrative programs been made more rigorous? At major universities the answer to this question appears to be yes. The work begun by the Kellogg centers in the 1950s has continued with the organization of the University Council of Educational Administration to which some fifty universities now belong. These institutions singly and in collaboration tend to set the pattern for ad-

---

36. See Jacob W. Getzels et al. *Educational Administration as a Social Process* (New York: Harper and Row, 1968) and Andrew W. Halpin, *Theory and Research in Administration* (New York: Macmillan, 1966).
37. Howard S. Becker, "The Nature of a Profession," in *Education for the Professions,* Sixty-first Yearbook, National Society for the Study of Education, Part 2 (Chicago: University of Chicago Press, 1962), ch. 2.

mission to and preparation for the superintendency. A majority of the doctorates given in educational administration are given by these universities. UCEA has also devoted considerable effort to the promotion of research and improved preparation programs in educational administration.[38]

UCEA has made a number of attempts to professionalize the field, including organizing career seminars for professors of educational administration. In 1976, for example, such a seminar, co-sponsored by the University of Virginia and UCEA, dealt with the study and practice of politics in education. These deliberations later appeared in a book edited by Mosher and Wagoner.[39] In 1977 the University of Rochester and UCEA sponsored a similar seminar devoted to the topic of "Problem Finding in Educational Administration." These deliberations were also published, under the editorship of Immegart and Boyd.[40] At both seminars participants included representatives from the basic disciplines and practicing administrators as well as professors of educational administration. Participants projected new research frameworks and considered changes in preparation programs for administrators.

Another attempt to professionalize educational administration was the establishment of a scholarly journal in 1963 and an abstracting service shortly thereafter. The first issue of *Educational Administration Quarterly* appeared in 1965 and has been published continuously since that time. *Educational Administration Abstracts* have been published since 1967.

In 1955 the American Association of School Administrators, assisted by a grant from the W. K. Kellogg Foundation, established a Committee for the Advancement of School Administration. This committee, or CASA as it was generally called, took as its first task the examination of the materials that had been developed in the various CPEA centers and attempted to interpret them for the superintendents. In *Studies in School Administration* Moore listed some 300 studies with a brief description of each.[41] CASA also prepared *Something to Steer By* in which 35 goals for the profession were set forth.[42] These goals dealt with standards of preparation, programs of in-service education, school board procedures for selecting superintendents, and some broad outlines for needed research. In 1960 a special AASA committee under the chairmanship of Hollis A. Moore, Jr., executive secretary of CASA, prepared a yearbook entitled, *Professional Administrators for America's Schools*.[43] Major sections of the yearbook dealt with the selection, preparation, and in-service education of superintendents.

After these early efforts, AASA took a further step to professionalize educational administration by creating in 1969 the National Academy for School Executives. NASE is guided by a 15-member board of directors and a relatively small headquarters staff.

38. Jack Culbertson et al., eds., *Social Science Content for Preparing Educational Leaders* (Columbus, Ohio: Charles E. Merrill, 1973), and Jack Culbertson et al., *Preparing Educational Leaders for the Seventies*, report prepared by University Council for Educational Administration for U.S. Office of Education, #8–0230, 1969.
39. Edith K. Mosher and Jennings L. Wagoner, Jr., eds., *The Changing Politics of Education* (Berkeley, Calif.: McCutchan, 1978).
40. Glenn L. Immegart and William L. Boyd, *Problem Finding in Educational Administration* (Lexington, Mass.: D.C. Heath, 1979).
41. Hollis A. Moore, Jr., *Studies in School Administration* (Washington, D.C.: American Association of School Administrators, 1957).
42. *Something to Steer By* (Washington, D.C.: American Association of School Administrators, 1958).
43. *Professional Administration for America's Schools* (Washington, D.C.: American Association of School Administrators, 1960).

Since its inception, more than 30,600 school administrators have participated in 796 NASE programs.[44]

The Superintendency as a Career

March and March have provided a sobering note about the superintendency as a career.[45] In a carefully designed study of the school superintendency in Wisconsin over a 32-year period the authors examined 1,528 individuals who held the office as superintendent in all districts having high schools. Of these persons, only four served in a superintendency for the entire period of the study. The data included 2,516 matches or superintendencies during the period of which only 353 existed continuously over the 32 years. In these 353 positions there were from 2 to 11 matches with a mean of 4.5 matches over the period. The median match or term of a superintendent in one position was four years and the median length of career in the superintendency was about seven years. Using a chance model in the analysis of their data, the authors found that superintendency careers are almost random. Two factors appeared to keep the career from being completely random: up to age 58 the promotion rate of the superintendent decreased slightly with increasing age, and school districts with larger enrollments had longer matches. Two of the conclusions drawn by the authors follow:

> . . . most of the time most superintendents are organizationally nearly indistinguishable in their behaviors, performances, abilities, and values. This is partly a consequence of the filters by which they come to the role, partly a consequence of the ambiguity of inference in educational settings, partly a consequence of the long-run stability of educational activities and organization, partly a consequence of a lifetime spent in educational institutions.[46]

> . . . the same behaviors, abilities, and values that produce successful careers at the top will, on the average, produce unsuccessful ones also; that little can be learned about how to administer schools by studying successful high-level administrators that could not be learned by studying unsuccessful ones; and that the stories we tell each other about success and failure in top management, like the stories we tell about success and failure in gambling, are in large part fictions intended to reassure us about justice and encourage the young.[47]

March and March have given us a rather accurate picture of the Wisconsin superintendency over the 32 years covered by the study. Wisconsin over much of that time, however, was a rural state with many small schools. Therefore, with respect to size, the data may be skewed. The mean enrollment in Wisconsin was 862, and 78 percent of the districts had enrollments below the mean. The results might have been somewhat different had the study been conducted in Ohio, Illinois, California, or some other state with a larger number of school districts with sizeable enrollments.

Carlson's picture of the superintendency is not quite so gloomy. While Carlson did not use the term "almost random," he did characterize the superintendency as an "open elite," meaning that superintendents come and go with some ease. Carlson also

---

44. AASA, "Annual Report, 1982," *The School Administrator* (March 1983).
45. James C. March and James G. March, "Almost Random Careers: The Wisconsin School Superintendency, 1940–1972," *Administrative Science Quarterly* 22 (September 1977): 377–409.
46. Ibid., 405.
47. Ibid., 408.

divided superintendents into two categories: career-bound and place-bound. Using Seeman's data,[48] he found that the average term of office was 4.6 years for the career-bound and 8.3 years for the place-bound. He also found that the mean years in office for his own sample of superintendents was 7.9.[49] Carlson also noted an AASA study of 859 superintendents where the mean time in office was 9.1 years.[50] In 1982, Cunningham and Hentges found that the superintendents in their sample remained in the superintendency a median of 7.6 years.[51]

Even with these possible modifications in term of office, the Wisconsin study still challenges us. While it does not represent a national sample, there are nevertheless many states with a large number of small schools. The Wisconsin data strongly suggest that selection procedures for superintendents, at the time of employment and also at the time of admission to graduate study, should be more rigorous. In addition, preparation programs for the superintendency may require considerable revision if they are to help superintendents acquire distinctive knowledge and skill.[52]

The Role of the Superintendent

Place in the Organization

In most school districts the superintendent of schools is the formally recognized chief executive. He is the most visible, most vulnerable, and potentially most influential member of the organization. There are still a few city school districts where the superintendent is coordinate with a business manager or superintendent of business, and there are still some rural districts where the school clerk, in practice if not in name, exercises a role coordinate with that of the superintendent. But for the most part the superintendent is the chief executive.

In sparsely populated school districts, as noted earlier, the superintendent may also double as high school principal and even as part-time teacher. In middle-range school districts the superintendent will ordinarily work directly with school principals and a few central office personnel. In large city school districts the superintendent may have scores and even hundreds of central office, regional, and individual school administrative subordinates. Despite these differences in size and complexity, the superintendent stands at the top of the hierarchy of the organization.

With respect to the board of education, the superintendent of schools is usually recognized as the chief executive officer. In some instances the board may turn to a business manager or a clerk as a coordinate executive in the realm of business management. But business decisions in an educational organization are finally related to the educational program which is the realm of the superintendent even in dual organizations. Hence, the pivotal nature of the superintendency in these organizations, as well as in unit organizations, is apparent.

Much of the writing on board-superintendent relationships suggests that the differentiation of function between the board and the superintendent is a very simple one: the board is to formulate policy, the superintendent is to administer it. This

48. Melvin Seeman, "Social Mobility and Administrative Behavior," *American Sociological Review* 23 (December 1958): 642.
49. Richard O. Carlson, *School Superintendents: Careers and Performance* (Columbus, Oh.: Charles E. Merrill, 1971), 140–41.
50. Ibid., 153.
51. Cunningham and Hentges, *The American School Superintendency, 1982*, 23.
52. See *Guidelines for the Preparation of School Administrators.* 2nd ed. (Washington, D.C.: AASA, 1982).

formulation has a certain gross usefulness, but upon examination it becomes apparent that most superintendents influence policy and that most boards have some voice in administration. Houle has suggested that the board and the superintendent are partners in the management of the enterprise, each with distinctive contributions to make.[53] This concept is generally more useful than strict ascription of policymaking to the board and administration to the superintendent.

To the extent that the staff of the school organization and the board of education hold different expectations for the superintendent, he or she is "caught in the middle." This is often the case in negotiations between teachers organizations and boards of education on salary and other welfare matters. While the superintendent might wish to assist each group in understanding the position and reasoning of the other, in the end the superintendent must represent management.

What Superintendents Do

Most accounts of what superintendents do are based on self-reports. There are, however, an increasing number of studies based on the actual observation of superintendents at work.

Pitner studied the everyday activities of three suburban superintendents.[54] Focusing chiefly on the superintendent as a manager of information, she raised questions about how superintendents spend their time; their role behavior as they deal with different groups; the comparability of their behaviors, abilities, and values; and the rules, strategies, and tactics they employ. Her data came from direct observation, five days for each superintendent, and from interviews with them. She found that superintendents spend about 80 percent of their time in verbal contact with others. Five types of information were processed: technical information, legal rules and regulations, past activities of the district, preferences of persons in and outside the school system, and probable reactions of different constituencies to decisions and conditions. Superintendents did differentiate their behavior with different groups, and they appeared to have considerable influence in making policy. Superintendents' activities proved to be largely desk work, phone calls, and scheduled and unscheduled meetings. In terms of tactics, superintendents were seen as interpreters of organization history, interpreters of contemporary events, managers of meaning, and managers of organizational myths or sagas.

In another study, Feilders examined in depth the activities of one urban superintendent, Robert Alioto of San Francisco.[55] Consideration was given to where he spent his time, with whom, at whose initiative, at what time, for how long, and what medium prevailed. The study focused not only on the superintendent's manifest behavior, but on his thoughts, feelings, and intentions. Drawing on techniques used by some ethnographers, Feilders shadowed the superintendent for three days per week over a ten-week period. He recorded his observations and interviews in a journal and made a time study of his activities similar to the one made by Mitzberg.[56]

53. Cyril O. Houle, "The Functions of Governing Boards in the Administration of Large Enterprises," in *Excellence in Administration: The Dynamics of Leadership*, ed. H. Thomas James (Stanford, Calif.: School of Education, Stanford University, 1962), ch. 3.
54. Nancy J. Pitner, "Descriptive Study of the Everyday Activities of Suburban School Superintendents" (Ph.D. diss., Ohio State University, 1978).
55. John F. Feilders, "Action and Reaction: The Job of an Urban Superintendent" (Ph.D. diss., Stanford University, 1978).
56. Henry Mintzberg, *The Nature of Administative Work* (New York: Harper & Row, 1973).

Some of the explicit features of the job that were discovered were: the work week of the superintendent was long; he spent most of his time in the office meeting with staff members for brief periods of time; he initiated less than half of his activities; face-to-face communication was the main medium; the discussion usually centered on issues related to personnel; the main purpose of his activities was to process information; and the superintendent's predominant role was that of spokesperson for the administration. Feilders noted some methodological limitations in his study, but his extended description and interpretation of the superintendent's activities are very revealing.

Also influenced by Mintzberg, Duignan did a structured observation study of eight superintendents in the province of Alberta.[57] He supplemented his observation notes with data collected through interviews and information provided by each superintendent on the pattern of his activities for the week prior to the observation period. He found that the superintendents averaged 8.2 hours of working time each day. This time was divided into 38 different activities, each lasting an average of about 13 minutes. Approximately one-quarter of a superintendent's daily working time was spent in unscheduled meetings and another one-quarter in scheduled meetings. The remainder of his time was spent at desk work, telephone calls, travel, evening meetings, and visits to the schools. A superintendent averaged 26 verbal contacts each day and these contacts represented about 70 percent of his working time.

> These and other findings led Duignan to conclude that the superintendent, works in a world of action where uninvited verbal encounters and externally imposed deadlines play havoc with his attempts to bring order to his work behavior. Instead of the calm and controlled practitioner who diagnoses problems and potential problems, generates alternatives and then chooses the optimum solution, one sees a more frustrated individual who is faced with an array of problems and crises of varied composition. Confronted with the myriad tasks and responsibilities of his job, the superintendent rarely finds sufficient time to analyze his problems and plan his strategies.[58]

To summarize, major studies of superintendents have concentrated on different aspects of the position. Pitner concerned herself with the nature of the information processed by the superintendents. Feilders concentrated on descriptions of manifest behavior and also attempted to get at the thoughts and feelings of the superintendent. Duignan gave particular attention to the need of the superintendent to control his time, to the ways others participated in the decision making of the superintendent, and to the relatively little time the superintendent gives to items strictly categorized as instruction.

Also suggested by these studies is the beleaguered nature of the superintendent's day. It is interesting to note that Willower and Fraser, after interviewing 50 superintendents came to the conclusion that superintendents deal with a wide range of problems, are irked by the paperwork demands of state and federal agencies, regret not being closer to the classroom, and feel the pressures of the job but are ready to do it over again.[59] Willower and Fraser also concluded "that school superintendents are not

---

57. Patrick Duignan, "Administrative Behavior of School Superintendents: A Descriptive Study," *Journal of Educational Administration* 18 (July 1980): 5–26.
58. Ibid., 25.
59. Donald J. Willower and Hugh W. Fraser, "School Superintendents and Their Work," *Administrator's Notebook* 28 (1979–80): no. 5.

quite as beleaguered as is sometimes claimed and when they are, they appear to have come to grips with it rather well, often with good humor."[60] Perhaps the term *beleaguering* is, at least in part, in the observer's eye.

In a quite different study of what superintendents do, Cuban made historical case studies of three prominent urban superintendents, Benjamin Willis of Chicago, Carl Hansen of Washington, D.C., and Harold Spears of San Francisco, all of whom served during the late 1950s and for most of the 1960s.[61] In analyzing his data, Cuban derived four concepts of the superintendency: the teacher-scholar, the negotiator-statesman, the corporate administrator, and the rational school chief. In characterizing his three superintendents, Willis was seen as a rational school chief and corporate administrator, Hansen was seen as a rational school chief and teacher-scholar, and Spears was seen as a rational school chief and negotiator-statesman. Common to all three superintendents was the designation rational school chief, but each person combined with that approach a unique approach of his own. Cuban then asked why his three superintendents exhibited the approaches described. His explanation included three factors: a historical residue of beliefs and practices, shared by the three men; individual socialization within the school enterprise as a teacher and administrator, also shared by the three men; and conflicting organizational role demands, again largely shared by the three men. It also is significant to note that the role common to all three superintendents, the rational school chief, was very much a reflection of the structural approach to administration, characteristic of both administrative thought and practice during the time of tenure of these superintendents.

Administration and Leadership

Another significant area of study of the role of the superintendent concerns the extent to which the superintendent attempts to maintain the organization or to change it. Lipham contends that in this distinction lies the difference between administration and leadership.[62] To keep an organization moving in its customary direction, he suggests, is administration; to change the goals or procedures in the organization is leadership. This distinction does not prohibit the administrator from being a leader, but it does suggest that, for the most part, administrators attempt to maintain their organizations.

The role of the administrator as a maintainer of the organization is given further support in the Hemphill study.[63] The principals who were strong in analyzing situations received negative ratings from their superintendents and teachers. One gets the impression from these data that superintendents and teachers cherish principals who "keep the lid on," who do not have too many "fool notions," and who keep things running smoothly.

It might seem that most organizations cannot stand up under frequent and extensive attempts to change goals or procedures. At the same time, there are periods in the life of organizations when new goals and new procedures are direly needed. Thus, when organizations become ripe for change an administrator who is also a leader should be sought. After a period of innovation, an administrator who is strong on consolidation and short on innovation may then be needed.

60. Ibid.
61. Larry Cuban, *Urban School Chiefs Under Fire* (Chicago: University of Chicago Press, 1976).
62. James M. Lipham, "Leadership and Administration," in National Society for the Study of Education, *Behavioral Science and Educational Administration,* Sixty-third Yearbook, part 2 (Chicago: University of Chicago Press, 1964), ch. 6.
63. John K. Hemphill, Daniel E. Griffiths, and Norman Fredericksen, *Administrative Performance and Personality* (New York: Bureau of Publications, Teachers College, Columbia University, 1962).

The Superintendent and the Environment

Superintendents work not only with their organizations; they must also relate their organizations to the larger society. Legitimization of the organization must come from the larger society and, in the case of a public service such as education, financial support of the organization clearly rests with the larger society. In the external relationships of the organization to its environment, the distinction between maintaining and changing an organization can be further elaborated. The administrator might accept the decision of society with respect to resources, or he or she might bargain, manipulate, and fight to obtain greater resources for the organization. Accepting the resources society offers cannot be called leadership; maneuvering to get additional resources would be considered leadership.

Many superintendents are greatly occupied with manipulating the environment in which the school is located to the end of winning support for education. In many city school districts where there is great diversity among people with respect to occupation, income, origin, race, and religion, the superintendent lives a life of constant struggle. Different groups of city school patrons may want better education for the gifted, more opportunity for the handicapped, extended preschool education in impoverished neighborhoods, more vocational education, the establishment of junior colleges, and many other diverse programs. At the same time, taxpayer leagues, some business groups, and real estate associations may be insisting that school taxes are already exorbitant. Blacks may be arguing that integration of the schools is not moving along or that it should be abandoned. It is in a welter of such demands that the superintendent must strive for wide public support.

The problem takes a slightly different form in the upper-middle-class suburb. The population is often much more homogeneous, most adults have a college education, and professional or managerial occupations are common. But these circumstances make every resident his or her own educational expert. Adults read the literature on basic education. Admission of their children to prestige colleges becomes paramount. The results of College Board examinations and the percentage of National Merit Scholarship winners are accepted as convenient yardsticks for measuring the quality of high schools. Teachers find that high living costs force them to reside outside the community in which they teach. For a superintendent to marshall support for public education from a population of this kind is no easy task.

Even the rural center presents many problems for the superintendent. Here schools have small enrollments, and because of farm mechanization and better roads, enrollments continue to go down. Combinations of schools, particularly at the high school level, are obviously needed, but local residents fear that losing the high school may mean the end of their community identity. For example, they would no longer have their own basketball team. Many farm residents and small-town merchants have little interest in college preparatory programs; hence, they see no great need to improve teaching in science, mathematics, or foreign languages. The employment of local teachers, even though they are less well prepared for their posts, may be seen as a way of keeping the community intact, particularly if they are willing to work for slightly less than teachers from outside the community. Superintendents may feel that to accept this situation is cheating the younger generation with whose tutelage they are charged.

The social and educational changes of the last few decades require a new set of management skills for the superintendent. He or she must be a social analyst, an organizational diagnostician, a planner, and a mediator, all rolled into one. The first two of these roles are conceptual and analytical; the last two are also conceptual, but the action components are generally more apparent. As a planner, the superintendent must be a logical analyst; as a mediator, the superintendent must be a skilled power broker. Administrators, particularly at the top of the heirarchy, must do much thinking before acting.[64]

Obviously, the superintendent has a political role, but it is a political role with educational underpinnings. As long as education remains as decentralized as it is in the United States, there is no alternative. If the superintendents of schools do not make the case for public education and wage the fight for community support, there will be a serious void in many communities. This is not to suggest that the superintendent is without allies. Cultivating lay leadership for education in the community can be a major part of the superintendent's job. Board members and other lay citizens may become community spokespeople for education, but behind them a catalytic agent is needed and for that role the spotlight is on the superintendent.

If adequate educational programs are to be developed and supported, superintendents must attempt to manipulate the environment. Such a course of action is not easy. Many superintendents, despairing of the rigorous professional life, will simply follow the will of the community. Even that course is not without hardship and conflict, however, for in time some minority will lose patience with the status quo.

As chief executive of the school system, the superintendent interacts with a variety of people on school matters both inside and outside the school organization. Most of the superintendent's time and energy is spent maintaining the organization, but at times he or she may be compelled to exert leadership to change the goals or procedures of the organization. Superintendents are confronted with the question of accepting the resources society offers to support the organization or working within the environment to win greater share of the resources. They also will have to continue to demonstrate considerable political acumen in order to foster in the larger society the conditions necessary to support viable educational programs.

The Influence of the Superintendent

Influence on the Board

As the chief executive officer of the board of education, the superintendent seems initially to have a position of power. Indeed, many superintendents speak of a honeymoon period early in their tenure when the board grants almost every request. But honeymoons end, and superintendents soon find their boards less tractable. To be sure, boards vary a great deal in this respect. Some boards become completely dependent upon the superintendents and in a sense become little more than a rubber stamp. Other boards regard the superintendent as a hired hand. One extreme is as undesirable as the other.

Several studies help to explain the influence superintendents may have with boards. To begin with, we need to recognize that the superintendency is not the same everywhere. Many factors can alter, to some extent, the context within which the superintendent operates. For instance, McCarthy and Ramsey, on the basis of their

---

64. See Roald F. Campbell, "Time for Vigorous Leadership," in *Bad Times, Good Schools*, ed. Jack Frynier, Kappa Delta Pi Monograph, 1983.

research, posited four types of communities which produce four types of school boards, and they suggested four corresponding roles for the superintendent. These roles include the functionary, the political strategist, the professional advisor, and the decision maker.[65] Carlson has also dealt extensively with career-bound and place-bound superintendents and the effect each type has on the school organization. For instance, the career-bound superintendent seems to have a mandate for change whereas the place-bound superintendent is expected to keep things pretty much as they are.[66]

The nature of the influence superintendents have with boards was the focus of considerable research conducted by Ziegler and his associates.[67] In essence, Zeigler found that most boards of education rely upon their superintendents for policy recommendations. Boards, rather than governing the schools, legitimatize the programs of their superintendents. Zeigler puts the matter as follows:

> Board members, lacking a meaningful relationship to an external political constituency, fall easy prey to the superintendent's claim for "expertise." The recruitment process—looking to the civic-business world for the pool of eligibles, *virtually guarantees that the notion of lay control will be subverted*. We do not have lay control because, among other reasons, school board members do not want to control educational policy. Their background and experience compels them to look toward the superintendent's office for leadership. As the ideological descendant of the nineteenth century reformers, today's school board member is doing a good job: he is leaving the governance of the schools to the experts.[68]

Zeigler's work and a number of related studies have been carefully reviewed by Boyd.[69] He finds the matter much more complex than might be inferred from the conclusions set forth by Zeigler. Boyd summarizes his main contention in the following statement:

> I have argued that if schools are not merely the "mirror images" of the communities they serve, neither are they almost completely insulated bastions dominated by unresponsive and self-serving professional educators. Instead, I have proposed that while educators tend to dominate local educational policy making, they usually operate within significant and generally neglected or underestimated constraints imposed by the *local* community and school board—not to mention those imposed by state and national forces. These constraints (or, put another way, the influence of the community and the board) are likely to vary primarily with the type of school district and the type of policy issue that is faced. The local citizenry and the board will tend to have more influence in *external, redistributive,* and *strategic* policy decisions, and in *smaller* and more *homogeneous* communities where the professionals tend to anticipate or reflect (especially in middle and upper middle class communities) community demands. The professionals, on the other hand, will tend to have more influence in *internal* and *routine* policy decisions, and in *larger* and more *heterogeneous* communities.[70]

65. Donald J. McCarty and Charles E. Ramsey, *The School Managers* (Westport, Conn.: Glenwood, 1971).
66. Carlson, *School Superintendents.*
67. For instance, see L. Harmon Zeigler and M. Kent Jennings with the assistance of G. Wayne Peak, *The Governing of American Schools* (North Scituate, Mass.: Duxbury, 1974).
68. L. Harmon Zeigler, "Creating Responsive Schools," *Urban Review* 6 (1973): 40.
69. William L. Boyd, "The Public, the Professionals, and Educational Policy Making: Who Governs?" *Teachers College Record* 77 (May 1976): 539–77.
70. Ibid., 572–73.

Superintendents in many school districts have considerable influence on their boards of education, and this influence is a product of the person who occupies the superintendency as well as the settings within which the superintendent and board operate. While many board decisions appear to merely rubber-stamp the superintendent's recommendations, most superintendents take pains to anticipate how board members will receive their recommendations and often adjust their opinions to the board's favor in advance. Consideration of these anticipated responses represent a kind of board control which is not easily observed and indeed may have been overlooked by Zeigler. While we suspect that most boards do not view the recommendations of their superintendents critically enough, the balance between professional expertise and lay judgment may not be tipped as far to the professional side as some have maintained.

Influence on the Staff

The superintendent of schools may influence his staff by exercising the prerogatives of the office and by developing prestige with the staff. Office is conferred, but prestige must be earned. These concepts will be discussed more fully in chapter 10, but let us see now what they may mean for the superintendent.

The superintendent usually selects subordinate personnel in the central office. In large organizations the superintendents will, of course, select only their major subordinates, but in small organizations their preferences will probably determine selections of all personnel. This prerogative means that the superintendent has great influence in defining job expectations, in seeking people who can meet such expectations, and in clarifying the assignments made to such personnel after they join the organization. To be sure, most administrators inherit part of their personnel, but even so, the opportunity to build an organization in whole or in part with people of his or her own choice gives an administrator, initially, great potential influence.

Ordinarily, too, the administrator has some control over salaries and promotions. While formal salary schedules lessen this control, there is often a way in which the administrators can channel additional pay to those in their organizations who, in their judgment, deserve it. Promotions to supervisory and administrative posts in the organization, like selection, are often at the descretion of the administrator.

As a further official prerogative, superintendents have some control over the allocation of material resources in their organizations. They often determine which buildings, which departments, and in smaller school systems which teachers, receive more books, more supplies, more equipment. To be sure, if these decisions become completely idiosyncratic there are ways, both formal and informal, in which an organization can seek redress. However, within limits the superintendent can, by the allocation of resources, determine which areas of the curriculum and which student activities will be promoted and which deemphasized.

But the power of office is hollow unless the superintendent has earned the respect of members of the organization. Prestige might come through the capacity of the superintendent to clarify purpose and direction for the school system both inside and outside the organization. Prestige might come through the demonstration of insight by the superintendent on program requirements to meet certain purposes. Prestige might be earned if the superintendent were able to provide appropriate participation for the staff on questions of importance to them. The superintendent might also acquire prestige with staff members if they become convinced that he or she influences the larger society favorably toward the school system. This influence could take tangible expression in the willingness of the community to provide money for school operation. But just as important is the way in which the superintendent stands behind the staff when representing them to the community. Unless the superintendent acquires some of the power of prestige, the power of his office will begin to erode.

According to the concept of authority suggested by Simon, the superintendent has authority only when subordinates permit their behavior to be guided by the superintendent's decision without independently examining the merits of that decision.[71] This concept should help superintendents recognize that the sanction of office, powerful though it is, must be supplemented by earned prestige and influence. With the increase in teacher militancy, the earning of prestige and influence by the superintendent will be more difficult to achieve, and indeed in some school systems this effort has been abandoned altogether.

The superintendent's influence either through sanction of office or earned prestige, can be considerable, but the school system is a loosely coupled system. A loosely coupled system, as Weick has suggested, allows more room for self-determination on the part of the actors.[72] Thus, staff members may or may not be impressed with the power of the superintendent's office and they may vary appreciably in their willingness to be guided by the decisions of the superintendent.

The size of the school system can affect the ways in which a superintendent exercises the influence of office and of prestige. In large school systems the superintendent's influence on selection of personnel, salaries, and promotion would affect most directly the central office staff and school principals while in small school systems that influence would affect teachers as well. In a large school system the superintendent's capacity to clarify purposes and comprehend programs would perhaps be most apparent to his immediate staff. The details of relationships with the community would also tend to be known only by his immediate staff.

But steps can be taken to make the superintendent visible and influential outside the central staff. This is largely a matter of communication. A willingness on the part of the superintendent to conduct an open school system and to keep staff, board, and community informed about problems, needs, successes, and failures would be a sound platform on which to operate.

Influence on the Local Community

Earlier in this chapter we noted that the superintendent is cast in a political role. Unless willing merely to accept what the community provides for school support, the superintendent must manipulate the environment in which the school exists in order to increase the resources for the school. Most communities, however, possess certain limiting characteristics which the superintendent cannot change. James and his colleagues have suggested that these limits are found in the expectations of the people for education, in the wealth of the school district most often expressed in assessed valuation, and in the government arrangements controlling access to money for schools.[73]

71. Simon, *Administrative Behavior.*
72. Weick, "Educational Organizations as Loosely Coupled Systems."
73. H. Thomas James, J. Alan Thomas, and Harold J. Dyck, *Wealth, Expenditure and Decision-Making for Education,* Cooperative Research Project 1241 (Stanford, Calif.: School of Education, Stanford University, 1963).

In open systems such as the schools, the expectations of the people for education in many communities are subject to some change. Wealth, however, barring some fortuitous circumstance such as the establishment of new industry, is not subject to change. Limited wealth can ordinarily be offset only by state or federal financial assistance of some kind. Obviously, state restrictions on tax levies, voting requirements, and other access arrangements can only be changed by the state legislature. Thus, at any point in time each superintendent works within a set of limitations in his community.

Within these limitations, however, there is ordinarily some leeway. The superintendent must find ways to exploit that leeway and in the long run must give attention to ways of reducing the limitations. Since the board of education is officially the intermediate body between the school organization and the community, the superintendent must begin with the board. Frequently board members become emissaries for carrying the school message to the community, but to be effective emissaries board members must understand the purposes behind school programs and something about the nature of the programs themselves. Inevitably, the superintendent becomes the chief agent for providing board members with such information.

In many communities the superintendent must work not only with the board of education but with other lay leaders. These people may be found in business, the professions, labor groups, ethnic societies, civic organizations, and other places. Ways must be found to acquaint these people with school needs. If needs seem important to interest-group leaders, they may be able to help marshal community support for programs to meet those needs. Leadership appears to be dispersed in terms of both people and issues.[74] Nevertheless, certain people in a community do influence the thinking of others, and they must be reached and enlisted in the support of school programs if those programs are to be adequately supported.

As an outgrowth of the civil rights revolution, most city superintendents in recent years have had difficulty interpreting the will of communities made up largely of blacks or other minority groups. At times minority group leaders insist that the schools be desegregated. At other times they accept segregated schools and demand that they have more control over them. When more community control is sought, white teachers and white principals are often not acceptable. Superintendents must develop ways of working with leaders of minority communities just as they do with leaders of other community groups. We should note, however, that not all superintendents now are white; a few blacks and other minority group members have recently been selected for the position.

To influence the community, it seems quite clear that the superintendent must have a program, must be aware of the limitations within which he is working, must build understanding and support with the board of education, must enlist, with the help of board members if possible, the support of lay leaders in the community, and must utilize mass media and other means to inform the community about school programs, desirable directions, and necessary resources.

Influence on the Larger Community

No school district exists in a vacuum. Actually, as noted in chapter 3, the district exists as an instrument of the state legislature to carry out certain state purposes.

74. Robert A. Dahl, *Who Governs?* (New Haven, Conn.: Yale University Press, 1961).

Even the federal government controls much of what schools can do (chapter 2). Every district, however, is also subject to many extralegal influences. Agencies such as the accrediting associations and the College Entrance Examination Board are examples of influential bodies. No school district is required legally to comply with these programs, but accreditation is important to most communities. College board scores are now demanded by hundreds of colleges as part of the entrance requirements for students. Thus, every local community is part of a larger state, regional, national, even world community.

It may be that the folklore of local school control has blinded some people, superintendents included, to the realities of the world in which they work. At the same time, many superintendents find that in order to assure adequate resources locally they must join in statewide efforts to augment school support. Most superintendents have also come to realize that they must be vigorous in seeking federal aid. In the future, superintendents of schools will be required to operate in the state and national as well as the local arena.[75]

Summary and Future Prospects

Influence of the Superintendent

Legally most states confer few prerogatives on superintendents. For the most part their legal powers are derived from those ascribed to the board of education. Despite this lack of legal status, traditions in each situation and the personal characteristics of the officeholder combine in some fashion to affect the influence of the superintendent. Also, it may be appropriate to apply here the injunction offered by Cohen and March, that college presidents should not take themselves too seriously.[76] But recognizing these limits should not suggest that superintendents have no influence. While most superintendents can no longer dominate school systems, they can in most places influence them in the following ways:

1. *The power of office.* The top administrative official can ordinarily exercise sanctions by way of appointments, assignments, promotions, and levels of salary. Perhaps even more important is the confidence people have in the holder of the top position in the organization. Unless this confidence is seriously abused, it is assumed that organizational decisions will emanate from that office.
2. *Information.* The capacity to develop, control, and use information is a second source of influence. The top administrator can largely determine what problems need study, can recruit and direct a staff for the studies deemed necessary, and can use or not use the data derived from the studies as he or she sees fit. Only the person at the top of the hierarchy can bring together into a coherent whole the results of formal inquiry with experience and intuition.
3. *Analysis.* The superintendent is an analyst of the school's social milieu and the school organization itself. Analysis obviously goes beyond mere information gathering and arrives at the meanings of the facts through interpretation. To be sure, the superintendents will need help from persons inside and outside the school organization for these analyses, but the capacity of superintendents

---

75. Roald F. Campbell and Tim O. Mazzoni, Jr., *State Policy Making for the Public Schools* (Berkeley, Calif.: McCutchan p. 1976).
76. Michael Cohen and James G. March, *Leadership and Ambiguity* (New York: McGraw-Hill, 1974).

to recognize and use such help to determine meaning for their organization enhances their influence.

4. *Planning.* In a sense, planning is the logical application of the analyses noted above. It is a rational and systematic process. Goals are established, alternative ways of achieving the goals are considered, the best way of reaching the goals is selected, and then the plan is implemented. Clearly, staff assistance is necessary for planning. Even if certain plans are never fully implemented, the capacity of superintendents to think through and communicate long-range plans to others greatly increases their influence.

5. *Mediation.* While planning is a very rational activity, mediation, or acting as a power broker, is clearly a political activity. The superintendent is continually called upon to exercise political skills within the organization and within the environment in which the organization exists. Frequently, the question is, what is possible under current conditions and what kinds of coalitions can be formed to support the possible? To achieve working agreements, compromise is frequently necessary. The influence of superintendents is determined by their skill in fostering successful negotiations (often with the help of others).

Outlook for the Future

Fewer Superintendents. While the rate of change has slowed, the combination and reorganization of rural school districts will probably continue. In addition, some new school districts will probably be formed around each of the major cities, areas where major population increase is projected. Also some school districts in our largest cities may need to be subdivided.

These developments portend a modest decrease in the number of school districts and in the number of superintendents. Conceivably, most of the superintendents in school districts with less than 40 or 50 staff members will disappear. This could mean that nearly all of the part-time superintendents—positions combined with high school principalships and with part-time teaching—will disappear.

With the reduction in the number of superintendents, there will probably be an increase in the number of subordinate administrators, particularly directors or assistant superintendents who serve in the central office. In suburban school districts particularly, the number of schools will also probably increase, hence there may be some increase in number of principals, at least full-time principals. The route to the superintendency will probably be through one or more of these subordinate positions with central office experience being seen as a stepping stone, but better training programs may modify this career route.

Better Selection Procedures. The selection of the superintendent occurs at two major points: when the university admits a candidate to the preparation program and when a board of education actually names a superintendent. Both of these processes will probably become more rigorous.

With fewer superintendents to be prepared and with preparation programs more definitive, as will be discussed next, it seems likely that fewer universities will offer preparation programs for the superintendency. This could mean an increase in the number of collaborative arrangements among universities so that programs for the principalship in many universities would be tied to fully developed programs for the superintendency at just a few universities. In any case, with fewer superintendencies to fill and with their preparation consolidated in fewer universities, selection procedures can become more rigorous and more manageable.

Fortunately, studies on the role of the superintendent, the relationship between personal characteristics and the performance of that role, and the development of procedures for identifying appropriate candidates provide universities with some help in the selection process. These studies will continue and their usefulness to university selection committees will continue to grow. As part of the selection process, universities must rely to a considerable extent upon practicing superintendents for nomination of candidates for admission to the preparation program. Programs for identifying promising candidates among teachers and subordinate administrators will probably be more highly developed and more commonly used. In addition, the pool from which superintendents are drawn may be enlarged to include persons in law, government, and business, as well as those in education.

With fewer school districts and with most rural districts combined into larger units, boards of education will be composed more and more of able lay people. Moreover, with the reduction in the number of school districts, more prestige will probably be attached to board membership. Under these circumstances, boards of education, more universally than now, can be expected to be more scrupulous in the selection of superintendents. The practice of a board enlisting the aid of professional consultants to establish criteria for the position, set up selection procedures, and actually screen candidates will probably increase. In any case, it seems probable that the boards of education will increasingly seek superintendents with professional strengths.

Improved Preparation Programs. Trends toward improved preparation programs for superintendents seem to be clearly established. Major universities, such as those affiliated with the University Council for Educational Administration, have taken the obligation seriously and are actively engaged in strengthening their programs. Two years of graduate study is considered a minimum program, and a program culminating in the doctorate is becoming more common. A number of experimental programs have also emerged. For instance, The National Program of Educational Leadership (composed of seven universities and a state department of education with U.S. Office of Education support) was chiefly concerned with broadening the recruitment base, decreasing formal academic requirements, and increasing field experience. Nova University continues to place great stress on field experience in preference to traditional academic requirements such as formal residence study.

In the more traditional settings as well as in the experimental programs, certain emphases are emerging. There will probably be considerable reliance on the basic disciplines, but these disciplines will not be taken in undigested chunks. Rather, harder questions will be asked about the relevance of the concepts the disciplines provide. The theory movement is an expression of this trend; school experts are realizing that many theories of human behavior may be useful in evaluating the role of the school administrator. In large part, these applications are still undeveloped. A parallel emphasis, and in many cases the dominant emphasis, will be on making greater use of field experience in training programs. Field experience may take several forms varying from brief periods of observation and participation to long periods of internship. At least one other notion is receiving considerable attention—perhaps it is an old notion with new emphasis—the idea of defining carefully the competencies required of administrators and building a training program around those competencies. Care must be taken, however, that this movement not promote a narrow or mechanistic definition of competence.

Realistic Role Definition. Projecting the future role of the superintendent is an extremely difficult task. Some maintain that current demands on the position make it completely untenable. Others insist that the present generation of superintendents is a failure and what we need is a new breed. The setting in which superintendents of the future will operate will be a difficult one. Many of the problems confronting the larger society will find expression in that setting. These problems emanate from our pluralistic culture in which there is often little agreement on basic values; blacks and other minorites are searching for ways to participate fully in our society, and many feel the conflict between a desire for self-determination and the push of our culture toward uniformity.

In a somewhat different vein, March has noted that education is a declining industry.[77] He suggested that in a declining industry management tends to age, there is some loss of *joie de vivre,* and there is an oversupply of administrators. Perhaps even more significantly, March contends that as it becomes clear that schools can make only a limited contribution to the solution of our social problems, social pressure on schools and school administrators will actually give way to indifference. Current developments may provide more optimism than is found in the March position. Recent studies of education, including *A Nation at Risk,*[78] all reflect a renewed attention to the significance of schooling. This seeming change in attitude coupled with a willingness of the private sector to invest more in education may do much to make education, once again, a growth industry.

Whatever view one takes of the future, there remain a number of dilemmas for the superintendent. Some maintain that the leadership of the superintendent is more vital than ever; others, because of increasing teacher and community power, assign much less importance to the superintendent's leadership. Many superintendents believe that their occupation must be further professionalized through training and certification procedures while many lay persons would like to dispense with professional requirements and open the occupation to able persons generally. There are movements afoot which would make the job of the superintendent much more rational through the application of cost-benefit and similar analyses, and at the same time there are some voices insisting that the great need is for humanizing the schools and the people who run them.

From one point of view, it seems clear that the superintendent of the future must give more attention to the external or community factors in school operation. Indeed, in the recent AASA study of the superintendency,[79] one of the challenges of the future dealt with the civic responsibility of the superintendent. Civic leadership was seen as a way of providing a broader view of how schools fit into community life. Moreover, it would also provide an opportunity for the superintendent to deal with the ever broadening constituencies found in the community.

77. James G. March, "Analytical Skills and the University Training of Educational Administrators," *The Journal of Educational Administration* 12 (May 1974): 17–48.
78. National Commission on Excellence in Education, *A Nation at Risk* (Washington, D.C.: U. S. Department of Education, 1983).
79. Luvern L. Cunningham et al. *The American School Superintendency, 1982* (Arlington, Va.: AASA): ch. 9, in press.

At the same time, teacher militancy and demands for better teaching suggest that the internal aspects of school operation must have priority. The need for superintendents who can use sophisticated techniques particularly in seeking resources at state and national levels is clear, but at the same time local problems demand constant attention. As a professional person the superintendent feels the need for considerable autonomy, but by the nature of the job, there is pressure to become a pawn of community and faculty.

These and other dilemmas document the complex task of the superintendent in the future. In the larger social context, as David Tyach and Elisabeth Hansot have noted "the political and idealogical disarray of the 1980s suggest that the major task today is to secure a new common ground for the common school."[80] Clearly, the superintendent has a role to play in that demanding task. Some of the best talent of the nation must be attracted to the position. Problem analysis and courageous action, not the application of ready-made solutions, will be necessary. We are encouraged that Cunningham and his colleagues found "vitality" in the American public school superintendency. We look to the future with some optimism.

---

80. David Tyack and Elisabeth Hansot, *Managers of Virtue.* (New York: Basic, 1982): p. 217.

10

The Administrative Hierarchy

School systems, particularly as they increase in size, employ not only a superintendent but also numerous subordinate administrators, and we now turn to this hierarchy.[1] This chapter discusses the kinds and numbers of these administrators, the problems growing out of the development of such a work group, and the nature of power exercised by administrators.

Kinds and Numbers of Administrators

Central Office Staff

We have already noted that there are over 14,000 superintendents of schools in the nation. Estimates, based on U.S. Office of Education statistics, suggest at least an equal number of assistant superintendents. Superintendents, assistant superintendents, and other central office administrators and supervisors together number over 65,000 people. These administrators, with their many responsibilities and titles must, at times, seem a rather formidable group to teachers who do the actual work of the school.

These administrators have a wide variety of titles: assistant superintendent for instruction, assistant superintendent for business, assistant superintendent for personnel (staff), assistant superintendent for pupil personnel services, administrative assistants to the superintendent, director of elementary education, director of secondary education, director of curriculum, director of special education, director of adult education, director of instructional materials, director of audiovisual education, director of publications and information, director of planning, director of research, director of evaluation, director of finance, director of buildings and grounds, director of health services, director of cafeteria services, director of transportation, elementary supervisor, primary supervisor, music supervisor, art supervisor, physical education supervisor, mathematics consultant, science consultant, and foreign language consultant.

1. See James G. March, "American Public School Administration: A Short Analysis," *School Review* 86 (February 1978): 223.

Staffs of Single Schools

School districts, as noted in chapter 6, are often divided into attendance areas, and a single school serves in each area. Ordinarily each school has a principal as its administrative officer. In schools with small enrollments the principal may also teach part-time, but increasingly the principal is becoming a full-time administrator. In schools with large enrollments the principal may also have one or more assistants or vice-principals who are also full-time administrators. In large high schools the principal may have a registrar, a director of guidance, and other administrative personnel.

The National Center for Education Statistics reports that there are a total of 74,000 elementary schools in the country, 61,000 of them public and 13,000 non-public.[2] The center also reports a total of 23,000 secondary schools, 21,000 public and 2,000 nonpublic. In another report from the center the total number of elementary and secondary principals and assistant principals is given as 107,000.[3] When central office and single school administrators and supervisors are combined, the total is about 155,000 people. This group comprises the administrative hierarchy which we will discuss in this chapter.

Generalists and Specialists

Administrators can be described by title and by their location in the central office or in a single school; they can also be classified as generalists or specialists. Superintendents and especially principals by the very nature of their assignments are generalists. Their responsibility is for the entire school system or the entire school. While teaching and learning are the main business of the school, many activities are required to carry out this function. These activities include goal determination, curriculum planning, personnel selection and supervision, organization of students into instructional groups, provisions for physical facilities, financial management, and accounting to the public. Inevitably, the line officer, whether superintendent or principal, has overall responsibility for fitting these pieces together.

In large school systems and large schools, the administrative organization may call for other generalists. For instance, at the district level some large cities have established regional or subdistrict superintendencies. Administrators who occupy these posts are held responsible for all or most of the functions pertaining to school operation. In somewhat similar fashion, some large high schools have divided the total school into subschools or houses, and a principal or vice-principal has been placed in charge of each unit.

In contrast with these line positions, large school systems and large schools often establish administrative positions which are essentially staff or advisory in nature. Administrators in some of these posts may become specialists. The director of business affairs in the central office, for instance, can be a specialist in budgeting, accounting, purchasing, and other business functions. Likewise, the director of guidance in a large high school can be a specialist in the psychology of human behavior, who might help principal and faculty alike understand individual students and the treatment they need.

A school system needs among its administrators both generalists and specialists. The generalist has a very important role to play. In fact, as many school positions

2. National Center for Education Statistics, *Digest of Education Statistics, 1982* (Washington, D.C.: Government Printing Office, 1982), 13.
3. Ibid., 53–54.

become more specialized, the need for the insightful generalist increases.[4] Conversely, each generalist must rely on information and insights which only specialists can supply. Administrative staffing in most school districts does not reflect an appropriate balance of generalists and specialists.

Reservations About the Hierarchy

Teachers, school board members, and the general public often express reservations about the administrative hierarchy. At times each of these groups feels ambivalent about its administrators; they find them necessary at some points, detrimental at others. Some of these reservations will now be examined.

Lack of Expertise

To many people it seems strange indeed that the administrator who heads an organization devoted to teaching and learning is often not a master of any particular subject. The administrator is neither scientist, social scientist, nor humanist. The first-grade teacher knows more about reading than the principal. The high school mathematics instructor knows more about mathematics than the superintendent.

Traditionally this has not always been so. In Europe and in early America, the headmaster, particularly in secondary schools, was indeed a master teacher and knew a particular subject in depth. Frequently he had a firm grasp of human knowledge in general. Two circumstances have contributed to the diminishment, if not the demise, of this ideal situation. The first is the great increase in the quantity of and the specialization of human knowledge. The disparity between how much was known in a discipline and how little was commonly being taught in school and college classrooms caused nearly every disciplinary group to mount a national curriculum reform movement during the late 1950s and early 1960s.[5] If keeping abreast of developments is difficult for teachers in one field of knowledge, it is next to impossible for the administrator who must deal with several fields of knowledge.

A second circumstance preventing the administrator from being a scholar is the demanding nature of the administrative position itself. The unrelenting demands of administrative work have been documented by Mintzberg.[6] The central task is one of establishing with lay people purpose or direction for the school, procuring professionals who can help implement that purpose, and then securing from the public the resources that will permit teaching and learning to flourish. These demands seem to leave little time for subject specialization.

Line administrators, such as principals and superintendents, not only find it impossible to become specialists in academic subjects, they cannot even be specialists in a single area of administration. These areas may include curriculum development, staff personnel, student personnel, school plant, and finance and business management. Inevitably chief administrators of school systems or single schools must deal with the institution as a whole, and this means cutting across many basic areas of operation.

4. See Jack A. Culbertson et al., *Preparing Educational Leaders For the Seventies* (Columbus, Oh.: University Council for Educational Administration, 1969).
5. See John I. Goodlad, *The Changing School Curriculum* (New York: Fund for the Advancement of Education, 1966).
6. Henry Mintzberg, *The Nature of Managerial Work* (New York: Harper & Row, 1973), 29–30.

The chief administrator can, however, in situations where size justifies an administrative staff, organize the staff so that the insights of specialists in the various aspects of administration can be brought to bear on decision making. The concept of line and staff, developed first by the military and so quickly dumped into the ash can during the so-called democratic period of administration, has a vital usefulness. Most superintendents and principals could improve their operation if they surrounded themselves with people who have specialized knowledge or skills that could be utilized as needed in giving the organization direction.

With more attention given to developing specialists in some area of administration, some of the concern about lack of expertise may have been mitigated. But even the generalist can perform expertly. The expert generalist has the ability to see the organization as a whole, to relate the organization to the larger society, and to give direction to the organization. Even though the administrative role has become common in every institution in our culture, there are still many people who do not quite understand it and are skeptical about supporting it. Some of these people are found on school boards and on school faculties. Perhaps more careful explication and more skilled demonstration will help to clarify the unique role of the general administrator.

Unproductiveness

Many people regard the administrative hierarchy as unproductive. In an organization that exists for teaching and learning, administrators do not teach. Why must principals of elementary schools with 15 or 20 teachers be freed from all teaching? What would they do with their time? Such questions are frequently asked, and admittedly some principals do use their time in ways that do not seem to promote the productivity of the school. Too many principals find themselves caught in a morass of detail and paperwork, much of which seems unnecessary or of such a nature that it could be performed by a clerical staff.

The principals, to continue to use them as an illustration, are not entirely free agents. At least four groups of people hold expectations of the principal. These groups include the central office staff, the teachers in the school, the students in the school, and the parents of these students. For instance, the central office expects reports on school progress; teachers expect the principal to provide materials and conditions which make better teaching possible; pupils expect the principal to be friendly and available; and parents expect the principal to listen sympathetically when they raise questions about school operation. These and similar expectations demand the principal's time and energy. No single reference group comprehends very well the extent of the total demand. Principals themselves often have difficulty in distinguishing between the necessary and the trivial. So the suspicion of unproductiveness persists.

Even more serious than the feeling some people have that administrators are unproductive is the opinion that administrators actually hinder teaching and learning. Over three decades ago, Goodman decried administrative excess in colleges and suggested that professors rid themselves of boards, presidents, deans, business managers, registrars, and other impedimenta, and go off in small groups to begin anew.[7] Every teacher, whether in college or high school, would at times, no doubt, be happy to join in such a revolt, but the realities of the world tell us the matter is not that simple.

7. Paul Goodman, *The Community of Scholars* (New York: Random House, 1962).

Parsons offered a concept which helps to explain organizations, including educational organizations.[8] He suggests that every organization has three levels: the technical, the managerial, and the institutional, or community, level. The work of the organization is done at the technical level and is performed by the teachers. Administrators perform chiefly at the managerial level but inevitably articulate between the managerial and institutional levels and between the managerial and technical levels. In this articulating role, administrators have much to do with what Parsons calls the procurement and allocation of resources necessary to organizational survival.

Clearly administration is instrumental to teaching and learning, the major functions of the school. Administrators can be seen as productive only when they help establish viable instructional programs, procure competent personnel, give appropriate motivation to the staff, help provide suitable physical facilities, and secure needed financial resources in such a way as to enhance the instructional program. These are stringent criteria for judging administrative productivity. Moreover, measuring the impact of these instrumental activities upon student learning is very difficult. Indeed, after examining the studies in this area, March came to the following conclusion: "Although there are some pieces of contrary evidence, the bulk of most studies and the burden of current belief is that little perceptible variation in schooling outcomes is attributable to the organization and administration of schooling. . . ."[9]

Despite this rather gloomy picture, there is reason to believe that administration can make a difference. Sarason, drawing on first-hand observations of schools, found that the principal was a major influence in establishing the culture of the school.[10] In 1981, Shoemaker and Fraser synthesized a number of reports on effective schools and noted the significant role ascribed to the principal in these schools.[11] More recently, *A Nation at Risk* and other national studies have stressed the crucial leadership role required of principals in implementing school reforms.[12]

Too Much Power

Many people believe the administrative hierarchy has excessive power. Administrators do participate in decision making and these decisions often affect other people. Thus, administrators may be seen as exercising power over other people. Like Lord Acton, many suspect that, "Power tends to corrupt."

Lieberman was one of the first to suggest that the power of administrators is inconsistent with the development of a teaching profession. He said:

> The prevailing theories of school administration make the superintendent of schools responsible for the operation of the school system. The school administrator's responsibilities should not exceed his powers; hence, if he is to be responsible for the operation of the school system, it is necessary that he be given power to control the

8. Talcott Parsons, "Some Ingredients of a General Theory of Formal Organization," in *Administrative Theory in Education*, ed. Andrew W. Halpin (Chicago: Midwest Administration Center, University of Chicago, 1958), ch. 3.
9. March, "American Public School Administration," 221.
10. Seymour B. Sarason, *The Culture of the School and the Problem of Change* (Boston: Allyn and Bacon, 1971).
11. Joan Shoemaker and Hugh W. Fraser, "What Principals Can Do: Some Implications from Studies of School Effectiveness," *Phi Delta Kappan* 63 (November 1981):178–82.
12. The National Commission on Excellence in Education, *A Nation at Risk* (Washington, D.C.: U.S. Department of Education, 1983); Ernest L. Boyer, *High School* (New York: Harper & Row, 1983); and John I. Goodlad, *A Place Called School* (New York: McGraw-Hill, 1984).

behavior of teachers. It is difficult to see how such power can be reconciled with professional status for teachers. The teachers will be too subject to administrative control to be regarded as professionals. They will lack the direct and personal responsibility of professional workers to their clients if primary responsibility for the quality of their services is lodged with educational administrators. The doctor, the lawyer, and the dentist are responsible directly to their clients. Placing the primary responsibility for the quality of professional services on the shoulders of administrators undermines the right of the practitioners to make the professional judgments. The practitioners are auxiliaries rather than professional workers in their own right. Simply stated the alternatives are to modify prevailing conceptions of the appropriate powers and responsibilities of school administrators or abandon the notion of a teaching profession.[13]

Lieberman has oversimplified the matter somewhat; the power of any administrator is subject to many limitations. Still, Lieberman does give voice to the concern of many teachers and students of education about administrative power.

The whole concept of hierarchy is sometimes contrary to Americans' traditional commitment to egalitarianism. We like to think that every individual is equal to the next individual. But our actions often seem to contradict that belief. On the one hand, we seek for our organizations people who will be strong leaders, and on the other hand, we feel the need to circumscribe leadership as soon as it is asserted. Often people do not oppose vigorous decision making by administrators as long as the decisions are consonant with their own desires. Within the organization, too, expectations for the administrator vary, and no administrator can meet all of these diverse expectations. When the administrator behaves contrary to one set of expectations he or she may be perceived as exercising too much power.

Many teachers, board members, and lay citizens do not recognize the difference between personal power and organizational power. Most administrators have little personal power, but they may have considerable organizational power. The principal of a school, for instance, will have the power of the office. As the principal, he or she is expected to implement certain policy decisions made at the level of the central office. As the principal, he or she is expected by the staff to implement policies and procedures which have grown out of staff discussions. In both cases, the administrator is to carry out organizational imperatives, not his or her own personal wishes. Power thus resides much more in the office than in the individual.

There are some who would dispense with the hierarchy altogether. If this were done, two alternatives would be available. The first is administration through group process, perhaps exercised by one or more committees. Our experience with this procedure suggests that committees may be fully as arbitrary as a single administrator. Moreover, the workforce requirements for committee administration can be staggering. The second alternative is complete anarchy: each member of the organization doing as he or she wishes. It is unlikely that society would long permit any function it deems important to be conducted in such loose fashion. The hierarchy seems to be with us for good—and for our own good. Our task is to make it work as well as possible.

13. Myron Lieberman, *Education as a Profession*, 1956, 485. Reprinted by permission of Prentice-Hall, Inc., Englewood Cliffs, N.J.

Growth of Specialization

The schools of the future will be more specialized than the schools of today. Some of the conditions which appear to contribute to increased specialization will now be examined along the implications of this development for school organizations.

Increase of Knowledge

It is an accepted fact that we live in a day of exploding knowledge. Some scientists claim that over a period of ten years all that we know in science becomes obsolete. Medical educators are concerned that by the time students complete the program for the M.D. much of what they have learned is already out of date. Knowledge in the humanities and social sciences may not be changing as rapidly as it is in the sciences, but anyone who tries to keep abreast of new developments in the building of nations, for example, will find the task an arduous one.

The rapid expansion of knowledge has brought us new disciplines, such as biochemistry and psychosomatic medicine, and hybrid disciplines, such as econometrics. Each new discipline attracts its own body of scholars, and the search for new knowledge continues.

This increase in knowledge also brings an increase in the applications of knowledge. A number of disciplines have made widely accepted contributions to education. For decades, psychology has been thought to have important implications for teaching and learning, and the area of educational psychology has been rather well developed. But scholars continue to be concerned with theories of learning, to do experimental work based on these theories, and to make application of their concepts and findings to school practices.[14] There is also the long-held belief that philosophy has a unique contribution to make to educational practice, particularly in the area of the purposes of education. Again, educational philosophy has become a recognized field of study and a part of most teacher education programs.

But scholars in a number of other disciplines have more recently suggested that their respective disciplines also have relevance for education. Numerous sociologists have begun to study education. Havighurst and Levine have drawn upon sociology and social anthropology for material to help school people understand how an individual becomes a cooperating member of a complex society.[15] Major sections of their book deal with the social structure in the United States, with the child's social environment, with the school as a social system, and with the social role of the teacher. Lortie, using empirical studies of teachers, attempted to define the ethos of the teaching profession, its pattern or organization, and the sentiments peculiar to teachers.[16]

Reconsideration of Functions

In light of increased knowledge about schools and new demands in society, schools expanded their basic functions. This expansion has had a number of dimensions. Schools began serving a greater age range of the population; preschools and kinder-

---

14. Gordon H. Bower and Ernest R. Hilgard, *Theories of Learning* 5th ed. (Englewood Cliffs, N.J.: Prentice-Hall, 1981)
15. Robert J. Havighurst and Daniel U. Levine, *Society and Education,* 5th ed. (Boston: Allyn and Bacon, 1979).
16. Dan C. Lortie, *School Teacher: A Sociological Study* (Chicago: University of Chicago Press, 1975).

gartens became much more common, as did programs for adults, often organized in community colleges. Schools also attempted to serve a more diverse population. High schools, particularly, once rather selective, began enrolling every youth of high school age. In large cities, where most of the children of the poor lived, this great diversity in terms of social-economic class, interest, and ability created problems that many schools found almost insurmountable.

These conditions help explain the expansion of the school curriculum, particularly at the high school level. Previously, high schools devoted attention almost exclusively to college preparation programs but societal demands led to the creation of many vocational and technical programs. Programs such as music and speech, once seen as essentially extracurricular, were expanded and made part of the regular curriculum. Societal problems such as traffic fatalities and pregnant teen-age girls prompted the organization of courses in driver education and parenting. With some encouragement from the colleges, high school athletic programs were expanded and intensified. In time, these new programs, particularly athletics, helped create a new atmosphere in the high schools. Academic achievement as a major goal often gave way to athletic prowess. Not only were athletes involved in this new emphasis; many other school activities, such as the pep club and the band, served as auxiliaries to the main events until the whole school became infused with a new ethos. Nor was this enthusiasm limited to high school youth; nearly always there were organizations of adults such as band parents and athletic boosters who encouraged the young, provided extra money when needed, and badgered school officials who thought such activities might be getting out of hand.

In recent years a number of studies have examined the American high school. The National Commission on Excellence in Education entitled its report, largely focused on the high school, *A Nation At Risk*.[17] Dimensions of that risk included such conditions as declining student achievement from 1963 to 1980, persistent widespread adult illiteracy and, the necessity for costly remedial instruction in the basic skills in industry and the military. The Commission blamed these conditions on such practices as a smorgasbord curriculum, lowered standards and expectations, too little time on task, and inferior teaching. These observations led to a number of recommendations, the basic one having to do with more rigorous high school graduation requirements. These more strenuous requirements were to include four years of English, three years of mathematics, three years of social studies, and one-half year of computer science. In addition, for college-bound students, two years of foreign language were strongly recommended. Other recommendations included higher grading standards, more selective college entrance requirements, a longer school day and school year, and steps to improve the quality of teaching through preparation programs, higher salaries, and rewarding career opportunities.

A more detailed study of the organization and instructional program of the high school, sponsored by the National Association of Secondary School Principals and the National Association of Independent Schools, has been directed by Theodore Sizer. Sizer, while a sympathetic critic, finds, in an early report of his study,[18] a number of problems with high schools. Since many of these are interrelated he suggests that there are no simple remedies. Instead, the times demand the complete restructuring

---

17. National Commission on Excellence in Education, *A Nation at Risk*.
18. Theordore R. Sizer, "High School Reform: The Need for Engineering," *Phi Delta Kappan* 64 (June 1983): 679–83.

of high schools. Some of the changes he advocates include a shorter list of goals, mastery of the basic skills, a focus on the higher-order thinking skills, teaching that cuts across departmental lines, a simplified curriculum and schedule, programs for students to progress at their own pace, reduction in teaching loads, more autonomy for teachers, and enhancement of teaching career opportunities through differentiated staffing and salary recognition.

These two studies suggest that the schools need to respond not only to new knowledge but to the need to recognize and select that knowledge which is basic to understanding our world and providing help in developing higher-level thinking processes.

Although the current movement to reexamine the purpose of the high school is a step in the right direction, the demands on schools to serve an expanded age range of the population, to deal with the increased diversity of students, and to teach emerging social needs—such as computer skills—still remain. This means, we think, that schools will become more diverse organizations.

The Carnegie Foundation study, reported by Boyer, has recommended that the high schools of the future require all students to devote a substantial period of time to community service.[19] In addition, high schools are urged to greatly strengthen their relationships with colleges and with business. The implementation of these or similar programs will require that some teachers and coordinators have close working relationships with the world beyond the school. Again, this will result in more diverse school organizations.

In all probability the differentiation between professionals and nonprofessionals in school organizations will be extended. The use of teaching aids, for instance, will probably be extended. Teaching teams, once looked upon as a panacea, may become a fruitful way of organizing professionals and semiprofessionals in an attempt to achieve school goals.[20] Hopefully, teachers will be seen less as replaceable cogs in the machinery of learning and more as unique individuals, each with some special talent to be fully utilized to achieve the purposes of the organization.

Moreover, when schools take on new functions or give more specific focus to academic excellence, as we've suggested, the organization of schools will become more complex. This complexity will be, in part, a function of increased size. There will be fewer school districts. Small rural school districts will give way to large consolidated districts, but most of the development of which we have been speaking will take place in urban school districts. These districts will be found in our central cities and in the rings surrounding the central cities. These school districts will tend to be populous ones. Despite loss of population in many central cities and some decrease in school enrollments, most city schools will remain relatively large as will their central office staffs.

Still another factor affecting the complexity of organizations is the need for change. New knowledge and new functions both suggest that business cannot go on as usual. Somehow, organizations must learn to keep many operations running smoothly while they at the same time assess the need for change, try out and evaluate changes on a small scale, and where justified, institute changes on a broad scale. Smith and Keith have shown what a demanding process this is in their careful analysis

19. Ernest L. Boyer, *High School* (New York: Harper & Row, 1983).
20. See David G. Armstrong, "Team Teaching and Academic Achievement," *Review of Educational Research* 47 (Winter 1977): 65–86.

of the establishment and first-year operation of a new elementary school.[21] There were liabilities as well as advantages in newness. Open-minded teachers, new use of space, freedom from curriculum restrictions, team teaching, use of temporary systems, and sensitivity training did not insure perfection. There was still the conflict between the "institutional plan" and "democratic" participation. There was still the inordinate amount of time needed for invention. There was still the need for the accounting of the school to the community. Moreover, staff commitment, desirable as it is, was not an adequate substitute for expertise in dealing with the learning needs of pupils. Perhaps change on the scale and within the time frame of this case is unrealistic. Nonetheless, changes of great magnitude will be required of school organizations and these changes will contribute to their complexity.

Some Organizational Problems

Having looked briefly at a variety of organizational problems, let us look now more deeply at three major questions. These might be posed as follows: How can divergent views of administration be combined? How can growth in bureaucracy and professionalism be reconciled? How can administrators cope with conflicting environmental influences?

Differing Views of Administration

Four basic views of administration have influenced the concepts surrounding the superintendent of schools (chapter 9). Those four views affect how one perceives the administrative hierarchy. The idea of hierarchy is a key concept in the structural view of administration and the idea of a chain of command permeates most school organizations. While the industrial management view of administration dealt chiefly with the shop level of industrial organizations, the concept of hierarchy and the separation of those who labor from those who supervise was always present. The human relations approach to administration provided a new challenge to the hierarchy: the superordinates were no longer simply to direct or command; they were to stimulate and inspire. The open systems view brought still another challenge to the hierarchy. All previous views of administration had assumed that the organization was essentially a closed system. With the open systems approach the interdependence of the organization and its environment was clearly recognized. The political forces in the environment, for almost the first time, were seen as legitimate and not abberrant factors.

A recent treatment of management, *In Search of Excellence,* reports lessons from America's best-run companies.[22] In one sense, the book might be seen as a revival of the human relations movement in administration but the book is more than that. Managers in the best-run companies do indeed treat employees as human beings but those managers can also be tough as nails in seeing that the central values or purposes of their companies are understood and in guiding the behavior of employees at all levels in the organization. Instead of relying on hierarchy to sustain their leadership, these managers work to command respect. They are patient coalition builders, altering agendas so that new priorities get attention. Peters and Waterman said of such managers, "like good parents, they care a lot and they expect a lot." [23]

---

21. Louis M. Smith and Pat M. Keith, *Anatomy of Educational Innovation: An Organizational Analysis of an Elementary School* (New York: John Wiley & Sons, 1971).
22. Thomas J. Peters and Robert H. Waterman, Jr., *In Search of Excellence* (New York: Harper & Row, 1982).
23. Ibid., 96.

Bureaucracy and Professionalism

How do we reconcile the growth in bureaucracy and professionalism? As we view the developments on the horizon, there seems to be no way of doing away with hierarchy and bureaucracy.

Blau and Scott have noted that the professional and the bureaucratic forms of organizational life have a number of things in common.[24] Professionalism is characterized by universalistic standards, by special skill and experience, by effective neutrality in client relationships, and by emphasis on client, not practitioner, needs.

It is mainly in the control structure that the two orientations differ. Professionals typically organize themselves into voluntary associations for the purpose of self-control. Each professional as a result of a long period of training is expected to have acquired a body of knowledge and to have internalized a code of ethics which governs his or her conduct. This self-control is subject to the surveillance of one's peers as the only group assumed to be qualified to make professional judgments. At least in the ideal, professionals in a given field constitute a group of colleagues, each with equal status.

Notwithstanding the current criticism of teachers,[25] there is a movement toward the professionalism of teachers. Teachers are now expected to acquire a larger body of knowledge than they were in the past.[26] The period of training is being increased. The need for in-service education in order to keep abreast of new knowledge is more generally recognized. Obviously, some teachers in our best schools and many teachers in colleges meet the professional criterion of having acquired a specialized body of knowledge and skill. The extent to which college professors are called upon as consultants in many enterprises in our society is clear testimony of their expertise.

Teachers are seeking ways to exercise more control over decisions which affect them. Most teachers agree that they should be participants in decisions pertaining to their job conditions, duties, and prerogatives. One example of this position is the push for "self-governance of the teaching profession," particularly through the establishment in each of the states of what has come to be called a teacher standards and practices commission. According to a recent report, such commissions exist in forty states.[27] Most such bodies are advisory to state boards of education, but in five states these commissions have been given some statutory autonomy.

Teaching is generally moving toward a professional status, but certain factors are hampering this movement. Pay scales are so low in many of our school systems that many teachers have found it necessary to supplement their income through part-time jobs. Moreover, the low salaries mean that teachers (and would-be teachers) are often attracted to other fields. To make matters worse, there is some evidence that the more able teachers are the first to move into other fields.[28]

Basing teachers' salaries on merit is frequently suggested as one way of attracting and retaining other teachers. This proposal seems to meet with considerable public support as shown in a *Newsweek* poll.[29]

24. Peter M. Blau and W. Richard Scott, *Formal Organizations* (San Francisco: Chandler, 1962), 66–74. See also Ronald G. Corwin, *Education in Crisis* (New York: John Wiley & Sons, 1974), ch. 1.
25. National Commission on Excellence in Education, *A Nation at Risk*
26. For a historical treatment see Willard S. Elsbree, *The American Teacher* (New York: American Book, 1939).
27. *Standards & Certification Bodies of the Teaching Profession* (Washington, D.C.: National Education Association, 1983).
28. Garry Sykes, *Teacher Preparation and Teacher Workforce: Problems and Prospects for the Eighties* (Washington, D.C.: National Institute of Education, 1981).
29. "The Merits of Merit Pay," *Newsweek*, 27 June 1983.

An important question concerning teacher professionalism is, How can the source of discipline be shifted from the administrative hierarchy to the colleague group? This shift cannot occur until teachers are professionally ready for it, but teachers may never become professionally ready until they feel obliged to accept greater responsibility for the control of teaching. Some give and take on the part of teachers and administrators will be necessary to achieve some movement on this issue. Still somewhat uncertain is the role teachers unions and other organizations will play in helping teachers assume more professional responsibility.

It seems likely that teachers and special service personnel will become more and more responsible for decisions having to do with the technical aspects of their practice. Actually, in many school systems this procedure is rather well developed. Many principals, for instance, seek the advice of teachers, school psychologists, guidance personnel, and even social workers on decisions having to do with the placement of and programs for students. As another example, many superintendents have found it desirable to have teachers in their own system examine the curriculums developed nationally in science and mathematics.

Despite these developments, teachers have relatively little to say about who will enter teaching, what the composition of the program will be, and what the conditions of employment will be. Interestingly, school administrators do not have control over many of these matters either. Decisions on some of these questions are made by the larger society. In the years ahead, however, society and the administrators will have to concede greater control over teaching to the teachers themselves.

Conflicting Environmental Influences

A third problem for administrators is the impingement of the environment on the organization. No administrator at any level of the hierarchy can escape environmental influences. Forces external to the organization may include other levels of government such as state and federal governments as they impinge on local school districts. These external influences may emanate from administrative agencies or from the state or federal courts. Or, the external forces may represent one or more interest groups that have a stake in school operation in areas ranging from citizenship training to the use of local vendors for the purchase of school equipment.

The concepts of open systems and loosely coupled organizations go hand in hand. Thus, not only do external forces impinge on the organization, but since the organization itself is not tightly structured, some parts of the organization may give covert, or even overt, support to the external forces. Teachers unions, partly inside and partly outside the organization, illustrate this play of influences.

Conflicting environmental influences are at the heart of many of the problems facing the school principal. On the one hand, an alert group of parents may be insisting that the law for the education of the handicapped be strictly enforced and that an individualized program be developed for each handicapped student. On the other hand, teachers may not be fully prepared or willing to implement such a plan. To complicate matters further, budget limitations set by the central office may make complete individualization of student programs fiscally impossible. In short, parents say yes; teachers say no, unless the teaching staff can be increased; and the central office, which can offer only minor support from federal sources, says few if any additional staff can be provided. There is no way the principal can completely satisfy all three groups. The principal must become a mediator. Parents as part of the environment must be taken into account. To what extent can their demands be altered? Teachers and teachers organizations are loosely coupled to the principal. To what extent can their position be moderated? Finally, to what extent can the central office increase its budget? If public funds are not availale, are private funds possible? If money cannot be found for additional staff, can volunteer staff be used to supplement the regular staff? Questions such as these become legitimate when the principal sees himself or herself as a mediator and not merely the executor of central office policy.

Models of Administrative Power

Greater understanding of the organizational problems of administration can be achieved by placing them in a theoretical context. Let us consider two models, one largely of historical interest and the other reflecting the open systems view, both of which help clarify organizational behavior.

An Early Model

An early model, reflecting largely the human relations and the structural views of administration, was formulated by Guba in 1960 and is shown in Figure 10.1.[30] Note that power was defined as the actuating force of the administrator in the organization. Power is seen as having two major dimensions or expressions. The first had to do with role or office. Power of this kind resides in status and legal authority. Thus, in a school system the superintendency and principalship are seen as positions of power. Certain powers are considered to be inherent in these offices regardless of who the incumbents are at any particular time. This kind of power is most often considered by those who detect great conflict between administrative and colleague control.

The second source of power had to do with the person of the administrator. In this case the power is not conferred by office; it must be earned. This power is most often referred to as prestige or influence. Clearly some administrators have little prestige and influence, others have a great deal. Administrators who have little influence may find it necessary to invoke status and authority frequently; those who have much influence will seldom resort to such formal expressions of power.

Administrators cannot hide the fact that they occupy a formal office and that the office itself represents power. An administrator who ignores status and authority would be only half-powerful. Likewise the administrator who ignores prestige and influence is also only half-powerful. A recognition that at least a portion of administrative power is conferred upon or withheld by the work group may mitigate, in part, the concern held for the power of administrative hierarchy.

The model suggested further that conflicts between the role expectations of an organization and the personal needs and dispositions of the people in the organization constitute alienating forces. Indeed, if organizational demands and personal dispositions become too disparate, the organization will cease to be productive or the members will leave the organization. Countering these alienating forces are integrating forces in the form of shared goals and values. If the administrator and members of his work group can agree on goals and if they hold certain values in common, organiza-

---

30. Egon G. Guba, "Research in Internal Administration—What Do We Know?" in *Administrative Theory as a Guide to Action,* ed. Roald F. Campbell and J. M. Lipham (Chicago: Midwest Administration Center, University of Chicago, 1960), ch. 7.

tional demands may be seen in a different context and organizational procedures may be more acceptable.

Finally, the model suggested that if administrative power is composed of both status and prestige, and if agreement on goals and values exceeds conflicts between role expectations and personal dispositions, the behavior of organization members will help the organization achieve its goals. Obviously, agreement on goals and values implies a great deal of communication and participation within the organization. Guba offered the model as a convenient way of summarizing what had been learned from both conceptual and empirical work with organizations.[31]

Guba's model had a number of implications for administrators and organizations in 1960 and many of those implications are still pertinent today. To begin with, administrators need to recognize that power is both vested and entrusted. Vested power resides in the office, what Guba referred to as the role dimension. Entrusted power

FIGURE 10.1

A Model of Internal Administrative Relationships

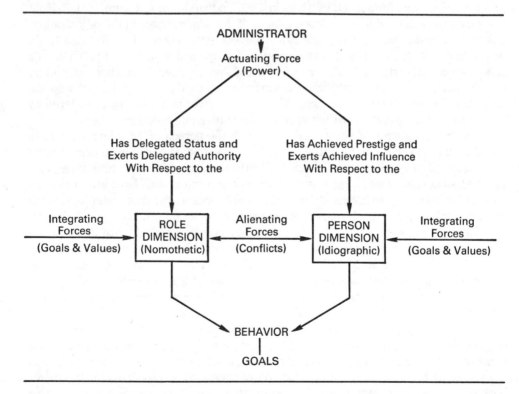

SOURCE: Egon G. Guba, "Research in Internal Administration—What Do We Know?" in *Administrative Theory as a Guide to Action,* ed. Roald F. Campbell and J. M. Lipham (Chicago: Midwest Administration Center, University of Chicago, 1960), ch. 7.

31. The work from which the model emerged is more completely explicated in Jacob W. Getzels, James M. Lipham, and Roald F. Campbell, *Educational Administration As a Social Process* (New York: Harper & Row, 1968).

is granted to the superordinate by the subordinate and is referred to as the person dimension. In a sense, vested power is delegated while entrusted power must be earned. Some administrators may need to give greater recognition to the power of office. Others, and probably a greater number, need to consider ways to earn prestige among their work groups.

In some cases, this prestige is largely a matter of charisma, but generally it will be grounded in sound administrative behavior. Most teachers are ready to rank an informed administrator higher than an uninformed one. The willingness of the administrator to consider alternative solutions is also admired by members of an organization. This capacity may be closely related to what many would call fairness, or a capacity to examine each question on its merits. Even though a decision may not be entirely to the liking of the work group, most people will respect the administrator who gives careful consideration to a question and then takes a position and stands by it. An adverse decision is often more acceptable than no decision at all or vacillation from one position to another.

Administrators also need to realize that the behavior of organization members is influenced both by organizational expectations and personal needs and dispositions. The organization can and should have certain goals and norms of behavior for its members. These will be reinforced by the administrator. But just as important is the recognition that each member of the organization brings the organization a unique background, unique personal characteristics, unique dispositions, even a unique set of perceptions of what the organization is about. Unless administrators can understand and take into account these personal idiosyncrasies, they have no way of knowing what organizational directions mean to the individual member.

A very common experience will illustrate. A principal sends a bulletin with instructions to a group of teachers. Some teachers read it; some do not. Some keep it for future reference; some toss it out. Some of those who read it understand the message the principal intended to transmit; others perceive other meanings. If the message is not acknowledged, is it because of carelessness, inability to read, or insubordination on the part of teachers? Not necessarily. One teacher may have a need to be orderly and thus files the message, but a teacher with no such need might lose track of the message. One teacher may have a need to be deferent thus pays careful attention to any message from a superior, while the teacher without such a need attends to other demands. The principal should be aware not only of what the bulletin says but how the bulletin is likely to be received by various teachers.

Another implication of the model is the crucial nature of goal reinforcement on the part of the administrator. If goals and values do indeed constitute the integrating forces in an organization, many administrators may find that they take too much for granted regarding the understanding members of their staffs have about goals and purposes. Obviously, goals cannot be imposed on the members of an organization. Frequently, goals will be consonant with the values held by organization members themselves. Even in such cases, however, goals need to be explicated and justified. Goal clarification by the administrator seems to be a major motivating activity in the organization.

We have noted some of the possible implications for the administrator growing out of the idea that the power of administration consists of both authority conferred by office and prestige earned by the office holder. Other members of the organization can earn prestige and thus exercise power, but only when official status is joined with earned prestige does one become fully powerful. This kind of power always carries with it responsibility, a fact not always appreciated by those who wish to shift power from the hierarchy to the colleague group.

The Open Systems View

Guba's model is very useful, but it does not deal with the external environment of the organization. It is this limitation which the open systems view addresses. The open systems view, as we have noted, is based on the idea that an organization and its environment are in constant interaction. The open systems view, as set forth by Easton, fits neatly with the concept of loosely coupled systems, as set forth by Weick. The notions of interdependence between organization and environment and loose coupling within the organization itself extend and in some instances modify the understandings gleaned from the Guba model.

The power of the administrator is not merely a combination of his or her status and prestige in the organization; that power is also a function of the political forces in the environment and, indeed, in the organization itself. Consider the case described by Smith and Keith earlier in the chapter.[32] The conflict between the "institutional plan" and "democratic" participation might well be seen as an illustration of loose coupling. Had the organization been tightly coupled, the institutional plan would have prevailed without question. The principal and the staff worked vigilantly to develop an innovative school and in the end there was much agreement between the principal and his staff on many aspects of a new program and fresh operating procedures. Despite these hard-won agreements, the program ran aground. Despite some meetings with school patrons, all organizational actors, principal included, paid relatively little attention to the concerns of the parents. When those parents learned of the new operation, they objected that their children were being made the subjects of experimentation. The parents were not at all impresssed with open classrooms, team teaching, temporary systems, and sensitivity training. Instead, the parents wanted a school like other schools and a curriculum devoted to the basic subjects.

This is not to say that the parents could not have been convinced that the new school was a better one. It is to say that the parents, as part of the environment of the school, cannot be ignored until the new school is already in operation and then be expected to give automatic approval and support. It may be that if parents had been part of the invention process from the beginning, parent support would have been secured easily, though there is no guarantee of this outcome. Earlier parent involvement would probably have slowed the whole process. It is also possible that parent participation would have precipitated parent-school disagreement much earlier in the process. In any case, parents were a part of the total picture with which the school had to cope. This example illustrates that open systems depicts reality more fully than the views of administration which preceded it.

Summary and Future Prospects

Influence of the Hierarchy

In many respects, what has been said about the power and influence of each member of the hierarchy corresponds to what was said about the power and influence of the superintendent; that is, power is based on the office, information, analytical capacity,

---

32. Smith and Keith, *Anatomy of Educational Innovation.*

planning know-how, and political skills in mediation. But there are some differences between the power of the superintendent and that of members of the subordinate hierarchy.

1. *Power of Office.* While there is only one superintendent, there may be several supervisors and principals, no one of which serves as chief administrator. Furthermore, in the hierarchy there are both line and staff officers. Line officers, generally principals, head at least a subunit in the organization and hence may have considerable power of office. Staff officers, often supervisors, provide information and counsel to the total organization but usually have no subunit of the organization for which they are responsible. Advisors ordinarily have less power of office than those who command. Two other factors affect the power of office of the principal. The first is the degree of autonomy granted to each of the schools in the system. With greater building autonomy the principal's power of office increases. The second factor, a related one, involves the degree of support extended by the superintendent and the board of education to the principal. If superintendent and board sustain the principal and staff in their decision making, the principal's power of office tends to increase.

2. *Information.* With respect to plans for and operation of the total system, principals and supervisors may be only partially informed, and hence less influential than the superintendent. Again, however, if there is considerable building autonomy, at least in that part of the system, the principal may be informed. Another kind of distinction in the area of information may exist between the superintendent and the specialists, supervisors, and staff in the central office. In many instances, the specialist may have more complete information about a particular field, be it reading instruction or long-range planning, than the superintendent. In these cases, the specialist has more influence.

3. *Analysis and Planning.* The power accruing from analytical capacity and planning know-how generally favors the superintendent, who must deal with the system as a whole, over principals and supervisors, who are frequently expected to deal with only part of the system. Again, however, if the superintendent has specialists working in these areas, such as might be found in a research division, their influence, though not always apparent, may exceed that of the superintendent.

4. *Mediation.* In the realm of mediation skill, principals and supervisors often have less influence than the superintendent. Once more, the degree of building autonomy may affect this generalization. Some principals, acting under a mandate of autonomy or assuming such autonomy, may indeed emerge as skilled political leaders with staff members and with community leaders. In some cases, a principal's influence may be welcomed by the superintendent, but in other cases such influence may threaten the position of the superintendent. In these cases the superintendent may take steps, such as transfer or promotion, to reduce the influence of the principal.

The variation in the influence of hierarchy administrators is evidence that schools tend to be loosely coupled organizations. Subordinate members of the hierarchy exert power and influence in many of the ways exercised by the top administrator, but the extent of the power and influence is contingent on other factors. In tightly structured organizations the power and influence of subordinate administrators tends to be reduced. In organizations which exhibit more loose coupling the power and influence of subordinate administrators may be increased.

Outlook for the Future

Focus on Instruction. There is an increasing demand, within and outside of the profession, that administrators, at all levels of school organizations, focus attention on those things that give promise of improving instructional outcomes. Within educational administration itself, it has long been recognized that school administrators engage in many activities that appear to have little relevance to the instructional program. In part, this may be written off as a narrow perception of what it takes to manage a school effectively. But, as Boyan has suggested, there is also a "renewed determination to extract, compile and synthesize data about what actually happens in and around schools". . .[33] This new resolve includes an attempt to see what administrative behaviors are related to instructional outcomes.

Outside of educational administration, there is also the call for more effective schools, illustrated by the report of the National Commission on Excellence in Education.[34] There, the shortages in student achievement are clearly set forth and principals and superintendents are charged with playing crucial roles in developing school and community support for the academic reforms set forth.

Increased Specialization. In the years ahead there may be further consolidation of school districts and thus some reduction in the number of school superintendents. At the same time, as districts become larger, there may be some increase in assistant superintendents and other central office personnel.

More significant than the number of administrators is the growing differentiation of the administrative staff. The need for generalists in the positions of superintendent and principal will remain. But increasingly those line officers will attempt to surround themselves with a specialized staff. This specialization will probably take three forms. The first development, and one which is already under way in larger school districts, is specialization in terms of the operating areas or functions of administration. There will be more assistant superintendents and directors in charge of instruction, business affairs, staff personnel, and student personnel. As staffs become specialized and schools take on new functions, positions such as directors of school-community coordination, early childhood education, technical education, education of the handicapped, and adult education may take on increased importance.

A second development in the differentiation of the administrative staff is the addition of people trained in disciplines thought to have great relevance to school operation. Thus, persons with strong backgrounds in psychology, social psychology, political science, economics, and other disciplines may be hired to provide additional insight on school operation. In all probability, staff members with competence in such fields of study as planning, research, and evaluation, will also be sought.

A third form of administrative staff specialization may develop in curriculum subjects. Schools which can attract few highly trained teachers in the various subjects may find it necessary to provide directors, supervisors, or coordinators who have

---

33. Norman J. Boyan, "Follow the Leader: Commentary on Research in Educational Administration," *Educational Researcher* 10 (February 1981): 13.
34. National Commission on Excellence in Education, *A Nation at Risk.*

special competence in science, social science, or the humanities. Even greater specialization may occur if special scholarship is sought in the areas of reading, mathematics, the foreign languages, art and music. Obviously, these specialists would not only advise administrators but also serve as resource people to teachers.

These three developments may merge in some very interesting ways. A director of instruction might emerge among the specialists in one subject group, or a director of staff personnel might find that social psychology provides many of the insights needed in the office. All of this means that there will probably be much more intercourse between education and other disciplines than has occurred in the past several decades. Conceivably, the school will seek to utilize knowledge from every discipline, and representatives from each discipline will feel some obligation toward the school.

Each line administrator will need to build a knowledgeable and diverse command staff. This staff will vary in size based on district size and resources. In small school districts some of these specialized personnel may be obtained through the regular use of consulting services. In any case, administrators, board members, and citizens will realize that decision making in education is too crucial to be carried on without the expertise of specialists.

Role Clarification. As school organizations become larger and more complex, there will be a need for greater diversity among administrative personnel, teaching personnel, and nonteaching personnel. In other words, there will be an increase in the number of roles found in school organizations. A consultant in mathematics, for instance, represents a new role for most school systems. An instructorship in Russian is a new role for most high schools just as a nursery school teaching position is for most elementary schools.

This development will be necessary to school organizations of the future as they take on new and more diverse functions. There is, for example, a growing need for people in school systems who really understand the labor market. Many city high schools will need instructors who can work with students of low academic potential in work-study programs. The schools of the future cannot meet diverse aims without enlisting people of diverse interests, preparation, and competence.

With more diversity among school positions, it should be possible to attract to these positions people of diverse talent. Also, it is more likely that school workers will be able to find roles that are compatible with their own needs and dispositions. For some, teaching adults may be more satisfying than teaching young people. For others, social work activities may be more rewarding than teaching activities. Schools of the future should be able to match the individual to the job more effectively than they have in the past.

As roles become more diverse, the need for role understanding and clarification will be intensified. Ways must be found to help all who work in a school system understand something about the work of others in the system. This will require more effective communication than in the past. It will also require ingenious organization of faculties and small work groups so that role understanding can grow through face-to-face contacts. These sorts of changes will call for astute administration. In addition, administrators themselves will have to define roles much more carefully than they do now.

There is a genuine danger in such advances, however. Formal organization could, with a dull or lethargic administrator, take the place of a working organization. Or, intermediate functionaries could become merely makers of paperwork or builders of small empires, and contribute little to the achievement of major objectives. Thus, the line administrator must not only define roles, but also appraise the performance of role incumbents.

Not only will administrators of the future find the job of role definition for members of their staff more demanding, they will also find it more difficult to delineate their own roles in the administrative hierarchy. Superintendents and principals will find it increasingly necessary to rely on staff expertise in their decision making. In fact, in professional organizations the line-staff relationships may even become reversed. As the science of administration develops, those who can analyze situations and predict with some accuracy the outcomes of administrative decisions will be increasingly needed as members of the administrative group.

Improved Selection and Preparation. The administrators of the future will be more carefully selected and more adequately prepared. Selection occurs at two major points: when a candidate is admitted to the preparation program of a university and when he or she is actually hired in an administrative capacity by a school district. Both of these entry points are being scrutinized and steps taken to improve present practices. Universities are no longer accepting for administrative preparation every candidate who appears in the doorway. Moreover, universities are beginning to recruit candidates for administrative training from many fields such as law, business, and government instead of limiting themselves to candidates with experience in education.

School districts, too, are building programs to control the entry of candidates into administrative posts. For example, the Cincinnati public schools have for years looked upon the assistant principalship as the point of entry to administrative posts in the school system. Consequently, careful appraisal procedures have been applied to all candidates for assistant principalships. The Chicago schools consider the principalship as the major point of entry, and they have developed a system of examination procedures designed to help identify the best candidates for the principalship.

Fortunately, research on administration has shed light on screening procedures, whether done by a university or a school district. For instance, there is evidence to show that mental ability and knowledge make a difference in administrative behavior.[35] One program designed to improve selection is sponsored by the National Association of Secondary School Principals. Initiated in 1975, with assistance from the American Psychological Association, NASSP has now established 12 pilot projects throughout the country to identify persons with high potential for success in school administration.[36]

Preparation programs for school administrators are also being strengthened. The components of these evolving programs were suggested in chapter 9. When the entire administrative hierarchy, not just superintendents, are considered, it becomes even clearer that the resources of the entire university are necessary to provide adequate preparation programs in administration. Administration itself is now a recognized part of the study of political science, psychology, sociology, and other disciplines.[37] With further specialization in administration, many other areas of human knowledge become

35. John K. Hemphill, Daniel E. Griffiths, and Norman Frederiksen, *Administrative Performance and Personality* (New York: Bureau of Publications, Teachers College, Columbia University, 1962).
36. Paul W. Hersey, "Validation: New Developments, Assessment Center Project," (Reston, Va.: NASSP, 1982).
37. Jack Culbertson et al., eds., *Social Science Content for Preparing Educational Leaders* (Columbus, Oh.: Charles E. Merrill, 1973).

pertinent. The school of education of the future will find one of its main tasks that of coordinating resources of the entire university into the preparation programs for administrators.

Improved Political Skills. Members of the school hierarchy will become more astute as political actors. In part, this will be a matter of survival. Schools are on the defensive. Many citizens are ready to join in movements against taxes and against government. Also, the case for alternatives to the public schools is being made more frequently and more persuasively.[38] These conditions are forcing school people to play political roles. Acceptance of the open systems view of administration will also contribute to more political action as administrators seek to improve their understanding of behavior in organizations and of relationships between organizations and their environments.

Individual schools within each school system are becoming more and more autonomous. Thus superintendents and school boards will have to become more active politically, in large districts especially. As more people in the school environment insist on having a part of the action, demands on the central office for the entire system will become unmanageable. Only as individual schools begin to respond to those demands will school-community interaction become effective.

---

38. For instance, see John E. Coons and Stephen D. Sugarman, *Education by Choice* (Berkeley, Calif.: University of California Press, 1978).

11
The Teachers

As recent widely publicized national reports on American schools have stressed, the quality of education in any nation is related to the quality of men and women who serve as teachers and administrators in its school systems.[1] The professionals themselves exercise subtle controls over education—what it is and what it can become—through their training, experience, and aspiration. Teachers exercise further control over schools through their behavior as members of formal and informal groups. Both of these forms of control, that which is reflected in what teachers are and that which is manifest in formal and informal behaviors, will be explored in this chapter which discusses the dramatic changes which have come about through the more active role many teachers now play in the governance of education.

The Teacher in America: Past and Present

Statistics show that about 2,370,000 teachers were employed in the public schools in 1982[2] and another estimated 275,000 were teaching in nonpublic schools. The number of K–12 teachers in public and nonpublic schools rose from 1,354,000 in the fall of 1956 to 2,019,000 in the fall of 1966.[3] Then, for the first time in decades, a perceptible decline in teacher demand occurred in the early 1970s. The recent slackening in teacher demand has been attributed largely to enrollment decreases and financial constraints. This declining demand for new teachers continued into the early 1980s but demand is expected to rise in the latter part of the decade as enrollments increase.

1. National Commission on Excellence in Education, *A Nation at Risk: The Imperative for Educational Reform* (Washington D.C.: Government Printing Office, 1983), 30–32 and Task Force on Education for Economic Growth, *Action for Excellence* (Denver, Colo.: Education Commission of the States, 1983), 10–11.
2. National Center for Education Statistics, *The Condition of Education* (Washington D.C.: Government Printing Office, 1983), 180
3. National Center for Education Statistics, U.S. Department of Health, Education, and Welfare, *Statistics of Public Elementary and Secondary Day Schools, Fall 1972* (Washington D.C.: Government Printing Office, 1973), 270.

This slackening in teacher demand in both public and nonpublic schools has had a dramatic impact upon not only the schools themselves, but also upon enrollment in teacher training programs on campuses throughout the nation. For years it had been assumed that additional teachers would be required to meet growth needs, cover retirements, and replace dropouts from the profession. Declining pupil enrollments and the fiscal restraints confronting numerous school systems, however, have compelled a reassessment of the teacher supply and demand situation and a reconsideration of education's long prevalent growth syndrome. This development surfaced in the early 1970s and will continue to have a profound impact upon teachers and their organizations. For example, the cumulative demand for additional teachers declined from 896,000 in the period from 1971–1975 to 749,000 in the 1976–1980 period.[4] For the five year period ending in 1985 only 670,000 additional new teachers were expected to be hired. As enrollments increase in the late 1980s, however, it is projected that 983,000 teachers will be hired for the period from 1986 to 1990.[5] This dramatic decline in teacher demand in recent years, not surprisingly, has precipitated marked decreases in the numbers of graduates completing teacher preparation programs. The number of newly qualified graduates of teacher preparatory programs declined from 314,000 in 1971 to 144,000 in 1980. These figures indicate that of the number of people receiving bachelor's degrees, 37% received degrees in education in 1971 but in 1980 this percentage dropped to 17%.[6] Teacher supply is least adequate in areas such as mathematics, the natural and physical sciences, vocational-technical subjects, and agriculture. The greatest oversupply of teachers is found in the social sciences, physical and health education, art, music, and foreign languages.[7] We will return to a discussion of the issue of teacher supply and demand in some detail later in this chapter.

Teachers, like the schools in which they serve, are a heterogeneous group. There are wealthy ones and poor ones, old ones and young ones, special ones and regular ones, and good ones and poor ones. The latter distinction of course is the most controversial. No one would deny the power of the great teacher in molding the minds of students. Nor would anyone deny the social significance of a nation's teaching force. Almost all children have contact with several teachers during their school experiences. Nearly every child develops a strong bond with one or more of them, based on respect, admiration, or love. Whether experiences were positive or negative, most citizens of this nation have had a more intimate acquaintance with teachers than they have with doctors, dentists, lawyers, engineers, and even clergymen.

Teachers in America reflect the spirit of America. Their origins are humble, and through time they have elevated their status to one of social significance, if not yet one of genuine public respect and appreciation. As far back as the first months and years of colonization in North America, certain individuals set themselves up as teachers and even organized their own private schools. Other persons, such as ministers and even shipbuilders, were sometimes prevailed upon to teach and to share whatever knowledge they possessed with children from the farms and villages. The principal credential for many of these early schoolmasters was the ability to read and write; in some cases charlatans passed themselves off as schoolmasters while possessing only the most rudimentary skills.

4. National Center for Education Statistics, *The Condition of Education,* 172.
5. Ibid.
6. Ibid., 173.
7. Ibid., 177.

The colonists of Virginia, imbued with missionary spirit, established schools for Indians and orphans in the very first years of settlement in the New World and sometimes imported their schoolmasters from Europe. The Puritans of New England, moving early for a system of publicly supported schools, sought university-trained teachers when they could find them. Many were ministers, and some, like Ezekiel Cheever, head of the famed Boston Latin School for a third of a century, achieved a highly revered status. The Dutch settlers were interested in education too, but their capacity to find and support schoolmasters did not match that of the New Englanders.

Professional Criteria

Progress in the selection and training of teachers likewise advanced rapidly in New England, but the first record of the establishment of "certification" for teaching appeared in New Amsterdam.[8] There the privilege of teaching had to be sanctioned by civil and ecclesiastical authorities, and one Jacob von Corler, who failed to seek and gain such approval, was prohibited from conducting his own private school until he had gained a license to pursue his calling. Thus, inadvertently, the practice of having lay citizens certify teachers was introduced—a practice which leaders among teachers have been seeking to overturn every since. The practice of empowering committees of citizens to examine teachers was adopted by the colonies and eventually was assumed by the states of the United States under their plenary power over education. Despite the vehement objections of men like John Swett, State Superintendent of California, lay control over licensing has been perpetuated. Swett argued that lawyers would not submit to licensing on the basis of an examination by a citizens committee any more than blacksmiths would stand for postmasters sanctioning the practice of blacksmithing. In a celebrated appearance before the NEA in 1872 Swett attacked the existing systems of certification and cited conditions which perpetuated the status quo in teaching: teachers as a group were made up of a procession of young girls anticipating marriage, young men working their way through college, and traveling Ichabod Cranes keeping school rather than teaching school.[9]

The certification of teachers continues to be a function of government. In most states the legislatures have delegated the task of determining specific qualifications for teaching to state boards of education or to special committees on teacher certification. The administration of certification and the decisions relative to qualifications in individual cases are now for the most part in the hands of certification divisions within state departments of education. Despite the fact that legislatures are now mostly out of the certification business, they still impose some restrictions upon teaching and the right to teach. The loyalty oaths, which many states imposed as a condition of employment shortly after World War II, constitute a type of restriction on the freedom to teach not unlike the provision for certification. The oath became a condition of employment much as the license itself. The requirement of the loyalty oath, imposed by legislatures and not state boards of education, is an excellent example of the reluctance of the states to relinquish completely their control over those who teach in the nation's classrooms.

8. Edwin Grant Dexter, *History of Education in the United States* (New York: Macmillan, 1922), 15–16.
9. For an account of Swett's views on certification see R. Freeman Butts and Lawrence A. Cremin, *A History of Education in American Culture* (New York: Holt, Rinehart and Winston, 1953), 398–99. Swett's presentation to the NEA appears in John Swett, "The Examination of Teachers," *NEA* Proceedings, 1872, 71–82.

Those who teach today are not unlike those who practice medicine, dentistry, or law. As a group, an occupational group if not a professional group, teachers are a much improved lot over those who were teaching a century or more ago. And so are doctors, dentists, and lawyers. The right to practice teaching, medicine, dentistry, or law is still guarded—maybe even safeguarded—through government or some instrumentality of government. None has achieved complete control, nor is it likely that any professional group ever will achieve complete control. Each profession is going through its own evolution; some are further along than others, but none has "arrived," so to speak. Because most teachers in America are public employees, they experience quite a different client relationship than do the doctors, dentists, and lawyers. Admission to practice for most doctors, dentists, and lawyers is a matter of licensure, and then they either "hang up a shingle" or join some private organization which has use for their professional services. Not so with teachers—the alternatives are few. Either they identify with a nonpublic school where licensing by the state may or may not be required or they become licensed by the state and seek employment in a public school system. Thus, in the latter case admission to the profession comes through licensing, but admission to practice is dependent upon some public employer of teachers, a school district, admitting the licensed teacher to practice.

Public concern about teacher qualifications is reflected, for example, in recent proposals in Virginia and New Jersey which would substantially reduce and change the professional education content required by prospective teachers for state licensure.

Among the criteria used to judge whether an occupation is or is not a profession is the existence of a body of specialized or esoteric knowledge upon which the occupation is based. Becker argues that an occupation must possess a monopoly on such knowledge and must assume responsibility for protecting and extending its knowledge.[10] Furthermore, asserts Becker, that which is esoteric does not consist of technical skills and the fruits of practical experience, but of abstract principles arrived at by scientific research and refined analysis. Such knowledge can only be applied by those who are privileged to possess it, and then its application must be wise and judicious.

Still another symbol of a profession is the confidence with which its clients receive its professionals' services. The client must trust the professionals completely and feel assured that the professionals put no other interests ahead of their professional activities.

Considered against the single criterion of custodianship over an identifiable body of knowledge, teaching does not yet begin to constitute a profession. Teachers, if they genuinely aspire to become professionals, must concern themselves as a group with what knowledge is exclusive to teaching. Careful analysis of the teaching profession probably will lead to the conclusion that there really is not a teaching or an education profession, but rather professions of teaching or of education. Controversy over issues like competency-based teacher education reflects the divisions even within the ranks of the educators themselves as to how teachers should be trained and certified. If the "professionals" within a field have such basic philosophical and substantive differences about not only the content but the control of teacher preparation,

---

10. Howard S. Becker, "The Nature of a Profession," in *Education for the Professions,* ed. Nelson B. Henry, Sixty-first Yearbook of the National Society for the Study of Education (Chicago: University of Chicago Press, 1962), 35–37.

is it any wonder that the general public is skeptical about teaching's status as a professional field?[11]

Characteristics of the Teacher Group

During the period 1945–1970 employment opportunities for college-trained men and women were unprecedented. With few exceptions, the economy was expanding; the nation was preoccupied with growth and growth-related problems. One of the disquieting features of much of this period was the high demand for talented youth and the realization that the supply, at least of trained or developed talent, in the nation was far short of needs and demands. For the most part, increasing demand for highly trained men and women, coupled with an awareness of the talent shortage, stimulated vigorous competition. The result has been that occupations such as nursing, teaching, and some religious vocations, have found it difficult to compete. Although there has been improvement in teachers' salaries, teaching is still running far behind in terms of lifetime earnings.

What is the teacher like? The National Education Association attempts to answer this question every five years by publishing a monograph on the status of the public school teacher in America.[12] The most recent report summarized data collected during the 1980–1981 school year. Most of the information in the paragraphs to follow is drawn from that report. The large majority of the nation's public school teachers are women—two-thirds are women with a median age of 35 years, 69 percent of whom are married. Male teachers have a median age of 38 years and 80 percent are married.[13]

Today's teachers come from the families of farmers, managers, the self-employed, professional and semiprofessional workers in larger proportions than is true of adult Americans in general. Fewer teachers than might be expected come from families of the unskilled, clerical, and sales worker groups. Many teachers are from families where one or more other members of the family have been teachers at one time. About 73 percent of the teachers have children of their own. Many of the married women who have children are beyond the age of 35 and have returned to the classroom following one or more absences for child rearing.

The level of teacher preparation is improving. More than 99 percent of our teachers now have bachelor's or higher college degrees. About 49 percent have master's degrees, and many have completed a year or more of work beyond the master's degree. Teachers employed in urban districts have higher levels of preparation than teachers employed in rural and small-town districts. Teachers have been trained for the most part in publicly supported colleges and universities. More than three-fourths of all bachelor's and master's degrees held by teachers in 1981 were earned in public institutions. Teachers continue to attend colleges and universities after earning degrees and initial teaching certificates. Most advanced work is taken at summer schools or through evening and Saturday classes during the school year.

11. See for example Robert R. Spillane and Dorothy Levinson, "Teacher Training: A Question of Control, Not Content," *Phi Delta Kappan* 57 (March 1976): 435–39, and Ralph L. Spencer and William E. Boyd, "CBTE Is Succeeding in the State of New York," *Phi Delta Kappan* 58 (May 1977): 677–79.
12. Research Division, National Education Association, *Status of the American Public School Teacher,* 1980–81 (Washington, D.C.: National Education Association, 1982).
13. Ibid., 15.

The income levels of teachers continue to improve although inflation seriously erodes these increases. Indeed, in the period from 1970–1971 to 1980–1981 teachers, unlike in the previous decade, actually lost buying power since the percent change for the Consumer Price Index (CPI) was larger than the percent change for teacher salaries during this period. For the decade ending 1980–81, for example, the CPI increased 57 percent while teacher salaries increased only 43 percent.[14] The base salaries of teachers are being raised everywhere, but more than one-half of all American teachers earn additional income. Nearly three-fourths of all male teachers have one or more part-time outside jobs. According to the NEA, teachers rely upon three sources of supplemental earnings: (1) a second school job, such as evening or summer school teaching or summer maintenance work; (2) earnings from salaries or wages outside the school system; and (3) dividends, rents, royalties, or any other type of nonsalary income. In addition to the individual incomes of teachers, the family incomes of married teachers are frequently increased through the earnings of the spouse. Most of the husbands of married female teachers are employed full-time, and 50 percent of the married men in teaching have wives who are employed full or part-time.[15]

Kershaw and McKean note that salaries motivate persons to enter occupations or jobs and that the nation can attain an appropriate allocation of its manpower through its compensation systems.[16] Since most teachers must rely on their teaching salaries as their basic source of support, these figures are very important. Teaching cannot continue to be a part-time occupation if it is to achieve the status it deserves.

In the early 1980s, as wrenching economic changes and recession beset the country, great public attention was focused upon the long neglected issue of the status of teachers in American society. It became clearer to the nation's political, business and civic leadership that our national survival as an international competitor in an increasingly technical world would depend upon improving the quality of our schools and teachers. As we will discuss later, numerous recommendations for improving the status and salaries of teachers emerged at every governmental level and the very directly related and long neglected issue of quality education became a major national issue in the presidential election of 1984 and an issue at local and state levels nationwide.

Salaries and salary schedules are often complex matters. School boards confronted with mounting pressures for strengthening the quality of public education encounter forceful teacher groups who argue for sharply increased levels of compensation without giving assurance that education will be better. To date most teachers are paid on the basis of salary schedules linked principally to preparation and experience. The merit pay concept has been for years flatly rejected by teacher groups in the face of growing public interest in professional accountability.[17] Growing political pressure, however, may well override these objections and some prominent teacher leaders, perhaps sensing the mounting tide of public opinion in favor of eliminating the almost exclusive dependence on the single salary schedule mode of remuneration, recently have begun to be more flexible on this sensitive issue.[18] Teachers maintain that there

14. National Education Association, *Status of the American Public School Teacher,* 1980–81, 79.
15. Ibid.
16. Joseph A. Kershaw and Roland N. McKean, *Teacher Shortage and Salary Schedules* (New York: McGraw-Hill, 1962), 6–7.
17. Dan C. Lortie, "The Balance Of Control and Autonomy in Elementary School Teaching" in *The Semi-Professions and Their Organization,* ed. Amitai Etzioni, (New York: Free Press, 1969), 40–41.
18. Michael Oreskes, "Shanker Urges Teachers to Aid School Reforms," *New York Times,* 1 May 1983: 1, 39.

should be a respectable base salary for all teachers before the quality performance argument is even introduced. They point out that the average teacher salary (about $17,000 in 1981) is not comparable to that of engineers, pharmacists, home economists, accountants, and business executives. There has been improvement in salary levels in most of the nation's school districts but these gains have not kept pace with increases in other occupations which are not locked into fixed salary schedules. Salaries in other occupations have risen to accommodate the inflationary spiral of the 1970s that has so eroded the purchasing power of fixed income groups like teachers.

Teachers Organizations

Organizations and associations in American society are numerous. The largest single organization is the National Education Association. For more than a hundred years this association has seen itself as representing the teachers of the country; at present its membership numbers almost 1.65 million teachers most of whom are teaching in public schools. There are 59 state affiliates and thousands of units at the local level. The American Federation of Teachers claims 580,000 members and purportedly has state federations in approximately one-half the states. The total AFT membership thus is much smaller than that of the NEA. Many teachers are members of both the NEA and the AFT, where these organizations exist side by side at the local district level. Other significant national organizations of teachers are The National Catholic Educational Association, the Jewish Education Association, and the Lutheran Education Association, though this by no means exhausts the list.

National Groups

Within the past two decades the NEA and AFT have dramatically altered their *modus operandi* and in the process have reshaped the governance of American education. Teacher militancy, a national phenomenon which surfaced only in the 1960s, has sharply altered traditional organizational alliances and educational decision making. Competition for membership between the NEA and AFT has affected profoundly the organization and control of schools. Both of these influential teacher groups have undergone major internal transformations in recent years as they have attempted to serve more aggressive and more dynamic constituents.

The NEA celebrated its centennial in 1957. Never an influential organization politically in the same way as the National Association of Manufacturers or the AFL-CIO, the NEA is nonetheless an organization to be reckoned with. The NEA through its extensive nationwide network of organizational affiliates and associates has a pervasive support base which reaches from the grassroots to the pinnacle of power in Washington D.C.

In the late 1960s the NEA was compelled to make significant internal changes as the result of escalating teacher militancy which estranged teacher organizations from administrator as well as school board groups. Until this time more than thirty autonomous national education associations were "departments" of the NEA which attempted to serve the entire education profession. NEA departments focused upon the special interests of groups representing the several levels of education (kindergarten-primary, higher education, adult education); the responsibilities of specific positions (school superintendents, principals, supervisors); and various instructional specializations (science, mathematics, social studies). These diverse departments for many years made up a relatively unified education family and held considerable autonomy under the NEA banner enjoying its financial and logistical support. NEA's departments had their own executive secretaries and budgets, elected their own officers, and had the freedom to establish their own policies, programs, and qualifications for membership.

Rising teacher militancy generated teacher-administrator rifts and the old NEA umbrella collapsed as major members of the educational family found themselves in adversary positions. In the late 1960s the NEA dropped its affiliate unification efforts and reorganized into departments, national affiliates, and associated organizations. The few organizations which chose to remain departments, including the Association of Classroom Teachers, which constitutes more than 90 percent of the NEA's membership, committed themselves to support the NEA policies and programs and to adhere to the requirement that all their members belong to NEA. More than 15 former NEA departments opted to become national affiliates which subjected them to the same requirements as the departments except for having to pay for their office space and assuming the responsibility of raising their own funds.

The ten or so departments which chose the status of associates were those most incompatible with NEA's new militant tactics. Associated organizations are independent and tied to the NEA only through their common professional goals and orientations. Not surprisingly, powerful administrator groups such as the American Association of School Administrators and the National Association of Secondary School Principals opted to become independent organizations. In the course of a few years, then, all remnants of even the illusion of a unified education profession were shattered.

Not all American teachers had been satisfied to let the teachers associations (NEA and affiliates) act as their representatives. At the turn of the century and shortly thereafter, small groups of teachers, principally in larger cities, began building alliances with organized labor. They were disenchanted with existing teachers organizations, dissatisfied with the economic conditions under which teachers were working, and discouraged by the status granted to teachers as individuals. Local teachers unions were organized into the American Federation of Teachers in 1916. From modest beginnings in a few cities the AFT grew until it could claim by 1976 a membership of nearly 450,000 teachers; in the early 1960s its membership had numbered barely 50,000.

What were some of the conditions in the 1960s which precipitated the growing militancy of the AFT and the new bellicoseness of the NEA? Of central importance, of course, were the pressures emanating from the nation's troubled city school systems. Racial conflicts, discipline problems, overcrowding, antiquated facilities, citizen pressures, and inadequate administration all contributed to rising teacher dissatisfaction in the large cities. Teachers were unhappiest in these districts and thus were particularly amenable to supporting organizations which would vigorously attempt to better their salaries and working conditions.

The AFT was traditionally strongest in these urban centers of discontent and unrest, and the union breakthrough occurred in New York City, the country's largest school system. One of the early controversies in which an AFT local was involved arose in New York City in 1961. There the 49,000 New York City teachers were faced with the prospect of selecting an organization to represent them in bargaining with the New York City Board of Education. In June of 1961 the teachers had voted overwhelmingly (3–1) in favor of collective bargaining. The New York City local, the United Federation of Teachers, was engaged in a fight for its very life during the latter half of 1961. Lieberman, a strong proponent for a single, powerful national teacher organization, described the vote taken by the New York teachers as a landmark in the history of American education.[19] The teachers, in December of 1961, selected the United Federation of Teachers to be their bargaining agent with the New York Board of Education. The United Federation of Teachers, acting as bargaining agent, entered into negotiations with the New York City Board of Education early in 1962. A breakdown in bargaining led to a teacher strike on April 12, 1962—an action which was in violation of New York State law as well as the bargaining agreement between the Union and the Board.

The strike in New York City was indeed a landmark because not only did teachers discover that they could strike successfully without suffering dire consequences, but they also found that militancy yielded dividends at the bargaining table. In just one contract, for example, the United Federation of Teachers was able to achieve for its constituents a sizeable salary increase, guaranteed duty-free lunch periods, a reduction in teaching load, 45-minute preparation periods for elementary teachers, a reduction in class size, a liberalization of sick leave policies, reimbursement for service-incurred injuries, and the provision of teacher aides to relieve many teachers from nonteaching responsibilities.

Other factors also encouraged teacher militancy in the 1960s. Organized labor recognized how crucial teachers were to efforts to organize white collar workers. Membership in the AFL-CIO had remained stable at a time of general population growth. Blue collar jobs were disappearing in an age of growing automation and labor's political viability and future rested on the success of efforts to unionize the white collar segments of the work force. School teachers, long frustrated by low salaries and minimal professional recognition, were an obvious wedge to the organization of other white collar workers. Thus, during the AFT's difficult struggles to survive, organized labor kept the teacher's union afloat with both financial and staff resources. The expertise of experienced AFL-CIO organizers was a significant factor in many of the numerous runoff elections against NEA affiliates as interorganizational rivalry intensified in the 1960s.

The number of governmental employees continued to increase in the decades subsequent to World War II. The public work force contained more lawyers, doctors, accountants, and other professionals who were employed by local, state, and federal governments. These better-educated employees wanted a voice in the determination of their working conditions and salaries and were less than tolerant of paternalistic personnel practices. A few cities and states in the late 1950s and early 1960s had sanctioned collective bargaining or negotiations for governmental employees, but the significant breakthrough occurred in 1962 when President John F. Kennedy issued Executive Order #10988. This order established the right of federal employees to organize and negotiate with their employing units regarding personnel policies and working conditions. Federal workers, however, were not permitted to strike. This executive order facilitated the growth of collective action by public employees at the state and local level as the federal example was emulated by a number of state and

19. Myron Lieberman, "The Battle for New York City's Teachers," *Phi Delta Kappan* 43 (October 1961): 8.

local governments. President Kennedy's action was thought by some to represent a Magna Carta for governmental employees, accomplishing for them what the National Labor Relations Act of 1935 had done for workers in private industry.

Other developments also converged in the late 1960s to help teachers organizations develop more aggressive tactics. The continuing growth of urbanization and the necessities of urban life facilitated the acceptance of collective action in all segments of an increasingly interdependent economy. Romantic notions concerning the virtues of rugged and unbridled individualism, the hallmark of America's early pioneering frontier days, were vanishing as three-quarters of the population was now living in urban areas. More teachers were better educated and thus less tolerant of paternalistic school boards and administrators. Educational requirements had increased and by 1965, 92 percent of the nation's teachers held degrees while only one-third possessed them only two decades earlier.

Since World War II more males have entered teaching. Traditionally, men have been more career-oriented and concerned with salaries and related benefits than were their female colleagues. Men accounted for less than one-fifth of the teaching force in the early twentieth century. In only a ten-year period (1954–1964), however, the number of male teachers increased by 93 percent. The number of women in the profession increased only 38 percent during this same decade.[20] The male-female ratio has stabilized within the past decade or so with men constituting about one-third of the teaching force. The overwhelming majority of elementary teachers are women with men comprising slightly more than one-half the number of secondary school teachers.

As federal programs for the disadvantaged were implemented in the mid-1960s and pressures mounted from civil rights groups, teachers were placed on the defensive and had to share decision making, to a greater extent than before, with parents, community leaders, and state and federal officials. This broadened base of participation in educational decision making and the resulting erosion of what many deemed to be professional prerogatives made teachers feel vulnerable. The resentment felt by growing numbers of teachers about being made defenseless scapegoats for societal problems like racial prejudice and poverty strengthened both the AFT and NEA in their organizing efforts. As their schools became focal points of criticism and controversy, teachers felt more and more acutely the need for powerful organizations to protect their interests.

The early 1960s were years of struggle between the AFT and the NEA. The 1961 vote in favor of the United Federation of Teachers to serve as bargaining agent for all New York City teachers precipitated national interest among lay people as well as teachers. The New York teachers strike in April 1962 fanned the flames of unrest. Boycotts and sanctions, as well as strikes, were used by the NEA and its affiliates in response. The 1968 statewide teachers strike in Florida, led and supported by NEA, was evidence that the NEA was matching the AFT stride for stride.[21]

The NEA and AFT battles of the 1960s were viewed from several different perspectives. School boards were anxious about the rapid spread of collective bargaining and professional negotiations across the country. The competition between aggressive

---

20. James W. Guthrie and Patricia A. Craig, *Teachers and Politics* (Bloomington, Ind.: Phi Delta Kappa Educational Foundation, 1973), 15.
21. For a discussion of the AFT-NEA power struggle see Alan Rosenthal, "Pedagogues and Power," *Urban Affairs Quarterly* 2 (September 1966): 83–102.

national organizations accelerated the adoption of these practices. Other public employee groups took heart from teacher group successes, applauded those achievements, and launched boldly into their own bargaining encounters with public bodies. Citizens were oblivious to the distinctions between the NEA and AFT by and large; strikes, sanctions, and boycotts all looked alike to taxpayers. Lieberman predicted in 1968 that a merger of the NEA and AFT was inevitable.[22]

The conflict continued into the 1970s and 1980s; energies were consumed in minor skirmishes as well as major strikes which attracted national attention. As the tactics of the competing organizations grew more belligerent, the purported ideological differences between the AFT's "unionism" and the NEA's "professionalsim" have become blurred. The issue of administrator membership, for example, was often cited as one of the significant differences between the AFT and the NEA. The AFT argued that administrators were a separate breed with responsibilities for selecting, directing, assigning, appraising, suspending, and terminating teachers. Because of these differences in duties, administrators could never be expected to represent teachers in collective bargaining or work with teachers in the same professional body. The NEA position was that because teachers and administrators work together even though they perform different functions, they needed to hold membership in the same professional organization. This argument has been blunted. The militancy of the NEA has forced the reexamination of the membership of administrators within the NEA at all levels. New tensions arose within the professional community causing associations of principals as well as superintendent groups to reappraise and restructure their relationships with teachers associations. Indeed, the traditional organizational linkages between teachers groups and administrators organizations have been severed in most states. Long-standing affiliations have been maintained in a few states located for the most part in the South and Southwest.

As the differences between the NEA and AFT narrowed, extensive efforts were made for a time to merge the two groups. Although teachers have demonstrated considerable political muscle in recent years, financial constraints, shrinking enrollments and the concomitant decrease in employment opportunities, and mounting public criticism of both the schools and teachers organizations, have made both the NEA and AFT somewhat uneasy. These apprehensions have been exacerbated by the powerful public and political support which proponents of educational alternatives like tuition tax credits and vouchers have been able to muster. Support for these widely discussed alternatives to traditional schooling, along with escalating public criticism and demands for accountability, has caused considerable consternation among teachers at a time of reduced demand for their services. The more aggressive political tactics pursued in recent years by both NEA and AFT affiliates, while undeniably effective in securing improvements in salaries and working conditions, have triggered a backlash among many citizens and politicians who want to see cost-quality justifications for increased educational expenditures. Numerous teachers see public disenchantment both with their performance and the quality of public schools as an ominous sign.

Thus we have an apparent paradox concerning the recent manifestations of teacher power. While the teachers organizations have exerted unprecedented political muscle in achieving their objectives at the local, state, and federal levels, they are becoming apprehensive about public criticism. Job security frequently replaced salaries and fringe benefits as their major area of interest at a time of declining enrollments and fiscal retrenchment. Teachers and administrators are also concerned that their political position is being eroded by the fragmentation of their once unified profession. Cleavages between teachers and administrators over negotiations at the local and state levels have weakened efforts to close ranks on issues on which there is agreement. Many statewide educational coalitions, for example, which once articulated a unified position for educators on the paramount question of state aid, have either disappeared or lost leverage because of bitter divisiveness on other issues.

NEA and AFT leaders, despite these external threats and continuing ideological differences, began to discuss merger possibilities. Prior to the 1960s such merger talks would have been virtually inconceivable because of the divergent philosophies and tactics. The first tangible steps toward merger were modest.[23] In 1969 the teacher organizations in Flint, Michigan merged. A year later in Los Angeles the Association of Classroom Teachers (ACTLA) combined with AFT local 1021 to create the 14,000-member United Teachers of Los Angeles.[24] Numerous merger efforts were made in the early 1970s at local and state levels. Illinois, Massachusetts, and Rhode Island were three of the states where merger possibilities seemed to be particularly viable.

It was in New York, however, that a major breakthrough occurred. On June 5, 1972, the NEA-affiliated New York State Teachers Association approved merger with the AFT-affiliated United Teachers of New York. Lieberman, in discussing the implications of this historic merger, described it as a development that was "likely to have the most profound effects, not only in teacher organizations and education but in labor relations and politics as well."[25]

The merger, however, was short-lived. In the spring of 1976 the shaky four-year alliance ended when the New York State United Teachers severed its dual affiliation and remained affiliated only with the AFT. The teacher leaders in New York as elsewhere were unable to resolve the seemingly intractable issues which for so long had precluded mergers between NEA and AFT affiliates. The major deterrent was and still is, as we shall see, AFT insistence upon maintaining close ties with organized labor or the AFL/CIO. The NEA and its state and local affiliates representing the viewpoints of hundreds of thousands of members have been adamant about preserving the independence of teachers from other organized groups. The NEA in taking this posture no doubt reflects the sentiments of many, if not most, teachers who fear that extra-educational ties will weaken the unique status of the teaching profession. Links with the labor movement are also opposed by many educators who are apprehensive lest their already shaky professional status be further diminished by association with blue collar workers. Leaders of the AFT, on the other hand, believe with equal conviction that only through building coalitions with millions of working people can the teachers generate a broad enough political base to accomplish not only their specific professional goals but their objectives for improving society at large.

This fundamental ideological disagreement could not be permanently resolved in New York even after the 85,000-member union and the 105,000-member NEA affiliate merged into what was called the New York State United Teachers (NYSUT). NYSUT

23. For a succinct review of the history and implications of the merger movement see Myron Lieberman, "The Union Merger Movement: Will 3,500,000 Teachers Put It All Together?" *Saturday Review* 24 (June 1972): 50–56.
24. Ibid., 52.
25. Myron Lieberman, "NEA-AFT Merger: Breakthrough in New York," *Phi Delta Kappan* 54 (June 1972): 622.

locals were compelled to maintain unified memberships in both the NEA and the AFT as well as in the NYSUT. NYSUT itself was to be affiliated with the NEA, AFT, and the AFL-CIO. This New York compromise was hailed inaccurately by many as auguring subsequent merger breakthroughs in other states. It was believed that teachers in other states would look at the political leverage wielded by New York's unified 200,000-member teaching force and expeditiously move to emulate their example.

The expected scenario, however, did not develop and the New York merger, of course, was aborted. Bitter competition between the AFT and NEA surfaced again in New York immediately after the merger terminated in 1976. The merger movement in most other states ran aground earlier for a number of reasons.[26] A primary factor was, and is, the substantial membership advantage enjoyed by the NEA. Whereas in New York the union represented a substantial percentage of the teaching force, elsewhere the NEA's numerical advantage is overwhelming. Union teachers make up 10 percent of the total instructional staff in California, Connecticut, Delaware, Indiana, Maryland, Massachusetts, and Pennsylvania. In only five states—Hawaii, Illinois, Minnesota, Michigan and Rhode Island—do unionized teachers account for 20 percent or more of the total teaching staffs, Rhode Island being the highest with 37 percent.

AFT teachers are heavily concentrated in the bigger cities. For instance, nearly 18,000 of the 31,000 union teachers in Illinois are from Chicago, 15,000 of the 19,000 in Pennsylvania are from Philadelphia and Pittsburgh, and 11,000 of the 19,000 in Michigan are from Detroit. Without the cities and without New York State—which accounts for nearly half the AFT's current membership of about 400,000—the national teacher's union would hardly exist.[27]

The NEA, of course, is very much aware of this still highly significant numerical advantage and sees little need to compromise, particularly when its relatively new militancy is virtually indistinguishable from union tactics. The NEA affiliates at the state and local levels can represent their membership not only as effective bargainers which produce at the table but also as maintainers of professional identity untainted by union affiliation.

These differences persist and the failure of the merger talks has caused the open rivalry between the two teachers organizations to continue. Numerous and imminent mergers at the local and state levels, projected earlier, have not materialized. Although hopes for organizational unity had been dashed at the time of this writing, economic and political conditions and recent membership losses adverse to teachers could quickly revive merger efforts. In any event, some feel that the organizations are now so similar in their goals and tactics that national merger would not significantly alter the status quo in education. A national merger occurring concurrently with increased statewide funding, however, could dramatically and quickly alter educational decision making. Meanwhile competition between the two organizations persists despite their agreement on issues like opposing tuition tax credits, supporting improvement of public education, and strengthening the position of teachers in the bargaining process. Indeed, the organizations continue to challenge each other throughout the country. Late in 1982, for example, the NEA was expected to challenge the AFT in Dade County, Florida while the AFT was expected to challenge the NEA in San Francisco.[28]

26. For a cogent analysis see John Mathews, "The States Eye NEA-AFT Merger," *Compact,* (January–February 1974) 33–35.
27. Ibid., 33–34.
28. *Special Report: Labor Relations in Elementary and Secondary Education, 1981–1982,* Government Employee Relations Report, Bureau of National Affairs, (October 1982): 41:611.

As the conflict continues, the question of its impact upon pupils enrolled in schools must be raised. What are the immediate as well as the long-range effects of such intra-occupational rivalry? The pupils enrolled in schools centrally involved in teacher strife may be affected markedly, but no one really knows. On the other hand, if the end result is the hammering out and shaping of an occupational group that is aggressive about improving its own performance, then the results may be salutary.

State Teacher Organizations

Thus far we have focused our attention upon recent developments in the two major national teacher organizations. Now we will turn to the state level and discuss education associations which are far less visible than their parent, the NEA, but which have had very influential roles in shaping educational policy within their own jurisdictions.

It is extraordinarily difficult to measure the effect of a group or an organization on one of society's institutions. Few would deny, however, that state education associations have had in most cases substantial impact upon the course of educational history in the 50 states. The state associations have exhibited many of the altruistic, humanistic characteristics of the parent organization, and like the NEA, they have not been totally unmindful of the personal needs of the teachers themselves. In recent years they have become exceedingly aggressive, matching union groups in strategy and toughness, and are perceived by legislators to be as effective as almost any other interest group in having their way.

Although AFT state affiliates exist in a number of state capitals, their relatively small membership and big-city focus have minimized the unions' political influence in rural- and now suburban-dominated legislatures. Elected officials as well as state agency personnel understandably have to be more responsive to the much larger NEA-affiliated teacher associations. These associations represent the great majority of school districts in which most of the children of the constituents of elected officials are educated. There have been a few exceptions, notably in industrialized states like Rhode Island and Michigan, where the AFT state affiliates have wielded considerable political influence. Even in a heavily unionized state like Michigan, however, the teacher union is outnumbered heavily by its NEA counterpart.

Several of the state associations, such as the one in Illinois, antedate the NEA. The Illinois Education Association was initially called the Illinois State Teachers' Institute at the time of its organization on December 26, 1853.[29] From very humble beginnings the association went through periods of vigorous activity and periods of decline. Early in its history the association helped to create the office of Superintendent of Public Instruction, to establish a state normal school, and to support the movement for a state university. In more recent years the Illinois Education Association has been the prime mover on much of the important education legislation in the state. The association has been relied upon by the Illinois General Assembly and other policymakers for information to help members make up their minds on educational questions. Similar case histories for teachers associations exist in other states.

While associations have supported better educational opportunities in the form of special programs, pupil transportation, higher standards of instruction, curriculum re-

29. George Propeck and Irving F. Pearson, *The History of the Illinois Education Association* (Springfield, Ill.: Illinois Education Association, September, 1961), 32.

forms, certification improvements and the like, they have not ignored the need for higher salaries, retirement benefits, sick leave provisions, and other welfare benefits. The fight for teacher tenure legislation, of interest also to the American Federation of Teachers, has been led frequently by state education associations. For example, the 20-year fight for a tenure law in Ohio was waged primarily by the Ohio Education Association.[30]

The state associations communicate with their memberships through state education association journals, in most cases long established. In Illinois, the *Illinois Teacher* is the official publication; in Nebraska a weekly newspaper serves this purpose. The character of these periodicals has changed sharply. A few years ago their focus was on broad educational issues; now it is on teacher actions—strikes, boycotts and negotiations—as well as other items relative to teacher welfare. The writing is pointed, the headlines are harsher; the content is organization oriented.

The policies of the state associations are made at state conventions of the associations or at special delegate assembly meetings of representatives chosen by local associations to represent them at state meetings. Some state associations have created state-level educational policies commissions patterned after the former national commission of the same name. Efforts are made to name prominent educators as well as a few noneducators to these bodies; the purpose of the policy commissions is to create a deliberative group and charge it with responsibility for examining the problems of education within the state and articulating long-range directions for the teachers of the state to follow.

The executive secretaries of state associations are key figures in most state-level educational developments. The history of any state association is linked closely to the kind and quality of leadership provided by the occupant of this office. Almost every state can point to one or more vigorous executive secretaries who were responsible for certain kinds of progress within the state. This office sustains the continuity of the state associations, and through the efforts of the executive secretary the internal structure of the association is kept intact. Now in the larger states at least, the state education offices are big, quite bureaucratized, and often populated with young, aggressive former teachers. The political activities of the association are maintained through the full-time staff of the associations. These persons are intimately familiar with the political life of the states; they are called on to testify before legislatures, committees of legislatures, special commissions, state boards of education, and other policy groups. In the American system of state government, association representatives perform an essential information-giving role for government officials. Inherent in this function is the exercise of considerable influence on American schools.

Local Teacher Organizations

An individual American teacher can belong to the NEA or to the state education association in his or her state without holding membership in a local association. But the person who belongs to the NEA without either state or local membership is disfranchised; likewise, the teacher who holds membership in a state association and not in a local affiliate is denied the privilege of participation and representation in policy matters of the association within the state. Nearly all NEA and state association members

---

30. La Vern Rasmussen, "Development, Operation, and Evaluation of the Ohio Continuing Contract Law" (Ph.D. diss. University of Chicago, 1961).

therefore are also members of local associations. The NEA approved its present representative assembly plan of organization in 1921 after a bitter struggle within the top echelons of the association. The adoption of the delegate assembly scheme was successful immediately—all states but four, with a total of 463 local associations, became affiliated in 1921 with the NEA.[31] Members of local and state associations are represented at the NEA annual conventions by colleagues elected locally to serve as delegates to the convention.

The local associations may draw their membership from a single school district, a combination of school districts, or an entire county. The affairs of the locals are completely in the hands of the local membership and the officers they elect. Locals traditionally have been weak organizations; this seems to stem from an absence of strong, committed leadership, and more basically, from the absence of a vigorous *raison d'être*. The locals usually worked through committees, the most active of which was the salary committee. The associations met several times a year; at these meetings they listened to speakers, heard committee reports, selected delegates to the representative assemblies, planned subsequent programs, heard minutes of previous meetings, and adjourned. It was rare that local association meetings were stimulating or well attended. The business of the local usually fell back on a hard core of long-time believers in the association and a cadre of new recruits who were asked to do some of the more onerous chores of the organization.

Increasingly, however, more locals have been influenced by the escalating teacher militancy of recent years and have begun to recognize the potential power which they possess. Among those local association leaders who realize that they have extraordinary power, increasing numbers are attempting or succeeding in using their capacity to influence local policy decisions. Less frequently does the do-good nature of many teachers and administrators interfere with their assuming a more active political role in the affairs of educational policy in their own communities. Such reluctance in the past has caused education to suffer in many places and has worked against the personal interest of teachers as well. Unlike the historical NEA pattern in which locals usually displayed low political profiles, AFT locals traditionally have been more active politically.

A strong local teachers organization can, of course, affect local policy in several ways. Through voicing positions on crucial educational issues, the group can guide the local board in making up its mind. Second, the local group through its committees can study local problems and report to the community and the school board on its findings. Frequently these reports have been on salary and welfare matters only. Third, the local can exercise unusual strength for or against issues brought before the voting public. Many school districts with small turnouts at the polls for educational referendums can sometimes have the issue decided by the teacher vote itself. Fourth, the local teachers group, possibly with the help of state organizations, can intervene in the political affairs of the local school district. Some locals, as illustrated above, have instituted recall elections of school board members and succeeded in unseating an entire school board or certain members of the board. This active involvement in politics, of course, has become more common as local as well as state teacher groups mobilize to support particular candidates for public office.[32] Fifth, the local group can

---

31. Edgar B. Wesley, NEA: *The First Hundred Years* (New York: Harper & Row, 1957), 44.
32. James Browne, "Power Politics for Teachers, Modern Style," *Phi Delta Kappan* 58 (October 1976): 158–64.

support vigorously its own local members for leadership posts within the state or national organization. The prestige of national and state leaders residing in a local may improve the posture of the local in the home district, including its political position with local school officials. Further implications of the political role of local organizations will be outlined in the discussion of collective bargaining.

Associations, Unions, and Control

Political Activism

Quite logically, teacher groups have become more active politically at the federal as well as at the state and local levels. Both the NEA and AFT have maintained for some years active lobbies in the nation's capital and have tried to maintain a constant liaison with leading legislators and administrative officials. Staff members have developed considerable political sophistication as a consequence of being on the Washington scene over a period of years. Despite this presence and the political potential inherent particularly in the vast NEA membership network which covers the nation, educators historically have had minimal impact on policy planning at the federal level.[33] In the presidential elections of 1976 and 1980, however, both the NEA and the AFT strongly supported President Carter. The NEA and its state and local affiliates spent millions on various campaigns during these elections. Much of the power of both unions came from the sheer number of registered voting members. The AFT with concentrated voter registration efforts in major electoral states like Michigan, New York, Illinois, Ohio, and Pennsylvania claimed that 85 percent of its members registered to vote. The NEA projected that more than 90 percent of its members voted. The two unions estimate that they delivered over 2 million votes in 1976, most of which presumably would have been heavily supportive of the Carter–Mondale ticket. The NEA and AFT efforts obviously had impact; Carter defeated Gerald Ford by slightly more than 1.8 million votes.[34]

The two unions also were involved actively in a series of other elections in 1976 and supported selected Republican as well as Democratic candidates. Indeed, the NEA endorsed 37 Senate and House Republican candidates, 30 of whom were elected. The AFT, through the efforts of its Committee on Public Education (COPE), backed ten Republican candidates for the House, nine of whom were successful in the 1976 campaign. Overall, Congressional victory percentages reflected impressive figures of 83 percent and 72 percent for the NEA and AFT respectively.[35]

The political record of teacher groups, however, is hardly unblemished. In 1980, despite the NEA's strong organizational endorsement of Carter, almost 40% of the rank-and-file membership voted for Ronald Reagan. Teachers constituted by far the largest single bloc of delegates at the Democratic nominating convention in 1980. Teachers learned that such active engagement in partisan politics exacts a price when their candidates lose.[36] Reagan, of course, after his landslide victory over Carter had no political obligations or debts to the NEA and proceeded to cut a host of educational

33. James E. Russell, "Realities of Policy Making for Education at State and Federal Levels of Government," in *Government of Public Education for Adequate Policy Making,* ed. Willaim P. McLure and Van Miller (Urbana: University of Illinois Press, 1960) 77–89.
34. "Newsnotes," *Phi Delta Kappan* 58 (January 1977): 440–41.
35. Ibid.
36. Stanley M. Elam, "The National Education Association: Political Powerhouse or Paper Tiger?," *Phi Delta Kappan* 63 (November 1981): 169–74.

programs which the teachers and other organizations had supported vigorously for years. Indeed, the Reagan Administration initially sought elimination of the Department of Education which had been reportedly created by President Carter as an act of gratitude to the NEA for its political support of the Carter-Mondale ticket.

Educators at the federal level have also been attempting to remedy a major long-standing political weakness—their failure to present a unified front. In the past there have been few agreements among the widespread segments of educators. The NEA and its affiliates, the Council of Chief State School Officers, the National School Boards Association, the American Association of University Professors, the American Council on Education, and many, many others speak out for education but the chorus of voices not only has lacked harmony but frequently has been caught singing quite different tunes. Those who fear "professional" control of education could gain some reassurance from the knowledge that frequently the "profession" has been so fragmented that it poses little real threat to lay control of education. In recent years, however, greater efforts have been made by the major national educational organizations to act consensually on issues where there is agreement. The Forum for Educational Leaders (FEOL), for example, recently has been created. This group consisting of the NEA, the AFT, the American Association of School Administrators, the National School Boards Association, The Council of Chief State School Officers, the National Association of State Boards of Education and other national education associations meets regularly to discuss issues of mutual concern and has' begun the tedious process of attempting to gain consensus on complex issues among the diverse groups. Many of these same organizations including the NEA and AFT formed the Coalition for Public Education to oppose the tuition tax credit proposals promulgated by the Reagan Administration.

At the state level the picture is somewhat clearer. Although most states still have a welter of professional organizations speaking out for teachers and education, there is evidence that teacher organizations in many states have increasing influence on educational legislation. Aufderheide found in a sampling of twelve broadly representative states (California, Colorado, Florida, Georgia, Massachusetts, Michigan, Minnesota, New York, Nebraska, Tennessee, Texas, and Wisconsin) that teachers groups because of their large memberships and staffs, financial resources, informational bases, and growing political activism wielded considerable political power.[37] Indeed, among educational interest groups Aufderheide's data showed clearly a pattern of teacher domination in influencing governors and legislators; legislators unanimously assessed the teacher associations as being the most influential educational organizations in the twelve states.[38]

Legislators and the other elected officials are even more annoyed and apprehensive about the direct and large-scale interventions of teacher groups in elections at the local and state levels. In California, for example, the California Teachers Association (CTA) created a Political Education Department in 1971 to increase the political influence of teachers. The CTA affirmed its goals in a statement of purpose which reflects the philosophy of large numbers of teacher organizations in states throughout the country:

37. J. Alan Aufderheide, "Educational Interest Groups and the State Legislature," in *State Policy Making for the Public Schools,* ed. Roald F. Campbell and Tim L. Mazzoni, Jr. (Berkeley: McCutchan, 1976), 176–216.
38. Ibid.

We call for the change we need in the highest traditions of citizenship. We accept the challenge of honest and open participation in politics. As teachers we welcome the responsibility of being a profession in service to the communities of California, and we intend to be involved in the legitimate process of law making, both in Sacramento and the electoral districts. We believe that it is in the best interests of California and California's children that we do so.[39]

The implications of this direct political activity of teacher groups have been indeed profound. Statewide teacher-groups with ample resources provided by large numbers of dues-paying members organized in the grassroots of virtually every community have tremendous political potential. At this time of fiscal crisis and special consciousness of job security teacher groups in many states have become more active in elections.

The Bargaining Role

For years it had been customary for the representatives of the teachers organizations to meet with school boards to discuss salary and teacher welfare matters. In thousands of school districts the superintendent had been the spokesperson for teachers in the presentation of teacher requests to the board. The superintendent frequently worked with salary and welfare committees of teacher groups as they prepared their cases for higher salaries or improved fringe benefits. Most superintendents worked conscientiously at this most difficult assignment; they knew that teachers trusted the superintendent to represent their interests adequately, and they knew that the board of education expected the superintendent to keep the teacher requests within bounds. The practice of collective bargaining as described above is of long standing. It stands in sharp contrast to practices which emerged in the 1960s.

As early as 1950 in Illinois, the West Suburban Teachers' Union, Local 571, made a bargaining agreement with the Proviso Township High School School Board of Maywood, Illinois. Features of this agreement included the expressed recognition by the school board of the union as the collective bargaining agent for all teachers in the district, no discrimination against teachers who were members of the union, the right of the union to meet in the school building after school hours, and the right for disputes between the union and the board to be considered and decided between representatives of the union and the board. The union agreed to not enter into union activities during school hours, to adhere to the policies articulated in the agreement, and to give their best efforts to their teaching duties. There was no statute in Illinois which prohibited this kind of agreement.

Edwards pointed out three decades ago that the law governing the right of teachers to strike or the authority of school boards to negotiate was still in the process of development.[40] Sharp acceleration in this process began with the passage of the 1961 Wisconsin statute which recognized and protected the right of public employees to organize and insisted that school boards negotiate with teachers organizations. The same Wisconsin law denied the right to strike to public employees. This legislation signaled the rapid examination of bargaining in the public sector in many other states.

---

39. *Statement of Purpose*, CTA Political Education and Action Committee, December 1971.
40. Newton Edwards, *The Courts and the Public Schools* (Chicago: University of Chicago Press, 1955), 473–74.

Within five years, six additional states (California, Connecticut, Massachusetts, Michigan, Oregon, and New York) had negotiations laws in force. The legitimacy of public sector bargaining was rapidly established at the state level.[41] Similarly a snowball effect was noted by Lieberman and Moskow at the local district level.[42] They pointed out that every time a teacher organization and a school board negotiate collectively, they make it more difficult for a neighboring school board to refuse to do so. The trend toward rapid acceptance of the bargaining concept at all governmental levels has continued its accelerated pace. Indeed, by 1975, according to Education Commission of the States data, mandatory collective bargaining laws existed in 31 states.[43]

The arrival of bargaining in the public sector has forced changes in attitudes toward negotiations on the part of citizens, board members, administrators, and teachers. There have been concomitant rearrangements in the locations of power. Roles of administrators have been altered. Principals have in many cases been threatened by the arrival of negotiations; they accuse superintendents and teachers of leaving them out of the process.[44] An extensive glossary of fresh terms, for the educator at least, has appeared. New careers have been spawned such as arbitration specialist and professional negotiator. A new coterie of consultants has been marshalled from the fields of education, law, and labor relations. Some consultants have profited substantially from the negotiations movement as they have worked both sides of the bargaining street. The confusion about negotiations which was widespread in its early history has been somewhat clarified in recent years. The rules of the game are more specific and the players have become more proficient with experience.

Informal Organization

Many teacher influences on learning and therefore education can be traced to the informal relationships among teachers that exist in every school system. Informal associations within schools become patterned over time, and identifiable structures of these relationships emerge. The existence of informal organizations within formal organizations has been known for some time. Attention was focused on the importance of understanding informal organization in the Hawthorne studies of the 1920s and 1930s. Later, Chester I. Barnard described and defined informal organization in his landmark volume *The Functions of the Executive*.[45]

Since these beginnings, interest has grown rapidly in understanding more clearly the nature of informal organization and its relationship to behavior of workers within a formal organization. One focus of observation has been on the relationship between informal organizational structures and decision making. In early writing on informal organizations, there was a tendency to classify organizational behavior as being either strictly formal or strictly informal. Subsequent investigation suggests that such polar

41. Myron Lieberman and Michael H. Moskow, *Collective Negotiations for Teachers* (Chicago: Rand McNally, 1966), ch. 2.
42. Ibid., 59.
43. *Update: Collective Bargaining in Education: A Legislator's Guide,* Education Commission of the States (Denver: Education Commission of the States, 1976), 5.
44. For a review of principals' concerns see Bernard C. Watson, "Role of the Principal in Collective Negotiations," *North Central Association Quarterly* 42 (Winter 1968): 233–43.
45. Chester I. Barnard, *The Functions of the Executive* (Cambridge, Mass.: Harvard University Press, 1938).

separations do not describe what really occurs; rather it is more useful to think of organizational behavior as existing along a continuum with formal behavior at one extremity and informal behavior—probably friendship groupings—at the other extreme.[46]

The classification of schools based upon the general nature of the relationships, formal and informal, that prevail within them was achieved by Halpin and Croft.[47] These researchers were able to identify several organizational climates which reflected the qualitative aspects of the professional interactions within elementary schools. Six climates were described: open, autonomous, controlled, familiar, paternal, and closed. Subsequent research will reveal what relationships there may be between school climates and school outcomes. If clearcut relationships are found, they will tell us much about the effects of organizational life on organizational achievements.

Still another example of teacher impact on the formal structures of the school is presented by Lortie.[48] Over a period of months Lortie interviewed in depth a large population of elementary teachers. He was seeking to ascertain what makes them tick as professionals. He wanted to understand more clearly teacher perceptions of teaching in relation to school organization. He posited a control system of three parts—hierarchical, collegial, and teacher autonomy—which coexist in all school systems. It is Lortie's contention that the strength of the autonomy impulse within the teaching occupation has been undervalued, especially as it affects what happens in schools. He argues that teachers protect their autonomy through whatever means they can devise. They are especially wary of attempts to differentiate among teachers either in rewards or specializations. They strive to retain equality of treatment in salary as well as status. Merit pay and teaching teams are often opposed because teachers believe that each of these diminishes their own freedom and transfers more control to superordinates.

Much remains to be learned in this area.[49] School administrators can profit most by keeping an open mind on the nature of organization itself and the relationships of formal and informal structures. They will detect many informal groupings within their own school systems. These groupings may be based on similarities in values, locations of teaching stations, age, experience and tenure, car pools, grade levels, subject fields, and so on. Some staff members may be active in many informal groupings; some few staff members may be part of no informal group. Informal group leaders are important opinion leaders, and the promotion or change in assignment of informal leaders can affect markedly the informal structure of a school system. A deliberate movement of an informal leader into a formal position of leadership is one clear-cut example of the formal organization affecting the informal structure.

46. See Daniel E. Griffiths et al., *Organizing Schools for Effective Education (Danville, Ill.: Interstate Printers and Publishers, 1962)*, 285–93, and Laurence Iannaccone, "*An Approach to the Informal Organization of the School*," in *Behavioral Science and Educational Administration*, Sixty-third Yearbook of the National Society for the Study of Education ed. Daniel E. Griffiths, (*Chicago: University of Chicago Press,* 1964), 223–26.

47. Andrew W. Halpin and Donald B. Croft, *The Organizational Climate of Schools* (Chicago: Midwest Administration Center, University of Chicago, 1963).

48. Lortie, "The Balance of Control," 1–53.

49. For valuable sociological insights into the profession of teaching and the dynamics of schools as organizations see Dan C. Lortie, *School-Teacher* (Chicago: University of Chicago Press, 1975),

Summary and Future Prospects

Teachers' Influence

Teachers are finding themselves in a somewhat ambiguous position in regard to their role in the organization and control of the educational enterprise. There is little doubt that their power within school systems has increased vis-à-vis administrators and school boards. Collective bargaining has given teachers greater influence over the educational program as well as their own working conditions. Teachers also have become much more visible and influential participants in the political process at every level of the governmental system; their human and financial resources and organizational base cannot be ignored by elected officials. Despite these gains, however, teachers are uneasy and apprehensive about their power and future status because of the larger demographic, political, and economic factors which are impacting so forcefully upon schools. The economic crisis, inflation, declining enrollments, and public demands for accountability represent an imposing configuration of concerns for teachers as they consider the influence they can exert upon the organization and control of American schools in the years ahead.[50]

The quality and status of teachers, because of their visibility and pervasive importance in the educational enterprise, have become matters of major public concern and debate as the result of recent national reports and the political saliency of issues such as merit pay. The need to improve the caliber of the nation's teaching force, in fact, was an issue in the presidential campaign of 1984. Despite this escalating public attention and recognition of the importance of teaching, tensions between teachers and citizens apparently persist as public disaffection and demand for accountability erode both the credibility and influence of teachers in a number of communities. Indeed, even supporters of Walter Mondale were somewhat ambivalent when he received an early endorsement from the NEA late in 1983. They were concerned that the backing of this major national teachers organization, despite all the resulting advantages of money and cohorts of workers that would accrue to the Mondale campaign, would boomerang with the general public and even hurt the former vice president's bid to become president.

Clashes between teachers and citizens on issues like professional competence and control, retrenchment policies, accountability legislation, teacher involvement in school board elections, and tax increases going largely to raise teacher salaries are generating considerable tension in communities throughout the nation. The outcome of these struggles will influence profoundly not only the organization and control of American education but also the ultimate power and role of organized teachers.

Outlook for the Future

American teachers may be on the threshold of a new and in many ways troubling period. The current visibility and criticism of schools and restlessness within the teaching ranks may lead to a change in teachers' conceptions of themselves and their professional status. This may require that administrators, school board members, and

---

50. Myron Lieberman, one of the earliest and most influential advocates of increasing the power of teachers organizations, has dramatically altered his position. See Myron Lieberman, "Eggs That I Have Laid: Teacher Bargaining Reconsidered," *Phi Delta Kappan* 60 (February 1979): 415–19.

the public in general modify their traditional views of teachers and teaching. The militancy of teachers unions and associations has in many cases led to improved compensation for teachers and better conditions for teaching. At the same time, teachers are becoming much more visible as a significant occupational group in our society and public expectations for their performance are being elevated accordingly. The recent militancy and political activism of teachers has created a strong backlash among more quality-oriented taxpayers in an uncertain economy. The public is understandably upset as the number of teacher strikes soared from 5 in 1965 to 218 in 1975 and the number of teachers involved in such activities burgeoned from 1,720 in 1965 to a high of 182,300 in 1975.[51] At the beginning of the 1978 school year there were some 120 public school teacher strikes in 21 states; 1,898,394 students had breaks in their education as a result.[52] By the fall of 1982, however, there were only 68 strikes in 7 states. These strikes affected 541,620 students and 29,858 teachers.[53] This dramatic reduction in the number of strikes in recent years not only reflects a more constrained economy but also an understandable reluctance on the part of teacher groups to engage in shutdowns of schools at a time when they are politically as well as fiscally vulnerable.

A persuasive argument can be made that despite their recent political gains, teacher groups are running scared in the light of growing indications that there is genuine public concern about the quality of their members. Many teachers have mixed emotions about this outpouring of concern. While the rekindled public interest certainly is viewed positively in the sense that the central importance of education and teaching to the society is being stressed as it has not been since the Sputnik era almost three decades ago, changes are being proposed and implemented which have caused considerable unrest and apprehension within the ranks of the nation's teachers. The national reports have provided concepts such as merit pay and differentiated staffing with unexpected momentum and political leverage. Teacher organizations historically have been reluctant to support merit pay or other types of financial reward plans which deviate from the traditional salary criteria based on years of academic training and/or years of experience.

Such proposals for merit or differential pay have been discussed and debated with little action being taken for more than 50 years.[54] A few school districts are exceptions to the generalization; systems like Houston, Texas; Ladue, Missouri; Seiling, Oklahoma; Lower Dauphin, Pennsylvania; and some others have operated on merit or similar pay systems for some time. What is so unique in the current environment, however, is the speed with which comprehensive changes are being promulgated and in a number of cases implemented. The U.S. Congress in 1983 created a Task Force on Merit Pay and countless school systems and many states have initiated studies or actually acted on a volatile issue which only a few months before would have been considered too politically sensitive and perhaps "untouchable" in many jurisdictions because of the opposition of powerful teacher groups. California, Florida, and Tennes-

---

51. National Center for Education Statistics, *The Condition of Education*, 182.
52. Richard G. Neal, "Newsnotes," *Phi Delta Kappan* 60 (December 1978): 327.
53. *Special Report: Labor Relations in Elementary and Secondary Education, 1981–1982*, 41:667.
54. For an excellent historical review and analysis of these issues, see K. Forbis Jordan and Nancy B. Borkow, *Merit Pay for Elementary and Secondary Teachers: Background Discussion and Analysis of Issue*, Congressional Research Service, Library of Congress, 33–541 S (July 1983) Mimeographed.

see provide three important examples of states which recently have either enacted or proposed major programs of merit pay or differentiated compensation for teachers.[55]

Teachers groups understandably have somewhat mixed feelings about these developments. They are certainly grateful for the new visibility given their enterprise and for the prospect of increased financial support to the schools to pay for changes like differential salary schedules and extended school days and years. In California, for example, $800 million will be raised in new revenue to pay for the recently enacted reforms. While these aspects of recent developments are certainly positive from the perspective of teachers, other facets are less appealing. The major initiative and impetus for the extensive legislative changes in both Florida and California were provided by government officials and businessmen, not by the teachers. In California, a new chief state school officer was elected on a reform platform which criticized the educational status quo and a powerful business group (The California Business Roundtable) consisting of the state's largest and most influential corporations played critical political roles in the passage of the comprehensive legislation. In Florida, reform-minded Governor Robert Graham and a change-oriented legislature provided the necessary clout for passage of the Raise Bill (SB 6B). Even in Tennessee where the teachers were barely successful in blocking passage of the Master Teacher Proposal, there was extensive support for the governor's initiative and the prognosis reportedly is favorable for its enactment in the near future.

The type of legislation proposed in California, Florida, and Tennessee may be replicated throughout the country and teacher groups in other states could be dealing with new and powerful coalitions which may push for changes similar to the ones proposed in the three states we have discussed. In other words, the state politics of education, for the immediate future at least, will be substantially changed. Teachers and their organizations with their rather deep and widespread apprehensions about merit pay, differential salaries, the subjectivity and dangers of abuse inherent in teacher evaluation plans, and other concerns related to these issues feel rather uncertain and insecure. The combined influence of civic, business, and governmental elites who have coalesced recently around the need to promote educational reforms is rather formidable to say the least. These influential groups are buttressed, as we noted earlier, by rather broad public support for change in the schools. Teacher groups, despite their entrenched and undeniable political strength in many states, could find it difficult to oppose changes which have such widespread and powerful backing.

The transcendent issue which will continue to drive the demand for reform is the deep public concern about the quality of the teaching force. The widely publicized recommendations of the aforementioned prestigious national study groups focused upon the central importance of improving the quality of teachers as the *sine qua non* of efforts to improve the schools. This emphasis on attracting and retaining better teachers was endorsed by prominent political leaders, notably numerous governors,[56]

---

55. Much of this discussion is derived from K. Forbis Jordan, *Comparison of the California Mentor Teacher Law, The Florida Merit Compensation Program, and the Tennessee Master Teacher Proposal,* Congressional Research Service, Library of Congress, (August 1983), Mimeographed.

56. Illustrative of the types of changes being suggested which are less than enthusiastically supported by teachers or their organizations is the recommendation of New Jersey Governor Thomas Kean that persons with college degrees without education courses be permitted to teach. See "New Jersey Governor Would Open Door for Teachers Without Teacher Ed", *Education Times* 4 (September 26, 1983), 3.

as well as by highly influential business and civic leaders. There was general consensus among these influentials as well as the public at large that any efforts to strengthen education would have to be predicated upon improving the socio-economic status and intellectual caliber of the classroom teachers who are at the core of the educational enterprise. In recent years because of the constraints on governmental spending, there has been a continuing drain of talent from the public sector and service fields in general. Teaching without question is not attracting or retaining the "best and brightest" young people.[57] It is generally agreed that attempts to replenish and strengthen the ranks of educators will have to be made in order to ensure the development of our nation's future intellectual capital.[58] Central to such efforts, of course, would be the need to elevate and differentiate teacher salaries in new and substantial ways.

The problem is most acute, of course, in areas like math and science where the economic and status rewards of teaching cannot begin to compete with the salaries and recognition available to talented individuals in business and industry. It is widely recognized that we have a crisis of national proportions because only approximately one-half of our math and science teachers are appropriately certified. Throughout the country, as we have noted, numerous proposals are being made to differentiate roles and salaries, develop merit pay schedules, and recruit part-time instructors from the private sector as efforts intensify to attract and retain talented teachers. The particularly acute problems in the math and science fields and the natural relationship of these realms to economic development may become a major lever for change.

The quality issue has been exacerbated by the fact that women, who still constitute approximately two-thirds of the nation's classroom teachers, now have expanded career options. Talented and intellectually able women who in the past entered teaching because it was one of the few occupational fields open to them are now entering other professional fields. Within the past decade or so, a "perverse form of indentured servitude" has been clearly weakened as our most talented women select from a much broader range of career options. For example, in 1965 only 6.5% of medical school graduates were female while in 1980 the percentage soared to 23.4%; comparable figures for law school graduates were 3.2% in 1965 and 30.2% in 1980. In 1950, only an infinitesimal .3% of the engineering graduates were women, by 1980, 8.8% were female.[59] It is reasonable to assume that many of these women doctors, lawyers and engineers would have been school teachers in prior years. Losing women to other fields because of the continuing expansion of career opportunities for women, historically the largest pool of prospective teachers, further compounds the problem of attracting adequate numbers of our most intellectually able young people to the teaching profession.

The serious economic and political problems confronting the public sector in the difficult period ahead, however, may lead to more formal organizational linkages between teachers and other public employees. The teaching profession is saturated with associations. The roughly 2 million members of the NEA and AFT now represent a no-growth or even declining market as enrollments stabilize or decline in the immediate future. Indeed, the AFT, faced with its first membership decline in two decades,

57. Phillip C. Schlechty and Victor S. Vance, "Institutional Responses to the Quality/Quantity Issue in Teacher Training," *Phi Delta Kappan* 65 (October 1983): 94–101.
58. C. Emily Feistritzer, *The Condition of Teaching: A State-by-State Analysis* (Carnegie Foundation for the Advancement of Teaching, New Jersey: 1983).
59. Feistritzer Associates, *The American Teacher* (Washington D.C.: Feistritzer Publications, 1983), 31.

expanded its membership to noneducational employees at its 1977 annual meeting. The resolution adopted at the meeting added the words "and other workers" to the constitution but President Albert Shanker somewhat narrowed this definition by saying that only workers with "kinship" with teachers such as librarians, nurses, and lawyers would be asked to join the AFT.[60]

These expanded membership standards may not be as farfetched as they seem if one places any credence in Senator Richard Lugar's analysis of labor's current political problems:

> The motivations of the national labor leadership are grounded in the unspoken fear that the tide is ebbing for trade unionism. Total union membership has been dropping consistently as a percentage of the work force and recently, for the first time, in absolute numbers. Public-opinion barometers have indicated further storm warnings. Measurements of the credibility of union leaders, the degree of blame assigned unions for inflation, animosity to union power and other indices of public sentiment have become increasingly negative. In this hostile environment the sense of need for means of reversing the membership numbers, if not the opinion-poll numbers, has become imperative.[61]

There is in prospect expansion of the scope of bargaining to include new protections for parents, students, and the larger society. In the past most of the concessions or compromises have been made by school boards and, indirectly, communities. The philosophy held by many teacher organizers that everything is negotiable may be taken much more seriously by boards in the future. Recent contracts in some districts have contained explicit agreements on discipline and so-called problem children. Some agreements have allowed teachers new freedoms in determining which children they will teach. These contractual features have been exacted in the face of rising expectations about the quality of education for everyone. It is possible that citizen pressure will force school boards to specify minimum performance criteria for individual teachers as well as districts' teaching forces.

As bargaining extends beyond the primary personal interests of teachers such as salaries, grievances, and welfare to other questions of educational policy, the existing system of local lay control of education may be placed in serious jeopardy. Teachers organizations may need to reconsider the nature and extent of the political activity in which they engage. Some critics of the recent political activism of teachers point to the drawback of the NEA's role in the creation of the Department of Education which many feel was President Carter's repayment of a political debt to the group. The NEA, these critics contend, was so enmeshed with Carter and his losing 1980 campaign, that it was unable to have any credibility with the Reagan Administration and even may have been largely responsible for the decline of the department during the Reagan administration. Some teachers favor a much more aggressive political posture, while other teachers cling to the thesis that the people must continue to make the important decisions about our schools. The truth of the matter is that "the people," broadly conceived, have seldom made many of the decisions about schools by themselves. The opinions of the teacher and administrator have either been sought out or freely offered with the result that most educational decisions at all levels reflect both

60. Ari L. Goldman, "Teacher Federation Opens its Rolls to Nonteachers," *New York Times,* 28 August 1977, 30.
61. Richard Lugar, "That Labor Bill," *New York Times,* 20 June 1978, A 17.

lay and professional judgment. The point at issue is whether this balance is to be maintained. There is little doubt that given present conditions teachers' organizations will attempt to exert more influence over the future of education. Administrators, those with managerial responsibilities, will need to recognize that as teachers take on more characteristics of professional associations, the role of administrators will change. Close-knit professionalism will introduce a type of collegial self-government within teaching that has not been present to date. The appearance of such self-government will increase sharply the need for new and more refined leadership skills.

Teachers, like members of other professions, will be challenged vigorously on the validity of licensing and tenure provisions in the near future. General public, student, and parent unrest will force external reviews of these matters if the profession does not itself lead in their reexamination. Recent events, especially in large cities, have caused school authorities to employ new types of personnel such as teacher aides without reference to formal qualifications. Past teacher shortages, often affecting rural areas more than others, have led to the employment of persons as teachers who are not licensed. The success of many such individuals brings into question not only licensing procedures but also teaching's rather tenuous professional status. Our need for better qualified math and science teachers will provide perhaps the most significant test of the validity of teacher licensing practices.

A concerted effort needs to be made to consolidate and integrate the many organizational segments within the broad institution of education. It is important that this be done quite apart from any consideration related to making the profession a more potent political force. Such consolidation would contribute to more uniform opinion about the essential problems of teaching and learning and dispel the current image of an undecided and internally divided profession. The achievement of unity within a profession of education will not come about easily. There are forces at work which act to fractionate the profession, such as the trend toward specialization in administration and guidance services and the elevated status of certain groups such as science and mathematics teachers as a consequence of economic and security needs and National Science Foundation programs. The objective of the profession must be to achieve consensus on important questions confronting the profession as a whole and at the same time to maintain an internal governing structure that can tolerate the emergence of powerful subdivisions within itself.

12
The Students

One of the most time-honored principles of American education is that schools exist to meet the needs and serve the interests of their students. It follows from this proposition that student interests are represented in the development and implementation of school policies. For the most part, this representation has been indirect in that lay citizens and school personnel have noted the characteristics of students and made decisions on the basis of these traits. In the late 1960s, however, students in many locales became involved more directly in school decision making.

In this chapter we will discuss the impact of students upon the control of schools. In the first section, we will look briefly at some general characteristics of students which influence decisions made by boards of education, administrators, and teachers. Then we will examine student efforts to participate in policy development and implementation.

Some Characteristics of School Students

Numbers

The early 1970s marked the crest of a steady increase in school enrollments. However, a larger proportion of American children spends more time in school than ever before. Enrollment figures for public and nonpublic elementary and secondary schools were presented in chapter 1. Including students enrolled in institutions of higher education, the total 1981 fall enrollment was 57.5 million which is an increase of approximately 23 percent since 1961 but a decrease of nearly 3,000,000 students since 1976.[1] Thus more than one-fourth of the slightly more than 223 million people in the United States are students. The percentage of the total school-age population enrolled in regular schools in October 1961, October 1971, and October 1981 is shown in table 12.1.

---

1. W. Vance Grant, "The Demographics of Education," *American Education* 17 (August-September 1981): 7.

During the past 20 years the percentage of young people in school increased considerably. As of October 1981 more than 98 percent of American children between the ages of 6 and 15 were enrolled in school. The most notable increases during the period under review were among 3 to 6 year-olds and students 16 and older. The former reflects an increase in the number of states which provide financial support for kindergarten. Moreover, 50 percent of 3–5 year old children were enrolled in either nursery school or kindergarten in 1980. This represented a 29 percent increase over 1966.[2] It also reflects significant societal changes such as growth in the number of working mothers, changes in family structure, and a dramatically altered economy. The higher figures for students 16 and older indicate both a decrease in the percentage of students who drop out before the completion of high school and an increase among those who enter and complete college.

The number of students enrolled in elementary and secondary schools declined in the 1970s as products of the post World War II baby boom moved through schools. Projections for the 1980s include an increase of pre-school and elementary age students from approximately 30 million in 1980 to 35 million by 2000. The population of 14 to 24 year olds is projected to decline from 45 million in 1980 to 38 million in 1990 and then increase to nearly 41 million by 2000.[3] Fluctuations in the numbers of students at various levels often pose difficult decisions for boards of education and school administrators.

Examples of decisions affected by the sheer numbers of students include determination of how many buildings and teachers are and will be needed, new patterns of staff utilization, and in some states the establishment of thirteenth- and fourteenth-grade programs. Declining enrollments have created serious policy problems for school boards and administrators. It is very difficult to win public acceptance for de-

TABLE 12.1

School Age Population Enrolled in Regular Schools (in percents)

Age Groups	YEAR			
	1960	1970	1980	1981
Total	56.4	56.4	49.7	48.9
3–4	N.A.	20.5	36.7	36.0
5–6	80.7	89.5	95.7	94.0
7–13	89.5	99.2	99.3	99.2
14–15	97.8	98.1	98.2	98.0
16–17	82.6	90.0	89.0	90.6
18–19	38.4	47.7	46.4	49.0
20–21	19.4	31.9	31.0	31.6
22–24	8.7	14.9	16.3	16.5
25–29	4.9	7.5	9.3	9.0
30–34	2.4	4.2	6.4	6.9

SOURCE: U.S. Bureau of the Census, *Statistical Abstract of the United States,* 102nd edition (Washington, D.C.: Government Printing Office, 1981), p. 139. Figures for 1981 are from *Statistical Abstract,* 103rd edition, 1982–1983.

2. *Characteristics of American Children and Youth: 1980* (Washington, D.C.: Bureau of the Census, 1982), 1.
3. Ibid., 2

cisions to close neighborhood schools even when such actions are taken as economy measures.

Distribution

Like the general population, students are not distributed evenly across the nation. Moreover, approximately 20 percent of the population moves annually. This rate is even higher among the school age population. For example, 50 percent of the American population of ages 5 to 24 moved between 1975 and 1980.[4] Although much of this was attributable to past 20 year olds establishing new households, it is clear that school age children move frequently. It is important therefore that substantial commonality exist among school programs in various parts of the country in order to provide some continuity for mobile students.

Population shifts also mean that some districts face teacher shortages and demands for new classrooms while others dismiss surplus faculty members and close schools. The current decade is witnessing dramatic population shifts from northeast and midwestern states to the Sun Belt. Another population trend is the movement out of major metropolitan centers to small towns and semi-rural areas. These trends result from economic relocation and improved communications and transportation.

The consolidation and decentralization of school districts has done little to equalize district enrollments on a national basis. For example, while there are about 16,000 local school districts in the country, approximately 27 percent of the national public school enrollment is in only 181 of them.[5] Further evidence of this disequilibrium is presented in table 12.2 where it is shown that more than 60 percent of public school students are enrolled in 11 percent of the districts in the nation. It also indicates that more than half of the districts in the nation enroll fewer than 1,000 students each. The scope of school programs is often related to the size of schools in which they are

TABLE 12.2

Number and Percentage of Public School Districts by Size of Enrollment, Fall, 1979

Enrollment/Size	School Systems		Pupils Enrolled	
	No.	%	No. (in 1,000s)	%
Total	15,944	100.0	41,882	100.0
25,000 +	181	1.1	11,415	27.3
10,000–24,999	478	3.0	7,004	16.7
5,000–9,999	1,106	6.9	7,713	18.4
2,500–4,999	2,039	12.8	7,076	16.9
1,000–2,499	3,475	21.8	5,698	13.6
600–999	1,841	11.5	1,450	3.5
300–599	2,298	14.4	1,005	2.4
1–299	4,223	26.5	521	1.2
None	303	1.9	0	0

SOURCE: National Center for Educational Statistics, *Digest of Educational Statistics, 1982* (Washington, D.C.: Government Printing Office, 1982), 61.

4. Ibid., 2.
5. National Center for Educational Statistics, *Digest of Educational Statistics, 1982* (Washington, D.C.: U.S. Government Printing Office, 1982), 61.

found. In other words, school districts with larger enrollments can afford to employ more teaching specialists than can much smaller districts. For example, a high school with an enrollment of 2,000 students is large enough for teachers of five different foreign languages to teach full schedules in their specialities. This would not be possible in a high school of 400 students. Thus, board of education members and administrators who make program decisions for two such schools do so within different sets of constraints established by enrollment figures.

Socioeconomic Composition

The spatial distribution of the population and widespread adherence to neighborhood school policies mean that student bodies are often segregated by socioeconomic characteristics. For example, there are small rural schools in which most students come from farm backgrounds, schools in well-to-do suburban neighborhoods where most students come from professional or managerial families, schools in working-class neighborhoods where most students come from low- or middle-income blue-collar families, and inner-city schools where virtually the entire student body may be eligible for public welfare assistance.[6] Generally speaking, the socioeconomic status of a student body reflects the education, occupation, and income of adults in the community.

The correlation between social class and academic success is well-known.[7] Students from middle- and upper-class backgrounds are more likely than lower-class students to do well on achievement tests, graduate from high school, and go on to college. On the other hand, lower-class students are more likely to enter school with severe educational deficiencies, behave in ways which middle-class teachers consider inappropriate, and leave school at an early age.

Probably the best-known decisions based upon socioeconomic characteristics of students are those dealing with Chapter 1 of the Elementary and Secondary Education Act and other compensatory programs. School eligibility for these programs is determined on the basis of student socioeconomic characteristics. Many other programs are also affected. Expensive program options such as summer tours in Europe are offered more often in neighborhood schools where parents can afford them. Similarly, some high schools in high-status neighborhoods offer virtually no vocational preparation because it is assumed that almost all students will go on to college. High schools in poor neighborhoods are less likely to offer advanced courses in mathematics and foreign languages than their suburban counterparts because of expectations based upon social class and achievement. There is also some evidence that many city teachers prefer to teach in middle- and upper-class schools.[8] As a consequence, teachers with experience and seniority often transfer from lower-class schools leaving younger and relatively inexperienced teachers to provide most of the instruction for lower-class children. The Houston Public Schools recently began to offer financial incentives to teachers willing to teach in difficult settings in an attempt to counter such actions.

In addition, the socioeconomic composition of the student body can determine the relative emphasis teachers and administrators give to instruction and pupil control in the school. For example, Havighurst concluded that the teachers of Chicago

6. For a discussion of various school types see Grace Graham, *The Public School in the New Society* (New York: Harper & Row, 1969), 21511, and Robert J. Havighurst, *The Public Schools of Chicago* (Chicago: Board of Education, 1964), 31–56 and 143–73.
7. Large-scale evidence on this point is presented in James S. Coleman et al., *Equality of Educational Opportunity* (Washington, D.C.: Government Printing Office, 1966).
8. See Howard S. Becker, "The Career of the Chicago Public School Teacher," *American Journal of Sociology* 52 (March 1952): 470–77, and Robert E. Herriott and Nancy Hoyt St. John, *Social Class and the Urban School* (New York: John Wiley & Sons, 1966), 206.

naturally give priority to the academic orientation if they can do so. This they can do in a high status school and in a main line school. They do not have to spend much time controlling the behavior of their pupils. In the common-man and inner-city type of school, the control of behavior becomes more of a problem. The school tends to adopt a behavioral orientation with the academic orientation subordinated to it. Many of the quotations from interviews with teachers of inner-city schools showed their preoccupation with the control of behavior. Teachers say they cannot teach because they are so busy trying to control their pupils' behavior.[9]

The fact that many schools are still racially segregated continues to influence decision making in some school systems. Apparently some decisions to assign black teachers, counselors, and administrators to predominantly black schools are still being made on this basis. Also, some school systems hesitate to assign a black principal or "too many" black faculty members to certain all-white schools. By the same token, some teachers are influenced in choosing the school where they prefer to teach by the racial composition of its student body. In terms of the school curriculum, the heritage and contributions of minority groups are more likely to be emphasized in schools where members of those groups are enrolled.

Many school districts which implemented desegregation plans several years ago have become resegregated due to population shifts and differential fertility rates. Hodgkinson points out that minority birth rates have stayed about the same while that of Caucasians has declined since the postwar baby boom.[10] As a result, the minority proportion of the school age population is increasing and will reach more than 30 percent for the nation as a whole by 1990. Immigration of Spanish-speaking young people also has had substantial effect on the school age population in many states. These two factors in combination with the disproportionate attractiveness of nonpublic schools to white students has resulted in increasing minority enrollments in the public schools of many states. For example, in 1980, minority students constituted 52 percent of the public school enrollment in Mississippi, 43 percent in Louisiana and California, 46 percent in Texas, 33 percent in Florida and Maryland, and 32 percent in New York.[11]

Another set of socioeconomic trends which affects the nature of the student body in a school involve changes in family structure. An increasing number of children spend a significant amount of their life in single parent homes and of those with two parents at home, an increasing number have mothers in the labor force. The 1980 U.S. Census estimated that of the children born that year, 48 percent would live "a considerable time" with one parent.[12] Also, in that year, the mothers of 53 percent of children who lived in two parent families were in the labor force.[13] There are at the present time literally millions of "latchkey" school children who let themselves into an empty house at the end of the school day. Schools with large numbers of children from single parent or two parent-earner families often face different problems. For example, it is much more difficult to close school or send children home early because of snow accumulations. Moreover, there is some evidence that children from single parent homes do less well in school than their peers.[14] Some schools are responding to

9. Havighurst, *Public Schools of Chicago*, 171.
10. Harold L. Hodgkinson, "Guess Who's Coming to College: Your Students in 1990" (Washington, D.C.: National Institute of Independent Colleges and Universities, 1983, Mimeographed), 3.
11. Ibid., 6.
12. B. Frank Brown, "A Study of the School Needs of Children from One-Parent Families," *Phi Delta Kappan* 61 (April 1980): 537–40.
13. *Characteristics of American Children and Youth: 1980*, 1.
14. Brown, "Study of the School Needs."

changes in family structure by establishing extended day programs whereby parents can bring their children to school early in the morning and pick them up at the end of their workday. The additional time can be used for supervised study, clubs, music lessons, or sports activities.

Educational Needs

In the past decade society has become increasingly aware that students have different educational needs. Some of this awareness has been stimulated by court rulings on behalf of minority and handicapped students (chapter 7). The passage of Public Law 94–142 required school districts to improve educational opportunities for handicapped students. Two aspects of this law, the requirements to develop individualized educational programs and to place students in the least restrictive educational settings available to them have particular implications for general school programming. The fact that districts must not only provide programs for such students but integrate them to the maximum feasible extent with other students means that all students in the district will become more accustomed to interacting with handicapped children. It also means that local officials will necessarily give more attention to the needs of particular students in designing programs and that districts with large numbers of handicapped students may incur greater costs than other districts.

Responsiveness to the individual educational needs of other types of students can be costly too. For example, it is usually more costly to provide instruction in vocational education than in general college preparatory programs. Similarly, it usually costs more to teach advanced physics than beginning mathematics because of the higher equipment costs and smaller class sizes associated with physics. Thus districts which enroll large numbers of students with special educational needs and which seek to respond to them will have programs which are different and probably more costly than those in districts where officials see the needs of all students being alike. This fact has important implications for financing school programs and has been recognized in some states. For example, the Florida Educational Finance Program provides payments to school districts according to the number of students they enroll in each of 26 program categories. Between 1961 and 1981, the average pupil-teacher ratio in American public schools shifted from 25.5 to 1 to an estimated 18.7 to 1.[15] This change is due largely to the addition of programs designed to meet special learning needs of students.

Student Involvement in Policymaking

The Tradition of Student Government

The notion that students should be involved in decisions about their education dates back to at least the days of Plato and Aristotle. Both the Academy and the Lyceum made provision for student participation in operating decisions on a representative basis.[16] In medieval times, students formed guilds for protection, charity, fraternity, welfare, mediation of quarrels, and other purposes. During the Renaissance, students were organized to assume responsibility for athletics and other events and to monitor the performance of other students.[17]

15. Grant, "Demographics of Education", 8–9.
16. Harry C. McKown, *The Student Council* (New York: McGraw-Hill, 1944), 1–5.
17. Frederick C. Gruber and Thomas Bayard Beatty, *Secondary School Activities* (New York: McGraw-Hill, 1954), 1–2.

Similar monitorial systems were established in many early American schools and academies and were referred to as Lancastrian schools (after Joseph Lancaster, one of the founders). The first of these schools in which some students served as what now would be termed teacher aides was established in New York City in 1805.[18] The system was being used in the New York City Public High School by 1825 and subsequently spread throughout New England and as far as Georgia, Kentucky, Michigan, and Texas. However, it virtually disappeared by the middle of the nineteenth century as states assumed greater responsibility for the support of public schools.[19]

Gruber and Beatty note that considerable faculty and administration support for student participation in school control did not develop until 1890.[20] Influential examples of student self-government at this time were the School City at the Norfolk Street Vocational School in New York City founded by Wilson L. Gill in 1897 and the George Junior Republic at Freeville, New York, established by William R. George in 1894. McKown describes the latter model as a "sort of self-governing community patterned after the federal government."[21]

The idea of student government apparently spread rapidly during the first half of the twentieth century. Writing in 1944, McKown referred to a series of studies which indicated that of the secondary school student councils then in existence more than 50 percent were established since 1925, and few, if any, predated 1900.[22] The National Association of Student Councils was founded in 1931. By 1954 Gruber and Beatty were able to write "there is scarcely an American secondary school without some form of student government."[23]

As student government evolved in the high schools, it was seen as part of a broader program of student activities. Educators wrote books about the total activities program and included student government as a subtopic.[24] Similarly, textbooks on secondary school administration generally treated student government as one part of the activities program.[25] Elicker has pointed to another twentieth century transition. Noting that the "desire of [early advocates of self-government] to release their charges from subservient obedience" often resulted "in swinging too far to the other extreme," he explains that later educational leaders led in the "return . . . from the by-way of student self-government to the highway of student participation in school government."[26]

Many objectives have been set forth for the participation of student groups in school government. Those listed by Davis are typical.

1. Providing opportunities for students to learn democratic processes
2. Providing opportunities to develop leadership abilities

18. McKown, *Student Council*, 6.
19. Ibid.
20. Gruber and Beatty, *Secondary School Activities*, 4.
21. McKown, *Student Council*, 8.
22. Ibid., 13–14.
23. Gruber and Beatty, *Secondary School Activities*, 4.
24. Examples include Gruber and Beatty, *Secondary School Activities;* Robert W. Frederick, *The Third Curriculum* (New York: Appleton-Century-Crofts, 1959), and Franklin A. Miller, James H. Moyer, and Robert B. Patrick, *Plannig Student Activities* (Englewood Cliffs, N.J.: Prentice-Hall, 1956).
25. See Rudyard K. Bent and Lloyd E. McCann, *Administration of Secondary Schools* (New York: McGraw-Hill Book Co., 1960), and Glen F. Ovard, *Administration of the Changing Secondary School* (New York: Macmillian, 1966).
26. Paul E. Elicker, "The Development of the Student Participation Movement" in National Association of Student Councils, *The Student Council in the Secondary School: A Handbook for Student Councils and their Sponsors* (Washington, D.C.: National Association of Secondary School Principals, 1955), 4.

3. Providing opportunities for students to participate in the management of the school
4. Providing opportunities for better relationships between students and school personnel
5. Providing oportunities for better coordination of all school activities
6. Providing a better atmosphere for learning
7. Providing opportunities for the students to help sponsor worthwhile projects
8. Providing ways for new students to become better oriented to the school
9. Providing ways for needed organizations to come into being in the school
10. Assisting the student body in its evaluation of the extraclass program[27]

Student councils across the nation have undertaken a wide range of activities in pursuit of such objectives. For example, Van Pool identified 269 different projects in what he described as a partial list of actual council activities.[28] Many of these projects were of great benefit to both schools and students, but only a very few offered students a voice in the formulation of basic school policies and procedures or in the planning and evaluation of the basic instructional program.

The traditional exclusion of student participation in such vital school areas has been by design. Mathes has stated the point succinctly:

> In general, there are three levels of student participation in school administration. One area is that in which the students have no authority or power to act. A second area is that in which they have been given almost complete control. A third area is that in which they share certain responsibilities with the faculty and community. When a student council is organized, these three areas must be clearly delineated and understood by all students.[29]

These spheres of influence usually have not been defined explicitly, and the area in which students are theoretically dominant is frequently small and inconsequential. The provocative statement of one principal in a discussion with some student council leaders characterizes many local situations.

> Most principals are involved in a game called "student council" where they give the student council very little authority and they let them discuss only the peripheral concerns of the school. It's a kind of hoax which they have perpetuated; these principals convince the students that the councils are doing something important when in reality, the councils are just going through the motions of considering and acting on trivia.[30]

Not all student councils function this way. Indeed, many groups have dealt effectively in the past with issues of paramount importance to students and will continue to do so. However, there is evidence that many students doubt that student councils can deal effectively with their concerns. In some instances, they feel they are not

27. E. Dale Davis, *Focus on Secondary Education* (Glenview, Ill.: Scott, Foresman, 1966), 207.
28. Gerald M. Van Pool, "The Aims and Objectives of the Student Council" in National Association of Student Councils, *The Student Council in the Secondary School*, 94ff.
29. George E. Mathes, "Organizing the Student Council," NASC, *The Student Council*, 21–22.
30. Allan A. Glathorn et al., "Students and Principals Discuss Today's Issues," *The Bulletin of the National Association of Secondary School Principals* 52 (February 1968): 22.

represented in student government; in others, they view administrative dominance of the council as an insurmountable obstacle. Many simply are not interested in school governance. However, some are open to utilizing other means of influencing school policies; history provides some important lessons in this regard.

Student Activism in the 1960s

In the middle and late 1960s a wave of student unrest swept across the campuses of American colleges and universities. While the frequency and volatility of student protest diminished substantially after 1970, it had important effects upon school policies. Moreover, the rise and decline of student activism paralleled the course of confrontation politics in the broader society, thereby demonstrating the impact of the larger environment upon school affairs. The impact of this movement was so substantial that Katz and Sanford said about it as early as 1966:

> In the last eighteen months, one central fact has emerged, namely that students have arrived as a new power, a fourth estate which is taking its place beside the traditional estates of faculty, administration, and trustees. What is more, the situation is irreversible. Students have become conscious of their own power. . . . Above all, they have experienced success in making their presence felt and extracting concessions.[31]

The momentum of protest increased during the last half of the decade. Directing their attention to national and international questions of race relations and foreign policy as well as local campus conditions, students from coast to coast confronted school officials with demands and sometimes clashed with police and the national guard. By 1969 events had progressed to the point where a staff report to the National Commission on the Causes and Prevention of Violence devoted substantial attention to student protest.[32] This report noted that "the major campus that has not experienced a certain amount of turmoil and disruption is the exception. . . . On several campuses, massive student demonstrations have become a familiar and almost banal occurrence. Moreover, there has been a discernible escalation of the intensity of campus conflict, in terms of both student tactics and the response of authorities." [33]

Also by this time, it was clear that student activism was a prominent phenomenon on the campuses of junior and senior high schools. A national survey of 1,026 principals, by J. Lloyd Trump and Jane Hunt of the National Association of Secondary School Principals, revealed that 56 percent of those in junior high schools and 59 percent of the high school principals had experienced some kind of protest.[34] The same report indicated that two-thirds of city and suburban schools had experienced unrest. There also had been and continues to be scattered reports of elementary school incidents.

At the junior and senior high school levels, three general types of unrest have occurred. The first is interstudent conflict in which one or more students challenge

---

31. Joseph Katz and Nevitt Sanford, "The New Student Power and Needed Educational Reforms," *Phi Delta Kappan* 47 (April 1966): 397.
32. Jerome H. Skolnick, *The Politics of Protest: Violent Aspects of Protest and Confrontation,* staff report to the National Commission on the Causes and Prevention of Violence (Washington, D.C.: Government Printing Office, 1969). For a comprehensive review of student protest at college and university levels see pp. 63–96. Also available from Simon & Schuster, Inc. and Ballantine Books, Inc.
33. Ibid., 63.
34. J. Lloyd Trump and Jane Hunt, "The Nature and Extent of Student Activism," *The Bulletin of the National Association of Secondary School Principals* 53 (May 1969): 150–58. Another survey which also discusses causes and response strategies is Stephen K. Bailey, *Disruption in Urban Public Secondary Schools* (Washington, D.C.: National Association of Secondary School Principals, 1970).

other students. Arguments and fights growing out of such incidents have a long history in most schools. However, racial tensions and the temerity of student gangs often have escalated minor disagreements involving two students into large-scale disorders. The possibility of such disturbances continues to be so real in some schools that security officers are assigned to the buildings, and elaborate surveillance and communications procedures. (e.g., the use of walkie-talkie radios by hall guards) are employed. Because athletic contests between rival schools have sometimes culminated in group violence, it has become increasingly difficult to ensure the safety of spectators and participants. Indeed the atmosphere has been so volatile in some instances that games have been cancelled or played behind locked stadium doors without spectators. Often student violence of this type is stimulated by nonstudents who gain entry to school campuses. The problem of dealing with unemployed school dropouts who have disruptive tendencies seems especially severe in inner-city schools.

A second type of student unrest is aimed at protesting political conditions in the broader society. The war in Vietnam, draft laws, and the power of the national "military-industrial complex" were popular targets of politically-oriented protestors. These were clearly conditions over which school officials had no direct control, yet students sometimes called for specific changes to be made (e.g., termination of school visits by military recruiters). While political protest has occurred primarily at the college and university levels, a substantial amount took place in secondary schools in the early 1970s. Like inter-student conflict, political protest can sometimes precede or occur concomitantly with demands to change school policies, which is the third general type of activism.

Policy-oriented protest by students has had several objectives. The NASSP survey mentioned above found that in the 1960s dress codes and hair regulations were the most frequent subjects of protest. Other common complaints dealt with smoking rules, cafeterias, assembly programs, school and student newspapers, and various aspects of the school program.[35] Forty-five percent of the principals who reported activism, however, said that students protested against some part of the educational program such as the quality and assignment of teachers, content of the curriculum, grades, and examinations.[36]

Many observers currently believe that student activism is a thing of the past. Certainly, radical alternatives based on dissatisfaction with the "system" are not sought as frequently nowadays. Most young persons have decided to face modern society by preparing themselves for upward mobility and by joining with others who have similar interests in order to promote the reforms they desire. One corollary to the increasing complexity of society has been growth in the percentage of the population which is literate, articulate, and imbued with the success ethic. Schools are very important to these people for they are seen as a means to upward mobility in both social and economic terms. However, it is apparent that some groups that believe opportunities for social and economic gains have not been improved sufficiently by the educational system wish to change that system. Less apparent but perhaps equally strong is the determination of groups which have benefitted most from that system to maintain it substantially as it is.

Those who wish to change contemporary institutions in some way have learned that a strategy of confrontation in which like-minded persons organize to make de-

35. Trump and Hunt, "Nature and Extent of Student Activism," 153–56.
36. Ibid., 156.

mands and threaten sanctions is often effective. It is a strategy which has been used most notably by labor unions and has spread in recent years to teacher groups and various civil rights and neighborhood organizations. Schools have become an important target of such groups in recent years. Teachers, of course, have sought higher wages and improved working conditions in such confrontations. Citizen groups, as we will see in chapters 13 and 14, have presented a variety of demands to school officials including improved performance in schools with minority groups and poor children.

Television and other media have made today's students more knowledgeable than their predecessors. Television readily communicates the reality of racism, violence, poverty, war, and other social ills. Students as well as adults have come to appreciate the value of education more than before and are cognizant of the criticisms which have been directed at schools. Thus some students question whether schools, as they experience them, deal with questions of importance in the broader society and prepare them adequately for the roles they seek within it. Student activism can best be understood as the product of conflict felt by youth aware of and influenced by the changing nature of society and the traditional nature of school systems.

Violence and Vandalism in the 1970s

Although student protest waned in the 1970s, that decade was marked by a substantial increase in student violence and vandalism. A special United States Senate Subcommittee to Investigate Juvenile Delinquency reported a dramatic increase in school violence in the 1970s. Senator Birch Bayh released the committee report in 1975 saying that the survey on which it was based produced "a ledger of violence confronting our schools that reads like a casualty list from a war zone or a vice squad annual report." [37] This survey of 516 school districts with enrollments of more than 10,000 students found that betwen 1970 and 1973 school homicides increased by 18.5 percent, rapes and attempted rapes increased by 40.1 percent, assaults on students increased by 85.3 percent, assaults on teachers increased by 77.4 percent, school building burglaries increased by 11.8 percent, drug and alcohol offenses on school property increased by 37.5 percent, dropouts increased by 11.7 percent, and the number of weapons confiscated by school authorities increased by 54.4 percent. [38]

Acts of violence and vandalism were particularly frequent in large school systems. Albert Shanker told the Bayh subcommittee that "during the first five months of the 1974–75 school year there were 31 incidents involving handguns; there were 474 assaults on teachers . . . and 612 arrests in the schools of New York—an increase of 95.6 percent over the 313 figure of the previous year." [39] Large suburban districts have also experienced violence in schools. In addition to crimes against persons, property destruction is a serious concern in many school districts. Arson is a particularly widespread and costly problem. Evidence of general public concern about violence and vandalism is seen in the fact that national polls in 1981 and 1982 identified student discipline as the most serious problem confronting American schools. [40] Teacher concern is reflected in a 1980 survey by the National Education Association which found

37. Quoted in National School Public Relations Association, *Violence and Vandalism: Current Trends in School Policies and Programs* (Arlington, Va.: The Association, 1975), 5.
38. Ibid., 5–6.
39. Quoted in James M. McPartland and Edward L. McDill, eds., *Violence in Schools: Perspectives, Programs and Positions* (Lexington, Mass: D.C. Heath and Co., 1977), 79.
40. George Gallup, "The Fourteenth Annual Gallup Poll of the Public's Attitudes Toward the Public Schools," *Phi Delta Kappan* 64 (September 1982).

that 4 percent of teachers reported that they had been physically abused or threatened and more than 35 percent said they had felt unsafe in school.[41] In the mid 1980s President Reagan called for a renewed commitment to school discipline as a condition for school improvement.

Violence and vandalism have usually not been policy-oriented; that is, students do not engage in violent acts primarily as a means of protest or to persuade school officials to change school policy. Most explanations for violence and vandalism focus upon conditions outside the school. School violence and vandalism have been most prevalent in areas which have generally high crime and delinquency rates. The growth in youth gangs, unemployment, and teenage drug and alcohol abuse has also been said to contribute to violence. However, some explanations cite the decline in emphasis upon discipline in schools, and in the home, as a prime factor. Yet another perspective is that the lack of responsiveness by schools fosters student alienation and violence. McPartland and Dill note, "While the main sources of most serious offenses almost certainly lie in features of the broad society, we feel that schools can aggravate the problem or reduce it according to the way they organize themselves to dispense costs, rewards, and access to individual students." [42]

Although the perpetrators of school violence do not seek specific policy changes, their actions have clearly influenced school policy. Most school districts have taken steps to improve school security such as requiring all visitors to report to the office, issuing student identification cards, hiring special security guards and erecting special lights or fences. Measures to improve school security and student discipline are increasingly being considered in negotiations and teacher contract provisions. Such actions have had an additional, indirect effect upon school policies because they require the expenditure of funds which might otherwise be spent on educational programs.

Responses to Student Activism

Student activism has elicited responses from policy makers at the highest government levels. The rhetoric of the 1968 political campaign had a strong "law and order" emphasis which helped to focus public attention upon campus disturbances. Noting instances where students had occupied buildings and violence and property damage had occurred, many candidates for office criticized administrators, particularly at the college level where the problem was most visible, for granting concessions to protestors and advocated police and military action if necessary to maintain order on campuses. In some states problems related to student unrest became a prominent and volatile political issue. The specter of campus unrest continued to influence legislators in the 1980s. Legislative pressure for more accountability in higher education as well as in the public schools can be attributed partially to public dissatisfaction with campus activists. Similarly, many of the recommendations for school reform offered by state and national study groups in the 1980s were based on views of students that were shaped by the protests of the 1960s and 1970s.

Lawmakers have acted as well as spoken on the subject of student unrest. For example, efforts were made in Congress to deny federal scholarship or loan support to students who take part in college and university protests or refuse to register for

41. Cited in Ernest L. Boyer, *High School: A Report on Secondary Education in America* (New York: Harper & Row, 1983), 21.
42. McPartland and Dill, *Violence in Schools,* 22. See also National School Public Relations Association, *Violence and Vandalism,* 12–18.

the draft. Several states enacted legislation which specified conditions under which protests were unlawful or designated penalties for engaging in such disruptions. At the public school level, the California State Board of Education outlawed SDS chapters on junior and senior high school campuses. At the same time, some colleges and universities increased student involvement in policymaking by granting them representation on the board of trustees. In addition some states appointed students to the state board of education as advisory members. Many local boards of education also have done this. More recently, state and local boards of education have prescribed student discipline codes.

The courts have also become involved in matters related to unrest. Students have pressed a number of cases against school officials. Matters about which they have gone to court include suspensions, rules regarding dress and appearance, the right to protest school policies and general political issues, and the right to publish underground newspapers. Supported by the American Civil Liberties Union, Legal Aid Societies, or local advocacy groups, students have been successful in many of these cases. As a consequence, a body of case law has developed which extends the rights of students and limits what formerly were perceived as prerogatives of school officials. The landmark case was *Tinker* v. *Des Moines Independent Community School District,* in which the U.S. Supreme Court declared, "First Amendment rights, applied in light of the special characteristics of the school environment are available to teachers and students. It can hardly be argued that either students or teachers shed their constitutional rights to freedom of speech or expression at the schoolhouse gate. . . . " [43] Some subsequent cases have been decided in favor of students and others in favor of school officials.

Responses to activism by local school officials have taken two basic forms. On the one hand, school people have dealt with the physical outbreaks of violence; they have expressed great concern for maintaining order in school affairs and protecting students, teachers, and public property. To this end, they have often refused to tolerate student demonstrations or other activities which disrupt traditional school procedures. Students who act in this way have been treated as discipline cases and in some instances as criminals guilty of trespassing, disorderly conduct, and other charges subject to police control. Many school systems have prepared emergency plans for coping with disruptive incidents. These plans typically spell out elaborate procedures for isolating disorderly students, guarding strategic spots in the building, and summoning police help if needed.

Students in many schools are now being warned explicitly about the consequences of engaging in disruptive behavior. The decrease in disruptions during the 1970s was at least partially a result of these actions. As school personnel became more adept at dealing with disruptive behavior, would-be activists lost the advantage of surprise and realized that militant efforts were more likely to produce suspensions or police actions than policy changes.

A corollary to official concern for maintaining order and protecting persons and property has been concern for preserving personal authority. Some school people reacted to student activism with extreme defensiveness, denying the legitimacy of protest in virtually any form or on any subject. They adopted repressive tactics which sometimes caused moderate or uninvolved students to sympathize with and join the protestors.

43. 390 U.S. 942 (1968).

A second type of response by school officials has been to deal with the causes of protest. A fundamental reason that student disruptions have waned is that many of the causes for protest have been ameliorated. Recognizing the importance of due process and the fact that legal precedents have changed in recent years, many school districts have developed codes of student rights and responsibilities. General guidelines for dealing with student problems came from the National Association of Secondary School Principals which published a booklet that called for "student participation—to the maximum extent feasible—in the development of rules of conduct and of related disciplinary procedures." [44] The same booklet called upon principals to accept freedom of expression "unless its exercise interferes with the orderly conduct of classes and school work," freedom of school publications "from policy restrictions outside of the normal rules for responsible journalism," and the right "to present petitions to the administration at any time." [45]

A host of new mechanisms have been created which expand the opportunities for students to be heard and participate in school policymaking. A fairly common step in this direction has been to expand the agendas and revise the membership requirements for student councils. More innovative developments have included establishing a student ombudsman, involving students in curriculum studies, placing students on advisory committees, involving students in the selection of building principals, and allowing students to elect a representative to the board of education. In the last instance, the student representative participates in discussion but in most cases does not have his or her vote recorded.

Students have changed their behavior as schools have changed in the wake of unrest. While some students continue to rebel and protest, most have adapted to the schools as they now exist and work within legitimate channels to achieve further changes. To be sure, these students enjoy more freedom than their predecessors did, as nearly any adult visitor to a high school will notice. For some, however, the school remains an oppressive and unpleasant place. Many students who feel this way and are not sanguine about achieving further changes in the system have reacted by dropping out or simply not attending. Absence rates have soared in some places. In some inner-city high schools, it is not uncommon for nearly half the students enrolled to be absent on any given day. The difficulty of forcing students to attend schools has been acknowledged by many adminstrators. In many locales the truant officer is an institution of the past as school officials have stopped attempting to enforce school attendance requirements. Indeed the attendance problem is so great that some educators cite it as an important reason to repeal compulsory education laws. On the other hand, some districts have increased student attendance by exacting heavier penalties (e.g. academic failure) for excessive absence and/or by providing incentives for students to maintain good attendance records. An example of the latter occurred in Houston where school officials increased attendance enough in 1982 to generate an additional four million dollars in state aid by rewarding all students who have perfect attendance at the end of the year with a day at a local amusement park.

Schools have been more effective in responding to and coping with protest than they have been in dealing with violence and vandalism. As noted earlier, the increase in such behavior has led to more stringent security measures. For example, it is now commonplace for uniformed police to patrol the halls in some schools, and many dis-

44. Robert L. Ackerly, *The Reasonable Exercise of Authority* (Washington D.C.: NASSP, 1969). 6.
45. Ibid.

tricts employ police to help supervise special events. Nevertheless, violence continues at such a rate that fear of physical harm is a reality of school life for many students and teachers.

Redirection in the 1980s

Organized student protests were infrequent at the outset of 1980s because of the changes described previously. At the same time, however, thoughtful observers of high schools noted they are staging areas for cultural conflicts.[46] On the one hand, an aging teaching force is concerned about the lack of student and parent interest and about maintaining order in school while teaching. Student concerns are more likely to deal with peer pressure, popularity, drugs, and alcohol than with academics. Because they are more likely to gain popularity as a result of good looks or athletic prowess than academic success, they may devote more time to extracurricular activities or an after school job than to their homework. As a result of their different orientations, students and teachers often have relatively low expectations for one another. As Boyer observed, " . . . there is a kind of unwritten, unspoken contract between the teachers and the students: keep off my back, and I'll keep off yours." [47]

Most proposals for school reform in the 1980s ran counter to the prevailing student culture. Calls for greater academic rigor may fall on deaf ears of young people whose earlier success in school has been lackluster and who are more interested in sports or part-time jobs than Chaucer or calculus. The problem may be attenuated by demographic changes that will bring increasing numbers of low income and minority students into high schools. A corollary issue is the fact that the economic downturn from 1974 through 1982 stalled the "momentum of social and econimic improvement" made earlier by black Americans.[48] Thus the origins of future student protest may be triggered by the perceived irrelevance of academic pursuits to rapidly changing economic opportunities as well as persisting social justice or equity concerns of an ever-increasing segment of the student population. Moreover, any future protests about the effectiveness of schools for minorities must take into account that minorities represent not only a very substantial percentage (25% in 1983 and an estimated 35% by 2000) of the total student population but also the dominant group in our largest systems (23% of the 25 largest systems are "minority-majority").

Summary and Future Prospects

Students have had a substantial impact upon school policymaking. The major reason for this is that school officials have been guided by their understanding of student characteristics and needs as they made decisions. In recent decades students themselves have become more active participants in the policymaking process.

Student Influence

For the past several years students, educators, and other citizens have struggled to define appropriate roles for students in educational decision making. Conflict has developed in many instances where students have presented demands to school officials. Administrative intransigence in the face of these demands has sometimes been count-

---

46. John I. Goodlad, *A Place Called School* (New York: McGraw-Hill, 1983) 61–92 and Boyer, *High School.*
47. Boyer, *High School,* 16.
48. Cited in Robert Pear, "U.S. Finds Black Improvement Halted," *New York Times,* 22 August 1983, 12.

ered by demonstrations of varying magnitude, and harsh disciplinary measures including police action have often followed. On the other hand, administrative acquiescence to student demands has sometimes been met by teacher protests of insufficient support for their position. Schools have been closed in the wake of disruptive actions taken by both students and teachers. Moreover, the tense and volatile atmosphere which these incidents sometimes produce in schools has engulfed entire communities as citizens choose sides with the students or the "establishment."

The direct action of student protesters had impact upon school policy in many areas during the 1960s and 1970s. It led to laws, court decisions, and changes in school rules and practices. Moreover, these actions have left a legacy for the future; they have made clear to students that direct action is a strategy they can employ to seek change. While a resurgence of student protest in the 1980s is unlikely, educators should be mindful of its potential.

Students will continue to influence the interpretation and enforcement of school rules and policies through their informal interaction with teachers and administrators. The ways in which students, both individually and collectively, reinforce and discourage particular teacher behaviors constitutes a subtle form of control by students.[49]

A final and unfortunate form of influence upon school policy which shows no sign of abating in the future is juvenile violence and vandalism. Responses to such actions consume a growing amount of the time and resources of educational institutions. While greater security in schools may be achieved at some cost in dollars and personal freedom, it is unlikely that the problem will be solved until the broader society successfully addresses the underlying problems of alienation and unemployment.[50]

Outlook for the Future

Looking to the future, the declining number of students will have a substantial effect on educational policy decisions in some areas. Although pre-school and elementary enrollments will increase over the next several years, junior and senior high school enrollments will continue to decline. Enrollment trends will vary substantially by geographic areas with decline characterizing the East and Midwest and increases being realized in the South and West. These trends may generate further community strife for schools. Many citizens have come to view enrollment of their children in a school in their immediate neighborhood as a fundamental right. They strenuously resist efforts to close "their" school when enrollment declines. Other citizens believe the declining enrollments should be met not only with school closings but other economies in operating expenses as well. Thus enrollment decline has posed difficult policy issues which attract widespread community interest in many school districts.

Enrollment decline also affects decisions about staffing. Teaching positions are no longer as plentiful as they were in the 1960s. Not only are there fewer students to be taught, but persons who presently hold teaching positions are less likely to leave them to return to school, raise a family, or pursue a different career. Thus school officials will need to become more concerned in the future with how to achieve reductions in personnel without weakening programs and will need to develop more sophisticated procedures for teacher selection. They will also need to find ways to encour-

49. See Philip A. Cusick, *Inside the High School: The Student's World* (New York: Holt, Rinehart, and Winston, 1973).
50. See Bernard E. Anderson, "Youth Unemployment: The Issue and the Policy Response," *Cross Reference* 1 (January-February 1978): 11–22.

age some long-tenured teachers to be more responsive to changing societal and classroom situations. This will be particularly important as the generation gap and value differences between students and aging teachers become more pronounced.

While enrollment decline is the general trend, it is not occurring in all school districts. Exceptions are to be found particularly in Sun Belt states, in small towns which are experiencing new growth, and in some suburbs of large cities which are receiving new enrollees as families move to escape involuntary school desegregation in the cities. These kinds of growth, a result of population mobility, pose policy issues which differ from those in districts whose enrollment is declining.

The diversity of student needs will also influence educational policymaking in the future. Elementary and secondary schools are faced with the challenge of teaching both students preparing for higher education and students planning to move directly into the work force from school. In addition to helping prepare individuals to assume specialized vocational roles, the school of the future will need to emphasize at least two other goals. The first of these is how to get along with other people. The strains and interdependence of urban life require conscious efforts to improve human understanding and tolerance at all levels. The second and related goal is to help individuals learn to find satisfaction and benefit in leisure activities. In short, schools must help individuals develop humaneness.

We have reached a time when students can and do learn much more outside school than they have in the past. Boyer's proposal of credit for community service is consistent with this view.[51] The vast educational resources which exist outside schools combined with the growing diversity of student needs and interests suggests that the school role may increasingly be that of coordinator of educational opportunities. According to this role, the school would rely heavily upon organizations, agencies, and individuals in the surrounding community to supplement the efforts of teachers at school. Some schools have already begun to move in this direction.

51. Boyer, *High School,* 202–5.

13

School-Oriented Groups

The pluralistic nature of American society is clearly manifest in the variety of organizations which have an interest in educational matters. Some of these organizations exist only because of their interest in the schools while others are civic associations which only occasionally focus their attention on education. In this chapter we shall consider the former type of organization and the influences it may wield. We shall look first at some representative organizations which have state and national affiliations and then turn our attention to a more general discussion of locally based groups. In chapter 14 we will examine the education oriented activities of some organizations whose principal raison d'etre is in other areas.

Organizations with State and National Affiliations

The National Congress of Parents and Teachers

The PTA remains the largest volunteer organization in the United States with more than 5.3 million members in 1983 and with overseas branches in Puerto Rico, Guam, and on other military bases around the world. The headquarters of the National PTA is in Chicago, Illinois, and there are 52 branches, including a District of Columbia branch, a branch associated with the Dependent Overseas Schools, and a branch in each of the states.

The objectives, policies, and practices of the PTA at the local, state, and national level are closely related to its origins and its development over more than 70 years. Founded in 1897 as the National Congress of Mothers, the organization changed its name in 1908 to the National Congress of Mothers and Parent-Teacher Associations, and changed again in 1924 to the National Congress of Parents and Teachers.[1] The obvious reason for the last change was to encourage male membership and the total membership today includes many men, but there is little doubt that the organization is still dominated by women. Some local units have opened their memberships to high school students, extending to them all privileges and responsibilities but dues, and have changed the organization's name to Parent-Teacher-Student Association.

1. *A Teacher's Guide to the PTA* (Chicago, Ill.: National Congress of Parents and Teachers, 1957), 15–27.

To assess more accurately its impact on the operation of American schools, let us consider the organizational structure of the PTA and the policies by which it operates. The PTA is a network with approximately 25,000 local units concerned primarily with specific problems facing a specific school and concerned secondarily with problems facing the community: fifty-two branch units to provide guidance and services to the local units; and the national office, which attempts to strengthen and unite the efforts of the entire membership on problems affecting children throughout the nation.

The common goals of the National PTA and all of its constituent units are called the Objects and are found in the bylaws of every affiliated group. These are:

> To promote the welfare of children and youth in home, school, community, and place of worship.
>
> To raise the standards of home life.
>
> To secure adequate laws for the care and protection of children and youth.
>
> To bring into closer relation the home and the school, that parents and teachers may cooperate intelligently in the education of children and youth.
>
> To develop between educators and the general public such united efforts as will secure for all children and youth physical, mental, social, and spiritual education.

The affairs of the national PTA are governed by a Board of Directors. This body includes the officers of the national PTA, the immediate past president, the president of each state PTA and members of the three commissions on education, health and welfare, and individual development. Commissions are established by the board to promote the Objects and carry on the program of the PTA. They are designed to establish both short- and long-term objectives and to develop guidelines for achieving them. Much of the work of the PTA is done through the local units which are connected to the national organization through the 52 state branches.

The national PTA establishes a new theme every two years; the theme for 1983–85 is "The National PTA—Advocates for Children." This theme is symbolic of growing efforts by the PTA to more aggressively influence educational policies at all levels. One publication refers to PTAs as "shareholders in education" and asserts: "We are now exercising our rights and demanding the opportunity to participate in the decisions that shape the educational experience. Through our children's use of the public schools, we are also a consumer organization, seeking to protect our youngsters' well-being by making certain the quality of the educational 'product' is all it should be." [2] Issues which the PTA has indicated are of current concern include opposition to tuition tax credits and other types of public subsidies to private schools, violence on television, the impact of federal legislation and public policies on children and families, drug and alcohol abuse, child safety, adolescent pregnancy, health education, and reading improvement.[3]

A further sign of the PTA's intention to become a more agressive policy advocate was the opening of a Washington office for the organization in September of 1977. The national PTA legislative program is formulated through a process which provides for the submission of program proposals at local, state and national levels; consideration by the national legislative committee; approval by the National Board of Directors;

2. *PTA Directions, 1978–79* (Chicago: National PTA, 1978), 1.
3. Elaine Strenkenmeyer, *The National PTA: Advocates for Children* Chicago: National PTA, n.d.).

and ratification by at least 31 state PTAs or PTSAs. The program is implemented through the Washington office. An important part of this work involves coordinating a network which calls upon local PTA members to contact their congressional representatives regarding pending and proposed legislation. A legislative newsletter is sent to all local presidents six times a year.

The PTA has a long record of supporting legislation at the state and national levels designed to help children; such legislation has concerned increased financing for education, school lunch programs, dental clinics and other health measures, juvenile courts, and school safety patrols. National PTA initiatives were evident during the national energy crisis in 1974. The organization contacted the president and other government officials to urge that schools be given a high priority in the allocation of fuel. It also urged its members to involve themselves on the issue. In a similar vein and at about the same time, the national PTA was among the first organizations to announce opposition to year-round daylight savings time. Calling for repeal of this measure, the national PTA president, Lillie E. Herndon, cited members' "concern for the safety of children." [4] She added that the coordinator of legislative activity had been directed to make this position known to congressional leaders and that PTA members had been asked to urge congressional repeal locally.

More recently the national PTA claimed that a call to action to state and local PTAs was instrumental in persuading Congress to amend the School Lunch Act to provide for increased federal subsidies.[5] They also noted that the PTA was among the educational groups which lobbied successfully for override of the president's veto of the 1975–76 educational appropriations act. In 1977 the new Washington office led the formation of the National Coalition for Public Education, a group of 40 organizations which has worked successfully against tax credits to parents of elementary and secondary education students. Thus the national PTA has become both more aggressive and more effective in influencing policy at the national level.

At the state level, PTAs rely heavily upon volunteers to remain abreast of and speak to state and local policy developments. While PTA representatives often testify about pending state legislation, some observers believe that they have little impact on state policymaking.[6] On the other hand, the PTA has often been a part of coalitions of education interest groups at the state level.

At the local level, the PTA has traditionally been viewed as being supportive of existing policies at the district and building levels. Jennings even referred to local PTAs as "kept organizations" and noted that school boards often lead and influence the interest groups rather than vice versa.[7] The PTA's view of the ideal relationship with the school board is that of a partnership—"For this partnership to work, . . . both parties should have a systematic program for exchanging information and for involving parents in school policy making processes." [8]

There are signs that the PTA is becoming more assertive at local as well as state and national levels. The most prominent sign was a 1972 bylaws change which altered an article that read, "The organization shall cooperate with schools to support the improvement of education in ways that will not interfere with administration of the

4. PTA News Release, n.d.
5. *Why PTA—Instead of PTO?* (Chicago: National PTA, n.d.).
6. See John T. Thompson, *Policymaking in American Education* (Englewood Cliffs, N.J.: Prentice-Hall, 1976), 109.
7. M. Kent Jennings, "Patterns of School Board Responsiveness," in *Understanding School Boards*, ed. Peter J. Cistone (Lexington, Mass.: Lexington, 1975), 244.
8. *The School Board and the PTA, Partners in Education* (Chicago: National PTA, n.d.).

schools and shall not seek to control their policies." The revised version states, "The organization shall work with the schools to provide quality education for all children and youth and shall seek to participate in the decision-making process establishing school policy, recognizing that the legal responsibility to make decisions has been delegated by the people to boards of education." In 1982, the PTA published a revision of its workbook, *Looking in on Your School*, stating " . . . parents must become more involved in their children's education. That is why the National PTA is calling upon parents this year to look in on their local school—to study its operation; to determine its strengths and weaknesses; to join with administrators, teachers, and community members to improve their schools in order to better the lives and futures of their children." [9]

The local PTA has long been a training ground for prospective board of education members.[10] It provides an opportunity for individuals to take part in school events, become knowledgeable about school issues, and gain public identification as a person who is interested in and supportive of schools. Although the national PTA points out that locals are to support issues and principles and not support or oppose particular candidates," [11] it appears that the informal contacts established by working in PTA have been helpful to school board candidates in many communities.

A comprehensive examination of PTA efforts to influence school board policy was part of a national study by Ziegler and Jennings.[12] Like earlier observers, they noted the tendency of the PTA to support established school policy and to be on good terms with school officials. However, they also found that the PTA was the group most frequently named by board of education members as seeking to influence school policy and concluded that in comparison to teachers the PTA is "a more potent force." [13]

PTA documents, as we have noted, indicate that the organization may be seeking a stronger and more independent voice in future local policymaking. The national PTA has encouraged local units to urge their boards of education to oppose federal- or state-prescribed competency testing in favor of locally developed criterion-referenced tests, to campaign for local teacher in-service training in reading instruction, and to seek a voice in local curriculum development and collective bargaining processes.[14] If local PTA units become more assertive about such sensitive matters, however, the bridging relationships between teachers and parents traditionally fostered by the organization may be jeopardized.

The future of the PTA as a policy force at local, state, and national levels is clouded by at least two other factors. The first is the growing tendency of mothers to return to the work force. Working mothers (and fathers) in two-income families often have less time to participate in organizations such as the PTA which rely primarily upon volunteer activity. The second factor is the trend in some areas to reject membership in the PTA in favor of a local Parent-Teacher Organization (PTO). Advocates of PTOs point out that the organizations are entirely local and therefore pay

9. National PTA, *Looking in on Your School: A Workbook for Improving Public Education* (Chicago: National PTA, 1982), 5.
10. See Robert A. Dahl, *Who Governs* (New Haven, Conn.: Yale University Press, 1961), 155–59, and Harmon Ziegler and M. Kent Jennings, *Governing American Schools* (North Scituate, Mass.: Duxbury, 1974), 31–32.
11. *The School Board and the PTA, Partners in Education* (Chicago: National PTA, n.d.).
12. Ziegler and Jennings, *Governing American Schools*.
13. Ibid., 99.
14. *PTA Directions*, 1978–1979. Also see *The National PTA Handbook* (Chicago: The National PTA, n.d.).

neither dues nor allegiance to state and national organizations. The national PTA has recognized this challenge and responded to it by pointing to the benefits of affiliation.[15]

The National School Boards Association

The organizational structure of American education places heavy responsibility upon the local school board member. Because these board members are usually lay people rather than professionals in the field of education and because of the importance of the decisions they make, it was only natural for them to create organizations which could serve as clearinghouses and exchange centers for many experiences and activities in which boards are involved. The first state association of school boards was formed in Pennsylvania in 1896. By 1920 there were seven state associations; by 1940, twenty-seven; and by 1957, all states had organized.[16]

At the national level, organization came more slowly. The National Council of State School Board Associations was organized in February 1940, in St. Louis at a meeting held in conjunction with the annual convention of the American Association of School Administrators.[17] The war slowed the growth of the organization but it was revived in 1945. It was at the 1949 meeting that action was taken which would put the organization on its feet permanently. Edward M. Tuttle, about to retire as editor-in-chief of Row, Peterson, and Company, a textbook publisher, was selected to serve as the full-time executive secretary. By the fall of that year Tuttle had established a headquarters office, had incorporated the NSBA under the "Not for Profit" laws of the state of Illinois, and had distributed the first directory of the presidents and secretaries then in office.

The founders of the NSBA wrestled for some time over the type of organization which was needed. The early conflict was waged over whether or not the association should work directly with local boards in matters of membership, finance, and service, or whether it should work primarily with state associations of school boards. The original name of the organization, National Council of State School Board Associations suggests that the founders had the latter alternative in mind. Nevertheless, the question of direct board membership versus the federation of state associations was an issue in all of the early meetings. Tuttle commented:

> Not until the 1950 Convention in Atlantic City was the issue apparently settled by a unanimous vote of delegates from 28 states in support of a motion that:
>
>> The National School Boards Association be a federation of state school boards associations, and that the National Association serve the state associations, and indirectly local boards through the state associations.
>
> A constitution was adopted embodying this principle and eliminating the sustaining membership.[18]

The decision made by the NSBA in 1950 held for 20 years. At its 1970 convention the association amended its constitution to provide for direct affiliation by "any school board that is a member of an Active Member" (i.e., a member state association) on

---

15. See, for example, *Partners in Education: Teachers in the PTA* (Chicago: National PTA, n.d.).
16. Edward M. Tuttle, *School Board Leadership in America*, rev. ed. (Danville, Ill.: Interstate 1963), 169.
17. Ibid., 211–12.
18. Ibid., 214.

an additional fee basis.[19] The primary advantage of direct affiliation has been in the area of legislative information services. Recently the Association expanded policy and information services to direct affiliates, and by the end of 1982 more than 1500 school boards had gained this status. The concept of a federation has been sustained as the organization has developed and was reaffirmed in a 1982 governance study of the Association. One provision of NSBA Beliefs and Policies states:

> The National School Boards Association recognizes that it is the right and duty of each individual state school boards association and local school board to express to its representatives in the Congress of the United States the positions of the National School Board Association and its own position, with regard to educational issues, even if the two positions are different. However, it is the obligation of the state school boards association and local school districts to keep the National Association informed when they actively pursue a position which differs from the position of the National Association.[20]

While retaining its federated character, the association has changed its policymaking procedures to give proportionately greater representation to state associations which represent school districts with relatively large aggregate enrollments. It has also spoken out increasingly on national policy issues and taken a more aggressive lobbying posture. The organization appears to have grown stronger through these efforts both in membership size and perceived influence. Through its member organizations, NSBA includes 95,000 members in 16,000 local school districts who oversee the education of 97 percent of the nation's public school children.

The NSBA has overcome its early reluctance to become involved with national policymaking for education and is now perhaps the most aggressive of existing lay groups in this regard. It provides relevant information for its members and direct affiliates. The association has also established a Federal Relations Network which has up to three school board members from each congressional district serving as liaisons with congressional representatives. In addition, NSBA is active in coalitions with other national education groups regarding federal education issues.

By 1976 the organization had moved its headquarters to Washington, D.C., a step symbolic of its intent to influence national policy. In 1984 NSBA moved to new permanent headquarters to house its staff of 100 in the Washington area.

The objectives of the Association are to: "(1) advance the quality of education in the nation's public schools, (2) provide up-to-date information on education issues and training in school administration to local school boards and their state associations, and (3) strengthen citizen control of schools, whereby education policy decisions are made by those who are directly accountable to the community through election or appointment." [21] NSBA has also established internal councils through which members with particular interests can share specialized information and activities. These include the Council of School Attorneys, the Council of Urban Boards of Education, the Conference of School Board Negotiators, the Large District Forum, and the Forum of Federal Program Coordinators.

As the influence of the NSBA has increased in recent years, there is some evidence that the impact of the group on federal policy has been substantial. Granted,

19. Constitution and By-Laws of the National School Board Association, Article III, Section 3, as adopted 14 April 1970 and amended 18 April 1972 and 10 April 1973.
20. Beliefs and Policies of the National School Boards Association as adopted by the Delegate Assembly, April 7–10, 1973, Anaheim, Calif.
21. *National School Boards Association: A Profile* (Washington, D.C.: The Association, 1982) 1.

federal policymakers and certainly the Reagan administration have not been greatly influenced by traditional educational interest groups in recent years but recent legislative successes for NSBA have included working with other education groups to limit cutback in federal spending for education, retaining the Department of Education, opposing tuition tax credits, and achieving simplification in the guidelines for certain federal programs. Beyond this, the problem of finding a composite representation of the views of school board members persists. While school board members and professional educators have many common interests, some board members oppose the NSBA on certain issues. The same condition exits regarding some state associations and issues.[22]

The NSBA and the state associations have been very effective in providing a clearinghouse service to facilitate an exchange of ideas and information. For example, The *American School Board Journal,* the *Executive Educator,* and *School Board News* are widely read by board of education members and others interested in education.

The National Citizens Commission for the Public Schools

Although this organization no longer exits, its influence in the first half of this century was extensive. Its meteoric rise to prominence brought thousands of citizens into school improvement work, and its almost as rapid disappearance from the national scene left a legacy of progress and citizen interest that is still reaping dividends in many areas. Indeed, the recent manifestations of interest in public education by many of the nation's most prominent political, civic, and business leaders have generated some discussion about creating a contemorary analogue to the National Citizens Commission for the Public Schools.

James B. Conant[23] has been credited with founding the commission. In 1943 while president of Harvard University, he suggested that the Educational Policies Commission of the National Educational Association should explore the idea of a citizen-led, citizen-serving group to foster solutions to some of the problems facing education. A year later the EPC formally approached the American Council on Education to explore jointly the establishment of a "national commission of largely lay membership to build a public relations program for education.[24] A committee of nine educators finally recommended the formation of a commission of prominent citizens unconnected with education who could study the schools and seek the public's support in improving them.

In October of 1946 these educators met with nine carefully selected people who had indicated an interest in at least considering the next step. Two particularly relevant facts soon became apparent as this group studied the educational scene. The first was that many efforts to inform the public about the schools were already underway, but these efforts were primarily local, and there was little if any communication or coordination between groups. In addition, except for a lay group that provided advice on policies to the United States Commissioner of Education, all of the national organizations concerned with education were composed either solely or primarily of educators.

22. James D. Koerner, *Who Controls American Education?* (Boston: Beacon 1968), 100–101. Koerner asserts that the influence of state school board associations upon state policy is generally less than that of state teachers associations and state departments of education although he notes that potential for great influence exists within these organizations.
23. David B. Dreiman, *How to Get Better Schools: A Tested Program* (New York: Harper & Row, 1956), 68.
24. For much of this historical detail we are indebted to Dreiman, *How to Get Better Schools,* 63–82.

As these people studied the problems, they recruited additional members who had a similar commitment to the public schools. The mechanics of organization took time, but by May of 1949 the National Citizens Commission for the Public Schools (NCCPS) was incorporated. The initial financial support came from the Carnegie Corporation and the Rockefeller-endowed General Education Board.

The original commission had 25 members, none of whom was professionally identified with politics, religion, or education. An advisory panel of six educators was established to serve in a strictly consultative role on many of the technical problems of education. One theme dominated everything the commission did: there is no school problem a citizens committee cannot help solve if the committee is broadly representative of all interests and viewpoints, if it makes an objective continuing study of the facts, and if it is independent but works cooperatively with school officials.

To spread this gospel, the commission undertook a number of activities. Regional offices were established to provide consultative help to the many local and state groups which were organizing. Regional and national workshops, 28 in all, were held to discuss ways of implementing the Better Schools campaigns. A monthly bulletin was published by the commission. Fifteen "Working Guides" were distributed in great numbers. These Working Guides were pocket-size pamphlets which served as how-to source books.[25]

The impact of the commission was immediate and almost startling. When the NCCPS was organized in 1949, it knew of the existence of only 17 communities with citizen committees. In 1957 Henry Toy Jr., executive director of the commission, estimated that about 15,000 local committees were working actively for school improvement, and approximately 40 committees were operating at the state level.[26]

In 1956 the National Citizens Commission for the Public Schools ceased to operate, but a successor organization was soon in operation. This group, known as the National Citizens Council for Better Schools, which lasted until 1959, began with the same staff, many of the same citizen members, and much the same task. The accomplishments of the NCCPS and its successor were many.[27] They made the public aware of its right to participate in school affairs and of its obligations to make such participation constructive. They convinced educators that public interest in education could be exceedingly useful and need not be either destructive or meddlesome.

The National Committee for Support of the Public Schools

Three years after the demise of the National Citizen Council for Better Schools in 1959, another organization involving prominent laypersons at the national level in education was created. The National Committee for Support of the Public Schools was formed in 1962 by 39 individuals, many of whom had played an active role in the National Citizens Commission for the Public Schools and its successor organization. Like its predecessors this organization has dissolved, but it has left an important legacy.

Chairing the new group was Agnes Meyer, author, lecturer, and former trustee of the National Citizens Commission. Among the nationally prominent founders were novelist John Hersey, a former chairperson of the National Citizens Council; James B.

---

25. Condensations of the Working Guides are found in Dreiman, *How to Get Better Schools.*
26. Roderick F. McPhee, "The Administrator and Lay-Advisory Committees," *Administrator's Notebook 5* (May 1957).
27. For specific accounts of local activity see Dreiman, *How to Get Better Schools.* 6–59.

Conant; educator Harold Taylor; President Harry S. Truman; poet Carl Sandburg; and General Omar Bradley.

The original objectives of the National Committee were more specific than those of its predecessors. Whereas the earlier organizations sought "to arouse broad citizen interest and action" for the schools, this committee formed for one purpose—to stimulate more adequate financial support for public education. The committee subsequently broadened its concerns to include the allocation of resources within and among schools and accountability for achieving educational objectives. Thus, while the committee continued to urge higher levels of funding for education, it also sought ways of assuring that these funds would be used to the greatest public advantage.

In announcing the formation of the committee, Meyer said that it would not be a lobbying committee and it would not propose legislation. It would, said Meyer, "rely on the intelligence of the American people first to make the maximum effort locally, then to demand whatever help may be needed from their state governments, and from the federal government to supplement the resources of local school districts.[28] She added that this would not be just another paper committee, that they were "determined to get results."

The basic strategy of the committee was one of "fostering change through public education and information."[29] One technique was to serve as a clearinghouse for information on school needs, school finance, and the activities of state education groups. One member in each state served as a representative of the committee and was the agent for answering questions about educational matters in that state. State representatives also worked with members and other citizens to increase support for education in their representative states. In addition, the small central staff, headquartered in Washington, D.C., often responded directly to citizen requests for information or referred questioners to an appropriate source of information. The central staff gathered considerable information on its own in addition to urging action by state representatives and disseminating information to its members and interested citizens.

In its brief life the committee gained a national audience. In 1970 there were approximately 1700 active members in all 50 states. The group published a regular newsletter as well as periodic fact sheets and special reports. An early set of fact sheets was designed to help members evaluate the ability of their state in relation to others to finance public education. Special reports were published on topics such as "The Need to Build a New Sense of Community" and "Quality Education, Some Clues for the Citizen." A book sponsored by the committee, *Changing Demands on Education and Their Fiscal Implications*, was distributed to more than 30,000 persons.

Another effective means of dissemination employed by the group was its series of annual conferences. These conferences were regularly attended by more than 500 persons, and the proceedings were widely distributed. The group became an important force at state and national levels by calling the attention of policymakers and influential citizens to financial and program needs in education. The death of Meyer in 1971, however, precipitated an important change of direction. Meyer had provided much of the voluntary financial support which sustained the committee. The loss of her leadership and the lack of sufficient funds from other sources led the committee to reduce its program efforts for a period of time. Then, in 1973, a proposal to revitalize the organization was presented to the Ford Foundation. This proposal was ap-

28. National School Public Relations Association, *Education U.S.A.*, 5 April 1962.
29. Gerald E. Sroufe, Executive Director of the Committee, to Nystrand, 13 August 1969.

proved and in November 1973 the Committee Board of Directors reconstituted the organization as the National Committee for Citizens in Education.

The National Committee for Citizens in Education

The National Committee for Citizens in Education (NCCE) seeks to establish a much broader membership base and agenda than its predecessor organization. The organization strives to improve the quality of education in public schools and proceeds from the premise that "constructive involvement of parents and citizens in public education is essential." The goals of the organization are to: (1) provide its membership, and as many parent-citizens as it can reach, with intelligible, jargon-free information about current issues in public education through brochures, handbooks, filmstrips, and its newspaper, *Network,* (2) provide direct services to its more than 300 affiliated parent-citizen groups and other groups which request its help, and to assist individual parents and newly organizing groups through direct technical assistance and through its network of education and noneducation groups around the country, and (3) serve as spokespersons for parent-citizen concerns at the national and state levels and to assist parents and their organizations in monitoring education legislation which directly affects them and their children. A unique form of joint leadership for the committee has been provided by Carl L. Marburger, former commissioner of education for New Jersey; J. William Rioux, former president of the Merrill Palmer Institute in Detroit; and Stanley Salett, former director of education, Community Action Programs, Office of Economic Opportunity.

The committee issued its first newsletter in January 1974. Its initial efforts were directed at building a mass membership, and it was assisted by considerable publicity in the national news media. Indication that the committee intended to take an aggressive advocacy position at state and federal levels was given when they became the first education-related organization to join in a suit against the secretary of the U.S. Treasury and the commissioner of the Internal Revenue Service which would allow tax-exempt charitable and educational groups to lobby for legislative proposals in the same way that other tax-exempt agencies do.

During its early years, the committee was instrumental in providing information which helped secure passage of the Family Educational Rights and Privacy Act of 1974. The committee also testified before Congress regarding the low level of parent participation in Title I programs and along with other national organizations convened a National Conference of Title I Parents. The Committee has conducted hearings on public school governance across the country and has put forth a number of publications which suggest ways in which parents and citizens can become more knowledgeable about school issues, their rights in relation to schools, and how they can become more involved in school affairs. Further assistance in this regard is provided through the Parents Network which includes 200,000 parents in 43 states and Canada, and through a toll-free telephone hot line which parents can use to seek information and help.

Recent activities included a 12-state review of parent participation in developing individual education plans mandated by Public Law 94–142, research on school-based management, urging educational agencies to comply with public requests for information which fall under the Freedom of Information Act, calling for enforcement of public participation provisions in federal education programs and studies of the relationship between parent participation and student achievement, the special educational needs and problems of children in single-parent families, and the legal rights of handicapped children and their parents. A recent example of influence at the federal level was NCCE success in urging the establishment of the Office of Public Participation and Special Concerns in the Department of Education. However, a follow-up study by NCCE in 1982 determined that the new office had done little to improve parental or public involvement in education.[30] In its ten year existence, the committee has demonstrated the ability both to work with citizens at the grassroots level and to influence policy at the national level.

The National Association for Neighborhood Schools

The National Association for Neighborhood Schools (NANS) was formed in 1976 primarily to oppose forced busing of school children. Total membership figures are not available, but, in 1983, the group had national members in 31 states and 28 affiliate organizations in 16 states. As might be expected, the organization has been particularly successful in recruiting members in communities where court-ordered busing has been mandated or seems imminent.

The focus of the organization has been to provide public information and to exert citizen pressure upon government officials primarily at the national level. The articles of incorporation state that the purpose is "to stop forced busing as well as federal intervention in schools either by a Constitutional Amendment or by such other means as may be necessary to accomplish this objective." The organization has concentrated on mobilizing national opposition to forced busing for school desegregation. They currently urge Congress to pass legislation which they say would "strip federal courts of the jurisdiction to order busing as a 'remedy' in so-called school desegregation cases."[31]

An early activity of the organization was to send representatives to debate the merits of school desegregation with members of the United States Commission on Civil Rights over the Public Broadcasting System. NANS claims to have won this debate, which was aired on November 7, 1976, and has subsequently published a written version of it.[32] Subsequent activities have included testimony before several congressional committees and support of anti-busing candidates in congressional elections through a Political Action Committee in support of anti-busing legislation.

In 1978 the organization collected more than a million signatures in an effort to pressure Congress to consider anti-busing legislation which had not been reported out of the House Judiciary Committee. While this effort fell short of gaining the level of congressional support required to make a discharge petition effective, it demonstrated that NANS has potential to influence national legislation by rallying public opinion. It does this primarily by publishing "What You Can Do" letters and newsletters, by making fact sheets and bulletins available to members, government officials, and the media, and by speaking on local implications of the busing through the local news media. Although the organization has no regular paid staff, it has employed a Washington lobbyist since 1980. In 1982, NANS contracted with a direct mail firm to assist in fund-raising and disseminating information.

30. Anne Henderson, *Public Involvement in Education: Is Education on the Right Track?* (Columbia, Md.: National Committee for Citizens in Education, 1982, Mimeographed), 15.
31. William D. D'Onofrio, President, NANS, to Kathy Nystrand, 7 January 1983.
32. "Is School Desegregation Working" (New Castle, Del.: National Association for Neighborhood Schools, n.d.).

The Council for Basic Education

The Council for Basic Education was incorporated in the District of Columbia in July of 1956 by some of the people who had been involved in a national campaign for a return to educational fundamentals. Membership in the organization has never been large, and by the end of 1978 approximately 4,500 persons were on the membership-subscription list. While acknowledging that the group is not large, former executive director Mortimer Smith noted its special character: "We aim deliberately at key people, teachers and administrators, and lay leaders in the community who are in a position to influence the educational program. It is reassuring to know that many of those responsible for what goes on in the classroom find our publications appealing."[33]

The Council describes its purposes as follows:

> The Council for Basic Education is a non-profit, tax-exempt educational organization whose primary purpose is the strengthening of the basic subjects in American schools. The function of the Council is to initiate and support measures to ensure:
>
> 1. That all students, except the severely retarded, receive instruction in the basic intellectual disciplines, especially in English (including reading, writing, speech, and literature), mathematics, science, history, geography, government, foreign languages, and the arts;
> 2. That all students are given ample opportunity to develop their abilities to the fullest extent;
> 3. That clear standards of achievement are used to measure each student's progress and to govern promotion to each next level of the educational system;
> 4. That teachers are thoroughly competent, by training and temperament, to teach the subjects assigned to them;
> 5. That vocational training is offered only as a supplement to the primary effort of the schools, which is to give a discipline to the mind; and that standards of achievement are maintained as vigorously in vocational as in academic fields;
> 6. That school administrators are encouraged and supported in resisting pressure to make the schools assume miscellaneous responsibilities for the social and personal adjustment of students;
> 7. That proposed innovations in curriculum and methods are subjected to rigorous critical evaluation so as to determine whether they promote or hinder the achievement of the above educational goals.[34]

The Council devotes its energies to emphasizing the intellectual purposes of the schools and criticizing what it considers challenges to these purposes. It takes some credit for reducing the national emphasis placed upon "life adjustment" education in the 1960s.[35] During the late 1970s the views of the organization became popular with many citizens as the public showed support for the "back to basics" movement. While recognizing potential in this trend, the Council expressed concern about its relatively narrow focus. A. Graham Down, Smith's successor as executive director, set forth these views in the 1976 annual report of the organization:

---

33. Excerpts from the annual report of the executive director, *Council for Basic Education Bulletin* 18 (November 1973):3.
34. "Council for Basic Education," descriptive leaflet (Washington, D.C., n.d.), 1–2.
35. "Reflections after Fifteen Years," *Council for Basic Education Bulletin* 15 (June 1971):2.

The phrase "back to basics" suggests reaction. The old-fashioned school room, the paddle, and political reaction come to mind. Further some proponents of this movement tend to suggest that basic skills and basic education are the same. They are not . . . . While admitting that some subjects are more important than others, we must yet insist that the three R's are not enough and that only those who are conversant with the whole sense of a liberal curriculum can possibly possess the flexibility and imagination to deal with the demands of a world changing at an unprecedented rate of speed.[36]

The views of the CBE are communicated through a series of publications including books, occasional papers, and the monthly *Basic Education*. Recent CBE concerns, and some of the persons who have written for them, can be noted by the following occasional papers: "Uses and Abuses of Standardized Testing in the Schools" by George Weber, "Inner-City Children Can Be Taught to Read: Four Successful Schools" by George Weber, "Teaching Mathematics: What is Basic?" by Stephen Willoughby, "Education's Stepchild, Inservice Training" by Peter Green, and "Minimum Competency Testing: Guidelines for Policy Makers and Citizens" by Dennis Gray.

Compared to the view which says that the public schools are so ineffectual they should be abandoned, the basic reform orientation of the CBE seems moderate and perhaps even comforting to some educators. For example, in an article entitled "Are the Schools Worth Saving?" the CBE cited several specific characteristics of the structure and procedures of the public school which it considered "valid":

[It offered] a system of public education; formal organization of the curriculum; the authority of the teachers; large group instruction; and some form of segregation by ability. These ideas seem to us to be sound ones that can be pointed to as a part of "what's right with the schools." Within an organizational structure incorporating such ideas, it is possible, we believe, to effect reform that will vastly improve the quality of education offered by the schools to all students.[37]

The Council maintains both an "information-service" program and an "educational studies" program.[38] In addition to publishing *Basic Education* as an information service, the Council provides informal consulting assistance in response to all requests from educators, the media, and citizens. Workshops and conferences are also part of the Council program. The educational studies program involves conducting and publishing studies related to basic education. Some of these appear as occasional papers and others are published in book form. In 1982, the Council received support from the National Endowment for the Humanities to establish a program of independent summer study for high school humanities teachers. In 1983, the Council began Project ABCs—Action for Better City Schools. Supported by four major foundations, the project will emphasize improved academic achievement. The initial project site was Atlanta where CBE staff members joined with public school officials, parents, other citizens, and the business community in a series of activities that focus on school effectiveness. Another program begun in 1982 helps teachers utilize writing as a medium to teach thinking skills.[39]

36. *Annual Report of the Council for Basic Education, 1976,* 6.
37. "Are the Schools Worth Saving?" *Council for Basic Education Bulletin* 13 (January 1969):5.
38. "Council for Basic Education," 2–3.
39. See James Howard, *Writing to Learn* (Washington, D.C.: Council for Basic Education, 1983).

There can be little doubt that some of the basic concerns of the CBE have become central concerns of American education during the past years. The increased attention to intellectual tasks in the schools is a case in point. It is difficult, however, to find a direct cause-and-effect relationship between the activities of the Council and some of these changes. Sputnik, the NDEA, increasing pressure to attend college, and tax-conscious consumerism are just a few of the factors which may have had greater influence than the Council on the public's basic educational concerns. Nevertheless, in the past 20 years the values of the general public have grown closer to the values espoused by the Council. Indeed, the recent national studies which have focused upon improving the quality of education reinforce some of the major themes propounded by the Council for some time.

Locally Based Groups

In many communities one or more groups exist which are not officially affiliated with broader organizations and which are oriented to school programs. Well-known examples include committees of business executives and industrialists who advise on the development of vocational education programs and booster clubs which support school athletic programs. These groups are sometimes quite influential in the determination of school policies at the local level.

The past twenty years witnessed an increase in the number of such local ad hoc groups especially in urban school systems. In some cases, these groups have been created by school officials in much the same way that earlier citizen committees were formed. In other cases, they were formed independently of school sanctions and sometimes in opposition to school policies. This section will focus on newer forms of citizen participation in local school affairs.

Most citizens do not become actively involved in attempting to change school policies directly. Moreover, most tend to regard the performance of schools as satisfactory.[40] Most citizen participation is short-lived and oriented to a particular issue. It is most common in metropolitan area school districts, and persons who espouse liberal rather than conservative views tend to be more active as well as more successful.[41] Recently, however, a new wave of conservative groups has confronted school officials over issues such as sex education, school prayer, and the teaching of scientific creationism.

Background of the New Participation

The traditional belief is that education is a profession in which policy decisions are made by a representative board of lay persons and implemented by professionals. This ideology has been challenged on two grounds which, taken together, provide the rationale for new efforts in citizen involvement. The public has challenged (1) the effectiveness of schools and (2) the representativeness of school policymakers.[42]

Despite records of improved student achievement in some cities, few institutions have received more criticism in recent years than urban school systems. This has

40. See, for example, George H. Gallup," Fifteenth Annual Gallup Poll on Public Attitudes Toward Education," *Phi Delta Kappan* 65 (September 1983).
41. M. Kent Jennings and Harmon Ziegler, "Interest Representation in School Governance" in *People and Politics in Urban Society,* ed. Harlan Hahn (Beverly Hills, Calif.: Sage, 1972), 201–30.
42. A thoughtful treatment of the relationship of these factors is found in Leonard J. Fein, "Community Schools and Social Theory: The Limits of Universalism" in *Community Control of Schools,* ed. Henry M. Levin (Washington, D.C.: Brookings Institute, 1970), 76–99.

been manifest in the press and the popular literature as well as in academic reports and journals. While it has been said many ways and attributed to various factors, the basic conclusion is that schools have not been sufficiently effective. Widespread acceptance of this conclusion has made the public more willing to consider alternatives to present arrangements for schooling.

Citizens have also questioned the representativeness of those who make policies for schools, particularly in large urban districts. To many, the five, seven, or eleven persons elected or appointed to positions on the board of education seem remote and very much unlike themselves. As the vignette in chapter 1 illustrated, they may even believe that this body has interests and attitudes which are inimical to their own. At another level, they may be suspicious of the principal and teachers at the school attended by their children. Convinced that education is important to their children's future and dissatisfied with the results they see, angry citizens and their advocates may seek to intervene in school policymaking.

Over the past twenty years, a new breed of activist has mobilized city residents to confront the institutions close to their lives. These activists have been visible especially in poor and minority group neighborhoods. Their emphasis has been upon community determination and achievement of goals in contrast to the traditionally docile acceptance of the benefits offered by established institutions. In short, they have encouraged citizens to participate in decisions concerning their own destiny.[43]

An important force supporting citizen assertiveness has been the activity of certain foundations and government agencies. Most notable among these have been the Ford Foundation and the Office of Economic Opportunity. The Ford Foundation was instrumental in stimulating citizen participation in the New York City Schools in 1967–69. First by supporting Ocean Hill-Brownsville and other experimental districts during their earliest stages and then by contributing to plans for decentralizing the entire system, foundation officials attempted to influence school policy in that city. Ford Foundation encouragement of citizen involvement, however, predates the saga of Ocean Hill-Brownsville. Earlier efforts (although they emphasized the coordination of services more than participation) included the "grey areas" project which established new community agencies in Boston, New Haven, Oakland, Philadelphia, Washington, D.C., and several locales in North Carolina and the partial support of the Mobilization for Youth project in New York City.[44] Moynihan has written of Ford intentions in these activities that "it purposed nothing less than institutional change in the operation and control of American cities. To this object it came forth with a social invention of enormous power: the independent community agency. In effect, the Public Affairs Program of the Ford Foundation invented a new level of American government, the inner city community action agency."[45]

The notion of community action was central to the "war on poverty" financed by the Economic Opportunity Act of 1964. Indeed, Community Action Programs (CAP) were designed initially as the biggest weapons in the antipoverty arsenal. According to the statute, such programs were to be locally based, to mobilize and coordinate sufficient resources "to give promise of progress toward elimination of poverty or

43. Probably the best known community organizer was Saul Alinsky; see Saul D. Alinsky, *Reveille for Radicals* (Chicago: University of Chicago Press, 1946). For a description of Alinsky's tactics and the development of one community organization, see the discussion of the Woodlawn Organization in Charles E. Siberman, *Crisis in Black and White* (New York: Vintage, 1964), 308–58.
44. For discussion of these projects see Peter Marris and Martin Rein, *Dilemmas of Social Reform* (New York: Atherton, 1967).
45. Daniel P. Moynihan, *Maximum Feasible Misunderstanding* (New York: Free Press, 1969), 42.

causes of poverty," and perhaps most notably to be "developed, conducted, and administered with the maximum feasible participation of residents of the area and members of the groups served."[46]

The last requirement brought citizens face to face with city governments, school systems, and other institutions on which they had been dependent. As they learned to organize in support of their grievances, these poor citizens and the community workers who headed their agencies challenged the prerogatives of traditional decision makers. William Haddad, a former OEO official and later a member of the New York City Board of Education, has said of "maximum feasible participation" requirements:

> What this meant in political terms was soon apparent to members of Congress, to Governors and Mayors, and to the established social agencies whose power and influence has long been based on their beneficences to the poor. If now the poor were to be given not merely the money but a voice in expending it, would not their leaders become competitors for power?[47]

The history of CAP agencies was tumultuous in many respects. Our purpose here is not to evaluate their product nor their processes but to note their legacy. First, participation in CAP programs provided a type of training in citizen involvement and group leadership for thousands of poor and minority group citizens. In some instances, this training included "field experiences" with instruction in the tactics of conflict and confrontation. Second, and perhaps more important, such participation helped to raise the expectations which citizens have for institutions such as schools. Although CAP programs have been discontinued, in many cases a leadership cadre of citizens has survived who are determined to work with others in the neighborhood to press for improved services.

The early impetus which local CAP agencies and boards had to intervene in school affairs was augmented by guidelines for the Elementary and Secondary Education Act which required evidence of cooperation with CAP agencies in the development of Title I programs. Subsequent federal guidelines for programs such as Head Start, Follow Through, and Title I of the Elementary and Secondary Education Act have also contained various provisions calling for citizen involvement in program advisory roles.

An important factor in the growing demand for citizen involvement has been the development of a participatory ideology. In part, this ideology was a product of frustration adopted by persons tired of waiting for either integration or compensatory education strategies to be employed on a scale large enough to have some possible effect.[48] Thus some citizens castigate the system charging that its structure or the biases of those who run it make it unresponsive to neighborhood needs. The answer they say is to divide it into smaller parts, each of them being accountable to local constituencies.

The forces discussed thus far in this section have been those urging poor and minority group citizens to seek an expanded role for themselves in school affairs. It should be noted also that many school people have recognized that some citizens are

46. Economic Opportunity Act of 1964, 78 Stat, 508, Title II. Sec 202 (a).
47. William F. Haddad, "Mr. Shriver and the Savage Politics of Poverty," *Harper's* (December 1965):43.
48. David K. Cohen, "The Price of Community Control," *Commentary* (July 1969):23–32. See also Diane Ravitch, *The Troubled Crusade* (New York: Basic, 1983).

alienated from the schools and have sought to draw them closer to their programs. Hoping to increase their sense of trust in the schools and to direct their energies toward constructive support of their children, some teachers and principals have visited parents in their homes and invited them to school for various activities. Thus, in some instances school people have taken the initiative toward increasing citizen involvement in school matters. Similarly, concerned middle- and upper-class citizens sometimes have recognized the myriad of problems confronting the schools and have organized themselves to help resolve them. In other instances groups have organized to counter conflicting demands set forth by other citizen bodies.

Two developments in the 1970s fostered further expansion of local citizen involvement. The first was the increased pressure, including court orders, to desegregate many school systems. Efforts to implement or even develop desegregation plans were often met by the formation of hostile citizen groups. These groups frequently attracted a broad following and sometimes were successful in delaying further desegregation. In some instances their efforts led to the removal of local superintendents or board of education members.

A second development which led to expanded involvement was the growing emphasis on accountability. In an effort to respond to such pressures, school officials in all kinds of districts have sometimes established citizen advisory committees. Similar steps have been taken at the state level.

In 1973 the Florida legislature mandated an accountability program which required every school district to establish citizen advisory committees. This and subsequent legislation in Florida pointed toward development of a school-based management system which has been advocated as a strategy to increase accountability at the building level.[49]

Objectives of Citizen Participation

Many objectives have been noted for citizen participation. Burke holds that it is useful to view citizen participation as a strategy, or "basis for various strategies," for achieving various kinds of goals rather than as a goal in itself.[50] In keeping with this view, six general objectives for citizen participation in school affairs can be stated.

The first of these is to increase public understanding and general support for the schools. Fantini has argued for this purpose as follows:

> When people have a part in their institutions, they share responsibility for them and are more likely to pay close attention to the stated mission and actual performance of the institution . . . Participatory democracy in education should also give parents and community a tangible respect for the intricacy and complexity of the professional problem in urban education. It is not likely that parents who have gained admission as true partners in the process will oversimplify and lay the blame for educational failures solely on the professional.[51]

49. For a discussion of school-based management, see Lawrence C. Pierce, *School Site Management,* An Occasional Paper (Cambridge, Mass.: Aspen Institute for Humanistic Studies, 1977). Developments in Florida are discussed in Luvern L. Cunningham et al., *Improving Education in Florida* (Talahassee, Fla.: Select Joint Committee of the Florida Legislature, 1978),
50. Edmund M. Burke, "Citizen Participation Strategies," *Journal of American Institute of Planners* 34 (September 1968):287–94. Burke discusses five strategies of citizen participation which he calls "educational-therapy, behavorial change, staff supplement, cooptation and community power." Also see Don Davies, ed. *Communities and Their Schools* (New York: McGraw-Hill, 1981).
51. Mario D. Fantini, "Alternatives for Urban School Reform" (New York: Ford Foundation, 1968), 14.

During the late 1970s and early 1980s corporate and civic leaders became increasingly aware of the strategic importance of public education to the economic and social fabric of the nation. They sought greater involvement with the schools and were welcomed by school officials as advisors on technical aspects of management and as partners in the operation of some schools. For example, the New York Alliance for the Public Schools was founded in 1979 under the auspices of New York University. It is a voluntary civic organization which joins business and civic leaders with educators to support projects on behalf of the New York Public Schools. Similar groups can be found in a number of other cities including Atlanta, Boston, Dallas, Hartford, Memphis, Pittsburgh, and San Francisco.

A second objective is to provide instruction or assistance of some type for the participants. Burke calls this an "education-therapy" strategy.[52] Examples in the world of education include parent advisory committees to preschool programs in which an implicit if not stated function is to help parents learn about school programs and ways in which they can assist their own children.

A third objective of some citizen participation mechanisms is to co-opt potential opponents of the institutions sponsoring the mechanism.[53] The notion of cooptation has been developed by Selznick who defines it as "the process of absorbing new elements into the leadership or policy determining structure of an organization as a means of averting threats to its stability or existence." [54] For example, a school principal might invite community leaders who are dissatisfied with the school to serve on an advisory committee in the hope that this position would dissuade them from mobilizing opposition to the school program.

A fourth objective is to provide advice and counsel regarding program goals and practices. The extent to which those for whom this advice is intended feel obligated to accept it varies widely and has provoked controversy in many settings. Nevertheless, this is probably the most frequently stated objective for citizen involvement. It was implicit, for example, in the guidelines for Elementary and Secondary Education Act Title I programs which required that "the priority needs of educationally deprived children in the eligible attendance areas (target populations) were determined in consultation with teachers, parents, private school authorities, and representatives of other agencies which have a genuine and continuing interest in such children." [55]

A fifth objective is to increase the amount of human and material resources available to carry out educational programs and to coordinate the application of these resources. For example, a local social club may volunteer the services of its members to serve as library aides, or a group of parents may organize to watch over their young children as they walk to and from school in a busy neighborhood. There are currently more than 4.6 million Americans who provide a broad range of volunteer services to public schools. Since 1968, an increasing number of them have been associated with National School Volunteer Program, Inc., a non-profit association based in the Washington, D.C. area that provides technical assistance and information services.

In the early 1980s, a new social institution was invented to aggregate and distribute voluntary contributions to schools. Local education foundations were established

---

52. Burke, "Citizen Participation Strategies."
53. Ibid.
54. Philip Selznick, "Foundations of the Theory of Organization," *American Sociological Review* 13 (February 1948):31. As cited in Burke, "Citizen Participation Strategies."
55. ESEA Title I Program Guide 46, 2 July 1968.

in many school districts to receive financial contributions that local corporations and citizens wished to be used for the benefit of local schools. The foundation board is generally apprised of school district priorities and makes its funding decisions and allocations accordingly.

The sixth objective, the most threatening to established institutions, is to monitor the performance of the institutions and to force changes if that performance is viewed as unsatisfactory. It is within the context of this objective that the words "account-ability" and "community control" have meaning.

Any given citizen group may have more than one purpose. Moreover, groups of all types may be formed at the initiative of either school officials or citizens them-selves. Often those who formed groups and those invited to participate in them have had different views of the purpose of the group. For example, the solicitation of advice by school people has sometimes been interpreted as an invitation to community control.

Summary and Future Prospects

Citizens have demonstrated increasing interest in organizing to effect changes in school policy at national, state, and local levels. Recognizing this citizen interest, fed-eral and state officials have mandated citizen involvement in many programs. Local use of advisory committees has also expanded.

It is an irony of the past decade that the organizations with state and national affiliations described in this chapter have increased in strength but without concomi-tant effects upon state and national policy for education. There are two major reasons for this state of affairs. The first is a shift in national priorities away from aid to education, a trend which may be reversed in the near future as a result of the recent national reports on education. The second is the virtual demise of coalitions which had so effectively influenced legislation in many states.

The nature and effectiveness of such coalitions was described by Bailey and by Masters, Salisbury, and Eliot.[56] The coalitions included the major educational associ-ations and interest groups in a particular state, who came together to develop legis-lative programs which they all would support. Such groups included the Education Council in Michigan, the New York State Educational Conference Board, the Joint Committee on Education in Wisconsin, and the Princeton Group in New Jersey. A 1966 survey revealed that 27 states had some kind of "cooperating council of organi-zation for the purpose of advancing educational legislative aims."[57] In addition, infor-mal cooperative efforts were organized in many states.

The cohesiveness of educational coalitions has been shattered in most states. This is due primarily to teacher militancy which resulted in splits between teachers associations and other participating groups. Other factors viewed as threatening to coalition structures include the demise of rurally dominated legislatures to which many coalitions have geared their strategies, and demands from urban officials that their systems receive special state subsidies to cope with pressing city school problems.

The demise of the coalitions made clear the fact that unity as well as a large membership is important for citizen groups that wish to influence educational policy at

---

56. Bailey et al., *Schoolmen and Politics*, and Nicholas A. Masters, Robert H. Salisbury, and Thomas H. Eliot, *State Politics and the Public Schools* (New York: Knopf, 1964).
57. National Council of State Education Associations Information Service Report, *Promotion of State Leg-islation by Cooperating Organizations* 2 (November 1966).

any level. Such groups are much more likely to gain favorable responses from elected officials if other groups with similar interests are not plying them with counteracting information and opinions.

Information is an important control resource for citizen groups. Policymakers, particularly at state and national levels, are generally interested in knowing how proposed legislation will affect constituents in their home districts. Groups which have developed the capacity to marshal such information and make it available to policymakers can be influential.

Initiative is also important for such groups. Groups which initiate action without impetus from school people and sometimes even in opposition to them can often affect school policies. For example, publications of the Council for Basic Education have probably influenced leaders in some states and communities to deemphasize nonacademic aspects of the curriculum. Even in cases where educators themselves are not supportive of the council position, they have responded to influential citizens who advocate basic education. Likewise, local groups sometimes form without school encouragement and become influential in school affairs. Thus, pressure for change often comes from outside of school systems.

In contrast to the past few years when the efforts of education advocates focused primarily on avoiding budget cutbacks at local, state, and national levels, it appears that the mid-1980s may be a time of increased investment in public education. The report of the National Commission on Excellence in Education and similar documents have directed public attention to the significance of education at a time of economic change. The time is reminiscent of the post-Sputnik era as the nation once again rediscovers the relationship between education and economic development.

Despite the growing consensus that education is important and schools should be improved, there are strong voices which urge that solution of this problem "does not require throwing money at it." Moreover, public school advocates must still overcome the indifference, if not hostility, of the growing numbers of citizens who no longer have children of school age or who regard public support of nonpublic schools as the *sine qua non* of any change in the level of expenditure for public schools. Thus, new money will not come easily to the schools and a condition of its arrival may be fundamental change in how schools are organized. For example, there appears to be substantial support among citizens and politicians to compensate teachers on the basis of merit. Likewise, there is widespread agreement about the desirability of higher standards for student performance.

This changing public view of education poses two kinds of challenges to the kinds of groups discussed in this chapter. The first is to achieve sufficient unity among themselves and/or with others who share common interests to achieve changes through the legislative process. The second has to do with adjusting to what appears to be a change in public values. For the past twenty years, equity has been a fundamental concern in educational policy. Many of the groups discussed herein have been strong advocates of equity. Progress toward this value has been apparent and substantial. In the current scheme of things, excellence is now of higher priority with the public than equity. Excellence and equity are not necessarily contradictory. An important challenge to advocacy groups at all levels will be to preserve the gains made in the name of equity as they and others seek progress in the name of excellence.

At state and local levels in particular, professionals and lay citizens need to reexamine their mutual obligations and techniques for working together. Hostility has developed between citizen, teacher, and administrator groups in some areas regarding the question of who will control the schools. The spread of such hostility would be unfortunate. Neither lay citizens nor professionals can make their full contribution to education unless they are sensitive to and trusting of each others desires and capabilities. An important step in this direction is for professionals to acknowledge both the boundaries of their own expertise and their ultimate accountability to their public as well as to their profession. By the same token, citizens must find the most appropriate and responsible means to participate in the policymaking process. Such cooperative approaches will be even more vital to schools in the future as their traditional constituency of young people shrinks numerically in many sectors of the country.

14

Other Interest Groups

In chapter 13 we looked at organizations which have education as a primary concern. We shall now look at a sampling of groups which have as their primary interest something other than education but which do influence educational policy. Indeed, some of these groups seem perfectly willing to submerge the schools in deep social conflict if that is necessary to further their own goals. Such activities illustrate the fact that the school as a public institution has increasingly become the focal point for the resolution of social problems.

Support and opposition to the schools as demonstrated by these groups takes a variety of forms. Some is aimed at textbooks, some at curriculum, some at expenditures, some at educators, and some at the schools as a public institution. Some of the criticism is rational and well deserved, but some of it is not justifiable and is focused upon the schools because of their accessibility and resultant vulnerability. In either case, these groups do influence educational decisions and policy in a variety of ways.

Our analysis is not concerned with attempting to refute or answer the charges of groups which criticize the schools. Indeed, informed criticism of education should be encouraged; it can help educators to make those changes which are necessary for improving the schools. Some of the criticism in the past decade or so, however, has been neither informed nor helpful. Rather, at times it has been destructive in nature— destructive to people, to ideas, and to the concept of public education.

Groups Concerned with Ideology

Education is of increasing interest to the nation's major political parties. Both Republicans and Democrats have shown more interest as pressures on schools have mounted and educational institutions have been drawn into complex social, political, and economic controversies. In addition, a number of interest groups have expressed continuing concern with how schools treat a range of ideological issues. In this section we will discuss briefly a few of the groups which have expressed concerns about American education.

315

Curriculum issues have deep roots in our history. Nelson and Roberts have discussed the furor caused by textbooks since the Civil War.[1] So bitter were the feelings over texts dealing with that war that in 1897 publishers approached the problem by publishing regional versions, one textbook for distribution in the North and another one for the South.

Following World War I a similar problem arose, sparked in large measure by Hearst newspaper attacks on histories which the newspaper considered too friendly to our wartime ally, Great Britain. Such attacks led the members of the American Historical Association in 1923 to adopt a resolution which would be equally appropriate today. The resolution stated that "the clearly implied charges that many of our leading scholars are engaged in treasonable propaganda . . . is inherently and obviously absurd."

The textbook controversies have involved a variety of organizations and individuals. Among the well-known national organizations which have played an active role are the Daughters of the American Revolution and the American Legion, organizations whose patriotic activities have been based on a vigorous defense of the American way of life as they interpret it. Among the more active but perhaps less well-known groups also prominent in attacks on education and textbooks have been America's Future, the Minutemen, the Minutewomen, the Circuit Riders, Pro America, the Sons of the American Revolution, and various state groups such as the Texans for America, and the Parents for Better Education of California. The John Birch Society, of course, has attracted nationwide attention for its attacks on schools.

Book banning activities have been effective in a variety of ways. Books have been withdrawn from school libraries, not purchased by library officials because they appeared on the suspect list of one of the alarmist groups, or altered by publishers to become as unobjectionable as possible. A California publisher, for example, once deleted from an eighth-grade civics book an entire chapter on the United Nations.[2] Opposition to specific texts has on occasion reached ludicrous heights. In the mid-1950s a member of the Indiana State Textbook Commission suggested banning Robin Hood on the premise that his philosophy of taking from the rich to give to the poor was the pure Communist line. A healthy wave of laughter managed to dissipate this charge, however.

There have been recurrent examples of conflict concerning how the schools teach the origins of man. Vocal groups of citizens and diverse organizations throughout the country have argued, for example, the respective pros and cons in the seemingly perpetual and vigorous dispute between religionists and scientists. Indeed, in recent years the creation movement has become a consequential national force in articulating its demands to local boards of education that equal time be provided for teaching both creationism and evolution. Several states in 1981 enacted laws calling for balance between "creation science" and "evolution science" in the public schools. Similar legislation has been proposed in numerous states, and the courts have been involved as well.[3]

---

1. For a detailed analysis of attacks on textbooks see Jack Nelson and Gene Roberts, Jr., *The Censors and the Schools* (Boston: Little, Brown, 1963), and Mary Anne Raywid, *Ax-Grinders: Critics of Our Public Schools* (New York: Macmillan, 1962).
2. Raywid, *Ax-Grinders*, 22.
3. *Issuegram: Scientific Creationism,* Education Commission of the States, October 1981. See, for example, *Epperson* V. *Arkansas,* 393 (U.S.) 97 (1968).

Several other instances can be cited of more recent conflict over the curriculum and textbooks used in schools. In the Island Trees Union Free School District in New York, for example, the board of education removed nine books from the school library because they were considered to be inappropriate. This school library book censorship case was heard by the U.S. Supreme Court in 1982 with the plurality opinion, written by Justice Brennan, concluding that local school boards could not remove books from libraries simply because they dislike the ideas contained in them.[4]

Similar debates have continued in recent years in many other communities and states. In Idaho, for example, a school district fired a teacher who assigned *One Flew Over the Cuckoo's Nest.* In a Pennsylvania system, *Huckleberry Finn* is no longer required reading because of the objection of black parents who resented the alleged racial stereotyping. The rather variegated works of prominent authors such as Studs Terkel, Kurt Vonnegut, Issac Asimov, Bernard Malamud, Nathaniel Hawthorne, Ernest Hemingway, Aldous Huxley, and George Orwell continue to be assailed by some critics as being inappropriate for school children.[5]

This struggle quite predictably will continue to persist throughout such a diverse nation. On one side are alleged "liberal educationists" who resent encroachments of "doctrinaire conservative lay persons." On the other side are conservatives who seek to halt alleged permissive teaching methodologies which they believe erode basic academic standards and undermine fundamental American values. Underlying this ideological clash, of course, is the question of academic freedom: the freedom of teachers to utilize their own independent professional judgment and not to be shackled by political constraints.

Conservative elements commonly feel that the schools are the origin of much liberal bias, and conservative opposition to the schools is concentrated on the programs of the schools, what is or is not being practiced, rather than on expenditures for education. It is often focused narrowly upon the failure of the schools to support adequately the free enterprise system.

These controversies are likely to continue as our schools inexorably remain enmeshed in the political, religious, ideological, social and economic controversies which divide our pluralistic society on certain complex issues.[6]

Racial Minorities

In May 1954 the Supreme Court ruled against school segregation in its famous decision against the doctrine of "separate but equal" schools. In the years immediately following that decision blacks and civil rights sympathizers concentrated on breaking down the legal barriers in the South which contributed to segregation. Among their demands were the reorganization of schools without regard to race and the elimination of racial classifications.

In the early 1960s and after the civil rights movement shifted to the North and West, and civil rights advocates concentrated on de facto segregation. Such segrega-

4. Virginia Helm, "Book Censorship in the Schools: Conflicting Rights, Conflicting Courts," *The Executive Review,* Institute for School Executives, The University of Iowa, Vol. 3, No. 5, February 1983.
5. Connie Lauerman, "New Censors Are Emerging: But This Time Foes Are Ready," *Chicago Tribune,* 30 March 1982, sec. 2, p 1, 7.
6. Michelle Marder Kamhi, "Censorship vs. Selection—Choosing Books for Schools", *American Education,* (March 1982): 11–16 and "Censorship and the Public Schools: Who Decides What Students Will Read?" *American Education* (December 1982): 8–14.

tion results not from formal, legal classifications based on race but from residential distribution that has the effect of creating separate black and white schools. By the late 1960s some of the enthusiasm for fighting de facto school segregation had waned. New black groups and leaders were calling instead for "community control" of neighborhood schools.

Black activism in the 1960s was paralleled by a drive for equality on the part of other minority groups. Chicanos in the Southwest, Puerto Ricans in the Northeast, and American Indians all began to assert themselves more vigorously and like blacks strove for greater control over the institutions which served them. These once relatively invisible minorities have become visible as they attempt to improve their lives and the educational opportunities available to their children. Let us now see how these several minority groups have tried to achieve their goals and how these efforts will have even a more significant effect on the schools as minorities constitute an ever growing proportion of the youngsters enrolled.

Black Americans

The drive for equality by blacks has had considerable impact on the development of black organizations. Until the late 1950s nearly all black efforts were channeled through one of two prominent black civic associations, the National Association for the Advancement of Colored People (NAACP) and the Urban League. Both organizations received much of their financial support from whites, and they operated largely through the conventional procedures of litigation and negotiation. While it is true that the cases they had taken to court had been largely responsible for the gains made by blacks, it is also true that their patience and conventional tactics became intolerable to the blacks of the postwar generation.

Handlin pointed out some years ago that improvement leads to increased hope for more improvement among the oppressed, and this rising level of expectations makes intolerable the conditions which were previously accepted by the utterly hopeless. "The proximity to equality only increases the hunger for it. The black man is less willing to wait than before, because his goal has never before been so clearly visible." [7]

Events in recent decades have underscored the validity of Handlin's comment. Rising expectations and dissatisfaction with the rate of progress have led to the development of diverse black organizations, each with increasingly narrow claims as to what it can do for its members. A major factor in the changing nature of these organizations has been the organizational rivalry brought about by the rise of many black civic associations. These associations, dominated by young and aggressive leaders, openly competed with the older groups in a variety of areas: finance, membership, strategy, and tactics. Such competition often resulted in claims and counterclaims as to which group could be most effective.

Active national organizations in the 1960s included the Congress of Racial Equality (CORE), the Student Nonviolent Coordinating Committee (SNCC), and the Southern Christian Leadership Conference (SCLC). The SCLC was founded by the late Reverend Martin Luther King, the symbolic leader of many aspects of the black-revolution. These organizations were originally active in southern cities, but their activities soon became national, and they played a major role in changing the nature of the battle

---

7. Oscar Handlin, "Is Integration the Answer?" *Atlantic* (March 1964): 50.

for black equality. Because of their more aggressive image and their strength, the old agencies had to make major changes to keep pace.

The most visible of the new militants were those who advocated "black power," a slogan which summed up the determination of blacks to control their own destiny. This militant, almost separatist attitude, though far less prevalent now, was the dynamic force behind the efforts of blacks to build unity and strength outside of, and often in opposition to, white organizations. To Carmichael and Hamilton, black power was

"a call for black people in this country to unite, to recognize their heritage, to build a sense of community. It is a call for black people to begin to define their own goals, to lead their organizations and to support those organizations. It is a call to reject the racist institutions and values of this society." [8]

This militancy contrasted with the traditional early civil rights movement in several important respects. The guiding theme was liberation or complete freedom from white society rather than acceptance of it. The emphasis was upon self-help, solidarity, and independent action; relatively little help was expected from the government. The decision made by the charismatic Reverend Jesse L. Jackson late in 1983 to seek the Democratic presidential nomination reflected the continuing belief in self-help, solidarity, and independent political action within the black community. Leadership in the civil rights movement up to the 1970s came from a handful of national organizations; by the 1980s it had become a much more diffuse social movement in which numerous local groups addressed local concerns.

The organization that certainly illustrates this more recent self-help emphasis among blacks is People United to Save Humanity (PUSH). Founded by Reverend Jackson in 1971, PUSH at one time claimed 30 chapters throughout the nation and a membership of one million.[9] PUSH's goals are predicated upon self-discipline and the work ethic.[10] Education is the cornerstone of the movement which strives to create close parent-school relationships which will help to change the attitudes and motivations of students. Jackson's PUSH for excellence in education is designed "to bring the resources of (1) parents and other community residents, (2) teachers, (3) preachers and other community leaders, (4) principals and other school administrators, and (5) pupils together in a common cause." [11] Although the PUSH program has been implemented on a meaningful scale in only a few cities such as Los Angeles and Chicago, it has attracted considerable attention and support. Indeed, many believe that its self-help philosophy offers unique promise to a nation still afflicted with severe racial travail. Many blacks, however, do not support PUSH because they believe that the approach offers whites a convenient escape hatch. It is also argued that PUSH is just another way to put the burden of survival on the victims of oppression.

The black movement like any other mass movement is not monolithic. Differences of opinion exist among leaders with respect to tactics and both short- and long-range goals. While very few leaders actually advocate a permanent separation of the races,

8. Stokely Carmichael and Charles V. Hamilton, *Black Power: The Politics of Liberation in America* (New York: Random House, 1967), 44.
9. Robert W. Cole, "Black Moses: Jesse Jackson's PUSH for Excellence," *Phi Delta Kappan* 58 (January 1977): 378–82.
10. Jesse L. Jackson, "Give the People a Vision," *New York Times Magazine*. (18 April 1976): 71.
11. Eugene E. Eubanks and Daniel U. Levine, "The PUSH Program for Excellence in Big-City Schools," *Phi Delta Kappan* 58 (January 1977): 383.

a number of others continue to see separation as an interim strategy to be employed in building sufficient strength to achieve "viable coalitions between blacks and whites who accept each other as co-equal partners and who identify their goals as politically and economically similar." [12] Demographic trends have lent credence to the separatist point of view as proponents stress the great difficulties in desegregating a society which more and more is segregated residentially. Indeed, the withdrawal or pulling back in recent years of many liberal whites as well as blacks from the integration push of a decade or two ago has undeniably eroded the influence of the once very visible and influential biracial civil rights coalition of the 1960s and early 1970s. The courts currently are virtually the only major force in our society supporting desegregated schools.

As the civil rights thrust lost much of its momentum in the late 1970s and 1980s, the major black groups underwent considerable financial strain and organizational stress. The leadership turned over in both the NAACP and Urban League during a period when the civil rights struggle was shifting from the more targetable legal area to the less focused and definable realms of economic equality and social policy. The election of Ronald Reagan in 1980 was viewed by the great majority of blacks as well as other minority group members as a manifestation of national retrenchment in the area of civil rights and affirmative action. [13] To many minorities it represented what was tantamount to a functional repudiation of the Brown decision of 1954. [14]

Despite the impressive academic gains made by many black youngsters in public schools and the doubling of black college enrollment in the decade of the 1970s, blacks in the 1980s continued to lag in income, were increasingly pessimistic about the future, and were trying to protect their recent gains in vital realms like education and employment. [15] In addition to their limited educational and employment opportunities, studies continued to show that black children remained seriously disadvantaged in critical areas like health, nutrition, and family economic status, and were often exposed to more crime in their neighborhoods than their white counterparts. [16]

Cutbacks in human service and education programs in the early 1980s plus growing apprehensions about the commitment of the Reagan administration and the nation at large to equity and affirmative action issues helped to force new unity among minority organizations. The political and economic assaults on longstanding programs aiding the poor catalyzed the NAACP and others to coalesce more frequently with organized labor and other civil rights advocates to generate stronger political opposition to what was widely conceived to be a national retreat on efforts to equalize opportunities for minorities.

Thus, other minority groups have joined in the drive for greater equality. Mexican-Americans (Chicanos), Puerto Ricans, and American Indians become more active in the 1960s and 1970s and, like blacks, will continue in the 1980s to demand more forcefully greater social justice and participation in the political process.

12. Carmichael and Hamilton, *Black Power,* 84.
13. Robert Pear, "Civil Rights and Reagan", *New York Times,* 31 August 1983. A-15 and Felicity Barringer, "Studies Say U.S. Desegregation Support Fell Under Block Grant", *The Washington Post,* 18 September 1983, A-8.
14. The decline in the saliency of civil rights issues has been documented in a recent poll of school administrators. See Luvern L. Cunningham and Joseph T. Hentges, *The American School Superintendency, 1982* (Washington, D.C.: American Association of School Administrators, 1982), 62–65.
15. *The Status of Black America 1983,* (National Urban League, The League, 1983) 44 p. See also, Robert Pear, "U.S. Finds Black Economic Improvement Halted," *New York Times,* 21 August 1983, A-22.
16. *Portrait of Inequality: Black and White Children in America,* (Washington D.C.: Children's Defense Fund, 1981).

Hispanics

Among the minority groups which have recently become more assertive are Hispanic or Spanish-speaking groups. Individual nationalities, like the Mexican-Americans, Puerto Ricans, and Cubans have been organized for some time, but not until the 1960s did they become politically aggressive and nationally visible.

Hispanics are the nation's most rapidly growing population group and their political influence certainly will continue to expand in the decades ahead as they are projected to become the largest racial ethnic group by the end of the century. Hispanics, while constituting only 6.4 percent of the total population in 1980, accounted for 23 percent or 5.5 million of the total population growth of 23 million in the country between 1970 and 1980.[17] Population statistics pertaining to Hispanics, of course, are inexact because of the millions of undocumented workers and their families. Some analysts project that the Hispanic population might total around 20 million, not 15 million. In any event, the Hispanic population was estimated to have grown by 61 percent from 1970 to 1980 as compared to only an 11 percent increase in the overall population.[18]

The Spanish-speaking population in the country is a diverse and not an easily identifiable ethnic group. Of the nation's estimated 15 million Hispanics, 8.7 million are Mexican-Americans, 2.0 million are Puerto Ricans, 803,000 are Cubans, and approximately 3.1 million are of other Spanish groups, primarily from South and Central America. This population has a roster of common grievances such as police brutality, unilingual education, inferior housing, and job discrimination. Recent efforts have been undertaken to establish "unidos," or unity among the several Spanish speaking groups. Efforts to create a political coalition, however, have been hampered by the substantial socioeconomic differences among these groups. For example, census data indicate that in the Cuban-American population, the typical family earns almost 90 percent of the typical white family income. But among the Mexican-American and Puerto Rican populations the comparable figures were only 70 and 60 percent, respectively.

Many remain unaware of the full implications of this dramatic population growth of Hispanics because the Hispanic population is clustered in a small number of states. For example, two-thirds of American Hispanics are concentrated in only three states: California, Texas, and New York. Indeed, one-fifth of the residents of California, the most populous state, and Texas, the third most populous state, are of Hispanic origin. When the Hispanic population of Florida, Illinois, New Jersey, New Mexico, and Arizona are added to the aforementioned three states, the great majority of the nation's Spanish-speaking population is included. In other words, approximately 85 percent of Hispanics are residing in only eight states.[19]

This great increase in the number of Hispanics has particular significance for schools because for the most part the Spanish-speaking population is much younger in age composition. The median age of Hispanics is 23 years while the median age for all Americans is 30. Over 30 percent of the Hispanic population is between the school-going ages of five and seventeen while only 23 percent of the total population is of

17. Leobardo F. Estrada, "The Dynamic Growth and Diffusion of the Latino Population" (paper presented at the Southwest Regional Forum of the American Association of Higher Education, San Diego, California, April 1983, Mimeograph).
18. Ernesto J. Ballesteros, "Equal Educational Opportunity: Access vs. Outcomes" (Paper presented at the National Symposium on Hispanic Issues in Higher Education, Wingspread Conference, Racine, Wisconsin, June, 1983, Mimeograph).
19. Cheryl Russell, "The News About Hispanics," *American Demographics* 5 (March 1983): 15.

school age.[20] In addition, the Hispanic birth rate is 75 percent higher than the remainder of the population, according to the National Center for Health Statistics.[21]

These demographic data, of course, already are influencing the composition of public school enrollments and in a number of major states with substantial Hispanic populations like Illinois, Florida, and New York the percentage of minority public school enrollment is well over 25 percent. In states such as California and Texas, this percentage is close to 50 percent.[22] Indeed, in the 1983–84 school year Texas' public school enrollment was "majority-minority."

The U.S. Commission on Civil Rights in the sixth and final report of the Mexican-American Education Study, "Toward Quality Education for Mexican Americans," presented a decade ago an insightful analysis of the educational opportunities available to Mexican-Americans in the Southwest.[23] Much of the context of this report is still relevant not only to minorities in the Southwest but also to minority groups throughout the country. Most of the Mexican-American population is concentrated in the five southwestern states of Arizona, California, Colorado, New Mexico, and Texas; a large percentage of the public school enrollment in these states is Chicano. Indeed, the illegal entry of thousands of Mexican-Americans into the Southwest poses a very severe educational problem, as well as social, economic, and political problems.

Mexican-Americans have a catalogue of grievances which in many ways is analogous to the dissatisfactions of blacks, other Hispanics, and other minority groups. The U.S. Commission on Civil Rights report catalogued the ways in which the rights of Chicano pupils were being denied in schools of the Southwest. School districts allegedly were discriminating against Mexican-Americans and the federal government had not seen fit to intervene and firmly enforce basic constitutional guarantees of equal education.

The commission report emphasized the need for more funding, noting that only 70,000 or 1.7 percent of the 1.6 million Chicano students in the southwestern states received the $7.7 million at that time allocated for bilingual education in federally supported projects. Only a tiny fraction of Chicano students, approximately two percent, received instruction in Mexican-American history or in Chicano studies. Mexican-Americans, quite understandably with their growing numbers and influence, have intensified their political activities in order to ameliorate these conditions.

There are approximately two million mainland Puerto Ricans, the large majority of whom live in the Northeast. More than 250,000 Puerto Rican youngsters are enrolled in New York City Schools alone. At least one-third of New York City's public school enrollment is now Puerto Rican or of Hispanic origin. The historical complaints of Puerto Ricans against school systems have a familiar ring. In 1972, in New York City, for example, it was estimated that more than 100,000 Puerto Rican students spoke little or no English, 86 percent were below average in reading levels for their age and grade, and almost 60 pecent were school dropouts.[24] Like comparable statistics for other minorities, these figures are disastrous for a recently migrated group

20. Jose Hernandez, "Hispanic Migration and Demographic Patterns: Implications for Educational Planning and Policy", *Hispanic Migrations from the Caribbean and Latin America: Conference Proceedings,* ERIC/CUE Urban Diversity Series, 65 (August 1979) 1.
21. "Birth Rate Highest for Latinos in U.S.," *New York Times,* 26 May 1982, C4.
22. Harold Hodgkinson, *"Guess Who's Coming to College"* (Washington D.C.: National Association of Independent Colleges and Universities, 1983), 6.
23. U.S. Commission on Civil Rights, *Toward Quality Education for Mexican Americans* (Washington, D.C.: February 1974).
24. Iver Peterson, "Puerto Ricans: Teaching Juan His Name is John," *New York Times,* 30 July 1972, 9.

that is striving for a socioeconomic toehold. Indeed, recent U.S. Census Bureau data indicate that poverty is more widespread among Puerto Ricans than among blacks or any other minority group. Puerto Ricans living on the mainland reportedly had a median family income of $9,900 or 50 percent of the $19,661 median for all families in the country.[25]

In New York City and elsewhere, the educational plight of Puerto Rican and other Hispanic school children has galvanized their elders into political action. In recent years Hispanic groups have more aggressively pushed in legal and political arenas for the dramatic expansion of bilingual offerings and other program changes which would improve the quality of education offered their youth.

A concrete example of this growing concern and involvement was the formation late in 1983 of the National Commission on Secondary Schooling for Hispanics. Under the aegis of the Hispanic Policy Development Project, a foundation and corporate sponsored non-profit organization which focuses on public policy issues affecting Hispanics, a prestigious eighteen-member group planned to conduct a study of the condition of Hispanic secondary school education in light of the recommendations of the various national reports. This National Commission on Secondary Schooling for Hispanics planned to conduct widely publicized meetings in Los Angeles, San Antonio, Miami, New York City, and Chicago. In the news release announcing the creation of the Commission, the following recent data were stressed:

Hispanic children enroll in school at rates lower than those for non-Hispanic students, they fall behind their classmates in progressing through school, and their attrition rates are higher than for non-Hispanic students.

In California, Mexican Americans drop out of high school at twice the average state dropout rate. Overall, the 1980 high school completion rate for Mexican Americans 25 years and above was 43.2 percent, compared with 68.7 percent for whites. Those Hispanic students who did remain in school fell behind their classmates often. So much so, that close to one-quarter of the 14- to 20-year-olds enrolled were two grades behind their classmates, compared to only nine percent of white students who were behind their contemporaries.

In all but two of the 25 largest public school systems, more than half of the students come from minority groups. In Los Angeles, close to half the public school enrollment is Hispanic and in New York more than one quarter is. Thus, Hispanics continue to lag far behind the general population with respect to the pool of students eligible for college.[26]

Illustrative of Hispanic groups with growing interest and influence in education are organizations like the League of United Latin American Citizens (LULAC), the Mexican-American Legal Defense and Education Fund (MALDEF), the National Council of La Raza, the National Puerto Rican Forum, and the Congressional Hispanic Caucus. These Hispanic organizations buttressed by the marked growth of their constituency are in the forefront of efforts to improve the economic, political, social, and educational opportunities available to America's burgeoning Hispanic population.[27]

25. Ronald Smothers, "Puerto Rican Family Increase Found to Be Half U.S. Median," *New York Times,* 12 July 1981, A10.
26. "National Commission on Secondary Schooling for Hispanics is Created" (News Release of the Hispanic Policy Development Project, 1983, Mimieographed).
27. *A Guide to Hispanic Organizations,* Philip Morris Incorporated, 1983.

American Indians

Yet another ignored minority group has spoken up in recent years. The unique difficulties confronting the native American, or the American Indian, have begun to attract greater attention. Growing national interest in minority groups generally in the 1960s as well as substantial increases in Indian attendance both in their own schools and in public schools rather than in Bureau of Indian Affairs institutions have dramatized the need for comprehensive examination of the status of Indian education. The U.S. Office of Education funded the National Study of American Indian Education. Professors Robert J. Havighurst and Estelle Fuchs directed this study which was concluded in 1971 and reported their understandings and conclusions in "To Live on This Earth: American Indian Education." [28]

The failures of Indian education according to Fuchs and Havighurst's analysis, are quite similar to those articulated by other minority groups:

> With minor exceptions the history of Indian education had been primarily the transmission of white American education, little altered, to the Indian child as a one-way process. The institution of the school is one that was imposed by and controlled by the non-Indian society, its pedagogy and curriculum little changed for the Indian children, its goals primarily aimed at removing the child from his aboriginal culture and assimilating him into the dominant white culture. Whether coercive or persuasive, this assimilationist goal of schooling has been minimally effective with Indian children, as indicated by their record of absenteeism, retardation, and high dropout rates. [29]

Like other minority groups, American Indians in recent years have become much more forceful in stating their belief in the central significance of education:

> We conceive education not only in terms of classroom teaching, but a process which begins at birth and continues through a life span. Of all the studies, surveys, and research made of Indians, the inevitable conclusions and recommendations are that education is the key to salvation of whatever ills may be, wherever Indians reside. [30]

In the last two decades the American Indian population has tripled, from a half million to a million and a half. Indians are participating in the dominant non-Indian society more extensively than ever before. The number of young Indians attending colleges and graduate schools has grown dramatically and there is escalating pride in their identity and heritage. [31] American Indians like other minority groups will be exerting continuous pressure to ensure that their children receive equal educational opportunities in the years ahead.

The Issue: Equal Educational Opportunity

For many years American educators have considered the problems involved in providing equal educational opportunity to all children. Before the 1954 Supreme Court decision, however, the problems involved in achieving equality were largely problems of

---

28. Excerpts from *To Live on This Earth: American Indian Education* by Estelle Fuchs and Robert J. Havighurst. Copyright © 1972 by Estelle Fuchs and Robert J. Havighurst. Reprinted by permission of Doubleday & Company, Inc.
29. Ibid., 19.
30. Ibid., 20.
31. Alvin M. Josephy, Jr., *Now That the Buffalo's Gone: A Study of Today's American Indians* (New York: Knopf, 1982).

equal financial support. Witness, for example, the persistent concern of the proponents of federal aid to education with achieving equal opportunities. Proponents of federal aid pointed to disparities in financing across the nation and used *equal opportunity* to mean *equal expenditures.* In recent years, however, the phrase has been identified with the drive for equal treatment of minority groups.

A major factor which has contributed to increased militancy is the increase in population distribution of nonwhites in America. There are about 40 million nonwhites, which equals almost 20 percent of the American population. Blacks represent well over one-half of this nonwhite group. The migration of this segment of the population has been astonishing. In 1900 nearly 90 percent of the nonwhite population was concentrated in the South, largely on farms.

These population patterns began to shift somewhat in the late 1960s, and by the 1970s the movement from rural and small town areas into metropolitan areas had slowed down perceptibly. Whites, however, continued to move out of the cities in substantial numbers. The 1970 census indicated, for example, that most of the central cities were continuing to lose their white residents as well as decreasing in overall population. Alan Campbell comments on the significance of the demographic watershed reached in the mid-1960s when the suburban population became larger than that of the central cities; he also notes that "this change does not bode well for the political strength of cities in either state legislatures or Congress." [32]

Despite the fact that some improvement has been noted in the condition of central cities because of the decline in population density in poor areas,[33] the educational problems in the major core cities remain acute. Although blacks and other minority groups are moving into the suburbs in growing numbers, the core cities increasingly are populated by poor nonwhites. It is largely middle-income minority people who are following their white counterparts into the suburbs leaving poorer elements behind. These demographic patterns have concentrated disadvantaged minority groups in urban centers and have thus increased their organizational strength and political potential. Their awareness of the problems created by unequal educational opportunities has also increased.

Equality of educational opportunity is a very complex, subtle, and elusive goal. It is achieved "when each child of school age residing within a school district has equal access to the educative resources of the district essential to his needs." [34] When the educational problem is compounded by social problems based on housing patterns, employment opportunities, population mobility, and community feelings, to name just a few, the problem of determining educational policies becomes even more difficult.

The root cause of de facto segregated schools is the extensive racial segregation in housing. Black and other minority groups have held that educational segregation, whether it is deliberate or not, has harmful effects on the children involved, and therefore should be corrected immediately. In northern communities, minorities accuse educators of attempting to shirk their responsibilities by taking the attitude that no one within the school system helped to create the situation and that the responsibility for change should not fall on the school system, or at least not on the school system alone.

---

32. Alan K. Campbell, "Education in Its Metropolitan Setting," in *Metropolitan School Organization: Basic Problems and Patterns*, vol. 1, ed. Troy V. McKelvey (Berkeley, Calif.: McCutchan, 1973), 14.
33. Ibid.
34. Luvern L. Cunningham, "Equality of Opportunity: Is It Possible in Education?" *Administrator's Notebook* 16 (November 1967): 1.

One point of attack has been the neighborhood school concept, which has been interpreted by some civil rights leaders as a segregated school concept that must be eliminated (see chapter 6). Historically, the assignment of children to elementary schools in urban areas has generally been done on a geographic basis, with a child being assigned to the school nearest, or near, his residence. Transfers are frequently permitted but not encouraged. At the secondary level more options are usually possible because of the specialized schools available; plus, because high schools have more students, they draw from a broader geographic area. The neighborhood school, however, will generally and inevitably reflect the racial, social, economic, and cultural features of the area it serves. Since most urban minorities live in racially segregated areas, the schools their children attend are largely or entirely segregated.

Such schools have traditionally had a unique set of educational problems. Among these problems are overcrowding, fantastic student mobility (in some classrooms over 100 percent for the year, meaning that the teacher has none of the students at the end of the year who were enrolled at the beginning of the year or that the number of transfers in and out was greater than the number of students enrolled at the beginning of the year), a high dropout rate, poor physical facilities, and the crucial problem of getting competent teachers to work in these schools. Despite efforts to improve programs in most city schools since the early 1960s, there is little evidence that their effectiveness has increased significantly although there have been encouraging improvements in test results in a number of cities.

Neighborhood schools, however, even though they tend to be segregated, are not always opposed by minorities. The reaction of Los Angeles Chicanos to the city's busing program is an example. Chicanos were apprehensive lest the integration plan dilute the city's bilingual education efforts and cripple recent efforts that had been made to provide additional teaching jobs for Mexican-Americans. Raul P. Arreola, administrative secretary of the Mexican-American Education Commission which advises the Los Angeles schools on matters pertaining to Chicanos, was quoted as stating that "very few Mexican-American parents are interested in busing their children into white schools. We feel that we have much to lose if our children are bused out of the neighborhood." [35]

The Approach: Due Process and Direct Action

There has been disagreement among minority groups and leaders regarding proximate objectives for achieving equal educational opportunity. Some have emphasized school desegregation while others have stressed the need to increase accountability to the community. Advocates of equal educational opportunity, however, have generally agreed upon a number of ancillary goals. These include more minority group faculty members, greater attention to minority group culture and contributions in the curriculum, increased sensitivity to minority group student needs and interests by teachers and adminstrators, smaller classes, and more remedial and special instructional services. In recent years, for example, minority groups, particularly Spanish-speaking ones, have pushed vigorously and with some success to expand federal and state bilingual programs (Title VII of the Elementary and Secondary Education Act of 1965). [36]

35. "Los Angeles Chicanos Fear School System's Proposed Busing Integration Plan Will Hurt Bilingual Program," *New York Times*, 6 February 1977, 25.
36. For a persuasive argument in support of bilingual education see Jeffrey W. Kobrick, "The Compelling Case for Bilingual Education," *Saturday Review* 29 (April 1972), 54–58.

Groups and leaders have disagreed about the most appropriate means to be employed in seeking their goals. The traditional view has been that progress can be achieved best by providing information to the public, negotiating directly with school officials, and invoking legal sanctions when necessary and possible. These are strategies of due process. The NAACP, in particular, has maintained steady pressure on the courts for action against segregation. They have opposed de jure and de facto segregation with equal vigor, holding that regardless of intent there is a constitutional obligation for school officials to take whatever actions may be required and are educationally sound to achieve maximum desegregation.

Other approaches ultilizing procedures of due process include support of state and federal legislation which provides (1) financial assistance to schools attended by poor and minority group children, (2) incentives to desegregate schools or penalties for failing to do so, and (3) bases for reorganizing school districts to achieve greater community control. Legislation of all three types has been passed by various states, and Congress has enacted measures of the first two types (The Elementary and Secondary Education Act of 1965 and the Civil Rights Act of 1964 respectively). The efforts of black groups have influenced the passage of such measures.

Where equal education opportunity legislation exists, minority groups have worked for its implementation. For example, Title VI of the Civil Rights Act of 1964 prohibits the allocation of federal funds to any agency (including school districts) which practices discrimination. Minority group representatives have petitioned the federal government to withhold Elementary and Secondary Education Act funds and other monies from their school districts in attempts to force local officials to desegregate. This tactic, however, has at least two disadvantages. First, it seeks to withhold funds often designated for programs to aid the very children minority group leaders also want to help. Second, there has been considerable ambiguity about what constitutes compliance with the act; in particular, the government certainly in recent years has not always acted forcefully against alleged de facto segregation.

It is difficult to gauge the effectiveness which minority groups have had in shaping educational policies. Surely progress has been made toward some of their goals, as we will see, but there have been no bold or significant breakthroughs, and urban schools continue to be a pressing national problem. While sympathy for improved educational opportunities for minority group children continues, the tactics used by some groups have alienated some of those who previously gave support. Indeed, many believe that the backlash generated by the militant tactics of black power some years ago has seriously eroded white liberal support and thus weakened the political influence of the once powerful interracial civil rights coalition.

There can be no doubt that minority striving has had impact upon American education in recent years. Educators have become aware that schools need to play a major role in bringing poor and minority group children into the mainstream of American life. Considerable legislation has been enacted to this end. In addition to such federal programs as Head Start and the Elementary and Secondary Education Act, several states have passed compensatory education legislation.

Minority efforts also have had considerable impact at the local school district level. Many school systems have affirmed integration of staff members and students to be a policy goal. In general, staff integration has been achieved more easily than student integration. Even so, strong teacher organizations and traditions of internal transfer and promotion within the system through examinations have impeded staff integration in some large cities. The desegregation of students has also been most problematic in our largest cities. However, noteworthy desegregation plans have been implemented in many small and medium-size cities including Berkeley, California, and Evanston, Illinois. Measures employed to desegregate schools have included boundary changes, open enrollment plans, educational parks, new organizational arrangements (e.g., changing from junior high schools to middle schools so students from a broader attendance area will attend school together at an earlier age), pairing two or more schools of differing racial composition and reassigning students on an integrated basis, and "magnet schools" (schools with special programs designed to appeal to students from a broad geographical area).

Other areas in which minority demands have had an impact relate to the school programs. Within the last few years most city school systems have taken steps to offer more realistic learning materials to urban children. Textbooks which emphasize white, middle-class views of society have been supplanted by materials that appear to have greater relevance to poorer children of the city. Bilingual instruction and courses in minority history and cultures have been added to many curriculums. Many special and remedial programs and services, often funded by federal or special state legislation, are now in operation. Paraprofessionals who serve as valuable links between school people and neighborhood residents as well as help teachers with particular tasks are now found in many inner-city schools.

Finally, minority demands have stimulated the increased accountability of school personnel to parents and other citizens. Parents in the poorer city districts especially ask how well the schools are doing, and they are demanding a response. One form of response has been to grant a measure of community control or establish advisory committees and other mechanisms for citizen participation. Another type of response has been to provide more information about the schools. A pioneering effort in this direction has been the publication of school profiles in many districts. These documents present median aptitude and achievement scores for students in all elementary and junior high schools as well as data describing the student body and staff including racial composition, turnover, training, and experience.

The cumulative effect of changes resulting from due process and direct action has been the creation of an atmosphere of uncertainty. Confronted with a growing range of demands and expectations for schools, society finds it difficult to agree upon a definition of equal educational opportunity in legal or educational terms. The problem is also a political one. The demands of minority groups challenge the status quo in terms of how resources are allocated for educational purposes. Some white, middle-class parents whose children have difficulty reading cannot understand why inner-city schools should have priority in the assignment of remedial reading instructors. Similarly, teachers and administrators who have grown accustomed to making unilateral educational judgments with the security afforded by tenure may resent citizen demands for more accountability and community control. Moreover, it is difficult to tell whether the demands of the future will resemble those of today, and it is hard to predict the tactics which will be used to advance them.

Within the past few years growing numbers of minority group members, largely blacks, have assumed leadership positions in major urban school systems. Minority group members now constitute an increasing percentage of the school superintendents, key central office personnel, and school board members in large, predominantly minority urban school systems. There are great opportunities in this development. The movement of more minority group members into leadership positions in education has many positive by-products. Black superintendents, for example, frequently have credibility in interacting with many minority parents and students and can ease tensions in many situations more effectively than their white predecessors. The image of success which the minority leader represents and the sense of group pride he or she inspires are additional positive by-products of this movement. This movement of minority group members into educational leadership positions (with the exception of Spanish-speaking minorities who remain inadequately represented at the top levels) is long overdue. However, educational leaders in the cities continue to face overwhelming problems, and the recent decline in overt conflict and tension cannot be viewed with equanimity by the majority population nestled in comfortable suburbs. The threat of educational apartheid is growing in many sections of the country and the consequences of such a split in a racially pluralistic nation would be drastic.

White Ethnic Groups

As public interest and controversy have focused upon the multifaceted problems of racial minorities, there has been a tendency to ignore the interests of "white ethnics." Who are these ethnics whose frustrations and resentments have so recently been registered? They are generally defined as upper-lower-class or very marginally middle-class, blue-collar populations that reside in sizeable enclaves in urban centers. Public attention, these citizens believe, has been concentrated inordinately upon the plight of nonwhite minorities, and the serious social and economic problems of ethnic groups, they feel, have been ignored.

These ethnics consider themselves to be the forgotten Americans of contemporary society. They are a polyglot group broadly defined to include some 40 million Americans of European extraction. These ethnics reside largely in the older industrialized cities of the Northeast and Middle West. As indicated earlier, the growing attention being paid to the problems of blacks, Hispanics, and other minorities triggered in the late 1960s a sharp response from this large group of whites of immigrant background. The various federal programs, they felt, were directed only at assisting racial minorities, and the serious problems of economically marginal whites were being ignored by governmental authorities at all levels.

The ethnics, feeling betrayed, overtaxed, and underserved, began to regenerate their group identity and ethnic pride in their heritage. By the 1970s the virtues of ethnic pluralism were being extrolled and assimilation was no longer the desideratum of many Americans with immigrant heritages. The melting pot ideal was being questioned critically.

White ethnics were angered in the late 1960s both by the "radical" antiwar protest movement which they felt demeaned their country and by the stereotyping of them as "racists" by liberal elite groups. Andrew Greeley, former director of the Center for the Study of Ethnic Pluralism at the University of Chicago, has compellingly described the attitudes of many white ethnics:

> American ethnics are deeply troubled at what they consider to be the "changing of the rules," a phrase I have heard over and over again. They had to work to achieve the social position they presently occupy, but other groups in American society are demanding these positions as a matter of right. Their children had to pass entrance exams to get into college; other men's children (they think) do not. Their fathers had to work long hours to support their families; other men's fathers seemingly did not. They fought bravely to defend America in World War II and in the Korean War, and now it is being alleged that those who fight and die in wars are immoral or foolish. They lived according to the American ethic of sobriety and respectability, and now

they see on TV the spectacle of the drug smoking hippie at a rock festival. In other words, the white ethnic feels that he is being told that the rules no longer apply, that others are to achieve what he has achieved (frequently, it seems to him, with his picking up the tab) by doing exactly the opposite of what the rules prescribed.[37]

Greeley describes the inherent tensions existing between ethnic Americans and liberal elite groups:

The intellectual and moral strains among the liberal elite groups run directly counter to strains in the white ethnics and other members of middle America. Not to put too fine an edge on the matter, the liberal elites are strongly tempted to view white ethnics with profound contempt. The elites are far better educated, far more articulate, far better informed, far more sophisticated and, in their heart of hearts, convinced that they are far superior morally.[38]

The very diverse ethnic groups thus began to demand attention and became much more visible on the American scene. Italians, Poles, Greeks, Slavs, Irish, Jews, Germans, and others began to demonstrate great interest in their heritage, and the general society was compelled to respond.[39]

The federal government provided resources through the Ethnic Heritage Studies Act (Title IX of ESEA, Education Amendments of 1972) for the development and dissemination of curricular materials and programs pertaining to white ethnics as well as racial minorities. Funds were also made available for the training of personnel in ethnic studies. Slogans like "Italian Power" and "Polish is Beautiful" expressed the resurgence of ethnic pride and identity.

Ethnic projects proliferated in the 1970s as numerous school systems and colleges began to provide courses and instructional materials in ethnic studies. The states also began to respond. Illinois, for example, required the implementation of a statewide program of ethnic studies by 1975 which would focus upon not only blacks but also Poles, Irish, Hispanics, Bohemians, Albanians, French, Scots, Lithuanians and Czechs. The Ford Foundation, reflecting the growing national awareness that ethnic issues needed attention, funded the National Project on Ethnic America. The objective was to foster better intergroup understanding by providing resources for fellowships to encourage scholarship in ethnic studies and other similar programs.

The white ethnic groups for a time were rather active politically and utilized many of the protest tactics employed by nonwhites. The mass demonstrations in Boston against court orders to compel the city school committee to comply with the Massachusetts Racial Imbalance Act and the protests in New York City's Forest Hills section against a mixed-income housing project some years ago illustrate this often latent ethnic militancy. The ethnic movement within the past decade seems to have lost much momentum, probably because minority groups overall have been less vocal and aggressive. If minority militancy is reasserted, however, it is likely that white ethnic groups will again become quite visible and strident.

37. Andrew N. Greeley, "Turning Off the People," *The New Republic,* 27 (June 1970), 15. Reprinted by permission of *The New Republic,* © 1970 by the New Republic, Inc.
38. Ibid.
39. Robert Coles and Jon Erikson, *The Middle Americans* (Boston: Little, Brown, 1971).

The Feminist Movement and Women's Organizations

Women's organizations constitute another category of groups which sometimes become involved in school matters. In recent years the escalating activism of the feminist movement has brought a growing awareness of the role and influence of women in the organization and control of American schools. Indeed, the feminist movement, especially as it has been bolstered by Title IX of the Education Amendments of 1972 (which prohibited sex discrimination in any education program or activity), has certainly affected the entire educational enterprise.

The feminist movement began to burgeon in the early 1970s as the issue of sexism, or the inferior status of women, surfaced with increasing frequency both in education and in society at large. A rapidly expanding literature of women's rights began to develop, and education quite logically became a focal point of criticism for advocates of equal opportunities for females. For example, Phi Delta Kappa, historically an exclusive male honorary educational fraternity, was pressured late in 1973 to change its constitution and to admit women members. Phi Delta Kappa's well-known journal, *Phi Delta Kappan,* devoted an entire issue to the feminist movement's wide ranging implications for education.[40]

Howe cited more than a decade ago some of the far-reaching and still relevant aims of those striving to give women improved status in the male-dominated social order:

> Recently something new has occurred, something new not only for women's education but also for the education of minorities, female or male. The hegemony of white, male middle-class control over the education of diverse racial and ethnic groups of women and men continues to be challenged. The voices of women may be the last to be heard, but they are the most numerous "minority" in history. Like the blacks, Chicanos, and other ethnic groups before them, women are saying we must build a curriculum that 1) compensates for prior deprivation; 2) allows us to raise the consciousness of many women; 3) encourages the production of useful research; 4) aims to restore the lost culture and history of women; and 5) actively works towards social change.[41]

Howe also stresses the central importance of education in the efforts of the women's rights movement to equalize opportunity for females:

> What do we need? A parallel movement of elementary and high school teachers to change the sexism of texts and classrooms. Such a movement should grow out of the practice of teachers as they begin to analyze their own behavior, the attitudes they and their students bring to school, and the curriculum materials they have used unthinkingly.
>
> We need nonsexist texts on all levels. We need to revise all social science and literature and language curricula, and much that passes for health, science, physical education, biology, or sex education. We need to become alert to the sexist and nonsexist behavior of teachers in the classroom. We need to develop special strategies to reverse the procedures that turn some boys into nonreaders and most girls into nonmathematicians and nonscientists. We need special efforts to encourage girls

40. Myron Lieberman, ed., "Education and the Feminist Movement," *Phi Delta Kappan* 55 (October 1973).
41. Florence Howe, "Sexism and the Aspirations of Women," *Phi Delta Kappan* 55 (October 1973): 102.

also to enter vocational schools long denied them or to learn sports they have only been allowed to observe.[42]

Women in the 1960s and 1970s began to change their political attitudes and behavior substantially. Growing numbers of women recognized that they were " 'locked out' of the political process, that their brains and talents were not only unused but unwanted. And they began to realize that any society that ignores the ability of half its adult population cannot be functioning intelligently. Simultaneously, women's organizations realized that if they wanted political clout (and they do), they would have to go after it."[43]

The feminist movement, of course, has moved with persistent vigor to increase the political potency of women. The Equal Rights Amendment has been forcefully pushed at both the state and national levels by ERA America which includes 55 women's organizations ranging from the National Organization for Women (NOW) to the Girl Scouts. The National Women's Political Caucus strove to raise the female delegate quotas during recent national conventions and in 1980 the Republican Party for the first time wrote a women's plank into its platform. The number of female delegates at national conventions has increased substantially, and the nomination of Geraldine Ferraro as the Democratic Vice-Presidential nominee in the 1984 convention is dramatic evidence of the growing political influence of women.

Feminists have made educational institutions major targets of reform. Lyon and Saario more than a decade ago documented the gross underrepresentation of women in educational leadership positions; in public education, for example, while 67 percent of the teachers were women only 15 percent of the principals and 0.6 percent of the superintendents were female.[44] These statistics confirmed the existence of sexual discrimination in education which is paralleled in other major spheres of American life. Educational institutions of all kinds were compelled to comply more strictly with Title IX of the Education Amendments of 1972 which states that "no person in the United States shall, on the basis of sex, be excluded from participation in, denied benefits of, or be subjected to discrimination under any education program or activity receiving federal financial assistance."

Education policymakers at local, state, and federal levels have become far more cognizant of women's rights and concerns than they were in the past.[45] Specific examples of the greater political leverage of women's groups show that the feminist movement is maturing into a force capable of shaping public policy. For instance, the changes made in public school athletics and physical education programs have been dramatic. When the Title IX regulations went into effect in July 1975, secondary and postsecondary institutions were given a three-year transition period to comply fully. This transition period ended on July 21, 1978, but even with minimum enforcement very significant changes occurred. In 1971, for example, only 7 percent of high school athletes were girls; by 1976, 29 percent were female.[46] Girls' teams in a variety of

42. Ibid., 103.
43. Suzanne Paizis, "Frustrated Majority: Consciousness-Raising at the Ballot Box," *California Journal* 5 (March 1974): 82.
44. Catherine Dillon Lyon and Terry N. Saario, "Women in Public Education: Sexual Discrimination in Promotions," *Phi Delta Kappan* 55 (October 1973): 120.
45. See, for example, "Thought-Provoking Comments on the Status of Women and Girls and Boys and Men in Classrooms," Comment Section, *Education Times* (2 August 1982): 2, and National Advisory Council on Women's Educational Programs, *Women's Education: The Challenge of the 80's,* Sixth Annual Report (Washington, D.C.: The Council, March 1981).
46. *Update on Title IX and Sports,* Project on the Status and Education of Women (Washington, D.C.: Association of American Colleges, June 1978), 7.

sports are on the rise as school systems are being compelled to provide the necessary facilities and equipment after years of neglect. On national television and in communities throughout the country, women's sports are rapidly capturing enthusiastic public support. In the future, school systems will continue to be under public and legal pressure to provide equal athletic opportunities to women.

There can be no doubt that the multifaceted feminist movement has already played a major role in expanding the roles and diversifying the aspirations of American women. A national survey of female college freshmen sponsored by the American Council on Education and the University of California at Los Angeles indicated that one in four female college freshmen in the fall of 1980 planned careers in traditionally male fields such as law and engineering. This percentage represented more than a 400 percent increase since 1966.[47] Indeed, women made notable increases in entering professional fields in the decade from 1972 to 1982. The ranks of women professionals soared from 4,534,000 in 1972 to 7,650,000 in 1982; for example, for the period from 1972 to 1982 the proportion of women graduates in law rose from 7 percent to 33 percent, in medicine from 9 percent to 25 percent, in dentistry from 1 percent to 15 percent, and in optometry from 2 percent to 20 percent.[48]

A number of nationally significant projects on women in education in the 1970s kept Title IX and affirmative action issues very much in the public limelight. The Equal Rights for Women in Education Project, for example, was initiated by the Education Commission of the States, with support from the Ford Foundation, to help states ensure equal rights for women in education. Materials designed to promote sexual equity in schools were developed for state legislators, state education departments, and state boards of education. The Legal Defense and Education Fund of NOW, also with the assistance of the Ford Foundation, operated a Project on Equal Education Rights (PEER) which focused primarily on the enforcement of Title IX in public schools. PEER monitored and publicized efforts aimed at ensuring compliance with federal laws barring sex discrimination in education. These and other national, state, and local activities have kept the issue of equal rights for women in the forefront of public discourse, and school systems are under constant scrutiny in this regard. The dramatic growth of women's studies programs also has raised public consciousness of sexism in the schools and in society. The number of scholarly and popular publications on women's issues soared. Interdisciplinary women's studies groups have been organized regionally and in local communities as well as on college campuses. By 1969 there were 100 women's studies courses on 48 campuses; by June 1978 there were 276 such programs spread across all but nine of the 50 states.[49] In January 1977 the National Women's Studies Association was organized in an effort to strengthen and lend legitimacy to this burgeoning national movement.[50]

Despite these impressive gains, the advent of the Reagan administration in 1981 represented serious regression to many in the women's movement. The president's opposition to the Equal Rights Amendment, lack of enthusiasm for affirmative action; endorsement of bans on abortion, and support of budget reductions in programs of

47. "More College Women Pursue Traditionally Male Careers," *Higher Education and National Affairs*, 30, 13 February 1981: 4.
48. Kenneth E. John, comp., "The New Social Order for Women," *Washington Post Magazine*, 27 November 1983: 15.
49. *Women's Studies*, Project on the Status and Education of Women (Washington, D.C.: Association of American Colleges, June 1978), 5.
50. Gene Maeroff, "The Growing Women's Studies Movement Gets Organized, *New York Times*, 18 January 1977: 23.

particular importance to women such as education and support for the poor and elderly precipitated considerable resentment and opposition to Reagan among women's groups. Policy changes such as cuts in Title IX, women-oriented programs in fields such as nursing, the deletion of a women-in-science program, and retrenchment in or the elimination of other federally supported activities hearalded a serious threat to the women's movement.

These reverses and the perceived threat of losing recent gains galvanized the women's movement. NOW's new membership early in 1981 increased between 9,000 or 10,000 monthly, two or three times the earlier average. In March of 1981, 24 women's groups ranging from the League of Women Voters, the Federation of Business and Professional Women's Clubs, the Young Women's Christian Association, and the Planned Parenthood Federation, to NOW and the Women's Equity Action League issued a joint statement condemning federal budget cuts as inimical to their interests. Women's groups coalesced with other organizations in opposing the Reagan administration's perceived retreat from women's equity in dismantling the federal government's commitments not only to women but also its commitments to other programs pertaining to the undernourished, the handicapped, the environment, mental health, the aged, and minorities.[51]

These developments catalyzed the women's movement in the 1980s to focus energies on increasing the involvement of its constituencies in the political process. Particular efforts were made to elect pro-feminists to office in both the Congress and state legislatures. These efforts and strategies seem to be reaping tangible dividends as reflected in the numbers of women elected to public offices. Between 1975 and 1981, while still very small percentage-wise, the number of women holding public office increased approximately threefold from 5,765 to 17,552. The number of women in the U.S. Congress has increased from 15 or 2.8 percent of the total in 1971 to 24 or 4.5 percent of the total in 1983; the gains in female membership in state legislatures are somewhat more impressive and reflect growth from 344 women legislators constituting 4.5 percent of the total in 1971 to 991 or 13.3 percent of the total in 1983.[52]

The implications of the feminist movement remain of great importance both for American education and the society at large, and we can only briefly address these complex issues here. Although we will return to a discussion of the women's movement in a later chapter, we will focus at this point on its significant impact upon other women's groups which traditionally have been involved with public schools.

Although the feminist movement has attracted extensive publicity in very recent years, two well established, multi-issue women's organizations, the League of Women Voters (LWV) and the American Association of University Women (AAUW), have long been active on education issues. These organizations, of course, are very much part of the women's movement. Both support ERA and have strong women's rights positions. While their more outspoken allies in the movement may have made more headlines lately, the LWV and AAUW for years have exercised great influence throughout the nation. Both organizations have articulate, influential, and highly educated members and are based strategically in communities throughout the nation. Both organizations have manifested a keen interest in educational issues through the years.

A nonpartisan organization of men and women for political action (the 1974 National Convention of the LWV voted to admit men to full membership although the

---

51. Linda Charlton, "Sisterhood is Braced for The Reaganauts," *New York Times,* 10 May 1981, E-20.
52. "Women Hold More Offices," *USA Today,* 1 December 1983, 9A.

name remains the same), today's League of Women Voters bears little resemblance to its predecessor, the flamboyant National American Woman Suffrage Association, whose members perched on flagpoles and marched through saloons to win for women the right to vote in 1920. But despite the league's more dignified approach and relatively small size (111,000 members), many politicians think its campaigns on state and local issues constitute an important force in American politics.

Political observers attribute the LWV's influence partly to its following among women, including nonmembers who are playing an increasingly important role in public affairs. They also credit its ability to involve members in detailed studies of complex issues to the point where they sometimes have more facts at their command than professional politicians. Many politicians view with wonder and a degree of frustration the league's ability to assume a mantle of nonpartisanship (chapters cannot side with parties or candidates) while becoming deeply involved in highly controversial issues.

The LWV has some 1,200 state and local chapters. League stands on issues at all levels are reached through a process the league refers to as "consensus." Local and state league chapters attempt to generate such consensus after sustained study and group discussion which involves a substantial number of members, representative of the membership as a whole. Consensus does not necessarily imply either a simple majority or unanimity. Procedurally the league concentrates on only a few issues at a time. After a study of available facts and positions on a given issue, members discuss the issue at small and large meetings. When consensus is reached, the LWV works to implement the position through an intensive action program that includes testifying at public hearings, use of public forums, panel discussions, mass media, league publications, and letters to public officials. The League of Women Voters in 1978 for example, published a document which explicated the organization's position on issues such as tax reform, employment, and housing. In this document the LWV also declared its position on a number of specific education issues such as support for racial integration "as a necessary condition for equal access to education," support for school finance reform at the state level, and support for federal education programs "designed to meet the special educational needs of the poor and minorities."[53]

The League of Women Voters is active in education at the federal, state, and local levels. Since action by the league is nearly always taken in concert with other groups, it is difficult to isolate actions at these levels which can be directly attributed to the efforts of the league. Officials of the organization are among the first to admit this although in California and some other states the league increasingly is becoming a very active and visible participant in the debates on major finance and governance issues.[54]

At the state level most leagues conduct intensive studies before positions are reached. Such studies often result in publications which receive widespread distribution. In addition to publications, activities at the state level include active lobbying for bills supporting the position of the league. Communication from the state office to local officers is frequent and informative, with current information on the status of various pieces of legislation, dates of hearings, and suggestions for writing or telephoning legislators.

Local league projects have included comprehensive studies of local school systems. League chapters also sponsor meetings at which voters can meet candidates

53. League of Women Voters of the United States, *Impact on Issues*, 1978–80 (Washington, D.C., 1978), 7–8.
54. Paizis, "Frustrated Majority," 82.

for boards of education as well as other officers and publish nonpartisan information about candidates and issues. In many communities the LWV fact sheet provides more information about candidates in board of education elections than any other source. The influence of the league on educational policymaking seems to be the greatest at the state level, and the least at the national level. At the local level the activity of the league has been sporadic but occasionally quite effective.

The American Association of University Women, founded in 1882 in Boston as the Association of Collegiate Alumnae, took its present name in 1921 when the ACA merged with the Southern Association of College Women.[55] Its members number approximately 193,000 in some 1,900 local branches. All of the members are women who hold baccalaureate or higher degrees from colleges and universities which have met the institutional standards for membership set by the association.

The structure and operating procedures of the AAUW are quite similar to those of the League of Women Voters although it is not as action-oriented as the League. At the national level there is a study-action program dealing with several interest areas, one of which is education. For many years the legislative program at the national level, which is voted by the national convention, as with the League of Women Voters, has supported federal aid to education. At the local level, where groups are referred to as branches, the programs are worked out according to the interests of members and needs of the community. Many branches work for better public schools—studying local school budgets, analyzing the needs of education, and mobilizing public support to meet them. The state division is expected to provide leadership and coordinate activities necessary to carry out the AAUW program on the state level, including action on state legislation related to education. In addition, the association is organized into ten regions, each headed by a vice-president who serves on the national board and helps to coordinate local and national efforts.

To aid in keeping the members informed, the association publishes *Graduate Woman* which is distributed to all members. It often contains articles dealing with elementary, secondary, and higher education, so there is ample opportunity for members to keep up-to-date on educational issues. In addition, state and branch officers and committee chairmen receive copies of *Leaders in Action,* a publication aimed at assisting and informing these leaders. Traditionally the AAUW has emphasized study more than action, although the national board of directors passed in 1968 a resolution on "Action for a Unified Society" which encouraged state and branch leaders to increase the emphasis upon action, particularly through local projects. While there have been signs that the organization is becoming more action-oriented, it generally does not play a militant role. This does not mean that the AAUW is unimportant, for a pool of college graduates interested and knowledgeable about education is an asset in any community, particularly when these people are accustomed to studying the issues before deciding upon a position. Their contribution is indirect in most cases with respect to our concern for influences on educational policymaking.

AAUW and the League of Women Voters make their major contributions by arousing interest in the study of educational problems. Such interest can assist in the creation of a political climate favorable to educational progress. The active involvement of these organizations is somewhat more sporadic but is generally supportive of the proposals of the professional educators. This is not to suggest that they are rub-

---

55. Marion Talbot and Lois K. M. Rosenberry, *The History of the American Association of University Women 1881–1931* (Boston: Houghton Mifflin, 1931), 61.

ber stamp groups, but often their lack of cohesion is such that they usually become involved only in a supportive sense where the apparent benefits to the public schools seem quite clear-cut.

The AAUW and LWV are important components of the women's movement. They have held women's rights positions for many years, but they are multi-issue organizations and do not focus all their energies on the feminist movement. The women's rights movement has made women more politically active at all levels, and both the LWV and AAUW have become more action-oriented and politically sophisticated in recent years.

One area in which the women's movement has helped to trigger very consequential changes is volunteering:

> The changing role of the American woman is making an enormous impact on the world of volunteer service. As more women go back to school and work, the supply of volunteers is shrinking. Competition is keen, recruitment has become sophisticated and some traditional organizations have had to cut back on their services.[56]

Factors such as changing family life-styles, rising divorce rates, soaring inflation, and the growing ideology of self-fulfillment are pushing more and more women into the labor force. For the first time in history more than half of the women between the ages of 18 and 64 are working.

The volunteer world has been affected to some extent by the argument used by some feminists that women volunteers are being exploited and by donating their services are helping to sustain historical patterns of economic dependency. Service volunteer jobs such as hospital aides, cancer society walkers, and so forth have been most drastically affected. Many contend that volunteerism is currently undergoing a difficult transition. The attrition of volunteers is particularly pronounced among white, educated middle- and upper-middle-class women who historically have been the backbone of service volunteer jobs in organizations like the PTA, the LWV, and the AAUW.

Both the LWV and AAUW are adapting to the presence of competing interests, changing expectations, and reduced spare time by training leaders (thereby providing valuable management training to members), by adjusting meeting times to accommodate work schedules, and by joining with other organizations to accomplish mutual goals. It is clear that those women's organizations that do adapt to the changes brought about by the feminist movement will be more viable than those organizations that do not. In any event, the threat to volunteer organizations is serious. Ruth C. Clusen, past President of the LWV, was quoted as saying that her organization, like most of its counterparts, is now "an endangered species"; the League reportedly lost between 5,000 and 6,000 members in 1977–78.[57] Indeed, most women's organizations are losing members.

A likely scenario for the future is the creation of political coalitions among women's groups dealing with women's issues as well as with other major public policy matters such as education.

In New York City, for example, fifteen women's organizations recently coalesced to raise resources to support programs which had been reduced by federal budget

---

56. Steven V. Roberts, "Volunteer Services Suffer as Self-Image of Women Changes," *New York Times,* 6 August 1978, 46.
57. Efthalia Walsh, "Volunteers Now Are Getting Choosier," *New York Times,* 16 April 1978, 9.

cuts. In addition to the New York chapter of the National Organization for Women (NOW.), the coalition included the Women Office Workers, the New York Chapter of the Coalition of Labor Union Women, the National Congress of Neighborhood Women, the Pre-School Association of the West Side, and the Reproductive Rights National Network.[58] The coalition had as one of its major objectives the broadening of the choices of charities available to working women. As one of the leaders stated, "over the years women have been the main fund-raisers for churches, schools, and community organizations. Now we believe that working women want an opportunity to choose to give to programs that benefit women. That option is not available to us now."[59] More organizations like this New York City group are likely to come into existence and become influential political forces.

This coalition style of politics has already operated as women's groups united in efforts to eliminate sex discrimination in schools. NOW's PEER program monitored sex bias in city school systems in Chicago, Atlanta, Cleveland, and San Francisco. Groups of women vigorously reviewed each complaint of sex discrimination filed by women employed in or students enrolled in the public schools of these cities. Women from the LWV and the AAUW joined NOW members in constituting these monitoring teams.[60]

Interest Groups and the Political Process

The Function of Interest Groups

Interest groups perform a number of functions in government. To begin with, the interest group provides a rallying point for the individual. The simple division implied by the concept of the state and the individual is not a practical concept in the formation of policy in our society. The interest group is a vehicle through which individuals of like circumstances or convictions can collectively develop a position on an important issue and then bring influence to bear upon governmental policymaking. This emphasis on group action does not rule out individual leadership, but it does stress the fact of life in the world of politics that leaders ordinarily have followers organized into groups.

A second function performed by interest groups has to do with the delineation of the issues. Hamilton and Jefferson, as leaders of their respective groups, helped clairify the issues of strong versus weak federal government and executive versus legislative power. An explication of different positions helps clarify the issues involved in proposed legislation. Legislators and citizens alike often depend for their understanding of a program on the opinions articulated by official groups which favor and oppose a particular program.

As a third function, interest groups also provide information relevant to a proposed program. To be sure, this information is often biased or selective according to the group's own position. At the same time, every interest group knows that distorted information may in the end be self-defeating. For instance, the proponents for a state aid program for schools are aware of the fact that their own figures will be carefully scrutinized by the opponents of such a measure. Nothing would please the opponents more than to show that the proponents had been careless in their collection of statistics.

58. Nadine Brozan, "Women's Groups Join to Raise Funds," *New York Times*, 17 December 1981, C-5.
59. Ibid.
60. Nancy Hicks, "Women's Groups in Four Cities Monitor Complaints About Sex Bias in Schools," *New York Times*, 31 August 1976, 30.

The fact that interest groups on both sides of a proposal gather information and check the information gathered by the opposition gives legislators considerable confidence that they have a reliable base from which to argue the issues. Debate then centers not on the facts themselves but on what the facts mean. Some state legislatures have even asked lobbyists in whom they have confidence to present and discuss factual material on the floor of the legislative chamber. The information-giving function of interest groups is well established.

Perhaps the most important function of interest groups in government is the role they perform in the processes of compromise and consensus. In a pluralistic society almost any proposal will have advocates and opponents. The position of any group is clarified through the activities of the opposing interest groups. Frequently the formal governmental body, such as the legislature, becomes the arena in which these positions are drawn. Contrasting positions can be resolved only through compromise.

It is at this point that the politician becomes a decision broker. Ways must be found to achieve some kind of compromise, and as far as possible consensus must be achieved on the compromise. Ordinarily proponents have to settle for less than they think desirable. Opponents may have to yield on some aspect of the proposal. A politician who can report that the contending groups have reached an agreement feels a genuine sense of achievement. Moreover, the compromise can usually become the basis for official governmental action. Thus, interest groups, through their facing off and their final acceptance of compromise, facilitate the governmental process.

The functions served by interest groups in the governmental process can be illustrated in the politics of federal aid for education. Major support for federal aid came historically from the National Education Association, the American Federation of Teachers, and the Council of Chief State School Officers, all education interest groups. These groups have had allies in the National Council of Jewish Women, the National Federation of Business and Professional Women's Clubs, the American Association of University Women, the National Congress of Parents and Teachers, the AFL-CIO, and other groups. Opposition to federal aid likewise has been chiefly an interest group activity. The opponents have been the U.S. Chamber of Commerce, the National Association of Manufacturers, the Daughters of the American Revolution, and a number of other groups. Groups for and against federal aid for education were so numerous and so varied that the individual had no trouble finding a platform compatible with his or her views. In fact, as we will note later, interest groups may have done more to provide individuals with their views than the other way around.

Three major issues continue to dominate the long debate on federal aid. These issues are the question of control, aid to nonpublic schools, and the integration of schools. In the passage of the Elementary and Secondary Education Act of 1965 certain compromises on these issues were achieved, seemingly made for the sake of helping children from poor families.[61]

The hearings on federal aid proposals have produced literally tons of documents. These materials provide the information needed by legislators. While proponents and opponents have not always agreed on the figures, the data produced in these hearings provoke individual scholars and groups not prominently identified with the proposed legislation to examine the question and produce more objective information.

61. See Committee for Economic Development, *Raising Low Income Through Improved Education,* 1965, and *Innovation in Education,* 1968 (New York: The Committee). Also see Philip Meranto, *The Politics of Federal Aid to Education in 1965* (Syracuse, N.Y.: Syracuse University Press, 1967).

The century-long effort to secure federal aid for education which we discussed in chapter 2 illustrates the various interactions between interest groups and government. Interests groups are an integral part of the political process.

Summary and Future Prospects

A number of significant controls are imposed upon schools by groups which have as their primary interest something other than education. Demographic factors, such as a rapidly growing Hispanic population in several sections of the country, will influence both the programs and staffing of educational institutions located in such communities. Interest groups representing blacks, American Indians, and other ethnic groups will continue to focus on the schools as a major mechanism for equalizing educational, social, and economic opportunities for their constituencies.

Taxpayers groups, manifesting their concerns about periodic inflation, recession, and energy shortages in an uncertain economy, will continue to scrutinize school expenditures. These taxpayer groups may occasionally express interest in a program, but in nearly every case such interest is tied directly to the cost of the program. Such taxpayer groups spurred by the success of Proposition 13 and by frequent backlash against public expenditures of any kind, are likely to continue to monitor school spending. Indeed, widespread national support of efforts to limit taxation will continue to serve as a deterrent to public spending in every section, including education. These financial control factors (e.g. Proposition 13) will have a political and economic impact on every phase of public school operations in the years ahead.

Only a handful of the organizations which have some concern for educational policymaking have been described here. We have not discussed, for example, the influence of environmental, anti-nuclear and other groups which at times attempt to influence the curriculum of schools. We also have not focused any attention on the influence of the media and related organizations on education. We will discuss the growing interest in public schools of business groups in a subsequent chapter. Some of the major types of groups which are most active in school affairs have been presented, however. Some of the groups are sharply critical of one phase of education more than others. Moreover, even groups which generally support the schools often do so from the viewpoint that existing good programs must be improved. Criticism of the schools will continue, and educators should not anticipate any decrease in pressure. This pressure need not be dreaded, for education is finally receiving the concentrated public attention that educators have long sought.

Millions of American parents expect the schools to play a major role in preparing their children for future success. When the stakes are this high and definitions of success vary, controversy is to be expected. It is clear, for example, that criticism of the schools by blacks will be present for some time. Even with the current crash programs, so many problems remain that it will take a while to treat the overt symptoms of inner-city schools to say nothing of dealing with the root problems. Similarly, right-wing criticism will continue from those who fear the schools are undermining the patriotic and moral fiber of young people. A newer and more ominous type of right-wing criticism is the backlash which sometimes has appeared in response to attempts to improve educational opportunities for minority group students. This too seems destined to continue at least until substantial gains in interracial understanding are made.

It would be an error to portray any group as being in complete and constant support or opposition to what the schools are doing. Support or opposition for school policies tends to shift from issue to issue. Likewise, many persons belong to more than one group. Overlapping memberships tend to neutralize individual support or opposition when reference group positions conflict on a particular issue.

The overriding lesson of this chapter is that many groups have interests in school affairs and that these interests and the means used to pursue them vary considerably. As a consequence, educational questions are becoming increasingly controversial in many locales. School board and administrative decisions which used to be routine have become matters for debate. There often are more than two sides in such controversies, and communities sometimes become fractionalized as a result of them.

The life of the school administrator is increasingly one of attempting to resolve and live with public conflict. This is not necessarily a bad situation, but it does take a special kind of person to deal with it. Progress can often be achieved through conflict. Marks of a successful administrator appear to be the ability to help define progress, to work with local groups to recognize and achieve it, and to live with the conflict engendered by these activities.

Some of the groups we have discussed often do not direct their criticisms through what school people would consider appropriate channels. Designs to take over PTA groups or school boards, publication of unfounded charges, boycotts, threats of violence, and other ill-considered approaches defeat the purpose of channels provided in the administrative structure of a school system to receive and evaluate criticism and suggestions. Interest groups, however, should point out when these channels are inadequate. Ways must be sought to establish and refine legitimate channels for dissent and to direct dissatisfied individuals and groups to their use.

Probably the best effort administrators can make to ensure that most criticisms are constructive and that those which are not gain little public credence is to work hard at informing the community of the strengths and the shortcomings of the local schools. In addition, they must show that they are sensitive to the concerns expressed by citizens. Too often educators assume that because the schools have noble ends, they should be exempt from attack.

Administrators must anticipate issues before they surface and take vigorous steps early, rather than just react to problems when they explode and are much more difficult to handle. For example, public school administrators in the 1980s and beyond will continue to be challenged by women and minority groups in their persisting efforts to achieve equal educational opportunity. The issues themselves are predictable and school leaders should prepare themselves for this continuing pressure from minority groups. Earlier in the chapter, for example, we noted the particularly important implications of the rapidly expanding Hispanic population.

Another struggle foreseeable in the 1980s relates to women and minority groups. A retrenchment in education will be occurring at the very time when affirmative action efforts will be accelerated by minority group members and women. In other words, there will be declining employment opportunities for these presently underrepresented groups.[62] Declining enrollments, inflation, teacher oversupply, layoffs, and recession are all making it increasingly difficult for minorities and women to find jobs at the same time when affirmative action is a desired social objective. Policy alternatives to seniority and tenure must be found. Work sharing, hiring freezes, early retirement, new clientele, and affirmative retention strategies must be employed crea-

---

62. See *Retrenchment in Education: The Outlook for Women and Minorities,* Report no. F76–9, Education Finance Center and Equal Rights for Women in Education Project, Education Commission of the States (Denver, Colo.: May 1977), and Terry Tinson Saario, *Title IX: Now What?* (New York: Ford Foundation, 1976).

tively by educational leaders if these terribly complicated issues are to be meaningfully addressed.[63] Administrators will be caught in the middle of what may prove to be one of education's most intractable issues, namely, the need to create equitable trade-offs between the rights of tenured professional staff and the legitimate rights of aspiring and long-denied minority group members and women.

The administrator need not wait helplessly to be impaled on these issues. While there is no easy road to community support and understanding, continued participation in school affairs by the responsible citizens of a community can build understanding which will not be easily destroyed by emotional or irrational attacks. To foster such community participation is one of the major tasks confronting the school administrator. Many school systems have already established ombudsmen, community relations specialists, to encourage communication and broaden the base of participation in school affairs.

63. *Retrenchment in Education,* 30–32.

15

Availability of Resources

The availability of financial resources is often a limiting factor in the operation of schools. James and his colleagues, whose study gave impetus to a reform movement in school finance, identified three major clusters of variables which in combination seem to determine educational expenditures.[1] These variables included wealth, or the ability to pay; the decision-making process, or governmental arrangements for permitting school board members and citizens to express their preferences regarding proposed school expenditures; and the aspirations of the people, or demand for educational services. Wealth, governmental access, and aspirations for education vary from district to district and state to state.

Differentials in Wealth

Among School Districts

Most school districts must rely upon the general property tax as a major source of school revenue, and the assessed valuation of the property within the school district becomes the base upon which the general property tax is levied. When assessed value is expressed in terms of some unit of educational load, such as "per pupil in school attendance," a convenient index for comparing the ability of school districts to support education is derived. These comparisons are more accurate when limited to a single state or to a subdivision of a state where assessment practices are more uniform.

In Cook County, Illinois, there are 116 elementary school districts and 27 high school districts. In table 15.1 the assessed valuations per pupil in average daily attendance (ADA) for four of these elementary districts—two wealthy, two poor—are shown. Note that the wealthiest district is 19 times more able to support an educational program than the poorest district.

---

1. H. Thomas James, J. Alan Thomas, and Harold J. Dyck, "Wealth, Expenditure, and Decision-Making for Education," Cooperative Research Project no. 1241 (Washington, D.C.: U.S. Office of Education, 30 June 1963).

The variation among the high school districts is not as great but it is still note-worthy. The wealthiest district has four times the assessed valuation of the poorest district. In terms of area, most high school districts are appreciably larger than the elementary districts. This condition alone tends to decrease the variability found among the districts.

When assessed valuations per pupil for an entire state are calculated, the spread between districts with the lowest and highest assessed valuation per pupil is generally even greater than those shown for Cook County. The ability of local school districts to raise school revenue varies tremendously. This difference is chiefly a function of the great variability in the assessed valuation of property within the school district, particularly when expressed in terms of educational cost per pupil or per classroom.

Among States

There is also considerable variation in the ability of the states to support an educational program. Since assessment practices among the states differ considerably, assessed values per pupil or per classroom are not the best measures to use in comparing state expenditures. Personal income per capita is a more useful measure. As shown in table 15.2, personal income per capita varies from $10,368 in Connecticut to $6,070 in Mississippi, and the average for the United States is $8,637. The four top states have about one and one-half times the ability of the four bottom states to support an educational program.

This table, of course, only roughly indicates the relative ability to pay of various states. Higher average income does not necessarily mean more money is available to support education. New Jersey, New York, Illinois, and other industrial states, for instance, impose many taxes upon personal income, perhaps more than is found in states that still have large rural populations, such as Mississippi and Alabama. Moreover, cities everywhere, even in industrial states, are in critical need of more money if they are going to provide quality education.

TABLE 15.1

Assessed Valuations Per Pupil in Cook County, Illinois, by Selected Districts, 1980–81

	Pupils in ADA	Assessed Valuation Per Pupil
Elementary Districts		
#78	199	$395,164
#170	3,199	402,883
#140	2,043	31,053
#168	1,775	21,681
High School Districts		
#212	3,420	216,011
#219	4,514	246,340
#227	3,596	81,227
#228	5,569	61,106

SOURCE: Illinois State Board of Education, Research and Statistics Section

The Role of Federal Aid

Federal aid for education seems to be a logical way to alleviate the differences among the states in their ability to support schools. We have passed the period when the question of providing federal aid was an issue. There has been some form of federal aid to schools throughout American history, as shown by the land grant acts of 1785 and 1787, the Land Grant College Act of 1862, the Vocational Education Act of 1917, the National Defense Education Act of 1958, and the Elementary and Secondary Education Act of 1965. Nearly all federal aid programs, however, have been categorical in nature. Moreover, these programs have been administered by numerous agencies in the federal government.

Berke and Kirst examined federal aid from the standpoint of who benefits from such aid and who governs the process by which the aid is provided.[2] They assessed the impact of eight federal aid programs (Titles I, II, III of ESEA, Titles III and V-A of NDEA, vocational education, school lunch, and assistance to federally impacted areas) upon a sample of school districts across the country. While their findings illustrate the differential effect of federal aid among school districts, they also suggest why federal aid does little to reduce inequities among states. The differential effect is noted in the following:

1. Federal aid to education in the aggregate has only a slight equalizing tendency at best, and that within a number of metropolitan areas it displays distinctly disequalizing characteristics;
2. The degree of equalization, where it does exist, is usually too small to offset pre-existing disparities among school districts, and
3. Although Title I of ESEA does flow in greater proportion to poorer and higher need school districts, a number of other federal programs operate to help the rich districts get richer.[3]

TABLE 15.2

Personal Income Per Capita in Selected States, 1979–80

State	Income Per Capita
Connecticut	$10,368
Illinois	9,683
New Jersey	9,756
Wyoming	9,840
United States	8,637
Kentucky	7,052
Arkansas	6,756
South Carolina	6,577
Mississippi	6,070

SOURCE: National Center for Educational Statistics, *Digest of Educational Statistics, 1982*, (Washington, D.C.: Government Printing Office, 1982), 80.

2. Joel S. Berke and Michael W. Kirst, *Federal Aid to Education—Who Benefits? Who Governs?* (Lexington, Mass.: D.C. Heath, 1972).
3. Ibid., 22.

Even though federal aid for education was increased during the 1960s and the 1970s, it has leveled off at about $15 billion for all educational puposes. In 1979–80 about 9.8 percent of the revenue for public schools came from the federal government. As noted in chapter 2, this percentage is not likely to increase in the near future.

The percentage of federal aid varies among the states depending in part upon the number of programs for which a state is eligible. This variation is suggested in table 15.3 where percentages of revenues from local, state, and federal sources are shown for selected states. In Wyoming, for instance, expenditure levels are relatively high and federal aid accounts for only 5.6 percent of total revenues. In Mississippi, on the other hand, expenditure levels are relatively low and federal aid accounts for 25.1 percent of total revenues. Expenditure averages do not reveal the wide variations among districts in each of the states; this variation is likely to be even more pronounced in a state like Nebraska where little has been done to define a minimum or basic school program which the state would support.

In assessing the impact of federal aid on the public schools of the nation, a number of conclusions can be drawn. First, federal aid is rather meager. Second, federal aid does little to provide equalization among school districts or states. Third, the categorical nature of most federal aid has made it a vehicle for changing programs in many school districts. Fourth, federal resources have given local districts leverage to work on important and often emotional issues such as bilingual education, preparations for school desegregation, and citizen participation. Fifth, federal aid may be of minor importance to many school districts, but it is of major importance to an increasing number of districts. For instance Public Law 874 and Public Law 815, first passed in 1950, to aid federally impacted districts, in time came to provide assistance to some 4,100 school districts in which one-third of the public elementary and secondary school pupils of the nation were enrolled.[4] With so many school districts affected, the impacted aid

TABLE 15.3

Current Expenditures Per Pupil (ADA) and Percentage of Revenue by Source for Public Elementary and Secondary Schools in Selected States, 1979–80

State	Expenditure Per Pupil	Percentage of Revenues		
		Local	State	Federal
Nebraska	$2150	75.7	16.7	7.6
Connecticut	2455	66.1	26.8	7.0
Vermont	2049	62.5	28.7	8.8
Wyoming	2527	60.2	34.2	5.6
United States	2275	43.4	46.8	9.8
Washington	2568	21.5	69.5	9.0
New Mexico	2034	19.9	63.6	16.6
Kentucky	1701	19.8	64.2	16.0
Mississippi	1664	18.9	56.0	25.1
Hawaii	2322	0.0	84.7	15.3

SOURCE: National Center for Education Statistics, *Digest of Education Statistics, 1982* (Washington, D.C.: Government Printing Office, 1982), 74,81.

4. Committee on Education and Labor, *The Federal Government and Education* (Washington, D.C.: Government Printing Office, 1963), 63.

lobby was very influential in Congress, where the desire of every recent president to eliminate such aid has been thwarted.

What of the future? Is general aid apt to replace categorical aid? At one time, Munger and Fenno, after their study of the politics of federal aid, thought general aid unlikely.[5] Since that time there has been some use of block grants to states and the consolidation of some categorical programs. However, the consolidated programs are still categorical in nature, even though the categories have been somewhat broadened. For the most part, Congress will probably continue to identify national needs and to insist that federal aid appropriations be directed toward those needs.

Financial Resources and Control

State aid programs in most states do not counteract the differential ability of school districts to support school programs. Nor are federal aid programs able to provide poor school districts with adequate school revenue. Helpful as state and federal aid programs are to many school districts, the differential ability of school districts to support education still persists. Moreover, the categorical nature of federal aid has had limited effect in equalizing the abilities of the states to support education. Thus, differential ability to support education at both local and state levels is still a fact of life.

Variations in ability to pay give rise to two kinds of control. One type of control is a result of limited resources, and a second type is a product of state and federal assistance. These controls, while often not deliberate, do affect what is done to provide school programs.

Let us look first at shortage of money as a limiting factor in education. Inadequate funds often mean larger classes for teachers, meager libraries, few instructional supplies, cheap building construction, poor instructional equipment, few guidance and health services, and poorly trained teachers and administrators. Two school districts, each with limited available funds, however, could make quite different decisions about these matters. For instance, large classes may be less of a handicap with superior teachers than with mediocre teachers, high-quality instructional equipment may make more of a difference than ultramodern buildings, and a live-wire principal can stimulate average teachers to become good ones. The wise allocation of limited resources can make a difference in many poor districts.

Nevertheless, lack of money constitutes a limiting factor in most poor school districts. This was clearly documented in a Michigan finance study where it was found that the extent and quality of programs for libraries, gifted pupils, handicapped pupils, art, new mathematics, and other program elements were directly related to money expended.[6] To the extent that lack of money prohibits desirable programs, the control of deprivation is operating.

Poor districts tend to receive a great deal of state and sometimes federal aid, and another type of control is inherent in this situation. Most state aid programs are designed to make money available to school districts contingent upon certain types of school district performance. Often school districts must establish a certain tax rate in order to be eligible for state aid. Or, if the aid is for a particular purpose such as transportation, certain standards must be met in order to receive aid. In other words, the provisions of most state aid programs are designed to guarantee that no district

5 Frank J. Munger and Richard F. Fenno, Jr., *National Politics of Federal Aid to Education* (Syracuse, N.Y.: Syracuse University Press, 1962), 184.

6. J. Alan Thomas, *School Finance and Educational Opportunity in Michigan* (Lansing: Michigan Department of Education, 1968), ch. 2.

in the state will fall below certain minimum operating standards. When districts strive to meet these standards, the state is exerting control.

The control inherent in federal aid is somewhat different. Since most federal aid is for categorical purposes such as vocational education and education of the children of the poor, the amount and kind of control depends on the definition of the program. For instance, a district must operate a vocational education program, often at considerable local cost, in order to qualify for the federal aid. Federal assistance for the disadvantaged requires that the disadvantaged be identified and that programs designed to improve their education be developed.

Both school districts and states, then, vary in their ability to support education. Despite substantial state aid programs in most states and a variety of federal aid programs, these differentials are only partially eliminated. There are controls inherent in the shortage of resources and in accepting assistance from a higher level of government, and these controls are more pronounced in poor than in wealthy districts.

Differentials in Governmental Access

Each of the 50 states has a body of law, often expressed in the constitution and always in the statutes, governing the expenditure of school funds. These provisions, which deal with both operating and capital outlay funds, vary greatly among the states, and these variations determine the ease of access of school funds.

Operating Funds

Some of the governmental arrangements regarding current expenditures for school purposes in selected states are shown in table 15.4. The table suggests that local access to school revenues may be relatively open or closed. If assessment practices and other governmental procedures keep the assessed value of property at a very small proportion of the market value of the property, then school revenue tends to be hard to obtain, or "closed." Conversely, when assessed values represent a fair proportion of market values, access to school revenue is relatively "open." In table 15.4, 31 percent or more of the market value, the U.S. average, was used as the dividing line between open and closed access.

As a second access factor, we have assumed that school districts in states with generous state aid programs have access to more revenue. In table 15.4 the median level of state support, 50 percent, was used as the cutoff point between open and closed access. States above that level are given an additional access score. Access is also influenced by the percentage of state aid distributed on an equalized basis. The average for all the states is 68 percent, hence that figure is the cutoff point. Again, states above that figure are given an additional access score.

Power given to boards of education to determine revenue needed for current expenditures or to establish tax rates needed to raise such revenues is another access factor. As shown in table 15.4, boards operate under three different arrangements. The most restrictive or closed arrangement is found in Alabama where the local board of education can increase the school levy by no more than three mills. In all other states the board appears to have more power to increase school levy rates, but in most states the legislature has set the limits for such authority. In Maryland and South Carolina there is no limit to board power in this regard, and for this access factor this seems to be the most open arrangement.

TABLE 15.4

Local Governmental Access Arrangements for Current School Funds in Selected States

State	Percent Assessed Value of Property to Sales Value	State Aid As Percent of State and Local Revenues	Percent of State Aid Equalized	Authorization of Local Board to Increase School Levy	Authorization of Local Electorate to Vote School Levy	State Supervise Local District Assessment	Ascribed Access Score
Alabama	10.8	75	87	3 mills	No provision	No	2
Illinois	26.0	52	80	12–20 mills	36–48 mills	Yes	5
Maryland	36.6	42	47	No limit	No provision	Yes	3
Michigan	40.6	41	82	15 mills	50 mills	Yes	5
Minnesota	21.5	70	76	30 mills	No limit	No	4
Mississippi	9.6	75	81	25 mills	3 mills	No	3
New York	27.0	40	98	Non-city, none; city, 12–25 mills	No limit	Yes	4
Oregon	71.5	20	18	Not more than 6% above prior level	No limit	Yes	4
South Carolina	3.3	65	Not given	No limit	No limit	No	3

SOURCE: 1977 Census of Governments, *Taxable Property Values and Assessment-Sales Price Ratios*, vol. 2, part 2, U.S. Dept. of Commerce, Bureau of the Census (Washington, D.C.: Government Printing Office, October, 1978); Esther O. Tron, *Public School Finance Programs, 1975–76*, Bureau of School Systems, Office of Education (Washington, D.C.: Government Printing Office, 1976).

Still another local access factor is the power the people have to vote for additional taxes for operating purposes. Again, there is wide disparity among the states. Most closed are the arrangements in Alabama and Maryland where there are no provisions for such referendums. Several of the states do have legislative limits beyond which taxes may not go even with the consent of the electorate of the district. Most open are the provisions in Minnesota, New York, Oregon, and South Carolina where there are no legislative limits on local school district electors.

The final access factor is state supervision of school district property. State supervision would be expected to provide more uniformity in assessment throughout the state and to guard against the tendency at the local level to keep assessments low. States with state supervision are given an additional access score.

Combining these six access factors, we have ascribed a local access score for each of the states. Illinois and Michigan have access scores of five out of a possible six factors and in these states the will of the people in a local school district regarding school revenues seems to be easily expressed. Assessed values are reasonably high in Michigan, less so in Illinois; state aid programs are relatively high in Illinois, less so in Michigan; and in both states the percent of state aid distributed on an equalized basis is high, local school districts have considerable power to set school levies (still higher school levies may be set by the electorate), and assessment of property is under state supervision. In Alabama, Maryland, Mississippi, and South Carolina, on the other hand, local access is limited on several factors. For Minnesota, New York, and Oregon local access falls between these two groups of states.

The analysis presented above is intended to be illustrative and not definitive. We have considered six significant access factors; there are many other access factors, some of which may be as significant as the ones we have employed. Under these circumstances, the access scores we have ascribed to each of the states should also be looked upon as suggestive only.

Governmental Access and Control

The governmental arrangements under which current and capital outlay funds are made available to school districts obviously impose controls or limitations upon American schools. The nature and extent of control is a function of the number of decision points required, the prescriptions surrounding each decision, and the levels of government involved in the decisions.

The greater the number of decision points the more complex control becomes. A simple arrangement is represented by a local board of education which has complete freedom to determine the school budget and to certify the tax levy needed to raise the money required. Somewhat more complex is the situation in which the board of education has discretion only up to a certain point, and additional taxes require the approval of the voters of the school district. Still more complex is the arrangement in which the school budget must be justified to some city, county or state agency. In the first instance, there is one decision point while in the last there may be three or more decision points and thus that many more opportunities to restrict educational expenditures.

Government may prescribe specific procedures or conditions for making the above decisions. For instance, a school district referendum may require a simple majority or a two-thirds majority for passage. Or, as found in the practice of a number of states particularly on bond issue elections, only those who own property in the district may qualify as electors. Even the requirement that a school issue be decided at a regular, in place of a special, election may make the issue more difficult to carry.

In addition to multiplying decision points, requiring decisions to be made at more than one level of government may present other problems. For instance, the people of a school district may believe firmly that higher taxes are necessary to support an educational program of high quality. If this decision must be approved by a county or state review board of some kind, other interests may be injected into the picture. A county or state representative may see no point in one district taxing itself far beyond what other districts do. This view might, of course, be encouraged by a few large property holders in the district who recognize that they cannot influence their neighbors but that they can, indeed, influence key officials at the county or state levels.

Governmental access in the local district, as we have seen, may be open in some respects and closed in others. Dyck has noted that the dichotomy of dependent and independent school districts is a distinction too gross to be useful.[7] Moreover, he suggested that dependence might be political, fiscal, or administrative in nature. Dyck conceived 32 models of local school government characterized by different combinations of variables associated with dependence and independence. Most school governments can be placed on a dependence-independence continuum with few, if any, school districts at the extreme ends. Most school districts are dependent to a greater or lesser extent on other levels of government and on the multiplicity of decision points. Under all of the various arrangements access to school funds may be relatively open or closed, and controls upon schools may be few or many.

Differentials in Aspiration

The third major variable affecting expenditures for education is the level of aspiration people hold for their schools. This variable has been conceptualized by James and others as demand for education.[8] Since the actual operation of schools is essentially a local function, evidence of this aspiration level can be noted in the purposes espoused by local superintendents of schools, in the budget adoptions of the local boards of education, and in the responses of local electorates at the polls. At the state level, evidence of aspiration may be noted in state aid provisions, particularly as expressed in the state foundation program. Congressional action on federal assistance may also suggest national aspirations for education. We shall give attention here to the nature or kind of education and the quality of education desired in different school districts.

Kind of Education Desired

Downey, Seager, and Slagle studied the tasks of public education as perceived by various subpublics in the United States and Canada.[9] Sixteen tasks or purposes, four each under the major categories (intellectual, social, personal, and productive,) were conceptualized and an appropriate instrument developed for permitting respondents to order these tasks according to their perceived importance. Almost 4,000 respondents, including educators and noneducators in four regions of the United States and one in Canada, rated these tasks. All groups of respondents agreed that the intellectual tasks

7. James et al., "Wealth, Expenditure and Decision-Making," ch. 7.
8. Ibid.
9. These studies are summarized in Lawrence W. Downey, *The Task of Public Education* (Chicago, Ill.: Midwest Administration Center, University of Chicago, 1960).

(possession of knowledge, communication of knowledge, creation of knowledge, and desire for knowledge) were the most important tasks of the school.

There were, however, subtle variations in the amount of emphasis placed upon intellectual tasks versus other task areas. For instance, there were regional differences. The western region (California) favored more than any other region the socializing aspects of education; the South (Alabama and Georgia) stressed physical education and personal development; the East (Massachusetts) emphasized moral training; and Canada (Alberta) stressed the intellectual and aesthetic tasks. In many respects the Midwest (Illinois and Wisconsin) stood in the middle with respect to its expressed preferences. The study also found that certain social and personal characteristics predicted various educational viewpoints:

> Occupation and amount of schooling were the best predictors of educational belief. Perhaps these are related, but the relationship does not explain the whole phenomenon. These two variables emerged more or less independently as consistent indicators of perception of the task. The higher one's position on the occupational continuum, the greater the importance he assigned to the intellectual, the aesthetic, and the world citizenship aspects of the task, conversely, the less importance he assigned to the physical, the moral, the consumer, and the vocational aspects. Similarly, the more schooling respondents had themselves, the more they tended to emphasize the intellectual aspects and minimize the social, physical, and vocational aspects of education.
>
> Age was a somewhat less reliable predictor, as were race and religion. It was rather surprising to note, however, that the older the respondent, the more he tended to favor the physical, the patriotic, the moral, and the family aspects of education; the younger the respondent, the more he tended to favor the intellectual and related aspects. Catholics, as a group, placed greater emphasis upon the patriotic, the civic, and the moral elements than did Protestants. Negroes, as a group, placed greater emphasis upon the physical, the social, and the moral than did whites.
>
> Community-type, income, sex, and proximity to school did not prove to be variables closely associated with educational viewpoint.[10]

More recent evidence on demand for public education can be found in the Gallup polls on education, conducted annually for the past several years. The following statistics are excerpts from the 1983 report and some references will be made to earlier reports for comparative purposes.[11] In 1983, 31 percent of the national sample of respondents gave the public schools an A or a B rating on a five point scale. In 1974, 48 percent of the national sample of respondents gave the public schools an A or a B rating. This change, over a period of nine years, appears to represent a serious loss in public confidence. Attempts were made to see what factors might help explain these ratings. Sex, age, community size, and level of education, did not appear to make much difference in the ratings given by the Gallup respondents. Race, on the other hand, seemed to be a significant variable. Thirty-three percent of the white respondents gave the schools an A or B rating, while only 20 percent of the nonwhite respondents gave such ratings. There also appeared to be some important regional differences. Thirty-six percent of the respondents from the Midwest gave the schools A or B ratings, while only 23 percent of the respondents from the West gave such ratings.

10. Ibid., 65.
11. George H. Gallup, "The 15th Annual Gallup Poll of the Public's Attitude Toward the Public Schools," *Phi Delta Kappan* 65 (September 1983): 33–51.

Two other factors may have been even more important in explaining the findings. The first of these has to do with the perceptions respondents had of the public schools nationwide as contrasted with perceptions of schools in their own communities. Public schools in the nation were graded A or B by 19 percent of the respondents, while 31 percent gave schools in their own communities an A or B. The other important factor had to do with whether or not respondents were parents with children in the public schools. Forty-two percent of the parents gave the public schools A and B ratings, whereas only 28 percent of respondents with no children in school gave the schools A and B ratings. While parents are still quite supportive of the public schools, it is interesting to note that even parent support has decreased over the past nine years. In 1974, 64 percent of the parents gave the public schools A or B ratings. Clearly, factors, such as those already noted, need to be taken into account as information about schools is made available to the public. In 1983, when those polled were asked how much they knew about the schools, 22 percent said, "quite a lot," 42 percent said "some," 29 percent said "very little," and 7 percent said "nothing."

While the Gallup poll did not consider respondents' occupational level and years of education to be factors which influenced their attitudes, these factors are generally useful indicators of the kind of education people demand. Citizens in professional or managerial occupations and with college educations want schools to stress the academic tasks and give less attention to vocational or personal tasks. On the other hand, citizens who are blue-collar workers and who are not college graduates place more importance on the vocational and personal tasks of the school. In a sense, both groups stress vocational education, but in one case this means preparation for the professions and in the other case it means preparation for skilled or semiskilled occupations. In terms of the school curriculum, however, the two demands have quite different impacts. Those who stress the academic, for instance, are more concerned with securing teachers with liberal arts backgrounds, having adequate libraries, and diagnosing reading disabilities. Those who stress vocational skills are more supportive of shops, home economics laboratories, gymnasiums, and other facilities that foster personal development and work skills.

Quality of Education Desired

The citizens of different school districts not only have different demands regarding the content of the school program, they also have different demands regarding the quality of the school program. If current expenditures are used as a rough index of quality, this differential demand is illustrated in table 15.5.

In table 15.5 the schools in the highly ranked socioeconomic communities have greater assessed values, spend more per pupil, and have higher tax levies than do schools in the low socioeconomic communities. The average expenditures per pupil are not as great as might be expected. While data to confirm this do not exist, state and federal subsidies appear to make up a larger proportion of the expenditures in the "low" communities than in the "high" communities. The most notable difference between the two groups of schools appears to be in the average tax rates. In the "high" communities, even with their greater wealth, the average tax rate is 62 percent above the average for the "low" communities. If citizens of the "low" communities brought their tax rate up to those found in the "high" communities, their expenditures could have equaled or exceeded those in the "high" communities. The table does suggest that wealthy and poor school districts have different levels of demand for quality of education.

As suggestive as the data in table 15.5 are, a more extensive study of this matter is required before one can be confident of a relationship between social class and school expenditures. Plus, the relationship will probably never be a perfect one since the variables of wealth and governmental access also affect expenditure levels.

Early but still useful case studies of two contrasting communities shed further light on this matter. Hills examined the educational expectations held for schools in two diverse communities.[12] Community A was an upper-income, residential suburb of 11,500 people while Community B was a lower-income suburb of 3,400 people. The two communities were compared on a number of characteristics. In terms of income, schooling, home values, and occupational distribution, Community A ranked high and Community B low on the socioeconomic scale. Each community was served by a township high school.

As part of the study, teachers were asked to give their perceptions of community expectations for the school. In Community A, teachers were convinced that school patrons expected the school to provide a highly specialized college preparatory program. One teacher's comment was:

> By and large, the majority of the parents think their children should go on to liberal arts colleges. I teach a low-ability section in my subject field. Parents feel that being placed in a group of this kind precludes going to college. Several have requested that their youngsters be transferred to the regular section even though they know they'll get lower grades there.

TABLE 15.5

Socioeconomic Characteristics of Selected Communities in Cook County, Illinois, 1975, and Operating Expenditures in Corresponding Elementary School Districts, 1976–77

Community	Socioeconomic Rank* (1-201)	Operating Expenditures per Pupil	Assessed Valuation per Pupil (1976–77)	Total Tax Rates (1977)
Kenilworth	1	$1,886	$44,479	4.49
Glencoe	3	2,472	53,013	3.83
Winnetka	6	2,410	50,272	4.21
Wilmette	11	1,862	42,388	3.76
Northbrook	12	1,756	37,595	3.46
Average		2,077	45,549	3.95
Chicago Heights	176	1,636	36,809	2.64
Blue Island	185	1,636	39,006	2.67
Steger	188	1,429	26,108	2.32
Posen-Robbins	193	1,959	19,162	2.14
East Chicago Heights	200	2,007	31,050	2.71
Average		1,733	30,427	2.46

*Based on income and home values.

SOURCE: Chicago Association of Commerce and Industry, "The Socioeconomic Rank of Chicago's Suburban Municipalities in 1975" (Chicago, Ill.: The Association, 1975); Research Reports, Cook County Superintendent of Schools, 1976–77.

12. R. Jean Hills, "The Relationship Between the Educational Expectations of Social Class Groups and the Role Expectations Within the Public High School" (Ph.D. diss. University of Chicago, 1961).

For many parents, just any college or university will not do. Several of the teachers interviewed were aware of the tendency of some parents to insist that their youngsters be prepared for enrollment in a college in the East considered to have prestige. The following is typical:

> They want a college prep course so they can get into a prestige school—an Eastern school. Occasionally students who are not doing as well as they might are taken out of school here and placed in a military or prep school. When parents contact you, it's because they are upset about grades—they're afraid their kid won't be able to get into the right college.

The following sentiment was shared by several teachers:

> There's a growing emphasis on suburban values—monetary position—social status—are terribly important here. Kids are unbelievably practical-minded; there's far too little idealism, very materialistic. Students here exhibit a strong tendency to examine critically their own motives and attributes. As a father, I question how long I want to stay here. I'm concerned about whether we can shield our children against these pressures. Everything is planned to be emblematic of success and prestige. I can't see bringing up my children in the competitive race for social status.

In light of the above comments it is not surprising that 65 percent of the teachers were aware of a high degree of community interest in school affairs. Nor is it surprising that 35 percent of the teachers in Community A commented specifically on the high degree of community pressure on the school.

The comments of teachers in Community B revealed a very different sort of community interest in the school. One teacher noted:

> The great majority of parents don't take a particular interest. They want a high school diploma; they're not concerned about grades or grade averages. When they ask, "How's my boy doing?" they mean, "Is he passing or failing?"

Fifty-two percent of the School B faculty specifically mentioned the absence of community pressure on the school. One teacher reported that:

> There's no parental pressure here—Johnny gets what he deserves and the parents stand behind the teacher. We get no pressure to give special privileges—people are willing to let the teachers run the school.

This evaluation is confirmed by the fact that 56 percent of the teachers in School B reported a high degree of professional freedom while only 22 percent of the School A sample gave a similar report. Community B does place certain restrictions on the school. For the most part, these center on what one teacher termed their "fundamentalist religious beliefs." One English teacher reported that he had been criticized severely for using *Macbeth* in a literature class because it was said to be obscene.

There were distinct differences between the two communities. Community A, a high income, residential suburb, preferred a highly academic, college preparatory high school program. Community B, the low-income suburb, preferred a terminal, vocation-oriented type of high school program. But these are not the only differences that existed. In addition to preferring a college preparatory program, Community A residents actively demanded that such a program be provided. Community B residents, however, despite their preference for a terminal program, were not especially interested in making their views known to the school.

Aspirations and Control

The aspirations people hold for education form a kind of control over education. First, community expectations influence the nature or kind of education offered. Some people insist that the program be highly academic, and they have little tolerance for courses designed to improve vocational or socal skills. Other people feel that training in the vocational and social areas is as important as, if not more important than, preparation for college. The people who favor the academic program usually insist that their demands be met.

Aspiration may also affect the level of education a community is willing to pay for. While not uniformly the case, school districts that support high expenditures per pupil and high teacher salaries tend to be those districts that rank high on the socioeconomic scale. It is not entirely by accident that Winnetka and Glencoe are among the Cook County districts with the highest expenditures. The people in those districts, even though conservative in many respects, are not conservative in their aspirations for schools. Willingness or unwillingness to provide money for schools is a significant form of control that citizens can and do exercise upon schools.

Lower aspirations for schools and even indifference, however, may not result in a drastic reduction in the quality of the schools. Traditionally, citizens with lower socioeconomic status have been more willing than citizens of higher socioeconomic status to leave school matters to the professionals. Thus, the nature and quality of the schools in places like Community B tend to reflect the aspirations of the professionals more than the citizens. In the Hills study it was found that the professionals in the two communities were more alike than different. This may have been fortuitous, but more likely it showed that teachers and administrators are agreed on many educational purposes and programs.

In terms of control of schools, it appears that in communities of high socioeconomic status citizens exercise more influence while in communities of low socioeconomic status school people exercise more influence. This phenomenon seems to be changing, however, particularly in black and other ethnic communities, and this development is placing new demands upon professional school workers.

Somewhat contrary to the generalizations above are the findings by Minar.[13] He found that school boards in lower status districts tend to restrict the authority (decisional latitude) of the superintendent more than those in higher status districts. He hypothesized that boards in lower status districts were less likely to defer to the superintendent's expertise than were boards in higher status districts where there are a disproportionate number of people with organizational and management skills and associated attitudes, who tend, to a greater extent, to understand and respect specialization, expertise, and the delegation of authority. By restriction of the superintendent's authority, Minar meant that boards in lower status districts tend to question and focus on minor policy issues, personnel, and administrative matters; boards in higher status districts deal with these routine matters with dispatch, allowing their

---

13. David W. Minar, *Educational Decision-Making in Suburban Communities,* Cooperative Research Project no. 2440 (Evanston, Ill.: Northwestern University, 1966).

superintendents great latitude in these areas and focusing their attention on more substantive concerns such as finances and building plans.

Boyd provides a still more comprehensive view of the matter.[14] After a careful analysis of his own and related data, Boyd suggests that citizens and the school boards, especially in smaller and more homoegeneous communities, tend to have more influence over external, redistributive, and strategic policy decisions whereas the professionals, especially in larger and more heterogeneous communities, tend to have more influence on internal and routine policy decisions. Perhaps in view of the findings of these studies, a distinction needs to be made between which professionals, the teachers or the superintendents, are influenced more by citizens in lower and higher status districts.

Recent Trends

Three recent movements, the reform of state school finance programs, tax limitation, and the current highly publicized reexamination of American education, have implications for the availability of resources to school districts. Each of these movements will be treated briefly.

Reform of State School Finance Programs

In the past 50 years state aid programs have been developed in most states. These programs have been motivated by a number of objectives, including the following: to stimulate improved programs, to compensate local districts for unusual programs, to guarantee a minimum program to all districts, to provide an incentive for local tax effort, and to broaden the tax base for school support. Paul Mort gave considerable emphasis to the equalization objective, while Harlan Updegraff tended to emphasize the reward-for-effort objective. These programs have been scrutinized by scholars and have been found inadequate in a number of ways. For instance, Berke and others suggested that the New York equalization program had five shortcomings:

> (1) structural limitations: (2) inadequate measures of educational need; (3) failure to relate educational finance to municipal or noneducational finance; (4) no consideration for cost differentials among districts; (5) too great a reliance on the local property tax.[15]

The courts have also examined state programs for financing elementary and secondary schools and in some instances have found such programs unconstitutional. Court initiatives suffered a setback when the U.S. Supreme Court reversed the lower court ruling on Rodriguez. Since then, state courts in California, New Jersey, and Connecticut have mandated new school funding systems. But these mandates are not automatic or universal, as Callahan and Wilken note, for state courts in Idaho, Washington, and Oregon affirmed the constitutionality of the existing programs.[16] The issue continues to be examined in state courts.

---

14. William L. Boyd, "The Public, the Professionals, and Educational Policy Making: Who Governs?" *Teacher's College Record* 77 (May 1976): 573.

15. Joel S. Berke et al., *Financing Equal Educational Opportunity* (Berkeley, Calif.: McCutchan, 1972), 23.

16. John J. Callahan and William H. Wilken, eds., *School Finance Reform: A Legislator's Handbook* (Washington, D.C.: National Conference of State Legislatures, 1976), 10.

Callahan and Wilken contended that the central features of the new state role in public school finance are as follows:

1. Budget surpluses have been tapped and traditional state taxes have been increased.
2. Local school tax rates on property have often been reduced.
3. The distribution of school aid has taken account of unusual needs and costs.
4. Most revised programs have placed systematic controls on the growth of local school budgets.[17]

Callahan and Wilken compared the state share of state-local expenditures in the last year before reform and the first year after reform in 18 reform states. The average state share before reform was 39 percent while after reform it was estimated to be 51 percent.[18]

Another characteristic of states that have effected reform programs has been the increasing diversity of actors participating in the process. Frequently, these reforms have been initiated by court actions. In many instances, governors have played leading roles in the support of proposals aimed at such reforms.[19] Since augmented state revenues are nearly always required, legislators who are concerned with overall state tax policy have been involved. In many states new configurations of political power have emerged at the state level as school issues have been sucked into the political mainstream. Governors and legislators have superseded the traditional custodians of educational legislation—the state education agencies, the teachers associations, and the superintendents and school board associations.

Tax Limitation

While the prospects for continued school finance reform are good, another movement which swept the country in recent years, is in many ways an anathema to reform. This is the tax limitation movement, particularly in the form represented by Proposition 13 in California and Proposition 2.5 in Massachusetts. While these states and others may have been ripe for tax revolt, the imposition of arbitrary tax limits, coupled with an economic downturn, have had drastic consequences for school finance. The nationwide interest in these movements suggests that many citizens are fed up with big government and with its insatiable appetite for tax revenues. Thoughtful citizens everywhere will find it difficult to espouse rational tax changes in face of bold and simplistic tax cutbacks.

Ironically, as Guthrie has noted, the most significant outcome of Proposition 13 in California may be a side effect, the substitution of a state school system for a system that has built on local school control.[20] As the percentage of revenue for schools accrues increasingly from state sources and as local school districts are more and more restricted in both raising and expending funds, such an outcome is not hard to visualize.

When one backs away from the specifics of Proposition 13, some general inferences are possible. As Kelly has observed, the fiscal conflict between special govern-

17. Ibid., 1.
18. Ibid., 8.
19. Roald F. Campbell and Tim O. Mazzoni, Jr. *State Policy Making for the Public Schools* (Berkeley, Calif.: McCutchan, 1976), ch. 4.
20. James W. Guthrie, "Proposition 13 and the Future of California's Schools," *Phi Delta Kappan* 60 (September 1978): 12–15.

ment for education and general government has sharpened over the last decade or so.[21] Because at least some overlapping of function between schools and other community agencies exists, many mayors and city councils question the "separateness" of school district finance. The fiscal conflict between general and special government is also intensified as the proportion of state aid to the total school budget is increased. State legislators, much more than local board members, place school demands within the context of total state demands for all state services. Many legislators want to see schools get their fair share, but they do not fancy starving other state services in order to feed the schools. These developments will also intensify overt competition between education and other public services.

School Reexamination

Particularly since the 1950s questions regarding the purposes and the performance of the public school have been raised. These questions prompted no less than seven substantial examinations and reports on the public school during the past few years. These included *A Nation at Risk, Making the Grade, Action for Excellence,* "High School Reform: The Need for Engineering," *High School: A Report on Secondary Education in America,* and *A Place Called School,* the culminating report of the comprehensive study of schooling directed by Goodlad.[22] While these reports differ in the assumptions they make about schools, in the approaches they followed in examining schools, and in the extravagance of the rhetoric employed in depicting the plight of schools, they do tend to make a number of common recommendations. For instance, they insist that the schools should establish higher standards for students including English literacy and more knowledge of science and mathematics. They also stress the need for attracting and holding better talent in the teaching ranks through such means as increased salaries, including merit pay, and improved working conditions.

For our purpose here, these reports seem to place education once again at or near the top of the national agenda. Not since the 1960s have the president, Congress, governors, state legislators, and other national leaders seemed as much in agreement that public education can and must make significant contributions to the public weal. If these convictions are, or come to be shared, by citizens generally, the public can raise aspirations for education across the land. We expect at least some movement in this direction. As we've noted, heightened aspirations frequently lead to increased resources for the schools.

Summary and Future Prospects

Expenditures for schools are influenced by wealth, governmental access, and aspiration. Lack of wealth results in control through deprivation and through stipulations which ordinarily accompany financial aid received from state or federal sources. The increase of governmental structure, particularly the multiplication of decision points,

21. James A. Kelly, "The Public Policy Context of Education Finance," in ed. J. Alan Thomas and R. K. Wimpelberg, *Dilemmas in School Finance,* (Chicago: Midwest Administration Center, University of Chicago, 1978), 45–51.
22. See the following: National Commission on Excellence in Education, *A Nation at Risk* (Washington, D.C.: U.S. Department of Education, April 1983); Report of the Twentieth Century Fund Task Force on Federal Elementary and Secondary Education Policy, *Making the Grade* (New York: Twentieth Century Fund, 1983); Task Force on Education for Economic Growth, *Action for Excellence* (Denver, Colo.: Education Commission of the States, June, 1983); Theodore R. Sizer, "High School Reform: The Need for Engineering," *Phi Delta Kappan* 64 (June 1983): 679–83; Ernest L. Boyer, *High School: Report on Secondary Education in America* (New York: Harper & Row, 1983); and John I. Goodlad, *A Place Called School* (New York: McGraw-Hill, 1984.)

imposes additional controls on schools and school districts. Controls growing out of levels of aspiration are obviously a reflection of the values held by lay citizens or professionals connected with the school. There is some evidence, as Boyd has noted, to suggest that in some communities and on some issues lay values dominate while in other communities and on other issues professional values dominate. Let us consider now some likely developments and try to discern how these may influence wealth, governmental access, or aspiration for education.

If state aid programs continue to be reformed, and this seems likely, the major variables affecting expenditures for schools will be altered. Many school districts in the low and middle ability-to-pay ranges will have more wealth or at least more potential revenue to spend for schools. Some controls nearly always inhere in state aid programs; hence it might be that local governmental access would become even more difficult. Moreover, with increased state support, even at the classroom level, more fiscal controls will be placed on local school districts. Improved state aid programs will provide no panacea for rising expectations, but such programs, particularly if they contain a reward-for-effort feature, will at least encourage greater aspirations. Moreover, the aspirations of the state at large tend to be substituted for the very low aspirations found in some districts.

The movement toward tax limitation is clearly an attempt to make governmental access more difficult, particularly for school districts and other units of government largely dependent on the property tax. When citizens vote for such limitations, they may also be expressing something about their aspirations for school programs or their doubts about the necessity of such programs.

Perhaps the most serious problems for the future are the diverse aspirations people have for schools and the fragmentation of public support for school programs. There are several conditions that contribute to this state of affairs. To begin with, many citizens are disenchanted with government and with governmental agencies, including the schools. The schools have their own special problems. For instance, greatly increased federal aid, particularly for the children of the poor has brought modest and often disappointing results. Moreover, beginning in the mid-1960s and lasting for more than a decade there has been a decline in achievement test scores, particularly the SAT scores of high school students. While one can find extenuating circumstances to explain both of these developments, in the minds of many people they suggest that the school is not doing its job, and providing more money to an inept institution does not make sense to them.

A second condition contributing to differential aspirations and fragmented support is the fact that a smaller percentage of parents now have children in the public schools. As noted earlier, parents with children in the public schools give higher approval ratings to the schools than do adults with no children in the public schools.

A third factor affecting aspirations and support for the public schools is the advocacy of alternatives to the public schools. The alternative movement is described in a book by Coons and Sugarman, *Education by Choice*.[23] The subtitle, *The Case for Family Control* and the following excerpt make their position clear.

> We . . . argue that the interests of children are best served in a decentralized polity giving maximum scope to free, chosen, communal relationships that are generally

23. John E. Coons and Stephen D. Sugarman, *Education by Choice* (Berkeley, Calif.: University of California Press, 1978).

organized on a small scale. Systematic domination of education by large enterprises (public or private) ought, therefore, to be disfavored. This suggests to us the strengthening of the family's role in education and the growth of a teaching fraternity which is related to the family as professional to client rather than as master to servant.[24]

In their treatment of school finance Garms, Guthrie, and Pierce, while not going as far as Coons and Sugarman, also advocate an alternative to the present system.[25] They would like to see a basic education, through full state funding, guaranteed to every child. Basic education would include reading, writing, arithmetic, and some knowledge of our democratic government and would ordinarily be completed by the end of the eighth grade. For the rest of elementary schooling parents might purchase "educational coupons" at differential rates, perhaps 10 cents on the dollar for poor parents and 90 cents on the dollar for wealthy parents, to be spent on such subjects as music, art, language instruction, remedial reading, or vocational education offered by either public or private schools. In addition, each student would receive a "portable grant" which would entitle him or her to a maximum of six additional years of schooling at any public or private school at any time during a person's lifetime.

A fourth factor in this complex arena of aspirations and support is the growing concern and support for segments of the school program as opposed to the total school program. This is perhaps most pronounced in federal support given to vocational education and to education of the handicapped, both of which are discussed in chapter 2. One aspect of the law on the handicapped illustrates the selective nature of provisions in special education: each student is to receive an individually prescribed program. Regardless of cost and regardless of the impact of such cost on the total school budget, each student is to receive such service. One can hardly deny the desirability of an individually prescribed program for a handicapped person, but what about an individually prescribed program for other students? Aspirations and support for certain types of special education have grown tremendously, sometimes at the expense of education for all.

Some of the conditions related to public aspirations and support have been affected by recent actions on the part of the Reagan administration. As noted in chapter 2, expenditures for equity programs were sharply reduced under the Educational Consolidation and Improvement Act. Moreover, the overall decrease in federal expenditures for education has shifted an even greater part of the total financial burden to state and local sources. These financial strains are being exacerbated by growing minority group populations and their increasing political pressure that government attend to equity problems. These conditions are forcing states to consider ways of increasing resources for education and some states, notably California and Florida, have enacted major financial reforms. It seems likely that these pressures the widespread reexamination of schools, now under way, will help build a consensus in most states favoring more adequate resources for the operation of the public schools.

24. Ibid., 2.
25. Walter I. Garms, James W. Guthrie, and Lawrence C. Pierce, *School Finance—The Economics and Politics of Public Education* (Englewood Cliffs, N.J.: Prentice-Hall, 1978), 241–46.

16
College Influences

Colleges and universities have always exerted influence upon the policies and programs of American schools, but the nature of this influence has varied considerably; some of it has been direct, some indirect; some of it has been purposeful, some accidental. The colleges' greatest influence has obviously been on that segment of the secondary school program to which such high status has been attached—the college preparatory program. For a time, this influence appeared to be lessening. However, the national concern for educational reform which emerged in the 1980s has been accompanied by a resurgence of college interest in and influence upon secondary school programs. Much of this interest and influence stems from a new spirit of cooperation between schools and colleges that is rooted in their recognition of common concerns.

In speaking of college influences "college" in this chapter will refer to colleges as individual institutions, groups of collegiate institutions in concert (as in the College Entrance Examination Board), and college administrators and faculty members, both in the field of education and in other disciplines.

The Historical Relationship

The Latin School

College influence was the most direct in the early days of American society when the sole function of the secondary school was preparation for college. An interesting but often forgotten fact is that the first secondary school in America was, in a sense, a vocational school with the exclusive function of preparing boys for the ministry. This school, the Boston Latin School, was founded in 1635, a mere five years after the city of Boston was settled. It was created to provide the same classical training that Latin grammar schools in England had offered.

This school, like other grammar schools found primarily in the northern colonies in the seventeenth and eighteenth centuries, was established to provide the necessary background in Latin, Greek, and mathematics for admission to the colleges. The most influential early secondary schools were in Massachusetts for the Massachusetts Act of 1647 demanded that every town of one hundred families maintain a Latin grammar school. As in Boston, these schools were supported by local taxation and were largely locally controlled. Despite considerable variety in these schools, they did have one thing in common: a strict and narrow classical curriculum, totally knowledge-centered. Justified primarily by long use in European nations, this curriculum was designed to provide a direct and essential road to higher education. Some towns with this type of school never sent a boy to college, but the curriculum remained the same until early in the eighteenth century when emphasis on the classical curriculum began to decline.

The influence of this early school is still with us. Spears has pointed out that the Latin grammar school bequeathed two major patterns to American secondary education: (1) the tendency of the college to dictate to the school below and (2) the concept of public support and control.[1]

Strange though it may seem, the preparatory school was created one year before the college that was to receive its students came into existence. Harvard was founded in 1636 and was the only college in New England until Yale was established 65 years later. Thus, for an extended period one institution set the scholastic standards and thus the curriculum for all Latin grammar schools, with this entrance requirement:

> When scholars had so far profited in the grammar schools, that they could read any classical author in English, and readily make and speak true Latin, and write it in verse as well as prose; and perfectly decline the paradigms of nouns and verbs in the Greek tongue, they were judged capable of admission in Harvard college.[2]

The Growth of Colleges

The growth of colleges in America was quite slow until the early nineteenth century, at which time many institutions of varying quality were established across the country. Regardless of the quality of the institutions, however, they all had an effect on secondary education: by requiring certain subjects as prerequisites for admission, they set the curriculum for the lower schools.[3]

Of course this influence worked in a variety of ways. If a certain standard of Latin and Greek was demanded by a college, schools with students interested in attending that institution developed curriculums to meet this standard. If a college admitted students without much attention to their prior scholarly achievements, secondary schools in the area languished and the college itself was in effect the secondary school. Other colleges developed their own "preparatory departments" which trained boys just out of the common schools, a practice which stifled the public or independent secondary school. Thus, the school that trained students for college had "a course of study . . . fashioned by the influence of the college to suit the purposes of the college."[4]

The Academies and the Common High Schools

With the rise of the middle class in the early eighteenth century, the Latin grammar school and the curriculum it offered began to lose favor with large sections of the

1. Harold Spears, *The High School for Today* (New York: American Book, 1950), 289.
2. Elmer E. Brown, *Secondary Education,* Education in the United States, monograph no. 4, ed. Nicholas Murray Butler (Albany, N.Y.: J. B. Lyon, 1900), 147.
3. Theodore R. Sizer, *Secondary Schools at the Turn of the Century* (New Haven, Conn.: Yale University Press, 1964), 55.
4. A. F. Bechdolt, "The High School as a Fitting-School," Addresses and Proceedings of the National Education Association (1890), 622.

society. Other types of secondary schools began to emerge. The proposals put forth by Benjamin Franklin in 1743 for the education of youth in Pennsylvania stimulated the development of the Public Academy in the City of Philadelphia in 1751. The diversified or differentiated programs of the modern high school have their roots in this academy as Franklin's liberal views on education were reflected in this school.[5] Franklin's recommended curriculum was far broader than that of the Latin grammar school, with emphasis on English, geography, history, even ancient and modern languages, but only as they were thought useful to the individual. Included as electives were such heretofore ignored subjects as surveying, merchants' accounts, gauging, navigation, and drawing perspective.

The concept of the academy as a publicly supported institution spread quickly, particularly among those people to whom the Latin school did not appeal. Academies grew rapidly in all parts of the country after the Revolutionary War until about 1850. They were established most often by private or local initiative, chartered by the state, and financed by taxes, endowments, state grants, and fees. There was a great variety of institutions. Some academies, like Phillips Andover which was one of the first, were hardly distinguishable from Latin schools. Others provided secondary schooling for girls for the first time. Some emphasized commercial work, others teacher training.

Despite this diversity, a basic assumption of most of the academies was that many of their students would go on to college, and thus the curriculum for college entrance remained very important, if not predominant, and continued to be controlled by college entrance requirements. The academy, however, had introduced "practical" studies, it had provided education for children from many different social groups, and it had broadened the aims and content of education.[6]

In the latter half of the nineteenth century, the influence of the academy declined. With the fight for free primary education won by 1850 and with the public high school the dominant form of secondary education by 1890, the role of the academy was destined to undergo an ironic shift. This role was articulated in 1885 by the NEA Commission on Secondary Education; it commended the academy for its important works and pointed out there was still room for the academy but stated that the high school was taking over many of its important functions. In considering the task of the academy in American education, the Commission stated, "This work will be largely, though not exclusively, in preparing youth for college." Thus the institution which was created because of dissatisfaction with the college preparatory character of the Latin school was destined to evolve into the kind of school against which it had made its original protest. In recent times the nation's independent secondary schools, directly descended from the early academy, have sent nearly all of their graduates to college.

Although there were many other types of schools and many variations within these types, the Latin grammar schools on the one hand and the academies and common schools on the other illustrate the two distinct traditions in American secondary education, one classical and linguistic and the other practical and vocational. The colleges and hence the Latin schools equated education with mastery of Greek, Latin, and mathematics in the tradition of Western education since the Renaissance. The academies and the common schools saw education more in terms of direct application and provided training in subjects that appeared to be immediately useful to the students of the day. The public high school drew on both of these approaches. As an

---

5. Newton Edwards and Herman G. Richey, *The School in the American Social Order*, rev. ed. (Boston: Houghton Mifflin, 1963), 174.
6. Sizer, *Secondary Schools*, 3–4.

extension of the common school it reflected the practical demands of its sponsors on local school boards and therefore provided training in English, commercial subjects, and history; as a school preparing students for college and as an institution aspiring to the social status of the Latin school, it provided course work in the classical languages and mathematics. Thus the public high schools that emerged contained elements of both of the traditions of secondary education.[7]

With the growth of colleges and secondary schools, no one college could ever again have the direct influence over the lower schools that Harvard had exerted in the late seventeenth and early eighteenth century. A number of collegiate forces, however, continued to have strong influence on the elementary and secondary schools.

New Disciplines

In the late nineteenth century industrialization and the rapid growth of cities led to major changes in the nature of American society. The growing importance of science as an intellectual movement also was affecting society, albeit in a different manner. Darwin's *Origin of Species,* published in 1859, and other works that followed, particularly those of Herbert Spencer, had significant impact on education as well as on American life.[8] The work of Spencer in linking evolutionary theory to social institutions, G. Stanley Hall in child development, William James in psychology and philosophy, among others, provided the theoretical underpinnings for the subsequent progressive education movement. At the same time the scientific approach was gaining acceptance and other scholars were producing new knowledge in the physical, natural, and social sciences. Even seminars on "scientific history" were being given by Herbert Baxter Evans at Johns Hopkins University. These developments caused problems for the schools. The scholars in many of these new disciplines sought time for their subjects to be offered in the lower schools—time that had to be taken from the old and time-honored subjects.[9] The ultimate question then, as now, was: what should the school teach?

One way to handle this question was simply to expand the number of subjects offered, and this is indeed what happened in the public high schools between 1865 and 1900.[10] As new subjects were added to the curriculum and new course organizations were devised to cope with the needs of an increasingly diverse high school population, the program of the high school became chaotic. With no model to provide order to the work of the high school, each community selected features that seemed best in the local situation, some operating a high school with a four-year program and others providing for three or even two years of study. As Edwards and Richey point out, the entrance requirements of the college served to bring some degree of uniformity to high school programs,[11] although there was a growing need for a more highly standardized institution.

The Committee of Ten

This state of disorganization prompted the National Education Association to appoint the Committee of Ten in 1892 to consider problems confronting secondary education.

7. Ibid. 5.
8. For discussion of these developments particularly as they pertained to the rise of progressive education, see Lawrence A. Cremin, *The Transformation of the School* (New York: Random House, 1961), ch. 4.
9. Sizer, *Secondary Schools,* 13.
10. See Edwards and Richey, *The School,* 546–52.
11. Ibid., 547.

Once again Harvard was to play an important role through the efforts of its president, Charles W. Eliot. He spoke at the NEA convention in St. Paul in 1890, calling for major reforms in the high school, including strict supervision by state inspectors and the adoption of a uniform system of examinations in college preparatory courses. Eliot said that "the schools need to be brought to common and higher standards, so that the colleges may find in the school courses a firm, broad, and reasonably homogeneous foundation for their higher work."[12]

Eliot, easily the most powerful voice in higher education of the day, was selected as chairman of the Committee of Ten. The charge given the committee was to consider the problems of secondary education. The composition of the committee suggests the dimensions of the problem seen in 1892 for five of the ten were college presidents, one was a college professor, and two others were headmasters of eastern preparatory schools.

Not surprisingly, their report concentrated on the problems of preparing students for college entrance. They stated that the committee recognized that the secondary schools, taken as a group, do not exist solely for the purpose of preparing students for college and that, indeed, only an insignificant percentage of the graduates would go to college. However, the recommendations made no distinction between the college-bound and the terminal student. The report declared that "every subject which is taught at all in a secondary school should be taught in the same way and to the same extent to every pupil so long as he pursues it, no matter what the probable destination of the pupil may be, or at what point his education is to cease."

The Committee of Ten suggested the following subjects were appropriate for the high schools: (1) languages—Latin, Greek, English, German, and French (and locally Spanish); (2) mathematics—algebra, geometry, and trigonometry; (3) general history and intensive study of special epochs; (4) natural history—including descriptive astronomy, meteorology, botany, zoology, physiology, geology, and ethnology; and (5) physics and chemistry. The committee also made three recommendations with respect to the organization of the secondary school curriculum: (1) organize a number of different curricula, such as classical, Latin-scientific, modern languages, and English; (2) introduce the elective system; and (3) define a unit of instruction in terms of the number of hours of instruction given per week in the subject.

The publication of the report caused a considerable stir in educational circles. Numerous articles assessing the findings appeared. The British government even sought the advice of the committee on comparable British problems. Schools throughout the United States changed their courses to conform wholly or in part with the committee's recommendations.

For better or for worse, the report had great influence, influence that has persisted to the present day.[13] In transmitting the report to the secretary of the interior for government publication, Commissioner Harris called it "the most important document ever published in this country." Many others of the time agreed.

Some, however, were dubious and even caustically critical of the report, believing that the committee, in using armchair methods, had served only to increase the traditionalist viewpoint in secondary education and had overlooked the fact that American society was undergoing radical changes.[14] Writing in 1950, Spears admitted the far-

---

12. Charles W. Eliot "The Gap Between the Elementary Schools and the Colleges," Addresses and Proceedings of the National Education Association (Washington, D.C.; The Association, 1890), 525.
13. For a discussion of this report and its effect, see Sizer, *Secondary Schools.*
14. E. P. Cubberley, *Public Education in the United States,* rev. ed. (Boston: Houghton Mifflin, 1934), 543–44.

reaching influence of the report with these bitter words: "National educational bodies, the Commissioner of Education, College presidents, and complacent school administrators were apparently willing, at the turn of the century, to sell the birthright of the American public high school for a pot of college-preparatory pottage."[15]

Sizer observed more recently,

> The fractional curriculum that the high schools have inherited from the 1890s serves us poorly. To reconstruct it will infuriate many academic scholars, scare many teachers who have been trained by those scholars, and send shivers of apprehension down the spines of parents. The core academic structure of high school, legitimized by the Committee of Ten in 1893 maintains a ferocious hold on our thinking.[16]

This college-dominated committee thus had a profound and long-lasting effect on the secondary schools, the most influential outcome perhaps being the standardization imposed upon the high school. Its influence is still apparent in the curriculum recommendations of national study groups and institutions of higher education. Whatever the merit of Sizer's lament, it and his suggestions for reform are less likely to be heeded by state and local boards of education than the recommendations of college officials for additional academic units.

The Cardinal Principles

A shift to an emphasis which reflected broader social concern was effected by the Commission on the Reorganization of Secondary Education which presented the famous "Cardinal Principles of Secondary Education" in 1918. This commission set the following as the main goals of education: (1) health, (2) command of fundamental processes, (3) worthy home membership, (4) vocation, (5) citizenship, (6) worthy use of leisure, and (7) ethical character.

The composition of this commission indicated that the influence of the colleges had diminished. Eleven members made up the commission, which was chaired by Clarence D. Kingsley, Massachusetts State High School Supervisor. The U.S. Commissioner of Education, P. P. Claxton, was a member. One college president was included, Edward O. Sisson of Montana, but he had spent most of his professional life in the public schools. Three men were professors of education, and the rest were involved in the administration of secondary schools. Spears, who was so caustic in his criticism of the college-dominated Committee of Ten, spoke of the commission in the following manner: "The work of this group came from the active field of secondary education itself, not from the easy chairs in a college conference room far removed from the give-and-take of a public secondary school."[17] Although the "Cardinal Prin ciples" have been criticized for being too general, nevertheless they have been very influential in the development of curriculums at the elementary and secondary level down to the present day.

---

15. Spears, *The High School for Today,* 306.
16. Theodore R. Sizer, "High School Reform: The Need for Engineering," *Phi Delta Kappan* 64 (June, 1983): 682.
17. Ibid., 314.

College Influences on School Programs

The College Entrance Examination Board

Many of the people who had been influential in the Report of the Committee of Ten were also to play a major role in the formation in 1900 of the College Entrance Examination Board. This board was "in its origins an attempt to introduce law and order into an educational anarchy which towards the close of the nineteenth century had become exasperating, indeed almost intolerable, to schoolmasters. The basic trouble lay in a lack of cooperation among colleges as a group and between colleges and secondary schools on the matter of college admissions."[18]

In 1877 President Eliot had suggested, with no apparent effect, that the colleges should cooperate to standardize admission practices. In 1894, speaking to the New England Association, he made the specific suggestion that the colleges organize a board of examiners to conduct admissions examinations all over the country.

The most scathing indictment of the general disorder in education, however, was made by a secondary school administrator, William Farrand of Newark Academy, in his 1895 inaugural address as president of the Schoolmasters Association of New York and vicinity. In a speech titled "The Reform of College Entrance Requirements" he ridiculed the inconsistencies in the entrance requirements of Harvard, Yale, Princeton, and Columbia, and he illustrated how influential these requirements were on the curriculum on his school. Fuess has abstracted his remarks as follows:

> The more closely we examine the details, the more marked are the differences. For instance, Princeton and Columbia call for six books of the *Aeneid:* Yale requires, in addition, the *Eclogues.* These do not count for maximum standing at Princeton unless combined with the *Georgics.* The elementary Algebra requirement at Harvard is less than is exacted of students at Princeton and Yale; her advanced requirement is greater. . . .
>
> When we come to the Scientific Schools, the discrepancies are even greater. Princeton requires Latin of candidates for one course, but not for the others. Yale demands it of all, Columbia of none. Princeton names five books of Caesar and four orations of Cicero; Yale names four books of Caesar and three books of Virgil. . . . Yale calls for Botany, Columbia for Physics and Chemistry, Princeton for no science. Princeton and Columbia demand both German and French, while Yale is satisfied with either. On the other hand, while Princeton and Columbia demand only American History, Yale calls also for that of England. . . .
>
> For our Princeton boys we must include a review of Arithmetic and carry Algebra farther than is required by Harvard or Columbia; for Yale we must read the Bucolics and study Logarithms and their applications to geometrical problems; for Harvard we must supply a thorough course in Physics. . . . Look again for a moment at the requirements in science. Harvard puts on a stiff requirement in Physics and Chemistry, Yale calls for Botany, Cornell for Physiology.[19]

Farrand was named as one of the original secondary school representatives of the CEEB in 1900 and was actively involved with the board until his death in 1942. According to Fuess, the original idea for the board came from President Eliot, but trans-

---

18. Claude M. Fuess, *The College Board: Its First Fifty Years* (New York: Columbia University Press, 1950), 3.
19. Ibid., 17–18.

lation of it into action was largely due to the spirit and work of Nicholas Murray Butler. In 1960 the president of the CEEB pointed out that the premise on which the original board system was based was the concept of college control of the curriculum.[20]

The first examinations, prepared by representatives of both colleges and the secondary schools, were given in June of 1901 to 973 candidates who wrote 7,889 papers. At that time twelve institutions of higher learning were members. By 1977 there were more than 2,400 members of the CEEB.[21] Secondary schools have been eligible for full membership since 1959. The board's membership and services have grown to include meetings and conferences throughout the year, the development of an extensive program of tests and examinations, the supervision and sponsorship of numerous research projects in the field of measurements, testing, and psychology, the support of the College Scholarship Service, and the publication of informational and interpretive guidance materials. Since 1947 the operational phases of the College Board's testing have been conducted by Educational Testing Service.

The best known activity of the College Board is probably the various college entrance and guidance examinations which it administers to secondary school students. In 1980–81 the board gave approximately 1,800,000 admissions tests through its Scholastic Aptitude Test (SAT) Program to prospective college students. An important addition to the program in 1971–72 was the Student Descriptive Questionnaire (SDQ) which enabled prospective students to share information about their interests, experiences, and future plans with colleges to which they made application. This addition reflects the understanding of the College Board that institutions are increasingly concerned with personal factors in addition to test scores in making selection decisions.[22]

Thousands of students take other tests each year in addition to or instead of the SAT. For example, nearly one million high school seniors are examined by the American College Testing Program (ACT) every year. Schurdson notes that the ACT's examination measures similar skills as the College Board aptitude tests and that scores from it are utilized most often by colleges and universities located in the Middle West and parts of the South and West.[23]

Although the rise of the testing movement is by no means solely the result of efforts of college personnel, use of the tests is important in college and university decision making. The selection patterns established by colleges do also provide a record which can be useful to students in determining the particular colleges to which they will apply.

Testing Programs

One facet of the tendency toward national standardization is the desire to have students do well on the various tests and therefore to attempt to "teach to the test." Early evidence on this point was provided by Brickell's study of change in New York State. Serving as a Consultant on Educational Experimentation to the Commissioner of Education he reported the following observations:

20. Frank H. Bowles, *Admission to College: A Perspective for the 1960's* (Princeton, N.J.: College Entrance Examination Board, 1960), 24.
21. *College Board News* (April 1977): 7.
22. *Individuals and Their Options* (Princeton, N.J.: Educational Testing Service, 1973), 19.
23. Michael S. Schurdson, "Organizing the Meritocracy: A History of the College Entrance Board," *Harvard Educational Review* 42 (February 1972): 62.

The Regents Examinations, beyond any question whatsoever, inhibit change in the State of New York. Serious students of the matter could hardly debate the point.

During May and June of 1961, the Consultant visited hundreds of high school classrooms, heard what was being discussed by teachers and students, saw what was written on the blackboards, looked at the books being used in the class, noted the other books students were carrying under their arms to other classes, talked briefly with many teachers and at length with many administrators. He offers this observation based on those visits: *Copies of previous Regents Examinations constitute at least ten percent of the curriculum* in the typical high school course (the old examinations are the material studied for approximately four weeks out of forty). The hesitancy of many schools to break this successful pattern of preparing for Regents Examinations tends to dampen their enthusiams for innovations which are distinctive in content or in approach.[24]

Thus we have, in effect a double indictment of the influence of examinations. Not only do the schools explicitly teach on the basis of previous examinations, but they tend to avoid experimentation with new materials or methods because such innovations might involve knowledge not covered by the examination and conceivably could result in a poor record for the school on the tests. Others assert that tests are not sufficiently valid and reliable to be used as readily as they are in making decisions of great significance to both individuals and society.[25]

A study by La Vigne on the impact of the National Merit Scholarship Program on the public high school revealed that this impact has assumed several expressions.[26] One of the most well-known results of participation is the rating of high schools by patrons in the district. Such a rating turns the program into an external measuring device to determine the relative quality of the high schools. Partially because of the impact of such ratings, a second result has been the use of a variety of coaching methods designed to "produce" scholars.

Another reaction of school personnel is the recognition of the National Merit Scholarship Program as a part of the multitest approach to college admissions and scholarships. High school staff members questioned the wisdom of so many tests. However, because community expectations required them to participate in this program, they felt the freedom to withdraw has been curtailed.

The program was accepted as a key to other scholarship possibilities and as an aid to college admission. The value of the National Merit Scholarship Qualifying Test as a guidance tool, however, was quite limited, apparently because of the variety and numbers of tests already available for such purposes, but it was considered valuable for raising the academic incentive of some students. Finally, La Vigne discovered that respondents disagreed with some of the program's policies and procedures, particularly with respect to the selection process, which removes the selection of scholarship winners from the control of local school personnel. We know of no follow-up to La Vigne's study which was completed twenty years ago. Our impression, however, is that her findings continue to be applicable. The National Merit Scholarship Program is

---

24. Henry M. Brickell, *Organizing New York State for Educational Change* (Albany, N.Y.: State Education Department, 1961), 40. Italics in original.
25. See Andrew J. Strenio, Jr., *The Testing Trap* (New York: Rawson, Wade, 1981).
26. Lorraine La Vigne, "Impact of the National Merit Scholarship Program on the Public High School" (Ph.D. diss., University of Chicago, 1962), as reported in *Nationalizing Influences on Secondary Education,* ed. Roald F. Campbell and Robert A. Bunnell (Chicago: Midwest Administration Center, University of Chicago, 1963), 41–56.

firmly established; in 1980–81, nearly 1,300,000 students took the qualifying examination.

Scores on the SAT declined on a national basis in recent years until 1982. Public notice of this decline has resulted in considerable pressure upon public school systems. College and university personnel in particular decry the alleged low ability levels of entering freshmen and the resulting growth in demand for remedial courses at the college level. While a comprehensive study of this phenomenon found that the causes for test score decline were complex and rooted in the general society,[27] many persons and national study groups nevertheless point to these scores as evidence of school failure.

Decline in SAT scores has also fueled the argument for statewide competency testing. More than 30 states have enacted legislation which deals with competency testing. Perhaps the most far-reaching legislation of this type exists in Florida where all students must now pass a state-designed test in order to receive a high school diploma. In the first year that the test was given, many students failed and criticisms were levied at the test as well as at the schools.[28]

The idea of using standardized achievement tests in the nation's high schools has long been favored by a large majority of the American public according to a survey conducted by the American Institute of Public Opinion. According to one early proposal, tests would be given to all freshmen and seniors to measure their degree of achievement and to compare this with achievement levels of other high schools throughout the country. Proponents of the plan said it would stimulate greater effort in those communities where scores fall below the national average. Those opposed feared it would control the local school curriculum by creating widespread conformity and would put those schools which deviate from the subject matter on which tests are based at a disadvantage, according to institute director George Gallup. The proposal was favored by 77 percent of a representative cross section of the public, opposed by 13 percent, and 10 percent had no opinion.[29] More recent evidence suggests that the public continues to believe that such testing is a good idea. A 1983 Gallup survey found that 75 percent of the population favored national tests of educational achievement, 17 percent opposed such tests, and 8 percent had no opinion.[30]

Whether the influence of tests on curriculum is a trend to be applauded or deplored, it is a force that cannot be ignored. Those responsible for the construction and administration of such tests are among the most vocal critics of those practices whereby teachers "teach for the tests" and are constantly seeking ways to construct examinations to minimize this possibility.

Nevertheless, the pressure to consider test results is always on the schools. Increased opportunities to attend community colleges and the freedom to consider options to university attendance may have decreased the visibility of this pressure

27. *On Further Examination: Report of the Advisory Board on the Scholastic Aptitude Test Decline* (New York: College Entrance Examination Board, 1977). Among the factors noted by the panel in addition to those related to school curriculum were changes in the population taking the test, the impact of television on learning styles, changes in the family, and a decline in younger people's motivation to learn.
28. For discussion of the Florida Program, see Thomas H. Fisher, "Florida's Approach to Competency Testing" and Gene V. Glass, "Minimum Competence and Incompetence in Florida," *Phi Delta Kappan* 59 (May 1978): 599–605. Also see Arthur E. Wise, *Legislated Learning* (Berkeley, Calif.: University of California Press, 1979).
29. *School Boards* 6 (January 1963): 3.
30. George Gallup, "The Fifteenth Annual Gallup Poll of the Public's Attitudes Toward the Public Schools," *Phi Delta Kappan* 65 (September 1983): 38.

somewhat in recent years. A more recent development which may offset this, however, is renewed college and university interest in awarding scholarships on the basis of merit rather than need. Insofar as institutions of higher education employ test scores as indicators of merit, secondary schools may experience increased pressure from parents to prepare students who do well on the tests.

The Advanced Placement Program

Another activity of the College Board which has had considerable influence on the lower schools is the Advanced Placement Program, which provides examinations for gifted students who have completed college level work in high school. Students who pass these examinations enter college at the sophomore level in the appropriate subject areas. The number of students who take this test has increased from 1,229 from 104 secondary schools in 1955 to 141,626 students from 5,525 schools in 1981–82.[31] The tests are offered to students in 23 percent of the nation's high schools, and nearly two-thirds of American colleges and universities offer some kind of advanced placement credit. These facts bear out Howe's observation that the Advanced Placement Program has more potential for a permanent effect on secondary education than any of the other activities of the College Board.[32] He saw three major advantages to the program: the secondary schools involved have a new grasp of what colleges want; colleges have a new respect for what can be accomplished in secondary school; and many able students have new opportunities for a more stimulating education. He went on to point out that the Advanced Placement Program is a graphic demonstration of the influence of the college on the secondary school. However, because the ends are worthy and the means have involved cooperation rather than dictation, he says that the issue of undesirable control by the colleges has never been a major problem. The tests are offered in a broad range of subjects and are taken most often in English literature and composition, American history, calculus, biology, European history, and chemistry.

Changing Admissions Standards

During the 1960s and 1970s, a number of colleges and universities relaxed their admission standards. Other state institutions have traditionally maintained a policy of open admissions toward graduates of high schools in their respective states. Societal pressures and incentives to attend college have led increasing numbers of high school graduates with lackluster academic backgrounds to enter these colleges and universities. Some took academic courses in high school and did poorly. Others focused their high school preparation in vocational subjects or "soft" electives either because they made a late decision to attend college or, knowing that a high school diploma would assure them of admission to college, they sought an easier curriculum that would enable them to get better grades and have more time for a part-time job or extracurricular activities. One consequence of these developments has been an increase in the number of students who require remedial instruction at colleges and universities. At

31. Sheppard Ranbom, "Schools' Interest in Advanced-Placement Classes Increases" *Education Week* II, 13 April 1983: 14–15.
32. *College Board News* (April 1977),7, and Harold Howe II, "Educational Controls Exhibited by the Colleges," *The American Secondary School* (Princeton, N.J.: College Entrance Examination Board, 1959), 39.

some state institutions, more than 50 percent of the freshman class enrolls in pre-college level English or mathematics classes.

Faculty members, administrators, and boards of trustees have expressed growing concern at the number of students who enter college with insufficient preparation and the corresponding need to offer pre-college course work to these students. The result has been sweeping changes in admission requirements to state colleges and universities. A 1982 survey by the National Association of Secondary School Principals found that the state universities in 27 states had recently increased their admissions requirements or were reviewing the possibility of doing so.[33] Some of these changes reflect increased test score, class rank, or class average requirements. However, most of them focus upon course requirements and call for students to take additional credits in mathematics, science, English, and social science. For example, the new pre-college curriculum in Kentucky will require students to complete four years of English rather than three, three years of mathematics rather than two, two years of science, and world history in addition to American history.

Such changes have implications for the budgets as well as the curricula of secondary schools. Increasing requirements for science and mathematics will require some small schools to add courses they do not presently teach; to teach them they may have to add faculty members. Virtually all schools will find their response to these changes complicated by the shortage of science and mathematics teachers.

These changes, though expensive initially, should have long-range benefits, according to experts. Thomson points out that the changes may have a "salutary effect upon student attitudes" and he encourages parents to be more vigorous advocates for improved academic standards.[34]

New Developments in Curriculum

Another arena within which the college influence is dominant is the development of new curriculums in many areas. An important catalytic agent in creating organizations to stimulate and support new curriculum developments has been the National Science Foundation. Though a relatively recent force (established in 1950), the resources of the NSF have had a profound impact. Its budget for educational purposes grew from $1.5 million in 1952 to approximately $116 million in 1981. By the early 1960s the Foundation was supporting extensive programs in the following areas: (1) financial aid for graduate students, advanced scholars, and teachers in seven basic fellowship programs; (2) supplemental training of teachers of science, mathematics, and engineering through an institute program; (3) improvement in the subject matter of science and mathematics, particularly in the high schools, through financing major curriculum studies; and (4) identification and motivation of talented high school and undergraduate science students through a variety of special programs.

The policy of the Foundation lends support to university scholars and professional scientists and has thereby greatly strengthened the role of these groups in effecting educational change. The Foundation also provides support for the continuing education of elementary and secondary school teachers. For example, more than 12,000 science and math teachers took part in NSF training programs during 1981.[35] More recent

---

33. Scott D. Thomson, *College Admissions: New Requirements by the State Universities* (Reston, Va.: National Association of Secondary School Principals, 1982).
34. Ibid., 7–8.
35. *National Science Foundation Annual Report: 1981* (Washington, D.C.: Government Printing Office, 1982), 86.

concern about science and mathematics teaching resulted in NSF funding of additional teacher institutes beginning in the summer of 1984. In addition, NSF provided five million dollars of increased support for research on teaching, learning, and cognition beginning in 1983–84. This allocation was a direct response to congressional and public concern about mathematics and science education. In 1983, NSF published the report of the National Science Board's Commission on Precollege Education in Mathematics, Science and Technology. The report called for a "series of major strategic actions" and heavy federal involvement in responding to the nation's mathematics, science, and technology problems.

The National Endowment for the Humanities was established in 1965. While it has had much less money than NSF, the Endowment has awarded grants to strengthen teaching and curriculums in the humanities for elementary and secondary schools as well as colleges and universities. Grants are available to provide teacher institutes, develop new curricula, and to support demonstration projects for a limited period of time. In 1981–82, NEH allocated more than 5 million dollars to such activities.[36]

Most of the developmental work in these new approaches has been done by or in collaboration with college scholars from the appropriate disciplines. Teachers in the secondary and elementary schools were involved in a variety of ways both in the development and tryout of materials, but the major thrust undeniably came from college personnel. These new programs have exerted strong and direct influence particularly in the sciences.

Accrediting Agencies

Another source of rather direct college influence on the secondary school is the accrediting agency, which over the years has been motivated by the desire to create more uniformity and standardization in the kinds of programs provided by the public schools. Accreditation simply means that a given school meets the criteria for a "good" school as determined by a particular agency. Historically, three dominant groups, through accrediting, have had a direct influence on the educational programs of the schools. These groups are universities, national and regional accrediting associations, and state departments of education.

The growth of the high school and the corresponding increase in the number of applicants to colleges created a need for the colleges to standardize the subject requirements for entrance as well as to measure the qualifications of the teachers offering these subjects. Thus in 1871 the University of Michigan introduced a system of admitting without examination the graduates of high schools that had been inspected and approved. Soon after this, regional and national accreditation grew as a voluntary movement because universities could not visit out-of-state schools from which graduates were seeking admission. Leadership in this process of voluntary accrediting was given by the state universities, and they have continued to play a dominant role.[37]

At present there are six regional associations. These associations, and the year of their creation, are as follows: The New England Association of Colleges and Secondary Schools (1885), the Middle States Association of Colleges and Secondary

---

36. *National Endowment for the Humanities Annual Report: 1982* (Washington, D.C.: Government Printing Office, 1982), 176.
37. Lee M. Thurston and William H. Roe, *State School Administration* (New York: Harper & Row, 1957), 310.

Schools (1892), the North Central Association of Colleges and Secondary Schools (1895), the Southern Association of Secondary Schools and Colleges (1895), the Northwest Association of Secondary and Higher Schools (1918), and the Western Association of Secondary Schools and Colleges (1930).

Clearly, accrediting agencies have had a visible impact on the program of the secondary school, particularly in their early years. At first, accreditation focused solely on the college preparatory program, and the universities exercised inordinate control by specifying entrance requirements so detailed that there was no room for local initiative. This university influence was so pervasive and indeed oppressive that the state departments of education joined the high schools in a resistance movement. In midwestern states resistance took the form of admission provisions to state universities which were under the control of state departments of education. In a study of state standardization, Henry H. Hill identified two main issues which he said have been fought out among the universities, high schools, and state departments of education.[38] First, who shall accredit, or standardize, the university or the state department? Second, who shall determine the high school curriculum, the university or the high school?

On the first issue, the movement at the state level has been almost entirely in the direction of the state department. On the second issue, there is still no final answer. The accrediting associations today, while still strongly influenced by collegiate personnel, have granted extensive participation in policy decisions to representatives of the secondary schools.

In addition, the original purpose of accrediation has undergone a significant change. No longer is the sole, or even major, concern college preparation. Rather, standards are set for total school operations to meet the needs of all pupils. Among the areas in which standards are considered are: housing, libraries, length of class period and school year, graduation requirements, teacher qualifications, equipment, guidance, administration, teaching load, and records. Through these standards, agencies seek to ensure overall program quality rather than specific college entrance requirements.[39] The standards are not goals to be sought but really represent floors to be maintained. The determination of these floors is not a matter of local initiative but a matter of outside authority. The local educator is perfectly free to rise as far above this foundation as is possible.

James B. Conant noted the influence of accrediting standards in the enforcement of teacher certification standards and regulations.[40] After examining state department action, he reported that Ohio has revoked high school charters because schools have poorly prepared faculties, Missouri will restudy a school's classification if too many teachers are not adequately trained, and Illinois will threaten loss of accrediation if too many faculty members have been granted temporary approvals. He also specifically cited the Commission on Secondary Schools of the North Central Association; he said this group, with its authority to accredit schools in 19 states, wielded tremendous power and has its own certification requirements.

38. *State High School Standardization,* Bulletin of the Bureau of School Service, vol. 2, no. 3 (Lexington, Ky.: University of Kentucky, College of Education, March, 1930).
39. Thurston and Roe, *State School Administration,* 312.
40. James B. Conant, *The Education of American Teachers* (New York: McGraw-Hill, 1963), 246.

Preparation of Teachers and Administrators

Schools depend upon colleges and universities to supply them with their professional employees. This practice is legitimated across the 50 states by professional certification requirements which are embodied in state codes. As noted in chapter 3, the enforcement of certification standards is an important responsibility of state education officials. Certification standards generally require prospective educators to hold college or university degrees and to have credit for particular courses in professional education. In one state, for example, a prospective elementary teacher must have a bachelor's degree and credit for at least 29 semester hours in course work dealing with (1) the learner and the learning process, (2) the school in relation to society, (3) elementary school curriculum methods including the teaching of reading, and (4) laboratory experiences including student teaching. The same requirements specify particular general education areas (e.g., visual art, English and communication arts) in which candidates must amass at least 60 semester hours.

Such requirements ensure that teacher education institutions have considerable impact upon professional employment in schools. School systems share in teacher preparation to a limited extent through the supervision of practice teaching and other field-based components in preparation programs. For the most part, however, teacher preparation tends to be campus based. Indeed, some critics have charged that the way in which teachers are educated in colleges and universities is one of the most fundamental problems in American education.[41]

In addition to providing education for prospective teachers and administrators, colleges and universities also serve as screening or selection agents for the profession. This screening function was not very prominent in the case of teachers for many years. As long as there was a teacher shortage, institutions of higher education were relatively open in allowing students to acquire teaching credentials. More recently, some institutions have become more selective in their admission policies in an effort to reduce the oversupply of prospective teachers. Such action naturally raises the question of criteria for entry to preparation programs and the effect of such screening upon the choices available to school districts as they select teachers. Programs to prepare administrators are graduate programs and, as such, have traditionally been more selective than teacher preparation programs. The impact of such selection procedures is largely unknown, but they determine the pool from which school districts select their leaders.

The influence of teacher education institutions upon the selection and preparation of prospective educational leaders has been strongly criticized from two different perspectives. Some charge that certification requirements and college education courses are unduly parochial and serve primarily to prevent persons whose education and experience may be in fields outside education from holding positions for which they may have the abilities. The basic argument is that teaching or administration involves skills which can be learned apart from colleges of education and that those who possess such skills should be allowed to use them. Persons who hold this view are often more critical of state certification arrangements than college preparation efforts and seek to have them changed.

A second kind of criticism comes primarily from teachers themselves, who, often through their professional associations, claim that control over preparation of educa-

41. See, for example, Charles E. Silberman, *Crisis in the Classroom* (New York: Random House, 1970).

tors should shift from the campuses and state certification departments to the profession itself. To this end, some now advocate the establishment of professional practice boards comprised primarily if not entirely of teachers to oversee preparation programs in the respective states. They have also been strong supporters of federally-supported teacher education centers which provide in-service preparation for teachers under the aegis of teacher-dominated policy boards.

Criticism of teacher education reached a new crescendo following the 1983 reports of the National Commission on Excellence in Education and other commissions. These reports noted that students entering teacher education programs during the past decade had low ACT and SAT scores in comparison to students entering other fields, and that the most able graduates of teacher education programs do not remain as classroom teachers.[42] They also noted that the nation faces a serious shortage of qualified science and mathematics teachers. Officials in some states including New Jersey and Virginia have responded to this situation by proposing that liberal arts graduates who pass certain examinations and complete internships or similar experiences be certified to teach despite their lack of formal teacher education. Other states have mandated competency examinations for prospective teachers, and at least two (Alabama and Florida) require the closing of any teacher education program that graduates substantial numbers of students who fail these examinations.[43] It is too early to assess the implications of those policies already in place or to determine what other changes are likely in teacher education. However, there is little doubt that the capacity of schools to respond to particular demands or curriculum opportunities is dependent upon the presence of able teachers. Whatever changes occur in teacher education, colleges and universities will probably continue to be involved in this process.

Colleges and universities also have an impact on teachers already in service as well as on persons preparing for the role. Many take courses at night during the school year or attend special workshops or summer sessions. Attendance at such sessions is often stimulated by salary schedules which reward teachers for extra course work, but many attend primarily to improve their teaching skills and understandings. In recent years, colleges and universities have redirected substantial resources to in-service programs for existing teachers. At the same time, teacher associations have lobbied successfully for changes in certification requirements and salary schedules that reward teachers for district or teacher center in-service activities as well as for university credits. One consequence of this may be to help redirect college and university resources to reflect greater concern with the day-to-day problems of the schools.

Further impetus for university attention to public school problems is the growing recognition by university presidents that colleges and universities have an important stake in helping to strengthen public schools. For example, the presidents of Stanford, Harvard, the University of Chicago, Columbia University, the University of Wisconsin and the University of Michigan showed their concern for and commitment to public schools by meeting in the summer of 1983 and issuing a joint statement, which said:

> . . . universities must play an active role if we are to ensure excellence in a full
> system of primary and secondary schools. As university educators, we have a special

---

42. See Victor S. Vance and Philip C. Schlechty, "The Distribution of Academic Ability in the Teaching Force," *Phi Delta Kappan* 64 (September 1982): 22–27.
43. Hope Aldriels, "Few Blacks Passing Georgia Teacher Test, Study Finds," *Education Week*, 9 November 1983: 6.

concern for the centrality of academic objectives in the schools, and for the importance of teaching as an activity. We therefore welcome a role as partner and advocate for our colleagues in the public schools.[44]

Summary and Future Prospects

The controls which colleges and universities have exercised in the past over public schools have been of three basic kinds. They have established expectations, developed curriculum materials, and prepared personnel to work in the schools. College and university expectations for schools have often been formalized through admission requirements. College admission controls are in a state of flux. As more and more students sought higher education, colleges and universities became more selective in their admissions policies. For example, some state universities which formerly admitted any graduate of an accredited high school in their state began to limit enrollment in the 1960s to students who achieved a particular class rank or certain scores on standardized examinations. Many private schools also became more selective. However, the end of the postwar baby boom, escalating college costs, and the pursuit of other alternatives by students have lessened the competition for admission to many institutions. Indeed, some have been forced to close for lack of students. At the same time, some institutions continue to be selective, and the competition for scholarship assistance is mounting as merit again becomes a criterion for such aid. These developments suggest that standardized admissions tests will continue to be important.

One response to the growing public interest in and growing cost of higher education has been the expansion of community and junior colleges. By making higher education available to virtually all high school graduates who wish it, these institutions are now fulfilling one of the original purposes of the land grant colleges which in many instances have become more selective in admissions policies. The presence of two-year colleges and the pressure for open admissions in some public institutions are evidence of American unwillingness to have a system of higher education which serves only an elite. Financial factors as well as demands to expand enrollment possibilities will probably increase the prominence of these institutions. The rising costs of colleges and universities have led to an upward spiral in tuition rates in public and even more so in private colleges and universities. As further increases are likely, students will probably try to economize by attending nearby public institutions.

Many public as well as private institutions of higher education are presently experiencing financial difficulty. Like some elementary and secondary school districts, these four-year institutions of higher education are confronted with rising costs but declining enrollments. Particularly as opportunities to obtain federal and foundation support dwindle, these institutions will place more pressure upon state legislatures for financial support. This may bring them into greater and more open competition with elementary and secondary schools for state tax dollars. Thus the need for improved interlevel cooperation will become more apparent.[45]

Part of the competition for state resources between institutions of higher education and public schools involves college and university claims for money to support developmental or basic education. In making this claim, institutions of higher education point to the deficiences in basic skills which characterize large numbers of incoming

---

44. "University, School Links Urged," *Education Week*, 24 August 1983:17.
45. Michael D. Usdan, David W. Minar, and Emanual Hurwitz, Jr., *Education and State Politics* (New York: Teachers College Press, Columbia University, 1969).

freshmen. By calling attention to declining SAT scores and low scores on local placement tests, colleges and universities help structure public expectations for schools. To a considerable extent, it has been college and university personnel who have made the public aware of the problems in teaching basic skills. The public response has been to demand improved performance by the schools.

Despite the aforementioned competition for state resources, an increase in programmatic cooperation is likely between schools and universities. Such cooperation will focus on improving teaching and learning to alleviate the basic skills' deficiencies of entering college freshmen and to provide enrichment opportunities for especially able students. A number of schools and universities have already established cooperative relationships to foster curriculum development, teacher preparation, part-time jobs for high school students, and high school courses for college credit.[46]

The final kind of control which colleges and universities have exercised over public schools has been in the preparation of teachers and other school personnel. For many years higher education has had a virtual monopoly over both preservice and inservice preparation of educators. There are signs that this may be changing. One response of public school personnel to criticisms of their efforts has been to blame colleges of education for inadequate preparation. Thus tension has developed between school and university personnel over questions of how teachers should be educated and by whom.[47] Another response of teachers and administrators, however, has been a growing tendency to look away from the university and toward their peers for inservice education. The establishment of teacher education centers has been an important development in this area.

As we look to the future, it is tempting to predict that competition for scarce resources and the continuation of educational problems which are more readily criticized than remedied will produce further strain on school-university relationships. To be sure the university dominance which characterized early twentieth-century relationships has deservedly been put to rest. What remains to be firmly established, however, is the kind of balanced relationship in which school and university personnel recognize that they have common concerns and that both parties can contribute to their resolution. Some important steps have been taken in this direction in recent years. Continued progress should be a matter of high priority for all educators.

---

46. See Gene I. Maeroff, *School and College: Partnerships in Education* (Washington, D.C.: Carnegie Foundation, 1983).

47. An example of school district dissatisfaction with teacher education programs and state certification standards has been the introduction of school district testing of potential teachers. See Richard Mitchell, "Testing the Teachers: The Dallas Experiment," *Atlantic* (December 1978), 66–70.

17

Nonpublic Schools and Other Alternatives

In this chapter, we will examine educational alternatives, some public, some private, some traditional, and some nontraditional. We will use the terms *private* and *nonpublic* to refer to elementary and secondary schools not supported by taxes. The term *alternative* is applied to both institutions not supported by taxes and to various forms of schooling within public school systems.

The post-World War II period has been marked by the extension of conventional forms of public and private schooling as well as new alternative schools that developed in 1960s and 1970s. On initial inspection, these alternative institutions seem to have much in common with conventional schools. Structural characteristics of both, such as length of school year and school day, class size, professional staffing, and organizational structures, are much the same. What is new are the forms and varieties of educational alternatives available to persons of all ages. Moreover, parents in several states have acquired legal rights to educate their children at home and private home tutorial programs have been developed to augment instruction received in the public schools. Opportunities for participation in formal and informal learning programs abound for everyone from the age of two through the advancing years. The rhetoric of lifelong learning has moved closer to reality.

In the mid-1960s the public schools, as well as the society's other major institutions, were subjected to a torrent of criticism. Reactions against the war in Vietnam and racism triggered overt demonstrations against the status quo. Basic questions were asked about the efficacy of public education, particularly in larger cities where the schools were proving to be inadequate in meeting the needs of minority and low-income youngsters.

The civil rights movement, in particular, precipitated growing criticism of American public schools as education, like other fundamental institutions of the society, was accused of suppressing the poor and disadvantaged in order to perpetuate a military-centered and exploitative economic system. The dissatisfaction of the disadvantaged was politically buttressed, if not ideologically supported, by criticism of the schools from another socioeconomic stratum of the society. The nation's most privileged students were accusing the schools of stifling creativity and self-expression. Numerous "alienated" middle- and upper-middle class youngsters protested what they considered to be sterile, uninspiring, and rigidly designed secondary school programs. This chorus of dissatisfaction reached full volume in the late 1960s, continuing though somewhat muted through the 1970s and into the 1980s. Educational alternatives burgeoned throughout the United States partly in response to parent and other citizen unhappiness with traditional public schools.[1]

For the most part the spotlight in American education has been on public education. There has existed throughout our history, however, a companion group of nonpublic schools comprising a substantial segment of our total educational system. Not as much is known about these schools because the focus has been on public schools and because the collection of data about nonpublic schools has been sporadic, poorly coordinated, and even ignored. Public school educators are not well informed about how nonpublic schools are financed or controlled, nor are they always interested. Nonpublic school educators are, in turn, not well informed about the public schools.

Nonpublic Schools Yesterday and Today

Despite the early colonial interest in public schools, especially in New England, considerable support existed for the establishment of nongovernmentally related schools. Butts and Cremin point out that private efforts by individuals and groups of like-minded people appeared early on the American scene and came to be the dominant method of promoting schools in many of the colonies.[2] A U.S. Office of Education survey indicates that 2.6 percent of the nonpublic secondary schools now operating were founded before 1850 and another 16 percent between 1850 and 1900.[3] Most of the older schools are located on the eastern seaboard.

In our early history the lines of demarcation between the management of nonpublic and public schools were often difficult to distinguish. This was particularly true in those colonies where the church and the state were allied. Frequently individuals gave private donations to town schools or to public authorities for the use of public schools. In other instances, public funds and other forms of public aid were turned over to private agencies and religious groups for the support of nonpublic education. Early nonpublic schools were endowed by individuals, established as denominational schools by churches and religious societies, developed by individual teachers as their own, or were created as private academies by corporations which served as their governing boards.

Nonpublic schools enjoy the protection of the law in the United States.[4] The states in the exercise of their plenary power over education require all children to attend school and compulsory attendance laws have been enacted in all of the states, but the power of the state does not include the right to determine which schools, public or nonpublic, children must attend. The courts have upheld the right of parents

1. For a useful overview of opinions regarding education over this period see Stanley M. Elam, "The Gallup Education Surveys: Impressions of a Poll Watcher," *Phi Delta Kappan* 65 (September 1983): 26–32.
2. R. Freeman Butts and Lawrence A. Cremin. *A History of Education in American Culture* (New York: Holt, Rinehart & Winston, 1953), 108–13. For a more recent and comprehensive overview of nonpublic schools including their origins see Otto F. Kraushaar, *American Nonpublic Schools: Patterns of Diversity* (Baltimore, Md.: Johns Hopkins University Press, 1972).
3. Diane B. Gertler, "Statistics of Nonpublic Schools," *School Life* 46 (October 1963): 31.
4. Martha M. McCarthy *A Delicate Balance: Church, State, and the Schools* (Bloomington, Ind.: Phi Delta Kappan Educational Foundation, 1983), ch. 7.

to make this determination. The celebrated case of *Pierce* v. *Society of the Sisters* removed all doubt about the right of parents to send their children to nonpublic schools.[5] In this case, the United States Supreme Court held that an Oregon statute, the Compulsory Education Act of 1922 requiring all children to attend public schools, to be in violation of the Fourteenth Amendment. A private military school joined the Society of the Sisters in bringing the suit, and thus the Supreme Court's declaration upheld the existence of not only sectarian or religious schools but nonsectarian private schools as well.

A democracy does not need a single system of public schools in order to survive. On the contrary, alternatives are desirable, and parents should have the opportunity to survey a range of educational opportunities for their children and the right to select the type of school which in their view offers the best education. Competition, to the extent that it exists, is desirable and contributes to the dynamism we have grown to cherish. A public school system is obligated to be responsive to the society which sponsors it, and a nonpublic school is prized precisely because it need not be responsive to the total society but chiefly to that constituency which supports it. The nonpublic school is prized precisely because it need not be responsive to the stereotype. It can innovate, define goals which may not be the same as other schools, specialize, and discriminate within legal limits in its choice of clients.[6]

Controls on Nonpublic Schools

Nonpublic schools for a time operated in a relatively free environment in this country. There was only limited competition from public schools and few controls were imposed by public authorities. Now, however, nonpublic schools function within a body of constitutional, statutory, and case law, both federal and state, which to some extent limits them. Some states regulate or govern nonpublic schools much more rigorously than do others, as we will see.

There are several state and local public agencies which "regulate" nonpublic schools. Nonpublic schools must abide by public controls which apply to buildings, safety, zoning, and public health. In those instances where the states exercise little or no jurisdiction over nonpublic schools, county or municipal officials have actually closed down nonpublic schools that have failed to meet fire safety codes or health standards.

The most far-reaching constraints are applied by the states. It is generally accepted that the states have the right, within reason, to regulate nonpublic education. These regulatory rights include inspection for the purpose of determining the adequacy of the curriculum and teaching staffs, the enforcement of compulsory attendance laws, and the requirement that students fulfill certain state expectations especially those for good citizenship. Although there is agreement on the regulatory rights of the states on these matters, there are widespread differences among the states in the stipulation and enforcement of those rights.

To some these restrictions are unnecessarily severe. Erickson, a strong advocate of nonpublic educational alternatives argues that, "Perhaps educational reform would come more quickly if public and private agencies were encouraged to specialize on

---

5. *Pierce* v. *Society of the Sisters*, 268 U.S. 510 (1925).
6. For a summary of recent issues in regulation see, Patricia M. Lines, "State Regulation of Private Education," *Phi Delta Kappan* 64 (October 1982): 119–23.

particular aspects of education, unburdened by the total welter of often contradictory custodial, instructional, and 'character building' goals that most schools are asked to achieve simultaneously." [7]

Nonpublic School Statistics

Complete, accurate data on private schools are nonexistent. Enrollment figures are at best rough approximations because not all of the states compile private school enrollment statistics. Past, present, and projected future enrollments of public and private schools are provided in table 17.1.

The enrollment growth patterns, in both public and private schools, that marked the twentieth century shifted to decline during the 1970s. There were nearly six million fewer public school students in 1980 than there were in 1971. Private enrollments declined 100,000 for the same period but the nature of private school enrollment experience was different from the public schools. Although the overall trend for private schools over the ten year period was downward, there were slight increases in the last half of the decade. Public schools did not experience this enrollment increase.

The ratio of private school to public school enrollments is not uniform over the United States. Higher percentages of private school enrollment occur where there are concentrated populations of Catholics or long traditions of independent school attendance among many families. It is evident from table 17.2 that large numbers of private school students are found in New England, the Mideast, the Great Lakes, and Plains regions. In ten states, 1979–80 private enrollments totalled more than 15 percent of total enrollments. Enrollment in those states (Delaware, Hawaii, Illinois, Louisiana, New Jersey, New York, Pennsylvania, Rhode Island, Wisconsin, and the District of Columbia) contrasts sharply with states such as Idaho, Utah, and Oklahoma which have nonpublic enrollments of less than 3 percent.[8]

In 1980–81, there were 21,000 nonpublic schools in operation (see table 17.3). Of these 77 percent were church-related; 23 percent had no religious affiliation. The largest number of church-related secondary schools (46.0 percent) were affiliated with the Roman Catholic Church. Catholic high schools range from small single-purpose schools to large multicurricular institutions. The second largest group of church-related secondary schools was Lutheran, followed by the schools of the Seventh Day Adventists.[9] The distributions of church-related schools by denomination and their enrollments are included in table 17.4.

The slight increase in enrollments in nonpublic schools has been paralleled by an increase in the number of nonpublic school teachers. During the 1970–71 school year there were 216,825 nonpublic school teachers. By 1980–81 that number was 281,000.[10] The plateau and decline in nonpublic enrollments which began in 1967 will

7. Donald A. Erickson, "Legal Impediments to Private Educational Options" in *The Courts and Education* Seventy-seventh Yearbook of the National Society for the Study of Education, part 1, ed. Clifford P. Hooker (Chicago: University of Chicago Press, 1978), 116–39. See also Helen M. Jellison, ed., *State and Federal Laws Relating to Non Public Schools* (Washington, D.C.: U.S. Department of Health, Education, and Welfare 1975).
8. National Center for Education Statistics, *The Condition of Education, 1983 Edition* (Washington D.C.: U.S. Department of Education, Office of Educational Research & Improvement, 1983), 17.
9. *Digest of Education Statistics 1982*, (Washington, D.C.: National Center for Education Statistics, 1982), 48.
10. Ibid., 48.

TABLE 17.1

Enrollment in regular elementary and secondary day schools, by control and organizational level of institution: 50 States and D.C., fall 1970 to 1990 (in thousands of pupils)

Year (fall)	Total public and private			Public			Private		
	K-12	Elementary	Secondary	K-12	Elementary	Secondary	K-12	Elementary	Secondary
1970.......	51,272	31,553	19,719	45,909	27,501	18,408	5,363	4,052	1,311
1971.......	51,281	31,588	19,693	46,081	27,688	18,393	5200[1]	3,900	1,300
1972.......	50,744	31,023	19,721	45,744	27,323	18,421	5,000[1]	3,700	1,300
1973.......	50,430	30,135	20,295	45,429	26,435	18,995	5,000[1]	3,700	1,300
1974.......	50,053	30,082	19,971	45,053	26,382	18,671	5,000[1]	3,700	1,300
1975.......	49,791	29,340	20,451	44,791	25,640	19,151	5,000[1]	3,700	1,300
1976.......	49,484	29,255	20,229	44,317	25,430	18,887	5,167	3,825	1,342
1977.......	48,716	28,751	19,966	43,577	24,954	18,623	5,140	3,797	1,343
1978.......	47,636	28,749	18,887	42,550	25,017	17,534	5,085	3,732	1,353
1979.......	46,679	28,551	18,128	41,579	24,851	16,728	5,100[1]	3,700	1,400
1980.......	46,095[2]	27,987	18,108	40,995	24,287	16,708	5,100[1]	3,700	1,400
				Projected[3]					
1981.......	45,189	27,555	17,634	40,189	23,955	16,234	5,000	3,600	1,400
1982.......	44,544	27,286	17,258	39,544	23,686	15,858	5,000	3,600	1,400
1983.......	44,165	27,106	17,059	39,165	23,506	15,659	5,000	3,600	1,400
1984.......	44,039	27,113	16,926	39,039	23,513	15,526	5,000	3,600	1,400
1985.......	44,166	27,338	16,828	39,166	23,733	15,428	5,000	3,600	1,400
1986.......	44,556	27,936	16,620	39,456	24,236	15,220	5,100	3,700	1,400
1987.......	45,004	28,660	16,344	39,804	24,860	14,944	5,200	3,800	1,400
1988.......	45,358	29,389	15,969	40,158	25,589	14,569	5,200	3,800	1,400
1989.......	45,905	30,205	15,700	40,605	26,365	14,300	5,300	3,900	1,400
1990.......	46,667	31,022	15,645	41,267	27,022	14,245	5,400	4,000	1,400

1. Estimated.
2. Preliminary, private figures rounded to nearest 100,000.
3. For methodological details, see Volume II of *Projections of Education Statistics to 1990–91*.

NOTE: Because of rounding, details may not add to totals.

SOURCE: U.S. Department of Education, National Center for Education Statistics publications: (1) *Statistics of Public Elementary and Secondary Day Schools;* (2) Bulletin: *Selected Public and Private Elementary and Secondary Education Statistics,* October 23, 1979; (3) *Statistics of Nonpublic Elementary and Secondary School;* and (4) unpublished NCES tabulations.

SOURCE: This table is drawn from *Projections of Education Statistics to 1990–91, Vol. I: Analytical Report,* (Washington, D.C.: National Center for Education Statistics, 1982), 35.

TABLE 17.2

Comparison of Public and Private School Enrollments by Geographic Region 1978–79 and 1970–71 (in thousands of pupils)

Region	Total Public and Private		Private		Percentage of Total	
	(1978–79)	(1970–71)	(1978–79)	(1970–71)	(1978–79)	(1970–71)
North Atlantic (New England and Mideast)	10,828	13,111	1,665	2,075	6.5	15.8
Great Lakes and Plains	11,777	14,697	1,380	1,734	8.5	11.8
Southeast	10,620	10,753	914	656	11.6	6.1
Far West, Rocky Mountains and Southwest	12,276	12,483	925	677	13.2	5.4
Total 50 States and Washington, D.C.	45,502	51,046	4,885	5,143	9.3	10.0

SOURCES: U.S. Department of Education, National Center for Educational Statistics, *A Comparison of Selected Characteristics of Private and Public Schools*, 1982, *Digest of Education Statistics*, 1982, and *The Condition of Education*, 1983 Edition, 16.

TABLE 17.3

Number of Schools and Enrollments by Type of Control, 1980–81

		Public		Private	
	Total	Number	Percent	Number	Percent
Schools	107,199	86,199	80.3	21,000	19.6
Enrollments	45,945,848	40,984,093	89.2	4,961,755	10.8

SOURCES: U.S. Department of Education, National Center for Education Statistics, *A Comparison of Selected Characteristics of Private and Public Schools*, 1982, *Digest of Education Statistics*, 1982, Washington, D.C.: National Center for Educational Statistics, 1982, p. 59, and U.S. Department of Education, National Center for Education Statistics, preliminary data from the survey of private elementary and secondary schools, 1980–81.

TABLE 17.4

Private School Statistics by Affiliation with Selected Church Denomination: U.S., 1978–79

	Enrollment	Percent Change Since 1977
1. Roman Catholic Schools	3,269,761	−3.3
2. Lutheran Schools	217,406	2.3
3. Seventh Day Adventist Schools	148,157	34.1
4. Calvinist Schools (National Union of Christian Schools)	47,269	8.0
5. Jewish Day Schools	101,758	5.2
6. Episcopal	76,452	2.9
7. Friends (Quaker) Schools	14,611	1.3
8. Eastern Orthodox Schools	2,682	0.9
9. Other affiliations*	231,317	5.4
10. Non-affiliated	746,730	−1.5

*includes schools affiliated with Amish, Christian, Mennonite, and other denominations

SOURCE: *Private Schools in American Education*, Washington, D.C.: National Center for Educational Statistics, 1981, p. 17.

be reflected naturally in the numbers and distribution of persons teaching in nonpublic schools in the future. The changing enrollment patterns within the several types of nonpublic schools described in the following section, have implications for many public school districts.

Types of Nonpublic Schools

To avoid arguments over definitions of nonpublic schools, we will use the definition of the U.S. Office of Education.

> *Non-public schools* are schools supported by means other than public taxation or public grants. They include parochial schools, privately operated non-sectarian schools (profit-making or nonprofit); privately operated schools for the deaf, blind, mentally retarded, or students with other types of physical or mental exceptionality, for whom education equivalent to that of the public elementary or secondary schools is provided; private college preparatory schools or military academies; secondary level "finishing"

schools; laboratory schools of private colleges and universities; and evening schools offering the equivalent of a high school education.[11]

The principal distinction of one of support and, with support, operational control.[12] The examples of nonpublic schools above are full-time day schools. Not included are the many schools which offer part-time special training in such areas as reading, foreign language, business, vocations, charm, art, and music. Many American youngsters, particularly from middle-class families, who are enrolled during the day in full-time public or nonpublic schools, supplement their day school work with evening and Saturday instruction in these other private schools. No one knows exactly how much part-time, nonpublic education is available in the nation. Nonpublic schools are most often divided into two groups—sectarian and nonsectarian—and these classifications are sometimes further divided.

Sectarian Schools

Among the array of sectarian schools, systems of school control vary. Data are quite unreliable on the numbers of schools that are maintained and controlled by local churches that have no denominational or other central organizational connection. Thus we know practically nothing about how these schools are governed. A distinction is frequently made between the parochial type and the parent-society type of school. The parochial group outnumbers the parent-society group. In the parochial school, control is tied directly to the local church, parish, or diocese whereas the control of parent-society schools remains in the hands of a group of parents who may be affiliated with one or more churches.

Many Roman Catholic elementary and secondary schools and most elementary Lutheran schools are of the parochial type. Others in this classification are most of the schools maintained by the Seventh-day Adventists, Jewish schools, all the Los Angeles Baptist City Mission Society schools, and a large number of the schools affiliated with the National Association of Christian Schools. Parent-society schools include schools in the National Union of Christian Schools of the Christian Reformed Church, New England Association of Christian Schools, and many Mennonite schools.

The precise patterns of church-related school control are difficult to discern. The two classifications above are crude for within each class there are variations. Roman Catholic schools, classed as parochial above, are themselves mixed in terms of control because of their close linkages to local parishes or orders. Catholic schools are all, theoretically, under the direction of the Ordinary (cardinal, archi-bishop, or bishop) of the diocese, according to the limits set by canon law.[13] But within dioceses there are private Catholic schools operated by religious orders, and the lines of authority between order and diocesan school officials frequently are not clear.[14] The distribution of power and control within sectarian schools is extremely varied. Historically, headmasters and headmistresses were powerful, controlled their schools, and seldom sought advice and counsel from boards, faculties, students, or parents. More recently, the patterns of control have shifted somewhat. In some cases, boards are powerful and faculties influential. Parent and student involvement in governance occurs and

11. Diane B. Gertler and Leah W. Ramsey, *Non-public Secondary Schools: A Directory, 1960–61* (Washington, D.C.: Government Printing Office, 1963), 1.
12. Ibid.
13. Raymond F. McCoy, *American School Administration* (New York: McGraw-Hill, 1961), 112–13.
14. Edward B. Smith, S. J., "Policy Making in Jesuit High Schools" (Ph.D. diss., University of Chicago, 1962).

decision making is a shared responsibility which is a distinct break with the past.[15] We now turn to a brief examination of three systems of sectarian schools.

Catholic Schools. A large majority, 63.4 percent, of all nonpublic school students were enrolled in Catholic schools in 1980–81, a decrease from the 1975–76 figure of 75.9 percent.[16] The numbers of students enrolled, schools, and teachers increased steadily through 1964. In 1965–66, 80.7 percent of all secondary school students in nonpublic schools were in Catholic high schools; an even higher percentage (88.6) of the total nonpublic elementary school population attended Catholic elementary schools. Catholic elementary school enrollment increased 171 percent during the decade of the 1950s, making it necessary for Catholics to nearly double the number of teachers and classrooms to keep pace. Catholic enrollments continued to increase through 1964 when total Catholic school enrollment reached more than 5,600,000. The 1964 total represented 12 percent of all school enrollments in the United States but after that year Catholic school enrollments began to decline. By 1967 there were 5,250,000 pupils enrolled in Catholic schools, representing 10.7 percent of all enrollments.[17] By the 1980–81 school year, the number of students had declined to 3,106,000. Such decreases have substantial policy implications as we will see.

The current state of the Catholic schools can be placed in sharper perspective by taking a look at their past. The number of Catholics in America prior to 1776 was small and rather insignificant, and the status of the teaching orders was precarious.[18] Catholic schools in the colonial period did not form a "system" of schools, and they persisted primarily through the zeal of the orders that sponsored them. No centralized support or even interest existed at this time; Catholic immigration later spurred the development of a system of Catholic schools. In 1884 the bishops and archbishops of the Third Plenary Council of Baltimore ordered that by 1886 parochial schools were to be constructed and maintained near all the Catholic churches of the United States.[19] The bishops stipulated clearly the duty of every pastor to erect and develop a school and to apprise parents of the obligations to send their children to Catholic schools. The duties of Catholic parents were dramatically reiterated in the 1929 Encyclical of Pope Pius XI when it was stated that the only acceptable education was "Catholic education in Catholic schools for all Catholic youth."[20]

The prospect for reversing the downward trend in Catholic schools is dependent on a number of factors, not the least of which may be the availability of public support. The costs of Catholic schools have grown enormously, and considerable debate has been generated among Catholic leaders as to the future of Catholic schools in America. Obviously policy decisions about Catholic schools made within the Roman Catholic Church have rather sharp implications for public schools. Some of these are explored later.

The diocese is an important unit in Catholic educational control, and in some respects the diocese resembles the local school district. A bishop of a diocese is the chief teacher of the diocese, and he is ultimately responsible for all diocesan schools

15. Otto F. Kraushaar, *American Nonpublic Schools* Baltimore, Md.: Johns Hopkins University Press, 1972).
16. *Digest,* 48.
17. Ibid., 50.
18. James A. Burns, *The Catholic School System in the United States* (New York: Benziger Brothers, 1908), 109.
19. Neil G. McCluskey, S. J., *Catholic Viewpoint on Education* (Garden City, N.Y.: Doubleday, 1962), 18.
20. *Christian Education of Youth,* 1929, official text published by the National Catholic Welfare Council (Washington, D.C., 1930).

in his jurisdiction and has, to some extent, control over the Catholic order schools located in his diocese. At the parish level the local pastor has traditionally been the responsible administrator of the parochial school in his parish.

The growing problems of school administration within the dioceses have led to the structural changes within many diocesan school adminstrations, including the creation of a diocesan superintendent of schools and a diocesan school board. In a 1981 survey of 167 dioceses conducted by the National Catholic Educational Association, there were 130 diocesan boards of education reported. All those boards function in accord with the canonical structure with authority coming from the bishop.[21] As McCoy points out, each of these boards is the creation of the diocesan bishop and they are no more or less than what he chooses to make of them.[22] Another change is the expansion of lay involvement in parochial education which McCluskey describes as revolutionary.[23]

In contrast to public schools, where the duties and responsibilities of school boards, and to a lesser extent school superintendents, are prescribed by law, canon law makes no mention of such administrative creations. The influence of both the diocesan superintendents and diocesan boards has mushroomed as Catholic schools struggle with enormous problems. Administrative problems have been magnified because roles and responsibilities are not clearly defined and differentiated. However, the roles of the diocesan school officials are being clarified as the dioceses gain more experience with the new administrative and policy structures.

Beyond the problems associated with ambiguous roles, finances present another difficult issue confronting diocesan school officials. Diocesan superintendents have little or no control over school finances. In fact, they often have had little knowledge of local parish school budgets and very limited resources for the operation of the diocesan school offices. Sources of support for the diocesan superintendent's activities come from levies on parish elementary schools, special collections, and in some cases, income from the sale of textbooks, courses of study, or workbooks.

Roman Catholic schools have encountered teacher problems that are not easily solved. The supply of religious teachers—nuns, priests, and brothers—has not been adequate, forcing Catholic administrators to employ lay teachers. In 1979 there were about 18,500 more elementary lay teachers than in 1969, and approximately 11,500 more secondary lay teachers; the elementary staff was approximately one-third religious and two-thirds lay. This shift from religious to lay teachers seemingly has not affected the essential character of the Catholic school. School boards, parents, and lay teachers continue to maintain the same conscientious concern exemplified by the religious community members who led the way and still hold key administrative positions.[24]

Lutheran Church, Missouri Synod. Several Lutheran denominations in addition to the Missouri Synod body sponsor nonpublic schools. Among these are the American Lutheran Church, Augustana Lutheran Church, Evangelical Lutheran Church, United Lutheran Church, Lutheran Joint Synod of Wisconsin and Other States, and the Nor-

---

21. The National Association of Boards of Education/NCEA, *The Flowering of Catholic Boardsmanship,* 9 (June 1981): 14.
22. McCoy, *American School Administration,* 113.
23. McCluskey, *Catholic Education Faces the Future,* 115.
24. *Catholic Schools in America 1978–1979* (Washington, D.C.: National Catholic Education Association, 1979), 18. ERIC ED168 215.

wegian Synod of the American Evangelical Lutheran Church. We have selected the Missouri Synod Schools for elaboration because they are the second largest group of sectarian schools in the nation.

The Missouri Synod stems from the religious family which predominated in northern Europe, the Lutheran Church. The Synod was organized in 1874 and had 12 parishes in five states. By 1959 the Synod had grown to more than 6000 congregations and a membership of over 2.5 million.[25] When the Synod was organized all of its parishes had schools, but this is not true today. In 1970–71 the Synod enrolled 163,386 students; by 1982–83 the enrollment had increased to 181,568. The total 1982 enrollment for all Lutheran schools (Missouri Synod, Wisconsin Evangelical Lutheran Synod, American Lutheran, Lutheran Church in America, Association of Evangelical Lutheran Church) in junior high, elementary, and pre-school was 258,405 and, for high schools, 22,681.[26]

The synod is organized into some thirty-four districts in the United States, with a Synod Parish Board of Education overseeing education in the districts. Each of the districts has its own officers, boards, commissions, and committees to administer the work within the district. One of the district boards is the Board or Committee of Parish Education, and the synod's role in education is to advise and serve the district board. The district boards of parish education promote and supervise the various agencies of Christian education such as day schools, Sunday schools, vacation bible schools, and other educational activities for children and adults. The Synod Board of Parish Education serves the district boards, the district boards serve the congregations within their geographical boundaries, and in most cases the congregations have parish boards of education.

The Missouri Synod has historically placed considerable power in its local congregations and allowed them considerable autonomy in local affairs. Thus the services of boards, counselors, and district superintendents, with respect to the schools, have been considered to be advisory and service-oriented for the most part. Beyond this function, the district boards and superintendents have been concerned with advancing, improving, and promoting Lutheran parochial schools. They have helped their schools meet the requirements imposed by the states on nonpublic schools and at the same time have watched for legislation that would be inimical to Lutheran schools.

The Missouri Synod enrollments have grown in recent decades; the elementary enrollment in fact has doubled since World War II. The greatest growth has been in the eastern, southeastern, and western parts of the United States. The enrollment in Lutheran high schools has also increased appreciably. Administrative roles appear to be more clearly delineated in the Missouri Synod districts than in the Catholic dioceses. Pressures exist, however, for more centralization of school control and supervision.

Jewish Schools. Jewish day schools have grown rapidly in the United States since World War II. In 1935 there were 4,600 students enrolled in 16 Jewish day schools in New York City and one in Baltimore. Nearly 102,000 students were attending such schools in 1978–79 and most of these students were from orthodox congregations.

Among the reasons cited for this phenomenal growth is the intense interest within

---

25. William A. Kranier, *Lutheran Schools* (St. Louis, Mo.: Board of Parish Education, The Lutheran Church, Missouri Synod, 1961), 5.
26. *Information Bulletin* (1982–83), No. 33982, (St. Louis, Mo.: Board for Parish Services, 1983), 7.

the Jewish community in the perpetuation of Jewish values.[27] Jews generally have not expressed the dissatisfaction with the public schools that members of other religious groups often have. Considerable emphasis is placed on Jewish studies in most Jewish day schools. Three or four hours per day are given to the Hebrew language and Jewish law and literature. The usual curriculum sometimes runs until 5:00 P.M., and in some instances students attend on Saturdays too.

Most schools have been operated on a community basis with supervision and support of a local responsibility. There is no central agency in charge of coordinating, organizing, or supervising Jewish day schools. In New York City some cooperation among schools is effected through the Jewish Education Committee of New York; outside of New York the National Society for Hebrew Day Schools has been instrumental in the founding of some schools.

Financial problems have plagued these schools as they have all schools. The shortage of dedicated Jewish teachers has been a problem as well. Because of money difficulties, few schools have been established away from urban centers. A very small percent of eligible Jewish children attend these schools and future enrollment trends are unclear. On the basis of post-World War II growth, however, and assuming the solid support of leaders in the Jewish community, there may well be continuing increases in the number of Jewish day schools and in enrollments as well.

Nonsectarian Schools

Several types of schools are included in this group—privately owned and operated kindergartens, elementary and secondary schools, academies, special schools for students with physical or mental deficiencies, laboratory schools associated with private colleges and universities, and evening schools which provide the equivalent of high school education.

Independent Schools. Many of the prominent, long-established independent schools are located in New England. Many of these have superb records of performance and are in fact national in terms of their drawing power, prestige, and influence. The headmasters and their faculties, like their schools, frequently are national leaders, giving expression to the values these select schools perpetuate. Larmee found many independent school staff members to be influential in the College Entrance Examination Board program as well as in national curriculum developments.[28] Andover, Punahou, St. Paul's, Groton, Lawrence, Choate, and Francis Parker are prominent private schools. Their contributions to the education of national leaders are well known. For instance, James B. Conant attended Roxbury Latin, Franklin D. Roosevelt attended Groton, and John F. Kennedy graduated from Choate.

The problems of finance, which plague most American schools, are present in the nonsectarian sector as well. Inflation and uncertainty regarding enrollments haunt trustees and headmasters annually. Costs of attending such schools increase each year causing parents to consider carefully their decisions to send children to nonpublic

---

27. One measure of the effect of Jewish education is the greater religious involvement of adults who have attended Jewish schools. For an important analysis of such effects see Harold S. Himmelfarb, "The Non-Linear Impact of Schooling: Comparing Different Types and Amounts of Jewish Education," *Sociology of Education* 42 (April 1977): 114–29.
28. Roy A. Larmee, "The Relationship Between Certain National Movements in Education and Selected Independent Secondary Schools" (Ph.D. diss., University of Chicago, 1962).

schools.[29] In 1978 Senator Daniel P. Moynihan (Dem.-N.Y.) cosponsored a bill which would allow taxpayers to take tax credits equal to 50 percent of their tuition and fee expenditures up to a maximum of $500. Since 1978, other tax credit proposals have been advanced by members of Congress as well as by President Reagan. Strong objections have been made to tax credits on constitutional grounds, specifically the First Amendment. Others have argued that the legislation would undermine public education and lead to further segregation of schools.

The high costs of attending nonsectarian schools have produced an image of snobbishness which may or may not be accurate. Independent school leaders argue that their student bodies are much more democratic than they were in the past. Even where only top students are admitted, they come from all income groups, races, religions, and parts of the country. High priorities are placed on academic achievement, but not to the complete exclusion of training in the social graces, physical education, the arts, and citizenship.

Despite the faculty resources available to many good independent schools, there is little evidence that they are demonstrably superior to those in good public schools. In general, the quality of independent school education is sufficiently high that states need not be concerned unduly about supervising them.

Kindergartens and Primary Schools. Nonpublic kindergartens are numerous in those sections of the country where public kindergartens are not provided. Even more universal are the nonpublic nursery schools and preschools which deal with three-, four-, and sometimes five-year olds. Supervision of such schools and the growing number of day-care centers is almost nonexistent in many cases. State departments of public instruction exercise only minimal supervision if any. State health agencies which oversee health and safety regulations are more prominent as are departments of welfare in looking after some aspects of preschool, day-care center, and nursery school operations. Such supervision is exercised under the police power of the state.

Some nonpublic school kindergartens have grown into full-blown private elementary schools. Teacher-entrepreneurs, having experienced success with kindergarten programs, have gradually added grades until their schools have become at least primary schools (K–3) and in some instances complete elementary schools. Parental satisfactions with kindergarten training have led apparently to pressures for extending the scope of these schools. Little data are available on the numbers of such schools and their enrollments.

Laboratory Schools. Several private colleges and universities have laboratory schools designed originally as first-rate experimental schools. Schools such as those associated at one time with Teachers College, Columbia University, and currently with the University of Chicago, have been looked upon as leading centers for educational research and experimentation. Laboratory schools in public and private university settings are not the potent forces they used to be. Innovations and research in other educational settings, public and nonpublic, have surpassed the contributions of most laboratory schools.[30]

29. Information regarding programs, tuition costs, fees, and other expenses of private day schools and residential institutions can be found in J. Kathryn Sargent, *The Handbook of Private Schools* (Boston: Porter Sargent, 1978).
30. William VanTil, *The Laboratory School: Its Rise and Fall?* (Terre Haute, Ind.: Indiana State University and Laboratory School Administrators Association, 1969), 14.

The laboratory schools' research and development function has been impaired in some cases because they have been expected to serve as student teaching centers; and their effectiveness as laboratory schools has been limited sometimes by parental resistance to experimentation. Many laboratory schools are much more like good prep schools than experimental centers. Despite attempts to be selective in clientele and to enroll a heterogeneous student body, some laboratory schools have acquiesced to pressures to admit children of university faculty members and children of their friends. The student bodies then are often homogeneous, high-ability groups.

The Alternative School Movement

The late 1960s saw a variety of alternative schools come into being. Some were openly nonsectarian protest schools; they were the product of adult and sometimes student frustrations. They carried many labels: freedom schools, storefront schools, black power schools, free schools, and street academies.[31] Their sponsorship was sometimes vague, feeble, and temporary. In other cases, where groups such as the Urban League sponsored street academies, the backing was clear, strong, and continuing. Disenchantment with the "system" was not confined to the United States. Canada too experienced a "free school" movement; in the late 1960s forty-five such enterprises were noted.[32]

Although the overt catalysts which triggered the harsh criticisms of public schools were proximate political and social issues like the Vietnam war and racial injustice, the seeds of disaffection with American education had been sown some time prior to the protests of the mid and late 1960s. Postman and Weingartner trace the genesis of one stream of indictments back to the attacks which had been launched for decades against John Dewey's progressive education for its alleged "gooey, precious, romantic philosophy which stressed permissiveness and life adjustment."[33] These long-standing attacks on the schools for their alleged failure to stress intellectual development and rigorous thinking crested in the late 1950s and 1960s after the Russian launching of Sputnik I. Much of this criticism centered on the need to eliminate "frills" from the curriculum; it was argued that disciplined scientists and highly trained technicians were needed to meet the Soviet challenge.

By the mid 1960s a much larger number of critics entered the fray with a different set of criticisms. Social critics like Paul Goodman, Edgar Friedenberg, and Jules Henry pointed out that, despite the much hearalded curriculum reform movement, the schools were in deep trouble with dropout rates rising among all social classes. They noted the gap between "the official rhetoric about the purposes of school (for example, to widen the horizons of students) and the real purposes of school, and they found it enormous."[34]

A few early critics including teacher-writers such as John Holt triggered between 1965 and 1970 a deluge of assaults against the schools as repressive institutions which destroyed children's spontaneity and natural love of learning. Hundreds of books and

31. Mario D. Fantini, "Alternatives for Urban School Systems," *Harvard Educational Review* 38 (Winter 1968): 160–75.
32. John C. Croft and Arnold J. Falusi, "Superschool: A Canadian 'Free School' Experiment," *Education and Urban Society* 1 (August 1969): 441–51.
33. Neil Postman and Charles Weingartner, *How to Recognize a Good School* (Bloomington, Ind.: Phi Delta Kappa Educational Foundation, 1973), 7.
34. Ibid., 11.

articles quickly appeared. These critics included practicing teachers like Jonathan Kozol, Herbert Kohl, and James Hernton; writers and journalists like Charles Silberman, George Leonard, Nat Hentoff, and George Dennison; and social scientists like Marilyn Gittell, David Rogers and Frank Reissman.[35] Within a very few years a large network of organizations and publications sprouted up that assaulted the conventions of traditional schooling in the United States.

In 1971 the New Schools Directory Project listed 346 non-tax supported alternative schools. By 1980 that number had increased to 504, with enrollments of approximately 40,000 students. Forty-seven states had at least one such school.[36]

Postman and Weingartner contend that sometime around 1970 the "romantic phase" of criticism of the public schools came to an end.[37] Some of the critics, who protested against the processes of schooling more than its basic structure, became frustrated with the system's incapacity to change. Others who were not basically educators moved into other activities. The remaining "romantics", who believed that schools had the potential to function humanely if governance procedures were restructured and democratized, faced a new wave of critics who were almost totally disillusioned with the schools. This development, called "Panic Phase II" by Postman and Weingartner, represented "the second coming of the idea that our schools are a betrayal and an abomination."[38] Interestingly, this assault came from not the political right which had launched earlier attacks on education, but from the political left.

Ivan Illich was the prime exponent of the point of view that the schools were not salvageable. The "romantic" critics, although harsh in their indictments of education, at least believed that there was some hope for reform. Illich, however, in his *Deschooling Society* called for the total elimination of schools and urged "replacing them with an informal, noncompulsory network of educational resources."[39]

Is this trend another faddish, evanescent educational innovation influencing only a tiny portion of American youth or will the movement lead to major revisions in the American school system which will affect substantial numbers of young people?

The ferment concerning schools continued through the 1970s and early 1980s. Marilyn Ferguson, a newcomer to the ranks of educational critics, noted in 1980 that "innovations in education have crisscrossed the sky like Roman candles, and most sputtered quickly out, leaving only the smell of enchantment in the air."[40] The cacophany of strident voices was joined by some of the nation's most respected educational leaders who called for improvements in the system which in many cases they had helped to shape. Ralph Tyler wrote of reconstructing the total educational system, specifying the responsibilities of the school as well as those of other partners in the educational process.[41] He noted too, however, that a revolution in the total educational system was not possible nor even desirable given the destructive side effects of revolution and the tremendous redirection of energy required.[42] Lawrence Cremin

35. Ibid., 12–13.
36. These data provided directly by the National Center for Education Statistics, 400 Maryland Avenue, S.W., Washington, D.C., 20202, December, 1983.
37. Postman and Weingartner, *How to Recognize a Good School*, 14.
38. Ibid.
39. Ivan Illich, *Deschooling Society* (New York: Harper & Row, 1971).
40. Marilyn Ferguson, *The Aquarian Conspiracy* (Los Angeles: J. P. Tarcher, 1980), 286.
41. Ralph W. Tyler, "The Total Educational Environment," in *Education for Responsible Citizenship*, ed. Louis Rubin (New York: McGraw-Hill, 1977), 15–25.
42. Ralph W. Tyler, "Dynamic Response in a Time of Decline," Phi Delta Kappan 63 (June 1982): 655–58.

called for fresh debate of the means and ends of education as a step toward the restoration of public confidence and commitment.[43] Cremin, while urging reconsideration of the specific aims and content of education, emphasized the contribution of American education to the advancement of liberty, equality, and fraternity.[44]

Status of Alternatives Within Public Schools

What, then, is the status of alternatives within the public schools which are attended by almost 90 percent of the nation's children? What have been the reactions of the professional educators whose work has been subjected to such scathing criticisms?

Cities like Berkeley, Philadelphia, and Minneapolis were pioneers in alternative education by developing 50 alternative learning environments at the secondary school level. These options were directed at the unique educational needs of individual students and offered a wide range of alternatives such as open classrooms, mini-schools, and work-study programs.[45] The Berkeley and Minneapolis public schools developed alternatives on a systemwide basis. Both school districts received substantial support from the federally funded Experimental Schools Program.

The Berkeley Unified School District created some 23 alternative schools which fell into the four broad patterns of multiculture schools, community schools, structured skills training schools, and schools without walls.[46] Thirty percent of Berkeley's parents selected alternative schools for their children. The Minneapolis Public Schools implemented a regional Southeast Alternatives Program which enabled elementary students to attend either a contemporary school, a continuous progress school, an open school, or a free school.

The swing of the political pendulum away from the social activism and institutional experimentation of the 1960s, however, has been of great concern to advocates of alternative education. Change inevitably engenders conflict which in turn produces political confrontation. Fantini enumerates some basic ground rules which he feels are not only good politics but which also maximize the chances for institutionalizing the philosophy and concepts of the alternative school movement:

1. Alternatives are not superimposed, but are a matter of choice for all participants-teachers, parents, and students.
2. Alternatives are viewed as another way of providing education alongside the existing pattern, which continues to be legitimate. They are different from special programs for dropouts, unwed mothers, and so forth.
3. They do not practice exclusivity.
4. They do not make exaggerated claims of accomplishments that may be deceptive in the long run.
5. They are aimed at a broad, common set of unlimited educational objectives. Alternative public schools are responsible to the public for comprehensive,

---

43. Lawrence A. Cremin, *Public Education* (New York: Basic, 1976), 96.
44. Lawrence A. Cremin, *Traditions in American Education* (New York: Basic 1977), 127–28.
45. See *Secondary School Alternative Programs: January 1973* (Philadelphia, Pa.: Board of Education, Alternative Programs Office, 1973).
46. For an analysis of the Berkeley program see Sherwood Davidson Kohn, "Getting Attention in California," *National Elementary Principal* 52 (April 1973): 90–93. Further evaluation of the Berkeley experimental schools appears in *Education R & D and the Case of Berkeley's Experimental Schools* (Washington, D.C.: National Institute of Education, 1976).

cognitive, and affective goals that cannot be compromised; these include basic skills, learning-to-learn skills, talent development, socialization of basic societal roles (citizen, consumer, worker), and self-concept development.

6. They do not cost more money than existing per student expenditures.[47]

Despite some growth in the alternative school movement in the 1970s, it was not without its casualties. Ravitch reported that the Experimental Schools Program of the Nixon administration which cost $55 million essentially failed. She cited the Berkeley experience as partial evidence. Only one of the 24 alternative schools in the Berkeley district survived even with a $5 million infusion of federal dollars.[48]

Alternative schools, however, were given a boost early in 1974 when the influential North Central Association of College and Secondary Schools after three years of discussion adopted standards for formally accrediting them. The Southern Association of Colleges and Schools, another major regional agency, has also adopted procedures, but not standards, for accrediting alternative schools.[49]

Alternative schools have also played a role in school desegregation in many cases. Survey data, in the early 1980s from the U.S. Department of Education confirmed the value of magnet schools for school desegregation.[50] Early in 1984 desegregation plans constructed around magnet school concepts were approved in courts in Ohio and California. Milwaukee, Houston, St. Louis, Dallas, Cincinnati, and Boston are among the cities that have emphasized educational options as a primary mechanism for achieving school desegregation. The Dallas Independent School District developed several magnet high schools, early childhood education centers, academies, and vanguard schools as part of their court-ordered remedy plan. The names of some of the Dallas schools tell the story: Health Professions High School, Transportation Institute, Sidney Lanier Center for Expressive Arts, Mark Twain Fundamental School, and the Business and Management Center. The Dallas citizens were extensively involved in the development of options, and many patrons of the school district were dismayed when the court of appeals in the summer of 1978 found the remedy plan inadequate and directed the Dallas Independent School District to prepare a more comprehensive approach to school desegregation.

Raywid surveyed public secondary alternative schools in 1982. Her work was a part of the Project on Alternatives in Education (PAE), supported in part by the National Institute of Education. She identified more than 2,500 alternative public secondary schools, but estimated that there may be two to four times that many in existence. Two-thirds of them have 200 students or less. Most such schools are in cities with some population growth occurring in suburban districts.[51]

The PAE-sponsored survey yielded interesting findings including the fact that per student costs in 62 percent of the responding schools are the same or less than those at other schools. Morale was found to be extremely high and the quality of

---

47. Mario Fantini, "The What, Why, and Where of the Alternatives Movement", *The National Elementary Principal* 52 (April 1973): 17.

48. Diane Ravitch, *The Troubled Crusade* (New York: Basic, 1983), 258–59.

49. "North Central Decides to Accredit Optional Schools," *Education U.S.A.*, (Washington, D.C.: National School Public Relations Association, April 8, 1974): 177.

50. For a description of the Dallas options see Daniel U. Levine and Nolan Estes, "Desegregation and Educational Reconstruction in the Dallas Public Schools," *Phi Delta Kappan* 59 (November 1977): 163–67, 221.

51. Mary Anne Raywid, "Schools of Choice: Their Current Nature and Prospects," *Phi Delta Kappan* 64 (June 1983): 684–88.

teacher/student interaction to be unusually fine. Attendance is excellent and faculty work hard in meeting high expectations which students have for them. Graduates succeed as well or better in college than those who attended traditional public secondary schools.[52]

Raywid believes that schools of choice are gaining ground and that the movement which began in the 1960s is alive and well. Furthermore, the trend toward tougher standards that developed in the early 1980s has not diminished respect for alternative programs.[53] Erickson, who studied climates of private schools and the two types of public schools, traditional and alternative, found substantial differences between the social climates of private schools and traditional public schools, but fewer differences between private schools and public alternative schools.[54] Erickson urged that more attention be given to alternative program development within public systems. He described the movement as the "privatization" of the public schools.[55]

National Calls for Reform

Prestigious groups began to call for reform in the early 1970s. As noted earlier, reports of such bodies were joined by a spate of critical documents in 1983 including *A Nation at Risk: The Imperative for Educational Reform,* the work of the National Commission on Excellence in Education.[56] Most of these documents had implications for alternative schools.

In 1973 a report of national significance called for reducing age segregation and for eliminating the insulation of young people from adults and the world of work.[57] The National Commission on the Reform of Secondary Education, established by the Charles F. Kettering Foundation and chaired by B. Frank Brown, made a series of recommendations which encouraged alternative routes to high school completion and the funding by local school boards of acceptable alternatives to the comprehensive high school:

> A wide variety of paths leading to completion of requirements for graduation from high school should be made available to all students. Individual students must be encouraged to assume major responsibility for the determination of their educational goals, the development of the learning activities needed to achieve those goals, and the appraisal of their progress.[58]

The Commission even made the rather radical recommendation that because of the earlier maturity of contemporary adolescents the states should reduce the formal age to leave school to fourteen.[59]

The report of the Panel on Youth of the President's Science Advisory Committee

52. Ibid., 686–87.
53. Ibid., 688.
54. Donald A. Erickson et al., *The British Columbia Story: Antecedents and Consequences of Aid to Private Schools* (Los Angeles: Institute for the Study of Private Schools, 1982), ch. 15.
55. Ibid.
56. See National Commission on Excellence in Education, *A Nation At Risk: The Imperative for Educational Reform* (Washington, D.C.: Government Printing Office, 1983).
57. *The Reform of Secondary Education: A Report to the Public and the Profession,* National Commission on the Reform of Secondary Education (New York: McGraw-Hill, 1973).
58. Ibid., 16–17.
59. Ibid., 21.

appeared in 1974.[60] It called for the design of educational environments and opportunities which would permit youth to become adults in all ways, not just intellectually:

> Our basic premise is that the school system, as now constituted, offers an incomplete context for the accomplishment of many important facets of maturation. The school has been well-designed to provide some kinds of training but, by virtue of that fact, is inherently ill-suited to fulfill other tasks essential to the creation of adults. Indeed, it would be unreasonable to expect any institution to suffice as the exclusive environment for youth. Signs of dissatisfaction abound, from parents and taxpayers who have an inarticulate sense that something is amiss, from school administrators and teachers who are experimenting with methods and objectives and forms that differ from those of the established system, and from youth themselves, many of whom are showing individual initiative in the search for extra-curricular experiences.[61]

The panel was critical of American secondary education and noted rising problems with the existing institutional arrangements whereby most students attend large neighborhood comprehensive schools. Some of these problems were: "little consumer choice, the heavy weight of bureaucracy and professional controls; the large size of single-grade student strata; segregation by class, race, and ethnicity; overloading of institutional capacity by an excess of expectations and functions; and the institutional blandness that can follow from ambiguous purpose and amorphous structure."[62]

The panel also suggested four routes of change which are very consonant with the underlying philosophy and goals of the alternative school movement. These strategies are (1) greater school diversity and student choice; (2) reductions in the size of large schools; (3) greater role diversity for youngsters in school; and (4) greater role diversity for the school as a multipurpose agency facilitating young people's participation in other social institutions and not as a single purpose agency responsible only for their intellectual development. In other words, schools should facilitate the overall growth of students as responsible participating citizens in the larger social setting.[63] The panel avowed the importance "in the design of environments for youth, to have an orchestration of such partial institutions, rather than the total and encompassing institution that the school has become."[64]

Willard Wirtz, chairman of the National Institute for Work and Learning and former U.S. secretary of labor, became one of the nation's most vocal spokespersons for improving employment-oriented education.[65] He deplored the growing numbers of young persons who were unemployable or underemployed. Wirtz urged closer cooperation between schools and their communities, especially local business and industry. Community Education-Work Councils were established in several cities and were devoted to solving the problems of education and unemployment. Several important proposals were offered by Wirtz including the establishment of more Community Education-Work Councils, increased career-work counseling, a break in the sequence of education to allow for one or two years of work experience, integration of education

60. *Youth Transition to Adulthood,* Report of the Panel on Youth of the President's Science Advisory Committee (Chicago: University of Chicago Press, 1974).
61. Ibid., 2.
62. Ibid, 151–52.
63. Ibid., 152–57.
64. Ibid., 148.
65. Willard Wirtz, *The Boundless Resource* (Washington, D.C.: New Republic 1975).

and work policy at state and federal levels, encouragement of adults who had not completed high school to do so at public expense.

The Paideia Proposal, authored by Mortimor Adler, appeared in 1982.[66] It was forerunner to more than twenty major analyses of American education, most of which included recommendations for change. *The Paideia Proposal* emphasized an academic education for everyone constructed on the belief that all children can learn, there are no unteachable children, education is lifelong, and schooling is only part of education. The proposed curriculum closely parallels the offerings of many private schools.

A Nation at Risk attracted considerable publicity when released in April, 1983.[67] This report was the product of a commission named by Terrel H. Bell, U.S. Secretary of Education. Weaknesses were identified in education at all levels and recommendations were made regarding curriculum, teachers, teaching, school organization, and school management. Suggestions were offered regarding specific steps to be taken to achieve improvements. John Goodlad published *A Place Called School* in 1983; his book contained a summary of nearly eight years of research.[68] *High School* authored by former U.S. Commissioner of Education Ernest Boyer, appeared at about the same time.[69] Boyer and Goodlad prepared their work from considerable data acquired from extensive observations in schools. Their reports, like many to follow, contained recommendations for reform including basic policy revisions such as school entering and leaving ages, length of school year, and larger blocks of time for instruction in specific subjects.

Public interest in education skyrocketed at local, state, and national levels as these reports were released. Education loomed large in the 1983–84 presidential campaign. Governors, especially in southern states, launched large-scale educational improvement efforts. In other states, legislatures, state boards of education, and professional organizations climbed on the band wagon. Since most of the public's attention was riveted on public schools, what are the implications for private schools and alternate schools within public systems?

Private schools may, in the short run, pick up additional students as parents' awareness of public school deficiencies are publicized. In the long run, the impact on private schools will depend upon improvements made in public schools. If, as a result of reforms at all levels of public education, public schools in fact become better institutions, they will be competitive with private schools. In time enrollments in nonpublic schools may dwindle. Many of the reports contained recommendations that teachers be better paid. Should this occur, private schools would then be placed in a more difficult competitive position, especially in regard to employing science and mathematics teachers. Many private schools have reputations for academic excellence; such schools may be challenged seriously by more and more public schools in the years to come.

Vouchers and Tuition Tax Credits

For two decades, the voucher concept has been debated within Congress and at the local school district level. Tuition tax credits for parents of children enrolled in non-

66. Mortimer Jerome Adler, *The Paideia Proposal* (New York: Macmillan, 1982).
67. National Commission on Excellence in Education, *A Nation at Risk*.
68. John I. Goodlad, *A Place Called School: Prospects for the Future* (St. Louis, Mo.: McGraw-Hill, 1983).
69. Ernest L. Boyer, *High School: A Report on Secondary Education in America* (New York: Harper & Row, 1983).

public schools, although equally controversial, have been prominent since the mid-1970s.[70]

As the 1970s gave way to the 1980s, discussions of educational options intensified. In Michigan voters rejected voucher proposals. In so doing, they reaffirmed, for the time being at least, belief in the traditional concept of public education. Had the voucher proposals been accepted, parents would have had several options for the education of their children. Public monies could have been expended for educational options other than those available through traditional public schools.

Several scholars at the University of California at Berkeley led the reexamination of the voucher concept. Some proposals regarding educational finance were developed essentially within the Childhood and Government Project supported by Ford Foundation and Carnegie Corporation grants. Sugarman advocated that more responsibility should be placed with parents and teachers for determining how significant portions of the school budget would be spent.[71] One of his proposals would establish a teacher-trustee plan. A teacher participating in the plan would be responsible for a trust account which would be available to enrich the educational experiences in her or his classroom.

A nontraditional approach to school desegregation, with some voucher overtone, was advanced by the Berkeley group. Apprehensive about the effectiveness of court-ordered school desegregation, Abrams, Coons, and Sugarman developed a financial incentives program to stimulate voluntary desegregation plans.[72] Basically, the incentives approach would involve the paying of financial bonuses to school districts that are able to develop high-quality integrated educational opportunities. The idea is similar to Wisconsin school desegregation legislation which provides incentives for urban students to attend school in suburban districts and for suburban youngsters to enroll in city schools. Families would be involved in the choices which would include nonpublic schools if they met the criterion of effective integrated education.

In 1978 Coons and Sugarman published a widely discussed book, *Education by Choice*.[73] The appearance of the volume stimulated discussions of the voucher concept among educators and lay people. The debate intensified regarding the issuance of vouchers to parents for the purchase of educational services in either the public or private marketplace. The basic voucher philosophy remains essentially the same as that first voiced by economist Milton Friedman in the 1950s. However, Coons and Sugarman added considerable detail to Friedman's initial concept particularly by dispelling many of the operational and procedural uncertainties that characterized early proposals.

Wise and Darling-Hammond argued that the sponsors of voucher proposals must demonstrate how public and private schools will achieve the state's goals efficiently and effectively when they said, "They must be prepared to explain how we will achieve public and private purposes in private settings with public money."[74] They

---

70. For a comprehensive review of the literature on vouchers (and tax credits) see "Vouchers and Tax Credits—A Special Issue," *Private School Monitor* 4 (Fall 1981).

71. Stephen D. Sugarman, "Education Reform at the Margins: Two Ideas, *Phi Delta Kappan* 59 (November 1977): 154–57.

72. Carol Abrams, John E. Coons, and Stephen D. Sugarman, "School Integration Through Carrots, Not Sticks," *Theory Into Practice* 17 (February 1978): 23–31.

73. John E. Coons and Stephen D. Sugarman, *Education by Choice* (Berkeley, Calif.: University of California Press, 1978).

74. Arthur E. Wise and Linda Darling-Hammond, "Educational Vouchers: Regulating Their Efficiency and Effectiveness," *Educational Researcher* 12 (November 1983): 9–18.

note that private control over the public interest has been avoided throughout our nation's history. Public funding of the private sector without public accountability is not likely to occur.[75] Tuition tax credits are quite another matter. This proposal has been before Congress for a decade or more. Opponents of tax credits breathed easier when the Packwood-Moynihan tuition tax credit bill was defeated in August, 1978.[76] The matter is far from resolved, however. The matter came before the Senate again in 1983 in the form of an amendment to other legislation but was defeated once more. Senator Daniel Moynihan doubts that it will go far in Congress but it is likely to be debated again in the 1980s. Moynihan forecasts reduced opposition during national election periods with an improved prospect for passage. Public school advocates see the measure as a substantial threat as do its opponents in Congress.[77]

In 1983 the U.S. Supreme Count approved a Minnesota tuition tax deducation law in a 5–4 decision. The Minnesota case, *Mueller vs. Allen,* allows parents to subtract from their taxable income up to $500.00 for grades K through 6, and $700.00 for grades 7 through 12, for tuition, textbooks, and transportation. It is important to note that the deduction is available to parents of public school children as well as those who have children attending private school.

Tax credit legislation was introduced in Illinois, Wyoming, and Minnesota in 1981.[78] A tax credit referendum was defeated in Washington D.C. in November of that year.[79] Similar initiatives are likely to take place at the federal and state levels where, if successful, they may lead to litigation on several points of constitutionality.[80]

Home Schooling

To this point, our attention has been directed to institutions—schools both public and private. Education however, takes place in many contexts including the home. In recent years, many people have converted to the practice of home schooling. Reliable estimates of the numbers of such parents do not exist, although the figure of 10,000 is cited.[81] Teaching children at home, under a variety of conditions was a prominent part of early American educational history. Distance and remoteness often forced parents to teach at home even if they would have preferred to have their children attend school.

Compulsory education laws were enacted to ensure the state's interest in an educated citizenry. The state's interest is now clashing with parent rights to determine the form and substance of their children's learning. In recent years both local school districts and states have searched for ways to accommodate both interests.[82] Divoky has indicated that many home schoolers are religious fundamentalists who are disappointed with the failure of public schools to teach moral and spiritual tenets.[83] Where

75. Ibid., 18.
76. Daniel Patrick Moynihan, "The Case for Tuition Tax Credits," *Phi Delta Kappan* 60 (December 1978): 274–76.
77. Ernest F. Hollings, "The Case Against Tuition Tax Credits," *Phi Delta Kappan* 60 (December 1978): 277–79.
78. Private School Monitor
79. "Tuition Tax Credits Pro and Con: A Case Study, Washington, D.C. Referendum," *ERS School Research Forum* (Arlington, Va.: Educational Research Service, 1982).
80. Donald N. Jensen, "Tuition Tax Credits: Has the Supreme Court Cleared the Way?" *IFG Policy Perspectives* (Stanford, Calif.: School of Education, Stanford University, June 1983): 12.
81. Martha McCarthy, *A Delicate Balance: Church, State, and the Schools,* 149.
82. Ibid., 52–54.
83. Diane Divoky, "The New Pioneers of the Home-Schooling Movement" *Phi Delta Kappan* 64 (February 1983): 395–98.

state law or local district policy prohibits home schooling, parents are using various subterfuges to teach their children at home. Some enroll their youngsters in private schools that will then allow the children to stay home. Others hire state certificated tutors or acquire state teacher certification themselves.[84]

Attitudes of educators toward home schooling are mixed. Some local districts have adopted a friendly, facilitative posture toward the phenomenon; others are hostile. Of major concern to public school administrators is loss of state aid when students fail to enroll and/or attend their schools. John Holt, a strong advocate for home schooling, urges school superintendents to abandon their opposition and develop local policies that will permit both home schooling parents and school districts to benefit.[85] This can be achieved by redefining attendance to include attendance at home.

Home schooling may grow moderately in the immediate future although a few observers believe it will become widespread or become a parental option which will threaten public or private schools. Home tutoring programs, on the other hand, may assume more acceptance since they are supplements to the offerings of public and private schools.[86]

Summary and Future Prospects

The future of alternative schools is less distinct than in the recent past. Many of the traditional issues will persist, especially the scope of public control over private schools.[87]

An expansion of private schools sponsored by fundamentalist religious groups has occurred in recent years. The growth has been rapid, so rapid in fact that the precise number of such schools is not known. These schools have produced problems in some states where their existence has run afoul of state regulations. In 1981 a fundamentalist school in Nebraska for example challenged the state's regulatory authority over personnel certification and curriculum materials. The Nebraska state supreme court upheld the authority of the state to regulate private schools and the U.S. Supreme Court refused to review the case upon appeal.

Earlier it was pointed out that the states vary widely in the extent to which they control various areas of instruction. Few states have comprehensive statutory provisions governing nonpublic schools while in others there are many regulatory requirements established by state departments or state boards. In some instances, even where statutes or regulations exist, enforcement is weak. Should states' rights to regulate be challenged more frequently states may respond by increasing the scope of their regulatory powers.

If non public schools should receive more direct public support regardless of the forms in which it is available, it seems clear that there may be increased controls on nonpublic schools. The same standards that are expected of public schools may be extended to nonpublic schools that receive public support. If the states provide the

84. Ibid., 398.
85. For a comprehensive overview of home schooling see John Holt, *Teach Your Own* (New York: Delacorte/Seymour Lawrence, 1981): 369.
86. Edward E. Gordon, "Home Tutoring Programs Gain Respectability," *Phi Delta Kappan* 64 (February 1983): 398–99.
87. Two sources for the analyses of governmental role and responsibility in regard to private or nonpublic schools are Donald A. Erickson *Public Controls for Nonpublic Schools* (Chicago: University of Chicago Press, 1969) and Otto F. Kraushaar, *American Nonpublic Schools* (Baltimore, Md.: John Hopkins University Press, 1972), ch. 11, 12, and 13.

same services to nonpublic schools that are offered to public schools, the programs of state visitation, school reporting, and inspections logically should be uniform for all schools.

The extension of public control has advantages, especially in insuring uniform levels of performance, but there are costs too; nonpublic schools will necessarily forego many of the freedoms that they have cherished. Carried to extremes, controls could lead to the disappearance of nonpublic schools and the substitution of quasi-public schools. If state supervision and control were carried to the extreme, nonpublic schools might retain only the privileges of determining the constituency which they would serve and deciding whether to include religious teachings in their curriculums. Increased communication between leaders in public and nonpublic schools, including the new alternative institutions, is both necessary and inevitable. Within the American culture the acceptance of public and nonpublic education is well established. Therefore, more is to be gained than lost as a consequence of cooperation and collaboration. There appears to be increased receptivity to dialogue on the part of leaders on both sides. However, additional court action will probably be required before legislatures and other policy bodies take many initiatives in this area.

A final issue of control concerns the expansion of learning opportunities outside and beyond the traditional public and private educational institutions at the elementary, secondary, and higher levels. Many of the settings, institutions, and delivery systems are described in chapter 18. They serve persons of all ages in contrast to the K-12 institutions that serve essentially the age range of five through sixteen. The control issue involved is subtle. Historically, public school leaders presided over a monopoly. Today they still control the school systems that enroll ninety percent of the K-12 group. What has gone relatively unnoticed is the emergence of a vast and highly differentiated body of learning opportunities about which public school officials are not well informed and over which they have no control. The presence of these options implicitly reduces the power and significance of traditional educational institutions.

The intense interest in education on the part of the American public may take several directions. In the mid-1980s it appears that the momentum of public judgment favors the continuation of public education as historically conceived. The concept of public education is consistent with the American commitment to small "d" democracy but that commitment has been and will continue to be subjected to reexamination. Should public schooling slip into further decline, Americans may shift their loyalties to a new balance between public and nonpublic schools. The challenge is real for leaders of public and nonpublic institutions. Expectations will remain high and continued public confidence and the resulting economic and political support cannot be taken for granted.

18

Extended Educational Programs and New Collaborations

Throughout this book an open systems perspective on the organization and control of American schools has been stressed. We have emphasized how schools are heavily influenced by many social, political, economic, and demographic factors. Such multiple environmental influences are currently at work shaping the potential extension of educational programs. These prospective programs will be designed to meet the needs of an array of constituencies that historically have not been served extensively by the public schools. Thus, as the enrollment of young students (ages 5 to 18) continues to decline in the 1980s in many areas of the country, shrinking education's traditional constituency, school systems may consider expanding their responsibility for different populations such as senior citizens and preschool children by providing new programs or by cutting back on certain existing programs and intensifying others. In this chapter, we explore the rationale for extending the educational program to meet the needs of diverse groups of citizens.

These opportunities for expanding educational programs have important political as well as substantive implications for the schools at a time of declining resources and significant economic change. The recent attention which has been focused upon education by the various national reports and the new interest manifested by political and business leaders provides a unique opportunity for the schools to broaden their political constituency through more concerted collaborative efforts. Closer partnerships must be forged not only with preschool or child-care interests and senior citizens, but also with the private sector to capitalize on the growing recognition of education by business as an essential investment in human capital that must be made if the nation's economy is to flourish in an increasingly interdependent and competitive world economy.

Adult Education

While public schools have long provided adult educational programs (Massachusetts permitted such programs as early as 1847[1]), retraining and reeducation has become

1. George C. Mann, "The Development of Public School Adult Education," *Public School Adult Education: A Guide for Administrators*, 2d ed. rev., John H. Thatcher (Washington, D.C.: National Association of Public School Adult Educators, 1963), 2.

increasingly important in our fast-changing technological society. Education has become more and more an unfinished task as knowledge proliferates in virtually every academic, vocational, and technical field. Adult education programs under the aegis of public school systems historically have responded to major social change. Circumstances surrounding World War I, for example, helped to launch vocational, agricultural, and Americanization programs. Needs generated by the depression in the 1930s produced emergency employment opportunities for teachers, and World War II created the need for a large number of programs in defense production. More recently, the 1960s and 1970s produced a host of adult-focused educational activities to meet the needs of the disadvantaged. Indeed, the traditional adult education programs offered for many years by hundreds of school systems throughout the country have performed a number of major functions such as providing remedial work for adults deficient in basic skills, retraining adults for different jobs, creating supportive programs and activities aimed at improving the home environment of school children, developing social studies offerings structured to increase knowledgeable participation in the democratic process, offering courses in areas such as art, music, and theater to enhance aesthetic appreciation of the physical and cultural world.[2] Superior adult education programs generally have been characterized by effective state leadership and commitment, necessary financial support, qualified staff, and flexible and diverse programs that have been responsive to ever-changing community needs.

The public schools historically have been logical delivery systems for adult education programs. They are dispersed geographically and penetrate the grassroots of virtually every community. They are widely accessible and are financially supported by the entire community. Trained staffs and established structures and organizations exist for handling funds and educational programs. Some observers contend that future political and economic support for public education may well depend on how successfully educators recruit new student constituencies to avail themselves of school facilities and services, and this in turn will depend on how creatively schools can become family service centers responding to the needs of adults and the elderly as well as children.

The recent wrenching economic transformations experienced by the country have made these issues and the potential of the adult education realm for school systems more salient.[3] As the economy has been shifting from a manufacturing base to the service and information areas, the need for massive retraining programs for older workers in the steel, auto, rubber, and other major industries has become increasingly apparent and necessary. It is estimated that 90 percent of the 1990 work force and 75 percent of the 2000 work force are already employed in the marketplace. Thus, traditional schools will be dealing with only 10 percent of the new work force, approximately one-half of whom will be minorities. Indeed, it is estimated that by 2000, approximately one-third of the young will be economically disadvantaged.

These rather startling statistics reflect why education will have to broaden its base of political support. Because only 20 to 25 percent of the overall population will

2. William S. Griffin, "Public School Adult Education—A Growing Challenge," *Administrator's Notebook* 13 (March 1965).
3. A number of sections in this chapter are derived from Michael D. Usdan, "Programs in Educational Administration: Their Future in a Changing Environment," Walter Cocking Lecture, 37th Annual National Conference of Professors of Educational Administration, Missoula, Montana, August 1983 (Mimeographed).

have youngsters enrolled in the schools, measures will need to be taken so that public schools are viewed as a civic responsibility by the majority of the population which will not have children involved or a direct stake in the educational process.

A Broadened Definition of Education

Public school systems, if they are to respond more effectively and extensively to the needs of an older clientele, must realize that contemporary education cannot be identified exclusively with schooling. Learning must be broadly defined as a lifelong activity, and it must be accepted that knowledge is provided by the family, the church, the media, and the job setting, as well as by the school. In other words, education occurs in many interrelated institutions—of which schools are only one.[4]

The federal Education Amendments of 1976 continue to be a significant landmark in the history of adult education. They legitimized the concept of lifelong learning and made provisions for the establishment of educational information programs to meet the public's growing need for educational services. This legislation confirmed the need for better coordination of services within all of education and stressed how crucial lifelong learning is to the well-being of the citizenry and consequently the national weal. Implicit in this legislation was acceptance of the "fact" that knowledge was acquired not only in schools or colleges but also through the efforts of business, industry, and labor. Thus, schools were not viewed as the ultimate or exclusive formative force in the education process. It became a matter of public policy that other social institutions (e.g., the family, the neighborhood, and the church), work experiences, technologies like television and radio, and social arrangements of various kinds were all vitally important in providing information, skills, or understanding.

A number of analysts believe that this new attitude may alter the organization and control of educational institutions from the preschool years through advanced graduate work at universities. Meaningful educational change, it is contended, is more likely to occur as the result of changes in the larger society rather than from forces internal to the institutions themselves. Several basic assumptions undergird this perspective. One is that educational policy must be formulated in conjunction with other elements of public policy and program development, such as housing, jobs, pensions, taxation, and income transfers, as well as training and research. This assumption is certainly congruent with the open systems approach to how schools are organized and controlled. A second major assumption is the more widespread acceptance of both the conceptual and operational significance of the distinction between education and schooling. The latter is only one component of the educational process. Cremin makes this point eloquently:

> In sum, then, to think comprehensively about education, we must consider policies with respect to a wide variety of institutions that educate, not only schools and colleges, but libraries, museums, day-care centers, radio and television stations, offices, factories, and farms. To be concerned solely with school in the kind of educational world we are living in today is to have a kind of fortress mentality in contending with a very fluid and dynamic situation. Education must be looked at whole, across the entire life span, and in all the situations and institutions in which it occurs.[5]

4. See, for example, Lawrence A. Cremin, *Public Education* (New York: Basic, 1976).
5. Lawrence A. Cremin, "Public Education and the Education of the Public," *Teachers College Record* 77 (September 1975): 7.

Adult or continuing education cuts across every facet of American life. Thus, program responses are not the sole responsibility of professional educators but must involve representatives from key sectors such as labor, business, and industry, as well as the general public. Such a broadening of the decision-making and participatory base has profound ramifications for the organization and control of schools.

Educational leaders must also recognize to a greater degree than they have thus far the incredibly diverse and extensive array of nonmainstream educational service providers such as industry, labor unions, some 9,000 proprietary schools and colleges, 300 businesses with a site called "college" or "university," an extensive military educational system, hospitals which provide their own educational programs, major service agencies with educational programs such as the Girl Scouts and United Way, diverse day care centers, and so on almost *ad infinitum.*

Industry, for example, invests approximately $40 billion in education and training, a total which rivals the investment made in traditional public higher education. Control Data spends hundreds of millions of dollars in its Plato system and innumerable other corporations such as IBM, Xerox, and General Motors are allocating substantial resources to improve the quality of education and training received by their employees. The Rand Corporation, Wang and A.D. Little actually offer degrees under the aegis of their corporate educational activities. Such nontraditional post-secondary educational enterprises already are educating 75 percent of the adults in the nation. This is hardly an inconsequential shadow system and educators at all levels must be more cognizant of the collaborative opportunities as well as the potential competitiveness of this somewhat parallel and nontraditional system.

Demographic trends as well as public service goals suggest that educators should pay greater attention to new student markets. America's population is changing in ways that will affect not only schools but nearly every facet of our society. Low fertility and dropping mortality rates in recent years have combined to produce an aging population. By the year 2030 the median age of Americans will be 37.3, 8.4 years older than it was in 1977.[6] The median age of Americans increased from 20.0 to 28.9 in only a six-year period from 1971 to 1977.[7] Thus, after decades of inordinate influence by younger people in a youth-oriented culture, the pendulum apparently will be swinging back and the influence of older citizens will grow.

The demographic phenomenon of "gray power" will be of increasing significance as the population ages and the number of citizens 65 years of age and older rapidly expands. By 1990, the number of youngsters under 20 will fall below 30 percent of the nation's population for the first time in history. In fact, in 1983, there were more people 65 years of age or older than teenagers. The implications of these changes are brought forth starkly by an analysis of the ratio of working to retired people. In 1940, approximately 10 citizens worked for every retired person, in 1980 the ratio was 3 to 1, and for 1990 the projected ratio is 2 to 1. By 2010, a negative ratio of workers to retired persons is possible. Thus, growing numbers of retired individuals will be dependent upon a younger population, increasingly composed of minorities, to sustain the economy in general and to maintain the stability of a rather vulnerable social security system.

If public school systems more aggressively seek new and expanded adult educa-

6. Robert Reinhold, "New Population Trends Transforming U.S.," *New York Times,* 6 February 1977, 1.
7. Edward B. Fiske, "Advancing Median age in U.S. Believed Shaping Schools' Futures," *New York Times,* 30 November 1977, 27.

tion markets, such efforts would be consonant with the needs of a "learning society" in which schooling is only one component. In a learning society all individuals, regardless of their age, would be entitled to maximum educational opportunities; all citizens would have basic educational rights which would include training and retraining opportunities. Extensive use would be made of the mass media. Although innovative and nontraditional, nonschool-based instructional modes would be more widely used, the public school might remain the logical institution for providing such services. Indeed, such efforts might finally bring to fuller fruition the community education concept in which schools are the base of many interrelated social and economic as well as educational services offered to every segment of a community.

General awareness of the importance of adult education has grown markedly in recent years as our society has grappled with rapid social and economic change and the concomitant need to develop academic and vocational training programs. Indeed, adult education in the late 1960s and into the 1970s became a multibillion-dollar growth industry involving over 10 percent of eligible Americans. In the few years between 1957 and 1975, for example, the number of involved adults more than doubled, increasing from 8.2 to 17.1 million, that is from 7.6 percent to 11.6 percent of the eligible population.[8] This blossoming interest in and continuing growth of programs sponsored by public schools, institutions of higher education, proprietary and correspondence schools, government, industry, the military, churches, and other community groups has made issues concerning adult education the subject of numerous proposals for its expansion and support. Two major social purposes underlie these proposals. One is the need to redress past inequities and to give disadvantaged individuals a chance to maximize their educational opportunities; the second purpose is to retrain people in a highly technological economy.[9] Another, more pragmatic reason for the growing visibility of adult education, as we mentioned, is embedded in demography. There are more adults and more older people now than earlier in this century. In 1960, 108 million people were 21 years of age or older; by 1976 that number had risen to almost 137 million.[10] The population continues to age and, as discussed earlier, there will be a gradual shift to an older population in this country because of aging of the post-World War II baby-boom generation and the lowered fertility rates of the 1960s and 1970s.

Other more complex demographic changes, such as the changing role of women and the decline in the number of students in the traditional college-age cohort, have created greater public interest in adult education. O'Keefe, summarizing these new demographic realities, has presented a cogent rationale for the expansion of adult education programs:

1. Current participation patterns demonstrate that for certain subgroups within the adult population, barriers exist that inhibit participation in further education;
2. Current participation points to unmet educational needs of adults, which public programs should be designed to meet;

8. Edward B. Fiske, "Programs Bypass the Neediest," *New York Times,* 11 September 1977, 6 (sec. 4).
9. For a stimulating discussion of these developments and changes and their implications for education in our evolving technological and information based society see John Naisbitt, *Megatrends* (New York: Warren, 1982).
10. Michael O'Keefe, *The Adult, Education and Public Policy,* Occasional paper of the Aspen Institute for Humanistic Studies Program in Education for a Changing Society (Cambridge, Mass.: Aspen Institute, 1977), 1.

3. Demand for adult education programs will increase in the future for a number of reasons:
   a. the society will become more and more middle-aged;
   b. increasing amounts of leisure time will in turn lead to an increase in educational activities; and
   c. the increasing level of formal education also will lead to increases in adult education.
4. Equity considerations require that those who in earlier life were prevented by lack of opportunity from obtaining an education for which they were qualified should be given an opportunity to compensate for that earlier lack;
5. As the population moves upward in career paths, our society will experience a "promotion squeeze" and job mobility will more typically be horizontal than vertical; several effects of this phenomenon will increase the need for expanded adult education:
   a. the numbers of these people in our society who will change careers in mid-life will increase substantially;
   b. increased limitations on fulfillment in the world of work will move people to seek fulfillment in other activities, including education;
   c. with competition for higher level positions growing more and more fierce, those who would move upward will need to keep themselves as well trained as their younger competitors;
   d. for the younger worker competing for higher positions, the level of education and training will become increasingly critical as a criterion for promotion.[11]

Target Groups

The changing nature of the society puts schools in a unique position to serve additional groups of citizens. Let us now look at some of the groups whose special needs might be met by public school-sponsored adult education programs.

A substantial number of the women who enter or reenter the labor force are either single, widowed, divorced or separated, or have husbands with incomes of less than $3,000 per year; significantly, "the disparity in income which women suffer relative to men is less at higher levels of education, suggesting a positive economic benefit in additional education for women."[12] The employment status of female heads of households is particularly sensitive to economic fluctuations and thus educational and training opportunities are of particular interest to this group. Patricia Sexton has documented how the numbers of working women grew in the 1950s and 1960s:

Between 1950 and 1969, women in the labor force increased by twelve million, 62 percent of whom were older than 35 years of age. Among the age groups, the greatest gain in employment during recent decades has been made by women age 45 to 54. In 1940, 25 percent of women in this age group were employed; in 1950 the figure was 37 percent and in 1969, it was 54 percent.

Most of these mature women needed education and training to prepare them for the job market. The need was highlighted by the rise in school enrollments of women age 25 to 29 from 26,000 to 311,000 between 1950 and 1969—and of women age 30 to 34, from 21,000 to 215,000.[13]

11. Ibid., 3–4.
12. Ibid., 10.
13. Patricia Sexton, *Women in Education* (Bloomington, Ind.: Phi Delta Kappa Educational Foundation, 1976), 150.

This growth in the decades of the 1950s and 1960s has continued. By the 1970s more women than men were enrolled in adult education programs and their participation rate had increased at twice the rate of males. Sexton laments the fact that "so few of these courses have apparently been designed either for or about women— aside from the traditional home economics offerings. Little publicity is given to women's courses in adult education because they serve mainly noncollege women who have a low profile on the women's scene and in the media."[14] Sexton projects the potential for adult education programs that are designed more specifically

> for reaching deep into the communities of noncollege women, where the vast majority of American women live, and bringing to them skills and knowledge they can use to improve themselves, their families, communities, and the status of women generally.
>
>   In the past, adult education has too often focused on courses, subject matter, and narrowly vocational subjects—usually of a highly traditional nature—to the neglect of people and their needs, as individuals, groups, and communities. Rarely have adult education programs addressed themselves to the special needs of women, as an interest group, as a "minority," as people who can play a significant role, collectively, in consumer affairs, civic and community affairs, the world of work and of politics.[15]

A second important target group are individuals who have not acquired a high school diploma. There is a fallacious assumption held by many that high school graduation has become almost universal. Substantial numbers of American citizens, however, have not earned high school diplomas; Sexton notes, "In 1974, 14 million Americans over the age of 25 had not even completed eight years of schooling. Six million individuals who were between the ages of 25 and 34, with a substantial portion of their working life ahead of them, had no high school diploma. An additional 15 million were between the ages of 35 and 54."[16]

The unemployed represent a third promising special target group for adult education programs. With unemployment rates in some areas hovering over or close to 10 percent in recent years, there is obviously an acute need for special educational and training programs to increase the employability of the hard-core unemployed. Among certain subgroups, particularly young people between the ages of 16 and 19, the recent rate of unemployment has constantly stayed at approximately two times the overall rate for the general population and the unemployment rate for minority youngsters is even higher. Males constitute three-quarters of these unemployed teenagers.

There are great opportunities for public schools to sponsor more responsive work-study or distributive education programs which are tied directly to the needs of the local economy and that are less subject to the vagaries of federal funding. Indeed, approximately one-half of high school youngsters now work at least part-time and much more can be done to make their job experience more relevant to their school activities.

The adult education potential inherent in the senior citizens population, a fourth target group, merits some additional elaboration. As indicated earlier, our population is aging. Gerontology has become one of the fastest growing fields of study in the nation:

14. Ibid., 153.
15. Ibid., 154.
16. Cited in O'Keefe, *The Adult, Education and Public Policy,* 10.

> The growing interest in gerontology is rooted in demographic trends; increased lob-
> bying and influence by older voters; sharply increased federal aid for older people and
> more local aid programs; and the beginning of career opportunities in a new field.[17]

Despite recent federal reductions in support for the National Institute on Aging and cuts in agencies and programs serving the elderly at all governmental levels, special programs for the elderly will continue to persist and expand because of de-mographic imperatives. The 1980 census, for example, revealed that for the first time Americans older than 60 were a larger group than those under 10 and those between 11 and 19. In the next 55 years, it is projected that the number of persons 65 and older will more than double and the number 85 and older will more than triple while the general population is expected to grow by only 35 percent.[18]

These numbers make it apparent that the federal government as well as more and more states, cities, and counties will be dealing with the problems of older citi-zens. Consequently, there is demand for more professional personnel to administer these programs. Our society will need not only thousands of psychiatrists, clinical psychologists, psychiatric social workers, nurses, and other specialists for service to the aging but also numerous quasi-professional or paraprofessional workers.

This emerging "gray power" will be manifest at every governmental level, and organizations like the American Association of Retired Persons and the National Re-tired Teacher Association will become increasingly visible and important advocate groups.[19] These two groups claim a combined membership of more than 13 million. They represent organizationally an impressive political base for the Leadership Council of Aging Organizations, an umbrella group of advocacy organizations that claims to represent more than 16 million persons.[20] Citizens over the age of 65 now account for more than 10 percent of the population and approximately one-fourth of the elderly live below the poverty level. Thus, issues which affect senior citizens, such as man-datory retirement, conditions in nursing homes, social security payments, Medicare, housing, and nutrition will become more politically salient. Annually thousands of older citizens have been compelled to retire although they remained able and willing to work. In recent years vigorous efforts have been made to create more flexibility and multiple retirement policy patterns in corporations, education, and government service.[21]

These developments, of course, have consequences for public education. The elderly, in addition to representing a growing pool of potential learners and voters with vocational, social, or recreational needs, provide a valuable reservoir of instruc-tional talent. Their expertise and experience can be used in such roles as tutors for the young and advisors in various areas to the less mature. The late Margaret Mead, for example, envisioned grandparents playing a much more important role in the ed-ucation of young people.[22]

As the twenty-first century comes closer, it is likely that more and more educa-tional programs will be structured around the needs of the elderly. Many, if not most,

17. Robert Lindsey, "Gerontology Is Still A Very Young Science," *New York Times,* 19 June 1977, 9 (sec. 4).
18. Lawrence Meyer, "Aging Conference Reflects a New Militancy," *Washington Post,* 6 December 1981, A–2.
19. Nancy Hicks, "The Organized Elderly: A New Political Power," *New York Times,* 22 June 1975, 1, 37. See also Henry J. Pratt, *The Gray Lobby* (Chicago: University of Chicago Press, 1976).
20. Meyer, "Aging Conference," A–2.
21. See Harvey D. Shapiro, "Do Not Go Gently," *New York Times Magazine,* 6 February 1977, 36–41.
22. Margaret Mead, "Grandparents as Educators," *Teachers College Record* 76 (December 1974): 240–49.

of these activities will be locally based, in the neighborhoods or areas where the aged live or in areas nearby. School districts may turn out to be the most logical, locally based delivery system to coordinate these efforts. There will be growing numbers of storefront, livingroom, and apartment-house teaching programs. Business and industry, likewise, will be expanding their support of programs for the elderly.

School officials should anticipate the opportunities that will be available to work collaboratively with the elderly in a variety of service and volunteer programs and not necessarily view the elderly as adversaries competing for scarce resources. The demography indicates conclusively that the elderly will be an increasingly influential force and will be demanding as they did at the 1981 White House Conference on Aging that educators be sensitive to their special needs.[23]

Learning and Earning

A number of approaches for expanding educational opportunities have surfaced in recent years.[24] One particularly interesting model attempts to reshape and make more relevant the relationship between education and work. This restructuring of the role of work in our society and of the relationship of the individual to the total economic system is a vital conceptual task. It is a task that must be undertaken before any meaningful reorganization of schools can become substantively supportable or politically viable. Willard Wirtz, former secretary of labor, working with the National Manpower Institute (now the National Institute on Work and Learning), studied the nation's education and employment patterns, and generated proposals for a community-directed work-study partnership for bridging the dysfunctional "learning-earning" dichotomy in our society.[25]

Wirtz (along the lines suggested earlier by James Coleman and the Panel on Youth of the President's Science Advisory Committee), stressed the need for better integration of the traditionally separate worlds of education and work. He contended that groups such as 16- to 19-year-olds, women, and senior citizens are blocked by the bureaucracies of both education and work. The system is dysfunctional when 20 percent of teenagers and 40 percent of minority young are unemployed. In an age of automation and technological sophistication, the problem cannot be solved simply by creating more jobs. Attention must be given to the kind of jobs provided. Wirtz proposed "educational renewal" opportunities for youths and adults and envisioned Community Education-Work Councils as the mechanism through which such services could be provided most effectively.

Such locally controlled Community Education-Work Councils have been created in a number of communities and involve employers, labor union members, school officials, and members of the general public who cooperatively develop and operate education-work programs. Practical career counseling and guidance are stressed with employment options being presented to all high school and college students on an occupation by occupation basis. The maximum number of work-study options are made available to students. For example, students between the ages 16 and 20 might want to work for a year or two. Wirtz suggests that laws and regulations either be created or revised to facilitate movement between the worlds of work and education.

23. Warren Weaver Jr., "White House Aging Parley Adopts Agenda for Decade," *New York Times,* 4 December 1981, A18.
24. *Youth Transition to Adulthood,* Report of the Panel on Youth of the President's Science Advisory Committee (Chicago: University of Chicago Press, 1974).
25. Willard Wirtz, *The Boundless Resource,* (Washington, D.C.: National Manpower Institute, New Republic, 1975).

Public schools, if such recommendations were adopted, could also be utilized more fully by adult learners.

Wirtz's thesis is that "learning" and "earning" must be interspersed with each other in order to maximize employment and self-renewal opportunities. In his view, American life is still too largely "divided into the time traps of youth for education, adulthood for work, and old age for nothing."[26] Learning and earning in his view can no longer "pass as isolated chapters" in the individual's life cycle. Education must be viewed as a "lifetime venture" with students of all ages dropping in and dropping out of educational opportunities.[27]

Bridge-building efforts must be undertaken to join the presently bifurcated worlds of education and work. Such collaboration would not only enlarge and enrich human potential but would also enhance economic productivity and value. The widely accepted notion that young people must stay in school in linear fashion until they have graduated must be demolished. This lockstep approach to education has already been weakened somewhat as a result of increases in the number of alternative programs, but it remains deeply embedded because of tradition, administrative convenience, and false parental concern and pride.

Ernest Boyer in his recent study of the high school urged that schools connect more systematically with other institutions to better prepare their students not only for work and further education, but also to fulfill their social and civic responsibilities as citizens. He recommends closer ties between the school and the business community and suggests that high school students serve internships in the community for academic credit as a means of building more meaningful relationships between the school experiences of youngsters and the interdependent and ever-changing larger world in which they will be spending their lives.[28] Wirtz and Boyer's proposals to fuse education and work experiences would precipitate significant changes in school operation and governance. The traditional isolation and insulation of the educational enterprise would be modified. The provision of more work and service opportunities in the secondary schools, for example, would require the generation of new and closer relationships with business and industry. The achievement of these closer relationships may impinge upon many of the customary professional prerogatives of educators. The curriculum or program offerings would not be determined unilaterally by professional educators but through interaction with business people, labor representatives, and others involved in a much broader decision-making process. Resource allocation decisions and priorities would not be determined exclusively by school superintendents, their professional staffs, and board of education members but by a much wider range of a community's citizenry. Such an open-ended decision-making structure builds upon the community school movement which has been supported by the Mott Foundation and other groups for many years.

The supporting role and cooperation of school systems in the implementation of such an approach would be of fundamental importance because no other institution in our society is so broadly based. Indeed, no other institution is in a better position to be the delivery system to implement the potential of the lifelong learning movement,

26. Ibid., 112.
27. James M. Heffernan, Francis U. Macy, and Donn F. Vickers, *Educational Brokering: A New Service for Adult Learners* (Syracuse, N.Y.: National Center for Educational Brokering, 1976).
28. Ernest L. Boyer, *High School: A Report on Secondary Education in America* (New York: Harper & Row, 1983).

not only for its economic benefits but also for the overall enrichment of life it can provide for so many individuals.

Early Childhood Programs: The Family in Transition

Many of society's basic institutions are undergoing significant changes. One particularly significant change relates to the family. The American family is in transition in ways that are reshaping society; the following statistics illustrate:

> There are approximately 61.7 million children under age 18 in the United States. Over 18.9 million of them are under age 6, 31.0 million are age 6 through 14, and 11.8 are age 15 through 17.
>
> The vast majority of children—over three-fourths, or 47 million—live with both parents. Another 20 percent, or over 12 million, live with only one parent.
>
> During the 1970s, the proportion of children living with only one parent increased dramatically, from 12 percent in 1970 to 19.7 percent in 1980. The numbers of children in one-parent families increased from 8.4 million to 12.2 million.
>
> The total number of children in the United States will increase steadily during the 1980s. The increase will be the result of the increasing number of pre-school children. By 1990, there will be over 23.3 million children under age 6, a 23 percent increase from 1980.
>
> There are over 58.4 million families in the United States of which 30.5 million, or 52.2 percent, have children under age 18.
>
> Of all families, 82.5 percent are married couples while 14.6 percent are headed by a woman.
>
> Family size declined steadily during the 1970s, from 3.58 persons in 1970 to 3.28 in 1980. Similarly, the number of children per family declined from 1.34 in 1970 to 1.05 in 1980. Both trends are expected to continue during the 1980s.
>
> The number of households in the United States increased by almost 16 million during the 1970s. Almost 9 million of these new households were not families. A similar total increase is expected during the 1980s: almost 18 million new households, but only 10 million of them will be families.[29]

Although experts disagree in their interpretations of the social implications of these data, there can be little doubt that within the past decade or so men and women have been shaping new relationships and that the basic nuclear family of father working and mother at home raising the children is less dominant. The women's movement has motivated many women to work for other than economic or material reasons. A national survey by the National Assessment for Educational Progress indicated that only 3 percent of 17-year-old females selected "housewife" as their first-choice career. Almost all of these young women assumed that they would be working for a living.[30] A number of women feel unfulfilled in traditional housekeeping and maternal roles and thus seek the stimulation of outside work. These feelings, not surprisingly,

29. Children's Defense Fund, *Employed Parents and Their Children: A Data Book,* (Washington, D.C.: 1982), 49.
30. *Newsletter,* Project on the Status and Education of Women, Association of American Colleges, no. 20 (June 1978) 3.

are manifested particularly by the growing numbers of college-educated women. As a result, new styles of marriages and personal relationships are evolving, as well-educated women defer marriage for careers and opt for smaller families and flexible homemaking arrangements. More and more women are heads of households in families without men.[31] For various reasons then, women are entering the job market in huge numbers. Eli Ginzburg, a nationally renowned work force analyst, describes this development as "the single most outstanding phenomena of our century. Its long-term implications are absolutely unchartable, in my opinion. It will affect women, men and children, and the cumulative consequences of that will only be revealed in the 21st and 22nd centuries."[32]

What then are the implications of these developments for public education? Enrollment in nursery schools and kindergartens has increased significantly within the past decade despite declining birth rates and an actual decrease in the number of children under 5 years of age. A report by the U.S. Census Bureau shows that "the number of children ages 3 to 5 declined from 12.2 million in 1967 to 9.7 million in 1976 while the enrollment in kindergarten and nursery school increased from 3.9 million to 4.8 million.[33] The major reason for this growth, of course, is the continuing dramatic increase in the proportion of working mothers with young children. Forty-five percent of the 4.8 million children enrolled in kindergarten and nursery school in 1976 had working mothers. The comparable figure in 1967 was 35 percent. To meet the growing child-care needs of working mothers, large numbers of new part-time and full-time day-care centers and nurseries have been established. In addition, more non-working mothers have availed themselves of such facilities to pursue their interests outside of the home. Mothers with higher levels of formal education were more likely to enroll their children in preschool programs than were those mothers with less formal education. For example, "among mothers of 3- and 4-year-olds in nursery school, 27% had finished high school, 40% had some college and 63% were college graduates.[34]

The Children's Defense Fund reports that almost 5 million children between the ages of 3 and 13 have mothers who work full-time and also are the caregivers. Another 1.8 million children care for themselves while their mothers work. While there are 22 million children under age 14 whose mothers work, there are only 900,000 children enrolled in the nation's 18,307 day-care centers. In addition, there are only 122,000 center slots for infants under age 3 and 126,000 for after-school care. The Children's Defense Fund estimates that there are at least 3 million children under age 3 with working mothers, and another 14.5 million school-age children whose mothers work.[35]

These statistics pertaining to families and children indicate that there obviously is a huge pent-up demand for child-care and preschool education and unique opportunities exist for public schools to extend their programs and make collaborative efforts to meet the special needs of this particular constituency.

31. Heather L. Ross and Isabel V. Sawhill, *Time of Transition: The Growth of Families Headed by Women* (Washington, D.C.: Urban Institute, 1975).
32. Robert Lindsey, "Women Entering Job Market at Extraordinary Pace," *New York Times,* 12 September 1976, 1, 49.
33. William Dunn, "The Patter of Little Feet Swamps Nursery School," *Detroit News,* 20 February 1978.
34. Ibid.
35. Children's Defense Fund, *Employed Parents and their Children,* 89.

The Public Schools as Delivery System

Public schools are very logical agencies to become *a,* if not *the,* major delivery system for preschool education. As enrollments decline in many areas of the country, space will be available in existing school facilities, and the administrative and teaching staff infrastructure is already in place. Albert Shanker, president of the American Federation of Teachers, and other educational leaders have argued that schools as permanent institutions in every community should be "the prime sponsor for all early childhood and day-care programs" and that such programs should not be subjected "to the fragmented efforts and slipshod administration that characterize inexperienced community groups starting up new programs. Schools are permanent institutions in every community and should be used. If they are not performing well, they should be improved, not bypassed.[36] On a more pragmatic note, the reasons why some public school leaders support day-care and preschool programs is abundantly clear:

> Declining enrollments and tight budgets mean teacher layoffs; expanded day care and preschool programs, federally funded but controlled by the public school establishment, mean teacher jobs and continued higher membership roles for their unions.[37]

Critics of the public schools, however, have vigorously protested legislation or policy that would make the schools the exclusive or dominant delivery system for preschool programs. These critics, particularly many representatives of minority and civil rights groups, feel that the schools would be too bureaucratized and unresponsive to the special needs of very young children and their families. The latter need a comprehensive human services approach to their problems that will address the health, physical, and socio-emotional needs of parents as well as children. There is skepticism as to whether most school systems are prepared either operationally or philosophically to develop the close ties with communities and parents that are so essential to successful preschool programs. Marion Wright Edelman of the Children's Defense Fund has expressed her concern that the interests of children and parents may be subordinated to narrow educational interests:

> I am fearful that too many school boards, suddenly given a new pot of federal money, will simply put those funds where they can spend them most easily and with the fewest adjustments in the regular school program—in kindergartens, where they don't have them, and in day care programs, where there are empty classes or unemployed teachers.[38]

Testimony a number of years ago at a U.S. Senate hearing on proposals to shift the Head Start program to a proposed new cabinet level department of education reflects how apprehensive many political and preschool leaders are about the possibility of expanding the role of public schools in early childhood education. Many of those concerned about an enlarged preschool role for public school systems contend that the schools stress academic achievement too narrowly and that many teachers could

36. William V. Shannon, "Government and Families," *New York Times,* 14 September 1975, 27. See also *Putting Early Childhood and Day Care Services Into the Public Schools* (Washington, D.C.: American Federation of Teachers, 1976).
37. John Mathews, "Day Care: What Role for Public Schools?" *Compact* 9 (June 1975): 19.
38. Ibid., 21.

not tolerate the more relaxed and flexible approach of most preschool programs with their greater emphasis on parental and neighborhood involvement.[39] There is fear that Head Start programs would be swallowed up if they were to be offered under the auspices of public schools. In 1978 former Representative Shirley Chisholm of New York, for example, testified that moving Head Start to a new cabinet-level department of education, thus "placing it under the control of education interests," would "undermine" the program because it would wind up "at the very bottom" of such a department's fiscal priorities.[40] Nancy Spears, representing the National Head Start Association, testified that the possible transfer of Head Start to a public school-oriented education department posed "the most serious threat which Head Start has ever faced" because it would "lead to exclusive public school control" with its attendant bureaucratic and professional constraints. In Spears' opinion, the public schools had not manifested the "capacity, the willingness, the empathy toward diverse communities, and the actual ability to successfully carry Head Start's comprehensive goals."[41]

These deeply felt judgments, particularly among minority groups, that the schools are not able to effectively provide early childhood programs and worse, that they have failed to serve many families and children adequately, are and should be of concern to professional educators. A serious threat to the existing governance structure of public education will be posed if a broadly based, large-scale preschool movement were implemented independently or even semi-independently of the public schools. If preschool teachers could be hired without being certified or being members of teacher organizations, the existing education establishment could be seriously challenged. If preschool and day-care programs could be run with "cheaper" and "less qualified" personnel for 3- and 4-year-olds, why not use such "nonprofessional" or uncertified teachers for 10-year-olds and 17-year-olds?[42] These questions understandably cause concern among professional educators in an economy-oriented, inflationary period when governmental expenditures are being subjected to intense scrutiny. Indeed, in a labor-intensive enterprise like education the possibility of reducing personnel costs is viewed by teacher groups as a very real threat to their status and job security. Thus, nonpublic, education-based preschool programs pose a number of concerns to the existing educational establishment. Community controlled early childhood programs represent to many school people an end run, a usurping of their institutions and traditional prerogatives to determine programs. The possible existence of independent or parallel systems of delivering preschool or day-care programs also threatens the current educational structure by encouraging or legitimizing education options such as vouchers.

The public schools, regardless of which agency or agencies control preschool education, have an enormous stake in the possible growth of the early childhood enterprise. Public policy and services ultimately will have to respond to the dramatic changes in family life and social mores mentioned earlier. Although the public schools may not become the exclusive delivery system for early childhood services, they are likely to be active, major participants in providing preschool programs. Indeed, many believe that the advocates of enlarged preschool programs under public school auspices have only temporarily relented in their efforts to gain control of the early child-

39. "Should the Public Schools Be Entrusted with Preschool Education: A Critique of the AFT Proposals," *School Review* 86 (November 1977).
40. "Witnesses Blast Public School Threat to Head Start," *Education Daily,* 28 April 1978, 2.
41. Ibid.
42. Mathews, "Day Care," 20.

hood area. Current fiscal pressures on existing school programs have diverted interest from new activities which might siphon away increasingly scarce resources.

Recent political and economic developments may provide more opportunity for public school advocates and their critics in the child-care community to collaborate more closely to achieve common goals. The recent cuts in social and education programs by the Reagan administration have compelled former foes to coalesce to combat a perceived common adversary. The fact that there are many more black and other minority superintendents and high-ranking administrators in urban school systems and recent improvements in test scores have somewhat reduced or at least mitigated the minority community's alienation towards schools in some districts. In an increasing number of school systems creative partnerships are being forged between the schools and child-care advocates. Such coalitions will become more common because of the interrelated demographic, political, and economic factors that we have discussed. The continuing unmet child-care needs of working parents, particularly mothers, will compel the development of more responsive public policy in this neglected area as we shall now discuss.

Community Education

If the schools are to be successful with preschool children and their families, efforts must be made to develop closer ties with parents and their communities. This is particularly important with low-income and minority families who are often dubious about the depth of the commitment of public school personnel to the well-being of their children. The importance of working cooperatively with parents and supporting families becomes even more significant when there are greater numbers of children coming from single-parent homes or from households where both parents are working. Indeed, if child-care services are to be extensive enough to meet our society's burgeoning needs, the facilities, outreach, and resources of the public schools may be of great importance.

No other institution has comparable social penetration. The possibility of schools becoming comprehensive social and medical, as well as educational, service delivery vehicles for children and families is exciting. The need for such focused community services is as real in affluent suburbia as it is in the most disadvantaged urban area. Families need help. The incidence of infanticide, parent-perpetrated child abuse, juvenile delinquency and crime, and suicides among children is alarming.[43] Why are children and families under such stress? Scholars and social commentators have made a number of analyses. Urbanization and rapidly advancing technology have left many people with feelings of anonymity and rootlessness. These developments, according to some, have triggered more serious social pathologies, such as crime.

These social problems and social transformations call for significant changes in public policy and thought. The presumption no longer holds that the majority of mothers are at home rearing children as they were only a decade or so ago. The policies of school systems as well as other governmental and private agencies and institutions must be altered in order to better serve students who are growing up in family and community environments that have changed dramatically in recent years.[44] Indeed,

---

43. See Kenneth Keniston, *All Our Children* (New York: Harcourt Brace Jovanovich, Carnegie Council on Children, 1977).
44. *Toward a National Policy for Children and Families* (Washington, D.C.: National Academy of Sciences, 1977).

many of the major problems of families are due to circumstances beyond their control such as lack of employment opportunities and the economic constraints caused by inflation, automation, and other factors. Merely educating parents in areas such as consumerism, child rearing, and nutrition will not suffice. Support systems may be necessary for families and children. No other institution is in a better position to assume responsibility for integrated educational, economic, health, child, and family care services than the neighborhood schools and the concept of extended day programs being offered under the aegis of school systems may well receive increased attention.

The area of parent education, in particular, offers unique service possibilities for schools.[45] For example, many women, while happy to be working for economic or personal reasons, are somewhat troubled about their new role. Can they enjoy their status as job-holders and concurrently meet their family obligations? Can they do both well? This ambivalence is very understandable and poses serious problems and choices as family and work priorities and obligations are sorted out. Creative thinking and flexibility are needed. An institutional base of support should be available to help adults and children work through such important problems. With the role of the extended family decreasing in a transient, urban society, neighborhoods and communities must provide the necessary social and cultural infrastructure to offset the anomie which so frequently afflicts both children and parents in an impersonalized mass society.[46] Berger and Neuhaus, for instance, focus on the need to strengthen the "mediating structures" of family, neighborhood, church, voluntary associations, and ethnic and racial subcultures if citizens are to be effectively served in the areas of education, child care, social services, health care, law enforcement, and housing.[47]

Changes in family structure will make traditional, largely at-home child care increasingly unfeasible. Policy must be generated that will meet contemporary conditions by being more responsive to the needs of working mothers and inflation-affected families requiring dual incomes. The caliber and extent of society's responses to these child-care needs will affect public schools significantly. If, as many child development specialists believe, the plasticity of the first five years of life make that period crucial in the intellectual and emotional growth of children, then the quality of preschool education is of paramount importance.[48] If youngsters are so malleable in these early years, then their preschool experiences will influence significantly their ultimate performance and behavior when they enter the public schools. Thus, the public schools, even in the event that they are not extensively engaged in preschool programs, should be concerned with the type of experiences preschool youngsters receive.

There are currently millions of American families in which mothers with children under six work. What are the effects of day care and sustained separation from parents on these children? What impact does daily separation have on parent-child relationships? To date, research evidence is mixed as to whether day care is good or bad. The preliminary results of a study undertaken by Greta Fein at Detroit's Merrill-

45. *Families and Schools: Implementing Parent Education,* Education Commission of the States, report no. 121 (Denver, Colo.: 1979). See also James A. Levine, *Day Care and the Public Schools: Profiles of Five-Communities* (Newton, Mass: Education Development Center, 1978).
46. David S. Seeley, *Education Through Partnership: Mediating Structures and Education* (Cambridge, Mass.: Ballinger, 1980).
47. Peter L. Berger and Richard John Neuhaus, *To Empower People: The Role of Mediating Structures in Public Policy* (Washington, D.C.: American Enterprise Institute for Public Policy Research, 1977).
48. Benjamin S. Bloom, *Stability and Change in Human Characteristics* (New York: John Wiley and Sons, 1964).

Palmer Institute, indicate that "day care kids not only are more skilled in the social graces—game playing, pretending, bargaining and backing off—than home care kids, but also are more independent, and less compliant to mommy's and daddy's demands. Kids who have early group experience are more oriented toward their age mates then they are toward adults. What the data are suggesting is that day care kids are more independent of controlling adults."[49] If these initial findings are validated, the results will have important implications for kindergarten and elementary public school programs. School systems throughout the land should be gearing up both psychologically and operationally to accommodate growing numbers of children with day care and early childhood center experiences. If the research is confirmed, these children will be more challenging to adults and will be more "assertive, ascendent and dominating" than the youngsters who do not have comparable social or peer experience in a nursery or child-care center.[50] In other words, a newer, more aggressive cohort of students may be entering public schools in the immediate future.

Whether young mothers should work or not is no longer an issue. Likewise, the question of whether preprimary programs offer educational benefits for very young children does not warrant debate. Despite some ambiguous data regarding such benefits, there is a growing belief that educational advantages can be attained through such enrollments especially if the conduct and administration of such programs can be professionalized. Bronfenbrenner, however, is skeptical about allowing a pattern to develop in which the care of young children is delegated to specialists.[51] He fears the social consequences of further separating the child from the family and reducing the family's and community's sense of responsibility for children.

Bronfenbrenner believes the problems of the American family and those of children and youth warrant very careful consideration.[52] Before any enunciation of local, state, and federal policy, Bronfenbrenner suggests an intensive national research program directed at families and children. He believes that we should: (1) study comparatively the effects of child rearing in the home, family day care, and group day care; (2) examine the effects of parental involvement in teacher training; (3) experiment with student volunteers as support systems for single-parent families; (4) measure the impact of high-rise housing on socialization practices and effects; (5) arrange for and study circumstances where parents can be home when their children return from school; (6) introduce children to the world of work; (7) examine family and individual development as a function of position in the social network; and (8) analyze the impact of moving to a new neighborhood on families and children.

Each of Bronfenbrenner's proposals for study has policy consequences for the organization and control of schools. At issue is the principal locus of responsibility for preschooling, its delivery and administration as well as the extent of public control over both public and private sector programming. Even more important, however, is the generation of improved understanding of the effects of alternative forms of socialization on both children and adults, the results of which will shape other public sector policies and decisions. Improved insight into inter- and intra-institutional policy options and the relationships of one to the other is also necessary. For example, research focused on the meaning for children and youth of life in high-rise housing has implica-

49. Arielle Emmett, "Seeking to Build a Solid Case for Day Care," *Detroit Free Press,* 11 January 1979.
50. Ibid.
51. Urie Bronfenbrenner "Children in America: The Roots of Alienation" *Educational Reform for a Changing Society,* ed. Louis Rubin (1978), ch. 1.
52. Ibid.

tions for educational, health, juvenile justice, safety, and employment policy. Similarly, the analysis of the meaning for families of movement into new neighborhoods, given the fact that one in five families moves each year, will have significance for policy in most human services areas including schooling. Obviously Bronfenbrenner's proposals for research do not exhaust the prospects for useful study, but they do offer a direction and underline the necessity for a sound knowledge base upon which to construct public policy for the education of young children.

The importance of clarifying the role and responsibility of the school and the role and responsibility of the family in reference to learning is often stressed. The assumption is that if those roles and responsibilities were clear, better learning would occur and everyone would be happier.

Historically, the family and school were expected to complement and reinforce one another. Above all they were expected to work in harmony. That characterization of school and family relationships seems to be breaking down. Rather than harmony between home and school, there is tension. Rather than mutual respect, there is suspicion. Rather than collaboration and complementarity, there is faultfinding and finger pointing. The alienation of family from school is matched by the alienation of child from family. The traditional locations of socialization—the home, the community, and the school—are no longer as important as in the past. They have given way in large part to television and peer groups, both of which have powerful influence on the lives of persons of all ages.

Educators, as well as parents, seem to be unable to unravel the tangled web of present circumstances long enough to gain perspective. So much has happened, yet so much is about to happen; change seems to be the only constant. Bronfenbrenner and others have documented the alienation of children in American culture; this evidence cannot be ignored. The schools must respond to these interrelated social changes which are so profoundly influencing American youngsters and their families. If the schools do not assume extended responsibilities to accommodate to these changes, other agencies surely will and the schools may become less valued in the process.

School-Business Partnerships

The recent highly publicized and dramatic growth of school-business collaborations throughout the country certainly reflects a broader concept of the role of schools in society. In the 1980s there is widespread recognition that new perspectives are needed on the relationship between public education and the nation's business community. These critically important sectors of American life are too detached from each other and there is a growing awareness that the entire society as well as business has a profound interest in the strengthening of the public school enterprise. A scientifically and technically trained work force is essential in today's world, essential not only if we are to compete economically with productive nations like Japan and West Germany but also if we were to maintain an adequate defense establishment. National security is not enhanced if technical, multi-page training tomes on operating and maintaining sophisticated weaponry are presented to semi-literate soldiers and sailors who are unable to comprehend complex, sophisticated materials.

There is greater understanding that the schools must offer quality education to produce the educated, productive work force that is essential to sustain the country in an increasingly competitive world. Obviously, businesses, as well as the society at large, would suffer if our schools did not produce well-educated, adaptable young citizens who are able to operate in an increasingly technological world in which change is the only constant.

Indeed, more leaders acknowledge that the business stake in quality public education really is not distinguishable from the entire society's stake. More corporations recognize that buttressing our schools is not mere philanthropy and "do-goodism" but actually "enlightened selfishness." In other words, the business world can "do well by doing good." Also, corporations in the 1980s are more cognizant of their direct, bottom-line stake in the improvement of public education. As we indicated earlier, it is estimated that the private sector expends some $40 billion annually on training programs for employees. Much of this investment is spent on providing remedial work in the basic skills such as basic arithmetic and English usage which quite logically could be assumed to be the primary responsibility of our public schools. In fact, business is investing in duplicative, costly ways in providing a range of basic programs which should be provided as fundamentals under the aegis of school systems.

It is estimated, moreover, that employee recruitment, hiring, and turnover expenditures total more than $100 billion annually. General Motors, for example, was compelled to hire 9,000 employees to fill only 1,500 jobs in a single year. A widespread consensus has developed that too many entry-level training programs are not cost-effective because of rapid turnover, and it is more openly avowed that improved educational opportunities in our schools must prepare people more adequately in a changing economy to move to their second and third jobs which frequently are more important barometers of meaningful employability than entry-level jobs which too often have been dead-end in nature.

Thus, it has become more apparent that business has a rather obvious and tangible dollar-and-cents economic stake in strengthening the quality of public education as well as the more intangible but equally important interest it has in our democratic system's need to maximize equity, provide social justice, and preserve domestic tranquility. As changes in the economy continue to trigger profound and rapid alterations in the nature of the work force, the need to invest in human capital becomes more important if the country is to be productive, profitable and viable. Thus, more members in the corporate world recognize that they have an up-front political, economic and social stake in improving schools.

The 1980s are a propitious time for systematic and sustained dialogue to begin to occur between the business and public school worlds. There is an emerging national consensus that basic skills in areas like reading, writing and math must be improved; that both the quality and quantity of our math and science instruction must be strengthened; that the effectiveness of teachers and teacher education must be enhanced; and that education like other sectors in our society must be made more productive with greater attention paid to the utilization of new technolgies such as computers, video discs, and robotry as well as educational television.

The various national reports, which we have alluded to a number of times, make education in the 1980s a far more visible and publicized enterprise. Reports such as *A Nation at Risk, High School,* and *Action for Excellence,* as well as the new economic realities, spawn a new saliency for schools by integrating concerns about education into the mainstream of major public policy issues. President Reagan's declarations on school issues as well as education's importance in the presidential election of 1984

helped sustain public interest. However, some skeptics fear that the educational bal-
loon might be deflated as quickly as it was inflated once the political rhetoric in the
1984 campaign and the freshness of the highly publicized national reports abate.

The reports, however, did help to interest many of the nation's civic and political
elites in school issues. A growing number of the nation's most prestigious business
and governmental leaders now espouse the importance of the schools to the nation's
economic development and comprehensive reform legislation was enacted in the early
1980s in states such as Mississippi, California and Florida. Governors like James Hunt
of North Carolina, Pierre Dupont of Delaware, Charles Robb of Virginia, Lamar Alexander of Tennessee, William Winter of Mississippi, Martha Layne Collins of Kentucky, and others were in the forefront of political and economic efforts to strengthen
the quality of and support base for education. Business leaders from major corporations such as IBM, Control Data, Hewlett-Packard, the Bank of America, Proctor and
Gamble, and numerous other representatives from the private sector throughout the
country became engaged in school issues in unprecedented, varied ways.

Major national business organizations such as the Committee for Economic Development, the Chamber of Commerce, the National Alliance of Business, the Business Roundtable, and their counterparts at the state and local levels are increasing
their education-related activities. Education is viewed more commonly not just as a
consumer of resources but as a necessary investment in human capital and the nation's
economic viability.

For example, late in 1983, the Committee for Economic Development, a prestigious business group, which has served as an influential forum for policy development
on many major and controversial issues since 1942, initiated a study on business and
the schools. Those involved in the project, directed by Denis P. Doyle, Resident
Fellow in Education at the American Enterprise Institute, are planning to explore
issues such as education as an investment in human capital, student needs, excellence
in teaching and business-education collaboration.[53]

Other nationally significant business groups such as the Chamber of Commerce
have shown similar interest. The Chamber of Commerce, the largest federation of
business and professional organizations in the world representing more than 209,000
members throughout the country, reflects its concern in recent testimony to the
House Education and Labor Committee in response to a proposal to create a National
Summit Conference on Education:

> We support the creation of a National Summit Conference on Education, provided
> the legislation and corresponding program agenda include the following:
>
> Adequate business representation. We are not as concerned about the quantity of
> business representation as much as the fostering and nurturing of innovative business
> responses at the federal, state, and local levels. The previously mentioned examples
> of business activity in education provide a very good starting point for any national
> conference.
>
> Recognition of the need to help students develop "school-to-work" and/or
> "school-to-college" skills. To combat the severe functional illiteracy problem, not only
> is the business community spending billions of dollars in remedial education and train-
> ing programs; statistics show that enrollment in remedial mathematics courses at 4-
> year colleges is up 72 percent from 1975-1980. So, not only are high school graduates
> seniors not ready for work; they are not ready for college.

53. Committee for Economic Development, *Business and the Schools* (October 1983), (Mimeographed).

In summary, the business community has a proprietary interest in assuring that the current "crisis in education" is adequately addressed and the American educational system is improved. We will continue to support those national efforts that will provide "work-ready-college-ready" students. To that end, the Chamber stands willing to assist in the development of a National Summit Conference on Education.[54]

Thus, these initiatives and countless other examples of growing school-business interaction throughout the country at the local, regional, state, and national levels are direct responses not only to economic needs but also to the recommendations in the aforementioned major reports on education that the private sector become much more involved in schools:

"Action for Excellence" very strongly urges the involvement of business people and other leaders outside of education in improving our schools, and "High School," "A Place Called School," "Educating Americans for the 21st Century," "Action for Excellence," and "A Nation at Risk," all issue an invitation to business leaders to become more active, not only in supporting schools financially, but also in developing curricula and programs and in sharing nonfinancial resources.[55]

What was largely obscure rhetoric about the importance of business-school partnerships only a short time ago became transformed almost overnight into a "front-burner" public issue.[56] Hundreds of grassroots examples of these emerging partnerships can be cited.[57]

Local efforts to encourage private support of the schools are exemplified through the work of regional coordinating mechanisms such as the Pittsburgh area's Allegheny Conference, the San Francisco Foundation, and New York City's Economic Development Council. A rapidly expanding effort to create locally based private foundations through which business support can be funneled into school systems also illustrates the extent of the movement which is being unleashed in districts throughout the nation. In addition, activities like the President's Task Force on Private Sector Initiatives and the Education Commission of the States' National Task Force on Education for Economic Growth involve influential governmental and private sector leaders in public school issues and problems at all governmental levels.

Summary and Future Prospects

In this chapter we have identified a number of societal trends and factors which provide school systems with some unique opportunities for extending their educational programs as well as broadening their political, tax and tuition base of support. We also have briefly discussed school-business partnerships, an important new collaborative movement with significant implications for the schools. We will conclude with a discus-

54. Robert Martin, *Statement of the Chamber of Commerce of the United States,* Testimony to the House Education and Labor Committee on the National Summit Conference on Education (H.R. 3245), 15 September 1983, 4.
55. *A Summary of Major Reports on Education* (Denver, Colo.: Education Commission of the States, 1983), 10.
56. Much of the following is derived from Michael D. Usdan, "School-Business Partnerships," Guest Editorial, *The School Administrator* (March 1983): 64.
57. See, for example, Ian McNett, *Let's Not Reinvent the Wheel: Educational Profiles of School-Business Collaboration* (Washington D.C.: Institute for Educational Leadership, 1982).

sion of how these trends and factors will influence the organization and control of education.

Most school-age youngsters in the United States attend school during the state-determined compulsory attendance years, most often from age five through age sixteen. The states of the United States patterned themselves, at least in part, after Great Britain in the establishment and enforcement of school attendance policy. Policy regarding school attendance, a state prerogative, was determined in the nineteenth century. It was fashioned in response to public needs and now, a century later, new issues regarding the education of children in the preschool years are developing.

An expanded educational program raises a number of control issues. For example, should the states develop new legislation regarding the certification of personnel, the licensing and supervision of institutions providing preprimary programs, and the location of administrative and supervisory responsibilities? Currently the states vary in the scope and specificity of policy governing preprimary education. The states' interests in the lives of young children date back to the emergence of kindergartens, many of which were nonpublic. There was concern about the states' responsibilities for their supervision, especially on issues pertaining to the welfare of children and the absence of compulsory attendance laws covering this age group.

The number of children presently enrolled or likely to enroll in preschool is becoming so large that governance and control problems have a new immediacy and urgency. Approximately two percent of the nation's total population are presently in attendance in a preprimary setting. The problem is not simply one of numbers but one of substantial philosophical, educational, political, social, and economic dimensions.

An important political and governance issue is involved in the administration and supervision of preprimary programs. Should such responsibilities rest with state education, health, or welfare departments? Or do they belong elsewhere? Or should those responsibilities be shared? Certainly the administrative bureaucracies within each of these areas and the interest groups they attract have preferences regarding the place-placement of administrative and supervisory responsibilities. Those preferences are based in part on philosophical beliefs about what should be emphasized in the lives of young children and in part on the ever-present pressure to extend and sustain the bureaucracies themselves. The same issues are prominent at the federal level as questions of children's welfare surface within the Congress, the executive branch, and the federal courts.

Economic issues also raise policy problems in regard to preprimary school programs as well as other public interventions in the lives of young children. We have referred to the income requirements of single-parent families as well as those where both parents are employed to improve their family's standard of living. These trends appear to be irreversible, given the entrenched belief in the free enterprise system. Another economic issue is institutional ownership. Day-care centers, nursery schools, and other forms of preprimary schooling have become big business in recent years. There are strong private interests striving to keep public institutions from expanding their services to include the preschool age group. Ownership of nursery schools and day-care centers can be profitable. So much so that day-care and nursery school chains are developing.

School districts, it can be argued, are the logical local governments to assume public responsibility for preschool programming. Proposals for incorporating these responsibilities within the public schools, however, are challenged by those who oppose preschool programming itself, resist the expansion of public school control, and fight increased support for the public school system. In addition, private sector interest groups argue for educational options as well as for benefits to the taxpayer which accrue if such services remain within private sector management.

In the welter of post-World War II developments, educational leaders joined others in an almost total preoccupation with growth. The rapid expansion of population and enrollments, the attendant requirements of classrooms, teachers, books, and supplies, tended to detract from concerns with teaching and learning. With the exception of short-term emphases on education of gifted children, national curricular reforms in such areas as mathematics, physics, and biology, and more modest attention to reading and career education, the major investment of institutional energy has been in keeping pace with the needs for personnel and physical facilities. As a consequence, educational leaders, like the general public, did not take full account of how new social conditions were altering the basic needs of the children in school.

Our society immediately after World War II was highly youth-oriented if measured by public expenditures on their behalf. Year after year millions of young people entered and exited from the schools (public and nonpublic) to assume adult responsibilities. Two generations have passed through the formal school since 1945. Their children are now students. During the four decades since 1945 enormous transformations have occurred in our society and its subcultures, which have affected parents and children simultaneously. Television, for example, is often cited not only for its pervasive impact but also for its negative influence on the lives of children and youth. Usually overlooked is the realization that television also occupies many waking hours of today's parents throughout their lives. The effects of television should be measured not only in terms of its meaning for the young but for adults as well. The impact of television is so significant that schools and other educational institutions will have to become more concerned with and perhaps even involved in the medium's governance.

The school-business partnership movement, as we have noted, is a development which has profound ramifications for the organization and control of schools. School leaders should recognize the recent attention by business leaders as an opportunity to reemphasize education as the engine of our democratic system. "Invisible politics is poor politics," and a public reawakening to the importance of education spurred by private sector influentials can buttress the schools politically at a time when competition for scarce resources is keener and the political leverage of education is lessened in many parts of the country. Stated differently, educators, (for pragmatic as well as substantive public policy reasons) as we have stressed in this chapter, must build new coalitions to include the business community and groups such as senior citizens, whose influence is becoming stronger in terms of their numbers and political clout.

But we hasten to add that situations which present opportunities also pose problems; there are dangers inherent in today's environment. In addition to the longstanding fear that business involvement could lead to control of our schools, more subtle dangers merit attention. New or rekindled business concern for schools may be viewed as evanescent, a public relations fad that will go the way of team teaching, programmed instruction, educational television, and other "quick fixes." We believe that such an appraisal would be a disastrous misreading of the current situation.

Another related danger is that because of current economic uncertainty schools will be unable to acquire monies from the private sector and thus will get "turned off" and businesses will fail to recognize the potential of the more significant long-range, non-monetary stake and self-interest that they have in supporting education. Despite these dangers, we believe that school-business partnerships and other forms of multisector collaboration represent an excellent opportunity to buttress and solidify public support for schools.

As the expansion of educational programs and services escalates, schools will be reaching out to new clientele. The schools are uniquely positioned to capitalize on growing continuing education needs and the recent interest in education manifested by the private sector. Non-college educated women, non-high school graduates, and the chronically unemployed are among the groups that will benefit especially from expanded programs.

Massive, centralized service programs, unresponsive to local needs, have generated disillusionment and dissatisfaction. Locally based institutions such as neighborhood schools are very logical organizations to deliver a new range of human services and adult education programs. Their special grassroots base if buttressed by the support of the business community could allow schools to become much more effective vehicles of community education as they attempt to meet the needs of the entire citizenry from preschool children to senior citizens by extending their programs. This new, expanded educational approach will precipitate a variety of new financial, political, and curricular problems: the organization and control of the schools may be significantly altered as these issues are addressed.

19

Control Elements: Summary and Conclusions

We began in chapter 1 by declaring our intention of placing the control variables which appear to affect schools in an open systems context. We defined open systems in terms of interaction between an organization and its environment, largely following Easton, and in terms of loose coupling within the organization itself, largely following Weick. We discovered that a large number of institutions, conditions, and persons control in one way or another what schools are, what they do, and how as organizations they behave. Throughout the book we have used the word *control* in a broad sense to encompass the various expectations, constraints, and influences which affect schools. We have also used the term *schools* in a broad sense. Ordinarily, we have used it to mean a single public school or a public school district but at times we also considered nonpublic or alternative schools. From the previous discussion of the various types of school control, seven general categories can be derived.

The Control Categories

The control categories which follow have been developed inductively from the descriptions and analyses of the institutions, conditions, and persons which affect the schools. The open systems approach to administration has informed our analyses and in a sense this book represents an empirical test of the open systems concept in the area of education.

The establishment of these categories was a difficult task. First, there was the problem of terminology. The term *control constraints,* considered because some of these controls do constrain, was rejected because on balance *constraints* seems to emphasize the negative and leave little room for the positive. *Control influences* seemed redundant for we used *control* and *influence* as synonyms throughout this work. *Control determinants* suggested a tightness of relationship which hardly fits the notion of loosely coupled organizations. From the more neutral terms remaining, such as *control factors, control components,* and *control elements,* we have chosen to use the term *control elements.*

A second problem in developing categories was deciding what level of abstraction should be employed. At the highest level of abstraction one might simply say that organizations are affected by internal and external factors. But such a statement is too general to be useful. Therefore, we have categorized internal and external factors which affect schools into seven control elements which we will look at one by one. These are outlined below:

1. Demographic control elements
   a. Number and character of adults
   b. Number and character of students
   c. Cultural traditions and values
2. Legal control elements
   a. State and federal constitutions
   b. State and federal statutes
   c. State and federal regulations
   d. State and federal case law
3. Structural control elements
   a. Governmental arrangements
      (1) Levels
      (2) Decision points
   b. Organizational arrangements
      (1) Levels
      (2) Power of office
   c. Employee organizations
      (1) Professionals
      (2) Service workers
4. Ideational control elements
   a. Concepts of government, organizations, and schools held by lay and professional persons
   b. Purposes for the schools espoused by lay and professional persons
5. Knowledge control elements
   a. Information possessed by lay and professional persons
   b. Expertise possessed by lay and professional persons
6. Financial control elements
   a. Resources at state and local levels
   b. Categorical aid at state and federal levels
   c. Federal and state use of money to support professional and lay interest groups
7. Network control elements
   a. Relations of the schools and school districts to state and federal agencies.
   b. Relations of schools and school districts to state and national nongovernmental organizations
   c. Relations of schools and school districts to other local governmental and nongovernmental organizations
   d. Relations of school persons to other persons and organizations

Demographic Control Elements

Demographic control elements include the number and character of adults in a particular school or school district, the number and character of students in a particular school, and the cultural traditions and values of these adults and students. In most areas of control, demography appears to make a difference. Federal aid (chapter 2), for instance is frequently related to the nature of the people residing in certain school districts or school attendance areas. Federal aid is channeled to areas where the people are poor, to areas where minorities are in need, and to areas where segregation is a problem. Acceptance of the notion of equal opportunity means that the institutions can no longer be racially, economically, or culturally blind; that people do differ; and that these differences often indicate where financial assistance is needed. To some extent, these same considerations are found to affect state support of schools and school districts (chapter 3), particularly where states have been called upon to implement federal provisions for the handicapped and sex equality.

Even where school districts, intermediate units, and attendance areas are concerned (chapters 1, 5, and 6) demographic considerations form the basis for certain controls. School districts, for instance, may include a great many people or very few people. In large districts the population tends to be heterogeneous economically and culturally while in small districts the population tends to be more homogenous. These demographic (or socioeconomic) factors explain many of the differences among subgroups within school districts in their aspirations for schools, their ability to support schools, and their level of interest in school programs and policy. Attendance areas, since they represent subunits of school districts, may vary even more economically and culturally than school districts. For this reason, increasing attention is being given to channeling federal and state assistance directly to school sites rather than to school districts. Again, demographic characteristics prompt these efforts to control allocations of resources. Intermediate units represent response to demography. Through them, resources from several school districts or from the state itself are used to meet the special needs of students in schools and school districts where the cost of services would be prohibitive if only local resources were available.

Controls exerted by colleges and universities, (chapter 16) are also affected by demographic factors. Small school districts and attendance areas where a large proportion of the adults are college graduates have different expectations of the schools than do school districts and attendance areas where college graduates are few in number. In the first instance, college preparatory curriculums are demanded and college entrance requirements are given serious consideration. In the second, more demand often exists for vocational curriculums.

The characteristics of students, as well as adults, are important (chapter 12). Students who are college-bound respond to one type of curriculum while those who have other objectives favor other types of offerings. Students with special needs due to economic deprivation or physical and mental handicaps require special instructional programs. Some of these program requirements, such as individually prescribed programs and mainstreaming for the handicapped, affect in many ways the curriculum, personnel, and organization of the schools.

A somewhat different order of control has resulted from the decline of student enrollments found in many schools. Where enrollment has declined, teaching staffs have been reduced. Because few teachers are hired and mobility among the current staff is limited, the entire organization becomes less dynamic. These conditions may also give rise to teacher activism. Enrollment decline may prompt the community to demand a reduction in the school budget. Such reductions may be difficult to achieve because of inflation and because some overhead costs are not geared closely to enrollment decreases. An even greater problem stemming from enrollment decline is the need in many communities to close some schools. In some instances, schools are community centers or at least community symbols. Closing schools portends loss of identity and prestige and frequently means some inconvenience for students and parents. Little wonder that superintendents have lost their jobs and board members have been replaced because of school closings. Thus a demographic condition, enrollment decline, can influence many aspects of school operation.

The control exercised by the superintendent of schools varies greatly in different communities (chapter 9). Depending on the demographic characteristics of its citizens, a community may encourage the superintendent to employ rational problem-solving procedures, to rely on political skills, or merely to take orders. Indeed, demography can also influence the nature of the board of education with whom the superintendent works and can indirectly influence the kind of person who will be attracted to the superintendency itself. In short, the context within which the school operates is in large part demographic in nature.

Demographic control elements are also found in interest groups (chapters 13 and 14). In some school districts and school attendance areas, strong school-related interest groups are active in supporting school programs. School board members may actually be recruited from these interest groups. The school board, the superintendent, school principals, and teachers inevitably hear from such groups and are generally aware of their positions on school issues. These groups also may take the initiative in generating proposals for new or improved programs. In other school districts and attendance areas there may be few if any of these school-related interest groups. The absence of such groups reflects on one hand the nature of the community and on the other hand may reinforce community apathy toward school programs. Of non-school-related interest groups, the most vocal are often those interested in tax reductions. Communities with very few school-related interest groups may be influenced much more easily by the groups representing fiscal restraint.

Finally, demographic control elements will influence the extension of the educational program (chapter 18). That extension will be determined, in large part, by the increasing number of adults in the population and by their demand that programs be designed to meet their needs and or the needs of their preschool-age children.

In this consideration of demographic control elements the interrelatedness of controls becomes very clear. For instance, the demographic characteristics of a school district or attendance area are in large part a result of the structural arrangements which establish those units. Are they large or small? Does their size contribute to their heterogeneity or their homogeneity? This interrelatedness of controls is apparent in fiscal allocations too. The nature of communities and their student populations determine, in some measure, the amount and kind of monies receivable from state and national governments. Finally, the influence of school personnel—administrators, teachers, even students—is determined, in part, by the nature of the communities in which the schools are located.

Legal Control Elements

Legal control elements have to do with state and federal constitutions, state and federal statutes, state and federal regulations, and state and federal case law. The role of the courts (chapter 7) has grown in large part because many educational issues are also social issues. In particular the courts have endorsed the civil rights of minorities, women, teachers, and students, and such endorsements have frequently enhanced the control which these groups exercise over certain aspects of school operation.

During the 1970s federal intrusion into school operation reached a new high (Chapter 2). Using recent enactments by the Congress to illustrate, we noted that these controls reside in the increasing specificity of the language found in the statutes and also in the regulations; in the mandates of such legislation to establish state and national advisory committees, frequently made up chiefly of persons from lay and professional interest groups in a particular field; and in the powerful sanction of placing the enforcement of many of these provisions within the civil rights context. With the advent of the Reagan administration there has been an attempt to deregulate some programs but the basic statutes still remain in place.

Many of the legal controls noted at the national level pertain also at the state level (chapter 3). There are, however, some interesting differences at the state level. Whereas the federal constitution affects education by implication, state constitutions deal with it explicitly. Moreover, each state has an extended body of statutory and case law devoted to education. While state education agencies until recently have been loathe to exercise their full regulatory powers over school districts, three conditions have shifted control to state agencies and to governors and legislatures as well: (1) the increasing proportion of funding at the state level; (2) the demand by legislatures that the state agency exercise its control functions over school districts, often expressed in the form of accountability and competency testing legislation; and (3) the provisions found in much federal legislation that the state agency, with persons paid from federal funds, act as the enforcement agency for federal provisions. In some states, state legislatures appear to be disenchanted with state education agencies and these legislatures have attached legislative oversight provisions to some of the laws they have enacted.

Legal controls are exercised by school districts and boards of education (chapters 4 and 8). In each state, school districts are the legal entities created by the legislature for the purpose of operating schools, and the legislatures have delegated considerable jurisdiction to the districts. In each district a board of education has been established to exercise the powers given to school districts. While boards of education lament the loss of local control (and indeed there are increasing impingements upon local board control), boards still have the legal responsibility to establish schools, to draw attendance boundary lines, to determine curriculums, to employ personnel, and to set school budgets. To be sure, all of these prerogatives are exercised within a state framework, and interest groups peer over the shoulders of the boards as they take action, but the board does have broad grants of power. Some boards are coming to recognize the place of the school district in a federal system, where on many issues each partner, ideally, can influence but none can dominate. Many boards also now differentiate more clearly their role and the roles of the professionals whom they employ to assist them.

Affecting the operation of schools in school districts is the legally constituted intermediate unit (chapter 5). These intermediate units are found in states with many small districts, and such units are usually designed to provide services which are not available or not feasible in small districts. The degree of legal control residing in these intermediate units varies appreciably among the states. In some states specialized services are an option available to school districts while in others such services are mandated. More and more, states are establishing legal requirements for intermediate units.

While intermediate units tend to place school districts in clusters for the delivery of specialized services, a move in the opposite direction is also in evidence. More attention than ever before is being given to individual school attendance areas or school sites (chapter 6). Part of this change is discretionary on the part of boards of education and part of it, particularly in California and Florida, is mandatory. In the first case, the board decides basically how much autonomy should be granted to a principal, the staff, and the citizens residing in the attendance area. This type of decentralization has come, in part, from demands of citizens who want a greater voice in the operation of their own schools. In California and Florida, the legislatures acted to establish greater legal control at school sites.

Legal controls have taken another interesting turn. Already noted are federal requirements that state and national advisory committees, made up largely of lay citizens, be established for a number of federal programs. But some states, here too, are in the mandating business. Florida, for instance, requires as part of its school site management program that advisory committees of citizens be established at the local level (chapter 13). Clearly, lawmakers at both state and national levels are convinced that citizens should exercise a more direct role in the governance of schools and school districts.

Considerable legal attention is being given to alternative schools (chapter 17). The legal right for such schools to exist was established long ago, but legal provisions to encourage their development and even to provide some public support for them continue to receive attention at both national and state levels. This move is based partly on the argument that parents should have a greater voice in decisions concerning the schooling of their children. This kind of emphasis pertaining to alternative schools tends to carry over, in the minds of many parents, to the control of public schools. Should the public schools be required to take over at least part of the responsibility for preschool education (chapter 18), additional legal stipulations will be necessary.

All forms of legal control depend ultimately on the respect that most Americans have for the law. While certain laws and regulations may incur the displeasure of some, most people know that redress for unwise or unfair provisions is possible. Regulations may be changed at the agency level, laws may be rescinded at the legislative level, and the courts are available as a last resort. The courts, particularly at the appellate level, are seen by most people as sustaining basic legal rights and American values.

Structural Control Elements

Structural control elements include governmental arrangements, official organizational arrangements, and unofficial organizational arrangements in employee organizations. While there are limits to the controls derived from structure alone, frequently structure may permit or prohibit, encourage or discourage, facilitate or complicate actions desired by those concerned with schools. The controls exerted by state education agencies (chapters 2 and 3), for example, derive from the fact that federal money is used to staff state agencies with persons committed to the implementation of certain federal programs. In many states one-half or more of the staff in the state agency is supported through federal subventions. Obviously, this is a form of financial control, as we shall note later, but it also constitutes structural control. Schools must confront and deal with a state agency which is structured in large part around federal programs. For years, this condition has been prevalent in the divisions of vocational education. More recently divisions have been established to deal with sex equity, the education of the handicapped, and other federal interests.

Closely related to the structuring of state agencies is the establishment of new regional resource centers across the country. In the area of the education of the handicapped, for instance, 17 centers have been established under federal auspices. Each center is staffed with persons committed to the program for the handicapped and with expertise in that area. An obvious purpose of these new structures is to provide resource people and materials to schools and school districts. If schools do not solicit that help readily, such a center must find ways to make its resources appealing.

Structural controls are at work within school districts, intermediate units, and attendance areas (chapters 4, 5, and 6). In a small district, for instance, organizational structure may be simple, and face-to-face relationships among professionals and lay citizens encouraged; in a large district organizational structure can be formidable, and communication among professionals and lay citizens extremely difficult. In some states intermediate units are set up to be controlled largely by school board members or others from the component school districts. In other states, the intermediate units are allowed much more autonomy. The autonomy granted by school districts or by state mandate to single schools or school sites also represents structural control. A school district may set up a highly centralized structure or it may operate with a much more decentralized arrangement.

Territorial structures, whether school districts, intermediate units, or attendance areas, affect the actors who operate within them. Of primary importance are the structural relationships, formal and informal, between the board and the superintendent (chapters 9 and 10). While this relationship is affected by demographic factors, structural arrangements are also significant. Some superintendents dominate their boards, some boards dominate their superintendents, and in some situations a sensitive partnership has been established between the board and the superintendent. In such partnerships control may go beyond legal definitions; the board may delegate to the superintendent the responsibility for program development. When recommendations growing out of program considerations are approved by the board, the board then holds the superintendent responsible for their implementation. In such a situation the superintendent enjoys considerable power of office not only with the board but with the professional staff as well.

Teachers organizations (chapter 11) are relatively new structures, particularly in the form they have now assumed and in the role they now play. A decade or two ago school administrators belonged to teachers organizations and such membership seemed quite acceptable to both groups. Indeed, some administrators became representatives for teacher groups at both local and state levels. That day has virtually disappeared. Teachers organizations are now led by teachers. They see a major function of those organizations as the protection of the economic well-being of teachers, and they insist that decisions affecting teachers, economic or otherwise, be made only with the participation of teacher representatives. Moreover, teachers organizations have learned that most policy decisions affecting schools are made at the state level, chiefly in the state legislature. Thus the teacher lobby, an unofficial structure, exercises considerable influence at the state level in policy formation and considerable influence, chiefly through the bargaining process, at the local level in policy implementation. Few principals, superintendents, or school boards can now ignore this new structure.

Controls exercised by school-related groups (chapter 13) are frequently benign, but as more citizens raise questions about the school enterprise, that picture is changing. Even the Parent Teachers Association, long under the domination of school administrators, has decided to be more aggressive in its review of school policy. Its current organizational emphasis particularly at the state and national levels, is on a number of issues, such as alcohol, drugs, and pornography, which the PTA is convinced affect learning outcomes of children and youth in and out of school. Another item of interest is the extent to which schools and school districts structure their organizations to permit or encourage interaction with school-related groups. Where such structures are not fostered by the school, these groups may speak for the community at large and demand such participation.

Governmental access is generally a function of the number and levels of decision points (chapter 15). The multiplicity of decision points may discourage and even deter citizens trying to affect the school. For school or school district officials the multiplication of decision points may also prove burdensome. For instance, some boards of education can by themselves adopt a school budget. Other boards of education are required to have their budget proposals approved by a town meeting, or a city council, or a county board of some kind, or even by a state agency. As decision points increase, governing bodies must devote more and more of their time to procedural details. This point is well documented in state and national programs where citizen participation is mandated.

Clearly, schools are affected by a wide range of structural controls, both horizontal and vertical in nature. Horizontal arrangements frequently include impingements by city or county government. Vertical arrangements always include the demands of state and federal agencies. Nongovernmental structures, particularly teacher organizations, have both horizontal and vertical expressions.

Ideational Control Elements

Ideational control elements go beyond the more obvious controls imposed by legal provisions and structural arrangements and arise from the concepts and values people hold. People inside and outside the schools and school district organizations have concepts concerning government, organizations, and schools themselves. These same people also favor or explicitly espouse certain ideas and values which do influence school operation. For instance, long-standing federal programs, notably vocational education, contain provisions for the preservice and inservice training of teachers (chapter 2). Such teacher education programs are clearly an attempt to socialize teachers into a certain way of thinking about their teaching area; they instill in those teachers certain concepts and values. In the military this process is called indoctrination. By whatever name, the purpose is to shape a person's way of viewing the world.

In school districts, intermediate units, and attendance areas, the perceptions and aspirations of people inside and outside the schools make a difference (chapters 4, 5 and 6). In school districts, for instance, when there is a proposal to close a school, the strength of these perceptions becomes readily apparent. Frequently, when intermediate units are established which combine several small districts for certain purposes, persons in a small unit who have certain perceptions and values must deal with the perceptions and values of other persons in a larger context. Where this kind of interaction produces a new level of ideational agreement, the new structure generally succeeds. If a new consensus does not emerge, the new structure probably can do little to enhance school programs. In some cases persons in a particular attendance area may want to become or remain more homogeneous than is possible in the larger school district. They wish their particular perceptions and values about education to be given greater recognition and even to control their particular school.

Legal controls (chapter 7) are effective only to the extent that such provisions seem to embody concepts and values acceptable to most people. In periods of social change, certain legal provisions may become irrelevant to many people. Under these circumstances the provisions will tend to be ignored or they will be changed. New legal status accorded minority groups, women, and now students, reflect changes in attitudes which brought further changes in legal arrangements themselves.

The controls exerted by school boards and superintendents (chapters 8 and 9) are also, in part, ideational in nature. Board members have certain concepts and values regarding schools, and superintendents also have a set of concepts and values which influence their thinking about school operation. The superintendent has been subjected to professional training, through which certain concepts and values are taught. When the superintendent's professional viewpoint differs appreciably from that of board members, conflict will ensue. Or, when board members and superintendent espouse one set of beliefs and major groups in the community operate from another set of beliefs, conflict will also ensue. There is no way of escaping the old proverb: as a man thinketh in his heart, so is he.

Controls exercised by teachers and students (chapters 11 and 12) came about primarily through a change in thinking about teachers and students. Teachers see themselves in a new light. Legislative enactments and court decisions have established the right of teachers to organize and to bargain. People generally have accepted teachers in their new role, and teachers exercise greater control because people's perceptions of teachers have undergone a change. To some extent, the same is true for students. The courts, in particular, have developed the doctrine that students are people too and as people they have certain rights. For instance, due process is to be followed when students are disciplined.

The influence of school-related groups (chapter 13) and other interest groups (chapter 14) is also, in part, ideational in nature. Two developments are pertinent here. The first is a growing concern, even doubt, about the capacity of the school to achieve its purposes or at least the purposes traditionally ascribed to the school. The second development is a rejection of big government, which must necessarily be representative in nature, and a resurgence of direction participation in government. Many different interest groups espouse these positions and are determined to influence decisions affecting schools and other institutions in our society. In many cases these groups become preoccupied with single issues, such as the selection of textbooks, and give little attention to other policy issues. When several interest groups speak out on different individual issues, those who must operate public institutions find it nearly impossible to respond to all of them. The inability of a school to respond to conflicting demands tends to reinforce, in the minds of many, the perception of school failure and governmental inadequacy.

The aspirations people have for the school often influence the financial support they will give the school. If people believe that schooling is important, that schools are offering relevant programs to their children, they tend to support schools both morally and financially. On the other hand, if schooling itself seems irrelevant or if school procedures seem misdirected, moral and financial support will be withheld.

College influences (chapter 16) are, in large part, a matter of expectations. Admission requirements are one vehicle which permit colleges to exercise some control over the schools. Through admission requirements, they express their expectations for entering students. Schools, students, and parents may accept such requirements as useful and conform to them, or they may question such requirements and join in efforts to change them. In either case, the response is essentially an ideational one. Over the past few decades, some prestigious colleges maintained rigorous admission requirements but many colleges, particularly public institutions, relaxed their requirements. Most of the recent studies on education have urged more demanding admission requirements and many colleges, public and private, have responded to these recommendations.

Controls concerning alternative schools (chapter 17) again are largely a matter of ideation. Those who believe that public schools are too large, too impersonal, too godless, too integrated, or whatever, frequently support the move to establish alternative schools. The establishment of these schools, their support by many people, and increasing efforts by government to provide some financial support to such schools pose ideational problems for the public schools. Indeed, the whole idea of public education itself, once accepted by many as almost a secular religion, is brought into question. At best, however, alternative schools do provide competition for the public schools and can be seen as a way of accomodating the diverse values and interests of a pluralistic society. If this understanding comes to be shared by more people, both public and private schools may flourish.

The extension of the educational program (chapter 18) is in large part an ideational matter. The idea that public schools are for children in grades K–12 is deeply entrenched in our society. Education and schooling have been equated. Now social conditions are bringing both of these assumptions into question. Clearly, schools can serve preschoolers, adults generally, and older people in particular if people want them to. Indeed, highly innovative learning arrangements can be established if the extended educational program finds widespread support.

This nation is in a period when the ideational landscape surrounding schools and school governance is changing. While not all of the basic concepts and values of the Reagan administration have been implemented, they have made a difference (Chapter 2). One has only to consider such terms as federal-state, public-private, regulation, desegregation, tuition tax credits, or school prayer to recognize that values, once largely taken for granted, have been challenged.

To some, we have reached a point where our pluralism has produced so diverse an array of concepts and values that we can no longer find a common ground. If that were true, governance would be impossible. Our diversity does pose new challenges. Indeed, there are probably places where governance has been quite hopeless, but there are many instances where people have taken account of new conditions and where they have increased their efforts to make the system work.

Knowledge Control Elements

There is some truth in the old adage that knowledge is power. Knowledge control elements include general knowledge and special knowledge, or expertise. In either case, those who know are usually in a position to exercise some control.

Knowledge controls are in evidence at both federal and state levels (chapters 2 and 3). For instance, federally funded resource centers are established, in part, for the purpose of extending knowledge about particular programs in education and for bringing together a group of persons with expertise in that area. In similar manner, state education agencies frequently have research, evaluation, and development divisions for the purpose of learning more about the educational needs of the state and of ascertaining how certain programs are affecting schools and the students who attend them. The state agency can and does determine what knowledge should be uncovered, what methods should be used, and what use should be made of the knowledge including its availability to others. State agencies also exercise another kind of knowledge control. They usually determine what kinds of knowledge, at least as expressed in college courses, teachers and administrators should possess in order to secure certificates permitting them to work in a school system. In both state and federal agencies those who work constantly in a particular area tend to develop an expertise in that area which few others possess. These experts or technicians are frequently called upon, not only in their own organizations but in the world beyond, to offer informed opinions and to recommend courses of action.

Information is also generated, or at least organized, in other agencies. Most school districts must generate information about their own operation (chapter 4). Intermediate units (chapter 5), now found in many states, were formed, in part, to bring more information and expertise to the operation of small school districts. For instance, such intermediate units frequently provide health and psychological services, both requiring some expertise, to their component districts. Colleges and universities (chapter 16) are also in the business of generating knowledge and provide a base of operation for persons with specialized knowledge and interests. Schools, school districts, and related agencies often see the experts in colleges and universities as somewhat more objective than the experts in their own organizations. This perception tends to extend the influence of college people.

A rather dramatic example of the control exercised by experts is found in recent court procedures. Judges often seek the knowledge and recommendations of persons in specialized areas—including the areas of teaching and learning, organizational arrangements, and environmental influences—as part of the background needed to make legal determinations. Thus, the increasing control of the courts is, in part, based upon the expert testimony of knowledgeable people (chapter 7).

Knowledge control in school districts is exercised to some extent by the school board (chapter 8), the superintendent (chapter 9), the other administrators (chapter 10), and the teachers (chapter 11). Board members obviously come to possess some knowledge about school operation. Presumably they also have some knowledge of the world beyond the school and how that world and the school are related. But most boards feel the need to employ one or more persons, reputedly with some specialized knowledge, to help them understand the institution over which they preside and to give them additional advice on the decisions they have to make. For many boards the superintendent of schools is their chief or only expert. In a less complicated world that arrangement may have worked fairly well. In today's world with its many complex problems, the expertise of the superintendent alone is simply not adequate. Superintendents need to be analysts, but as such they need to call upon many others with special expertise.

This need for both special and general knowledge is frequently recognized in the organization of the superintendent's office. While in larger districts the superintendent may need line officers for assignment to major divisions of the district program, the superintendent also needs staff specialists whose major function is to generate information and to advise the superintendent, the board, and others concerned. Often staff advice is the most important ingredient in board and administrative decisions. Thus, the roles of decision makers and decision advisers have sometimes been reversed— dramatic proof that knowledge is indeed a control element. In addition, the more specialized knowledge becomes, the greater the need for competent generalists. The superintendent and board members, as generalists, need to rely on the unique contributions of specialists.

In many ways, the real experts on school operation are the teachers. Only the teachers have a day-to-day knowledge of student behavior, including student reaction to procedures and instructional materials. This argument is used by teachers organizations as they press for greater teacher participation in decisions made by schools and school districts. While these organizations frequently seem to be more interested in the well-being of teachers than in the well-being of students, the fact remains that competent teachers have a reservoir of knowledge which can and does make a difference in many school systems. Much of the conflict between teachers and administrators is based on the issue of professional versus bureaucratic control. Bureaucratic control has been too pervasive in most school districts, but there is no way for it to be eliminated entirely, particularly the hierarchical arrangements found in school districts. At the same time, the professional knowledge of teachers ought to be given a more prominent place in school decision making.

School-related and other interest groups (chapters 13 and 14) exercise considerable control in an open system, and their control depends on what they are able to know about the schools. For instance, more and more groups outside the school are insisting that the school release information about its operation. Movements for accountability and for competency testing are attempts by persons and organizations outside the school to force the school to study itself in order to tell the community how well it is achieving its purposes.

Citizens generally are better educated than ever before and are capable of raising more relevant questions about school operation. In a sense, this condition reflects the success of the schools as an institution over the last several decades. Schools must now deal with well-informed citizens, some of whom possess specialized knowledge in relevant fields. Schools can no longer claim that they have a monopoly on knowledge about learning, evaluation, organization, and finance. Experts in all these areas are found among parents and other school patrons, and they are using that expertise to affect the direction of the schools.

Many of our conclusions about knowledge control are based on the assumption that people are rational beings. Rational people would obviously be interested in generating information and in using information in decisions affecting their lives, but nonrational considerations often affect people's decisions. Schools, have, as a part of their mission, the extension of rational or problem-solving behavior.

Financial Control Elements

As other control elements have been discussed, financial controls have been mentioned. In this category are included financial resources or money made available at the local, state, and federal levels; categorical aids at state and federal levels; and the use of money to foster the development of lay and professional interest groups. Wealth has been identified as one of three major clusters of variables determining the level of expenditures in school districts (chapter 15). Obviously, there must be, in addition to the possession of wealth, a willingness to use it for school purposes. While there is not a one-to-one relationship between money and the quality of a school program, money does make a difference.

Both federal and state levels of government exert a number of financial controls over schools and school districts (chapters 2 and 3). For instance, nearly all money at the national level is for categorical assistance, thereby determining that specific aspects of the educational program will be supported. While federal financial assistance covers only about nine percent of the total cost of public education, the percentage of support for certain programs, such as those for the poor, is much higher; hence the inducement to many school districts to accept federal assistance is enhanced. Even so, few federal programs are supported entirely from federal funds, meaning that states and school districts must support such programs with additional revenues. The need for state and local contributions is dramatically illustrated in the law for the education of the handicapped. Categorical assistance at the federal level, then, means categorical assistance at state and local levels as well. While categorical programs may be entirely desirable, such pressure to fund them may prevent a balanced look at other programs supported by the school budget.

In addition to allocating federal monies and providing additional monies to match federal programs, state agencies may also sponsor certain categorical programs of their own. When that is done, budget control is again imposed upon school districts. State agencies also exercise another financial control over school districts: they interpret and implement the general state aid program. While most of the details of that program are ordinarily spelled out in the statutes, there is frequently some room for discretion at the state level. Moreover, state agencies are often given the power to cut off funds to local districts when such districts are found to be in noncompliance with the law or state regulation. These controls may appear to be completely justified and the categorical assistance at state and federal levels may be for worthy purposes, but the fact remains that substantial control is imposed upon schools and school districts.

Financial controls operate in school districts, intermediate units, and attendance areas (chapters 4, 5, and 6). School districts vary greatly in assessed valuation per child, the most common way of expressing their wealth or capacity to support schools. While state aid programs tend to alleviate these disparities, much variation remains. In poor districts lack of money may result in what might be called the control of deprivation. Intermediate units are often able to provide certain services, in such areas as health and transportation, on a more cost-effective basis than would be possible in small school districts. Where that is so, school districts ordinarily give up some control in return for the added benefits. These trade-off provisions vary greatly among the states. Attendance areas are almost entirely dependent upon school districts for financial support. Nearly all fiscal arrangements at the local level are made by school districts, and the districts also channel most state and federal money to attendance areas. While some attempt has been made to modify this situation, attendance areas have little control over financial matters. Since attendance areas may vary even more widely than school districts in assessed value per student, district discretion in finances may be a desirable condition.

The basic control instrument in the hands of the board of education and the superintendent (chapters 8 and 9) is the annual school budget. Ordinarily the superintendent, with the help of staff, formulates the budget and recommends its adoption to the board. To be sure, there are many constraints, other than program requirements, present in the development of the budget: the wealth of the district, the tax limits imposed by state statute, the nature and amounts of state and federal funds anticipated, the demands of employees for salary increases and for other benefits, and the perceived willingness of citizens to vote for a tax override. Even so, most boards and superintendents exercise some discretion in arriving at a total figure for expenditures and in allocating monies within that figure to various programs. Once the budget is adopted, allocations for various functions and for individual schools are ordinarily set for the year.

Teachers, whose salaries often represent 75–85 percent of the total budget, have considerable influence on the budget (chapter 11). In recent years teacher organizations have insisted upon recognition and the right to bargain with school boards on pay levels and other provisions. In many instances, where agreements were not reached, teachers have gone out on strike until boards were ready to resume bargaining. Increasingly, the local teachers organization, often with the help of staff from the state or the national organization, makes careful analyses of both proposed budget expenditures and budget revenues. As a result, the budget process in most school districts has become a more open process with information made available to both teachers and the public.

School-related and other interest groups (chapters 13 and 14) exert considerable financial control. When these groups concur with budget proposals their support becomes a positive element in budget adoption and in passing a tax override, if that is necessary. Where some or all of these groups find budget proposals unacceptable, the budget proposal is frequently adjusted. Such budget adjustments usually require that total expenditures be reduced, but specific budget provisions may also be altered. Tax limitation proposals, now popular with certain interest groups, get at budget reductions by limiting revenues that can be made available to school districts. In any case, citizens and citizen groups do exercise great control over the local school budget.

Financial support for alternative schools, (chapter 17), at least those outside the public school system, may present a challenge or even a threat to the support of public schools. More money for alternative schools may mean that less money is available for public schools. Perhaps more significant, in the process of establishing alternative schools, the role and performance of public schools may become devalued in many people's opinion. If that happens, the desire to support public schools will undoubtedly be reduced.

In many ways, financial controls are the means whereby other controls are imposed on the schools. For instance, when states and school districts do not respond adequately to certain educational needs, as perceived by congressional representatives, categorical aid for those specific programs may be established. Or, at the local level when citizens become disenchanted with some aspects of the school program, their chief recourse is to deny money to the school district, often through defeat of a tax override election.

Network Control Elements

No school or school district is an island. Schools as institutions are related to many other institutions. The conditions affecting schools are often pervasive in the society and affect other institutions as well. The people, lay and professional, who make the schools what they are, are connected with many other persons and organizations who have special interests. Network controls also include the relationships of schools and school districts to state and federal agencies, the relationships of schools and school districts to state and national nongovernmental organizations, and the relationships of schools and school districts to other local governmental and nongovernmental agencies and organizations. These relationships may be both vertical and horizontal, they may involve both governmental and nongovernmental organizations, and they may evolve into countless combinations and variations. In all of these relationships the potential for influence is present and in many of them that potential is realized.

Governmental networks exist at state and national levels (chapters 2 and 3). Most of the federal programs are channeled through state education agencies and then to local education agencies. Frequently these programs require that advisory committees be established at state and federal levels and that such committees take part in approving and monitoring such programs once they are in operation. These advisory committees are often composed primarily of persons who represent interest groups concerned with the particular program. The use of such persons on advisory committees extends the governmental network to nongovernmental interest groups and, in a sense, provides a sanction for those groups and for the viewpoints they espouse.

Another type of nongovernmental network is found in the relationships among schools, colleges, accrediting associations, and testing agencies. Colleges and agencies dominated by college personnel, have traditionally exercised great influence over the high school curriculum (chapter 16). That influence, while modified somewhat in recent decades by standards established by state departments of education, has been reaffirmed in the recent studies of education.

Still another set of network relationships is found in the school districts (chapter 4), intermediate units (chapter 5), and attendance areas (chapter 6). While school districts, as such, may have many or few network relationships, frequently school district officials will select a number of other districts of comparable size, or location, or wealth, or demographic characteristics on which they develop comparative data with respect to tax levies, teachers' salaries, expenditures per student, and so on. In many instances, these comparative data become most persuasive to school board members and the citizens of the community. Those concerned with the operation of schools in attendance areas also may make use of comparative data about schools in the same school district or in nearby or similar districts. The intermediate unit is deliberately established to encourage network relationships, first among a group of school districts, second with state and federal education agencies. Frequently the intermediate unit acts as agent to see that its component districts get "their share" of available resources from state and federal sources.

School personnel (chapters 8, 9, 10, and 11) have a wide range of network relationships. For instance, nearly every state has an active state school boards association and generally membership is extended to the board and not to individual board members. The National School Boards Association is essentially a federation of state school board associations but individual memberships are also permitted. Regardless of how official membership status is arranged, board members attend the state and national meetings of these associations by the tens of thousands. Board members also make use of the publications of these organizations. Frequently, attendance at such meetings and the materials acquired there influence board behavior back home. On some issues, board members have also been able to arrive at a common position and communicate that position to state and local government. Again, network influence may involve governmental and nongovernmental actors. Superintendents, like board members, have both state and national organizations and these affiliations also make some difference in the thinking and action of many superintendents. Those who serve in the administrative hierarchy also belong to many state and national organizations. These memberships may be quite diverse and each organization may represent a specialization in the field of education such as school law, curriculum and instruction, or evaluation; any number of subject specialities such as reading, mathematics, or science; or even some of the more recent emphases such as special education. In each case, members and organization materials provide justifications for particular views and concerns in education and thus influence those who operate school systems.

Teachers, like other school personnel, are tied into many networks. At the local level most teachers belong to a local association or a local union, with unions being most prominent in large cities (chapter 11). Most states have strong professional associations and some have strong union organizations. At the national level are the National Education Association and the American Federation of Teachers. These organizations at local, state, and national levels tend to emphasize teacher welfare issues. Teachers may also belong to organizations that focus chiefly on teaching and learning or on some specialty in the field of education. Teacher influence at all levels of government has grown in recent years. Many state legislators, for instance, aver that the teacher lobby is much more powerful than the school administrator lobby and generally more powerful than the school board lobby in influencing state legislation. Indeed, the teachers organization is considered to be among the most powerful of all lobbying groups in many states.

But teachers are not alone in their efforts to influence legislation and other aspects of policy formation. School-related and other interest groups (chapter 13 and 14) also have a network nature. The PTA, for example, has strong organizations at local, state, and national levels. In like manner, the U.S. Chamber of Commerce has local, state, and national expressions and a network linking all three levels. Similar network arrangements can be found in labor organizations, agricultural organizations, and other special interest fields. Most local school issues are not merely local issues. Whether the issue is textbook selection in West Virginia or the teaching of evolution in Arkansas, local groups are soon joined by their state and national counterparts. What began as a school or school district problem can become the basis for a state and even a national confrontation. Frequently many actors, governmental and nongovernmental, at all levels of our society become involved and their influence is felt in the local arena and beyond.

The network controls noted above are, in part, a result of our federal system of government. Major policy issues in education can seldom be confined to one level of government. Local concerns often get bucked up to the state or even the national level. National concerns must be bucked down to state and local levels for their implementation. These networks are also a product of interest group activity and the need of such groups to form coalitions in order to augment their influence. While most coalitions of teachers and school administrators came apart over the bargaining issue, in many states and school districts these groups are now considering ways of collaborating, at least on some issues.

Concluding Comments

Having examined the institutions, conditions, and persons that exert control over schools and school districts, and having categorized and summarized these controls, we can now draw a few conclusions about the nature of these controls.

Nature of Controls

In part, the wide range of controls on schools and school districts is a consequence of our federal system of government. In the beginning federalism represented a rough division of powers between national and state governments. Experience over nearly two centuries has brought a number of developments in federalism. First, there has been a move from dual to national federalism (chapter 2). Second, for many practical purposes not only two but three levels of government are involved. Indeed, with the new emphasis on school site management, there are in effect four levels of government. Third, despite the Reagan reversion, each level of government must be involved on many important policy questions. This inevitably means that government is more extensive, more complex, and more time-consuming.

The wide range of controls on schools and school districts is partly a consequence of the extensive development of interest groups and the role they play in the governmental process. Interest groups have proliferated more in America than in any other nation. In many ways interest groups have undercut and even replaced the political parties in taking positions on policy issues and exerting pressure upon local, state, and national governmental officials. While these pressures are sometimes lamented, the activities of interest groups are generally praised. Whether lamented or praised, attempted influence by interest groups is considered to be a normal part of governance even though it adds to the array of controls exerted on schools.

In some cases individuals and interest groups have resisted all governmental controls, to the point of making governance almost meaningless. For instance, some court orders to desegregate schools have been met with foot-dragging that has stalled implementation for years. And in some states where laws make strikes illegal, teachers have nevertheless gone out on strike. While some state laws and court directives may be ill-considered and even unfair, deliberate disobedience to such provisions is a serious matter. Some choose disobedience as a means of dramatizing the need to change the law and willingly accept the consequences; others simply ignore the law and expect to suffer no consequences, and their actions cannot be condoned, for in that way lies anarchy.

Controls over schools and school districts are complex. Some of those who write treatises on school operation do us a disservice when they ascribe control to a single person or group of persons. As this book and the summary of control categories demonstrate, controls emanate from many institutions, conditions, and persons. To be sure, in some situations a single person or group of persons may exert considerable influence but even in these cases institutions and conditions cannot be ignored.

Controls are also interrelated. Legal and structural arrangements are obviously shaped and reshaped by the perceptions of people. Demographic characteristics of people in particular jurisdictions determine, in large part, the knowledge they possess, the values they hold, and frequently the financial resources at their command. Financial controls, while fateful in their own right, are usually symbolic of the perceptions and values of those who impose financial conditions, be they penurious or generous. Network controls emphasize the fact that institutions, conditions, and persons do not stand in isolation; what others think and what other institutions do becomes very important.

Those who would influence schools and school districts need to take account of the complexity and interrelatedness of controls affecting these institutions. This means that such persons need to be knowledgeable, politically astute, and personally persistent.

Controls and Open Systems

Throughout this work we have tried to show that controls reside both in the institution—a school or school district—and in the environment in which the institution exists. The many interactions between institution and environment, make the open systems concept a useful one. Easton suggests that the relationship oetween a political system (i.e., an institution) and its environment is characterized by both inputs and outputs. The inputs are expressed in terms of demands and support. The outputs are expressed in terms of decisions and policies. This model is helpful but it is extremely general. Lawrence and Lorsch have defined environment more specifically for business organizations to include technological development and market changes.[1] These aspects of the environment appear to be pertinent to business organizations with which Lawrence and Lorsch were dealing. In education we also need to think more specifically about the environment that surrounds educational institutions. The seven control elements explicated at the beginning of this chapter may serve as a start in this direction.

A second limitation in applying the open systems view to schools and school districts, is that it is often difficult to distinguish sharply between what is outside (environmental) and what is inside (organizational). For instance, the board of education is, in one sense, outside the organization. Yet as board members become socialized to organization norms and as they place greater reliance on the "expertise" of the superintendent, they tend to become more a part of the organization and less a part of the environment. Or, take students. In one sense they are inside the organization. But students live at home, they participate in many nonschool community functions, and they obviously absorb many of the values of home and community, and are thus also outside the organization. Or, consider teachers. As individuals they are clearly inside the organization. Even the local teacher association, while not a formal part of the school or school district, might be considered to be inside the organization. But the local association becomes intimately tied to the state and even to the national association, both of which are outside the organization. This condition makes classifying the local associations even more difficult.

The difficulty of determining what is inside and what is outside the organization is alleviated by combining Weick's concept of loose coupling, with Easton's model of political systems. As noted earlier, according to Weick, "coupled events are responsive, but each event also preserves its own identity. . . . " In other words, a decision at the top level in the school hierarchy may or may not affect behavior at the bottom level in hierarchy. This kind of loose coupling or independence in a school organization brings to light vulnerable points in the organization on which forces in the environment may focus. For example, a teachers organization might choose to approach the organization or school district through teachers who are most disaffected from the organization and least inclined to accept organization directives. Linking the concepts of loose coupling and political systems makes for a comprehensive and useful model for understanding the organization and control of American schools.

1. P. R. Lawrence and J. W. Lorsch, *Organization and Environment* (Homewood, Ill.: Irwin, 1961).

Index